MW00623385

COMEBACK
PITCHERS

COMEBACK PITCHERS

The Remarkable Careers of
Howard Ehmke and Jack Quinn

LYLE SPATZ *and* STEVE STEINBERG

Foreword by Pat Williams

UNIVERSITY OF NEBRASKA PRESS

LINCOLN

Library of Congress Cataloging-in-Publication Data
Names: Spatz, Lyle, 1937– author. | Steinberg, Steve, author.
Title: Comeback pitchers: the remarkable careers of
Howard Ehmke and Jack Quinn / Lyle Spatz and Steve
Steinberg; foreword by Pat Williams.
Description: Lincoln: University of Nebraska Press, [2021] |
Includes bibliographical references and index.
Identifiers: LCCN 2020032183
ISBN 9781496222022 (hardback)
ISBN 9781496226624 (epub)
ISBN 9781496226631 (mobi)
ISBN 9781496226648 (pdf)
Subjects: LCSH: Ehmke, Howard, 1894–1959. | Quinn, Jack,
1883–1946. | Baseball players—United States—Biography. |
Pitchers (Baseball)—United States—Biography.
Classification: LCC GV865.E37 S63 2021 |
DDC 796.3570922 [B]—dc23
LC record available at https://lccn.loc.gov/2020032183

Set in Minion Pro by Laura Buis.

To people everywhere who face
obstacles and barriers in their
chosen careers and find the strength
to push ahead. May the stories
of Jack Quinn and Howard Ehmke
provide inspiration to carry on.

CONTENTS

ILLUSTRATIONS

FOREWORD

Jack Quinn and Howard Ehmke were exceptions to the old adage that most ballplayers hang on too long. The two pitchers were repeatedly told they were washed up, over the hill, too old, etc., but they kept coming back. Both men played in the 1910s and 1920s and were among the last active big leaguers to have played in the Federal League.

Quinn pitched until he was fifty and is still the oldest pitcher to start a World Series game. He held the record as the oldest pitcher to win a Major League game (at forty-nine) for more than eighty years, until the Philadelphia Phillies' Jamie Moyer, three months older than Quinn, broke it in 2012. He won eighteen games for the 1910 New York Yankees, who released him in 1912; he came back to star in the Federal League and then the Pacific Coast League.

In 1918 Quinn was the subject of a fierce "free agency" fight between the White Sox and the Yankees that permanently severed the friendship between Sox owner Charles Comiskey and American League president Ban Johnson. He excelled for the 1919–21 Yankees, who repaid his efforts by sending him to the lowly Boston Red Sox in December 1921. He was too old at thirty-six, they said. They did not realize he was actually thirty-eight.

Boston released him four years later, and A's manager Connie Mack picked him up. Quinn was an eighteen-game winner for the third time in 1928, as Philadelphia came close to winning the pennant, and he was a major contributor to the A's pennant-winning 1929 season. Let go by Philadelphia a year later, he was a top relief pitcher on the 1931–32 Brooklyn Dodgers.

Howard Ehmke attracted national attention as a twenty-year-old phenom in the Pacific Coast League with the 1914 Los Angeles Angels. Arm problems seemed to have ended his career just as it began, but after a terrible 1915 season in the Federal League, he came back to win thirty-one games for Syracuse a year later. Like Quinn, Ehmke then became the object of a battle between two teams for the rights to him.

Ehmke eventually signed with the Detroit Tigers and spent six years with Detroit, the last two of which Ty Cobb was his manager. Ehmke and Cobb clashed repeatedly. Cobb's biographers have painted him as everything from a devil to a saint. The authors see him as somewhere in between but question the extent of recent Cobb revisionism.

In 1923 Ehmke too was exiled to the Red Sox, where he became Quinn's teammate. That season he came one questionable scoring decision away from tossing back-to-back no-hitters. In 1926 the Red Sox traded Ehmke to Connie Mack's Athletics, where he and Quinn again became teammates. By 1929 the Athletics were world champions.

Howard Ehmke is best remembered for his surprise start for the Athletics in Game One of the 1929 World Series. The thirty-five-year-old Ehmke had appeared in only eleven games that season, and at one point manager Mack was ready to release him. But Ehmke assured Mack he had one great game left in him. And he did. His slow balls handcuffed the Chicago Cubs, thirteen of whom he struck out, a Series record that endured for twenty-three years.

This book is a tribute to all those in sports, and in life in general, who have overcome injury, ageism, undue criticism, and other obstacles to endure and to succeed.

PAT WILLIAMS
Former general manager of the Philadelphia 76ers and Spartanburg Phillies; founder of the Orlando Magic

PREFACE

In our previous books, *1921* and *The Colonel and Hug,* our focus was on some of the most memorable names in baseball history—immortals such as Babe Ruth, Jacob Ruppert, Miller Huggins, and John McGraw. Yet many of those who play for or manage Major League teams are not headliners but rather men who contribute to their teams' success while occasionally flirting with stardom. The two men whose lives we spotlight here personify those qualities.

Jack Quinn and Howard Ehmke were pitchers whose careers began in the Deadball Era and continued well into the Lively Ball Era. They were teammates for many years, with both the hapless Boston Red Sox of the mid-1920s and the world champion 1929 Philadelphia Athletics.

Athletes face many obstacles. Even those who have the talent to reach the highest level of play confront major challenges:

The risk of injury, which is always present and has ended many promising careers.
The aging of the body, accompanied by the inevitable erosion of physical skills.
Questions about whether their commitment to succeed matches their physical ability.

Time and again Quinn (aging) and Ehmke (injuries and commitment) faced and overcame these challenges. Had there been a Comeback Player of the Year Award when Ehmke and Quinn played, each would have been in contention several seasons.

Beginning as far back as 1912, when he was twenty-nine years old (and thought to be only twenty-seven), Quinn was told he was too old and on the downward side (if not at the end) of his career. Yet for the next twenty years he proved his critics wrong. Because of his determination, work ethic, positive outlook on life, and physical conditioning, he continued to excel. In his midthirties, then his late thirties, and then into his forties and on to fifty, he overcame the naysayers. When Quinn finally retired in 1933, after pitching his last game at the age of fifty, this "Methuselah of the Mound" owned numerous longevity records, some of which remain his to this day.

Ehmke battled arm trouble and poor health through much of his career. Like Quinn, he was dismissed by the experts and from his teams, only to return and excel. One of his managers, Ty Cobb, sneered at what he felt was Ehmke's lack of drive, and the two men had fierce battles when they later were on opposing teams. Ehmke compensated for his physical problems with the innovative use of new pitches and pitching motions. He persevered through the physical ailments and capped his career with a record-breaking performance in the 1929 World Series, one that still ranks among baseball's most memorable.

Both men played in the Federal League when that upstart group was challenging Organized Baseball, and both were spurned by the established Major Leagues when the Federal League disbanded after the 1915 season. Moreover, both were at the center of disputes over which Major League team owned their rights. One of those conflicts had far-reaching consequences for the leadership of Organized Baseball.

Jack Quinn and Howard Ehmke dealt with the doubters and the adversity by pushing forward. They played for some great managers. One of these stood taller than the others, a man who is considered one of the greatest judges of talent ever: Connie Mack. In the mid-1920s, when these two pitchers were written off by almost everyone, Mack saw the strength and potential of the aging Quinn and the sore-armed Ehmke. They rewarded him with key contributions as Mack's Philadelphia Athletics rose to the top of the baseball world. They showed the world they could still pitch.

ACKNOWLEDGMENTS

We want to thank Rob Taylor, our editor at the University of Nebraska Press, for his ongoing faith in our research and writing, and his assistant, Courtney Ochsner, for her support with the myriad of details that brought this book to fruition. We also are grateful for the foreword that Pat Williams provided. We thank our readers for their input: John Zinn, Gary Sarnoff, and especially Gabriel Schechter, who served as both reader and fact-checker. Gabriel did two separate reviews of the manuscript and provided many pages of suggestions and corrections.

The following people were generous with their time and knowledge: Judy Cash, Rick Huhn, Ian Kahanowitz, Jim Leeke, Norman Macht, John Matthew IV, Jennifer McCord, Jerry Nechal, Brian Richards, Richard Smiley, Bob Warrington, Bob Wiggins, and Marshall Wright. The members of the Society for American Baseball Research (SABR) continue to be an invaluable resource for expertise on baseball history. *Retrosheet*, led by David Smith, allowed us to examine countless box scores and even play-by-plays of games from a century ago. *Baseball-Reference*, led by Sean Forman, is our go-to database for Major and Minor League statistics.

The support of Jack Quinn's and Howard Ehmke's family members has been invaluable. Laurie Athmann and Lois Nevinski, grandnieces of Quinn, and Sheryl Lucas, grandniece of Ehmke, provided insight into and stories about the men, as well as remarkable photographs. Special thanks to the microform rooms of the Boston Public Library; the Carnegie Library in Connellsville, Pennsylvania; the Detroit Public Library; the New York Public Library; and the Free Library of Philadelphia for the microfilm that allowed us to get contemporary accounts and quotes that enrich this book.

We have assembled unique photographs, not only from the Quinn and Ehmke families but also from other collections. Dennis Goldstein once again has provided us with many seldom-seen photos, and coauthor Steve Steinberg drew on his collection. We also want to thank Mark Macrae; Michael Mumby; Paul Reiferson; the National Baseball Hall of Fame Library of Cooperstown, New York; the Chicago History Museum; the Garland County Historical Society of Hot Springs, Arkansas; the Leslie Jones Collection at the Boston Public Library; and the Special Collections at the Temple University libraries. These people and organizations help Jack Quinn and Howard Ehmke come alive on these pages. Our sincere thanks to all of them.

COMEBACK PITCHERS

Prologue

May 28, 1924. Connie Mack's Philadelphia Athletics had just split a home doubleheader with the lowly Boston Red Sox. This season had not started as Mack had expected. After seven consecutive seasons of last-place finishes, his Athletics had finally started to move up, to seventh place in 1922 and to sixth in 1923. Nineteen twenty-four was supposed to have continued that progression after Mack acquired Minor League hitting sensation Al Simmons from Milwaukee and promising first baseman Joe Hauser, who had by then emerged as a slugger. But after splitting their first twelve games, the A's went into a tailspin and dropped to last place. The May 28 split put their record at 12-20.

The Red Sox had gone in a very different direction, one that was the talk of the baseball world. After taking over last place from Philadelphia in 1922 and 1923, they were now in first place with a 20-12 record. The new ownership group that had bought out Harry Frazee in the summer of 1923 made many changes in personnel that seemed to be paying off. Two players they had not replaced in the pitching rotation, Ehmke and Quinn, continued to deliver.

It was an afternoon of high drama and pitching excellence in Shibe Park. Mack's starting pitchers were Dennis Burns and Roy Meeker, a pair of journeymen who would each win only eight games in his career. They pitched well, but Mack was more interested in the Red Sox pitchers who opposed them, veterans Howard Ehmke and Jack Quinn. They had piqued his interest for some time now, and today's games only intensified that interest.

Ehmke had been traded by the Detroit Tigers to the Red Sox after the 1922 season, primarily because of Tigers manager Ty Cobb's frustration with Ehmke's seeming indifference. The impassive pitcher did not project the intensity that Cobb expected of his men. Ehmke flourished in his new surroundings. He won twenty games in 1923 for a Boston team that won only sixty-one.

Ehmke had a baffling array of deliveries, underhand and sidearm, as well as the traditional overhand form. In the first game on May 28, he took a 1–0 one-hitter into the ninth inning, when a two-out home run gave the Athletics an improbable 2–1 win. "Ibsen could not have provided a more pulse-racing, breathtaking climax," wrote one Philadelphia reporter.[1] The usually unemotional Ehmke never even turned to watch the flight of the ball and threw his glove all the way to the dugout. It was the first time the A's had beaten him since he had been traded to Boston after the 1922 season. Eight straight times he had come out on top, including three shutouts and one no-hitter.

The veteran Quinn was one of the game's few remaining spitball pitchers. He had reached the Major Leagues in 1909 with the New York Yankees, who traded him in 1912 and reacquired him amid controversy in 1919. The Yankees unloaded the aging hurler a second time after they won the 1921 American League pennant. As a member of the Red Sox, Quinn had beaten his old club eight times since then, including a 1–0 win near the end of the 1922 season that almost denied the Yankees the pennant.

Quinn won the second game of the doubleheader, 1–0, to salvage the split for the Red Sox on the road. A home run was again the difference, though this one came by the game's leadoff hitter rather than the last batter of the game. Quinn, thought to be thirty-six years old, was now actually thirty-eight. Yet he continued to baffle opposing hitters with his spitball and confound sportswriters and fans with his performance.

It is not known precisely when Connie Mack first conceived of the idea of acquiring Howard Ehmke and Jack Quinn. But the events of May 28, 1924, surely reinforced in his mind that these two veterans were not done. They had both proved the naysayers wrong. They could still pitch.

1

Jack Quinn, Man of Mystery

Jack Quinn's life was shrouded in mystery. His date and place of birth were enduring enigmas and topics of conversation throughout his career and for decades to follow. Quinn contributed to the mystery with his vagueness and love of storytelling. Philadelphia sportswriter Stoney McLinn wrote in 1930, "Unconsciously, we believe, Ol' Jack stumbled over the fact that his age could become a matter of Nation-wide curiosity. So he shrouded the year of his birth in a veil of mystery that had everybody guessing. . . . The age mystery threw around him a blanket of color that kept him in the major arena."[1]

Sportswriters told their readers that his family came from Wales, Ireland, Poland, or even Russia, depending on Quinn's most recent comments on the topic. He usually accepted his own place of birth as somewhere in northeastern Pennsylvania coal country. On various governmental documents he listed his last name as "Picus"; his place of birth as either Hazelton or Mahanoy City, Pennsylvania; and his date of birth as July 5 in either 1883, 1884, or 1885.[2] In 1924 Quinn said, "I am a lot of things which nobody knows, and a lot of things which they knows [sic] about me ain't so."[3]

Will Wedge of the *New York Sun* wrote in 1924, "At present there is nearly as much dispute about Quinn's age as there is about his nationality."[4] That confusion continued for the rest of his life. Quinn's obituary in the *Sporting News* stated that he had taken part in the 1898 Spanish-American War.[5] Father John Whitney Evans, a Quinn family friend who researched the ballplayer's life, wrote, "Jack Quinn seemed to be living what spies call a cover story." He appropriately titled the paper he delivered in 1994 "Jack Quinn: Stitching a Baseball Legend."[6]

Columnist Joe Williams always took Quinn's stories with a healthy dose of skepticism. He jokingly told of reports that Quinn was Paul Revere's stable boy.[7] He wrote that Quinn "may also have enjoyed bamboozling members of the Fourth Estate. Of course, there is also the possibility that his memories were blurred."[8]

The more likely possibility is that Jack Quinn did not know where or when he was born. Almost a decade of genealogical research culminated in a paper presented by Michael Scott, a Quinn relative by marriage, in 2007 and published a year later.[9] Scott concluded that Quinn never "told" because he never knew. Scott pointed out that when Quinn applied for a Social Security card and a Delayed Birth Certificate, he was unable to give the name of his mother. Scott's research involved family members, various official records, and even a genealogist in Slovakia who found the record of Quinn's July 6, 1883, baptism—five days after his birth—at a Greek Orthodox church in Stefurov, Slovakia.[10]

The Quinn family's story is part of the mass migration of East Europeans to the United States in the late nineteenth century. Quinn's father, Michael Pajkos, was born in Stefurov, a town in the Slovakian region of the Austro-Hungarian Empire, in 1851. Michael's three siblings died in early childhood, and his father died in 1853. He and his wife, Maria, were of Rusyn ethnicity and baptized in the Greek Orthodox Church.[11] Their first three children were born between 1876 and 1881, and all had died by 1882. Their fourth child, Joannes (Janos or John), the future Jack Quinn, was born on July 1, 1883.[12]

Living conditions in the Slovakian region of the Austro-Hungarian Empire were abysmal for the lower classes since the nobility owned most of the land.[13] They were particularly harsh for non-Austro-Hungarians in the empire. Slovak emigration, which started after 1880, was driven by economics and oppression and was part of the "new immigration" (of East Europeans to the United States).[14]

Improved rail lines provided more access from Eastern Europe to German ports, and newer, faster turbine-powered ships made more frequent Atlantic crossings. Transatlantic steamship companies made the bulk of their income from the transport of immigrants.[15] U.S. anthracite mining companies, in turn, had arrangements with shipping firms whereby they provided free passage to America for men who would work in the mines.

Historian William Kashatus noted that the immigrants who were arriving to work in the coal mines of Pennsylvania were coming to a life only marginally better than the one they had in Eastern Europe.[16] They had to live in company housing and shop in company stores. And the work was far more dangerous than farming the land in Slovakia. "Increasingly, these Eastern Europeans became the backbone of the anthracite region. . . . The power of the coal companies was near absolute, being firmly rooted in a medieval-like institution of servitude. . . . Few of those who did survive escaped the dreaded black lung disease, suffering a fate more terrible than death itself."[17]

Anthracite coal was concentrated in eastern Pennsylvania. Coal historian Walter Licht has written, "The coal is prized because it burns longer and produces less acid rain pollutants since it has a high carbon and low sulfur content. But what makes this brittle and lustrous rock, often known as black diamond, so hard and pure is that it is often deeper and under greater pressure than other forms of coal, which also explains why it is expensive and dangerous to extract." Since 1870 these mines have accounted for more than thirty thousand deaths.[18]

Driven by the tragedy of losing three children in infancy, Jack's parents decided to emigrate. The passenger manifest of the ss *Suevia*, which arrived in New York from Hamburg, Germany, on June 18, 1884, listed Michael and Maria Paichus and their one-year-old son, Janos, from Hungary. Maria died only a few months later. Michael worked long hours in the mines and likely had a caregiver provided by the local ethnic community who looked after little Janos. This was likely Anastasia Tzar, the woman Michael married three years later in St. Michael's Ukrainian Catholic Church in Shenandoah, Pennsylvania.[19]

Lee Allen, the historian of the Baseball Hall of Fame in Cooperstown, seemed to clear up the enigma of Quinn's origin decades ago. In 1967 he revealed that he had located the July 5, 1884, baptismal certificate of Jack Quinn and that the baptism took place in a Pennsylvania church.[20] But after Allen's death two years later, that document vanished and has never again been located.

How can Allen's assertion be squared with Michael Scott's findings about Stefurov? The probable answer is that Michael Pajkos wanted a baptismal record for his infant son from a U.S. church. Less than three weeks after the family arrived in America and around the first birthday of baby Janos, he was given a "conditional" baptism.[21]

Michael and Anastasia had four children of their own. Their children and grandchildren, Jack's half-nieces and -nephews, related that Jack was the outcast child. His stepmother did not want to hear talk of Jack's mother, Maria, and Michael went along. At the age of nine or ten, Jack took a job in the mines as a breaker boy.[22] This was common for male youngsters in a mining family; the extra pay was needed to eke out a subsistence.[23]

Jack Quinn often told the story of his harrowing escape from a mine fire deep underground: "I can't tell how long I kept coming through the smoke. . . . I never went back to work in the mines."[24] Hall of Fame pitcher Ed Walsh, whose career started five years before Quinn's and who grew up in the town of Plains, less than sixty miles from Pottsville, where the Quinn family lived at the turn of the century, spoke of the lifeline that baseball provided to the fortunate and talented few men in coal country: "The shadow of the coal mines was on me, and I used to say to myself, 'It is make good or back to the mines,' and I certainly didn't want to go back to life in the underground."[25]

With unhappy home and work situations, Quinn decided to leave home while in his midteens. He does not appear in the 1900 census data of the Pajkos household in Pottsville, where his father and stepmother lived with their four children. He hopped a rail car and went as far west as Montana and then worked his way back to western Pennsylvania, where he settled around Dunbar and Connellsville, less than sixty miles south of Pittsburgh.

Quinn held various jobs that demanded and developed physical strength. He explained: "As a boy I worked in a blacksmith shop near Dunbar, PA. Working twelve hours a day at the forge made me hard as nails, and that strength built up in my youth has stood by me all through my later years."[26] He often told the story of getting off the train in Dunbar on a July 4, wandering over to a ballgame in progress, and making a perfect long throw of an errant ball back to home plate. "I was strong as an ox then and could throw pretty smart."[27] The toss so impressed the manager of the Dunbar club that he asked Quinn to pitch the game that afternoon against nearby rival Connellsville, with a $5 payday for a win and $2.50 for a loss. "I figured, 'What the hell?' I was hungry and without a dollar to my name. So I took him up on it,"

Quinn said.[28] He won the game, and inquiries about the "mysterious kid pitcher" started swirling about.

This chance encounter with baseball gave Jack Quinn his start in the national pastime. It certainly beat swinging a pick ax deep in a mine. Philadelphia sportswriter James Isaminger wrote, "In northeastern Pennsylvania, baseball and anthracite are synonymous. Those boys who delve into the bowels of the earth to snatch black diamonds from their beds . . . have no loose or idle idea about the game for the game's sake."[29]

Quinn often pointed out, "I had to fight to make my way. I got help from no one."[30] New York sportswriter Frank O'Neill later wrote, "The story of his development is pretty much on the order of one of Horatio Alger's novels."[31]

2

From Town Ball to the Big Leagues

Jack Quinn's pitching career before he entered Organized Baseball is lost to history. *Baseball-Reference* lists his first Minor League season as 1907, with Macon of the South Atlantic League. Other accounts confirm his pitching with Connellsville of the Pennsylvania State League for three or four seasons, starting in 1903.[1] Because that club and league were not affiliated with Organized Baseball, its records did not appear in the annual editions of the *Reach Guide* or the *Spalding Guide*. Baseball's governing body considered all such unaffiliated teams and leagues as "outlaws."[2]

Whether Jack Quinn was as young as fourteen years old when he got off the train in Dunbar that July 4, he probably started playing ball no later than 1900, when he was not part of the Picus household in that year's census. So what was he doing those years, before 1903? By Quinn's own accounts, he first played ball only once or twice a week while he held down regular jobs not only as a blacksmith but also in a brickyard and a boiler factory.[3] Some of his clubs may have been semi-pro teams, not professional ones.[4]

His biggest payday in those early years, said Quinn, was for Connellsville against the Pullman AC, a Philadelphia athletic club. "I got 60 bucks for that game. Gee, I thought it was a windfall. When they handed me those 60 plunkers I thought to myself, 'Holy smokes, if there's that much money in playing ball here, I can make a living out of this game without any trouble.' So I stuck around Connellsville and that part of the country for six or seven years."[5]

Just when he changed his name to Quinn and moved "Picus" (an Americanization of "Pajkos") to his middle name is unclear. Some accounts say he played under the name of Johnson in his early years.[6] Just why he changed his name—and changed it to Quinn—is more easily understood. There were hardly any East European ballplayers in the early twentieth century and very few Major Leaguers from that region even in the 1910s.[7] The first ballplayers from that part of Europe experienced discrimination and often Anglicized their name to be more readily accepted.[8] Social and urban historian Steven Riess has noted, "Because they thought so many players had Irish-sounding names, the public saw baseball as an Irish-dominated occupation."[9]

The game was indeed dominated by the Irish, who constituted a large portion of the mid-nineteenth-century immigration into the United States. Riess wrote, "The Irish familiarity with the sport and their opportunities to play the game proficiently enabled them to achieve great success in baseball. . . . By comparison, the new immigrant groups [from Eastern and Southern Europe] had very little success in breaking into the Major Leagues during this period."[10] By 1907, when he was pitching for Macon, John Picus had become Jack Quinn.

In 1907 former big league manager Bill Armour took over the Toledo Mud Hens of the American Association, as part owner, president, and manager.[11] In early March he signed Quinn and soon loaned him to the Macon Brigands, a Class C club in the South Atlantic League, for whom Quinn won six games.[12] Just a week after a *Sporting Life* reporter wrote of him, "When in shape, no pitcher has anything on him," Quinn tossed a one-hitter against Savannah.[13] More than twenty years later Quinn reminisced, "I breezed into Macon and blew out with a sore thumb."[14]

Quinn had a salary dispute with his manager at Macon, Perry Lipe, who did not pay him when he was sidelined with the injury for a couple of weeks. Quinn left the club and returned to his hometown of Pottsville, where he finished the summer pitching for that club's entry in the unaffiliated Atlantic League. Quinn was now flirting with professional danger: not only had he jumped his Macon team, but he then had also played for an outlaw team. It was one thing to do so before he started Organized Baseball, pre-1907. It was quite another to do so now, after Toledo had signed him.

Quinn laid out his case in a letter to John E. Bruce, the secretary of the National Commission: "I have pitched for seven years for Dunbar, Connellsville, Mt. Pleasant, Ursina, Berlin, Washington, and Pottsville, all in Pennsylvania." He suggested the National Commission check with any of those clubs, and it would discover he was not a troublemaker.

Defending himself against charges that he was "a drunkard, stubborn, independent," he wrote, "I still remain the same old Jack."[15] Quinn suffered no long-term penalty because he continued in Organized Ball the following year, but it is unclear if he recovered his salary.

Bill Armour was still interested in him and put Quinn on Toledo's reserve list for 1908.[16] But now Quinn's status got both complicated and controversial—and not for the last time. A few sentences in *Sporting Life* in January 1908 noted that Quinn had signed with the National League's Philadelphia Phillies. The National Commission overruled that move and gave "sole title to player J. J. Quinn, . . . under the name of Jack Picus" to Toledo. His claim of bad treatment by Macon (and by extension, Toledo, who had loaned him out) was ruled "unfounded."[17]

Quinn started the 1908 season with the Mud Hens. He appeared in a few games for the club before he was let go.[18] He said that Armour released him for "thumbing his curve" and told him he would never succeed as a pitcher.[19] Years later Quinn admitted, "He was right. I never would have been a pitcher with that 'sore thumb.'"[20]

Perhaps it was then that Quinn started to throw the spitball. In one account, he said Armour's criticism led him to develop the new pitch.[21] However, in other accounts, he said he had a sore arm at the end of the 1908 season: "Every time I tried to throw a curve ball, a terrible pain shot up my arm from the elbow to my shoulder. . . . Gee, I didn't know what to do." Then a Pottsville player showed him how to throw the pitch: "Well, I slobbered all over myself practicing that ball all during the fall, and I got so I could throw it pretty good."[22] It is likely this occurred late in 1907, not 1908, when he had no arm trouble.

Soon Quinn's "wet one" became quite dry, as he moistened just the ends of his fingers. Veteran sportswriter Sam Crane described it this way: "Jack is very dainty in his work with the freak ball, as he only delicately wets the leather."[23] And, unlike most spitball pitchers, he did not use tobacco juice or the bark of the slippery elm tree to generate saliva. "Sometimes there's enough perspiration on my hand to suffice," he explained later in his career.[24]

After Toledo released him, Quinn again returned to Pottsville—he said he was homesick and reconnected with his parents—where he claimed he won twenty of twenty-four decisions by July 4.[25] His Macon

1. Pottsville, Pennsylvania, in the coal-mining region where Jack Quinn grew up, had a team in the independent Atlantic League in 1907–8. Quinn played for the club both seasons. Quinn, seated on the ground, likely learned to throw the spitball from a Pottsville teammate. *Family of Jack Quinn.*

manager, Perry Lipe, was now the skipper of the Richmond Colts of the Virginia League (Class C) and had no hard feelings against Quinn. The two men put the previous year's dispute aside. This would be a propitious career move for Quinn. Richmond would propel him to the Major Leagues.

Quinn did not join the Colts until late July. He tossed a shutout against Danville, Richmond's main rival for the pennant, on July 28, and one-hit them four days later. In late August he went the distance in a thirteen-inning 0–0 game that was called because of darkness. He tossed a no-hitter against Norfolk on August 27.

Twenty years later Quinn said the last game of the 1908 season gave him his greatest baseball thrill: "When I walked out the door [onto the field], everybody in the park opened up on the noise. I walked in space all the way over to the bench. They had me so excited I hardly knew if I was walking on the ground or in the air."[26] He said he beat

Danville's Marty Walsh, Ed's brother, 2–1, to help Richmond win the pennant by one game.

Unfortunately Quinn's memory failed him, or his storytelling enhanced the memory. First off, Richmond had already clinched the 1908 Virginia League pennant; the Colts finished 12½ games ahead of Danville. The Labor Day doubleheader did draw huge crowds. Ten thousand fans showed up for the morning game, when Richmond's Dutch Revelle (not Quinn) beat Walsh, 2–1.[27] Quinn pitched the second game before fifteen thousand fans; it ended as a 1–1 tie after ten innings.[28] No wonder John Kieran of the *New York Times* said of Quinn's life story, "Undoubtedly, this is a matter for the Historical Research Society."[29]

Quinn started sixteen games for Richmond and won fourteen of them, without a loss. His earned run average was a sparkling 1.10. By the end of the summer he recalled that "Quinn for Governor" and "Quinn for Mayor" signs were all over town.[30] In September the New York Yankees drafted him, and their scout, Arthur Irwin, signed him. In one communication National Commission secretary Bruce confirmed the Yankees' signing of "pitcher Quinn, alias Picus, alias Johnson."[31] Irwin had an assist from former Yankees pitcher Al Orth, who had won twenty-seven games for the 1906 Yankees and managed the Lynchburg club of the Virginia League briefly in 1908. Orth predicted Quinn would be a sensation: "He is a wonder. He is the double of [nineteenth-century Hall of Fame pitcher] Amos Rusie on his best days. He has a graceful delivery, a great turn of speed, and is as fine a slow ball pitcher as I have ever seen. Moreover, he has a wonder of a spitter which he sometimes uses in a pinch."[32]

Yankees coach and former catcher Duke Farrell and New York sportswriter Mark Roth also compared Quinn to Rusie, who was known for his fastball, as was Quinn in his early career. A Richmond reporter wrote that Quinn's pitches in his no-hitter "had the speed of an 18-inch Krupp gun projectile, and his delivery was as full of action as the fire of a Gatling gun."[33] The comparison to the "Hoosier Thunderbolt," as Rusie was known, may have referred only to his fastball. Yet Quinn had a large assortment of pitches. A reporter for the *New York Sun* described the rookie this way: "He has a delivery that is a cross between that of [New York Giants pitcher] Joe McGinnity and Amos Rusie. His

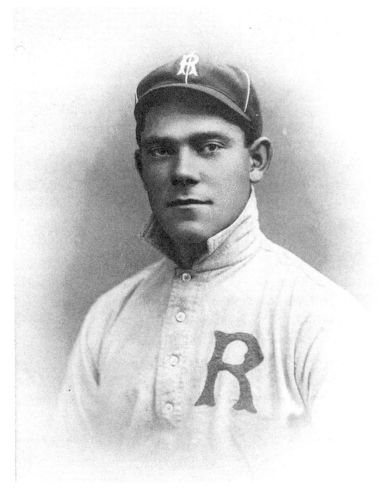

2. Jack Quinn's undefeated 1908 season with Richmond led the Colts to the Virginia League pennant and propelled Quinn to the Major Leagues. The Yankees bought his contract that fall, based in large part on the recommendation of Lynchburg manager Al Orth. Orth led the American League with twenty-seven wins for the 1906 Yankees and would be Quinn's teammate on the 1909 club. *Family of Jack Quinn.*

curves are quick, sharp and wide, while his control is remarkable. He has phenomenal speed and a puzzling slow ball, and above all he is the possessor of a cool head and iron nerve."[34] No wonder a New York sportswriter wrote in April 1909, "[Yankees manager George] Stallings is in high glee over the performance of the Richmond phenom."[35]

3

"I've Never Seen a Greater Pitcher Anywhere!"

The 1909 New York Yankees were a team in transition. They had two of the game's greatest players, but thirty-seven-year-old Willie Keeler, with more than 2,800 hits and a .345 career batting average, and spitball pitcher Jack Chesbro, who won forty-one games for the club in 1904, were nearing the end of their careers. The Yankees were also a team with dissension not far from the surface. Star first baseman Hal Chase had walked out on the club the previous September, when he was not selected to replace manager Clark Griffith. And truculent infielder Kid Elberfeld, whom co-owner Frank Farrell had chosen instead, was unhappy that Elberfeld had been replaced this season by George Stallings.[1]

In addition, the club had a major setback even before the season began. Early in spring training Chase, who had returned to the team, came down with smallpox, a deadly disease at the time. He was quarantined for a month in what was called a "pest house" in Augusta, Georgia.[2] The U.S. surgeon general sent public health doctors to intercept the Yankees' train to New York in Lynchburg, Virginia; everyone was vaccinated, a necessity that caused many of the players to have sore arms, and their clothes and equipment were fumigated. No one else on the club contracted the disease, but Chase did not return until May 3.

Into this mix came a fiery new manager, George Stallings. Yankees historian Jim Reisler wrote, "Stallings' hallmarks were supreme confidence, a good rapport with his players, and iron discipline. . . . Stallings was intense, hot-tempered, and spectacularly foul-mouthed on the diamond."[3] A half-century later Jimmy Austin, an exuberant rookie third baseman that season, told historian Lawrence Ritter, "Talk about cussing. Golly, he had 'em all beat."[4]

Another rookie on that 1909 club was the far less exuberant pitcher Jack Quinn, whose reputation for reticence was getting well established.

One story conveys this as well as any. A couple of his teammates were out drinking one night. "They stood and debated as to whether a third figure in the darkness was Jack Quinn or a cigar store wooden Indian. One of them interrogated the figure and reported back. 'He didn't say a single word.' 'Then it must be Quinn.'"[5]

Stallings and Quinn quickly made their marks on astute observers of the game. The team's pitching coach, Duke Farrell (no relation to team co-owner Frank Farrell), remarked early that season, "I will tip my hat to him as being the best manager I have met in my baseball career, and it has been a long one."[6] After Quinn won his first two Major League starts, giving up only two runs in eighteen innings, Farrell raved about "the Richmond phenom," and reporter Mark Roth noted, "His break into fast company has been so marked that Stallings has put a lock and chain on him."[7]

Joe Vila, a veteran New York sportswriter of two decades, was not easily impressed or prone to praise an unproven youngster.[8] But even he could not hold back on his opinion of the young pitcher from Richmond:

And Jack Quinn! Is he good? Is water wet? You bet! Why, kind sirs, this Quinn person is a jewel, a solitaire, a find of priceless value. . . . An iron man and a wonderful curve artist, who has mastered the intricacies of the spit ball until he has opposing batters at his mercy. I've never seen a greater pitcher anywhere! No, I'm not joshing! No more confident, skillful young box artist ever came out of the minor leagues. . . . He has the physique of a [wrestler Billy] Sandow, the arm of a blacksmith, the head of a philosopher and the nerve of a champion prize fighter! . . . If this iron man does not turn out to be the greatest find in years, then I'll be ready to treat all the correspondents of the *Sporting News* to new hats.[9]

Quinn's quiet confidence was evident early on. Before his first start, against the Washington Senators, he bet his teammates fifty-cent cigars that he would win. He collected on those bets.[10] Ed Grillo of the *Washington Post* wrote, "Quinn, judged on his work yesterday, is about as clever a youngster as has ever broken into fast company. . . . He had

3. Rookie Jack Quinn impressed observers from the start of spring training in Macon, Georgia, in 1909. He helped the Yankees' new manager, George Stallings, lift the club from last place to a fifth-place finish that year. Quinn was referred to as the "Richmond phenom" and a pitcher with "supreme confidence in himself." His origins were already a mystery: a Hearst reporter described him as "the Hungarian Irishman." *Steve Steinberg Collection.*

great speed, a spitball of which he had absolute control, and plenty of nerve behind it all."[11] Quinn's fastball and slow ball drew raves during his rookie season, but those were not his only weapons. Al Orth, now his teammate, said the rookie had the best spitball he had ever seen.[12]

After posting a 2-13 record for the Yankees in 1908, Orth was released in August and took over as manager of the Virginia League's Lynchburg Shoemakers in time to follow Quinn's sensational month with

Richmond. Stallings brought Orth back to New York, not for his pitching but for his pinch-hitting. Orth was a career .273 hitter with twelve home runs, a large number for the Deadball Era. He hit .265 in 1909, far above the American League's .244 average.[13]

Despite his early success, Quinn had long periods of inactivity his first season. He pitched only once in June and did not pitch the last two weeks of July, while he dealt with attacks of quinsy, an inflammation of the throat.[14] He returned to action with nine innings of strong relief against the Browns on August 3 and picked up the extra-inning victory. He appeared in twenty-three games, split almost equally between starts and relief appearances, and posted a 9-5 record. His 1.97 earned run average was a full half-run below the league average. Also promising was the team's 74-77 record, an improvement of twenty-three wins from 1908.

Both Quinn and the Yankees built on the promise of 1909 the following season. Chesbro (retired), Keeler (released and signed by the Giants), and Elberfeld (sold to Washington) were gone. The club finished May with a 23-10 record, capped off by Quinn's second win, a four-hitter against Senators pitcher Walter Johnson. That win pushed his record to 6-3. His spitter was especially good that day. A Washington reporter wrote, "Without any of the motion that is used by a drop ball pitcher, he was speeding the ball to the plate, or almost to it, when it would tumble toward the earth with as much rapidity as if a ton of coal had fallen on it from the top story of a skyscraper."[15] Even Quinn said his spitter had rarely been so effective.

Economy of motion was a trademark of Quinn's pitching style from early in his career, and he would later credit it as an important element in his longevity. He often compared his minimal windup and short stride to tossing stones as a youngster; that childhood activity helped him develop his pitching motion.[16]

Another signature trait of Quinn's pitching was his calm and steadiness on the mound. Years later he told F. C. Lane, the editor of *Baseball Magazine*, "Pitching is like any other work. You can make hard work of it if you want to, by getting nervous and fidgety, or you can get through a lot of work without much trouble if you will take your time and keep cool. . . . I never found that getting excited would help any."[17]

4. This spring 1910 Yankees team photo gives no indication of the turmoil that would occur near the end of the season, when star first baseman Hal Chase (*third from left, top row*) orchestrated the removal of manager George Stallings (*middle row, sport coat and bow tie*), despite the club's progress. Jack Quinn is kneeling at the far right, behind the first row. Yankees scout Arthur Irwin, who was a National League infielder in the 1880s and signed Quinn, is in the top row, far right. *Family of Jack Quinn.*

There was at least one instance when Quinn did seem to get a bad case of nerves. It occurred in Cleveland on August 3, 1910, when he took a 2–0 lead into the bottom of the eighth inning. "Picus the Pole, who is Jack Quinn on the payroll," wrote a reporter for *Sporting Life*, "had a fit of baseball intoxication."[18] With runners on first and second, a wild pitch moved them up. Then after his catcher, Lou Criger, yelled at him (just what Criger said was not reported), Quinn appeared rattled and threw another wild pitch. He followed by giving up a walk and two hits. Four runs were soon in, and a sparkling shutout had become a 4–2 loss.[19]

That the writer had called him "Picus the Pole" is an indication that the mystery of Quinn's origin was already present early in his career. The great fiction writer, Charles Van Loan, writing for the *New York American*, referred to him as "the Hungarian Irishman."[20] Another writer said that his real name was Picus and that he was Polish, but he was not "crazy of being classed with [pitcher Harry] Coveleskie [*sic*]."[21]

Another big reason for the Yankees' success in 1910 was their sensational rookie pitcher, Russ Ford. The twenty-seven-year-old Canadian put together a 26-6 record and a 1.65 earned run average with his devastating "spitball." But was his pitch really a spitter, as he claimed? Mark Roth wrote after Ford won his twenty-second game, "Only one man in the whole world knows that secret, and he is Russ Ford. . . . Whatever it is, it's a mystery."[22] It took a few years before he and his pitch were exposed. It was an emery ball. He had inserted a piece of emery paper (similar to sandpaper) in his glove, with which he was doctoring the ball.

The Yankees were knocked out of first place on June 16, a game Quinn left after he was hit on his left wrist by a Napoleon "Nap" Lajoie line drive. It was feared the wrist was fractured, but it was just a bad bruise.[23] The Philadelphia Athletics then put a serious crimp in the Yankees' season by sweeping four doubleheaders from them in the space of twelve days in late June and early July. "If the New York Yankees ever expect to regain the lead in the American League pennant race again," wrote a *New York Times* reporter, "they had better cut out playing double headers with the Athletics."[24]

It was a low point for Quinn too. He entered July with a 9-3 record and pitched only one inning on both July 1 and July 2, taking two of those eight losses.[25] Almost twenty years later Joe Vila revealed that Quinn was convinced he could not beat the 1910 A's, who would win the World Series that year. He complained of a "lame arm" whenever it was his turn to start against them. Quinn started seventeen more games that year—none against the Athletics.[26]

A couple of months later Quinn started against Walter Johnson in Washington. Since joining the Yankees, he had beaten the Senators eight times, without a loss. He had a no-hitter for five innings, but Washington rallied for a 2–1 win. New York was still nineteen games above .500 and remained in third place.

Sportswriter Fred Lieb wrote upon Hal Chase's death that he was "a player equipped by nature to be one of the game's immortals" yet was "more or less of a stormy petrel" his entire career.[27] Ballplayers and reporters raved about his fielding. Mark Roth wrote that he "can play first base the way Paderewski does the piano."[28]

In his *New Bill James Historical Baseball Abstract* James wrote, "No one ever saw [Chase] play without being left gasping for adjectives."[29] Here are a few comments from a writer for the *New York American* after a game in the spring of 1910: "He was like a Mercury, fast as a flash of light and as sure as fate. . . . He made two of the grandest stops, two all but impossible stops, ever seen on a ball field, and he made them so artistically that everybody gasped. The Hal Chase brand doesn't need any protection from the copyright law, because there can be no plagiarists."[30]

When George Stallings joined the Yankees, he said, "Chase is the best-looking ballplayer I ever saw in all my life, and I had Lajoie when he was at his best."[31] But Chase had a dark side. Charges that he was throwing ballgames first arose in 1908.[32] Chase was working to undermine his manager, with the goal of taking over the helm of the club himself. He had the ear of co-owner Frank Farrell. Initially almost all the players were in Stallings's corner. "Chase stands almost singlehanded in his fight against Stallings," wrote a reporter for the *American*.[33]

Things came to a head on September 19, after a 1–0 loss to Chicago. Quinn pitched a brilliant three-hitter, but Chase made some mistakes, including crowding into Quinn when he was fielding a bunt. Chase also called for a hit and run during three separate at bats and then did not make contact with the ball. Twice he failed to swing at "perfect strikes," and the third time, in the words of the *Sporting Life* writer, he "swung indolently a foot under the pitch."[34]

Stallings accused Chase of "carelessness or willful indifference" and almost came to blows with him on the bus after the game.[35] *Sporting Life* did not hold back: "Hal Chase, the pet of his employer, and the grandstand managers who have all but wrecked Frank Farrell's club year after year, has quit cold."[36]

The matter ended up in the hands of Farrell, who met separately with both Stallings and Chase. Before Farrell decided what to do, he consulted with the American League's president, Ban Johnson, who had a deep hatred of Stallings.[37]

In one of the greatest personnel blunders ever by a baseball owner, Farrell not only backed his star player over his manager, but he also appointed Chase as the new manager. "Chase is too great a player to have his reputation blackened by such charges," he declared.[38] Ban Johnson chimed in, "Stallings has utterly failed in his accusations against Chase. He tried to besmirch the character of a sterling player. Anybody who knows Hal Chase knows that he is not guilty of the accusations against him."[39] Johnson would avoid confronting gambling's influence on baseball until the repercussions from the 1919 Black Sox scandal permanently eroded his power.

Chase would repeatedly be suspected of fixing games over the next decade. Two more respected men who managed him, Frank Chance and Christy Mathewson, would openly accuse him, and a third, John McGraw, while mostly silent, would have the same opinion.[40]

Perhaps realizing Farrell had made the wrong decision, a *New York Tribune* writer tried to justify it this way: "First basemen like Chase are born, not made, and not born very often either, while managers like Stallings, so successful as he has been, can be replaced."[41]

Stallings departed New York in a dignified manner. "I had hoped to be the man at the helm of the Gotham flag winner, but the fates were against me. I am satisfied to stand on my record," he said. He noted that he had built the club into a "machine" that could compete for a championship, and "Now that they see what I have made of them, I think every man except two are for me strong."[42]

From the start of spring training in 1909, Stallings had been impressed with Quinn. The spitballer's 18-12 record and 2.37 earned run average in 1910 seemed to confirm his manager's belief that he had "one of the greatest pitchers in the business."[43] Their paths would cross again in a few years.

4

Quinn Gets Sent Down and
Brought Back Up

In one of his signature "It Seems to Me" columns, written in 1926, journalist Heywood Broun recalled what it was like to be a fan of the New York American League team in its early years. A fighter for the underdog in his adult life, Broun learned how it felt to be the "bottom dog" when he was a schoolboy:

In those days there were Giants. We who loved the American Leaguers made up a small minority ever so loyal. To be a Yankee fan was an exclusive thing, like belonging to the Brook or being a collector of rare Japanese prints.[1] Part of our joy lay in the fact that most of mankind despised us and went to the Polo Grounds. The very intimacy of the park [Hilltop Park, at Broadway, between 165th and 168th Streets] itself promoted intimacy.

Our Highlanders were champions of nothing but a lost cause and beleaguered in a gross city of roundheads. Sometimes I think my whole life was altered wholly by the fact that the old Yankees did not win very much. My mind was more plastic then, and I came to think of winning as a little vulgar. To be trampled on for the right was glorious.[2]

After the 1910 season Jack Quinn married his hometown girlfriend, Georgiana Lambert, in a Methodist Episcopal church in Pottsville.[3] He gave his name on the marriage certificate as "John James Picus." "They stole a march on their friends and had a quiet wedding," wrote a Philadelphia reporter before the couple went to Tampa for their honeymoon.[4]

Quinn slumped in 1911, as did many of the Yankees. He posted an 8-10 record, and his earned run average rose to 3.76, almost a half-run above the league average. With promising young starters Ray Caldwell and Ray Fisher available and with Russ Ford still doing well, 60 percent of Quinn's forty appearances were out of the bullpen.

But there were bright spots. Quinn led the league in games finished with nineteen. He was "the same Jonah" to the Senators and Walter Johnson on April 24, when he beat them, 5–3.[5] And he beat Johnson again two months later, when Washington's feeble hitting was reflected in Quinn's eight assists. When the Yankees won sixteen of nineteen games in a stretch in June, Damon Runyon wrote that the way they were playing "would drag an invalid from a bed of pain."[6]

On July 25 Quinn went six innings against the St. Louis Browns and did not get a decision. The Yankees rallied for a 3–2 win, and Runyon raved about Hal Chase's key play in the field. On a line drive toward the right field line, "where nothing but triples drop," the first baseman made a "copyrighted stab at apparent impossibility . . . leaped into the air, like he had been sitting on a suddenly released spring."[7]

Yet by early August, when the Yankees were just above .500, Runyon questioned whether Chase was "temperamentally suited for the leadership of men."[8] Chase had become increasingly weary of the dual responsibilities of a player-manager. While he remained the manager for the full season, he had already offered his resignation that summer. "I have found out," he said upon his resignation, "that a star ballplayer who can get a big salary is foolish to take up the responsibilities of leading a ballclub."[9]

When Chase passed away in 1947, Arthur Daley of the *New York Times* wrote, "One of the most gifted operatives the sport ever possessed, [Chase] lacked the moral stability to become the all-time standout his talents ordained. Quietly he was eased out of the game, departing under a cloud. Yet that cloud never has completely obscured his greatness."[10]

On September 11 the Philadelphia Athletics drove New York pitcher Hippo Vaughn out of the game in the second inning. Like Quinn, Vaughn, in his second year, was struggling this season; he too would finish with an 8-10 record. With the Yankees down 4–1, Chase assigned Quinn the long relief role, but he gave up eight runs. The only bright spot was his first career home run, a massive blast off future Hall of Famer Chief Bender.[11] "Certainly, few balls have ever been hit harder

5. This studio photo captures the camaraderie of ballplayers of an earlier era. Jack Quinn is with catcher Walter Blair (*center*) and pitcher Lew Brockett. Blair caught in eighty-four games for the 1911 Yankees but hit only .194. He reunited with Quinn at Rochester late in the 1912 season. His baseball career ended with Buffalo of the Federal League in 1915. Brockett never realized the potential of his twenty-three-win season with Buffalo of the International League in 1906 and won only thirteen Major League games. *Family of Jack Quinn.*

than that upon which Virginia Jack leaned for as clean a home run as ever graced a big-league score," wrote a reporter for the *New York American.* "Only once before in the history of the game on the crag had such a long swat been seen."[12]

Late in the season the Yankees put Quinn and Vaughn on waivers. A *Sporting Life* reporter wrote that while both had shown "flashes of form," they seemed to have "outlived their usefulness on the Hilltop squad."[13] The club was probably not ready to release them just yet but wanted to see what interest was out there. There was not much, and both men remained with New York.

The Yankees hired Harry Wolverton as their new manager for 1912. He had a nondescript eight-year Major League career. But he had developed a fine reputation as the manager of the Oakland Oaks of the Pacific Coast League in 1910 and 1911. Unfortunately the 1912 season for both the Yankees and Jack Quinn, as well as for Wolverton, was not successful. Wolverton managed to keep his job for the entire season, despite his club's 50-102 record. Neither Quinn nor Vaughn was so fortunate.[14]

Wolverton came into a difficult situation. W. J. MacBeth wrote in the *Sporting News*, "No manager was handicapped worse to begin with. . . . [Wolverton] took hold of a club that was absolutely demoralized as anything that ever played for major league patronage" under Chase.[15] The Yankees also struggled with a rash of injuries. Their best hitter of 1911, outfielder Birdie Cree, suffered a broken wrist on June 29 and missed the rest of the season.[16]

Before the season began, Wolverton warned both Quinn and Vaughn that they had to improve if they were going to remain with the club. After the Yankees opened the season with three straight losses, Quinn dropped a 1–0 decision to Washington's Walter Johnson. Just eleven days later "the Senatorial hoodoo" beat the Senators with a four-hitter. It was only New York's second win in ten games. It was also Quinn's thirteenth career win in eighteen decisions against Washington.

On May 11 at Hilltop Park, the usually unflappable Quinn was ejected by umpire Silk O'Loughlin and then suspended for arguing balls and strikes and throwing his glove at the umpire. O'Loughlin also tossed Wolverton and two other Yankees. A barrage of soda bottles then came his way, in a scene that had never occurred at this ballpark, according to the *New York Times* reporter. "The rumpus blew the smoldering wrath of the rabid fans into a blaze." The reporter added that if O'Loughlin had no bumps on his head, it was because "the wild-eyed hoodlums" were bad shots.[17]

Quinn's outburst was very much out of character for him. *Retro-sheet*'s evolving database shows he was ejected only one other time in his career, and that was in 1913 for bench jockeying. Years later Quinn spoke of his approach to the game, one that he adhered to virtually his entire career: "You can't pitch your best when you're 'tightened up,' and worry is bound to do that. I've never worried since I've been in baseball."[18]

Before the suspension Quinn was pitching "better than ever before."[19] But something happened to him after he returned to duty. In his next eleven appearances, by far the worst stretch of his entire career, he gave up more than one run per inning.[20] With injuries to other pitchers, Wolverton just left Quinn on the mound in several games, even after they were out of reach. Typical of this stretch of games was Damon Runyon's description of one of the beatings: "Quinn was simply mas-sacred. . . . Certainly Jack had nothing. The further he went, the worse he looked."[21]

Just what was bothering Jack Quinn that day and why he performed so poorly in the following weeks is not known. There was no mention of an injury or personal problem in any newspaper account we reviewed. Sometimes history does not reveal all the answers, and mysteries remain.

Quinn's final game as a Yankee was a July 4 loss to the Senators, 12–1, in which he pitched the entire game. He finished his shortened season with an ugly 5.79 earned run average. July 4 was also the day Wolverton levied his first fine and suspension, on wayward pitcher Ray Caldwell, for "not keeping in condition." When the Yankees' manager released Hippo Vaughn ten days later, the *New York Press* warned it was only the beginning of an overhaul of the club.[22] The team was 31½ games out of first place at the time.

The Yankees had an informal working relationship with the Roches-ter Hustlers of the International League, a league at the highest level of the Minors (Class Double-A).[23] Some former Yankees, including team-mates of Quinn, were on that club.[24] The manager, John Ganzel, was a regular on the 1903 Yankees in their inaugural season.[25] The past three seasons, he had led the Hustlers to three straight pennants.[26] Ganzel wanted to strengthen his pitching staff for the stretch run in 1912. At the same time Wolverton had his eye on Rochester shortstop Tommy

McMillan, and the Minor League partner in this club relationship felt obligated to let him go.[27]

A reporter for the *New York American* wrote what seemed to be Quinn's baseball obituary: "Few major league pitchers have proved such a sad disappointment as Quinn did to the Yankees. . . . Last season he was practically valueless to the club. This season he showed nothing of class." The reporter called Quinn part of New York's "dead wood" but then held out a glimmer of hope. He noted that the spitball pitcher had complained of lack of work. "If idleness is really the curse of his present baseball existence, he is likely to be back in the big show before long."[28]

Quinn immediately paid dividends for Rochester as he won four games in his first two weeks. A reporter who covered the league's Baltimore Orioles wrote, "Jack Quinn looks every inch a ball player. He is graceful and has the physique of an athlete. Quinn's strong point never was to hold his adversaries to few hits, but in the pinches, he seldom fails to tighten up. He had Baltimore at his mercy."[29] Quinn capped off the season with a two-hit shutout of Montreal. In his brief 1912 Rochester stint, he started twelve games and posted an 8-4 record with a 2.33 earned run average. He had stopped the slide in his career.

If it was work that Quinn needed, Ganzel gave it to him in 1913. And the pitcher responded. By the end of August he had started thirty-one games, pitched 267⅔ innings, and earned nineteen wins. After he beat Baltimore on Opening Day, a Rochester reporter wrote about his signature pitches: "Quinn's chief stock in trade, naturally, was his spitball, which broke nicely for him nine times out of ten. Just as effective was his slow ball, with a fake spitter effect."[30] Five weeks later Quinn went the distance in a thirteen-inning win over Jersey City. "Quinn was as cool as a cucumber," wrote one sportswriter about Quinn's presence on the mound.[31]

After shutting out Baltimore on August 10, with a career day at the plate—a home run and two triples—Quinn pitched both ends of a doubleheader against league-leading Newark. He went the distance in both and suffered two frustrating defeats, 1–0 and 3–2.[32] In his next start, on August 19, he earned a win, though it took a while. It was a twelve-inning, one-hit 2–1 victory.

After this spectacular stretch of pitching, a writer for the *Sporting News* declared, "Put pitcher Jack Quinn's name in the Hall of Fame."[33] While the Baseball Hall of Fame in Cooperstown would not come into existence for more than two decades, the phrase was often used when a ballplayer did something special. It was usually mentioned after a pitcher tossed a no-hitter.

George Stallings had been following the progress of his former pitcher. After he left the Yankees, Stallings managed the Buffalo Bisons, in the same league as Rochester, for two years. Late in the 1912 season Stallings saw Quinn pitch firsthand and surely kept abreast of Quinn's 1913 season. Stallings had been hired to manage the Boston Braves this season, and he led them to eighteen more wins than in 1912.

Following four years of last-place finishes in the National League, the Braves had climbed to fifth. As Stallings looked toward 1914, he wanted to reach higher. And he saw Jack Quinn in his plans. On August 22, 1913, he purchased the thirty-year-old pitcher from Rochester. Just over a year after he had been sent down to the Minors, Quinn was coming back up. He had proven his New York critics wrong. He could still pitch.

Stallings also purchased two of Quinn's Rochester teammates in late August, first baseman Butch Schmidt and outfielder Guy Zinn. Like Quinn, they were top performers with the Hustlers that season.[34] These deals signaled that the working relationship between the Yankees and the Hustlers had come to an end, and Stallings was certainly pleased to obtain them rather than lose them to the team that had let him go so unceremoniously three years earlier.[35] Prior to the deals' being finalized, one Rochester sportswriter pointed out that Stallings was "fast building a winner."[36] When the deals were consummated, he wrote that the new partnership between the Braves and the Hustlers was "the talk of the baseball world."[37]

Rochester sold Quinn for more money than the club would have received had he been drafted by a Major League team a month later.[38] More important for manager Ganzel, his Hustlers would also receive some Braves players the following season, in return for sending them Quinn, Schmidt, and Zinn. However, their names would not be revealed until they cleared waivers after the season.[39]

6. In late August 1913 Jack Quinn (*middle row, third from right*) joined the Boston Braves, where he was reunited with his former Yankees manager, George Stallings (*wearing suit*). Stallings appreciated Quinn's remarkable control. "It would just be my luck," he once said, "to go to hell and be chained to a bases-on-balls pitcher." Future Hall of Fame shortstop Rabbit Maranville is in the front row, far right. Quinn jumped to the Federal League in 1914 and missed the Braves' spectacular rise to the world championship that season. *Family of Jack Quinn.*

In his five weeks with the Braves at the end of the 1913 season, Quinn's overall performance was mixed. His fine control was becoming a feature of his outings: In 56⅓ innings he walked only seven men. He easily won his National League debut, 6–1, over Brooklyn. A week later he gave up only three hits and dropped a 1–0 decision, on an error by his shortstop, Rabbit Maranville. In his next start the Phillies drove him out of the box after he retired only one man.

When Quinn beat the Pirates in Pittsburgh a week later, two hundred noisy fans from Dunbar, where his career began, presented him with a silver chest before the game. He rewarded them by stealing home in his one-run victory. After the game they put him on their shoulders and circled the field.[40] In all, he started seven games and completed six for Boston, although he gave up five or six runs in three of those starts. The 1914 season would determine whether he could pitch consistently.

Sometimes a new manager concludes that the material he inherited is simply not good enough. A story, likely apocryphal, reflects on both Stallings and the weak Braves team he inherited. He yelled at one point during a game, "Bonehead, get up there and hit!" Six players arose and picked up their bats.[41] Yet as intense and unforgiving as Stallings was during a game, a Boston sportswriter noted that "The Big Chief is a lenient man when it comes to giving a ballplayer a thorough chance to make good."[42] Ernest Lanigan of the *Sporting News* wrote of Stallings's "celebrated system of trying out 19-year-old kids and 40-year-old vets."[43]

Stallings was determined to build a winner; he went through many players to find the right talent and mix. In his first season as Boston's manager, 1913, he used thirty-seven players, and in 1914 he used forty-six, large numbers for the Deadball Era.[44] In his history of Stallings's 1914 Braves, Charles Alexander pointed out that by early September 1913, only six men who had been on Stallings's opening-day roster were still with the club.[45] Quinn was one of the new players. Philadelphia Athletics star second baseman Eddie Collins felt Quinn's decline in New York occurred "after the Big Chief [Stallings] got out."[46] The 1914 season offered great promise for Quinn, reunited with his manager, and for the Boston Braves.

5

Howard Ehmke Hailed as Another Walter Johnson

The word "phenom," an abbreviation of "phenomenon," is defined as "a highly skilled or impressive person; a performing wonder."[1] Invariably referring to someone young, "phenom" has been a part of the language of baseball since as early as 1890. Phenoms do not come around very often, but when they do, they lend a special excitement to the game. Jack Quinn's 14-0 record with the Richmond Colts of the Virginia League in 1908 and impressive wins in his first two Major League starts with the 1909 Yankees had led to his being called "the Richmond phenom."

But when a phenom arrives directly out of high school and immediately begins to excel, a certain aura is attached to him. Such was the case with Howard Ehmke, a pitcher for the Pacific Coast League's Los Angeles Angels who early in the 1914 season was being hailed as a phenom by the West Coast press. Labeled "Kid Ehmke, the boy wonder," he quickly became the darling of Los Angeles baseball fans.

Yet despite both being labeled "phenoms," the circumstances in which Quinn and Ehmke grew up were almost diametrically opposed. Quinn grew up in a poor and unsettled immigrant family; he had little if any formal education and spent much of his youth working in the Pennsylvania coal mines. Howard John Ehmke, born in Silver Creek, New York, on April 24, 1894, was the sixth son and ninth child of the eleven children (seven sons and four daughters) born to Charles and Julia Ehmke.[2] Ehmke's father, Charles Gottlieb Ehmke, was born in Prussia in 1855.[3] He came to the United States in 1857, along with his mother and one brother. As has been the oft-repeated pattern throughout the history of the immigration of families, fathers came first. Charles's father had emigrated a year earlier, in 1856, and after getting settled in America, he sent for his family.

7. An Ehmke family portrait from the early 1900s taken in their hometown of Silver Creek, New York. Howard is in the middle row, far right. His eldest brother, Frank, an attorney and his guide in early contract negotiations, is in the top row, far left. *Family of Howard Ehmke.*

Ehmke's mother, Julia Emily (Green) Ehmke, was born February 7, 1856, in Chautauqua County. Julia's parents, Carl Johan and Caroline Hällgren, had emigrated with three sons from Kalmar County in the Swedish province of Småland, in 1852.[4] Julia was the second child in her family born in America. Charles and Julia were married in 1875. The next year, Julia gave birth to their first child.

While Ehmke was German on his father's side and Swedish on his mother's side, the press overwhelmingly referred to him as being Swedish or Nordic or Scandinavian. America's being at war with Germany— first diplomatically and then for real—in the early years of his career may have been responsible for that.

Ehmke was the star pitcher at Silver Creek High School. Silver Creek, a village about thirty miles south of Buffalo, is on the shores of Lake Erie in the town of Hanover in western New York's Chautauqua County. A year earlier, in 1913, Silver Creek High had defeated Jamestown High,

8. Howard Ehmke (*right*), who had six brothers and four sisters, is pictured with his brother Charlie and Charlie's wife, Blanche, in front of a barn on the Ehmke family property in Silver Creek, New York. *Family of Howard Ehmke.*

3–1, to win the high school baseball championship of western New York. Ehmke was the pitcher and also drove in all three runs.

Prior to entering high school, Ehmke had been a standout pitcher in grade school and for an amateur team that competed in and around Silver Creek. Ehmke, called "Bob" by all who knew him, came from a large family, as noted. Several of his older brothers had also starred for Silver Creek High and for the local baseball team, known as the Horseshoers. "My coach at high school said I had the ideal built [*sic*] for a pitcher, and I went ahead and paid as much attention to baseball as I did to my studies," Ehmke said in a 1928 interview. His father was strict about his children going to school, he recalled: "He made us study hard and at the same time he made me swing an axe in the forest until my hands were like leather. During summer vacations I used to contract with the town for the removal of dead trees."[5]

Henry P. Edwards, a reporter for the *Cleveland Plain Dealer*, wrote about his memories of playing against Ehmke when they were teenagers.[6] Edwards said he had always been an Ehmke fan and explained why. He had grown up in Dunkirk, New York, and played for a team known as the Dunkirk Defenders. Edwards remembered the Defenders' great rivalry with the team from Silver Lake, twelve miles away, the Silver Creek Horseshoers.

There always seemed to be an Ehmke on hand to pitch for them. There was Frank Ehmke who pitched for Brown University, played tackle on the eleven, was the heavyweight collegiate champion wrestler and a hammer thrower and shot putter. Then came Brother Charley, a lightweight wrestler who also pitched and played in the infield for Brown as well as for the Horseshoers. Then came Brother Harry. He pitched a no-hit game for Brown against Lehigh about twenty-five years ago and also proved a puzzle for adversaries of the Horseshoers. He played fullback for Brown. Next came Brother Lester. He was not a pitcher, however, but did win the middleweight wrestling championship of Brown and proved a very fair outfielder. Next in line was Howard Ehmke, and he had distinguished himself in high school by pitching a 1 to 0 game against Jamestown, N.Y. high, striking out twenty-three men with the first baseman having but one putout, a pop fly.[7]

The Silver Creek locals expected that their star athlete, Howard, would follow in his brothers' footsteps by pitching for Brown University and, later in the summer, for the Horseshoers. But the trajectory of Ehmke's future was changed in 1911, when his brother Frank accepted a position as the director of physical education and a teacher of mathematics at Glendale High School near Los Angeles.[8] Meanwhile, Ehmke's father, a heretofore successful mill owner, began neglecting the mill while he became involved with harness racing as an owner and driver. When this caused a rift with his wife, Frank persuaded his mother to come to sunny California to get away from the cold New York winters and to alleviate her stressful home situation.[9]

Ehmke was scheduled to graduate from Silver Creek High School in 1913. Instead he left without a diploma and enrolled at Glendale High, where he continued his studies in preparation for taking the entrance exams at Brown. He attended Glendale High from January to April 1914, living with Frank in Glendale. He played on the school's basketball team that winter and pitched in some baseball practice games in the early spring.

Ehmke showed so much promise that Frank wrote to Major League managers Connie Mack and John McGraw, asking each to give his tall and lanky young brother a trial. McGraw did not reply, but Mack wrote that he would keep the young man in mind and possibly give him a chance when he became a little older.[10] True to his word, Mack did give Ehmke a chance, but it would not come until 1926, when he acquired him in a trade. There is no way of knowing if Mack remembered that long ago letter from Frank Ehmke.

According to one source, the Pacific Coast League's Venice Tigers had the first chance at signing Ehmke. George Banks, the former pocket billiards champion of the Pacific coast, said Ehmke spoke to him that spring about getting a trial with one of the Pacific Coast League clubs. In addition to working at the Tigers' ballpark, Banks helped run W. L. "Happy" Hogan's billiard parlors. Banks introduced Ehmke to Hogan, who also served as the manager of the Tigers. But Hogan showed no interest in the youngster, claiming his pitching staff was oversupplied with veterans. "I was turned down without even a chance to show what I could do in batting practice," Ehmke said.[11] It would be the first time, but far from the last, that a club gave up on him prematurely.

Banks then brought Ehmke to the camp of the rival Los Angeles Angels and introduced him to Boots Weber, a former Chicago newspaperman who had recently become the Angels' secretary. Weber had seen Ehmke pitch for Glendale against other high schools and recommended him to Frank "Pop" Dillon, the Angels' manager. Dillon agreed to give Ehmke a trial during morning batting practice. Future Major Leaguer Ernie Johnson hit the first ball Ehmke threw on a line over the second baseman. But after that the Angels batted around a number of times without anyone making good contact.[12]

Dillon, who had a reputation for discovering and signing good pitchers, was so impressed he wanted to sign Ehmke before the workout session was completed.[13] A big league first baseman for five seasons (1899–1902, 1904), Dillon had managed the Angels since 1905 and played regularly for them until 1912. "An excellent judge of talent, he had little patience for those lacking it," wrote Pacific Coast League historian Dennis Snelling.[14] Ehmke held off signing, waiting to hear if McGraw's New York Giants or Mack's Philadelphia Athletics were interested in him.

Going from high school to the highest level of the Minor Leagues was a rare accomplishment, but Ehmke, with the confidence of youth, felt he was ready to compete at the Major League level.[15] Only when he realized the Giants and A's were not interested did he sign with the Angels.

On April 23, 1914, Dillon found an excellent time for Ehmke's professional debut. He brought him in to pitch against the San Francisco Seals, with the Angels already trailing, 9–0. On seeing the youngster's thin, gangly frame, many of the San Francisco fans greeted him with laughter. But when Ehmke started retiring one Seals batter after another and demonstrating the skills of a veteran in holding close the rare runner who reached base, the laughter ended.

It was an impressive performance, praised by Dillon and Angels owner Henry Berry. Once Ehmke learned some of the fine points of the game, said Berry, he will be a wonder. "He has the physique and the head and better than all, good control."[16]

The Angels fans' love of Ehmke took root on May 3, when he faced Venice in the afternoon portion of a Sunday doubleheader.[17] Venice won the morning game, giving the Tigers four straight victories over the Angels, before Ehmke, "a fuzzy-chinned boy who hasn't been playing professional ball long enough to have his name on file at league headquarters," beat them, 5–1.[18] He held the visiting Tigers to four hits, and only a pair of errors by his teammates prevented him from recording a shutout.

What made the win even more notable was Ehmke's mound opponent, Doc White, who had won 189 games in thirteen seasons in the Major Leagues, mostly with the Chicago White Sox. White had started his first year in the Pacific Coast League with six consecutive wins. "Just think of a mere stripling of a kid defeating a twirler, acknowledged as the best in the Coast league; a twirler who had spent 13 years or more in the big brush, where he defeated everything in sight," noted a reporter from the *San Bernardino Sun*.[19]

Los Angeles sportswriter H. M. Walker described Ehmke as "looking enough like Walter Johnson to be a brother and following closely the lines laid down" by the Washington ace.[20] Comparing a twenty-year-old, barely out of high school, to the greatest pitcher in the game could hardly be taken seriously; yet in Ehmke's early years comparisons to Johnson would be frequent.

Matt Gallagher of the *Los Angeles Evening Herald* described Ehmke as having "a cool, calculating brain, backed by a right arm of Damascus steel." Hollywood was coming into its own in 1914, and some movie men saw the local star pitcher as a fit subject. Gallagher described moving pictures of "Ehmke's delivery of his wonderfully fast underhand ball. He is shown beginning the pitch at the lower left. At the lower right the young pitcher has just let go of the speeding ball."[21]

People in Ehmke's hometown were following his career through the local newspaper, the *Silver Creek News*, which reprinted articles from the Los Angeles papers. One such reprint appeared in the paper's May 14 edition: "Howard Ehmke, that busher of recent origin, appears to be quite the talk of the town. . . . Ehmke is a New York person, having arrived here from there near the beginning of the present year. That he should have originated in 'New Y'wk' [*sic*] will not be held against him. Many others have done the same thing.[22] The kid has pitched two games and won them both. What more could a reasonable man ask? That is more than Walter Johnson accomplished in his first trial in Class AA company."[23]

On May 8 manager Dillon called on Ehmke in the eighth inning against the Portland Beavers, with the scored tied, 2–2. He responded with two scoreless innings, striking out the side in the eighth. When the Angels scored a run in the bottom of that inning, Ehmke was credited with the win. Two days later he beat the Beavers, 4–1, for his fourth win in a row. Number 5 came on May 15, when he shut out the Sacramento Wolves on three hits.

"What has young Ehmke got?" wondered a writer from the *Los Angeles Evening Herald* after Ehmke's five consecutive victories to start the season. "That is the question Pacific Coast League baseball fans have been asking each other since the young Glendale high school phenom started in the Coast league."[24]

One *Evening Herald* writer noted that Ehmke had an above average fastball, though it was not in Walter Johnson's class, while failing to add that neither was anybody else's. The writer called Ehmke's underhand fastball his best pitch, followed by his underhand curve ball. He also praised Ehmke's change of pace and his proficiency in mixing up his pitches to keep batters off stride. That skill, seldom found in young pitchers, was an early indication that Ehmke, barely twenty years old, had above average intelligence on the mound, an asset that would augment his physical talent as he grew older. "He has everything," said teammate Charlie Chech, a thirty-six-year-old pitcher who had spent four years in the Major Leagues.[25]

Ehmke continued to credit his brothers for his success. "I learned points from every one of my brothers," he said. "When I started out pitching I was as green as grass, but they were patient with me and soon I learned control. I realize that I have not obtained my full strength, but I believe I am capable of working in at least one game a week. I believe that baseball is just as much a profession as practicing law. There is more to it than the average fan imagines."[26]

It was becoming obvious that if Ehmke were to keeps up the pace he had set, he might not finish the season in the Pacific Coast League. Owner Berry was likely to sell him to a Major League team, probably Clark Griffith's Washington Senators, a club with whom the Angels had a working agreement.[27] Berry kept Griffith informed of Ehmke's early success; nevertheless, he claimed the working agreement did not bind him to sending all his talent to Washington.

With each win Ehmke's popularity with the local fans increased. In May he was voted most popular baseball player in a contest held at the Los Angeles Outing and Sportsman's show. On May 21 "that high school kid," as he was often referred to around the league, shut out the Seals, 1–0, for his sixth consecutive win. Moreover, he singled in the last of the eleventh inning to drive in the game's only run.[28] "Never before in the entire baseball world has there been a young pitcher raised from the cradle to the regular's berth in the same way as Ehmke," wrote Ernest A. Phillips in the *San Bernardino County Sun*.[29]

"Two runs scored off him in the last forty innings he has pitched constitute Ehmke's record," wrote Matt Gallagher. "Isn't that a mark of which even Walter Johnson would have been proud? . . . If Ehmke goes to Washington this fall, and—take the word of Cap Dillon, who has seen hundreds of heavers—he will be just as good there as he has been here."[30]

9. Twenty-year-old Howard Ehmke's great early success with the Pacific Coast League's Los Angeles Angels drew comparisons to Walter Johnson. "Experienced baseball men have pronounced Ehmke greater than Johnson at the same age," wrote *Los Angeles Times* columnist Harry A. Williams. *Mark Macrae Collection.*

Ehmke's early appearances were so impressive that they led his manager to believe he could develop into the greatest pitcher of all time. It also inspired veteran *Los Angeles Times* sportswriter and future Pacific Coast League president Harry A. Williams to move from reality to fantasy. If Ehmke was as good as he looked, wrote Williams, "he would be a second Walter Johnson, and then some." And if he were to pitch for the Senators in 1915, Williams continued, it would all but guarantee a pennant for Washington.[31] "Experienced baseball men have pronounced Ehmke greater than Johnson at the same age," Williams wrote. "Washington, it is believed, will have first claim on the youngster's services, as a result of its working agreement with the Los Angeles club."[32]

The Angels' arrangement with the Senators did not prevent other clubs from attempting to deal for the young phenom. "The fame of Howard Ehmke is not confined to the Pacific coast," wrote W. A. Reeve in the *Los Angeles Tribune*. "Major League clubs are already angling for the sensational kid hurler, and Berry has received from Pittsburgh an offer of $7,500 for the youngster. Berry promptly turned the bid down."[33]

Even Ty Cobb, the game's greatest hitter, believed Ehmke would be successful in the big leagues. The *Los Angeles Evening Herald* quoted Cobb as saying that "any underhand pitcher who can get something on the ball will prove a winner in the American League."[34]

At this point Ehmke's won-lost record was 6-0, with three shutouts; he never had been removed from any of his starts and had made three relief appearances. In addition to allowing only two runs in forty innings, he had not been scored on in the last twenty-seven.

According to Harry Williams, Ehmke had created the greatest furor felt in the Pacific Coast League since 1904, when future star first baseman Hal Chase joined the Angels fresh out of Santa Clara College.[35] "Chase was absolutely in a class by himself," Williams wrote, adding that "Ehmke begins to loom the same way."[36] All but three of the sixteen Major League teams made offers to the Angels for Ehmke, who had yet to lose a game. The offers reportedly ranged from $3,000 to $17,000, as well as the trading of as many as three players to Los Angeles.[37]

"I would not take $50,000 spot cash for Ehmke," said Henry Berry, explaining that if he sold Ehmke and the Angels did not win the pennant, he would never hear the end of it. "The fans would never forgive me. . . . And that would mean the loss of money, for in that case Venice might get all the patronage."[38] Manager Dillon said he was not the one to ask about such things: "That is a matter for Mr. Berry to decide. But my views coincide perfectly with his on Ehmke's valuation."[39]

Ehmke's focus remained on advancing his career, not on how much money the Angels would get for him. "I lack the baseball experience to talk in cash figures," he said. "Of course, I want to go to the big leagues, though. Every player who is conscientious wants to do that. But I couldn't say what I am worth. Mr. Dillon and Mr. Berry ought to know. They have seen me work."[40]

However high the estimates of his worth were, they were still much too low for his mother. "I don't know what fixes a man's value in baseball," she said, "but Howard is my son, and I wouldn't sell my interest in him for a million dollars."[41]

6

Ehmke's Tumultuous Season
Comes to an End

On May 7, 1914, at Portland, Howard Ehmke's season-opening winning streak reached seven when the Angels rallied for two ninth-inning runs to pull out a 6–5 victory. Ehmke had left for a pinch hitter in the top of the inning, and reliever Jack Ryan blanked the Beavers in the home half to preserve the victory. Ehmke had allowed only thirteen runs in his seven wins and six relief appearances and continued to be the most talked about player in the league.

While Ehmke's win streak attracted national attention, another Pacific Coast League pitcher was quietly compiling his own win streak. San Francisco left-hander Hub Pernoll, who had brief trials with the Detroit Tigers in 1910 and 1912, had begun the season with eight straight wins. But unlike the handsome, twenty-year-old, 6-foot-3, 180-pound Ehmke, Pernoll, twenty-six years old and a roly-poly 5 feet 8 inches and 175 pounds, had not captured the public's imagination.[1]

Yet an article in the *Sacramento Union* suggested that the fans throughout the league who were rooting for Ehmke to tie or break Pernoll's mark might not get their wish. The young Angels pitcher had been hit freely in win number 7 against Portland and again in his next two starts. "In his first eight appearances," noted the *Union*, "Ehmke allowed only thirteen runs and forty-two hits in fifty-five and one-third innings. In his last three appearances Ehmke has allowed fifteen runs and twenty-four hits in only fourteen innings."[2]

Ehmke seemed to regain his stride on June 9 with a 6–0 shutout of San Francisco, raising his record to 8-0 and tying Pernoll's win streak. "Howard Ehmke did it," wrote Matt Gallagher of the *Los Angeles Evening Herald.* "He stopped the tongues of the critics who have been claiming that he 'blew.'" Gallagher believed Ehmke's performance against the Seals "has proven to the Northerners that he is there with the goods."[3]

However, this would be the high point of the season for Ehmke, and before long the accolades would turn to criticism.

Ehmke's win streak ended at San Francisco five days later, when he lost to the Seals, 3–1. Four more losses followed in quick succession, including a 17–6 shellacking by Oakland, in which he lasted just 1⅓ innings and allowed eight runs and eight hits.

After losing five in a row, Ehmke finally got his ninth win, on July 9, against Sacramento. But his outings were mostly inconsistent after that, with a brief return to form in the final weeks of the season. While some attributed his slump to a lack of stamina and experience, team-mate Rube Ellis, an outfielder who had spent four years with the St. Louis Cardinals (1909–12), had a different explanation: "Ehmke's arm simply went dead on him during the season from overwork. Now he is showing more than at any time since joining the club."[4] He then added his name to those who were predicting greatness for the youngster. "I may be overestimating him," Ellis continued, "but I am willing to go on record as declaring that he will in time be the superior of Walter Johnson. He shows a lot more than Johnson did at his age.[5] Another year under [Angels manager Pop] Dillon will make him a finished pitcher, and he will then have the physical development to stand the strain of a hard Major League race. A lot of promising youngsters have been ruined by going to the majors before they were ripe."[6]

Ellis's concern that Ehmke was being rushed to the big leagues before he was ready was in response to the season-long speculation that the young pitcher would be joining Johnson on the 1915 Senators. "Is the Washington American League club to be blessed with two Walter Johnsons?" the *Sporting News* asked as early as the first week of June. The paper reported that experienced baseball men on the West Coast rated Ehmke a better pitcher than Johnson had been at the same age; manager Dillon still believed he would develop into the greatest pitcher of all time.[7]

Ehmke's height and wingspan made him an imposing figure on the mound. According to the *New York Evening Telegram*, his arm expansion was five or six inches longer than that of the average pitcher, and his hand was so big it could conceal a baseball. In the spring of 1913, it reported, Ehmke met Christy Mathewson and threw a few pitches for

10. Frank "Pop" Dillon managed the Pacific Coast League's Los Angeles Angels from 1909 to 1915. Dillon, who passed on signing Walter Johnson, cautioned Howard Ehmke against signing with Buffalo of the Federal League. "Next year he should he considerably stronger," Dillon said, "but not quite strong enough for the Major League grind." *Mark Macrae Collection.*

the great Giants hurler to evaluate. An impressed Mathewson wrote that Ehmke possessed everything needed to be an excellent pitcher: "He pitches among others an underhand ball, with a tremendous swing, which starts almost at the ground, rises steadily until nearing the plate, when it takes a quick jump with an outward turn."[8]

Two weeks later the *Evening Telegram* reported Washington was offering $20,000 for Ehmke. In addition to detailing his pitching accomplishments thus far this season, it stated: "Furthermore, he has so endeared himself to the fans of this California city that they say the manager will invite the severest censure if he sells the youthful player to any of the Major League teams which are now bidding for his services."[9]

Club president Henry Berry said he had rejected a big league club's offer of $20,000 for Ehmke (presumably from Washington's Clark Griffith).[10] "The offer called for immediate delivery, however," Berry said. "I could not afford to lay myself open to criticism for selling Ehmke in the middle of a hot fight for the pennant."[11] Nevertheless, Berry admitted it was practically settled that Ehmke would be going to the Washington club in the fall. "Washington can have Ehmke if it wants him," Berry announced on June 28. "Of course," he added some days later, "should anything befall Ehmke, Griffith might select another man."[12]

Meanwhile, Ehmke's midseason slump was adversely affecting the price the Angels could get for him. "One more cipher was knocked off the market price of Pop Dillon's $12,000 pitching wonder," wrote a reporter for the *Sacramento Union*.[13] The reporter's comment followed Ehmke's July 26 loss to the Sacramento Wolves and a previous July 14 drubbing by the Portland Beavers.

However, the advent of the Federal League in the 1914 season had given Ehmke and all other players added leverage in deciding where they would play.[14] On August 20, days after Berry's announcement, Ehmke, on the advice of Dillon, returned the contract Washington sent him, unsigned. He, his brother Frank, and Dillon felt the Senators were not offering enough money.

Several weeks earlier Ehmke had received an offer from the Federal League calling for a salary of $700 a month plus a $1,000 signing bonus, although he denied the offer influenced his refusal of the Washington bid. An unsourced article in Ehmke's Hall of Fame file claimed his brother Frank had sent a telegram to Griffith on his behalf, asking for an annual salary of $4,500 and a bonus of $1,500. Griffith later received a telegram from manager Dillon saying Ehmke would likely be joining the Federal League.

Some friends advised Ehmke against a move to the new league. Because he had not fully demonstrated he was ready to pitch in the Major Leagues, they reasoned, it would be unwise to desert Organized Baseball at this time. After all, they said, if Ehmke did not succeed with the Senators, he could always return to Los Angeles for more experience. However, if he failed to succeed with the Federals, that league had no Minor League affiliates to which he could return.

Washington Post sportswriter Stanley P. Milliken appeared confident Griffith would land his man. "It is not likely that Ehmke will sign with the Federals or be lost to the Nationals," he wrote.[15] Ehmke's mother hoped to see him pitch for Washington in 1915. She said she and Howard's siblings "want him to be a great ballplayer, but we would rather have him be a good, clean, manly boy than the greatest player in the world."[16]

In addition to dealing with an uncertain future, Ehmke continued to struggle on the mound. After a 7–1 loss to Portland on September 9, the Portland battery of pitcher Harry Krause and catcher Gus Fisher suggested they knew what was responsible for Ehmke's poor pitching. According to their analysis, Ehmke threw too many "curved" balls. They claimed that "if he had a little more steam on his fast one and used it more, he would be a better pitcher." They further claimed they could tell what Ehmke would be throwing from his windup.[17]

Late in the season sportswriter Harry A. Williams predicted that Ehmke, along with several other young Coast Leaguers, had star potential. Angels outfielder Rube Ellis was still convinced Ehmke would fulfill that prediction: "I knew that the kid had stuff, and I am now more convinced than ever that he will prove to be one of the greatest pitchers of all time."[18]

Clubs in the six-team Pacific Coast League played more than two hundred games per season, a schedule that translated into a lot of work for each team's pitchers. Seven Angels pitchers appeared in thirty-five or more games in 1914, and five appeared in forty or more. Ehmke, whose record was 12-11, appeared in exactly forty, pitching 232 innings as a starter and a reliever.

Negotiations between Ehmke and Griffith had come to a halt. Ehmke had not heard a word from the Washington club since returning his contract unsigned. While joining the Federal League remained in play, it was still a league outside of Organized Baseball, whose rules made him the property of the Washington club. Should Ehmke fail to sign with the Senators, he risked being suspended.[19] Keeping this dynamic young pitcher out of baseball was an unpalatable option for Organized Baseball, so it began to look likely that some arrangement would be made whereby he would be allowed to remain another season with the Angels.[20]

Matt Gallagher reported that Pacific Coast League players were united in their belief that Ehmke should remain in the Minor Leagues at least one more year before moving up to the Majors.[21] Henry Berry agreed. In his opinion Ehmke did not yet have the physique to stand the strain of a Major League campaign.[22] Pop Dillon, Ehmke's manager this tumultuous season, summarized the young man's ups and downs while making a strong case for him to remain in Los Angeles:

> It is laughable the way some persons regard Ehmke. Some of the fans look upon him as an exploded phenom. Nothing could be more ridiculous. The lad had a good winning streak at the start of the season, and when he ran into a little bad luck, there were plenty to say that he was only a morning glory. They do not figure that he pitched good ball during most of his losing period. He regained his effectiveness toward the latter part of the season and helped save a number of games for us during that part of the year. . . . Ehmke realizes that if he plays ball in the Coast league next year, where he will he handled right, that he would be a better pitcher a year from now than if he spent the same time in the big league. The reason Ehmke made a poor showing in the middle part of the season was because his arm was too weak to stand the strain. I aimed to pitch him only one game a week, but once in a while, because the other pitchers were sick or injured, I was forced to send him in the game. He could not stand it. Next year he should be considerably stronger but not quite strong enough for the Major League grind.[23]

Whatever influence these pleas to stay in the Minor Leagues had on Ehmke is unknown, but as the year neared its end, he appeared to be leaning that way. The sticking point, as it so often is, was money. Ehmke, or perhaps brother Frank, wanted a higher salary than the Angels were willing or able to offer.

7

A Wasted Year for Howard Ehmke

From Washington in the east to Los Angeles in the west and places in between, most noticeably Buffalo, much of the off-season talk centered on where Howard Ehmke would call home in 1915. The attention paid to Ehmke's eventual landing spot seemed out of proportion for a twenty-year-old pitcher with just one season of Minor League experience. But his sensational first half had been one of the biggest stories of the 1914 season. And while he faded in the second half, three teams, in three different leagues, were clamoring to sign him. Each potential destination had pluses and minuses.

The Los Angeles Angels of the Pacific Coast League for whom Ehmke pitched in 1914, would allow him to further develop his raw talent and stamina and better prepare him for a future in the big leagues. The drawbacks of remaining in the league were his desire to move up to the Major Leagues and the Pacific Coast League's salary cap, which would prevent him from earning the money he and his lawyer-brother Frank believed he deserved.

The Washington Senators of the American League, who had claimed Ehmke as part of their working agreement with the Angels, were members of Organized Baseball and would give him a place in the Major Leagues. But they had offered him a contract he and Frank, as well as Angels manager Pop Dillon, felt was below his worth.

The Buffalo Blues of the Federal League, which was challenging Organized Baseball by offering existing Major Leaguers and promising Minor Leaguers higher salaries than their current employers were offering, were also interested in Ehmke.[1] The foremost downside of jumping to the Federal League was the very real possibility of the league's going out of business sooner rather than later. In addition, the Federal League had no Minor League structure. Should a player not succeed, there would be no place to send him for seasoning or development. Furthermore, should the league fold, there was no guarantee Organized Baseball would take the player back.

A column in the January 27, 1915, *Los Angeles Evening Herald* accentuated the drawbacks of Ehmke's signing with the Feds. We cannot know whether Ehmke read that article, but a few days later Matt Gallagher, in the same newspaper, reported that Dillon had all but convinced him to remain in the Pacific Coast League for another season. "It is a certainty that if the Federals are willing to pay a pitcher big money, they want value for their money," Dillon said. "He is still a youngster, and the Feds would take the heart out of him by overworking him during the spring training trip and the first few weeks of the season."[2]

Another factor that contributed to Ehmke's 1914 success, according to Dillon, was his ability to get along with his teammates: "He has a good disposition, and all the older players were anxious to show him the fine points of the game."[3] At the same time, the *Buffalo Evening News* was telling its readers that it was looking ever more likely that Ehmke would be returning to western New York: "The Buffalo Feds have made him an offer of $700 per month and a bonus of $1,000 for signing, and close friends say he will sign with the Feds."[4]

On February 3 Gallagher reported that Ehmke would leave for Buffalo the following day. Frank, now teaching in a Buffalo high school, had telegrammed his brother that the Federals had made a good offer and he should come east as soon as possible. So despite Dillon's misgivings, when Ehmke left for Buffalo on February 4, his former manager figured the odds of his signing with the Blues were high. "The lad is all right," said Dillon, lamenting the almost sure loss of his young pitcher, "and I would certainly like to have him with me this season. If the matter was left to him, I am sure he would stay on the Coast. However, his brother, who is handling his affairs, is looking out for the big money, so I guess he will go after it."[5]

Dillon conceded that a man should not be blamed for seeking a higher salary but added that Ehmke was "still only a kid and not fully developed."[6] His wish to keep Ehmke in Los Angeles went beyond their professional relationship, Dillon said: "My desire to keep him here is as much for personal reasons as anything else. I like the boy and would like to develop him. I understand him pretty well, and we are good friends. It is very seldom that a lad of his age with the success in the game that he has had, does not get the swell head."[7]

Sporting Life weighed in on the side of those who believed Ehmke was making a big mistake: "Young Ehmke pitched remarkable ball for Los Angeles in his first 10 games and then blew up entirely, being afflicted, it is said, with an exaggerated opinion of himself. He is only 18 [*sic*] years of age and undoubtedly will make a wonderful pitcher, but he appears to have been very badly advised in all of his dealings since he became a star.[8] A brother living in the East is taking charge of his affairs, and it would be unfortunate if a great pitcher should be ruined by poor handling, yet such appears to be the case."[9]

Ehmke made it official on February 13, when he signed a contract to pitch for Buffalo in 1915.[10] The *Sporting News* reported on February 18 that "the Washington Senators had lost out to the Federal League for the coveted Los Angeles schoolboy wonder, Howard Ehmke."[11] *Washington Post* sportswriter Stanley T. Milliken reacted with surprise and outrage at Ehmke's choice: "If this be so, then Ehmke should have his head examined, for he is making a move that may put an end to his baseball career. Ehmke was offered a contract by manager Griffith of the Nationals calling for a sum in advance of what an ordinary pitcher breaking into Major League baseball would receive."[12]

Milliken directed his fury at Ehmke for the youngster's refusal to sign with Washington for anything less than $6,000: "Great guns, what is baseball coming to when a busher demands such a salary before even giving the slightest inkling that he would make good. It has been rumored that the pitcher was influenced by his brother. If this be so, then a major league is really no place for pitcher Ehmke. There are a lot of temptations in the majors, and if Ehmke is so easily drawn aside, manager Griffith may pat himself on the back that he is without the services of this young man."[13]

Several weeks later, however, the team with "the services of this young man" was delighted to have him. Reporting from the Blues' training camp in Athens, Georgia, the correspondent covering the team for the *Buffalo Evening News* wrote, "If there ever was a youngster who gives promise of developing into a 'find,' the Buffalo Federals have him in Bob [*sic*] Ehmke, who appears to have everything that goes to make him a first-class major league twirler."[14] He predicted Ehmke would be one of the regulars on manager Larry Schlafly's pitching staff this year.[15] He went on to describe Ehmke's unusual pitching style, one that many batters found confusing: "Bob [sic] has a most bewildering delivery. His six feet, three-and-one-half inches standing in the pitcher's box is enough to scare any batter into swinging at anything that comes anywhere near the plate. When Ehmke takes his position on the mound, all set to deliver, he faces third base and has that long overhand swing, it being impossible to tell just when he is to release the ball. His graceful style of delivery is quite an asset to a pitcher."[16]

In response to reports that Clark Griffith was still after him, Ehmke, speaking from the Buffalo team's training camp, assured the Blues he was happy where he was. "Their terms are much better than those offered by the Washington club," he said, "and I am satisfied that the Federal League is the real Major League of the world."[17]

At one point during spring training, Schlafly had indicated he planned to nurse Ehmke along for a season before giving him a regular turn on the mound. But Ehmke had been pitching well in practice, and Schlafly saw a great future for him. As the 1915 regular season approached, it appeared Ehmke, Hugh Bedient (recruited from the Boston Red Sox), and Russ Ford would lead Buffalo's pitching staff. Ford, a former Yankees teammate of Jack Quinn, had gone 21-6 for Buffalo in 1914. He had taken Ehmke under his wing and predicted the youngster would have a sensational year. One of the secrets Ford was imparting to Ehmke was how to throw the "emery ball."[18] The use of this pitch was the primary reason for Ford's previous success with the 1910–11 Yankees and with the 1914 Blues.[19]

Umpire Bill Brennan, who left the National League to become the chief umpire for the Federal League, claimed in a 1917 interview he had warned Ehmke not to use the pitch. Ehmke complied, said Brennan, and soon realized he had more than enough good pitches to be successful.[20]

Newspapermen are free to float rumors or to repeat them. Following the 1915 season, columnist Harry Williams repeated two regarding Ehmke. Both involved the emery ball. He wrote that Ehmke's poor season was attributable to his not being allowed to throw the emery ball. This seems puzzling in light of Ehmke's suffering a sore arm and spending a good part of the season away from the team. Williams also claimed that one reason Ehmke had been reluctant to sign with Washington was because the American League had banned the emery ball, and the Federal League had not. However, after he signed with Buffalo, the Federal League had followed suit.[21] This too seems puzzling. Ehmke had never been accused of throwing the pitch with the Angels in 1914 and experimented with it only after being tutored by Russ Ford at the Blues' training camp.

In the Blues' final intra-squad game before heading north, Ehmke pitched for the regulars, who beat the bench players, 4–3. When the team broke camp, Schlafly announced that Ehmke would be in the Blues' regular rotation. But that was not to be, as Ehmke told a Detroit reporter in 1917: "The fourth day before the beginning of the season we were playing an exhibition game in Atlanta, Georgia, and I slipped in pitching and tore a ligament in my right elbow. That ended my pitching there."[22]

Not exactly. Over the years Ehmke would sometimes exaggerate the extent of his injuries, so if he had indeed torn a ligament, it healed amazingly quickly. Nevertheless, he was likely not completely healthy when he made his Major League debut on the second day of the season, a 7–5 loss to the Brooklyn Tip-Tops. Ehmke relieved starter Gene Krapp in the second inning and was removed after the fourth. In 2⅓ innings he gave up three hits, walked five, and hit two but allowed just two runs.

On April 24 Ehmke made his home debut in relief of Ford in a game won by Jack Quinn of the Baltimore Terrapins. While Ehmke was just starting his Major League career, Quinn was coming off a twenty-six-win season with Baltimore, and he was among the leaders in several Federal League pitching categories. Ehmke gave up two earned runs in 3⅔ innings but again was wild, walking four, as Baltimore pounded Buffalo, 10–4. Yet he made a favorable impression on the fans and the local press. "Time and a bit more experience are all that the Silver Creek lad needs to be placed among Schlafly's regulars," wrote the correspondent from the *Buffalo Express*.[23]

Following three brief scoreless relief appearances, Ehmke made his first Federal League start, on May 13, against the Pittsburgh Rebels at the Blues' home park, the International Fair Association Grounds. He failed to survive the second inning, yielding six runs and seven hits. At 8-19, the last-place Blues were already 10½ games behind the first-place Rebels.

When the Blues dropped to 13-28, following a doubleheader loss to Brooklyn on June 3, Schlafly was fired. Catcher Walter Blair split the two games he managed, and third baseman Harry Lord, a recent addition to the club, was a respectable 60-49 over the rest of the season. "I accepted terms from the Buffalo club because there were no other offers to accept," said the thirty-three-year-old Lord, a former captain of the Chicago White Sox.[24]

Hampered by the spring training elbow injury, Ehmke was of little use to the Blues. He spent a good part of July and August trying to rehabilitate his arm by pitching for an independent team in Johnsonburg, Pennsylvania, a town located 115 miles south of Buffalo.[25] After having pitched well at Johnsonburg, he returned to the Blues and started at St. Louis on September 24. In his second, and final, start of the season, Ehmke pitched five innings, allowing five hits and five runs (three earned) in a 6–1 loss. He finished the season with no wins, two losses, and a 5.53 earned run average. Overall he appeared in eighteen games and pitched just 53⅔ innings for the sixth-place Blues.

Ehmke's arm injury was the first serious one he suffered. There would be many more, large and small, that would impede his progress during his career. But until the accumulation of arm injuries that led to his retirement, he always bounced back, pronouncing himself ready to pitch.

8

Another Pitcher Joins the Outlaws

The Federal League was an independent midwestern Minor League that began operating in 1913; it was not part of Organized Baseball, which considered it an "outlaw" league. Four of its six teams were in Major League cities, but none were on the East Coast.[1] As 1914 approached, the league brought in deep-pocketed investors, many of whom were independently wealthy and far richer than most Major League team owners.[2] The league added two more teams, relocated one, and placed franchises in Baltimore, Brooklyn, and Buffalo.

The league's leaders announced they were going to challenge Organized Baseball's hegemony in 1914 and become the nation's third Major League. They would follow the model the American League had used in 1901 and 1902: raid the established leagues for star players with the lure of higher salaries. Such men and the high quality of play would establish the league's legitimacy in the eyes of baseball fans. The escalation of salaries in the bidding war for talent would force the established leagues to sue for peace and recognize the upstart league as an equal, as the National League had done with the American League in early 1903.[3]

Under Organized Baseball's reserve clause, a player was tied to his team for his entire career, even after his contract ended. This system, which would not come to an end until 1975, depressed salaries because a player could never consider competing offers from other clubs. Now, for the first time since 1902, players were free agents in a bidding war.

In his history of the Federal League, Robert Wiggins noted, "While Organized Baseball decried the outlaws as 'pretenders,' most of the nation's newspapers printed the Federals' scores and standings on an even footing with the two established Major Leagues. Ironically, the Major Leagues' combative campaigns against the Federal League in both the press and in the courts gave credibility to the newcomers, though Organized Baseball never publicly acknowledged the outlaws."[4]

Salaries skyrocketed, as did lawsuits, as the legality of the reserve clause was argued in court. Ultimately many of the game's biggest stars, from Walter Johnson to Ty Cobb, did not jump, but they used the new league as leverage to extract larger salaries and longer contracts from their existing clubs. Enough big names and recognized players did sign with the new league to get it rolling. Jack Quinn was one of them.

As Howard Ehmke would do a year later, Quinn gravitated to the upstart league for money. Both pitchers had offers from Major League clubs, but each saw an opportunity to secure larger salaries. Both were trying to make comebacks: Ehmke, from the disappointing second half of his 1914 season with Los Angeles, and Quinn, building on his comeback from Rochester with the Braves. But there was quite a contrast between the two pitchers. Quinn was an aging veteran of thirty when he made his move in 1914, while Ehmke was a decade younger when he joined the new league in 1915.

The Braves tendered Quinn a contract, he later said, that called for a salary lower than he had in Rochester, but that is questionable.[5] Whether he signed a 1914 Braves' contract, only wrote a letter in which he agreed to do so, or had simply verbally agreed to terms is unclear. In January a *New York Times* headline announced that Quinn had agreed to terms with Boston for the 1914 season.[6]

A month later sportswriters reported Quinn had signed with the Federal League's Baltimore Terrapins. Ned Hanlon, the celebrated manager of the National League's Baltimore Orioles (1892–98) and Brooklyn Superbas (1899–1905), was a major investor in the club. Quinn signed a three-year deal (as opposed to the one-year contracts that Major League clubs offered almost exclusively) for around $4,800 a year (with an advance of $3,500), as opposed to the annual salary of $3,600 Boston had offered.[7]

James Gaffney, the owner of the Braves, was outraged. His starting catcher, Bill Rariden, had also jumped to the Federal League. Gaffney claimed that James Gilmore, the new league's president, had agreed not to go after Quinn since he had already "accepted terms" with Boston. The two men almost came to blows at an attempted settlement meeting in New York that spring.[8]

11. Jack Quinn (*front row, second from right*) joined the upstart Federal League's Baltimore Terrapins in their 1914 inaugural season. As the players gathered for spring training in Southern Pines, North Carolina, they were a motley group, wearing a variety of uniforms from previous teams. Manager Otto Knabe (*back row, third from left*), a veteran second baseman of the Philadelphia Phillies, was an intense and scrappy player and leader. *Family of Jack Quinn.*

A huge Opening Day Baltimore crowd of more than twenty-seven thousand turned out to see Jack Quinn beat the Buffalo Blues, 3–2. Hungry for a Major League team since they lost their National League franchise in 1900 and their short-lived American League one in 1903, the fans hurled their seat cushions onto the field when the home team scored its first run. "Quinn worked like a wonderful machine, and his steadiness and cunning were particularly noticeable in the pinches," wrote Starr Matthews in the *Baltimore Sun*.[9]

That same day, April 13, Gaffney brought a $25,000 lawsuit against Gilmore and his league, the leaders of the Terrapins, and "John Picus, also known as Jack Quinn." Gaffney charged that the executives had "willfully, unlawfully, and maliciously planned and conspired to induce Picus, or Quinn, to violate his contract with the Bostons."[10] He later said Quinn had offered to return if Gaffney would pay the $3,500 advance back to Baltimore. Gaffney turned down that offer. "I want to teach the Federal League a lesson," he said, and he added, "I don't want Quinn as a player."[11] Braves manager George Stallings had threatened Quinn with arrest if he took the mound on Opening Day, but no police action materialized.[12]

In his next start Quinn beat the Brooklyn Tip-Tops by the same 3–2 score. His tenth-inning home run won the contest, and the jubilant fans carried him off the field. His shutout of St. Louis a couple of weeks later pushed the Terrapins to within a half-game of first place. Quinn beat the Chicago Whales on May 21 to give the 17-7 club a 4-game lead over the Whales. That same day Stallings's Braves won for only the fourth time against sixteen losses. No wonder a *Sporting Life* reporter noted, "We can realize Stallings' feelings every time he peeks at a box score which contains the name of Jack Quinn."[13]

All season long Baltimore battled for the league's top spot with Chicago (led by former Cubs star shortstop Joe Tinker as player-manager) and the Indianapolis Hoosiers (with future Hall of Fame outfielder Edd Roush).

On August 4, when Quinn beat Chicago at home, for his seventeenth victory against only six losses, the Terrapins climbed into a first-place tie with the Whales. A Chicago reporter noted that Baltimore fans were "completely wild" about their team, "and such rooting has not been heard outside of a world series."[14] But when Quinn beat them again on September 21, the Terrapins were already fading. They would finish in third place, 4½ games behind first-place Indianapolis.[15]

In his last start of the season Quinn had to leave after a line drive hit his pitching hand. He finished with a 26-14 record, second in the league in wins, and was the club's workhorse with 342⅔ innings pitched and twenty-six complete games. He was also maintaining his superb control; Quinn walked about one man every five innings, close to his career mark and third best in the league. Years later he explained the connection between control and ease of pitching, as well as control and longevity: "Control is easy on your arm. If you can put the ball where you want to, you don't need so much stuff. . . . Some pitchers like to burn the ball over the plate when they get in a hole. I prefer to fall back on a change of pace. Slow stuff will stop a slugger more effectively than speed."[16]

As the season progressed, high salaries and low attendance led to financial losses for virtually every team in all three leagues. Harry Williams estimated the new league would lose $1,000,000, while Organized Baseball would lose only slightly less: "There are not enough two-bit pieces being piled up at the gates to meet it [payroll]. . . . It is apparent the Feds aren't going to quit. Some of them are in too deep for that."[17] Two International League teams were particularly hard hit by Federal League competitors in their cities: the Baltimore Orioles and the Buffalo Bisons.

While Gaffney's suit did not come to court during the season, other lawsuits over players revealed no clear-cut winner.[18] In the meantime, the Braves stunned the sports world when they rallied from last place on July 15, won the National League pennant by 10½ games, and swept the defending world champion Philadelphia Athletics in the World Series.

In December the Braves dropped their lawsuit against Quinn and the Baltimore organization. Boston could no longer argue that the Braves had suffered from the loss of Quinn "inasmuch as without him the team won the greatest possible honors in the baseball world."[19] Stallings later claimed that Quinn told him he had made a mistake by jumping, but the pitcher never commented publicly on the matter.[20]

Not only did Quinn's jumping not hurt the Braves, but it also really made their championship season possible. When Quinn did not report, Boston no longer had to compensate Rochester with the players it owed the Hustlers.[21] Years later veteran Philadelphia sportswriter Bill Dooly wrote that the players who were to go to Rochester in payment for Quinn were pitcher Dick Rudolph and catcher Hank Gowdy.[22] They were two of the stars of the 1914 Miracle Braves. Rudolph won twenty-six games for them, as well as two in the World Series. Gowdy hit .545 in the Series.

Stallings never talked about the deal that would have made him look bad, and he would not admit that a lucky break was crucial for his 1914 success. Such a transaction would not have been preposterous in August 1913. Gowdy was playing in the Minor Leagues at the time, and the Braves had a solid catcher in Bill Rariden. Moreover, Quinn seemed to be an equitable replacement for Rudolph, who was in his first full season in 1913. In early August, when Stallings was finalizing the Quinn acquisition, Rudolph's Boston record stood at 9-10.[23] Rariden subsequently jumped to the Federal League in 1914, and Gowdy became the Braves' starting catcher that championship season.

Nineteen fifteen was a disappointing season for both Quinn and the Terrapins. Baltimore scored ninety-five fewer runs than in the previous season and tumbled to last place with a disastrous 47-107 record. Quinn led the league in losses with twenty-two. His earned run average rose almost a full run from the previous year. Quinn was inconsistent all season. He was shelled in an Opening Day loss to Newark but easily beat Buffalo four days later. On April 24 he again beat Buffalo, whose starter that day was his former Yankees teammate, Russ Ford, and whose reliever was a future teammate, Howard Ehmke.[24] In May Quinn feared he had broken a bone in his hand and planned to visit Youngstown, Ohio, to seek treatment from the famous muscle and ligament specialist, Bonesetter Reese.[25]

After getting some rest, however, Quinn four-hit Kansas City on May 29 and canceled the visit to Ohio. After he was hammered by Chicago in late June, 11–4, Starr Matthews declared, "It is hard to tell just what Jack will do. One day he looks like a million dollars, and the next day he is batted all over the field."[26] On August 9 Quinn faced the former star of the Philadelphia Athletics, southpaw Eddie Plank. Just three weeks short of his fortieth birthday, Plank was approaching the milestone of three hundred wins. While Quinn pitched well enough to win, Plank's four-hitter made the Terrapins "look foolish, [with Plank] beating them yesterday with ridiculous ease," 3–0.[27]

Baltimore's heady and aggressive player-manager, Otto Knabe, led the club both seasons. A veteran second baseman with the Phillies from 1907 to 1913, his intensity seemed like a strong point his first season at the helm but may have worn on his men the second time around. A notorious umpire baiter and bench jockey, Knabe was known to taunt his own players.[28] When Grover Cleveland Alexander was a rookie in 1911, he criticized his teammate Knabe, who snapped back, "Listen, you fresh busher, when we get to the clubhouse, I'll show you how to talk to a regular."[29]

The Federal League became a victim of its recruiting tactics, and the Terrapins were a good example. They had attracted talent by signing many players to two- and three-year contracts. When men were not performing well, Knabe was stuck with them. There was no Terrapins Minor League team to which he could send them.

Beyond a thin veneer of name players, most of the Federal League rosters were filled with former Minor Leaguers and marginal Major Leaguers.[30] Nevertheless, in 1969 a Special Baseball Records Committee ruled that the Federal League was a Major League, and its statistics then became part of Organized Baseball's records. In a 2012 article baseball analyst Rob Neyer concluded that the committee made the wrong decision: "The best of the Federal League players, with the exception of [Benny] Kauff, were barely good enough to play in the real Major Leagues at all."[31]

After the 1915 season the Federal League settled with Major League Baseball and ended its operation. The two-year war had been extremely costly for all three leagues.[32] While the upstart league did not survive, Organized Baseball's victory was not overwhelming. Two of the eight Federal League owners bought Major League clubs in their Federal League cities, the National League's Chicago Cubs and the American League's St. Louis Browns. In addition, Organized Baseball agreed to pay hundreds of thousands of dollars to some Federal League owners.[33]

Organized Baseball also agreed that its owners could purchase Federal League players they wanted for their teams from the defunct league's main financial backer, oil tycoon Harry Sinclair.[34] This was a remarkable concession to the rebel league. During the war between the Federal League and Organized Baseball, the latter minimized its personnel losses by threatening to blacklist any player who jumped. Now not only was Organized Baseball allowing these players to come back, but it was also paying the "outlaw" league to get them back. However, there was still an informal blacklist of players whose desertion seemed particularly egregious.[35]

Quinn had abandoned the Boston Braves for the Federal League in early 1914. As noted, the club's owner, James Gaffney, was furious at the time with Quinn's behavior. Did this play a role in Quinn's being passed over by all Major League clubs for the 1916 season? Obviously Organized Baseball did not announce it was blacklisting a player, yet this may have been a factor in Quinn's not being proffered a contract.

For the third time in less than twenty years, Baltimore had been jilted. In 1900 the National League had contracted from twelve to eight teams, eliminating Baltimore and three other cities.[36] In 1903 the American League's Baltimore franchise became defunct and was replaced by one in New York. And now, while two Federal League owners joined Organized Baseball, the city was denied again.[37]

The Terrapins filed an antitrust lawsuit (they included other Federal League owners in their suit), and Organized Baseball was stunned when the Federal District Court in Washington DC ruled in the club's favor in April 1919. The $80,000 in damages was trebled under the Sherman Antitrust Act.[38] But Organized Baseball won on appeal in 1921, and in May 1922 the U.S. Supreme Court upheld the Appeals Court with its famous ruling that baseball did not constitute "interstate commerce" and therefore was not subject to the antitrust laws.

Jack Quinn's last victory of 1915 had come on August 13. His last start came a month later, when he allowed only three hits but lost to Kansas City, 2–0, on a throwing error. As the 1916 season approached, no Major League team showed any interest in him. At the age of thirty-two, when many ballplayers' careers were winding down, he was again being told that he was not Major League material. His mediocre 1915 performance did not help his cause. Teams were not keen on Howard Ehmke either, though he was not much more than a year removed from "phenom" status.

The thirty-two-year-old Quinn had already won seventy-nine games in the Majors, but many observers thought that he could not return to his 1910 form. He would have to prove that his brief career was not over. Ehmke, approaching the age of twenty-two, had yet to win a Major League game. He would have to prove that his career was about to begin. Both men would have to take the long way back.

9

Breaking Records in Syracuse

After suffering through a miserable year in Buffalo, a dejected Howard Ehmke spent the off-season at home in Los Angeles. After the first significant setback of his young career, he was exploring his options for 1916. They did not include returning to the Federal League, which ceased operations following the 1915 season.[1] Even before that season reached its halfway mark, Ehmke realized jumping to the Feds had been a mistake. He wrote to Walter Boles, his 1914 batterymate with the Angels, that he wanted to return to the Pacific Coast League.[2]

Shortly after New Year's, an article in the *Los Angeles Evening Herald* suggested Ehmke might get his wish. The arm injury he sustained the previous spring, which so adversely affected his season, had healed; nevertheless, no big league club had shown any interest in him. Meanwhile, several Angels players and most Angels fans were anxious for him to return. "He still is a youngster," noted the *Herald*, "and with proper handling, will go up to the big show once more."[3]

On January 7, 1916, Ehmke met with Boles and new Angels owner John F. "Johnny" Powers at Washington Park, the team's home grounds.[4] Ehmke told Powers he wanted to pitch for the Angels in 1916 and that as far as he knew, he was free to do so. His brother Frank, who had been instrumental in getting him to jump to the Buffalo team, had convinced him to sign only a one-year contract with the Blues.

Powers agreed to give him a chance with the Angels if he indeed was a free agent. But while Ehmke was sure he was free of any ties to Buffalo, he was unsure of his exact status with the Washington Senators. He thought he would have a hard time getting free if he was still on Washington's reserve list.[5] "When the Federal League expired," he explained, "I wrote to the Buffalo owners and asked how I stood. I received a reply saying I was a free agent. I wired to Washington asking for a reserve list of the pitchers and was notified that my name was not written there."[6]

Boles, who had played a major role in the young pitcher's development, said Ehmke would have no trouble in coming to terms with the Angels. He further predicted that Ehmke would be better than ever this coming season: "Ehmke has developed a new kind of a slow ball that should be a pippin with his underhand fast one."[7]

As he had the previous year, Ehmke spent the off-season not knowing for whom he would be playing in the new season. While he waited, he stayed busy pitching in "amateur" games in the Los Angeles area. He received an offer from an unidentified American Association team but decided if he did not receive an offer from a Major League club, he would sign with the Angels.

Powers was in favor of adding Ehmke, but the final decision would be made by Frank Chance, his new manager. Chance was the onetime first baseman and manager of the Chicago Cubs, where he won four pennants and two world championships. More recently he had spent two unsuccessful seasons (1913–14) as the manager of the New York Yankees. Chance had stated previously he did not think Ehmke was strong enough to stand up through the long Pacific Coast League season. He was looking for big, strong pitchers who could start at least twice a week, and it was not something he believed Ehmke could do. A March headline in the *Los Angeles Tribune* emphasized Chance's position.[8]

Chance thought Ehmke could be a big winner only if he worked one game a week. His criticism of Ehmke's stamina and durability, which echoed that of Pop Dillon, would follow Ehmke throughout his career. Still Ehmke wanted only the chance to prove himself, insisting he was in great shape and that his arm was strong. In the end the Angels gave him that chance. He signed a contract on March 14 and headed to the team's training camp in Elsinore, California.

"This lad Ehmke looks better every day," wrote W. A. Reeve of the *Los Angeles Tribune*. "I can't figure how he can be kept off the ball club, and neither can anyone else who watched him. He has more speed and more stuff than when he was out here before and has the additional quality that comes only with experience." Reeve recognized that the

Angels had a lot of good pitchers in camp, yet he thought it a near certainty that Chance would keep Ehmke, who "looks too good to let go."[9]

Ehmke had shown well early in spring training, but on March 30, three days after Reeve's article appeared, he had a disastrous performance in an intrasquad game. That one appearance was enough for Chance to release him. Or was it? Chance was heard saying he did not want any former Federal Leaguers on his team, and one poor outing may have been his excuse to cut Ehmke.[10]

A year later, in March 1917, Ehmke discussed his attempt to land with the Angels without ever mentioning that Chance had even given him a tryout. It is true Chance had been reluctant to do so, but he had, and Ehmke evidently had chosen not to remember that. He claimed Chance had laughed at him and said he was not good enough to pitch in the Pacific Coast League. "I'll show you," Ehmke thought. "I'll catch on, and I'll be in the big time in four months. I was mad clear through. I turned away, and I could hear Chance laughing even after I left. I tried to catch on with another Coast League club. I wanted to get back at Chance now. But they all turned me down. I referred to my record with Los Angeles a couple of years before, but that did no good."[11]

It was now the first week of April, and no team in the Major or Minor Leagues had a spot on its roster for Ehmke. If this had him concerned, he was not showing it outwardly. Matt Gallagher wrote that not only was Ehmke unworried, he also felt he had several potential landing spots in mind. One was in San Francisco, though Seals manager Harry Wolverton was satisfied with his pitching staff and had no interest in signing him.[12] Ehmke sent a telegram offering his services to manager Cliff Blankenship of the Salt Lake City Bees. Though the Bees were short of pitching, Blankenship did not respond. A few days later, hoping to be seen by potential managers and owners, Ehmke pitched in a game for the semi-pro Alhambra team of western Los Angeles County. To assure he would be in shape when the call came, he worked out at Washington Park almost every day.

Ehmke understood that after his wasted season in Buffalo, no Major League club would sign him. Both he and Jack Quinn had come off poor 1915 seasons. While Quinn's brief Major League career was thought to have come to an end, Ehmke's appeared to be stillborn. Now he had been turned down by three veteran Coast League managers: Chance, Wolverton, and Blankenship. Just two years earlier Ehmke had been a young phenom earning praise as a future pitching great, first on the West Coast and then nationwide. Now, at age twenty-two, it seemed no one wanted him.

Deliverance arrived from the other side of the country via an offer to pitch for the Syracuse Stars of the Class B New York State League. The *Los Angeles Tribune* reported that Ehmke, "the sensation of the Coast League in 1914," had reached terms with player-manager Mike O'Neill of Syracuse and would head east the next day, April 29.[13] The New York State League was familiar territory for O'Neill, as he had managed and played in the league since 1910. This would be his second year at Syracuse, following a fifth-place finish in 1915.[14]

Ehmke said his contract called for the lowest salary he had received in his three years of professional baseball, but he accepted it for the opportunity it might give him to get to the Major Leagues. To make up for the low salary, there was an understanding that if he were sold, he would get $1,000 of the purchase price.

As he had done with the Angels in 1914, Ehmke got off to a strong start. Only this time there would be no prolonged slump. He won his first three games, including a 7–2, ten-strikeout victory over the Albany Senators and an eleven-inning, 1–0, shutout over the Utica Utes, in which he allowed just two hits. By mid-June he was 7-2, with four of the seven wins by shutout. But an old charge arose that questioned the validity of his accomplishments. A report in the *Los Angeles Evening Herald* quoted a rumor from an eastern sportswriter that claimed Ehmke's success was due to his use of the emery ball.[15] Ehmke responded in a personal letter to the *Herald*, emphatically denying that he was using what he called the "preparedness" ball.

The rumor gained some credibility when the manager of a club Ehmke defeated protested that he had indeed used the emery ball in the game. The protest was disallowed by the league president, who said that the umpires would have thrown any such ball out of the game if there had been one in play.[16] Ehmke continued to deny that he had ever used the emery ball. At the same time, according to the *Herald*, reports in some eastern papers were predicting that Ehmke was likely to get a chance in the Major Leagues in 1917: "He has more stuff than he ever had before, and he also is working regularly."[17]

By mid-July Ehmke had a record of 17-5 and had beaten each of the other seven teams in the league at least twice. Big league teams had started paying close attention. Ehmke was not only winning games, but he was also dominating the opposition. Among his best outings was the July 23 game, in which he retired the first seventeen Harrisburg Islanders on the way to a thirteen-inning, 3–2 win.[18] He yielded only 4 hits, while striking out 14, raising his season totals to 136 strikeouts and 130 hits.

A pitcher with more strikeouts than hits allowed was extremely rare at any level, a feat that contributed to the *Syracuse Journal's* calling Ehmke "the best pitcher in the New York State League since Grover Cleveland Alexander."[19] Pitching for this same Syracuse club in 1910, the twenty-three-year-old Alexander had won twenty-nine games with just eleven defeats. Ehmke, who two years earlier had often been compared to Walter Johnson, the best pitcher in the American League, now was drawing comparisons to Alexander, the best pitcher in the National League.

Ehmke pitched another masterpiece on July 28, a one-hit, 4–0 shut-out against Albany that raised his record to 19-5. In its coverage of the game the *Syracuse Journal* reported that "Howard Ehmke . . . will join the Detroit Tigers at the end of the State League season on September 10."[20] Stars manager O'Neill and Tigers scout Larry Sutton had reached a deal that included cash going to the Stars, as well as the loan of Tigers pitcher George Boehler for the rest of the season. O'Neill had checked with his brother Steve, a catcher for the Cleveland Indians, who told him Boehler had a world of stuff and would be a successful pitcher in the New York State League.[21]

Sutton was a scout who would eventually spend fifty years in baseball. While working for Brooklyn, it was he who convinced owner Charlie Ebbets to take a chance on Dazzy Vance, a future Hall of Fame pitcher who had failed twice in the Major Leagues. Sutton recalled how he directed Ehmke toward the Tigers:

[Tigers owner] Frank Navin called me into his office one day and told me the Detroit club wanted a good pitcher with as little delay as possible. I bought a ticket for Syracuse, where I knew Ehmke was pitching, but I had to wait three days before I could see his wares. I might have been in Syracuse yet, had it not been for a friend whom I met and who told me Ehmke had a sore finger and was on the hospital list. Faced with such a tough break, I had just about decided to beat it when my friend phoned me at the hotel and told me if I'd stay over the next day, Ehmke would pitch—sore finger or no sore finger.[22]

Sutton stayed for the next day's game and watched as Ehmke struck out fifteen batters: "I couldn't help but wonder what he'd have done without his finger ailment, and I bought him for $2,500."[23] While Sutton listed the price as $2,500, no official sale price was announced. Mike O'Neill claimed the price was $4,000, which at the time would have made it the highest sum ever paid for a player in the New York State League. In addition, Syracuse would get to keep Ehmke until September 10, when the Stars' season finished.

There was, however, one additional proviso, Ehmke told his 1914 Angels teammate Charlie Chech. There was an agreement between the Detroit and Syracuse clubs that in case the Stars were either so far in the lead or out of the race, Ehmke would go to Detroit in late August. That would be time enough to make him eligible for the World Series should Detroit win the American League pennant.[24] As it turned out, Ehmke stayed with the Stars until the end of their season. He was the main reason they finished first, with an 81-52 record, 7 games ahead of the Scranton Miners. In compiling one of the greatest Minor League pitching seasons ever, he had a sparkling 1.55 earned run average and also led the league in wins (31), strikeouts (195), and winning percentage (.816).[25]

Ehmke's great 1916 season with Syracuse followed his awful 1915 season at Buffalo and his being laughed at by Frank Chance in the spring. It marked the first great comeback of his career and propelled him to the Major Leagues.

10

"A Fellow to Be Reckoned With"

The sale of Howard Ehmke from Syracuse to the Detroit Tigers would not go unchallenged. Believing Ehmke still legally belonged to his club, Washington's Clark Griffith immediately put in a claim for him. A reporter for the *Detroit News* explained why he thought the claim had no legal validity: "Ehmke jumped from Los Angeles to the Buffalo Federals while he was Washington property. After the Federal League dissolved, Washington refused to claim him, and he drifted to the minors. Washington, therefore, to every appearance, forfeited all rights to the player. But the Nationals are putting up a hard fight in the baseball courts to retain Ehmke and may succeed in taking him away from the Detroit club."[1]

The desire for Ehmke was a complete about-face for Griffith. "I don't want any of them on my team," he had said in December 1915, referring to Ehmke, Bob Groom, and Frank Laporte. Groom and Laporte had played for the Senators in 1913 and jumped to the Federal League in 1914.[2]

In a September 1, 1916, decision, the National Commission awarded Ehmke to Washington. Despite the sale to Detroit in July, the commission ruled that Washington had prior claim to Ehmke as he had been signed by the Senators in 1914. Still it was considered likely that Ehmke would end up in Detroit, with Griffith receiving some form of remuneration from the Tigers.[3]

Five days later Ehmke received a telegram from the Detroit club, confirming it had purchased his contract from Syracuse and that he was to report immediately. The Tigers would reimburse him for his travel expenses. Ehmke planned to stop in Silver Creek to pick up his brother Frank, who would accompany him to Detroit. The Washington club was scheduled to receive the purchase money the Syracuse owners thought would be coming to them, but instead the Stars received only the regular draft price.[4]

Minor League owners had often complained about their unfair treatment by the three-man National Commission in disputes they had with Major League teams. The *Elmira (NY) Star-Gazette* cited the sale of Ehmke from Syracuse to Detroit, where the $3,000 purchase price went to Washington rather than to the Stars, as an example of that unfair treatment.[5] Ehmke was apparently a free agent when he signed with Syracuse, and it was that club who deserved the money.

When Ehmke joined the Tigers, on September 10, 1916, the Boston Red Sox led Detroit by a game and the Chicago White Sox by a game and a half. The Red Sox had traded a disgruntled Tris Speaker, its best player, to Cleveland but retained the core of the team that had defeated the Philadelphia Phillies in the 1915 World Series. Boston's strength was its pitching staff, led by twenty-one-year-old Babe Ruth, who had emerged as the best left-hander in the game. Behind Ruth were left-hander Hubert "Dutch" Leonard and right-handers Carl Mays, Ernie Shore, and Rube Foster, who at twenty-eight was the oldest member of the staff.

The manager of the Tigers was Hughie Jennings, shortstop for the Ned Hanlon–led Baltimore Orioles teams of the 1890s that won three consecutive National League pennants and finished second twice. As his Baltimore teammates and friends—Joe Kelley, Wilbert Robinson, and John McGraw—had done, Jennings went on to a managerial career of his own. After replacing Bill Armour at Detroit in 1907, he won three consecutive pennants, although the Tigers lost the World Series each year.[6] They had not won a pennant since, not even in 1915, when they won 100 games but finished 2½ games behind Boston.

The Tigers' greatest strength was in their outfield, featuring Ty Cobb in center, flanked by Sam Crawford in left and Bobby Veach in right. Cobb, at age twenty-nine, was recognized as baseball's greatest hitter. He had won the last nine American League batting titles, including two seasons in which he hit better than .400. He was also a sure-handed fielder and gifted with speed on defense and on the bases. Jennings's two best pitchers were left-hander Harry Coveleski (19-10) and right-hander George "Hooks" Dauss (17-10). The two had accounted for thirty-six of the Tigers' seventy-seven wins thus far this season.

Jennings put his new pitcher to work immediately. The afternoon he arrived, the twenty-two-year-old Ehmke made his American League debut at League Park in Cleveland. He worked an inning and a third of mop-up relief, allowing two unearned runs in a game the Tigers lost to the Indians, 8–2. Ehmke's appearance, brief as it was, made a strong impression on the correspondent for the *Detroit Times*. He called Ehmke "a fellow to be reckoned with" and said that the Tigers were delighted by the class he showed. "Best of all, he had control and a cool, calculating attitude that indicated a cranium filled with . . . more than a little pitching knowledge." In short, he wrote, "Ehmke looked so good that it is predicted that he will be a winner right off the reel, and it is a cinch that Jennings must give him another chance, and a better one. The rookie right now is running strong as the candidate for the man the Tigers have been looking for lo, these many seasons."[7]

Two days later Jennings started Ehmke against the Indians' Stan Coveleski in the final game of the series. Backed by Cobb, Crawford, and Veach, who had a combined eleven hits, Ehmke pitched the Tigers to a 10–2 victory. Coupled with Boston's ten-inning loss at Washington, the win moved Detroit to within a half-game of the lead.

Ehmke's complete-game outing, which included holding Speaker, the league's leading batter, to one single, elicited this reaction from E. A. Batchelor of the *Detroit Free Press*: "You never would have thought, after watching Howard Ehmke perform on the mound this afternoon, that he was pitching his first full game as a major leaguer," wrote Batchelor.[8] "On the contrary, he had the aplomb and the equipment of a veteran in the big show. He was cool and collected at all times and put so much stuff on the ball that the Indians, reckoned a hard-hitting club, were as helpless as babes."[9]

In praising Ehmke's overall effort, the writer from the *Detroit News* took particular note of his fielding, citing the pitcher's four assists and two putouts. He also informed his readers that all of Ehmke's pitches were delivered sidearm, similar to Carl Mays, Boston's star right-hander.[10] Tubby Spencer, Detroit's catcher that afternoon, said that while Ehmke also had good overhand stuff, he saw no need to switch from a delivery that was working well.[11] In just his second big league game, Ehmke was already showing his penchant to change the angle

12. In September 1916, after his sensational season with the Syracuse Stars of the New York State League, Howard Ehmke made his big league debut with the Detroit Tigers. In his first start he defeated Cleveland, moving the Tigers to within a half-game of first place. *Dennis Goldstein Collection.*

of his deliveries from game to game or even from batter to batter. "He can pitch overhand, underhand, or sidearm," wrote H. G. Salsinger.[12]

On September 16 Ehmke made his home debut in a start against the Philadelphia Athletics, a team against which he would have great success in his career.[13] His first appearance at Detroit's Navin Field had been highly anticipated by the fans, who were hoping his spectacular season with Syracuse was an indication he would be the final piece in helping the Tigers win the pennant. Ehmke did not disappoint. He turned in his second complete game, and his infield single in the sixth inning scored Sam Crawford with what proved to be the winning run in Detroit's 4–3 victory.

Philadelphia scored a run in the ninth to get within one run of the Tigers and had runners at second and third with two outs. A hit would tie the game or, more than likely, put the A's ahead. But Ehmke bore down and struck out Socks Seibold on three pitches. "Ehmke not only has everything, but he has it when he gets into a game and particularly when he gets into a pinch," said veteran catcher and Tigers coach Billy Sullivan.[14] Combined with Boston's loss to Chicago, the win moved the Tigers into first place, a half-game ahead of the White Sox and a game ahead of the Red Sox. The win also came with an added bonus. Owner Frank Navin had promised his players $50 each with which to buy articles of clothing if they won the game.

It was still a three-team race when Boston came to Detroit on September 19 for a three-game series. The Red Sox led the Tigers by percentage points (.579 to .576), with the White Sox third, 1½ games back. Jennings had his two best pitchers, Dauss and Coveleski, slated for games one and three and bypassed the other veterans on his staff to go with the rookie Ehmke in game two. But it was the Boston pitchers that prevailed. Carl Mays defeated Dauss in the first game, 3–1; Dutch Leonard beat Ehmke in the second game, 4–3; and Babe Ruth topped Coveleski in the third game, 10–2. The sweep gave Boston a 14–8 edge in the season series and dropped Detroit to 3 games back and into third place.

More than sixteen thousand fans came out for the middle game, confident that their blossoming young star, whom *Boston Herald* sportswriter John A. Hallahan described as "a tall twirler with a sidearm delivery," would even the series. Ehmke's teammates, aided by a sloppy Boston defense, gave Detroit the early lead with three second-inning runs, but the Red Sox evened the game with a three-run fourth. Boston's third run scored on catcher-manager Bill Carrigan's hit, which center fielder Cobb allowed to get by him. "Ty Cobb made a sorry exhibition of playing the ball," wrote Hallahan. "He actually quit when the sphere bounded past him, and he refused to chase it. He just looked at it and allowed Veach to retrieve it."[15] By that time the slow-footed Carrigan was at third base, where he was awarded a triple by a kindly scorer. That Cobb would do this in a tight game, with the Tigers only one game out of first place, was both egregious and counter to his usual style of play. Throughout his career Cobb would castigate players he felt were not giving their best. One can only wonder if Ehmke ever brought up this play in the coming years when manager Cobb would question his devotion to the game.

For the next three innings Leonard and Ehmke held the opposition scoreless before Boston broke the tie in the eighth. Everett Scott was at second with two outs when Carrigan, the scheduled batter, called on the left-handed-hitting Olaf Henriksen to pinch-hit for him. The Danish-born Henriksen lashed a single to center that brought Scott home with the winning run.

It had been an all-around difficult day for the often obnoxious Cobb. He was doubling as the Tigers' third base coach until home plate umpire Brick Owens had had enough of Cobb's questioning his balls-and-strikes judgment and ordered him out of the coaching area. Cobb made a show of slowly making his way to the dugout, but he attempted a return to coaching at third when the Tigers came to bat in the ninth. The *Boston Globe*'s Edward Martin described what ensued: "Owens saw him and told him to get out, but he [Cobb] looked down at the grass and never lifted his head. After Owens shouted at him four times, he lifted his head, panned Brick properly, but refused to budge. Then [base umpire] Billy Evans got busy. He took two or three steps across the infield, yelled 'Get out of there, Mr. Cobb,' and Mr. Cobb got out."[16]

Ehmke made one final appearance in 1916, against Washington, at home on September 24. He pitched a complete game, winning 6–5, aided by Veach's ninth-inning throw to the plate that cut down what would have been the tying run. The losing pitcher was Walter Johnson.[17]

For those who followed the game closely, there was a dramatic backstory to what was otherwise a meaningless late-season encounter between two teams out of the pennant race. Two years earlier, when Ehmke was burning up the Pacific Coast League for the Los Angeles Angels, he was drawing favorable comparisons to Johnson.

And because the Angels had a working agreement with Griffith and the Senators, there was much speculation about Ehmke and Johnson being teammates in 1915. Now Griffith and Johnson were getting their first serious look at Ehmke. It is surprising that Stanley Milliken, who covered Griffith's two attempts to sign Ehmke, made no mention of any of this in his *Washington Post* story on the game.

Ehmke may have been ignored in Washington, but he was being amply praised in Detroit. He had been a bigger hit with Tigers fans than any newcomer in recent years, said Batchelor: "We believe that we have nailed one of the coming stars of the American League. The youngster has won his way into the hearts of the fans by his skill and gameness. . . . He proved in the few games he worked after joining the Tigers this fall that he knows how to pitch, that he has the control and the 'stuff' and that his heart is stout."[18] Opponents around the league had spoken equally enthusiastically about Ehmke, including Bill Carrigan, whose Red Sox team defeated him in that crucial September game.

Ehmke's success with the Tigers did not come without a monetary drawback. Before the season ended, Frank Navin informed him that he would be barred from playing winter ball, something many players did to pick up extra money in the off-season. Ehmke, at twenty-two, had pitched 302 innings for Syracuse and another 37⅓ for the Tigers in 1916. It is likely that Navin wanted him healthy and rested for the 1917 season. Unable to play winter ball, Ehmke spent the off-season at home in Los Angeles and supplemented his income working during the Christmas holiday as a floorwalker in a Los Angeles jewelry store.[19]

11

Ehmke and the Tigers Take
a Step Backward

After a brief holdout Howard Ehmke signed his 1917 contract in late February. He was reasonable in his demands, and there was little doubt he would sign, a significant change from his previous contract negotiations. In the recent past Ehmke had been ill advised by his brother in his contract dealings with owners Clark Griffith in Washington and Frank Navin in Detroit. In his anxiety to protect Ehmke's interests, Frank had antagonized both men. They resented the implication that they were trying to take advantage of his younger brother, and each sent Frank a sharply worded letter to that effect.[1]

Throughout the off-season Detroit sportswriters had been touting Ehmke as the man capable of turning the Tigers pitching staff into one of the league's best. H. G. Salsinger called him the "most promising hurler Detroit ever harbored."[2] Manager Hughie Jennings had shown great confidence in his rookie pitcher by starting him against the Red Sox in the heat of the 1916 pennant race. In addition, Ehmke had shown great confidence in himself. With a pitching repertoire that included speed, curve balls, and control, he seemed to need only experience to help him realize his potential.

Despite the praise he received from the press, Ehmke was not fully satisfied with his performance for the Tigers in 1916. "I did not have my curve ball working right for Detroit last fall," he said. "I guess my fast ball was good enough, but I did not have control. I know I can pitch better than I showed for Jennings, and I am going to give everything I have to prove it. I want to listen to something besides a laugh from Frank Chance. I saw him just a few weeks ago, and he congratulated me on my advancement. I asked him if he remembered the day I asked him for a trial. He said he didn't. But I know he did."[3]

In the early days of spring training, the talk around the different camps was that in Ehmke the Tigers had the American League's star pitching find. Such rave reviews were nothing new to Ehmke. In his brief career he had drawn comparisons to future Hall of Famers Walter Johnson and Grover Cleveland Alexander, premature as they were. Now another pitching great was being added to the list.

According to N. B. Beasley of the *Detroit Journal*, Ehmke was being called the probable successor to the late Addie Joss.[4] Making those comparisons were such long-time American Leaguers as Griffith, St. Louis Browns manager Fielder Jones, former Boston Red Sox manager Bill Carrigan, and umpire Billy Evans. After serving as the home plate umpire in a game Ehmke pitched the previous fall, Evans had said this about the young pitcher: "Ehmke comes as near to pitching like Joss as any man I have ever seen. Joss was my ideal of a pitcher. Fast, with a wonderful curve, a knowledge of what he was out on the diamond to do, and a thorough respect for the batsman along with a confidence in his own ability. Slight of build, much like Ehmke, and with a zipping underhand delivery that kept the batter from taking a toe hold and waiting for the break. That was Joss."[5]

Harold Wilcox called Ehmke the best of the Tigers' rookies in camp at Waxahatchie, Texas, and enlightened his readers on some things they might not know or were misinformed about him. For one, his weight. Expectations that he would add weight to his slender frame and that the extra weight would be good for him were not true. "It has developed," Wilcox wrote, "that Howard is not likely to take on more weight and that it would be a calamity if he did." Wilcox described him as all legs and arms and as being built like a piece of piano wire with muscles like whipcord. Of Ehmke's reputation as a modest, unassuming young man, Wilcox wrote, "That is the bunk. There isn't a cockier lad in baseball than he."[6]

Yet not everyone was enamored of Ehmke. During the off-season Yankees manager Bill Donovan told the New York press he did not think Ehmke would be a successful Major League pitcher. "Ehmke is a big awkward fellow like [Ernie] Shore," said Donovan, whose club had not faced Ehmke in his brief big league stay in 1916. "We beat

Shore by bunting. . . . We'll be at Ehmke the same way, [and] so will the other clubs."[7]

St. Louis Cardinals manager Miller Huggins had read Donovan's analysis and put it to the test when his club played the Tigers in a March 22 spring training game.[8] "Where do they get this stuff about Ehmke not being able to field?" asked an incredulous Huggins after Ehmke registered eight assists and a putout in five innings. "We tried everything on him without getting by. If that boy can't field, I want a corps of slouching pitchers such as he."[9]

During training camp Beasley questioned the Tigers' leading pitchers on what could be expected of them in 1917. It is not surprising that Harry Coveleski, Hooks Dauss, Willie Mitchell, Bernie Boland, Bill James, George Cunningham, and Ehmke each predicted a successful season. "I have plenty of confidence in myself," Ehmke responded. "I won three in four for the Tigers last fall. . . . Baseball owes me a lot of money, and the single method for getting it is to be a winner."[10]

Among those predicting a great future for Ehmke was New York Giants outfielder Benny Kauff, who played against him in the Federal League in 1915. "He's bigger, has more stuff, and will bother any batter he faces," said Kauff, the batting champion both years of the Federal League's existence.[11] Also on the Ehmke bandwagon was sportswriter J. C. Kofoed of *Baseball Magazine*, who gave his thoughts on all the rookies of 1917. "This boy emphatically 'has the goods,'" he wrote of Ehmke, "and with a little more experience, should be one of Jennings' best winners. The efforts of his lawyer brother to procure him a contract calling for $5,000 a season when he was an unknown youngster nearly robbed Howard of a big-league tryout. But since he secured it, he has shown himself to be one of the best men on the Detroit staff."[12]

The Tigers entered the season without any significant roster changes. After they lost the opener to Cleveland at home, Ehmke started the second game of the season, against Jim Bagby. He allowed just two runs, but the Tigers could score only one against Bagby, who would be one of the league's top pitchers in 1917.[13]

After losing his next start to the Chicago White Sox, 4–2, though only two of the runs were earned, Ehmke faced the Indians again, at Cleveland. This time he lasted only a third of an inning as the Indians reached him for four runs on the way to a 4–3 victory. The winner was Ed Klepfer, who was again his opponent when he faced Cleveland for a third time in the first game of a May 9 doubleheader at Navin Field. Ehmke got his first win of the season, 4–1, limiting the Indians to three hits.

He was even better in his next start, on May 13, the final game of a four-game home series against the Red Sox. Ehmke, like the rest of the Tigers' pitchers, had been receiving very little run support from his teammates. In the first three games Detroit scored one, one, and zero runs against Boston pitchers Dutch Leonard, Babe Ruth, and Carl Mays.[14] They managed to score two for Ehmke, just enough for him to defeat Ernie Shore, 2–1, in twelve innings. Ehmke gave up just five hits while holding Boston hitless in ten of the twelve innings. "His pitching," wrote Beasley, "went to prove what was said about him in this and other columns in the spring that he will win 20 ball games or better for Detroit this season if given decent support."[15] An article in the *Syracuse Journal* quoted E. A. Batchelor of the *Detroit Free Press*: "It was probably the greatest exhibition of pitching ever seen at Navin Field. One hurler sometimes has done better work than either of the duelists, but seldom if ever before have two turned in such a performance on the same day."[16] In June the *Silver Creek News*, Ehmke's hometown paper, reported on its native son's early-season success with the Tigers. It noted that he was being hailed as Detroit's greatest pitcher since "Wild Bill" Donovan.[17]

Following tough losses to the Senators and the Athletics, Ehmke raised his record to 3-6 with a 5–1 win at Cleveland's Dunn Field on Memorial Day. He followed with what looked to be another complete-game win but resulted in his most bitter defeat of the season. Facing the Yankees at the Polo Grounds on June 4, Ehmke had a 5–2 lead after seven innings. But the Yanks scored one run in the eighth and three in the ninth to win, 6–5.

The Tigers moved on to Boston, where they swept the three-game series from the league-leading Red Sox. The sweep allowed the White Sox to move past Boston into first place. Two of the wins were shutouts, one by Dauss (3–0 over Ruth) and one by Ehmke, with another win over Shore, 1–0. Ehmke had already beaten Boston four times

13. Howard Ehmke, pictured throwing overhand in 1916, also used sidearm and underhand deliveries throughout his career. *Dennis Goldstein Collection.*

this season (including three shutouts) when he faced them at home on August 26. But he was exceptionally wild in this game, and it was a major factor in the Red Sox 6–3 win. He walked a career-high nine batters in eight innings, with four of them eventually scoring.[18]

Ehmke had one other shutout in 1917, on September 22, at Washington. Making his final start of the season, he allowed just three hits in a 4–0 win over Walter Johnson, who had won twelve of his previous thirteen decisions. The win, impressive as it was, was just Ehmke's tenth against fifteen losses and concluded an overall disappointing season. He was unable to match his 4-2 record against Boston with similar success against the league's other six teams, compiling a dismal 6-13 mark against them. For the Tigers, with a 78-75 record and a fourth-place finish, it was a mediocre season as well and a step backward from the 1916 squad. The team had started poorly, losing six of its first seven, and was a season-worst nine wins under .500 on May 29. It was not until June 24 that Detroit, at 28-27, had a winning record.

Chicago and Boston had waged a fierce battle for first place all season. On the morning of September 2, as Chicago began a four-game series against Detroit, its lead over Boston was 3½ games. Detroit was at Comiskey Park for a makeup doubleheader on Sunday and the traditional Labor Day doubleheader on Monday. Tigers historian Dan Holmes wrote of these four games: "The Tigers were central in a plot that probably placed two games and possibly as many as four games into the win column for the White Sox."[19] Holmes continued:

When the Detroit team arrived in Chicago via train (from Cleveland) for their first doubleheader on Sunday, the club was in a foul mood. This was mostly a veteran team who had played much of their careers under manager Hughie Jennings, and the bloom was off the rose. Jennings knew his team wasn't going anywhere in the standings, his team knew their manager wasn't going anywhere, and most of them were mired in terrible slumps that had lasted nearly the season. Only center fielder Cobb (on his way to another batting title with a mark well over .380) and right fielder Bobby Veach were enjoying good seasons at the plate. The clubhouse was also split into two factions over the situation with veteran outfielder Sam Crawford. Jennings had benched Crawford in June for his poor hitting, handing his outfield spot to Harry Heilmann. Half of the team was pissed that Wahoo Sam had been so poorly mistreated in their view, while the other half was irked that Jennings allowed Crawford (in his diminished role) to skip several road trips that summer. The 1917 season would be Sam's last in a Detroit uniform. The ballclub in a sense was now Cobb's team.[20]

Sensing the discontent among several members of the Tigers, someone on the White Sox, likely first baseman Chick Gandil, sent word to the Tigers that they would receive money if they did not try to win these four upcoming games. Later interviews with Gandil, White Sox team owner Charles Comiskey, and three members of the Tigers confirmed the White Sox offer.[21] Moreover, Holmes believes most players on both sides were aware of the arrangement. The Tigers' poor play and seeming indifference led E. A. Batchelor to give his readers broad hints that something was amiss:

September 2, game one, a 7–2 White Sox win: "Hard hitting in the first and third innings, coupled with some very amateurish fielding by the Tigers in these rounds, made the first game a romp for the Sox."[22]

September 2, game two, a 6–5 White Sox win: "Bases on balls and failure to hold men on the sacks. . . . Three of the Sox's runs were scored by men who had walked, and there were six thefts, all due to long leads that [pitcher] George [Cunningham] allowed."[23]

September 3, game one, a 7–5 White Sox win: "But Ehmke couldn't get the ball over and, between putting men on and letting them run hog wild after they got there, tossed it off. . . . The wildness of the Detroit hurlers and the base-running of the Sox decided the first joust. Chicago stole seven [actually eight] bases and six of its seven (runs) were scored by men who had walked."[24]

September 3, game two, a 14–8 White Sox win: "No language that a respectable family newspaper would print would do justice to this carnival. It was a grand medley of bad pitching, loose fielding, and hard hitting."[25]

In the game Ehmke started, he pitched six innings, allowing six earned runs, seven hits, and six walks. He also threw a wild pitch and allowed most of Chicago's eight stolen bases. However, when a hearing concerning this series came before Commissioner Kenesaw Mountain Landis in 1927, Ehmke never was mentioned as one having received money in the alleged arrangement between the two teams. As a result of winning the four games with Detroit, the White Sox picked up three games on the Red Sox, and their lead over Boston was now a commanding 6½ games.

In his next start, at St. Louis six days later, Ehmke lasted just 2⅓ innings, allowing the Browns five runs on six hits in a 6–2 loss for the Tigers. Two relief appearances followed before he ended the season on a high note in his final start, a three-hit shutout against the Senators and Walter Johnson on September 22.

Ehmke did make one more pitching appearance in 1917, but it was in an exhibition game at Fenway Park on September 27. He pitched three scoreless innings in a game between the Red Sox and a team composed of Major League stars. The contest was played as a benefit to raise money for the family of Tim Murnane, a former player and longtime sportswriter for the *Boston Globe* who had passed away in February. Tigers manager Jennings managed the all-stars, and Ehmke's teammate Ty Cobb was part of an outfield that included Chicago's Joe Jackson and Cleveland's Tris Speaker.

The Red Sox could not do anything against the Yankees' Urban Shocker, who pitched the first three innings, or Ehmke, who pitched the middle three, allowing no runs and one hit. They scored the only two runs of the game in the eighth, against Walter Johnson. Babe Ruth pitched the first five innings and Rube Foster the final four for the winning Red Sox.[26]

The Tigers were not scheduled to play that day, allowing Ehmke, Jennings, and Cobb to participate in the benefit game.[27] However, Ehmke was also absent from the club for Detroit's last scheduled games of the season on September 29. While the Tigers were in Philadelphia playing a doubleheader against the Athletics, he was at the First Universalist Church in Mount Vernon, New York, serving as the best man at his brother Lester's wedding.

In June the *Silver Creek News* had reprinted an article by the *Detroit Journal*'s Beasley that quoted former pitching star and current American League umpire Bill Dinneen. "Ehmke is a great pitcher right now," Dinneen said, perhaps going a bit overboard in his praise. "He is one of the wisest youngsters I ever have come in contact with. He has exceptional ability and the principal reason for his effectiveness is that he never gives the batter the same thing twice. A batter may look at the same hook, but it is delivered in a different way, and the style of delivery puzzles quite as much as the stuff on the baseball. With any kind of hitting, Ehmke will win just about every game he pitches."[28]

While Dinneen's account establishes that Ehmke used different deliveries early on, game accounts throughout his career show that he sometimes used only one or two styles of delivery to a batter and even throughout a game. However, he often varied the angle of delivery within each style.

Dinneen's prediction, as well as predictions of bright futures for all young players in 1917, now came with an acknowledged caveat, however. The United States had entered the Great War in April, and the Tigers feared they would lose Ehmke to the draft. When Congress passed a bill favoring conscription, the twenty-three-year-old unmarried pitcher seemed likely to be called. "After searching for years for a pitcher with the promise of the class of Walter Johnson or Grover Cleveland Alexander, and finally uncovering one," wrote Beasley, "wouldn't it be just a little like fate if the long and purposeful arm of conscription reached in and jerked him away from Hughie Jennings?"[29]

12

Quinn Goes to the Pacific Coast League

Like Howard Ehmke, Jack Quinn had to lower his sights in 1916. As a result of his poor 1915 season in the Federal League, no Major League club offered him a job.[1] Instead Quinn signed with the Vernon Tigers of the Class Double-A Pacific Coast League, the Minor Leagues' highest level. Class Double-A rosters were filled with a fascinating mix of players: future stars on the way up, aging veterans hanging on, and a large group who would either never make it to the Majors or would be marginal contributors when they got there. Ehmke, by comparison, would compete in the lower-level Class B New York State League in 1916.

Quinn's teammates included twenty-two-year old shortstop Swede Risberg, who would go on to infamy as a member of the 1919 Chicago Black Sox, and thirty-five-year-old Charles "Boss" Schmidt, Ty Cobb's teammate and antagonist on the pennant-winning Detroit Tigers of 1907, 1908, and 1909.[2] Art Fromme, who had some success with the Cincinnati Reds and the New York Giants a few years earlier, led the club in wins with twenty-three. He would never return to the Majors.

The Coast League, with the temperate climate of its cities, played a much longer schedule than the 154 games Major League teams played. In 1916 the season started on April 4, and the final game was played on October 29. The longer season allowed teams to pay salaries close to those of Major League clubs. The 1916 Tigers played 206 games, and Jack Quinn was their workhorse; he appeared in fifty-one of them and won sixteen.

Vernon was a small community just five miles south of downtown Los Angeles; it was founded in 1905 as a factory town and remains so to this day. A 2011 *New York Times* article described it as a backdrop to David Lynch's bleak futuristic movie *Eraserhead*.[3] Its drawing card was that it was one of only two cities in the county that allowed the sale of alcohol in ballparks.[4] Boxing promoter Jack Doyle's huge tavern with its hundred-foot "longest bar in the world" was adjacent to his boxing arena and next to the Tigers' ballpark.[5]

The other "wet" town was Venice, a beach community where the Tigers played in 1913, 1914, and part of 1915. Owner Ed Maier wanted to host Sunday games, which Venice allowed and Vernon did not. Moreover, the Vernon ballpark, located in a saloon-infested neighborhood, was not conducive to family crowds. But Venice was simply too small a town to support the team.

A February 1916 article in the *Los Angeles Times* reported that the "celebrated" Federal League pitcher Jack Quinn might join Vernon, but he would bring with him a salary for "an unheard of sum of money," the final year of his three-year Federal League contract.[6] When Quinn did sign later that month, a reporter noted that Vernon assumed only part of his contract, $2,000–$2,500, and Quinn then settled with Baltimore for the balance.[7]

The Tigers battled Frank Chance's Los Angeles Angels for first place all season in the six-team league. The proximity of the Angels to the Tigers made for one of the best rivalries in the game. "Ball Games may come and go," a local journalist noted, "but Tiger-Angel ball games always have been and always will be the best of them all."[8]

The legendary Chance's return to baseball made headlines that spring. In addition to taking over as the manager of the Angels, he bought an ownership stake in the club.[9] After winning four pennants and two world championships as a player-manager with the Chicago Cubs from 1905 to 1912, he had a miserable time and poor results leading the New York Yankees after replacing Harry Wolverton in 1913. But he grew restless tending to his Glendora, California, orange grove and, despite numerous health problems, wanted to get back into the game.[10]

On April 13 Quinn three-hit the defending league champions, the San Francisco Seals, 11–0. With his spitter "breaking fast he had almost perfect control," reported the *Tribune*.[11] But Quinn hit a rough stretch in May, and one Los Angeles paper reported, "Indications point to the release of Jack Quinn today."[12] It did not happen, and at the end of the month, he turned his season around. Quinn, who was superstitious by nature, felt there was a jinx following him and therefore threw away his

14. Jack Quinn started for the Pacific Coast League's Vernon Tigers on Opening Day, 1916. Seen here that day are Tigers manager Ham Patterson, automobile maker Hugh Chalmers, and Los Angeles Angels manager Frank Chance (*left to right*). Chalmers, a baseball enthusiast whose cars were awarded to the Major League's best players from 1910 to 1914, provided a fleet of his cars for the opening day parade in Los Angeles. *Dennis Goldstein Collection.*

shoes and glove and got new ones.[13] Jinx or not, the new equipment coincided with his improved performance.

While the Tigers won 115 games (and lost 91) in 1916, they fell 8 games short of Los Angeles. The Angels made a key pickup late in the season, Doc Crandall, a longtime pitcher for the New York Giants and one of the game's first relief specialists.[14] He would pitch ten more seasons for the Angels and win at least twenty games five times.

Chance gave the credit for winning the pennant to his men. "The boys are showing me one real quality that every champion must possess," he told a reporter in July. "And that thing is nerve."[15] At the end of the season he noted that only once did a poor ball club win a pennant through the efforts of a good manager, and that was the 1906 Chicago White Sox, "the Hitless Wonders," led by Fielder Jones. That club stunned Chance's 116-win Cubs in the World Series.[16]

Ham Patterson, the nondescript manager of the Tigers, planned to beef up the club's batting attack in 1917, but he never had the chance. He had replaced one of the most successful and popular managers in the league's history, Happy Hogan, who died of pneumonia during the 1915 season at thirty-seven.[17] Hogan had been the club's only manager since its formation in 1909. When Ed Maier sold the club after the 1916 season, it became clear new owner Tom Darmody wanted his own man.

Vernon's new manager was George Stovall. Nicknamed "Firebrand," the hot-tempered Stovall had lost his job as manager of the St. Louis Browns in 1913, when he spit tobacco juice over umpire Charlie Ferguson. Before he could take the Vernon job, Stovall had to buy his release from owner and player-manager Roger Bresnahan's Toledo Mud Hens, of which Stovall was captain in 1916.[18]

The 1917 Tigers had a future star, twenty-year-old third baseman Bob Meusel, who would become an outfielder for the great Yankees teams of the 1920s. The Tigers also had a player on the way down who would never return to the Majors even though he was only twenty-nine: Fred Snodgrass.[19]

Vernon's best pitcher in 1917 was George "Chief" Johnson, who won twenty-five games that year after winning only forty games in his Major League career. Jack Quinn was not far behind. He posted a 24-20 record and pitched a yeoman's 409⅓ innings, often pitching every third day.

When he beat Los Angeles early in the season, Harry Williams gave a vivid description of Quinn's spitball: "Quinn was full of sap, and it was flowing freely. Never when he reached to his mouth for a fresh supply of saliva was he disappointed. He always managed to secure a handful, while holding a double handful in reserve for emergencies. Jack's face is a human freshet, and he could put out a fire with it in an emergency. Yesterday he used it merely to extinguish the Angels."[20]

This description of Quinn's spitter is very different from others, which often depicted it as a dry spitter. Just two years later *New York Sun* sportswriter Dan Daniel described Quinn with that pitch: "Unlike other pitchers, he does not decorate the ball with huge gobs of saliva. He needs only one little moist spot on the ball."[21] Perhaps in this Pacific Coast League game, Quinn was experimenting, or maybe he actually reduced the wetness of the pitch later in the 1910s. Or perhaps Williams was embellishing his account.

Throughout his career Quinn's positive thinking and calm demeanor were key elements of his personality, a steadiness that belied outside circumstances. Yet in the 1917 season he let circumstances affect his behavior, if not his pitching.

For the second time in three years, Quinn's team went from being a pennant contender to a cellar dweller. After the 115-win season in 1916, the Tigers followed with an 84-128 record and a last-place finish. There were games that Quinn pitched well enough to win, but he did not receive the needed run support. He became discouraged after a difficult stretch and left the team in July, when it departed for Portland. A headline in the *San Francisco Chronicle* told the story: "Jack Quinn Has Grouch; Can't Win, So Goes Home."[22] He told the team's owner that he wanted the break "to shake the jynx [sic]."[23]

The break helped his results, if not the team's overall direction, as he and Art Fromme won thirteen of fourteen starts in a stretch of July–August games.[24]

Quinn's bad luck still dogged him. In his last August start he went eighteen innings against Portland, only to lose, 3–2. Bob Meusel dropped a routine fly ball in the eighteenth, followed by another Tigers' error that led to Portland's winning run.[25] On September 11 the thirty-four-year-old Quinn (thought to be thirty-two at the time) faced thirty-eight-year-old Long Tom Hughes of Salt Lake City. In a game that showed "the old geezers are getting tight and stingy in their old age," as one reporter put it, Quinn's two-hitter topped Hughes's four-hitter, 2–0.[26]

San Francisco edged Los Angeles by 2 games to capture the 1917 pennant. Harry Wolverton was fired as the Seals' manager in June, although they were in first place at the time, and a couple of weeks later Frank Chance resigned as manager of the Angels.[27] "'The Peerless Leader' was sick, exhausted and finally ready to heed the desire of his wife to retire," wrote historian Dennis Snelling.[28]

Vernon finished 35 games back. George Stovall's temper erupted at times during the season, most dramatically on August 19. He was so upset with a call by umpire Ed Finney that he tore off Finney's chest protector and, according to one reporter, attempted to "disrobe" the arbiter. A suspension followed for Stovall.[29] Because of the Tigers' poor performance, his contract was not renewed. The Tigers would be looking for their fourth manager in four years.

No member of the 1917 Vernon Tigers was drafted by a Major League club. Jack Quinn's twenty-four wins, along with his sterling 2.35 earned run average and impeccable control (he gave up a walk only every 4.9 innings) were not enough to get him back to the big leagues. In November he asked for his release, but the Tigers wanted to keep him.[30] He would be thirty-five years old in 1918, an age at which most ballplayers were reaching the end of their careers, if they had not already done so. If he was not getting breaks on the playing field or in the scouting reports, he would have to make his own breaks.

Quinn was in terrific physical shape, a reflection of his off-season regimen. As early as 1912, *Sporting Life* noted that he spent most of the winter hunting bear and deer.[31] He had a cabin in the wilderness area of Roaring Creek, Pennsylvania, below Catawissa Mountain and about 115 miles northwest of Philadelphia, to which he and his wife returned year after year. Years later he told a reporter that he always wanted to keep his legs strong: "That's the reason I come up here every year, take out a hunter's license and stick around for several months."[32]

Vernon's new manager was Bill Essick, who had led Grand Rapids of the Class B Central League, where he was the club's part owner, business manager, and field manager since 1913.[33] Grand Rapids won pennants his first and last years there. Essick had been a "cup-of-coffee" Major Leaguer, a pitcher who appeared in only nine big league games.[34] He faced a new challenge in 1918, as did all of baseball: the entry of the United States into the Great War. While the nation had entered the war in April 1917, it was not until 1918 that the military draft had a major impact on society in general, and baseball was no exception.

A looming manpower shortage in baseball created an opportunity for Quinn, and he maximized it with a 1918 season that was so impressive that he simply could not be denied.[35] He was consistently sharp, game after game, allowing very few runs.

On April 9 Quinn shut out the Angels, 2–0, with a two-hitter. Reporter Edwin O'Malley wrote, "The ball whirred over the plate in all kinds of elusive dips from the twirl of a dancing dervish to the twist of a St. Vitus expert. . . . Any time a club spots Jack Quinn two runs, it's almost Kitty [sic] bar the door for his opponents."[36] Two weeks later he went the distance in a seventeen-inning loss to Oakland. Quinn did not walk anyone and struck out twelve. And he seemed to handle a tough loss better than he had the previous year. "It also would have been hard for him [referring to opposing pitcher Speed Martin] to lose," he said.[37]

On May 29, Quinn was one out away from a 2–1 win over San Francisco when Lefty O'Doul, a twenty-one-year-old pitcher, pinch-hit with a man on base and won the game for the Seals with a double and a subsequent Tigers throwing error. O'Doul would win only one game in the Majors but would move to the outfield and post a career .349 batting average.[38] He and Jack Quinn would be teammates more than once in the coming years.

On June 16 Quinn three-hit Oakland, beating Martin, 1–0. Ten days later he beat the Oaks again by the same 1–0 score, this time on four hits, and struck out nine men. The reporter for the *San Francisco Chronicle* noted the improvement of the Tigers. This year's team "is after [head of the Food Administration Herbert] Hoover's own heart, for it conserves everything, and a lead of one run means a lot in their style of play, so Jack has a chance."[39] On July 9 he two-hit Salt Lake, 6–0, and defeated the Bees again four days later, 3–1. In both games former Detroit Tigers star pitcher Ed Willett was the loser.[40]

Charlie Chech, who had been Howard Ehmke's teammate on the Angels in 1914, was now Jack Quinn's teammate. Chech had been a two-time twenty-game winner for Los Angeles, and now, at the age of forty, was still effective with a 2.11 earned run average in 1918. Chech's parents had emigrated from Bohemia and probably came from what is now the Czech Republic or Slovakia.[41] Whether he and Quinn ever talked about their similar ancestries is not known.

The Great War was now having an impact on many aspects of life in America. When the railroads raised their rates for Pullman travel, effective June 10, the Coast League's executives announced that the teams would travel by automobile.[42] The league had already replaced the Portland club with one in Sacramento, 579 miles to the south, to reduce travel expenses. The military draft of all able-bodied men between the ages of twenty-one and thirty was ramping up considerably as the nation was now sending large numbers of soldiers to Europe. As Steve Steinberg wrote, "After years of enormous casualties on the European front, it was evident that American manpower held the key to the Allied war effort."[43]

On June 24, when the Tigers moved to within 3 games of first place, a reporter predicted the pennant would be theirs: "Developments of the past few days make it a cinch for the Vernon club to win the pennant this year. The opposing clubs have been blown to pieces. The Tigers haven't been touched." The reporter noted that the draft would not be a problem for Vernon "unless our Uncle Sam takes a notion to grab a few veterans to amuse the boys at the front by telling stories or giving lessons in checkers."[44] The reason for the prediction was simple: the Tigers were an older club. Their top five pitchers were all over the age of thirty, as were two of their best hitters.[45]

But the terrain was shifting quickly. Provost Marshall Enoch Crowder, in charge of the military draft, issued a "Work or Fight" order on May 23. Young men either had to work in an essential industry (such as steelmaking or shipbuilding) or enter the military. In July Secretary of War Newton Baker clarified that baseball was a nonessential industry; there would be no exemption for the national pastime. With falling attendance and rising costs, the league's teams were losing a lot of money. On July 12 Vernon owner Darmody informed the league he did not have the resources to continue.[46]

The Pacific Coast League season ended on Sunday, July 14, after teams had played about one hundred games, half their typical schedule.[47] The league's officials decided a best-of-nine series between the top two teams would determine the league's champion, even though Vernon had finished 2 games ahead of Los Angeles. It would generate additional revenue for two struggling clubs, with minimal travel costs.

Though Quinn's record was just 13-9 in 1918, his control was spectacular: he walked one man every 10.7 innings. His 1.48 earned run average is still the lowest ever in the highest level of the Minor Leagues.[48] While Quinn did not create the furor that Howard Ehmke had generated with his 1916 season in Syracuse, he did show that he could still pitch. But would anyone in the Major Leagues give this thirty-five-year-old another chance?

13

"The Dynamite That Finally
Shattered Their Friendship"

When professional baseball shut down before the end of the 1918 season, the National Commission ruled players could sign elsewhere and compete in leagues that were still operating.[1] Even the Major Leagues were ending their season about a month early, on Labor Day, after it was clarified in July that ballplayers were not exempt from the military draft.[2] Organized Baseball had to let Minor League players become free agents to avoid their suing, on economic grounds, that they were entitled to earn a living. An adverse court ruling might threaten the reserve clause, a foundation of the game and major source of profit for the owners.

The government never required baseball to shut down. But with the requirement that all able-bodied young men had to work in essential industries or fight, the quality of play would decline, with resultant loss of fan interest and a fall-off in attendance. As early as late May, a Pacific Coast League sportswriter realized the impact the war would soon have: "We do not agree with the one or two magnates who express the optimistic opinion that 'enough bushers and old timers can be held together to keep the game going.' If the regulars are called, all public interest will follow them to their new field. There would remain no reason why the game should be carried along at a limping gait."[3]

The National Commission legislated to have it both ways. As leagues suspended play, the clubs did not pay their players for the canceled portion of the season.[4] But once play resumed, at the end of the war, the rights to the players would revert to their original teams.[5]

When the Coast League season ended on July 14, 1918, the Major Leagues still had more than six weeks to play. They were losing players, especially to war-related industries, and looked to the Minors to fill roster spots. Because of his performance that season in Vernon and because he was beyond draft age, Jack Quinn received a deluge of offers from independent and shipyard teams, as well as Major League clubs. This had to be a satisfying time for the man who had garnered no interest just two years earlier. A Boston sportswriter noted that Quinn "was recently resurrected on the Pacific Coast. It is beginning to look now as if Mr. Methuselah might be worth paging."[6]

Quinn had offers from eight big league clubs and was leaning toward one from one of his old teams, the Boston Braves.[7] "I had about made up my mind to accept the Braves' terms when I met a White Sox scout," he told a reporter. The scout talked to Charles Comiskey, owner of the defending world champions, who offered Quinn a better salary and agreed to provide transportation to Chicago for him and his wife.[8] Chicago also was where he and his wife lived during the off-season.

Before signing Quinn, Comiskey asked Garry Herrmann, the president of the National Commission, how he should handle the transaction. Herrmann told him to deal with Quinn directly since, like other Minor League players whose season had ended, he was a free agent.

But a complication arose, one that would have far-reaching implications for Organized Baseball. As noted in chapter 12, the Coast League decided that first-place Vernon and second-place Los Angeles would play a best-of-nine series for the league's championship. It would enable the clubs to make more money and the players to earn more of their contract salaries. On the day that Comiskey and Quinn had agreed to terms, July 18, the owner of the Angels, John Powers, wired the National Commission that the Angels were playing the series with Vernon and "until that period is complete, we have the right to dispose of players as we see fit."[9]

This extension of the season meant that Quinn was still a member of the Tigers on July 18, when the White Sox signed him—and not a free agent. That same day the New York Yankees reached terms to acquire Quinn directly from Vernon owner Tom Darmody. Just how much they paid is not known, but ten years later the *New York Sun* reported that Connie Mack, owner and manager of the struggling Philadelphia Athletics, was aware of Quinn's excellent 1918 season but was not convinced of Quinn's rejuvenation enough to pay the $10,000 asking price.[10] It later emerged that the Yankees sent three players to Vernon for Quinn.[11]

Los Angeles won the series, 5–2. Their star pitcher, Doc Crandall, who led the league with sixteen wins, beat Quinn in game two, 3–1. Quinn dropped another close decision in game six, 4–3.[12] After one of the championship games, manager Bill Essick informed Quinn that he had been sold to the Yankees. When Quinn got upset, Essick told him, "You report to New York, and they'll straighten it out. . . . Well, you better go to New York if you don't want to get in trouble."[13]

After the series, many of the Tigers joined the Los Angeles Dry Dock team, and Essick took over as its manager. Quinn ignored Essick's warning and reported to the White Sox, where Comiskey told him he would straighten the matter out with Ban Johnson. Quinn felt the matter had been—or would be—resolved and focused on pitching in the Majors once again.

In August Quinn started five games for Chicago and completed them all. He won four and picked up another victory with six innings of three-hit relief work against New York.[14] When he beat the Yankees for the second time, on August 19, a *New York Times* reporter wrote, "The funny part of it is that [Yankees] Manager Miller Huggins maintains that Jack Quinn is the property of the Yanks."[15] Quinn's 4–1 win that day came over his one-time Yankees roommate, Ray Caldwell.

Huggins and the Yankees had not given up on their claim to Quinn. Sportswriter Fred Lieb found the fight over Quinn amusing; he assumed the pitcher, now in his midthirties, was washed up. Musing about older former players manning lineups after regulars left for war industries, Lieb wrote, "Still more funny is the sight of the Yankees and Chicago White Sox scrapping for the services of John Picus, alias Quinn."[16]

On August 24, the day he won his fifth game in just eighteen days for Chicago, Organized Baseball awarded Quinn to New York. In his history of the White Sox, Warren Brown wrote, "In a decision that sets some kind of record for confused expression . . . the Quinn case was the final destructive blow to any hope of a reconciliation between [Ban] Johnson and [Charles] Comiskey."[17]

The ruling stated the following: "The controversy is rather unfortunate for several reasons. The advice given Mr. Comiskey in the matter

15. Charles Martin Conlon (1868–1945) was arguably the most famous baseball photographer ever. Rarely appearing in photographs himself, Conlon is seen here taking a photo of White Sox teammates Joe Benz and Jack Quinn (*in dugout, left and right respectively*) in August 1918. Quinn was on the club only for the final month of that war-shortened season before he was awarded to the Yankees in a controversial ruling. Benz, who won his final Major League game that month, had appeared in twenty-nine games for the 1917 world champion White Sox. *Paul Reiferson and Julie Spivack Collection.*

of the Commission was in line with the thought that was in its mind at the time. . . . Unfortunately, in this case, Mr. Comiskey, having followed the advice of the Commission, probably may have lost the opportunity to deal direct with the club and thus may have secured the player's release previous to the time that the New York club commenced to negotiate for him."[18]

It is not clear whether the three-man commission made the ruling or whether American League president Ban Johnson did it on his own since this was solely an American League dispute. Both Taylor Spink, the publisher of the *Sporting News*, and Fred Lieb reported that it was Johnson's decision alone.[19] However, the decision was signed by all three members of the commission, including National League president John Heydler and commission president and Cincinnati Reds owner Garry Herrmann.

Johnson likely wanted the other signatures to accompany his because he knew how controversial the ruling would be. A longtime friend of Comiskey, Johnson already had a strained relationship with the White Sox owner that had deteriorated over the years. Johnson had come under severe criticism from other owners for his shifting approach to baseball during the war. After supporting an early shutdown in the summer of 1917, he switched direction and requested an exemption from the military draft for all 288 Major League players. Many felt his first position was premature and his second was damaging because it portrayed baseball as unpatriotic.

When he did not secure such an exemption, Johnson reverted to his original position and recommended an immediate shutdown of the game in the summer. Historian Jim Leeke noted that just three weeks before the Quinn ruling, Comiskey and owners Harry Frazee of the Red Sox and Clark Griffith of the Senators had lashed out at Johnson. "He has bungled the affairs of his league in this particular case. . . . He has tried to close our gates several times this season. . . . But from now on, the club owners are going to run the American League."[20]

The National Commission's Quinn ruling infuriated Comiskey. The Chicago owner was reputedly overheard shouting at Johnson afterward, "I made you, and by God, I'll break you."[21] More than a decade later Johnson said, "Comiskey regarded it as something I was personally responsible for, and the final break in our baseball relations occurred."[22] The two men, close friends and the driving forces behind the rise of the American League in the early 1900s, never spoke again.

In his biography of Johnson, Eugene Murdock stated the decision to award Quinn to the Yankees "was no doubt right."[23] *Sporting News* columnist John B. Sheridan agreed: "I would have voted to give Quinn to New York—for the reason that it was wise, good business, good law, and good policy that the Vernon club should get the benefit of the sale of this pitcher."[24]

The decision seemed the correct one. The National Commission ruled that after the war, with the resumption of baseball, players would revert to their original teams. Therefore in 1919 a Major League club that wanted to acquire Quinn would have had to deal with his club, the Vernon Tigers. A chapter of Johnson's life story, serialized in newspapers in early 1929, was titled "Yankees Had Clearer Title."[25] Comiskey was simply caught in a unique and shifting set of circumstances.

Johnson also told his side of the story in another widely publicized newspaper article in the *Cleveland Plain Dealer*, also in early 1929. It prompted Comiskey to respond with a letter to the paper. This was his first public utterance on the matter, and he made some interesting points. He claimed that both Garry Herrmann and Ban Johnson had told him "to deal with the players direct and that if later on we wished to retain them for the season of 1919, we should pay the draft price to the Pacific Coast League clubs involved."[26] Comiskey added he was incensed because he felt the league's president was trying to curry favor with the owners of the Yankees, Colonel Jacob Ruppert and Til Huston. Unfortunately for Johnson, he lost their support in the summer of 1919, when he opposed their signing of Red Sox pitcher Carl Mays. Johnson's power base had eroded significantly.

Chicago sportswriter Hugh Fullerton was an outspoken critic of the National Commission long before the Black Sox scandal. After the Quinn ruling he wrote, "On just what grounds the decision was made, no one seems clear.... If it is within the power of the commission to make or to wreck ball clubs, to strengthen or to weaken teams at will, then the sooner the National Commission is put out of business, the better it will be for the game."[27]

Without Comiskey's backing, Johnson lacked the support to maintain his power after the 1919 Black Sox scandal broke in the fall of 1920. While there were many factors contributing to the demise of the National Commission and its replacement with a single commissioner, the Quinn case helped facilitate the change, and Commissioner Kenesaw Landis was able to marginalize and humiliate Johnson in the 1920s.

When Comiskey died in October 1931, a few months after Johnson, obituaries noted the conflict. Typical was the AP account: "As Damian and Pythias, they elevated themselves to powerful positions in the National Pastime; as bitter enemies, both fell from their pinnacles with broken hearts and shorn of their influence. . . . The fight over pitcher Jack Quinn in 1918 was the dynamite that finally shattered their friendship."[28]

Would a 1919 White Sox team that included Jack Quinn have changed baseball history? Black Sox historian Gene Carney wonders if the Black Sox scandal might not have occurred had Chicago manager Kid Gleason had another "clean" pitcher besides Dickie Kerr at his disposal.[29] With the arm trouble and illness of pitcher Red Faber, Gleason started Eddie Cicotte and Lefty Williams, both members of the plotting Black Sox, six times in the World Series.

In August 1918 Congress expanded the age range of men eligible for the draft to include men aged 18–45. While we now know the war was only three months from ending, that did not appear likely in the summer of 1918. In September Jack Quinn registered for the military draft as "John Quinn Picus," and he listed his occupation as "blacksmith."[30] There is no indication he ever changed his legal name to Quinn.

Quinn spent the off-season in Chicago and played some exhibition games in the area that fall. On October 6, before an enormous crowd, he pitched for a club called the Normals against the Fairbanks-Morse Fairies, which included Buck Weaver of the White Sox. Quinn lost, 2–1, on a tenth-inning squeeze play.[31]

"The thing they cannot fathom," wrote the *San Francisco Chronicle* about Quinn in late August, "is how he was ever allowed to remain in the Pacific Coast League so long when the world was being searched by high-priced scouts with unlimited bank rolls . . . if they could turn up a winning pitcher."[32] Quinn could not fathom it either. But now he was back. Ten years after a young phenom up from the Richmond Colts had turned heads in the Yankees' spring training camp at Macon, Jack Quinn was making his return to New York.

14

Navy Service and a Return to Detroit

Having avoided the military draft, Howard Ehmke spent the entire 1917 season with the Tigers. That would not be the case in 1918. Unlike Jack Quinn, Ehmke, because of his age and marital status, was squarely in the crosshairs of the military draft. But rather than waiting to be called, he acted first. The *Detroit Free Press* broke the news in January that the Los Angeles–based Ehmke had enlisted in the navy and was serving in California.[1] In all, twenty-four Tigers would serve in the Great War, the most of any big league club.[2] Tigers owner Frank Navin had heard rumors of the impending enlistment but hoped Ehmke would change his mind and take his chances with the draft. If he did, the Tigers would have his services for at least part of the 1918 season, if not all of it.

While praising Ehmke's abilities, the *Free Press* article brought up a quirk that often accompanied Ehmke's appearances: "Somewhere along the route of the majority of his games, Howard became submerged in the meshes of a bad inning that, if it didn't ruin him for the afternoon, usually made his eventual ascension to victory doubly difficult. . . . But the bad-inning bugaboo, over which he appeared to have no control, kept him from the glory that seemed to want to reach out and claim him."[3] Such criticism would follow him throughout his career.

Ehmke and his brother Lester were assigned to the submarine base at San Pedro, California, a community within the city of Los Angeles and the navy's first submarine base on the West Coast.[4] His first day at the base went smoothly until it was time to go to sleep. When he crawled into a lower berth, Ehmke, who was 6 feet 3 inches tall in his stocking feet, found the berth too short for him. After it was determined there was no bunk on the base long enough, a crew member was called on to add another foot to the length of the original berth. A satisfied Ehmke asked for and received a longer mattress to go with his extra-long bunk.[5]

Shortly after his enlistment, the *Los Angeles Herald* called Ehmke "the kind of lad that gets along with his teammates" and reported he would be playing the saxophone with the San Pedro sub base's band.[6] His saxophone playing aside, Ehmke spent his fourteen-month service time in the same manner as most ballplayers did: playing ball.[7] He was an immediate success for San Pedro, pitching four scoreless innings of relief in a combined 9–0 no-hitter against the Fort MacArthur army team, also located in San Pedro.[8]

Ehmke's San Pedro team was among the best of the service teams. It had won the West Coast naval baseball title in 1917 and would win it again in 1918. In addition to Ehmke, the ace of the pitching staff, its roster included many former Major and Minor Leaguers. Foremost among them were Harry Heilmann, Ehmke's teammate with Detroit, and future big league stars Bob Meusel and Lefty O'Doul. The team played against other service teams, Pacific Coast League teams, and a wide assortment of company and industrial teams from the Los Angeles area.

Two of the game's best pitchers, Christy Mathewson and Grover Alexander, saw action in Europe and had their postwar lives adversely affected. By contrast, Ehmke spent his entire service time in California. As a student of the art of pitching, he used the time to work on various deliveries and to further develop his underhand pitch, which at the time he called his "tunnel ball." Over the years, as noted in a 1928 interview, Ehmke would earn a reputation for "devising many and varied methods of pitching, most of which were dependent upon the surroundings in the park in which he pitched." In the interview Ehmke said his height and wingspan allowed him to make use of side-arm and underhand pitches. He would stand on the extreme third base side of the rubber, a position that caused his pitches to come at an angle that was difficult for batters to pick up.[9]

Ehmke's year in the navy was injury-free, though one late autumn headline suggested otherwise: "Ehmke, Big League Pitcher, Near Death in Crash of Autos." Despite this alarming headline, Ehmke was not seriously hurt in the two-car accident two miles east of Los Angeles. However, his car was wrecked in the head-on collision. Deputy sheriffs determined the other driver was drunk and took him to the county jail.[10]

16. Douglas Fairbanks, National League pitching great Grover Alexander, Chicago Cubs owner William Wrigley Jr., Yankees-pitcher-turned-chief-petty-officer Bob Shawkey, and Howard Ehmke (*left to right*) at a California fundraiser for the war effort. Five years later Ehmke and Shawkey would be the opposing pitchers in the first game played at Yankee Stadium. *Family of Howard Ehmke.*

Both men were in a Los Angeles courtroom in early December, where the other driver was charged with "driving a machine while drunk and colliding with Ehmke's car on the Whittier Road." The accused's lawyer argued that Ehmke had been paying more attention to the pretty girl seated next to him than to the road. But Ehmke told the judge that he always drove with two hands, even when accompanied by an attractive companion.[11]

Ehmke was discharged from the navy on March 5, 1919. He mailed his signed contract to Navin and included a letter informing the owner he had added some weight during his time in the service. The weight, in the form of muscle, came from months of physical training at the submarine base. The mention of the added weight pleased Navin, who believed Ehmke's lack of heft had worked against him in the past.[12]

"Recognizing the dislocation and social and labor upheaval the war had generated, baseball's owners believed a return to a full 154-game schedule would be both impractical and unprofitable. So, they decided on another shortened season for 1919, only 140 games."[13] But the owners badly misjudged how much peace would stimulate turnout at all levels of baseball. Major League attendance more than doubled from 1918, while in Detroit it rose from 203,719 to a league-high 643,805.

The Tigers' team to which Ehmke returned was very similar to the one he had left in 1917. Hughie Jennings was still the manager, and Ty Cobb was still the team's—and baseball's—biggest star. As someone who took a cerebral approach to pitching, Ehmke would be most affected by the hiring of Dan Howley as the team's new pitching coach. Howley, a former National League catcher, had managed in the International League the previous five seasons.[14]

The thirty-three-year-old Howley spent a good part of spring training encouraging Ehmke to work on developing his slow ball. "Howard, you should be a great pitcher," Howley told him. "You have good speed, use good judgment, and if you can perfect your change of pace with a good slow one, you will be hard to beat."[15]

Because of the shortened season, training camp started three weeks later than the usual March 1. And for the Tigers it would be in a new location. After three years in Waxahatchie, Texas, they moved to Macon, Georgia, a city the Yankees had abandoned.[16] In Ehmke's first workout he showed the batters more stuff than they would usually see this early in the spring. He attributed his advanced standing to having worked out three weeks on the West Coast and pronounced himself ready to start the season.

"Great," was manager Jennings's description of Ehmke's performance against the Boston Braves on April 4 in Columbus, Georgia. "Ehmke was great, not so much because he held the Braves hitless in his three innings, but because of his intelligent pitching. He mixed a fast one, which fairly sizzled, with a slow delivery that [Braves manager George] Stallings' men popped up."[17] Ehmke was three weeks short of his twenty-fifth birthday, an age at which pitchers are seldom described with the adjective "intelligent." But he had already earned that reputation and would carry it throughout his career.

Cold weather in Detroit twice postponed the Tigers' opener against Cleveland. Every team in each league had already played when Ehmke beat the Indians and their ace, Stan Coveleski, 4–2, at Navin Field on April 25.[18] Ehmke had been the team's best pitcher all spring, and manager Jennings chose him to pitch the opener despite his not having pitched in the league in 1918.[19] Weather conditions remained windy and frigid, making it especially difficult for the fielders. Cleveland had three errors, and the Tigers had two. Ehmke allowed only one earned run, and Coveleski allowed two.

Four consecutive losses followed Detroit's Opening Day win. After finally winning a game, the team continued to struggle. When Ehmke dropped an 8–2 decision to Washington's Walter Johnson on May 18, the team's sixth straight loss, the Tigers' record fell to 5-14, which would be their low point for the season.

A *Detroit News* reporter, while acknowledging Ehmke's natural ability, thought his worst liability was overconfidence. He believed it led Ehmke to underestimate his opponents and get careless. "Few pitchers who have come into the majors in recent years have displayed more natural ability, speed, curves and control than Howard Ehmke," he wrote. "He is a good pitcher now and is bound to improve, but he has one fault which he should overcome, a tendency to be careless."[20]

While Ehmke had lost four of his five starts since the opener, he had pitched extremely well in two of the games but was victimized by poor run support. One of the losses was to Chicago, 3–1, and another to New York, 1–0. Ehmke's one win was a 3–2 game against St. Louis. The Tigers had rallied after that May 18 loss to the Senators, winning twelve of fourteen to rise above the .500 mark. Ehmke's contribution was three wins and one loss, including a 2–0 shutout of the Browns.

After floundering for two weeks, the sixth-place Tigers began a hot streak on June 15. They went 29-15, rising to third place on July 24, 7½ games behind first-place Chicago. Ehmke won four consecutive games and seven of eight during that stretch to raise his record to 12-7. Two of his best efforts of the season came in back-to-back starts against the Indians and the Browns.

Facing Cleveland at home on June 29, Ehmke pitched a one-hit, 4–0 shutout, giving Detroit a sweep of the four-game series. Larry Gardner got the Indians' only hit, a second-inning infield single that shortstop Donie Bush was unable to handle. "The official scorer wisely and justly credited the batsman with a safety," wrote Harry Bullion of the *Detroit Free Press.* "Even if he didn't satisfy the ambition of all pitchers [a no-hitter], Ehmke treated the largest crowd of the season to the best performance on the hill turned in by any Bengal twirler [this season]."[21]

At St. Louis on July 3 Ehmke outdueled Urban Shocker, 3–1, allowing the Browns just three singles. The win was his fourth of the season against St. Louis, the team against which he had the most success in 1919. He would defeat the Browns one more time, giving him a 5-0 record against them. However, one of those wins was hardly an artistic success. In game two of an August 30 doubleheader at Sportsman's Park, Ehmke fell behind, 7–0, but the Tigers scored four runs in both the eighth and ninth innings to win, 8–7. Because Jennings kept him on the mound for eight innings, Ehmke batted four times and had the only four-hit game (4 for 4) of his career. Earlier in the season, on July 21, he had had a three-hit game against Boston's Babe Ruth. A better hitting pitcher than most, Ehmke easily led all Detroit hurlers in hits (23) and batting average (.253) in 1919.

Already in his young career, Ehmke had been criticized for both fragility and a lack of competitive spirit. Despite two heroic pitching efforts, seven weeks apart, such comments would continue to haunt him.

Facing the last-place Athletics on July 16, Ehmke took a 4–3 lead into the ninth inning, only to have the A's tie the score. Detroit failed to score in the home ninth, and the game went into extra innings. Ehmke and Scott Perry, in relief, kept their opponents scoreless until the Tigers pushed over a run in the fourteenth inning to win, 5–4.

Making just his second start after missing three weeks with arm problems, Ehmke showed even greater endurance in a September 2 win over league-leading Chicago. The Tigers staked him to an early 3–0 lead, but the White Sox rallied in the middle innings and after six, the score was tied, 3–3. For the next nine innings Ehmke (whom the *Chicago Tribune*'s I. E. Sanborn called the "human string bean") and Chicago's 5-foot-7-inch rookie left-hander Dickie Kerr (whom Sanborn called "the pygmy of the pitching world") put up zeroes on the scoreboard.[22] Ty Cobb opened the last of the sixteenth with his fifth hit of the day, a single, and eventually scored the winning run. In the sixteen innings Ehmke was constantly in trouble, as Chicago left nineteen men on base. He walked seven and allowed seventeen hits, with each of the nine White Sox batters getting at least one. The Tigers' defense did not help, making four errors, all the White Sox runs being unearned.[23] "There is no question today but that Howard Ehmke's arm once more is in good shape," wrote John C. Manning. "The lanky blonde star pitched as nervy and nice a game as anyone would care to see."[24]

Ehmke made only two relief appearances on the season. The first was at New York on August 2.[25] He replaced Dutch Leonard in the fifth inning before an estimated thirty-three thousand fans, a crowd the New York Times called the largest ever to see an American League game at the Polo Grounds.[26] It was "a flattering indication of the Yankees' hold on New York's interest."[27]

The score was 6–6 when Ehmke came into the game and 8–8 after nine, but the Tigers exploded for six runs in the tenth to win, 14–8. Ehmke earned his thirteenth win of the season. Yankees starter Jack Quinn, also going for his thirteenth win, pitched into the tenth, surrendered a grand slam to Harry Heilmann that inning (the slugging first baseman's second home run of the game), and took the loss.[28] Cobb drew the ire of the crowd when "he jumped into third base in the eighth inning with his spikes gleaming. . . . The crowd booed Tyrus long and vociferously, for his spikes cut [Frank] Baker's hand slightly."[29]

Cobb's overly aggressive style of base running and sliding surfaced again in Ehmke's complete-game, 9–4 win at Washington on September 14. Making his Major League debut for the Senators that day was twenty-four-year-old Jesse Baker. The 5-foot-4-inch Baker, nicknamed "Tiny," was Washington's starting shortstop. He was covering second base on Cobb's successful steal attempt in the second inning when the sliding Cobb spiked him. "Calling Cobb a lot of hard names," Baker left the game without getting to bat.[30] He never again played in the big leagues and is the only position player to start his only game in the Majors without ever making a plate appearance in that game.

After finishing seventh in 1918, the Tigers moved up to fourth with an 80-60 record, 8 games behind the pennant-winning Chicago White Sox. The offense was led by the trio of Ty Cobb, Bobby Veach, and Harry Heilmann. Cobb batted .384 to win his twelfth and final batting title; Veach led the league in hits, doubles, and triples; and Heilmann batted .320, the first of twelve straight seasons in which he would bat .300 or better.

Ehmke's win total jumped from ten to seventeen (he was 17-10), though his earned run average rose slightly from 2.97 to 3.18. Most of that increase came after he recovered from his arm problem. His being sidelined for three weeks in August, combined with the fourteen games lopped off the shortened schedule, may have cost Ehmke his first twenty-win season.

Yet the year 1919 had a happy ending for him. On October 21 in Los Angeles, Ehmke married Los Angeles resident Marguerite Poindexter, a twenty-five-year-old native of Oregon. Marguerite's parents, George and Genevieve Poindexter of Los Angeles, served as witnesses.

In a letter sent the next week, Ehmke informed his mother that he and Marguerite had married and that they were spending their honeymoon in a four-room, well-furnished bungalow in Avalon, on Catalina Island, fifty miles from Los Angeles. He assured his mother that his new wife "gets all the meals and knows how to care for a home."[31]

Just before the New Year Ehmke signed his contract for the 1920 season. A sportswriter for the *Detroit Free Press* hailed the signing: "That the tall fellow has the natural ability to win regularly in the big leagues has been attested ever since he became aligned with the Bengals."[32] The writer quoted late umpire Silk O'Loughlin's assessment of Ehmke. O'Loughlin, whom he called one of the best judges of ball players that ever lived, said Ehmke was "the best young pitcher he ever was privileged to look at in action," and he predicted a bright future for him.[33]

There had been a time during the 1919 season, however, when Ehmke's return with Detroit in 1920 was not considered a sure thing. Once during the summer he had requested that the Tigers trade him to another club.[34] He cited as his reason a misunderstanding with a teammate. While he mentioned no names, it is very likely, in light of later public statements by both men, that the teammate was Ty Cobb.

When Ehmke first joined the Tigers, his locker at Navin Field was next to Cobb's, and the young pitcher was impressed with Cobb's tutoring. "In the fall, he used to sit down and talk baseball with me before and after the games. The opening of every series he'd take a half hour and point out the weakness and strength of the opposing batters. Cobb knew just what kind of stuff to serve every batter."[35]

But the rapport between the two soured significantly since then and would continue to worsen over the years. The deterioration in the relationship between the stolid Ehmke, from upstate New York, and the fiery Cobb, from Georgia, was inevitable. They could not have been more different in their personalities and their approaches to the game. The cerebral Ehmke played with an even-tempered demeanor that some reporters and players, especially Cobb, often mistook for indifference. By contrast, Cobb's style of play has been well described by many, including journalist Jack Sher. "He was a fiery, unpredictable, bull-headed, daring, cruel, and brilliant performer," Sher wrote. "He was a lone wolf, fierce, combative, despised by many of his own teammates, always a center of storm and strife, one of God's angry men. But a ballplayer, a fantastic ballplayer."[36]

Almost a quarter-century after they had played their last game together, Ehmke spoke about Cobb with Philadelphia sportswriter Ed Pollock. He told Pollock that while he had a deep admiration for Cobb's competitive spirit and baseball skills, he never rated him high as a team player: "Cobb was an individualist. I doubt if any of the players liked him at the time I was with the Detroit club."[37]

15

"The Greatest Comeback in Baseball"

Jack Quinn must have felt an enormous sense of satisfaction when he arrived at the Yankees' spring training camp in Jacksonville, Florida, in March 1919. Ten years after he first joined the team in Macon, Georgia, he was back. And he was returning to a club with far wealthier owners than those of the 1909 Yankees.[1] Like Howard Ehmke, he was a survivor, a member of an exceedingly small fraternity of Federal League pitchers who were still in the Majors.

Just before Christmas 1918, Yankees manager Miller Huggins told reporters that he was counting on Quinn to be a regular in his rotation. "Quinn is a veteran, to be sure," wrote a reporter, "but he has remarkable speed, fine control, and a fast ball that promises much for the Yanks."[2] Just four days earlier Huggins had traded starter Ray Caldwell to the Red Sox, after he concluded that the pitcher's drinking problems and resultant disruptive behavior were not going away. When the Yankees were unable to sign Dutch Leonard, one of the Boston pitchers they received in return, Quinn's importance in the rotation became even greater.[3]

In 1918, Huggins's first year as the club's manager, he led the Yankees to a fourth-place finish, up two spots from 1917. Only two Yankees pitchers, George Mogridge and Slim Love, had double-digit wins in that war-shortened season, and Huggins had fought hard to acquire Quinn, first from Vernon and then from the White Sox.[4]

The harsh New York press had its skeptics about the veteran spitballer. One reporter said the "mad desire" for Quinn was "one of baseball's little mysteries."[5] But sportswriter Hyatt Daab called Quinn "the greatest comeback in baseball, a pitcher who sank to the depths of the Minors after one brief spree on the heights, but who has come back to brilliant rehabilitation."[6]

Quinn was no longer turning heads, as he had when he joined the Yankees in the spring of 1909. That attention now fell on two rookies, George Halas and Lefty O'Doul. Sportswriter Harry Schumacher wrote that if Halas, an outfielder, was even half as good as "supposedly competent judges of youthful talent persist in saying he is" (including veteran umpire Billy Evans), the Yankees' outfield should be set. Huggins himself was impressed with his prospect: "If I am any judge of a ballplayer, Halas is a star. He has every action of a great player."[7] Hampered by a spring hip injury, however, Halas hit only .091 in twelve games, and after a brief stay with the St. Paul Saints in 1920, he retired from baseball.[8]

O'Doul was a cocky twenty-two-year-old pitcher who also showed ability at the plate and in the field. One reporter wrote, "At the risk of being called an overenthusiastic booster, we will say that this boy O'Doul is the goods, even if he is left-handed. . . . He has speed to burn and a hop like a hula dancer's."[9] Huggins said that if the club's pitching held up, he would give him a chance to develop as an outfielder. "I want to hold onto this boy O'Doul," he said.[10] But the versatile athlete would not get much of a chance with the Yankees.

Jack Quinn was already one of the older pitchers in the game. While his exact age was not known, it was accepted that he was in his midthirties. (Later research showed he would turn thirty-five that summer.) References to his age, some jocular, began to reappear. Al Munro Elias, known as the "Longfellow of baseball statisticians," said, "Hardly a man is alive who saw Jack Quinn first arrive [in New York]."[11]

F. C. Lane, the editor of *Baseball Magazine*, explained why Quinn was able to pitch effectively as he got older: "A powerful physique, an iron endurance, an easy delivery, and a placid mind are the four cardinal causes of his prolonged activities in the big show."[12] Quinn had another key element that made him effective: his off-season regimen. While many players relaxed in the winter and reported to spring training out of shape, Quinn always took a different approach. "Baseball is my business," he said, "and keeping myself fit to play it is an all-year-round proposition with me." Besides a lot of hunting and hiking, he regularly got in front of a mirror and went through his pitching motions.[13]

Sunday baseball was not allowed in New York state until the spring of 1919, except in rare cases for charity games.[14] Upstate conservatives, with religious support, blocked legalization for years, even though fans in New York City clamored for legalization. Sportswriter Sid Mercer spoke for many when he wrote in early March, "When the ungodly who work six days a week in crowded cities arise and demand the right to play or witness the playing of games on Sunday, the wardens of the public morals assume the irritating paternalistic attitude, and there is trouble."[15] That May, after more than a decade of failed attempts, Sunday baseball became possible after a bill sponsored by state senator and future New York City mayor Jimmy Walker was passed.[16]

On Sunday, May 4, the Giants played at the Polo Grounds before thirty-five thousand fans. A week later the Yankees hosted the Washington Senators, and Quinn got the start against Walter Johnson. Only four thousand fans showed up due to the cold and damp weather and the uncertainty of whether the game would be played. The scoreless game was called after twelve innings, not because of approaching darkness but because Yankees co-owner Jacob Ruppert mistakenly thought no Sunday ball could be played after 6 p.m. He did not want to risk the wrath of political opponents of legalization and convinced umpire Bill Dinneen to end what was a brilliant pitchers' duel.[17]

Walter Johnson's biographer and grandson, Henry Thomas, called it one of Johnson's greatest games. Not only did he give up just two hits, but at one point he also retired twenty-eight Yankees in a row. While "the venerable Jack Quinn, in the full flight of as noteworthy a comeback as the annals ever have recorded," allowed fifteen base runners, none scored.[18] Hyatt Daab noted the game showed how valuable Quinn would be for New York.[19] His performance followed an impressive 5–1 win over the Red Sox.

On May 22, when the Yankees came to Chicago, where most of Georgiana Quinn's family lived, the White Sox organized a Jack Quinn Day. It seemed like a nice gesture for his first return to the city that believed he should still be playing for the White Sox. But baseball superstition said such attention jinxes the honoree. Indeed after Quinn was presented with a large floral horseshoe, he proceeded to lose a 1–0 decision to Lefty Williams, despite allowing only four hits.[20]

Fred Lieb noted that when Quinn pitched in Chicago and Philadelphia, "There were more big and little Picuses there than Quinns, but if John Picus wants to pitch as Jack Quinn, who can say him nay?"[21] But when Quinn applied for a passport that year, it was "John Quinn Picus" who signed the paperwork.[22]

In early June, after Quinn beat Williams in a rematch and then shut out the Detroit Tigers, his record was 6-2 and his earned run average a sparkling 1.32. New York pitching coach Paddy O'Connor's April prediction that Quinn would be "one of the leading lights of the league" was proving prescient.[23] The hard-luck pitcher dropped another 1–0 game on June 15 to Urban Shocker of the St. Louis Browns.

The Yankees were experiencing the same June success they had in 1918. When Quinn beat the Red Sox and Herb Pennock with a four-hitter on June 30, New York was in first place by 2½ games, with a 35-18 record.[24] But as in 1918, they faded in July, falling to fourth place by the end of a 13-21 month.[25]

Quinn had built a reputation as a cold-weather pitcher. He was said to have problems as the weather and the hitters heated up. Perhaps the issue was more mental than physical; after all, he grew up in the searing heat of the coal mines. Yet this season he ran off a five-game win streak in late June and early July. He beat the Cleveland Indians on July 10, finally prevailing in a 1–0 game, and led the American League with a 1.40 earned run average.

When Quinn beat the Tigers on June 11, New York fans booed the losing pitcher, Dutch Leonard, who had refused to sign with the Yankees. A month later, on July 14, Quinn again faced Leonard, this time in Detroit, and again pitched well. But the Yankees' offense slumped during a road trip that was becoming "a prolonged disaster," and Quinn lost, 3–0.[26] The game was also notable because the mild-mannered Quinn almost came to blows with Detroit's young first baseman and future Hall of Famer Harry Heilmann. When Heilmann mistook Quinn's inside pitch for a beanball, he had harsh words with the pitcher. Quinn came off the mound ready to fight, but veteran umpire Billy Evans stepped between them.[27]

On August 2 Quinn again faced Leonard, before thirty-three thousand fans at the Polo Grounds. When the Yankees knocked Leonard out of the game after four innings, Howard Ehmke took over for the Tigers. Both he and Quinn were going for their thirteenth win of the season. Heilmann's eighth-inning home run put the Tigers on top, but the game went to extra innings. Heilmann struck again in the tenth with a grand slam off Quinn, and Ehmke got the win in long relief, 14–8. Quinn's worst outing of the year (twelve runs, eleven of them earned) dropped the Yankees to fourth place.

As the Yankees fell from the top, Miller Huggins's detractors, in the press and among the fans, as well as in his own clubhouse, became more vocal and restless. During a difficult road trip in mid-July, Harry Schumacher wrote, "Never in their most degenerate days did the Yankees of 1916 and '17 display a greater facility in the art of losing than the present combination is now parading."[28]

Some criticized Huggins simply for not being the mixer, "the hale and hearty fellow" that his predecessor, Bill Donovan, had been. Others felt he was not getting the most out of his men. New York sportswriter Dan Daniel spoke out against the critics: "Propaganda, some of it outspoken, some of it insidious, is being carried on to undermine the position of the manager of the New Yorks."[29] Second baseman Del Pratt and pitcher George Mogridge were later identified as two of the "inside critics"; there was never an indication that quiet Jack Quinn was anything but supportive of his manager.[30]

While the Yankees faded from the pennant race by the end of July, they dominated the headlines for the next few weeks. On July 30 they traded for the Red Sox's talented but temperamental pitcher Carl Mays. When the American League's president, Ban Johnson, tried to stop the deal by suspending Mays, the Yankees' owners went to court.[31] Harry Schumacher sized up the acquisition well when he wrote, "It is almost certain that the Yankees will ultimately realize handsome dividends on their latest investment." However, he added, Mays is "a temperamental sort of a cuss."[32]

Schumacher also had a good grasp of the possible ramifications of the battle over Mays. After Johnson's falling out with Charles Comiskey over the Quinn case (discussed in chapter 13), he now had the Yankees' powerful owners lined up against him. They were "on the war path, with blood in their eye and murder in their hearts and will never be satisfied until they have taken Ban's umbrella away from him, jammed it down his throat and opened it to its widest spread."[33] That indeed they would do, first by obtaining an injunction preventing Johnson from interfering, then by suing him, and ultimately prevailing. Meanwhile, Mays would win fifty-three games for the 1920–21 Yankees.

While Boston's Babe Ruth set a new season's record with twenty-nine home runs, he hit none off Quinn. On September 24 Ruth was tied with Ned Williamson for the single-season record with twenty-seven, and Quinn fanned him twice. Ruth then set the mark off Bob Shawkey in the second game of the doubleheader when, "like the Colossus of Rhodes," in the words of the New York Times, he "catapulted the pill for a new altitude and distance record."[34]

While Quinn had some fine outings in the final two months of the 1919 season, he faded, as did his club, which finished in third place. He ended the season with a 15-14 record after sporting an 11-4 mark after his July 10 shutout of the Indians. His earned run average rose more than a full run from the midpoint of the season, to 2.61.[35]

When Quinn shut out Philadelphia, 9–0, on four hits on June 24, he overcame two old mental obstacles: hot weather and the Athletics. "Toiling under a torrid sun," said the account in the Philadelphia Inquirer, "the ancient muscles of John Picus became pliant and answered his every command."[36] The Athletics were now a last-place club; Quinn beat them three times in 1919 (against no losses) and had a 1.12 earned run average against them. Did Connie Mack consider that perhaps he should have bought the veteran when he had a chance to do so a year earlier?[37]

16

"Not Content to Accept Fate's Decree"

When the Yankees announced their acquisition of Babe Ruth from the Red Sox in early January 1920, the pennant expectations for Miller Huggins and his club quickly rose. The Babe's timing was impeccable. After a successful career as a pitcher, Ruth had become an everyday player in 1919. Now he was coming to America's sports and entertainment mecca as a slugger, just as the game's owners were introducing rules that would encourage hitting at the expense of pitching.[1] In 1929 Ruth looked back at the fortuitous timing of his career evolution: "I've been a pretty lucky fellow. . . . In the old days when defense was the big thing, I was a pitcher. . . . And when things switched over and hitting became the rage . . . [I was given] a chance to 'take my cut' with the rest of the sluggers. So I got a break going and coming. You can't beat that!"[2]

"The fight against the predominance of the pitcher is almost as ancient as baseball itself," wrote Chicago sportswriter I. E. Sanborn in 1920.[3] Before the start of that season, in order to introduce more offense into the game, trick pitches, which involved "doctoring" the ball and changing its aerodynamics, were banned.

Unlike the Babe, Jack Quinn (and almost all other pitchers) did not have the option of giving up pitching. And Quinn's best pitch, the spitball, was included in the list of banned pitches. Back in 1917 Washington Senators manager and future owner Clark Griffith (himself a former pitcher, ironically) declared, "Why encourage the stranglehold which the pitcher has on batting? . . . Batting is the most interesting part of the game. It ought to be encouraged."[4]

The only concession given to the spitballers (as opposed to pitchers of other doctored pitches, such as the shine ball) was a one-year reprieve. During the 1920 season they could still use the pitch as they developed replacements. Seventeen spitball pitchers, including Quinn, were registered with their league's office as permitted to use the spitter in 1920.

Harry Schumacher wrote about the uncertain future these pitchers faced: "Few confirmed spitballists have anything else to speak of, and a great majority of them will probably fade from the Major League picture when their only really effective delivery is taken from them."[5] The spitballers depended on that pitch to varying degrees. Some used it almost exclusively, while others used it sparingly. But the latter group often bluffed it to confuse batters. Some of them confused sportswriters as well.

An astute observer of the game, Harry Williams, who covered Quinn in the Pacific Coast League, wrote, "Jack Quinn is another whom prohibition of the spitball will hit in the solar plexus. . . . He is primarily a spitball pitcher."[6] Quinn himself was a bit coy at first. "I guess I'll get along [after the ban]. Maybe I don't pitch the spitball as much as a lot of people think," he said shortly after the ban was announced.[7]

But it may have been false bravado. In June Williams wrote, "Jack told me that he expects next season to take refuge in the Pacific Coast League, where spitball pitchers are permitted to pass their declining days in peace."[8] A month later a New York reporter wrote of Quinn in the *Sporting News*, "He is nearing the end of his career. Jack would not be the same cunning pitcher without the spitter that he is with it."[9]

Yet in Schumacher's opinion, "'Big Jack' never has been wholly or even largely dependent on his spitter for success. . . . It has been his custom to use it as a threat rather than a consistent aid. . . . [He] seldom dampens the ball except in an emergency or for strategic purposes. Once the 'threat' is established, he depends almost exclusively on speed, curves, and control, with the latter element predominating."[10] It is fascinating that reporters who cover the game have conflicting opinions of a pitcher's repertoire. Quinn seems to have used the spitter more often, especially as his career progressed and his fastball waned.

Quinn continued his rivalry with Walter Johnson when they split two games in the first three weeks of the 1920 season. On May 4 Quinn defeated Boston's "boy wonder," Waite Hoyt, 6–1. On May 15 Quinn had one of the most dramatic games in his career. He shut out the Indians, 2–0, and hit a two-run home run in the eighth inning off future Hall of Famer Stan Coveleski. Damon Runyon called it "a Polish affair up at the Polish Grounds yesterday. [Famed Pianist Jan] Paderewski would have enjoyed it."[11]

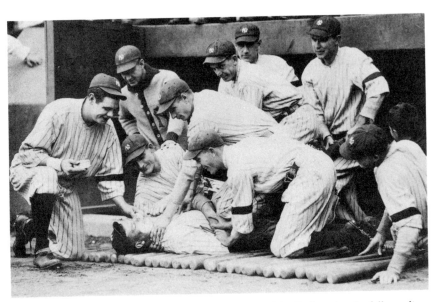

17. In 1920, Babe Ruth's first season as a member of the Yankees, he playfully applies shaving cream to Jack Quinn's face. This image reveals a lighter moment during a season with a high-pressure pennant race for the players, who fell three games short of the American League pennant. *Family of Jack Quinn.*

When Quinn defeated the Athletics on June 7 for his eighth straight win, he raised his record to 9-1, with a league-best earned run average of 1.68. On June 20 an overflow crowd in St. Louis, with fans on the field, necessitated ground rules for fly balls. The Browns, with eight doubles, took advantage of the rules more than the Yankees did. Though he gave up twelve hits, Quinn edged Urban Shocker, 4–3. The *St. Louis Post-Dispatch* reporter noted, "Quinn's exhibition of pinch pitching was one of the best witnessed in many a day."[12] He was gaining a reputation for excelling at "pitching in the pinch," being difficult to score against with runners on base.

July was a lost month for Quinn. He won only one game against four losses. Some reports said he was worn out from overwork; others said he had pulled a muscle on his side. Schumacher looked back to the weather: "Quinn is a great spring pitcher but peters out with the coming of hot weather."[13] As if to prove Schumacher wrong, Quinn bounced back in early August, shutting out the White Sox on August 2 and beating the Indians ten days later. In the latter game a *New York*

Times reporter noted Quinn's "great control and change of pace," as well as "his moist, tantalizing twists and jumps [that] obeyed his orders perfectly."[14] It was his sixteenth win. "Jack Quinn was at his best," wrote William Hanna. "He was steady, unruffled, and practically unhittable," especially when an Indian was on base.[15]

The victory brought the Yankees to within 1½ games of the first-place Indians and just a half-game behind Chicago. Babe Ruth's presence was felt in every game he played, as he drew large crowds, home and away. As sportswriter Paul Gallico put it, "The impossible was becoming the probable, and for the price of admission would take place before one's very eyes."[16] Ruth was so fearsome that pitchers were often walking him, if not intentionally, then semi-intentionally. When Coveleski faced him on August 12 in Cleveland, Ruth had already walked 106 times.[17] In addition to his .388 batting average, he had an incredible .538 on-base percentage and a slugging percentage of .878. Coveleski walked him twice that day, to limit his threat, but even Indians fans wanted to see Ruth swing away.

Quinn's return to his early-season form did not last. He pitched only one more complete game in 1920 and won only twice. On August 16 in Cleveland, a Carl Mays pitch hit popular Indians shortstop Ray Chapman and fractured his skull; he died the next day. Quinn later said he was the first man out of the dugout to tend to the fallen player and added, "It was a terrible tragedy, but an accident. . . . The truth is that poor Ray was at fault. He always crowded the plate when he hit, and he actually leaned his head over it."[18] Despite his reputation as a "headhunter," Mays hit only eighty-nine batters in his career; 127 pitchers have hit more.[19]

On August 29 Quinn hit his second home run of the year, off Shocker, to give New York a 2–0 lead in the fifth. Later in the game his spitter was neutralized—not by the St. Louis batters but by the drizzling rain. The spitball no longer generates an unpredictable break when wet weather dampens the entire ball. Quinn was able to retire only one man in the sixth and gave up three runs and the lead. The Yankees finally won, 4–3, when the opposing spitballer, Shocker, was touched for two late-inning runs. With the win, the Yankees again crept to within 1½ games of first place.

The Yankees came to Cleveland on September 9, just a half-game behind the league-leading Indians. Quinn got the start, but he did not

18. Jack Quinn won eighteen games for the 1920 New York Yankees. He had a 2.16 earned run average against the Cleveland Indians and Chicago White Sox, the league's top two teams. The Yankees wore black armbands that season after the Indians' Ray Chapman was killed by a pitch thrown by the Yankees' Carl Mays on August 16. *Dennis Goldstein Collection.*

survive the fifth inning. The Yankees were crushed, 10–4, and Miller Huggins's critics came out in force. Despite Quinn's poor performance, Huggins started him a week later, in a pivotal game against the White Sox. Quinn and Chicago starter Dickie Kerr had identical 17-9 records. The Yankees were in first place, 1 game ahead of Cleveland and 2½ in front of Chicago. This time he did not get out of the second inning, and Kerr went on to win number 18, 8–3.

In the second inning Quinn fielded a bunt after Joe Jackson doubled and was going to retire him at third base. But third baseman Aaron Ward had charged in for the bunt too, and shortstop Roger Peckinpaugh, the club's captain, did not cover third. In frustration Quinn did not throw to first to get the sure out either. One New York reporter called it a "stupid play" during which Quinn was "shooting killing glances at Ward."[20] The usually unflappable pitcher seemed rattled and then gave up four quick runs, as New York lost the game, 8–3. In an article titled "Huggins's Judgment Suicidal to Yankees," Schumacher wrote that "Quinn went stale some weeks ago," and the decision to start him was "a terrible blow to Yankees' pennant hopes."[21] Huggins could have started pitchers Hank Thormahlen, Bob Shawkey, or Carl Mays, reporters noted.[22]

The Yankees were swept by Chicago and never got back to first place. The sports editor of the *New York Evening Mail*, Sam Murphy, wrote after the series that Huggins lacked confidence and was indecisive. "Miller Huggins is through as manager of the Yankees if the pennant is lost to the Yankees," he declared.[23] Joe Vila had a very different evaluation: "Huggins, I hear, is a marked man. . . . Huggins is charged with manhandling the pitching staff, although he is not responsible for the evident lack of class in that department of the game." Vila felt that the New York manager "has accomplished wonders under the most trying circumstances."[24]

Quinn won his eighteenth game on September 26, but it came a month after he had secured his seventeenth, and the Yankees had already fallen three games behind Cleveland with just three games remaining. He finished with a record of 18-10, with a 3.20 earned run average. It was the same number of wins he had for the Yankees ten years earlier. References to his age and determination often surfaced this year. A Philadelphia sportswriter called him one of "the feeble old veterans" who were doing well.[25] Syndicated columnist Grantland Rice mentioned him as an example of an athlete who had been "tossed back" to the Minors but was "not content to accept Fate's decree."[26]

At times during the season Quinn was brilliant and dominant, yet his last few weeks were disappointing. Had he come close to his performances of early in the season, the Yankees might have won their first pennant in 1920. They finished in third place, three games behind the eventual World Series winners, the Cleveland Indians. The White

Sox finished two games back; when the Black Sox scandal broke in the last week of the season, Charles Comiskey suspended his eight suspected players.

Jack Quinn turned thirty-seven that summer. Even though his exact age was unknown, it was a given he was in his midthirties. Whether his decline late in the 1920 season was due to a lingering injury, ineffectiveness in hot weather, the strain of too heavy a workload, or simply the aging process, he would be a question mark when the Yankees set out for the 1921 season.

17

Yankees Win a Championship but Quinn's Future in Doubt

Jack Quinn received some good news early in 1921, and he played a key role making it happen. The National Commissions Rules Committee decided that the one-year reprieve for spitball pitchers would be a permanent one for that select group. The seventeen pitchers who had been registered as spitballers before the 1920 season could continue to use the pitch for the rest of their Major League careers.[1] The ruling was the result of an effective lobbying campaign by the spitballers and some fortuitous circumstances at the end of the 1920 season.

Columnist and former ballplayer Sam Crane called it "a very sensible plan."[2] Umpire and syndicated columnist Billy Evans estimated the registered spitball pitchers represented property value of almost $500,000, a point that resonated with the club owners.[3] The spitballers gained a further boost as a result of the 1920 World Series. The Cleveland Indians, led by twenty-four-game winner Stan Coveleski, faced the Brooklyn Robins, led by twenty-three-game winner Burleigh Grimes. Both were spitballers, and Coveleski won three games in the Series.

As early as May 1920, the seventeen pitchers began to organize, circulating a letter among their fellow spitballers. "Bar Spitter and We Starve" was the headline in a New York newspaper, quoting spitball pitchers Dana Fillingim of the Boston Braves and Spittin' Bill Doak of the St. Louis Cardinals.[4] The next day influential sportswriter Fred Lieb wrote that the abolition of that pitch was "a real sore spot" with Quinn. "Cutting out the spitball after permitting me to pitch it all my life," he told Lieb, "is like reaching into my pocket and taking money from me."[5]

The spitball pitchers took every opportunity to argue their case with club owners. They also submitted a petition to the two league presidents. By early July New York sportswriter Sid Mercer noted there was "a growing sentiment" not to throw these pitchers out of the game because that would be "an unnecessary sacrifice of property rights." Instead these men "should be permitted to yield gracefully to time."[6]

Major League baseball had achieved what it wanted: an almost complete ban on trick pitches that would fuel an increase in offense in the 1920s. Hitters now faced pitchers with fewer weapons. The spitball was included in the ban, except for its handful of existing users. They would maintain their "weapon" and "their advantage of about 10 percent fewer earned runs allowed than all Major League pitchers" in the 1920s.[7]

As early as 1923 the verdict was in about the new era of hitting. W. R. Hoefer wrote in *Baseball Magazine*, "Batting is king. All other departments of the game are now subordinate subjects. The increased crowds at the present games strongly indicate that the public likes the present era of free and fancy swatting. . . . And if the public prefers the new game, the magnates prefer it."[8]

With the eight Chicago White Sox players suspended by their club for the 1921 season (and banned by Organized Baseball that summer), observers saw the pennant race as a two-team affair between the world champion Cleveland Indians and the Babe Ruth–led New York Yankees. It proved to be exactly that, a torrid, back-and-forth race all season long.

After Quinn was ineffective in two of three April appearances, Joe Vila wrote, "Overworked last year, [Quinn] either has seen his best days or needs hot weather."[9] It was a sign of a struggling pitcher when reporters, at a loss for an explanation, resorted to writing that the weather was too warm or the weather was not warm enough. It was not the first time, nor would it be the last, that "experts" felt Jack was "through." A few days later, with former president Woodrow Wilson attending his first game since the spring of 1917, Quinn faced Walter Johnson, against whom he had a lot of success over the years. However, in this game the Senators chased him in the second inning.

The Yankees had a new pitcher this season, twenty-one-year-old Waite Hoyt, whom they acquired in an eight-player deal with the Red Sox in December 1920.[10] Hoyt had won only ten games for the 1919–20 Red Sox, as he dealt with arm trouble between flashes of brilliance. He bailed out Quinn and the Yankees in this game at Washington, going 6⅔ innings in relief for the 6–5 win. Babe Ruth's eighth home run of the season, the longest ever hit in the Senators' ballpark, helped New York rally from behind. After Quinn was unimpressive in his next two starts (a win and a loss), Vila's evaluation of him became more ominous. Quinn "is believed to have strained his salary wing to the extent that he will never be the same consistent performer who helped to land the New York Americans in third position [in 1920]."[11]

On May 25, after Huggins moved him to the bullpen, Quinn's ninth-inning wild pitch allowed the St. Louis Browns to push across the winning run. Five days later he had his best outing of the season, a complete-game eight-hitter against the Senators. But the Yankees managed only two hits against their former pitcher, George Mogridge, and lost, 1–0. A Washington reporter wrote, "Jack Quinn lived up to his reputation as one of the hardest-luck pitchers in the game."[12] Less than two months later sportswriter Frank O'Neill wrote that Quinn was "running in hard luck" this season.[13]

On June 9 Quinn got the start in the third game of a four-game series against the Indians. New York won the first two games to draw within a half-game of first place. Quinn could not get out of the first inning; he gave up four runs and retired only one batter. Three relievers were almost equally ineffective, prompting a reporter to write sarcastically that the Yankees tried everything "except playing baseball and hitting. There was another thing they might have attempted, too, and that was pitching."[14] Cleveland rolled to a 14–4 victory and won the next day to gain a split in the series.

Approaching age thirty-eight, Quinn again seemed to be nearing the end of his career. O'Neill could have been posting the pitcher's epitaph in July when he wrote, "Quinn has always been a good pitcher, with strains of greatness in his work at times. Always he has been a credit to baseball both on and off the field." In the same article O'Neill reported that Quinn had decided to end his playing career and become an umpire in 1922.[15] An article that appeared in many papers included the report that "There are plenty of folks in New York willing to testify that Quinn is through as a top-notcher."[16] Similar epitaphs had been written in 1912, when the Yankees sent Quinn to Rochester, and in 1916, when no Major League team showed interest in him after he led the Federal League with twenty-two losses.

In the six weeks after a July 10 defeat by the White Sox, Huggins called on Quinn to pitch only five more times, all in relief. He had become a non-factor in the fierce pennant race. When the Yankees began a crucial series in Cleveland on August 23, Huggins surprised everyone, perhaps including Quinn, when he started the veteran.

If Huggins was playing a hunch, he played it well. Quinn went the distance and quieted the Indians with a five-hitter; Ruth hit home runs number 47 and 48 off Ray Caldwell on the Yankees' way to a 6–1 win. The Yankees closed to within a half-game of first place. A copyeditor at the *New York Times* may have been talking over the heads of most of his readers with the headline "Yanks Ambuscade Speaker's Indians."[17] That Quinn "could step in and hold the Indians next to helpless for nine innings did not seem possible," marveled the *Times* reporter.[18]

The sports editor of the *New York World*, George Daley, saluted the spitballer: "Quinn, in his long career, has risen to many an emergency, but never did he perform such a sommersault [*sic*] in form as today. . . . Jack never was better. He had his spitter breaking low, and the result was the eager Indians whaled the ball along the ground."[19] Joe Vila wrote: "The Anti-Huggins Society let out a yelp when the mite manager sent old Jack Quinn against the Clevelands. . . . But Huggins made the chronic fault-finders look cheap. He knew what he was about when he selected Quinn."[20]

A month later, on the eve of another four-game series against the Indians, Quinn relieved an ineffective Bob Shawkey in a September 22 game against Howard Ehmke and the Tigers. Quinn shut out Detroit on three hits over 6⅓ innings, as New York blasted Ehmke and turned a 4–1 deficit into a 12–5 victory. While Quinn excelled in this meeting, neither man was having a good season. Ehmke's 4.54 earned run average was the highest in his career (for a full season, more than a full run higher). Quinn's rose more than a half-run from 1920, to 3.78, though the league average rose by almost the same amount.

When Cleveland pulled out a twelve-inning win in Boston that day, the Yankees remained in first place by percentage points. The game with the Tigers did not win the pennant for the Yankees, wrote a sportswriter, "but it certainly saved it."[21] A Detroit reporter marveled that Quinn "was in the midst of one of his old-time days."[22] And Quinn even got his only home run of the year, off Ehmke.[23]

The Yankees won two of the first three games from the Indians to take a tenuous 1-game lead in the pennant race. This only magnified the importance of the final game of the series: it would either give New York a 2-game margin with a handful of games to play or leave Cleveland still only a few percentage points behind. With his pitching staff overworked, Huggins was not sure whom he should start. He had used all his key pitchers in the first three games but not Quinn. Jack had not started a game for more than a month; that start was his August 23 gem against the Indians.

In his history of the Yankees, Frank Graham tells the story as if he were there in the home team's clubhouse before the game. Perhaps he was. Huggins kept his pitchers with him, as the others went out to warm up before the game. "'I'm up against it. I don't know who [sic] to pitch,'" he told them.[24] The players did not know what to say. "They all began to talk at once. The discussion lengthened, grew heated. It ended in a decision to pitch Quinn, an old man as ball players go . . . but crafty and stout-hearted and one of the last spitball pitchers. It was an unhappy choice." Quinn retired just two Indians and gave up three runs, albeit unearned ones because of an error by second baseman Mike McNally. He also walked one man and hit another.

Stan Coveleski, who had gone the distance in a 4–2 loss in the first game of the series, was almost equally bad; he departed in the third inning. Babe Ruth led the Yankees' comeback with a double and two home runs, numbers 57 and 58 for the year. A reporter for the usually staid *New York Times* wrote, "The titanic figure of Babe Ruth stood out in the triumph as the Leviathan would stand out in a flock of harbor tugs."[25]

New York barely hung on for an 8–7 win. In 1945 Fred Lieb, who would cover baseball for almost seventy years, called this game one of the ten greatest ever played.[26] The Yankees clinched their first American League pennant a few days later. Quinn ended the season with an 8-7 record and appeared in a surprising thirty-three games, though he started only thirteen. He was heading to the World Series, though he probably did not expect to start a game.

The Yankees met John McGraw's New York Giants, the city's dominant and favorite team since 1904. All the games were played at the Polo Grounds, the home of both New York teams. The Yankees won the first two games in the best-of-nine World Series, despite no extra-base hits from Ruth.[27] (He walked four times.) Carl Mays and Waite Hoyt pitched masterful shutouts, both by the score of 3–0. When the Yankees scored four runs in the top of the third inning to give Bob Shawkey a 4–0 lead in Game Three, a Series rout seemed at hand. But Shawkey became unnerved, and he walked three straight men after having given up two hits in the third inning. Quinn got the call to relieve him, and after the Giants had tied the game, he tossed three scoreless innings.

Heywood Broun envisioned a stirring story line: "By every theatrical and fictional law, Jack Quinn should have been assigned to a heroic role. He was the oldest man on the field. He came first to the Yankees 11 [actually 12] years ago."[28] In the top of the seventh, with the score still knotted at four, Quinn led off and hit a tremendous drive to deep left-center, "a slam that had triple emblazoned over it," in the words of one reporter.[29]

But this story line was not meant to be. Giants center fielder George Burns broke with the crack of Quinn's bat and ran to the fence. "When the ball appeared to be going over his head," wrote J. C. Kofoed, "he leaped in the air and speared it. From a spectacular point of view, that play was unequalled."[30]

In the bottom of the inning Quinn was hit hard. The Giants opened the frame with five hits, including two doubles, and a walk. Quinn was done; the Giants' bats had caught fire. They scored eight runs in the inning, a new World Series record, on the way to a 13–5 win. Fate, wrote Broun, "is supposed to be a great dramatist, but today the material at hand was muddled. . . . He [Quinn] was only a three-inning hero. Like Napoleon, he failed to make his exit in time."[31]

What happened to Quinn after three strong innings of relief? Hugh Fullerton felt it was just a matter of time until one of the two relievers, Quinn and Jesse Barnes of the Giants, "would explode first. It was Quinn who was out of luck."[32] But a couple of weeks later, Fullerton had much more to tell. He wrote that Quinn told him he was pitching well with his slow ball and curve and laying off his spitter, which was not breaking. However, in the fateful seventh inning Quinn was told to start throwing the spitter. "The indications are that the orders came from the catcher."[33]

The catcher, Wally Schang, had appeared in World Series with both the Philadelphia Athletics and the Boston Red Sox in the 1910s. The Yankees acquired him in the same December 1920 deal with the Red Sox that brought Waite Hoyt to New York. It is hard to know what to make of this account. Perhaps Schang wanted Quinn to "show" the Giants a pitch they had not seen most of the game. Evidently the veteran pitcher did not shake off his veteran catcher, despite his doubts about throwing his spitter.

The Giants stormed back to win the Series, five games to three, primarily because they had three strong starting pitchers, and the Yankees had only two.[34] Also Ruth had a serious elbow injury and missed the final four games, other than one pinch-hitting appearance. In the games he did play, the Giants' pitchers, as instructed by McGraw, stymied him with a diet of slow curve balls and limited him to one extra-base hit.

Jack Quinn was surely disappointed with his season. He had been on a pennant-winning team, but he must have realized that the Yankees' wealthy and impatient owners were going to bolster their pitching staff for 1922. That would mean there would be little opportunity and few innings, if any, for him. The possibility of turning to umpiring may have loomed in his mind.

18

"A Fellow of Gentle Soul"

In 1920, when the Detroit Tigers returned to Macon, Georgia, for spring training, manager Hughie Jennings was optimistic about his team's chances to overtake 1919's pennant-winning Chicago White Sox and capture the American League flag. Jennings said he expected his four top pitchers from 1919—Hooks Dauss, Dutch Leonard, Bernie Boland, and Howard Ehmke—to again make the majority of the team's starts. Dauss, a twenty-one-game winner in 1919, was the staff ace, though his earned run average for the season was higher than those of the other three. This quartet, along with the rest of the pitchers, would be tutored by Jack Coombs, the fourth pitching coach in Ehmke's four seasons in Detroit.[1] Coombs, winner of 158 games for the Philadelphia Athletics and Brooklyn Dodgers from 1906 to 1918, replaced Dan Howley, who left to manage the Hartford Senators of the Eastern League.[2]

Of greater long-range significance to the Detroit club was the change in ownership that took place during spring training. William Yawkey, the team's sole owner from 1903 through 1908 and the majority owner with Frank Navin since 1909, died in March 1919.[3] After Yawkey's death Navin became a half-owner of the Tigers.[4] Unlike most other owners, Navin had no income apart from baseball, a situation that in part explained his reputation for frugality.[5]

The Tigers opened the 1920 season at Chicago, with Dauss facing Lefty Williams. When last seen, in the eighth and final game of the 1919 World Series, Williams had lasted just a third of an inning in losing his record-setting third game of the Series.[6] The one-time Tigers pitcher won twenty-three games in 1919 and would win twenty-two this year. But Williams and seven of his teammates would be suspended by White Sox owner Charles Comiskey in September 1920 and expelled from Organized Baseball by the new commissioner, Kenesaw Landis, in the summer of 1921.[7]

19. George "Hooks" Dauss, Howard Ehmke's friend and teammate with Detroit, is the Tigers all-time winningest pitcher. H. G. Salsinger of the *Detroit News*, perhaps serving as manager Ty Cobb's mouthpiece, compared Ehmke's "mental attitude" unfavorably to Dauss's. *Steve Steinberg Collection.*

Unfortunately for Detroit, Williams was in midseason form this day, as he outdueled Dauss, 3–2, in eleven innings. Ehmke started the next day, and he was wild and hittable, allowing four runs, six hits, and five walks in four innings. The four runs were more than the White Sox needed, as Eddie Cicotte shut out the Tigers, 4–0.[8] Although Ehmke had walked a league-leading 107 batters in 1919, one pundit suggested his wildness this afternoon may have been due in some measure to the presence in the stands of his new wife. Marguerite had traveled from California and arrived in Chicago the night before the opener. The couple planned to live in Detroit during the season.[9]

For the thirty-six-year-old Cicotte it was a brilliant start, the first of his twenty-one wins in 1920.[10] In the opinion of the *Chicago Tribune*'s James Crusinberry, Cicotte, a twenty-nine-game winner in 1919, had been the primary target of the new ban on "trick pitches."[11] Cicotte was not known as a spitball pitcher, though he used just about every other trick pitch the owners banned, primarily the shine ball. He had no need for any of those pitches in shutting out the Tigers. "You can legislate against the thing a pitcher can do with his hands or his feet, but you can't legislate against his using his brain," Sox owner Charles Comiskey said when the legislation was passed.[12] "Using his brain," or some variant thereof, would be a description applied often to Ehmke over the course of his career.

Although Detroit lost its first five games, Jennings insisted he had a first-division team and expected his players to shake their losing ways soon. Neither he, Coombs, nor anyone on the Tigers' squad could have imagined those five losses would be the beginning of a Major League record-setting thirteen-game losing streak to start a season.[13] At 0-13 the Tigers were already 10 games behind the first-place White Sox. Three of the losses were charged to Ehmke. He was much stronger in his second start, also against the White Sox, but lost, 2–1, in ten innings to Lefty Williams. After nine scoreless innings, Chicago's Eddie Murphy singled home two runs in the top of the tenth, and the Tigers could manage only one in the home half.

"When a club is losing, the breaks go against it," said George Hildebrand, the plate umpire in the May 1 game against Cleveland that resulted in Detroit's twelfth consecutive loss.[14] The Indians scored four runs (two earned) in the first inning against Ehmke, who was replaced in the second. An incident in that inning reignited questions about Ehmke's ability to overcome those "breaks." Jack Graney opened the game with a double. Ray Chapman followed with a bunt to the right side that either Ehmke or first baseman Harry Heilmann could have fielded. But neither did, each expecting the other to make the play. "This one play got on Ehmke's nerve [sic], and Speaker followed with a three-run homer," Hildebrand said. Yet he noted that Ehmke "had a lot of stuff on the ball," and that he "never saw his curve breaking better."[15] Catcher Eddie Ainsmith said Ehmke's curve was breaking so sharply he had trouble catching it.[16] However, Indians batters had no trouble hitting his pitches. Five of the ten batters he faced in his one inning had hits.

Ehmke had been, and would continue to be, criticized for lacking the ability to deal emotionally with the inevitable in-game setbacks all pitchers face. In late May *Syracuse Journal* columnist Bob Kenefick quoted from an article H. G. Salsinger had written in the *Detroit News* about this perceived flaw in Ehmke's makeup.[17] "Howard Ehmke can no longer be depended upon," Salsinger had written. "The tall blonde is rather an enigma. Had he the same mental attitude that marks Boland, Dauss, Leonard, or [Red] Oldham, he would be one of the toughest men in the league to beat, but he lacks that thing they call 'heart.'"[18]

Salsinger had also referred to the mixup between Ehmke and Heilmann that allowed Ray Chapman's bunt to go for a single: "That play took all the nerve out of Ehmke; he was completely upset. Pitching to Speaker, he did not get a thing on the ball, and Tris drove it into the bleachers." In his next start, against St. Louis, Ehmke appeared distressed when third baseman Sammy Hale made a fourth-inning error on a ground ball, and before the inning was over, the Browns had scored eight runs. "As long as Ehmke gets the breaks, he will pitch wonderful baseball," concluded Salsinger, "but he goes to pieces as soon as the turn of the play is against him."[19]

Throughout baseball history certain reporters have taken a personal or professional dislike for a hometown player. That seems to have been the case with Salsinger, who seemed to go out of his way to criticize Ehmke. Usually the criticism was based on what he perceived as Ehmke's psychological makeup, which he felt was inimical to that of a successful Major Leaguer.

After Ehmke ended his five-game losing streak with an 8–2 win at Philadelphia, he defeated Carl Mays and the Yankees, 3–1, on May 24. He allowed just two hits, a single and a triple, both by Babe Ruth. It was the Tigers' best-pitched game of the season, wrote John C. Manning, Salsinger's colleague at the *Detroit News*, as he described how helpless the mighty New Yorkers looked against Ehmke. Yet he too raised the question of Ehmke's competitive spirit, wondering how great Ehmke would become if only he possessed the "heart" of a Walter Johnson:

Since he entered the league, it has been common knowledge among ball players, though not so generally appreciated by the baseball public, that the lanky, blond Tiger has as much natural "stuff" as any pitcher around the circuit. His battery mates [Eddie] Ainsmith and [Oscar] Stanage will tell you they scarcely can hold him when he is going right.

Opposing players say his curves are uncanny. Tris Speaker has declared it is almost impossible for a hitter to brace himself against one of Ehmke's shoots, so sharply bewilderingly do they break. Cicotte said last September, "If I had that kid's stuff I'd never lose a ball game."

But, notwithstanding all this, it is doubtful whether Ehmke will ever be a great pitcher unless he can manage to toughen his disposition. He is not indifferent. He likes to win as well as anybody. He simply appears incapable of surviving the buffets of ill fortune.

You have seen Johnson and Cicotte and—in the old days—Ed Walsh and Bill Donovan and [Addie] Joss and [Eddie] Plank. You will remember how those masters rose above themselves in the crises. Breaks of luck, bad support by their comrades, concentrated attack by the enemy, invariably acted as spurs to their pitching efforts. That was because they had heart. They were innate, fighting pitchers.

Ehmke is different. Almost you can sense it by talking to him once. He is a fellow of gentle soul, soft-spoken, diffident, shy. In personal habits he is as fastidious as a girl. He never has tasted liquor or tobacco. And he broods over fancied bad luck. Bill Donovan used to pull his mates along by his downright dominant courage. He bullied them into supporting him. Ehmke grows flighty and sulks if things go wrong.

Perhaps eventually he will harden. It's an unconventional statement, but the best possible prop to his diamond career would be to become a bit tough—a trifle rowdyish. Give him half the heart of a Johnson, and he should do wonders. Otherwise, he should seek some walk of life more sedate than baseball.[20]

In the rough-and-tough world of 1920s baseball, these were damning charges. But Ehmke was not the only Tigers player receiving criticism for his supposed lack of grit. Another writer for the *Detroit News*, using the nom de plume Old Timer, thought the whole team, except for Ty Cobb and Donie Bush, was soft. He imagined Jennings must have been frustrated when comparing his current team to the legendary Baltimore Orioles teams of which he had been a part in the 1890s or even the Tigers' teams he had led to three consecutive pennants in 1907, 1908, and 1909. "They are nice boys," the Old Timer summarized, "all of them fine upstanding lads, but the song of battle is not in their hearts."[21]

In any field of historical research, we seldom see such a clear delineation between the end of one era and the start of another as we do in baseball as it was played in 1919 and in 1920. By the time the 1920 season ended, it was obvious to all that the "inside baseball" of the Deadball Era, which had prevailed from 1901 to 1919, was over, and the game was entering an era where offense would be in the ascendancy. That fans seemed to prefer high-scoring games made the owners eager to promote the transition. Both leagues saw sharp increases in offense in 1920, particularly in the American League, where the slugging of new Yankee Babe Ruth was singlehandedly revolutionizing the game. Batting averages in the American League rose from a league average of .268 in 1919 to .283 in 1920; home runs rose from 240 to 369; and total runs rose from 4,593 to 5,868. Conversely the league's earned run average rose from 3.22 to 3.79.[22]

Other reasons were also being put forth for the increased hitting this season. Indians manager Tris Speaker attributed it to the banning of trick pitches, such as the emery ball, the shine ball, and the spitball. White Sox second baseman Eddie Collins thought the ball had been changed to where it jumped off the bat more quickly. Ehmke thought it was the result of new balls being constantly put into play after just the slightest scuff marks. "As it is now," he said, "a ball no sooner gets so a pitcher can use it effectively than the umpire throws it out. As a result, the pitchers cannot get their curveballs working right, and the batters slam them."[23]

New York's batters were certainly slamming Ehmke when they faced him at Detroit on June 9. They scored four runs in the first inning and three more in the third and went on to pound the Tigers, 11–3. Ehmke went all the way, allowing thirteen hits and issuing five walks. He had barely survived the third after dodging Ruth's vicious one-hopper back through the box. According to the *New York Times*, "Ehmke dropped in his tracks and in so doing wisely avoided being badly injured for the ball was traveling at bullet speed."[24] The Babe had this at bat in mind when asked a month later about his greatest fear. "I'm afraid that some day I'll kill some pitcher," he answered. "It is one thing I've always dreaded. My heart stood still in that game in Detroit when I almost got

Ehmke with that drive through the box. I thought for a certainty that the ball would hit him before he got his hands up to protect himself."[25]

Ruth's teammate Carl Mays expanded, and perhaps embellished, upon this incident in a 1958 interview. According to Mays, Ehmke would always knock down the Babe twice just to loosen him up. "Well, he nearly loosened Ruth from his head with one pitch," Mays recalled, "and the Babe came out of the dirt with fire spouting from his eyes and sweet little passages of profanity pouring from his lips." Glaring at Ehmke, Ruth warned him to be ready. "'I'm gonna slug this next one right back at ya, and it'll put a hole this big through that big mouth of yours!' Ehmke threw, and Babe swung," remembered Mays. "I thought it had killed Howard. He went down scrambling, and the ball crashed into his glove. When they picked a very frightened Ehmke off the ground, they found he hadn't been hit, but they found his glove in left field."[26]

On Sunday, July 11, Ehmke again faced the Yankees, this time at the Polo Grounds before an estimated thirty-five thousand fans, many of whom had come specifically to see Ruth hit a home run. Though the season was only half over, he already had twenty-six and needed four more to surpass his Major League record of twenty-nine, set with the Red Sox a year earlier. Ehmke was exceptionally careful in pitching to Ruth—much too careful in the eyes of the New York fans. They booed him when he walked Ruth on four pitches in the first inning, but he got one too close to the plate in the third, which Ruth blasted for home run number 27. Ehmke made sure nothing was close in the Babe's next two at-bats, walking him each time on four pitches, accompanied by loud booing from the fans.[27]

The correspondent from the *Times* summed up the feeling of the fans toward Ehmke: "Every last mortal in that gathering of 35,000 wanted to see Babe hit, and the idea of one man blocking the will of the populace was more than the crowd could bear. Ehmke reached a new mark in extracting jeers, hoots, and hisses from a Polo Grounds crowd."[28] Ehmke allowed just seven hits, but five went for extra bases, and the Yankees won the game, 6–5, dropping his record to 4-11.

In all, Ehmke had eight appearances against the Yankees in 1920, seven as a starter, winning four and losing three. Two were complete-game wins in the first and last games of a four-game home series in early August. He defeated Bob Shawkey, 7–1, on August 5, with the

Yanks' lone run coming on Ruth's second-inning home run. After New York's Jack Quinn and Carl Mays took the next two games, Ehmke came back to defeat Rip Collins, 1–0. It was one of Ehmke's best-ever games against the Yankees—a three hitter with eight strikeouts. Detroit scored the game's only run when Cobb raced home from third on a Collins wild pitch in the fourth inning. The game was played in one hour and thirteen minutes, still the fastest 1–0 game in American League history.

Ehmke's strong performances in this series would soon be part of a Yankees' complaint against the other American League clubs. During the series the Yankees alleged that some of the league's other teams were favoring Cleveland in the pennant race. They pointed to a recent series between the Indians and the Red Sox in which they claimed Boston made "an unusually large number of errors" in the late innings. Moreover, they said, the St. Louis Browns had used their best pitcher, Urban Shocker, and the Tigers had used their best one, Howard Ehmke, twice in their series against the Yankees and had done nothing similar when they played the Indians.[29]

The charge gained a degree of credibility when Yankees co-owner Jacob Ruppert also weighed in on it. "We shall watch the next series St. Louis and Detroit play against Cleveland," said the colonel. "We are anxious to see whether Shocker and Ehmke will each work twice against the Indians as they did against New York."[30] The general reaction in the New York press was that Ruppert and the Yankees should stop squawking and trying to dictate the way other managers used their pitchers.[31]

Ruth had already shattered his own home run record and was headed toward a previously unimaginable fifty. His total stood at forty-eight when Ehmke faced him at Navin Field on September 13. This time he chose to pitch to Ruth, retiring him on ground balls in his first two at bats. Ehmke "has been a stumbling block in the Yankees' path pennantward this season," noted the *Times*, and he seemed on his way to defeating them again this afternoon.[32]

The Tigers had a 2–1 lead when Ehmke faced Ruth in the sixth inning with two outs and Wally Pipp at first base. The count went to 3-2, and Ehmke's next pitch appeared to be low and outside. But Ruth swung and drove the ball into the right-field bleachers. His forty-ninth home run of the season gave New York a 3–2 lead in a game they eventually won, 4–2. "I give Ehmke credit for taking a chance," Ruth said in his ghost-written column the next day.[33]

Detroit closed out its season with four games against Cleveland. The pennant race was still undecided, with the Indians holding a 1½-game lead over Chicago. In the series opener Ehmke defeated thirty-game winner Jim Bagby, 5–4, in eleven innings. The win gave him a final record of 15-18, as the Tigers finished seventh, 37 games behind the Indians. With their pennantless streak now at eleven seasons, there seemed little doubt that someone other than Hughie Jennings would be managing the club in 1921.

19

Playing for Ty Cobb

As the baseball world focused on the 1920 Brooklyn-Cleveland World Series, Howard Ehmke headed to California. He and Ty Cobb boarded a train for San Francisco, where they, along with Harry Heilmann, Rogers Hornsby, George Sisler, and other big leaguers, would take part in two months of exhibition games. But Cobb had more pressing concerns on his mind. Frank Navin informed him that Hughie Jennings was stepping down as manager and that he and his two new partners wanted Cobb to be Jennings's replacement. Navin had been reluctant to fire Jennings after his fourteen years at the helm, despite the manager having become increasingly unpopular with his players. Jennings solved the problem by resigning.

Early speculation had former White Sox manager Clarence "Pants" Rowland and former Boston Braves manager George Stallings as the leading contenders to be Detroit's new manager. But Navin was set on Cobb and was able to convince him to take the job. On December 18, 1920, Cobb's thirty-fourth birthday, the game's greatest player signed a one-year contract to manage the 1921 Tigers.

Many baseball people questioned Navin's choice, wondering whether Cobb would be able to tame his temper enough to run a big league team. "They do not seem convinced that a man with the fiery disposition of the Jewel of Georgia can last through a campaign at the head of a ball club," wrote Damon Runyon.[1] However, Runyon pointed out that a fiery temperament was not necessarily a detriment to a manager, citing New York Giants manager John McGraw as his prime example. Runyon also mentioned the pride factor as something that likely would work in Cobb's favor: "Cobb dislikes failure as keenly as any man you ever saw."[2] But W. O. McGeehan, of the *New York Tribune*, was not so sure. "Unquestionably, Cobb is a great player," he wrote, "but whether he will succeed as a manager or not is for Cobb to demonstrate."[3]

The fans in Detroit were mostly pleased with the announcement; perhaps some of the players were too, but surely Ehmke was not among them. He and Cobb had not had an open breach in 1920, but both thought it best they stay apart. Ehmke had made it known he preferred to be traded and rid of Cobb; nevertheless, he swore devotion to his new manager. Meanwhile, Cobb, recognizing that Ehmke likely would be the ace of his staff, praised him as a man and as a pitcher.[4] "I think Howard will pitch better than ever before, for he has it in him to be a top-notcher," the new manager said.[5]

Sportswriter H. G. Salsinger, who had often criticized Ehmke's attitude, thought he would be among the best in the game if he were given the proper direction. "Umpires have told me," he wrote, "that they thought Ehmke had more stuff than any pitcher in the league, and if he ever gets going in the right groove, he will head the lot."[6] Much of the responsibility for getting Ehmke "going in the right groove," of course, would fall to Cobb. Salsinger reminded his readers that the two supposedly had settled their differences late in the 1920 season.[7]

Cobb had high hopes for Ehmke, perhaps too high. He expressed confidence he could turn the youngster into baseball's greatest pitcher. The previous summer Cobb had given Ehmke advice on how to proceed after getting two strikes on a batter, after which Ehmke won nine out of ten games. (He was 4-12 on July 14 and 13-13 on August 22.) Moreover, Ehmke, just short of his twenty-fifth birthday, appeared bigger, heavier, and stronger, leading Cobb to believe that confidence in his own ability was all Ehmke needed to become a great pitcher.[8]

At the start of spring training, Cobb said he hoped to improve over last season's seventh-place finish. However, the new manager did not place the bar very high: "Last year we finished seventh. This year I hope to be able to finish sixth. If we should be lucky enough to finish a little higher, I would feel very thankful. We have about the same team that finished seventh in the 1920 pennant race."[9] In what could be considered a slap at Jennings, he added, "The men who did not do well last year may be more successful under different conditions this year. As a result," Cobb concluded, "I must wait and find out the men who will attune themselves to my methods. If I should discover after two months or so that certain players cannot deliver the goods, then I would go about making changes."[10]

From Cobb's assertion about men attuning themselves to his methods, Ehmke likely realized that despite Cobb's continued praise of him, there would be problems ahead. He was right, and it did not take long for them to surface. On his first day in camp, in San Antonio, Ehmke warmed up his arm for five minutes and then started throwing at full speed.[11] Cobb told him what he was doing was very bad for him. He should go slowly in conditioning his arm and not cut loose for a few weeks. An unconvinced Ehmke replied that it was all right for him to cut loose. Cobb, firmly but gently, insisted it was not all right, not on the first day. But Ehmke still maintained that it was all right in his case. He said it was not his first day but the fourth week for him, as he had had more than three weeks' work getting his arm in shape in California before coming to San Antonio.

At a team meeting Cobb told his players what he expected of them, and many were loud in shouting their approval. "You know Ty has the right idea," said veteran pitcher Doc Ayers. "You cannot go too strong in boosting him. He realizes that the players of today are not the type we had in baseball 15 and 20 years ago. They are not chiefly a booze-and-fighting crowd. They are intelligent. . . . You will find few players who lack education," said Ayers, a spitballer whose Major League career would end when the Tigers waived him in May.[12]

Salsinger may have been serving as Cobb's conduit in a spring training column that was picked up by Bob Kenefick in the *Syracuse Journal*. "He has an underhand and sidearm delivery, which is the roughest thing imaginable on right-handed batsmen, but the trouble with Ehmke is that he does not use it [*sic*] enough," Salsinger wrote. "Ehmke prefers to twirl overhand, and Ehmke is not hard to hit when pitching overhand. If he depended upon his underhand and crossfire delivery, he would come near pitching greatness and probably would achieve it, but never with the overhand delivery." Ehmke needed careful tutoring, thought Salsinger, and "as long as he does not get his pitching hand above the level of his shoulders, he will be one of the leading hurlers of the pastime."[13] Kenefick recalled that when Ehmke had his great success with Syracuse, he depended entirely upon his sidearm delivery.[14] But Ehmke had his own theories on all aspects of pitching, including his delivery. He would use the method that best fit his physical condition, the opponent, the ballpark, and even the weather on any given day.

In his first league game under Cobb, following a Tigers' win in the season opener, Ehmke lost to Chicago's Red Faber, 3–2. His next start was on April 21, against the White Sox in their home opener. This game may have set the tone for the rocky relationship Ehmke would have with Cobb over the next two seasons. He blew an early 3–1 lead and left after six innings, trailing, 6–3. He walked six batters, and author Tim Hornbaker described the effect his wildness had on his manager: "Cobb became aggravated to his limits by the inability of Ehmke to throw with any semblance of accuracy."[15] "Manager Cobb wore a path from his position in center field to the rubber to remonstrate with Ehmke," wrote Harry Bullion.[16]

"The way he treated pitchers was awful," said Al Schacht, who pitched and coached for the Washington Senators and recalled Cobb's demeaning treatment of Ehmke. "I remember one day Howard Ehmke was pitching for the Tigers. He was getting hit, and Cobb called time to go to the mound and talk to him. Well, Cobb stood there on the mound showing Ehmke up in front of the whole ballpark. I mean Cobb was holding the ball demonstrating the grip, the stride, the release, and everything else. Imagine that! Talk about ruining a pitcher's confidence. I don't think Ehmke ever was the same after that."[17]

The Detroit press roundly criticized Ehmke's mediocre showing in Chicago. Bullion called it an indifferent effort and castigated Ehmke for what he considered an apathetic performance: "Memory cannot recall an exhibition by the elongated gunner that could equal, for its many offenses against sound ethics of baseball, the one of today." Bullion compared Ehmke's performance unfavorably with that of winning pitcher Dickie Kerr, who had persevered despite falling behind early.[18]

"Poor Pitching by Ehmke Loses for the Tigers," blared a headline in the *Detroit Times*, with an equally accusatory subhead: "Tall Slabbist Has Nothing, Not Even Confidence, and Score Is 8 to 3." The article contained the following sentence, which underscored Cobb's displeasure: "Cobb was deeply grieved over the defeat, not simply because it was a defeat, but because the pitcher he expects to make a star this sea-

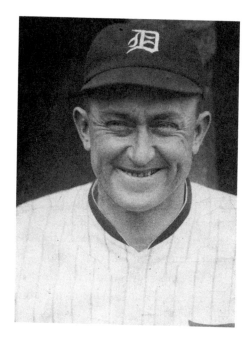

20. Manager Ty Cobb was not above running in from the outfield to remove a pitcher while humiliating him. "He shouldn't have gone near [the pitchers] except to tell which of them was to pitch the day of the game," said Howard Ehmke. *Dennis Goldstein Collection.*

son did not appear to be living up to his expectations or to be pitching the quality of ball of which he is capable."[19]

Cobb's reaction was to move Ehmke to the bullpen, from which he made five relief appearances, including two in which he was the winning pitcher. Ehmke returned to the rotation for a May 13 home game against the Yankees. He allowed all six runs in a 6–4 loss, though only three were earned. He pitched cautiously to Babe Ruth, walking him three times, but had no place to put him when Ruth batted with the bases loaded in the second inning. The Babe hit a long drive to center field that resulted in a bases-clearing triple. The three runners had all reached base on walks, three of the eight Ehmke allowed.

On May 20 Ehmke pitched his first strong game since coming back into the rotation, defeating the Red Sox, 12–2. The win moved Detroit past Boston and Washington into third place, a half-game behind New York and 2½ games behind league-leading Cleveland. The Tigers, Red Sox, and Senators would soon fade, and the race would develop into a grueling season-long battle between the Yankees and the Indians, with Ehmke playing an important role in games against both teams.

Despite a series of injuries, the Indians stayed in the lead. On May 23 they lost their leader when a pitch from Boston's Hank Thormahlen hit player-manager Tris Speaker on the wrist. Speaker's replacement in center field, Jack Graney, filled in successfully, helping the Indians compile an eight-game winning streak. The last of those eight wins, in the first game of a Memorial Day doubleheader at Detroit, was a costly one for Cleveland. Still battling control problems, Ehmke walked seven, and one of his sixth-inning pitches hit catcher Steve O'Neill in the hand, breaking one of his fingers. O'Neill, a key contributor offensively and defensively, would miss the next six weeks. When O'Neill returned to action in a series against the Yankees in July, a telegram from Ehmke was waiting for him. It read: "I wish to congratulate you on getting back into the game and wish you the best of luck the remainder of the season."[20]

Following complete-game wins at Philadelphia and Washington that evened his record at 5-5, Ehmke faced the Yankees at the Polo Grounds on June 13. Jack Quinn had just picked up a win in relief over the Tigers the day before, when Dutch Leonard had a disastrous relief appearance. Ehmke's mound opponent was Ruth, who went five innings before moving to center field. It was Ruth's only start of the season and one of his two appearances and two wins. Ruth was having the greatest offensive season of his career, one that still ranks among the best ever. Ehmke went the distance, giving up all thirteen runs in a 13–8 loss. He allowed sixteen hits, including four home runs, two by Ruth. It was the only time in his career Ehmke gave up more than two home runs in a game. Ruth's second home run, his twenty-first of the season, came in the seventh inning off one of Ehmke's "slowest little floaters" and landed in the center-field bleachers. Veteran New York sportswriters claimed it was the first ball ever hit into that territory.

In addition to the battering he took, Ehmke walked four, and in the third inning he hit Yankees catcher Wally Schang on the right forearm. The intense pain caused by the blow made Schang lose consciousness temporarily, but he was able to walk back to the bench. An X-ray showed that while the bone was severely bruised, it was not broken. Ehmke would lead the league in hit batsmen in 1921, one of five times in his career he would lead the league.[21] "Perhaps the most conspicuous trait about Ehmke is his lack of control," wrote F. C. Lane.[22] The

Yankees defeated the Tigers again the next day, to complete a four-game sweep and move to within a half-game of first place. The Tigers scored twenty-eight runs in the series and would lead the league with a .316 batting average. But they gave up for forty-one runs in the series.

When Detroit played at Cleveland on June 19, they had lost eight straight games. Ehmke was the loser of three of them. In addition to the one against the Yankees, he was the losing pitcher in both games of a June 17 doubleheader against the Red Sox—in the first game as a reliever and in the second as a starter. The losing streak was especially difficult for Cobb. "Ty Cobb never learned how to lose gracefully, or even decently," wrote Jack Sher. "Whenever a decision went against him, he retaliated with snarls and threats. He couldn't help it. He had a deeply rooted, sincere hatred for defeat."[23] "He was into every game the way [Jack] Dempsey climbed into a ring full of fury and blood lust, filled with a deep and burning desire to win at all costs."[24]

The Tigers appeared ready to end the streak on June 19, leading 7–4 when the Indians came to bat in the seventh. Cleveland loaded the bases against Suds Sutherland, who had relieved Dutch Leonard an inning earlier. A seething Cobb ran in from center field to replace Sutherland with Red Oldham.[25] But when Oldham walked Jack Graney to force in one run and then threw two balls to pinch hitter George Uhle, Cobb came rushing in again and grabbed the ball from Oldham's hand.

"One aspect that bothered Cobb was any semblance of indifference from his men. . . . He wanted his players to be as edgy as he was," wrote Hornbaker. "Additionally, he wanted his men more angry and aggressive than happy and passive."[26] Perhaps mistaking wildness for indifference, Cobb proceeded to "show up" his pitcher before the delighted Dunn Field crowd. As described by Ross Tenney, "He grabbed the ball, took his position on the rubber, and hurled the ball across the plate to show that strikes could be pitched." While waiting for Jim Middleton to relieve Oldham, Cobb called Harry Heilmann in from right field and had him throw a strike. "There," Cobb shouted, "if outfielders can throw strikes, you pitchers ought to be able to do it."[27] The Indians scored four runs in the inning to win, 8–7 (the final one on a walk by Middleton), and give the Tigers their ninth consecutive loss. Shortly after Ehmke retired, he said of Cobb: "He couldn't keep away from his pitchers, and he shouldn't have gone near them except to tell which of them was to pitch the day of the game."[28]

The Tigers played just above .500 in the month after they ended their losing streak, when they entertained the Yankees in a four-game series starting on July 16. They lost all four, including a 10–1 rout of Ehmke. A gargantuan home run by Ruth was again the highlight of the game, though this one did not come off Ehmke, who walked Ruth each of the four times he faced him in his seven innings.[29] When the Babe batted in the eighth inning, Bert Cole was on the mound for the Tigers. Cole, who the New York Globe suggested "has more courage than Ehmke or less sense," chose to pitch to Ruth. The home run he surrendered cleared the center-field fence and was reported to have traveled anywhere from 560 to 610 feet.[30]

Ehmke raised his record to 10-11 before injuring his side on August 2, in a complete game loss at Washington. He missed three weeks but came back on August 21 with a three-hit shutout against Philadelphia, the first shutout of the season by a Detroit right-hander. "Ehmke has rarely looked so good," wrote Salsinger. "His cross-fire delivery was effective, and he controlled it nigh perfectly."[31] Ehmke always pitched well against the A's, winning four of six this season. The Yankees were another story; he lost five of six to the eventual pennant winners.[32] One loss came in his next start, when the New Yorkers pounded him for fifteen hits in an easy, 10–2, win. Every Yankee hit safely except for Ruth. Ehmke, who pitched the entire game, walked him once and retired him four times, ending the Babe's career-high consecutive-game hit streak at twenty-six.[33]

Ehmke faced the Yankees twice more, as part of a four-game series in New York, beginning on September 18. Waite Hoyt pitched the Yankees to victory in the first game, vaulting them over the Indians and into first place by percentage points. The next day New York jumped on Red Oldham and had a 4–0 lead after three innings. Ehmke came on in the fourth and held the New Yorkers to two hits and no runs over the next four innings. It appeared to be a wasted effort, as Carl Mays held the Tigers scoreless through seven. But Mays, who sometimes weakened in the late innings, did so again. The Tigers erupted for eight runs in the eighth and two in the ninth to win, 10–6. The loss was so upsetting to Yankees manager Miller Huggins, already in a fragile state of mind resulting from the incessant attacks by several local sports-writers, that he wrote a letter of resignation to Jacob Ruppert. Ruppert did not accept Huggins's resignation and persuaded him to stay on.[34]

After New York won the third game, Cobb started Ehmke in game four, against Bob Shawkey. With Cleveland coming to town for a four-game set beginning the following day, this was an extremely important game for the Yankees. But Shawkey turned in a terrible outing, and Ehmke was no better. The Yanks won the slugfest, 12–5. Jack Quinn, in relief, was the winner, while Ehmke, who took a 4–1 lead into the bottom of the third and gave up six runs in four innings, was the loser. Quinn, who relieved Shawkey in Detroit's four-run third, pitched 6⅓ scoreless innings. This was the game in which he hit his only home run of the season, off Ehmke in the third inning.[35]

The loss, in his final 1921 appearance, dropped Ehmke's record for the season to a disappointing 13-14. His earned run average was 4.54, which would be the highest full-season ERA of his career. The fifteen home runs he allowed would also be a career high, while his games played (30) and innings pitched (196⅓) would be full-season career lows.

Harry Heilmann led the American League in batting with a .394 average. His manager and teammate, Cobb, was second with a .389 average. Heilmann also led the league with 237 hits, and his 139 runs batted in were second to Ruth's 168. Much of Heilmann's success, Cobb let it be known, was because of him. It was a valid claim; Heilmann had clearly benefited from Cobb's spring training advice on how to hold his hands and how to position himself in the batter's box. "Cobb was a great teacher of batting," Heilmann once said. "He taught me everything I knew."[36]

On taking the manager's job, Cobb had said he hoped to be able to finish sixth. He achieved that goal, as the Tigers won seventy-one games, ten more than Hughie Jennings's seventh-place club in 1920. Yet no one believed the fiery Cobb was satisfied with such mediocrity. As the 1921 season drew to a close and Detroit's slide grew steeper, Cobb's congenital rage widened, wrote William Curran. "A snarl became his habitual mode of expression."[37] Ehmke would spend the off-season hoping that the trade rumors involving him would serve as a rescue from his dictatorial manager.

20

Ehmke Endures a Season of Criticism

Without actual games to write about between the end of one season's World Series and the start of the next season's spring training, baseball writers must find topics to satisfy fans' hunger for news. No topic satisfies that hunger more than talk of trades and their possible effects on the new year's rosters. Amid these rumors of contemplated trades, the December 1921 American League owners' meeting, at New York's Commodore Hotel, allowed the press to feed that hunger. For those in Detroit the focus of attention was a deal that would send Howard Ehmke and veteran outfielder Bobby Veach to the New York Yankees for Johnny Mitchell, a twenty-six-year-old rookie shortstop and one of the Yankees' young pitchers. Manager Ty Cobb did not deny that Ehmke and Veach were available but said he would not trade them for Mitchell.

Harry Bullion thought either Veach or Ehmke might wind up in New York but not both. A trade between Detroit and New York, as well as a rumored deal between Detroit and Boston, reflected a significant change in relations among the owners of the league's teams.[1] "In large measure," Bullion wrote, "the spirit of animosity that existed between the insurgents and the loyalists [owners] in the American League has disappeared, and supporters of Ban Johnson in the long fight against [Harry] Frazee, [Jacob] Ruppert, [Til] Huston, and [Charles] Comiskey hold much less resentment for them."[2]

While pondering a possible Ehmke trade, columnist Bert Walker thought Howard's departure might be best for him and for the Tigers:

Ehmke is a good pitcher. Far better than his work in Detroit has shown. Howard himself believes he will do better elsewhere. . . . He has lost many magnificently pitched games, often losing the verdict when he outpitched his opponent. . . . If Howard, who can't win consistently for the Tigers, is traded for an inferior twirler who can win or for a second baseman who shall stand as an iron wall in the infield, the trade will be a good one, and that isn't taking anything away from Ehmke, for he is a high-class boxman destined to a long and useful service in the American League, with another club.[3]

Frank Navin and Cobb had been discussing a deal with their Red Sox counterparts, owner Harry Frazee and manager Hugh Duffy, but with no results. "Go home and go to bed. There will be no trade tonight," Frazee announced to reporters on December 14. "But there may be something doing tomorrow," he added.[4]

The Tigers had offered Veach in exchange for Red Sox shortstop Everett Scott, a deal Duffy and baseball people in general felt was one-sided in favor of Detroit. When Navin offered to send the seemingly always cash-strapped Frazee some money along with Veach, the possibility of the deal came alive again. There were also reports that instead of cash, Ehmke would accompany Veach to Boston in exchange for Scott and pitcher Sam Jones. Cobb's frequent clashes with the easygoing Veach made him eager to trade the thirty-four-year-old outfielder. Although Cobb said he would not include Ehmke in the deal, Boston writer Burt Whitman did not believe him. Whitman was confident the final deal would be Veach, Ehmke, and an infielder for Scott. It did not happen. The next day Duffy called the trade talks off, saying he would not give up Scott unless Boston received a decent shortstop in return.

The Tigers wanted Scott to replace Donie Bush, their shortstop since 1909, who had been sold on waivers to Washington in August 1921.[5] They lost out to the Yankees, however, when later in the week Boston traded Scott to New York in a multiplayer deal.[6] Cobb was not deterred. After the trade he offered Veach to New York, even up for Scott, but the Yankees were not interested.

Because Commissioner Landis had suspended Babe Ruth and Bob Meusel for the first six weeks of the 1922 season, the Yankees were not finished dealing.[7] The loss of the two sluggers for a month and a half led Ruppert and Miller Huggins to believe the team needed a hard-hitting outfielder to help them repeat, and they had targeted Veach.

"We are not yet through with our deals to strengthen the Yanks," said Ruppert. "Veach is a mighty good ball player, and he would look good on our club."[8]

Veach batted .338 with 207 hits in 1921 and was among the league leaders in most every offensive category.[9] But his calm, even-tempered manner did not please Cobb, who preferred his players to be more aggressive. Cobb had gone so far as to order Harry Heilmann to ride Veach and even to call him "yellow" to make him angry.[10]

Ehmke, much to his chagrin, would also remain in Detroit, playing for Cobb. Unhappiness with Cobb was undoubtedly the driving force in Ehmke's wanting to leave Detroit. "Nobody disputes the fact that Ehmke isn't in love with his berth here and prefers to play elsewhere," wrote Bullion. "It is admitted by those who have closely associated with Ehmke that he is a very indifferent fellow, a whale of a pitcher when he wants to be and just the reverse when the spirit seizes him. . . . It is a situation simply where the Bengal management is reluctant to dispose of his services to another club out of fear that he would prove to be a consistent winner and thereby reflect on any action that would send him away from here."[11] Bullion noted, "Every method of handling the pitcher has been tried without attaining the desired results; Howard refuses to be driven, and he balks when pleaded with. In a good many ways Ehmke is like the weather; good, bad, and indifferent, but mostly indifferent."[12]

Ehmke arrived at spring training determined to do all he could to help the Tigers win. He was forthright in describing how the constant criticism from various quarters affected him. "Some of the things said about me in the papers last winter hurt me, and that is one reason why I am determined to correct a wrong impression," he said. "If Cobb feels the same toward me as I feel toward him, I am certain there won't be any cause for the stories that got around last winter to be repeated."[13]

Donie Bush was not the only veteran the team had shed. "When Cobb took hold of the Tigers he assumed a difficult task," wrote Joe Vila. "The team had become thoroughly disorganized under Hughie Jennings, and Cobb had to begin building from the bottom."[14] Gone along with Bush were pitcher Dutch Leonard and several other veterans.[15]

As discussed in chapter 18, in 1920, Jennings's last season as manager, the Tigers opened with thirteen consecutive losses. Nineteen twenty-two was not that disastrous, but they did lose their first six. Ehmke had cautioned the press not to expect too much of him, a warning that seemed prophetic after he lost his first four decisions. It was not until May 2, at Navin Field, that he won his first game, a well-pitched 3–1 victory over St. Louis Browns ace Urban Shocker. "Howard introduced a splendid assortment of pitcher's wares, a fast ball when he deemed it good policy to buzz it under the Browns' chins, sometimes a hook that broke sharply, and the best change of pace any Tiger pitcher has exhibited this spring."[16]

The Tigers rebounded from their terrible start, and when St. Louis came to town for a four-game series on June 22, Detroit was in third place, 3 games behind second-place New York and 4½ games behind the league-leading Browns. Ehmke too had recovered from his season-opening losing streak and raised his record to 8-8. Cobb chose him to pitch the first game, which he won, 3–2, in eleven innings. Detroit also won the next day, but the Browns won the final two. The Tigers remained 4½ back, yet they felt confident they would win the pennant.

Over the next few weeks Ehmke continued to be a .500 pitcher. His 9–4 shelling by Philadelphia, on July 13, evened his record at 11-11. Ehmke's performance led several Detroit sportswriters to again question his dedication and once more to suggest that Cobb trade him.[17] "There is no doubt that Howard Ehmke has caused the Georgian considerable worry, particularly mental worry," wrote Bullion. "Cobb has just about despaired of getting the service Ehmke is capable of giving the Tigers, and Ty admits he would trade him for another pitcher of approved caliber."[18]

Bullion, who along with H. G. Salsinger was one of Ehmke's severest critics, continued: "Ehmke's case is the season's tragedy, another wasted baseball campaign and a year of his baseball career. Howard cannot with justice to the Detroit baseball club protest against the treatment tendered him. Few pitchers draw a heavier stipend than Ehmke, and a great many who have pitched much better ball in the league extract a whole lot less than he does."[19] Bullion continued, "It is common gossip on the club that Ehmke has no desire to do his best for Manager Cobb, just as he balked on Manager Jennings, and there can be only one remedy. Were Howard hurting only himself and his leader, things would not be so bad. But the club's morale is damaged when Ehmke, a pitcher on whom so much depends in a ball game, does not bend

21. Howard Ehmke's unhappiness with Ty Cobb was his major reason for wanting the Tigers to trade him. The team's management was reluctant to send Ehmke, seen here with a sidearm delivery, to another club out of fear that he would be a consistent winner. *National Baseball Hall of Fame Library, Cooperstown, New York.*

with a will to his task." Bullion was merciless in noting that Ehmke had lost a lot of games this year in ways of which other clubs were not aware: "Howard has lost many games simply because he toiled with half a heart whereas his achievements would have put him up near the top, had he displayed a different temperament."[20]

Bert Walker also came down heavily on Ehmke for his July 13 performance against the A's. "He gave the poorest exhibition of pitching he has shown since donning a Tiger uniform," wrote Walker, who wondered how long Ehmke would remain with the team. "After his poor showing here, it would not be astonishing if Ehmke was sent to other pastures before long. There is every prospect that he will figure in a deal of some kind before long."[21]

The Tigers moved from Philadelphia to Boston, where Herman Pillette shut out the Red Sox, 2–0. Walker drew a contrast between Pillette, who raised his record to 10-4, and Ehmke. It was a particularly unflattering comparison for Ehmke, as it was not their ability Walker was comparing; it was their courage and work ethic. "Howard Ehmke could pitch as well as Pillette if he had as much ambition and nerve," wrote Walker, who had suggested in the spring that the Tigers trade Ehmke. "But Howard can't stand prosperity, and if he gets a good start he grows careless and throws it away. Pillette gets better as he goes along, and when things look toughest he pitches the harder. He doesn't lose heart and therefore he doesn't often lose games."[22]

Ehmke was used to hearing his attitude and lack of competitiveness criticized, but Salsinger's latest fault findings concerned his ability. "Ehmke has what many claim to be the best fastball in the league today, but he had always had trouble controlling it," he wrote. "This season he had taken to throwing his fastball underhanded, but in recent weeks it had been a failure. It lacked the velocity he had when throwing overhand or sidearm, and it hadn't improved his control."[23]

The Tigers were in a close race with Chicago for fourth place, but both teams were still within striking distance of New York and St. Louis, who continued to battle for the lead. Four days after Ehmke's poor showing against the Athletics, he was effective in long relief and was the winner as newly acquired Red Sox starter Jack Quinn squandered a five-run first-inning lead, and the Tigers rallied to win, 16–7.

"If I could make a trade for [A's third baseman] Joe Dugan, and Howard Ehmke should pitch as he can when right, I think I could come through for the 1922 championship," said Cobb. "These two men, giving their best, would be all that the Tigers would need." Cobb emphasized how important Ehmke was to the team, while hinting at his lack of dedication. "Perhaps I can come through with Ehmke alone, but he must pitch 100 percent ball the rest of the season for me to absolutely feel that I have a chance." While still insisting Ehmke was one of baseball's best pitchers, Cobb complained, "He cannot win for the Tigers for some reason or other. My ball club has a punch, but when he goes to the box, it does not seem to be as effective as it is when other pitchers are working."[24] Cobb's last statement implied that the Tigers players let down in some way when Ehmke was on the mound. Whether true or not, such a statement coming from the team's manager was likely to sow discord between Ehmke and his teammates.

In Fred Lieb's history of the Tigers, he quoted Detroit sportswriter E. A. Batchelor on Cobb's relation to his players: "Like so many other great performers, he was impatient with stupidity, lack of ambition, and lack of what he considered normal baseball ability. The result was that he proved to be a poor teacher and that he could never get his team imbued with real team spirit."[25]

As July turned to August, Cobb was still complaining about his pitchers, especially Ehmke, who he claimed had been "indifferent." The only pitcher to escape Cobb's criticism was Pillette, while he threatened to trade all the others. "Bids will run pretty high for Howard Ehmke," according to an unsigned article in the *Sporting News*, "because managers in general consider him a pretty effective piece of pitching machinery, and there are some team leaders in the American League who calculate that this alleged temperamental pitching person won't be so hard to handle under different methods." The writer took exception to the accusation of indifference, noting that "the records show he has worked like a pack horse and that his percentage of wins equals that of his team as a whole."[26]

Ehmke's trade value suffered with his August 15 start against the Yankees at the Polo Grounds. Instead it served as an example of the charge made by some, including Cobb, that Ehmke became easily rattled when a break went against him. After the Tigers scored a first-inning run off Bob Shawkey, Ehmke held that 1–0 lead until there was one out in the ninth. Bob Meusel's high pop foul should have been out number 2, but catcher Johnny Bassler dropped the ball. The error gave the dangerous Meusel another chance, and he took advantage of it by homering into the left-field seats to tie the score. Ehmke retired Aaron

Ward, but yielded singles to Everett Scott and Shawkey. Cobb replaced him with Red Oldham, who got the third out. But with two down in the tenth, Elmer Smith reached Oldham for a game-winning home run.

It was a devastating loss for the Tigers and an exhilarating win for the Yankees, who remained in a battle for first place with the Browns. The Tigers improved their position with a doubleheader win at Boston on August 19. Pillette won the opener, 6–1, and Ehmke outdueled Benn Karr in the nightcap, 1–0. Bullion used Ehmke's wonderfully pitched game to indirectly remind his readers of the 1–0, ninth-inning lead he had blown in his previous start. "Ehmke pitched like he can when his mental poise suits the occasion," he wrote.[27] The sweep allowed the Tigers to gain ground on both front-runners; they now trailed New York by 7½ games and St. Louis by 7.

When Ehmke faced St. Louis at Sportsman's Park on September 11, the Browns trailed the Yankees by just 1½ games. His pitches were so effective that afternoon several batters complained about the way he was rubbing the ball. But after a close examination, umpires Bill Guthrie and George Moriarty could find no foreign substances on the ball. With the Tigers leading, 4–3, Ehmke retired the first two batters in the last of the ninth but walked Eddie Foster on a 3-2 pitch. That brought up George Sisler, the league's leading hitter, whom Ehmke had already fanned twice.[28] After Sisler fouled off the first two pitches, Ehmke was one pitch away from the win. But Sisler tripled on a liner to right-center that scored Foster with the tying run.

The standing-room-only crowd erupted. "Play was stopped for 10 minutes, while old faded straw hats, new fall headwear, and seat cushions were cleared from the field."[29] When play resumed, Ehmke walked Ken Williams and Baby Doll Jacobson to load the bases. The game ended when Marty McManus singled on the first pitch to bring Sisler home with the winning run.[30]

Nine days after St. Louis rallied late to defeat Ehmke, it was New York's turn to do the same. Ehmke went the distance but blew a 4–0 lead and lost, 6–5, on Meusel's ninth-inning home run. It was a tense game with much bickering among the players. Ehmke hit two of the visiting Yankees, Aaron Ward twice and Bob Shawkey, who yelled at his mound opponent for doing so.[31] In addition, players on both teams were knocked down, and Cobb and Wally Schang had to be separated from brawling at home plate during one of Cobb's at bats. It was in the fourth inning, after Cobb had asked umpire Brick Owens to examine the ball. The situation escalated from there, and several players from each team gathered around to pull their respective teammates away.

The 1922 Tigers finished third, 15 games behind the Yankees. "[Hooks] Dauss (13-13) pitched erratically, and Ehmke (17-17) as if he did not care," wrote Cobb biographer Charles Alexander; only Pillette, who won nineteen games as a rookie, was a dependable starter.[32]

A season that began with Cobb trying unsuccessfully to trade Ehmke would end with his succeeding in moving the pitcher he neither liked nor to whom he could relate. And the feeling was mutual. When Cobb resigned as manager of the Tigers after the 1926 season, Ehmke said of him, "For years [he] was Detroit's greatest pennant handicap."[33]

21

From the Pennant in New York
to the Cellar in Boston

Jack Quinn would not have a chance for another comeback with the Yankees. On December 20, 1921, he was sent to the Red Sox in New York's second consecutive year-end, multi-player trade with Boston.[1] One New York newspaper headline read "Biggest Trade in Baseball History."[2] The Yankees bolstered their pitching by acquiring two veteran hurlers, Joe Bush and Sam Jones, and gave up three pitchers: two young men who had not delivered on their potential, Bill Piercy and Rip Collins, and the thirty-eight-year-old Quinn. The other part of the deal was a blockbuster and a surprise to fans in both New York and Boston: the teams swapped their star shortstops, Roger Peckinpaugh and Everett Scott.

Insiders, however, were not surprised at the trade of shortstops. The Yankees' clubhouse had been wracked by an anti–Miller Huggins clique for several years, and Peckinpaugh was a convenient rallying point for the group. Babe Ruth and his unruly teammates figured they could operate with little discipline if their shortstop took over as manager from Huggins.[3]

There is no indication that Peckinpaugh encouraged Huggins's removal; he was a quiet and professional team man who would not undercut his manager.[4] Peckinpaugh was the last Yankee remaining from the 1915 club Jacob Ruppert and Til Huston had purchased. He carried himself both on and off the field with class, and many New York papers used the word "regret" in describing his departure.

Much of the newspaper coverage focused on which team got the better of the deal. Jack Quinn hardly figured in the discussion; he was almost an afterthought in the trade. Most sportswriters felt the Yankees had come out on top. They were said to have given up little to get much of the remaining talent on the once powerful Red Sox of the 1910s.[5] Boston's press and fandom were near despair, outrage, or both. Burt Whitman wrote that "the scrapping of the great Red Sox armada . . . reached the junk stage" with this deal.[6] Paul Shannon's headline in the *Boston Post* read "Frazee Junks His Ball Club."[7] While they all acknowledged Peckinpaugh's talent, they bemoaned the loss of a great shortstop in Scott.

Whitman pointed out that Quinn, like Piercy and Collins, had not been "good enough to do regular work with the Yankees" late in the 1921 season.[8] Another Boston reporter referred to Quinn as an "antique pitcher . . . who at best was a relief pitcher."[9] And Shannon called him "the ancient Mariner of the American League, once potent as an effective spitballer, but of late effective only against Boston."[10]

The harshest critique of the trade may have come from Joe Vila, who wrote for both the *Sporting News* and the *New York Sun*. He suggested that "Frazee was either chloroformed or hypnotized" to make this trade.[11] Perhaps he was hypnotized by the $150,000 cash the Yankees' owners gave him, a detail that was left out of newspaper accounts. While Frazee denied there was any cash involved, most observers doubted his claim. "Unquestionably, there is something about the trade that reeks of burning money," wrote Frank O'Neill.[12]

As for Quinn, Vila repeatedly dismissed him as "through."[13] Sam Crane wrote that Quinn had just been "hanging on" in 1921: "He had ambition enough, but age was telling on him, and he found that too big a handicap to overcome. Evidently he has 'run out' of big-league class, although he has a splendid record behind him."[14] Quinn seemed about to leave the Major Leagues with a respectable, if not impressive, number of wins, 125, against 105 losses.[15]

Quinn, who had heard all these criticisms before, did have one supporter in the New York press corps, Frank O'Neill, who saw a future for him. When the trade was announced, he wrote that Quinn was "making his last stand. He will be at least a good finishing pitcher for Boston. . . . He always gives his best."[16] In July 1921, when he referred to Quinn's "strains of greatness," he had written that the pitcher had "come upon evil times."[17] He pointed out that even when Quinn had been driven from the mound in the first inning against the Indians on September 26, he had been victimized by a bloop single and an error.

22. Hugh Duffy was a legendary star of the 1890s Boston Beaneaters, who won four National League pennants that decade. He averaged .332 for the Beaneaters, including a record-setting .440 in 1894. He managed the struggling Red Sox in 1921 and 1922. "The only straw at which [owner Harry] Frazee can clutch," wrote one Boston reporter when Duffy was hired, was that "out of this hodge-podge of material Hugh Duffy can make a winner." He was unable to do so but continued as a Red Sox scout for many years. *Steve Steinberg Collection.*

Hugh Duffy, a seventeen-year Major League veteran and Boston Beaneaters star of the 1890s, had taken over as Red Sox manager in 1921 and led the club to a surprising fifth-place finish with a 75-79 record. He declared that the trade, and another the Red Sox made the same day, as good for Boston: "I wanted a stronger batting team. I now think I have it."[18] Sam Crane felt Duffy was not merely supporting his beleaguered owner, but had also signed off on the deals.[19]

A *Boston Herald* sportswriter viewed the swap of shortstops as beneficial for the Red Sox. Of Peckinpaugh he wrote, "There is not a gamer ball player in the country. In the same breath it may be said that there is no better ball player in the country."[20] But Boston fans never had a chance to find out if this opinion was accurate. Just three weeks later, on January 10, 1922, the Red Sox traded Peckinpaugh to the Washington Senators for third baseman Joe Dugan and infielder Frank O'Rourke.

As 1922 approached, Quinn had to accept the fact that the Yankees had practically discarded him, as they had in 1912. He suspected his opportunities with the Red Sox would be limited. He told one reporter that he had written the Red Sox a number of times and received no reply.[21] The *Chicago Tribune* and *New York Times* reported in January that he had signed with a semi-pro team. Quinn told reporters, "Boston probably would have sent me to the bushes. Chicago is my home, so when this semi-pro offer came along, I figured the best thing for me to do was to take it."[22]

Duffy reached out to Quinn as spring training approached. He assured the pitcher that the Red Sox had no intention of sending him to the Minors.[23] He explained that with the departure of Bush and Jones, Jack would have the opportunity not only to pitch for Boston but also to be a starter. He signed for less money than the Yankees had paid him in 1921, a lot less with a World Series appearance not a realistic possibility.[24]

The Red Sox had been training in Hot Springs, Arkansas, for most of the past decade, and Quinn reported early to "boil out" in the town's mineral pools and take long hikes in the surrounding hills. For the rest of his career, he would spend time in Hot Springs before reporting for spring training, even when his club trained in a different city. He would hike ten or fifteen miles and then soak in the thermal waters of the town's spas each day. As a *Sporting News* reporter later wrote, Quinn "believes training of the legs is the most important of athletic conditioning, and that if the legs are sound, the throwing arm of a pitcher, with ordinary care, will take care of itself."[25]

"My arm is just as I want it, and I am sure of being a winner for Duffy this season," Quinn said in early April. "And if it stays the way it is now all season, I will beat the New York club every game."[26] Quinn impressed observers that spring with his approach to the game. "Pitcher Jack Quinn, although well over 30, works out with the pep of a 20-year-old youngster," wrote A. J. Rooney.[27] W. C. Spargo noted that after more than twenty years in Organized Baseball, "Ambition is Jack's middle name. . . . He will do a lot toward reviving the fans' pepper for the Sox."[28]

The doubters about the Red Sox were many, as were the doubters about Quinn. "The only straw at which Frazee can clutch," wrote Spargo, "is the hope that out of this hodge-podge of material Hugh Duffy can make a winner."[29]

Duffy followed through on his promise and made Quinn his starter on Opening Day. The veteran went the distance in a 3–2 loss to the Athletics. Three Boston errors—including one by Quinn—cost them the game. A week later he beat the Yankees, and on April 29 he had another fine performance against his former team. He pitched 11⅔ innings but had to leave the game when he was hit on his pitching hand by a Waite Hoyt line drive. The Red Sox went on to win in fourteen innings. The game drew attention because Hoyt scuffled with Huggins in the dugout after he gave up three runs in the fourteenth.[30]

When Quinn shut out the Senators four days later, helped by his own bases-clearing double, one Boston newspaper column had the giddy headline, "Present Pace Will Land Hub Hose in First Division."[31] But by early summer the only question was whether the floundering Red Sox could avoid finishing in the cellar.

Quinn again beat the Yankees on June 22, a five-hitter that prompted the *New York Times* reporter to moan, "All that Huggins has to do to discover a pitcher who can defeat the Yankees is to release one to another club, whereupon he immediately develops into a full-fledged jinx for the Mite Manager and his cohorts."[32] Four years earlier the

Yankees had traded Urban Shocker to the Browns, and he had beaten them with regularity ever since.[33]

On July 24 the Red Sox played an exhibition game in Connellsville, and a number of Quinn's former Dunbar teammates attended. The occasion was designated "Jack Quinn Day" to honor the pitcher who had starred in that western Pennsylvania area two decades earlier. Boston beat the Connellsville Independents, 9–2.[34]

Quinn had developed a reputation as a good early-season pitcher who lost effectiveness as the temperature rose. Typical was the comment of Harry Schumacher when Jack was a Yankee: "Quinn is a great spring pitcher but peters out with the coming of hot weather."[35] But as the 1922 season continued into the heat of summer, he showed no signs of wearing down. He three-hit the White Sox on July 26 and less than two weeks later went the distance in a twelve-inning loss to Stan Coveleski and Cleveland, 3–2. On August 25 Quinn tossed a two-hit shutout against the Indians.

American League president Ban Johnson was frustrated by the length of ball games in his league and announced on August 22 that nine-inning games must be played in less than two hours. A columnist for the *Sporting News* wrote, "These two-hour games wore on the nerves." He explained, "They made the Boss Bug [fan] late for supper, and when this happened, the real Boss Bug [his wife] peeved."[36] Umpires were now directed to remove stalling players and managers, who would then be suspended for ten days. "It seems that President Johnson has made a good ruling, and fans will enjoy faster games," wrote A. J. Rooney.[37] He felt the biggest reason for slow games was that managers were telling their young pitchers to take their time on the mound and not to rush their delivery.

Johnson was also concerned about nails that players were hammering into their bats to make balls go further. One Boston reporter wrote that more than 75 percent of Major League players had nails in their bats, with as many as sixty nails in each one. These bats were said to have generated more home runs and "heavy hitting."[38]

The Yankees and Browns had battled for the lead all season, and the Yankees needed just one win in their season-ending series with the Red Sox to clinch the pennant. But two former Yankees rose up to cause them problems. First, Rip Collins beat them on September 28 with a four-hitter.[39] The next day Quinn defeated them, 1–0, prompting Babe Ruth to mutter, "What the hell are those guys trying to do to us?"[40] Boston reporter Nick Flatley described Quinn's performance this way: "Ol' Jack, Yank discard, worked all afternoon with a million-dollar smile brightening his broad countenance. He nipped the first man at bat in every one of the nine innings, which is the real secret of successful pitching."[41]

The *Boston Globe*'s James O'Leary wrote that the Yankees had been beaten by New York's second team since so many New Yorkers were now on the Red Sox.[42] "Many of Hugh Duffy's present string have a lot of grievances to redress at the expense of their former New York teammates," wrote Paul Shannon, "and they got some measure of revenge."[43] The Yankees staggered to the pennant the next day, when they beat Boston in the final game of the series and edged the Browns by just one game. It was only their eighth win over lowly Boston in twenty-two games in 1922.

In late August Rooney called the 1922 club the worst Red Sox team ever.[44] The club finished in last place with only sixty-one wins, the fewest since 1907. As the season came to an end, Flatley wrote, "The only hope seems to rest in the league stepping in and buying Frazee out, for his club has become a dependent."[45]

Quinn was the club's "iron man" in 1922. He led Red Sox pitchers in most categories, including innings pitched (256) and complete games (16). His 13-16 record had a far better winning percentage than that of his club, and his 3.49 earned run average was more than a half-run lower than the league's average. The pitcher who was thought by many to be "through" had surprised the doubters again. He had shown he could still pitch.

22

———

Veteran Aces on the League's Worst Team

Reports of Howard Ehmke's liberation from Ty Cobb came shortly after the 1922 season ended. The actual date of Ehmke's trade to the Boston Red Sox remains a mystery. *Baseball-Reference* and *Retrosheet* list it as October 30, but H. G. Salsinger of the *Detroit News* had it in his story of September 29.[1] In addition, an October 5 story in the *Sporting News* claimed a trade was imminent, one that would send Ehmke and pitcher Carl Holling (described by Cobb biographer Charles Alexander as "two malcontents") to the Red Sox for pitcher Rip Collins and second baseman Del Pratt.[2]

When the trade was completed, Ehmke, Holling, second baseman Danny Clark, Minor League first baseman Babe Herman, and $25,000 went to Boston in exchange for Collins and Pratt.[3] At the time, the prize of the deal for the Red Sox may have been Herman, a nineteen-year-old left-handed hitter who had drawn comparisons to Babe Ruth. "Herman is bigger than Ruth, swings a heavier bat, hits them as far, is as good a first baseman or outfielder, and about as intelligent, according to all accounts," claimed the *Sporting News*.[4]

Detroit had kept Herman in the Minors in 1922, where he hit a combined .402 while splitting time between Omaha of the Western League and Reading of the International League. "If there is a real 'find' among the several promising rookies on the Red Sox squad, or a guy that fairly oozes colorfulness, that one is 'Babe,'" wrote one Boston sportswriter in March.[5] "My, what a future that kid has before him," said Sox pitcher Jack Quinn.[6] But Herman's Major League future would have to wait; he would not play his first game until 1926.

Salsinger also hailed the arrival of Collins, whom he expected to become a big star. A frequent critic of Ehmke and a close friend of Cobb, Salsinger added a farewell dig at the departing pitcher, hinting at the frustration felt toward him by so many in Detroit. "Always

23. Babe Herman's Major League debut did not come until 1926, with Brooklyn. But he appeared in spring training for the Tigers in 1922 and the Red Sox in 1923, both before he was twenty years old. Herman would gain fame with the Dodgers, batting .381 in 1929 and .393 in 1930. In his history of the Dodgers, sportswriter Tommy Holmes noted that he had a great throwing arm. "There was, however, always a question about where he would throw the ball." Arthur Daley of the *New York Times* put it more simply. "He was the delight and despair of a generation of Brooklyn Dodger fans." *Steve Steinberg Collection.*

Ehmke stood on the brink of a great season," he wrote. "He always had an unusual amount of stuff that, because of one reason or another, he never quite delivered in the style that his ability warranted."[7]

Most fans backed Cobb's decision to make the trade, which Fred Lieb would later call one of the worst the club ever made.[8] At the time, however, there was much speculation about how Ehmke would do with Boston. "Ehmke for several seasons gave promise of being a real 'great' in the American League, but his disposition has been against him, and he has fallen down," wrote K. W. Hall in the *Sporting News*. "Yet he is a good twirler who may find himself while working under new ownership. Howard developed a fine underhand ball while with the Tigers, and when using it, was very effective, but when he switched to his overhand delivery, which he frequently did, the opposition hit him."[9] According to Hall, "Cobb worked long and hard in an effort to convince Ehmke that he should use this underhand style at all times, but Ehmke persisted in following his own ideas in the matter and lost many games through his obstinacy."[10]

As discussed in chapter 20, Cobb explained that while Ehmke had enough stuff to be one of the game's greatest pitchers, he intimated that Ehmke lacked courage. There can be no greater denunciation of an athlete than such a charge. Ehmke did not let this and Cobb's other criticisms of him go unanswered. In addition to describing how he had to look toward center field (from where Cobb was signaling instructions) while he was pitching to the batter, Ehmke claimed Cobb had thrown him off his stride and destroyed his poise by insisting he resort to intentionally hitting batters.[11]

Baseball historian Larry Amman wrote, "Ty wore a path from the outfield to the pitcher's mound, giving advice. Or he would whistle with his fingers and give hand signals to the pitcher and catcher, embarrassing both."[12] Amman, who studied Cobb's career, called him "the quintessential bad pitchers' manager. There was no pattern to his rotation," he wrote. "He might pitch a man with five days' rest or with one. He would warm up two or three starters and decide which one to use minutes before game time."[13]

Outfielder Joe Hauser, who played with Ehmke on the 1928 Philadelphia Athletics, also had negative memories of Cobb as a teammate.

Cobb alienated himself from the team, often dining alone, Hauser said in a 1997 interview.[14] Once when Cobb offered to buy some players drinks in New York, he was told, "No thanks, Cobb, it's too late. You've been a bastard for too long."[15]

Rip Collins, who came to Detroit in the Ehmke trade and pitched for Cobb's Tigers from 1923 to 1926, thought his manager had an excellent grasp of the game. "Where he lost out," Collins told *Baseball Magazine* in a 1930 interview, "was in antagonizing his own men. His very ability as a player made him irritable and hard to work for. He could grasp a play instantly that other players couldn't see at all. When he tried to explain it to them, some of them didn't follow him any too closely. Their dumbness used to exasperate him," Collins said. "But he stirred up bad blood on the team. A good many players detested him. And I was one of that misguided bunch."[16]

At training camp in Hot Springs, Boston sportswriter Fred Hoey predicted Ehmke, the Red Sox's new acquisition, would be their best pitcher in 1923. He based his prediction on what Ehmke had accomplished at Detroit in 1922, despite his early season illness: "Last year a week before the Detroit season opened Howard was 19 pounds under weight, due to a malaria attack."[17]

Ehmke said the trade to the Red Sox was the best thing that happened to him since he reached the Major Leagues. He said he had not felt well in 1922 and was unable to perform up to his standard but added that he now felt fine. "This former Detroit star has a barrel of stuff and should go good for the Sox. He has been anxious to get away from Detroit for two years" (since Cobb became the manager).[18] An unsigned column in the *Boston Herald* mentioned the well-known difficulties Ehmke had faced pitching for Cobb: "Tyrus has the habit of bothering his pitchers so much that a few of them, notably Ehmke, cannot win for him. They want more freedom and independence and a little bit of encouragement and appreciation."[19]

The trade reunited Ehmke and Frank Chance, with whom he had had a checkered relationship during his time as a Minor Leaguer. Boston owner Harry Frazee had made a flashy signing when he hired Chance, the first baseman-manager of the great Chicago Cubs teams of 1906–10. As Fred Lieb wrote in his team history of the Red Sox,

"Having wrecked the Red Sox, Frazee tried to restore favor with his fans in 1923 with a managerial name."[20] Some of the sheen had rubbed off Chance's stellar reputation after his unsuccessful stint as manager of the New York Yankees in 1913–14.[21] Despite fighting blood clots on his brain from his many beanings, he was restless to return from his California orange grove to big league action. He sounded positive as he assumed the helm of the Red Sox: "If I saw no hope of climbing out of the cellar, I never would have signed a contract for, you see, I myself am staging a baseball comeback."[22]

One Boston writer said of Chance's return, "He is getting so much delight out of it. . . . His smile has been working overtime, and he has been kidding and joking as much as anybody."[23] Just before spring training, Chance met with Jack Quinn in Chicago and said of the veteran pitcher, "He looks as good as he did when I first saw him ten years ago. Jack is a wise old bird."[24] Chance planned for Quinn to assist him with Boston's young pitchers.[25]

While no longer considered young, at twenty-nine Ehmke was new to the Red Sox and now a teammate of Quinn. But while Quinn would have preferred to stay with the contending Yankees, Ehmke welcomed the opportunity to go to this second-division team. Anything to get away from Ty Cobb.

New managers tend to be optimistic, no matter the quality of the club they have joined. Frank Chance was no different in sizing up his Red Sox at the start of spring training. "I feel confident we will amount to something this season," he said of a team that finished last in 1922. "I saw Ehmke in California before I left, and he is pleased with his transfer to the Red Sox. He is heavier than last year." (The assumption was that the extra weight would help Ehmke.)[26] Chance said, after a workout at Hot Springs, "It is a fine arm, one of the rubber arms that will stand a lot of work and doesn't get lame."[27]

Former Sox manager Hugh Duffy stayed on with the club as a scout. One account noted that a smile had returned to his face now that he was relieved of leading "nondescript athletes tossing ball games away."[28] The change in managers changed the atmosphere in the clubhouse. Chance was a disciplinarian and a fighter who did not tolerate stupidity or lackadaisical play. "I have always insisted on discipline," he said during spring training, "and it is necessary in order to attain success in baseball."[29]

But even before the end of spring training, Chance realized how lacking in talent his team was. "It is a sad-looking baseball team. . . . Chance has told Frazee that the bunch won't do. Frazee has given him permission to clean house. But where are the players coming from? It takes money to build a ball club. You can't pick up ball players in [discount variety stores] Woolworth's or Kresge's," wrote Hoey.[30] New York sportswriter John Kieran wrote that Chance predicted a last-place finish for his team. Kieran agreed and wrote that winning games with this roster would be "just as easy as throwing watermelons through keyholes."[31] With so little talent left on the club, Chance would manage the 1923 Red Sox to only sixty-one wins, the same number as the previous year.

On April 8 the Red Sox were in Owensboro, Kentucky, for their exhibition series with the American Association's Louisville Colonels. But the weather was so frigid the game was called off. Louisville manager Joe McCarthy wanted to play, but Chance said it was too cold. Chance also got the bad news that Jack Quinn's injury in a game the day before had resulted in a small broken bone in the back of his right hand.[32] A week earlier Chance had told reporters that Quinn was the club's "best-looking pitcher . . . Jack is in great shape."[33] The injury was likely to keep him out for a couple of weeks and meant he would not pitch the opener at the new Yankee Stadium. That had been Chance's plan, but he would open instead with Ehmke. Fred Hoey lamented the bad luck that befell Quinn because "No man on the squad has worked harder than the veteran to get into condition."[34]

The magnificent new Yankee Stadium opened on April 18, 1923. More than sixty thousand fans attended, while an additional twenty thousand were turned away.[35] It was by far the largest crowd ever to see a Major League baseball game.[36] Yankees manager Miller Huggins gave the honor of pitching the opener to Bob Shawkey, who was the Yankees' all-time leader in wins, with 120, and second only to first baseman Wally Pipp in length of service with the club. Boston first baseman George Burns got the first hit in the new stadium, one of only three hits Shawkey allowed in a 4–1 win.

24. On April 18, 1923, Howard Ehmke made his Red Sox debut opposing New York's Bob Shawkey in the first game played at Yankee Stadium. Babe Ruth's three-run home run in the fourth inning, the first at the stadium, was the difference in the Yankees' 4–1 victory. *Steve Steinberg Collection.*

The distinction of hitting the first home run in the new park went, as if willed by the baseball gods, to Babe Ruth. It came against Ehmke in the fourth inning, with Whitey Witt and Joe Dugan on base. "Grinning as he followed Witt and Dugan around the bases, he waved his cap to the fans, who responded with the loudest roar of the day. Given the size of the crowd, the ovation Ruth received following his home run may have been the biggest ever heard at a ballgame" to that time.[37]

In mid-August Ehmke spoke of the Yankee Stadium opener with Ed Cunningham of the *Boston Traveler*. Ever since Ruth had come into the league, pitchers had tried to figure the best way to pitch to him. Ehmke thought he had the answer, and for one stretch of 28 at bats, dating from September 1921 through all of 1922, the Babe had managed only one hit against him, a single.

"Babe loves a fastball," Ehmke said, "and long ago I decided never to treat him to one of his favorites. . . . I resolved to give him nothing but slow curves. Because of my underhand delivery, this ball rises while it is breaking and when delivered properly, is a difficult ball to hit far."[38] He recalled that when Ruth batted in the fourth inning of the opener, there were two men on base: "I got the count down to three and two on him, and he refused to nibble. Then I was determined to pitch to him, as Bob Meusel was coming up, and he always has been bad news to me. Unfortunately for me and the Red Sox the ball did not break high enough. . . . Babe gave it a belt, and it sang on a line into the right field bleachers. Those three runs beat me as the final score was 4 to 1."[39]

Ehmke called it a good strategy to walk Ruth if the situation called for it, but added "it seems almost like jumping from the frying pan into the fire with Meusel coming up." He considered Meusel the toughest Yankees batter he had to face: "He broke up two games on me last year with home runs. Every pitcher has a batter somewhere along the line who likes his stuff. Big Bob has showed a marked preference for mine. He is far more effective against me than the Babe."[40]

Following three more loses to the Yankees, the Red Sox moved on to Philadelphia, where on April 26 Ehmke pitched them to a 9–6 win, their first of the season. Far from overpowering—he allowed thirteen hits—he was helped along by nine A's errors. Three days later Ehmke faced the Yankees again in Boston's home opener. He went 8⅓ innings but left after putting the tying run aboard. Lefty O'Doul got the final two outs and picked up his only Major League victory when Boston scored in the home ninth.[41]

Ehmke, having defeated Philadelphia fourteen times in twenty-two decisions as a Tiger, continued his mastery over the A's by striking out ten in a 5–4 victory on May 1. It was not an easy win, as the Athletics had jumped to a 4–0 lead. Boston won by scoring three in the sixth and two in the eighth. On May 5 Ehmke got his third consecutive victory, a twelve-inning, 4–1 win over Washington's Tom Zachary, raising his record to 3-1. Ehmke allowed just five hits, while he himself had two hits and a run batted in.

Quinn's injury-delayed first appearance of the season came on April 27, in relief against the Yankees. He showed no signs of rust, allowing only four hits in 7⅔ innings. A week later he was "as steady as a church" in an efficient complete-game 3–1 win over the Athletics.[42] On May 20 he suffered a tough loss to Cleveland's Stan Coveleski, 1–0, as Boston's record fell to 8-16.

The Yankees were on their way to a third straight pennant in 1923. When the Red Sox came to Yankee Stadium on May 31, New York was already in first place by seven games. Yet the Boston players felt a special rivalry with the Yankees because so many of them were Yankees castoffs.[43] "Rivalry between Red Sox and Yankees," wrote Ed Cunningham, "make Harvard and Yale antipathy toward each other look like a flock of sheep in a pastoral setting."[44] Jack Quinn, whose career included seven years with the Yankees and four with the Red Sox, experienced the rivalry from both sides. And while Quinn did not have the fiery personality of Urban Shocker, the pitcher who had sworn revenge on the Yankees for trading him away, he did gain satisfaction in beating the team he believed had given up on him. "Ever since Jack was traded to the Red Sox," noted Fred Lieb, "his greatest pleasure in life has been to beat the Yankees."[45]

Joe Vila gave a vivid account of Quinn's June 1 performance, when he shut out the New Yorkers, 5–0: "The Yankees were as harmless as a bunch of armless and legless swimmers. The Ancient Quinn, with moist balls, speed balls, and slow balls, all perfectly controlled, made Hug's famous sluggers look like mummies from King Tut's tomb."[46]

On June 26, when Quinn beat the Yankees again, 3–1, for his fifth win, he was repeatedly applauded during the game. One New York reporter wrote, "When Quinn is right, he still retains much of the old-time cunning. . . . He was right today."[47] His record against the Yankees now stood at 5-2 since he had come to Boston.

Meanwhile, Ehmke continued to be Chance's most reliable pitcher. A Peekskill, New York, reporter imagined that whenever Ty Cobb looked at the pitching records, he likely threw a fit. Cobb had traded Ehmke to the Red Sox because "he did not agree with Howard in their personal relations." Neither Del Pratt nor Rip Collins, whom Detroit received for Ehmke, had lived up to expectations. "Pratt has been collecting splinters on the bench, and Collins hasn't won many games for the Tigers."[48]

Yet Cobb had been eager to trade Ehmke, noted F. C. Lane. "The bond of affection existing between Ehmke and Cobb has long been conspicuous by its absence. Cobb, swayed somewhat by his feelings, doubtless found it difficult to rate Ehmke at his true worth. Ehmke, on his part, found it difficult, if not impossible, to do his best work under the direction of Tyrus Raymond Cobb."[49]

23

Ehmke and Cobb Get Physical, and
the Red Sox Get New Owners

On May 18, 1923, Howard Ehmke faced the Tigers in Detroit for the first time since his trade to Boston. His mound opponent was his former teammate and close friend, Hooks Dauss, who came into the game with a 6-0 record. The game was tied after nine innings, but the Red Sox scored four runs in the tenth to win, 6–2. Ehmke contributed three singles, including one to lead off the tenth inning. The result was a disappointment for Ty Cobb, Ehmke's former manager and longtime antagonist. Cobb was eager to prove he had made the right decision in trading Ehmke. He loaded his lineup with left-handed batters, and when he was not batting, coached at first base, where he yelled at Ehmke and attempted to distract him.

In his plate appearances Cobb went 0 for 3, walked once, and was hit by a pitch in the seventh inning, one of three batters Ehmke hit in the game. The crowd, which had greeted Ehmke warmly when he took the mound in the first inning, assumed he had hit Cobb intentionally and began razzing him. "He [Cobb] made gestures of throwing the bat at me and swore I hit him on purpose," Ehmke recalled to sportswriter Ed Pollock in 1952. When he went under the stands after the game, Ehmke found Cobb waiting for him. "He took a shot me, and we scuffled around," Ehmke said. "It was a typical baseball fight. . . . Cobb won all right. . . . We beat Detroit that day, and I'd still rather be the winning pitcher than the winner of the fight."[1]

"Cobb was very vicious along those lines," said pitcher Waite Hoyt, a contemporary of both Cobb and Ehmke. "And as I heard it . . . Cobb went into the clubhouse and didn't shower but came out and hid. Then when Ehmke came out he sneaked up behind him and hit him with a roundhouse punch. Cobb had several incidents like that."[2]

Ehmke did not deny he hit Cobb deliberately and was scolded about it by one Boston sportswriter. "Ty Cobb can take care of himself on and off the ball field, as many a player knows," wrote Herman Nickerson of the *Boston Traveler*. "If what was reported is true, that Ehmke deliberately hit Ty, then what he [Ehmke] got was not half enough. This 'beaning' of players is not in the game and should figure as a common assault and be treated as such."[3]

When New York sportswriter Joe Williams mentioned to Cobb in a 1941 interview that one of his pitchers with the Tigers had said he sometimes ordered his pitchers to bean dangerous hitters and fined them if they failed to do so, Cobb disputed the claim. "I know who you are talking about," Cobb said. "That was Howard Ehmke. All I can say is that Ehmke wasn't speaking the truth."[4]

A month after the Ehmke-Cobb confrontation at Navin Field, the Tigers came to Boston for a three-game series. They beat Bill Piercy in the first game and Jack Quinn in the second and would have loved to beat Ehmke for the sweep. A Saturday crowd of close to fourteen thousand fans was at Fenway Park on June 16. They saw Ehmke and Detroit's Herman Pillette match each other with three scoreless innings before the Tigers scored a run in the fourth. But that would be the total of their scoring. Meanwhile, the Red Sox bombarded Pillette and Rip Collins for seven runs in the home fourth and coasted to a 9–1 win. "From the moment the game started, there was a tenseness noticeable among the players on both sides," wrote the *Boston Globe*'s James O'Leary.[5]

Manager Cobb was again coaching at first when he wasn't batting and again took the opportunity to taunt and deride Ehmke all afternoon. Cobb had doubled in the fourth inning and scored the Tigers' only run, but Ehmke handled him in his other three at bats. In his last plate appearance, Cobb hit a weak pop fly to shortstop Johnny Mitchell that he did not bother to run out. When Boston catcher Al DeVormer laughed at him, the easily provoked Cobb responded with words that led DeVormer to start after him. Nothing further occurred, though Cobb was said to be "boiling over" after his team had scored just one run against Ehmke.[6]

In his 1952 interview with Ed Pollock, Ehmke recounted his memories of that game. He remembered DeVormer as "a tough fellow who loved to fight." He and teammates Piercy and Ira Flagstead wanted DeVormer to fight Cobb and offered to buy him a suit if he did. They never did fight, but that was more likely Cobb's choice. Ehmke recalled that after DeVormer had a good laugh when Cobb popped out to Mitchell, Cobb glared at him as he headed out to the field. "Want something?" DeVormer said in a challenging way. "But Cobb just continued heading to his position."[7]

The Red Sox had briefly emerged from last place after a mid-June series with Chicago. Moreover, the crowds at Fenway Park were getting bigger, as the fans warmed to the fighting spirit Chance had instilled in the team. He lambasted them when they played poorly, and that was thought to have made a difference. But Gus Rooney, who covered the Red Sox for the *Sporting News*, believed much of the credit should go to Ehmke. He called Howard's June 12 victory over Chicago's Red Faber an inspiration to the team's other pitchers. "Ehmke is not only the best pitcher on the Boston team," Rooney wrote; "he seems to be about the best we have had here since the days of George [Rube] Foster and some of those former [manager Bill] Carrigan champion hurlers, and the Boston fans are strong for him."[8]

Fred Hoey also gave much of the credit for the team's rise to Ehmke. "If one or two of the other pitchers should come through to balance Ehmke's work," he wrote, "the Sox might rise in the standing to dizzy heights."[9] The effusive praise of Ehmke by the Boston press was in sharp contrast to the criticism he had received in Detroit, where he was so often faulted for what reporters perceived as indifference and lack of heart.

Ehmke's three-hit, 4–1 win against the Browns on June 20 gave him ten of Boston's twenty-one wins. He now had at least one victory against every team in the league. "Three more Ehmkes, and the Red Sox would win the A. L. pennant and World Series," wrote Bob Dunbar of the *Boston Herald*. "If Ehmke were working for a first division nine this year, the chances are that he would have had a most phenomenal record. With the eighth-place Red Sox, he has won 10 and lost four, showing remarkable effectiveness."[10]

On June 28 Ehmke hooked up in a pitching duel with Washington's Tom Zachary. Like the May 5 game at Griffith Stadium, each pitcher allowed just five hits, but Ehmke won again, 4–1. He followed with a win against the A's, after which Burt Whitman wrote: "Howard Ehmke strikes us as one of the most hustling pitchers even seen on the Fenway stretch, and that makes it all the more difficult to understand why Ty Cobb thought so little of the Viking athlete."[11]

Around this time—late June, early July—talk of trading Ehmke was bandied about again. No doubt recalling the long list of Red Sox stars who had ended up being sold or traded to New York, Bob Dunbar said sarcastically, "Howard Ehmke is getting too good for the Red Sox. He is going well enough to be promoted to the Yankees."[12]

Ehmke may have preferred being traded to a contender, but instead he said words he had not been truly able to say while playing in Detroit under Cobb. He pronounced himself very happy in Boston with manager Chance, his teammates, and the fans. "It was the best move I ever made when I came to Boston," he declared. "I could not ask for anything better this year." He called Chance "the squarest man I ever worked for in baseball. All the boys admire him and will do anything possible to win for him."[13]

On July 1 Jack Quinn turned forty. While his exact age was not known at the time, not even by Quinn himself, he was recognized as one of the league's oldest players. Just two weeks earlier manager John McGraw of the New York Giants had made an astute observation about Quinn's success: "Jack Quinn simply has an unusual constitution and an unusual pair of wrists. It is when the wrists lose their snap that a pitcher begins to slow up. The ball loses its jump. That is the first sign."[14] Jack Quinn was showing no indications of that sign.

As Quinn grew older, there were more frequent comments about his durability. While he often explained how he stayed in shape year round, this season he talked about the importance of a pitcher's understanding his body: "I know what my arm will stand and what it will not stand, and nurse it along accordingly."[15] If a pitcher does have a sore arm, he explained, he must admit it and not try to pitch through it, a move that could endanger his career. Quinn felt that Chicago's great spitball pitcher, Ed Walsh, had probably shortened his career by such self-denial.

On most teams pitchers have always been a club within a club. More than position players, they seem more aware of what their fellow hurlers are doing, an awareness that even includes opposing pitchers. It is not surprising that Quinn had an opinion on what had shortened Ed Walsh's career. While naming no one in particular, the Yankees' Carl Mays also held forth on his fellow hurlers. "There are lots of queer pitchers," he said. "I know, for I am a pitcher myself. But the oddest one in the bunch, to my way of thinking, is the fellow who can't win with a strong club but goes great with a loser. How do you figure him out?"[16]

There were several pitchers that fit this description, noted F. C. Lane, who offered Ehmke's 13-8 record for the last-place Red Sox as the best example. "Ehmke served for some years with the Detroit Tigers," he wrote. "True, the fielding of the club left something to be desired. But they were known through all the circuits as the greatest bunch of hitters and run scorers baseball has seen for a generation."[17]

When asked about his success in Boston, Ehmke told Lane, "I don't care particularly to discuss affairs at Detroit. It is no secret that things there were not pleasant for me." Ehmke emphasized his wish that fans not believe he had failed to give his best in Detroit: "Most of the time while I was with that club, Dauss and myself carried the main pitching burden. We were sent against the strong clubs. Naturally, we had the hardest opposition to overcome."[18]

But "Cobb did not have confidence in Ehmke's ability to win ball games," according to Lane, a stance that naturally upset Ehmke. "Cobb is hot-headed, exacting, a terrific driver. Ehmke is quiet, studious, a gentleman in every sense of the word." Lane concluded that although Cobb had seemingly made a terrible trade, it is likely that Ehmke would never have become the pitcher he now was while Cobb was his manager.[19]

Owner Harry Frazee had traded away most of his talented players, many of whom had helped the Red Sox win the World Series in 1918. The deals usually included a significant amount of cash coming his way, with the talent usually going to the Yankees. Ed Cunningham wrote,

"Boston was the capital of baseball. . . . Then Harry Frazee started to make capital out of baseball by moving the capital over to New York."[20]

Red Sox fans desperately wanted Frazee out as the club's owner. The problem was finding a buyer. Nick Flatley lamented, "With nothing left to sell . . . it's doubtful if anybody can be discovered sufficiently philanthropic to kick in with more than half the price that will be asked."[21] But in the summer of 1923 a wealthy prospective buyer surfaced: Palmer Winslow, an Indianapolis glass manufacturer.

Baseball executives, led by American League president Ban Johnson, were thrilled by the impending change in ownership. "As a sportsman he was a total failure," said Johnson of Frazee, "and as a trouble maker he was a huge success."[22] The sale was completed on August 1, and Frazee received slightly more than one million dollars, a very large sum for a struggling, losing franchise.[23] "Frazee sent over [to the Yankees] everything except the stands," wrote Cunningham. "Frazee received a fortune for these players. He stripped the Sox of every valuable asset with the single exception of Howard Ehmke."[24]

Bob Quinn, the respected business manager of the St. Louis Browns, led the Winslow group and would be the club's president.[25] He had built the Browns team that had come within a game of the 1922 American League pennant. Quinn put his life savings into the Red Sox purchase. "My heart and soul are in this ball club," he told Boston fans. "Ever since I was a kid I have been in baseball. All that I have now is due to baseball. . . . I want to give Boston a winner."[26] Knowing a seasoned executive like Bob Quinn would run the club made the Winslow purchase look even more attractive to Johnson and the league's owners.

Quinn's group took over after the June 15 Major League trade deadline, so his focus was on acquiring Minor League talent. He went on a $250,000 shopping spree. He bought slugging outfielder Ike Boone from San Antonio of the Texas League, where Boone batted .402 with 241 hits. Quinn's most expensive acquisition was highly touted shortstop Dud Lee from Tulsa of the Western League, for starting shortstop Johnny Mitchell and $50,000.[27] Former Sox manager Hugh Duffy whetted the fans' appetite when he said, "Boston fans are going to go crazy over the boy [Lee]."[28]

The Philadelphia club continued to be an easy target for Ehmke, who defeated the A's, 8–1, on August 30. It was his fifth win against them without a loss and his sixteenth win for the season.[29] The game was not without controversy. Perhaps because Connie Mack had seen Ehmke defeat his Athletics so many times over the years, he decided to try a new tactic. Aware of Ehmke's reputation of being easily ruffled, Mack and catcher Cy Perkins accused him of roughing up the ball. Umpire Tom Connolly decided the roughness had come from a foul ball hit by A's batter Heinie Scheer, and Ehmke did not let it affect his pitching.

Similarly Ehmke was unaffected by *Sporting News* columnist John Sheridan's view of his pitching arsenal. Sheridan claimed that overhand pitchers usually had better control than underhand or sidearm pitchers. He used Ehmke as an example: "I saw Howard Ehmke work a game, underhand, sidearm, the other day. He had stuff galore, hard to hit. Hits made off him were lucky hits, but hang it all, Ehmke had no control. Against a team of free swingers, batters who would hit at anything, he was effective, but when a few hitters waited him out, he was not so effective. Free swinging at balls off the plate make it easy for Ehmke. The team that makes Ehmke pitch will beat him."[30]

The *Boston Herald*'s Bob Dunbar disagreed with Sheridan's assessment. "The secret of Ehmke's effectiveness," he wrote, "is not in any illegal thing he does to the ball to make it break suddenly or sail erratically, but rather lies in his unusual delivery. His style is a combination of Grover Cleveland Alexander's side-arm stuff and Carl Mays's underhanded concoction."[31]

But no matter from what angle he threw the ball, Howard Ehmke was still the best pitcher on a 1923 Red Sox team that was, in short, dreadful. Nevertheless, the Tigers did well without him. Though Del Pratt and Rip Collins, the men for whom he was traded, did not contribute much, the Tigers finished second, a distant 16 games behind the Yankees.[32]

24

"The Toughest Break a Pitcher Ever Had"

In September 1923, as Boston's miserable season wound down, Howard Ehmke took part in three of the most memorable games of his career. The first was Friday, September 7, at Shibe Park in Philadelphia.[1] Ehmke held the Athletics hitless through six innings, but in the seventh, pitcher Slim Harriss ripped a drive into the gap in left-center field that hit the scoreboard on one bounce. By the time the ball was returned to the infield, Harriss was at second with what appeared to be a two-base hit. However, the Red Sox appealed to first base umpire Red Ormsby, claiming that Harriss had not stepped on first base. Ormsby had seen him miss the bag as well and ruled Harris out, maintaining Ehmke's no-hitter.

An inning later A's right fielder Frank Welch hit a knee-high liner to left that Mike Menosky failed to catch. "He fumbled the drive, and it was at first ruled by the official scorer as a hit," reported the *Boston Globe*, quoting a special dispatch from Philadelphia. "Later," the dispatch continued, "a consultation of players and the scorer took place, and Menosky was given an error."[2] Saved for a second time, Ehmke went on to complete the 4–0 no-hitter.[3] He celebrated by treating all his teammates to taxi rides back to the hotel and later footed the bill for a sumptuous dinner.[4]

"Technically or otherwise, I'm glad I got credit for a no-hit game," Ehmke said. "It's every pitcher's ambition. I needed a few breaks." He recalled that he would have had a no-hitter except for a bad break in the second inning of a June 29, 1919, game while pitching for Detroit against Cleveland at Navin Field. "With two out, Larry Gardner hit a high grounder over my head. It was a play for Pep Young at second. Shortstop [Donie] Bush tried for the ball and missed it, the scorer recording the play as a hit. That was even closer than yesterday's performance; so I certainly do deserve a break."[5]

Four days after his no-hitter Ehmke faced the Yankees in New York. His mound opponent was rookie George Pipgras, making his first Major League start.[6] Pipgras matched Ehmke with six scoreless innings before Boston scored three runs in the seventh to win, 3–0. Ehmke contributed to the scoring by singling home the first run and later scoring on Val Picinich's inside-the-park home run. This game is still remembered not for what Ehmke did on offense but for what he accomplished as a pitcher.

Yankees center fielder Whitey Witt led off the bottom of the first inning with a "ground ball that Red Sox third baseman Howard Shanks knocked down with his glove hand, picked it up and threw to first baseman Joe Harris, but not in time to get the speedy Witt," wrote Fred Lieb in the *New York Evening Telegram*.[7] Lieb, in his role as the official scorer, ruled the play a hit for Witt. The only other Yankee to reach base that afternoon was catcher Wally Schang, who drew a second-inning walk. When Ehmke was asked after the game to what he attributed his season-long success, he could not resist taking an indirect dig at Cobb. "I am winning," he said, "because Frank Chance lets me pitch the way I want to. He never bothers me."[8]

The Yankee Stadium crowd was a big one for a Tuesday because it was a Jewish holiday (Rosh Hashanah). As the game wore on, the fans began calling for Lieb to reverse his call on Witt's first-inning grounder. Several of his fellow reporters in the press box also suggested the change to Lieb, who was also the *Evening Telegram*'s beat writer for the Yankees. Replacing Witt's hit with an error charged to Shanks would allow Ehmke to become the first Major League pitcher to throw consecutive no-hitters.[9]

But Lieb was firm in responding to the writers who were urging him to change his ruling: "No, it's a one-hit game in my book, and it's going to stay that way."[10] While Lieb's refusal to change the call caused Ehmke to miss throwing back-to-back no-hitters, Ehmke set and still holds the American League record for the fewest hits allowed in consecutive complete games: one. "One hit in eighteen consecutive innings is not merely miraculous pitching; it constitutes the greatest exhibition of box-work in the history of baseball," wrote the correspondent from the *New York Times*. "Trot out your Mathewsons and Waddells and Miner Browns and Walshes and Youngs and all the other heroes of the 'good old days,' and you still won't match the exhibition that the lean and lanky Ehmke completed at the Yankees Stadium yesterday."[11]

Howard Ehmke is largely unknown to modern fans. Some may remember he once held the record for most strikeouts in a World Series game. Trivia buffs know he is the answer to the question, "Who yielded the first home run at Yankee Stadium?" However, had Fred Lieb scored Whitey Witt's first-inning ground ball differently, Ehmke's name would likely still come up whenever a pitcher made his next start following a no-hitter.

Lieb's awarding of a hit to Witt was widely criticized. "Howard Ehmke, the Red Sox sensational side-arm pitcher, would have had a world's record, but for the hasty judgment of the New York official scorer," wrote Boston reporter Gus Rooney. "Perhaps if the New York scorer could make a second guess on the play that took two consecutive no-hit, no-run games away from Ehmke, he would give him the benefit of the doubt."[12]

Tom Connolly, a twenty-five-year veteran who umpired at first base that day, said: "If ever a pitcher worked a no-hit game, Ehmke did against New York. If ever an infielder made an error, Shanks did on Witt's grounder. It was a great pitching exhibition that will fail to get its proper place in the Hall of Fame because the scorer erred."[13] Connolly had worked Ehmke's no-hitter against Philadelphia and had gotten him to autograph a ball from the game. He did so again after this game, saying, "If you didn't pitch a no-hit game today, I shall never live long enough to see one."[14] Bill Dinneen, the former pitcher who umpired at third, agreed: "I have made lots of bad decisions but never one that compared with scoring Witt's grounder to Shanks a base hit. It was a bad error on an easy chance."[15] According to Lieb, some friends of Ehmke petitioned Ban Johnson to change the verdict, but the American League president upheld the official scorer.

That fall F. C. Lane wrote about the game, titling his article "The Toughest Break a Pitcher Ever Had." He wrote that Grover Alexander had once said the toughest break a pitcher can have is to lose a no-hitter with two outs in the ninth inning and two strikes on the batter. But Lane thought losing a no-hitter the way Ehmke did was even worse.

The toughest break, he wrote, "is to have the first batter who faced him hit a little bouncing grounder which the third baseman messes up and plays ping pong with and finally throws too late to catch the runner" be scored a hit. "Had that first ball . . . been the last play of the game," Lane wrote, "the odds are a million dollars to a German mark that it would have been called an error." Lane revealed that he had gone to the game with Ehmke that day and wished him luck, adding that "the pitcher who got this send-off generally won." Ehmke laughed and said he hoped it would be true in his case and that he ought to pitch a no-hit game.[16]

Fred Lieb was thirty-five years old when he covered Ehmke's near no-hitter. He would go on to a fabled career as a baseball writer and author, but his decision that afternoon haunted him for the rest of his life. "Through the years, Ehmke has been unhappy over this decision, and I have been unhappy that it was my lot to make it," Lieb wrote in 1957.[17] "Several years later [in 1925], when Shanks came to the Yankees, he said to me, 'Fred, I think it should have been called an error,' and ever since I've had the play on my conscience."[18]

In his 1977 memoir, *Baseball As I Have Known It*, published when he was eighty-nine, Lieb wrote at length about this game. He called it "the saddest decision I ever made, for it prevented Ehmke from becoming the first pitcher ever to throw two successive no-hitters."[19] Lieb went on to describe the play much the same way as he had for more than a half-century:

> So [Witt] hit a chopper down the third-base line to Howard Shanks, a former outfielder who was playing third. The ball took an odd hop, and Shanks muffled it against his chest. By the time he was ready to throw, he saw there was no chance to get Witt, and so he didn't throw.[20] Considering all these things—the ball took a strange hop, and Witt was the fastest man, I think, in the American League at that time in getting down to first base—I decided it was a hit, however scratchy. There was no murmuring over my "score" in the press box at the time.[21]

Around the sixth inning, Lieb recalled, some of the Boston writers were suggesting he change the decision. Lieb again said no. "I scored it a hit then, and it's a hit in the early edition of my paper, and it's a hit in my scorebook."[22] Lieb did admit, however that "it *was* a doubtful call on my part, and if it had happened later in the game I just might have scored it as an error for Shanks."[23]

The day before Ehmke's gem, the Yankees' Sam Jones had beaten Boston, 8–1, allowing only two hits. Among the onlookers who had seen two days of such dominant pitching was the former great Cubs trio of Joe Tinker, Johnny Evers, and Frank Chance. Chance watched from the dugout as the manager of the Red Sox, and Tinker and Evers were in New York to see Jack Dempsey defend his heavyweight title against Luis Firpo at the Polo Grounds on September 14. "I guess that young fellow pitched some game," said Chance of his ace. "I've never seen better pitching," added Tinker. "I've been here two days and seen Jones pitch a two-hit game and Ehmke a one-hit game. That's the best pitching I've seen in a long time." Johnny Evers asked, "What have they done with the rabbit ball?"[24]

Ehmke was not nearly as effective in his next start, an 11–6 win over Cleveland, but returned to top form in defeating Chicago, 2–1, on September 19. The one run he allowed was unearned, and he appeared headed for a hard-luck loss before Boston scored two in the last of the ninth to win. The victory was Howard's twentieth of the season, the first and only twenty-win season of his big league career.

The first two of Ehmke's memorable September 1923 games had ended in glory and near glory. The third, on September 28 against the Yankees at Fenway Park, resulted in the most lopsided defeat of his career. Led by Babe Ruth and Wally Schang, who each had five hits, and rookie Lou Gehrig, who had four (including three doubles), the Yankees pounded the Red Sox, 24–4.[25] Ehmke pitched six innings, allowing seventeen runs—sixteen earned—and twenty-one hits. The game accounted for just over 10 percent of the runs he allowed in 1923. In all, the Yankees had thirty hits, which set an American League record that lasted for sixty-nine years.[26]

New York scored four in the first, single runs in the third and fifth, and then eleven runs in the sixth, turning a 6–3 game into a 17–3 rout. Despite Ehmke's allowing all eleven runs, Chance kept him out there for the whole inning. Perhaps he was upset by club president

Bob Quinn's previous day's announcement that Chance would not return as manager in 1924. Yet leaving a pitcher in to "take his lumps" was not an unheard-of strategy for Chance. He had done it earlier in the season. On July 27 he failed to replace Lefty O'Doul, who gave up thirteen runs (all unearned) in the sixth inning at Cleveland. O'Doul, then, and Ehmke, in this game, each tied the modern Major League record for most batters faced in an inning (16).[27]

The blowout loss to the Yankees was Ehmke's final appearance of the season. With a record of 20-17, he became the third pitcher in the twentieth century to win twenty or more games for a last-place team.[28]

While Jack Quinn did not throw a no-hitter or a near no-hitter in 1923, he did have several impressive outings. When he tossed a three-hitter to beat the Senators, 3–1, on July 24, a Washington reporter wrote, "Jack Quinn gave father time another thump in the thorax."[29] Less than two weeks later he again pitched a complete game to edge the Tigers, 3–2. On September 14 Quinn went the distance in a twelve-inning win over the Indians. It was the fourth time he pitched more than nine innings for the Red Sox this season. This game caught the attention of fans nationwide because Boston first baseman George Burns, a former Indian, executed an unassisted triple play, the first ever by a first baseman.[30] On September 29 Quinn won his final start of the season, against his twice-former club, the Yankees. It raised his Red Sox record against them to 7-4.

Umpire-columnist Billy Evans featured the ageless Quinn in two syndicated columns that summer. While most ball players were "has-beens" over the age of forty, Quinn was a notable exception. There was never a spitballer who threw as Quinn did, Evans wrote: "He goes through exactly the same maneuvers in delivering the curve and fast ball as the spitter."[31] Evans also quoted Quinn's approach to the number of pitches he threw: "Don't waste a ball that isn't necessary. The fewer balls you pitch in each game, the more games you will pitch."[32]

Ellery Clark Jr., son of a famous Olympic rowing champion, befriended many ballplayers as he grew up in the 1920s. He wrote of Quinn, "One reason for his durability was his minimum pitching motion. He had no exaggerated windup—he just raised his hand to his lips to moisten the ball, and he was ready to let it go."[33]

In addition to Quinn's being a key member of Boston's rotation, Chance used him in both long and short relief during the season—often enough for him to be retroactively credited with seven saves in 1923, the second most in the American League.[34] He finished the season with the same number of wins and complete games he had in 1922, thirteen and sixteen respectively. While the pennant-winning Yankees won ninety-eight games, with eighty-two of those wins coming from former Red Sox pitchers, Boston won only sixty-one games. Ehmke and Quinn had more than half of the team's wins. They also had more than half the complete games and pitched more than 40 percent of the club's innings.[35]

The Sox descended into last place after a June 18 loss in St. Louis and stayed there for the remainder of the season, finishing 37 games behind the Yankees. They hit 34 home runs as a team, scored the fewest runs in both leagues, and their pitching staff allowed a league-highest 804 runs and had a league-worst 4.20 earned run average.

Almost forty years after Boston's horrendous season, Lefty O'Doul told historian Lawrence Ritter, "Well, in 1923 we ended dead last. Just proves if you haven't got the horses you haven't got a Chance."[36]

25

A New Beginning for Boston

Inevitably the result of new ownership's taking over a last-place team is change. Late in 1923 Red Sox president Bob Quinn decided to make a clean break with the past. His first step was to not renew the contract of manager Frank Chance. Herman Nickerson was one of the sportswriters who urged Quinn to stick with the current skipper, "to give Chance an opportunity to show what he can do with better material."[1]

But Quinn had other plans. A *Sporting News* editorial in October acknowledged the fan resentment over Chance's departure but noted that Quinn wanted to give Boston "a new deal, from top to bottom." He was "fearless in his moves," willing to defy "the Chance propaganda." The editorial concluded that Quinn's track record of success, in St. Louis and before that with Columbus of the International League, gave him the benefit of the doubt for the changes he was making.[2]

Quinn hired Lee Fohl, his manager with the St. Louis Browns for the past three seasons, to lead the Red Sox.[3] Fohl had played and managed for him in the Minor Leagues as early as 1907.[4] A taciturn man known for improving clubs in general and pitchers in particular, Fohl had turned around the Cleveland Indians in the late 1910s.[5] The sports editor of the *New York World* wrote in admiration of Fohl, "If he had a middle name, it would be 'Tenacity'—a never-say-die spirit that defies all obstacles and overcomes all setbacks. Truth crushed to earth rises again, and so does Lee Fohl."[6] Ed Cunningham described Fohl's style as very different than that of Frank Chance. He tells his men to "do the right thing," with an honor system away from the ballpark. "He treats all the players squarely, is not a driver, and they are willing to play their heads off for him."[7]

Fohl made it clear he would not "crowd" his pitchers with a short hook; he would win or lose with his starters.[8] He praised the veteran mound leadership of his club as early as January 1924: "Don't make any mistake, the Sox are going to have a good pitching staff. . . . Everyone

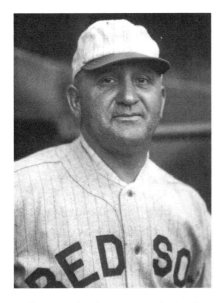

25. Lee Fohl, a former catcher, was hired as the Red Sox manager in 1924. The taciturn Fohl had a reputation as a developer of pitchers and a man with a sharp baseball mind. He was once called a "doctor of hopeless teams" for the work he had done with the Cleveland Indians in the late 1910s and the St. Louis Browns in the early 1920s. Both teams fell just short of the pennant (in 1918 and 1922 respectively). Fohl's Red Sox stunned the baseball world the first two months of the 1924 season before reality set in. *Dennis Goldstein Collection.*

will concede that Howard Ehmke is quite a pitcher. They will make the same admission regarding the veteran John Quinn."[9]

The Browns' best pitcher during Quinn's and Fohl's time in St. Louis, and one of the best in baseball, was Urban Shocker.[10] The headstrong pitcher had clashed with Browns owner Phil Ball and was suspended for the last month of the 1923 season. So it was perhaps only a mild surprise when reports surfaced that the Browns were considering a trade of Shocker to Boston for Howard Ehmke after the season.

John B. Sheridan, for one, greeted the possibility with strong disapproval. "Shocker is a really very great pitcher," he wrote. "I read something about trading him for Howard Ehmke. Ehmke had more 'stuff' than any pitcher I saw work last year, but he is not so enduring as Shocker is, has been pitching about as long as the Browns' ace, depends more upon natural ability, less upon device than Shocker does. Just now I would not trade Shocker for two Ehmkes. When they are declining from their peak, Shocker will remain the more useful man for the longer time."[11]

The Shocker deal, if there ever really was one, never materialized, and Ehmke remained with Boston. He reported to training camp in San Antonio appearing underweight, but after three weeks he had pleased manager Fohl by working himself into excellent shape while setting an example for all the other pitchers with his hard work.

"I am looking forward to having one of the best seasons of my career," Ehmke said shortly after arriving. It was the type of statement most ballplayers make during spring training. Ehmke had done it before and would do it again, but almost always with an addendum regarding his health. "Of course, I have not fully regained my strength that my illness of about a month ago took away from me," he said. "I cannot see why I will not be more successful this season. In the first place I will have a far better club behind me. . . . Bob Quinn certainly did some fine trading during the winter. I did not think it would be possible to work such a change in the team in a single season."[12]

President Quinn decided to go with veterans as position players too. On January 7 he traded for two Cleveland Indians from the 1920 championship team, men Fohl had managed in Cleveland as early as 1915. Boston acquired catcher Steve O'Neill (age thirty) and second baseman Bill Wambsganss (almost thirty). The Red Sox also acquired outfielder Bobby Veach (almost thirty-five) from the Tigers in early May. Veach joined Shano Collins (thirty-eight) as the team's leading backup outfielders. Joe Harris (almost thirty-three), who also played for Fohl in Cleveland, moved from the outfield to first base.[13] If Quinn was rebuilding the Red Sox, he was certainly not doing it with young players.

Manager Fohl had a reputation for spotting flaws in pitchers' deliveries and helping correct them. "Ehmke and Bill Piercy pitch properly," he said one day at training camp. "They go on through with their pitches, get their body into every delivery, and are firm on their feet when they finish, and thus are ready for anything they have a chance to field."[14]

After his usual stop in Hot Springs, Jack Quinn reported to spring training looking "like a schoolboy," wrote Ed Cunningham. "The 21 pounds he lost in Hot Springs make him think he is getting younger."[15] Quinn made a point to his namesake president that he expected to start games and not be merely a reliever.[16] But many observers had their doubts, even Cunningham. Toward the end of spring training, he wrote, "Quinn will give them some help, but he is a kid no longer and cannot stand the gaff."[17]

According to his tax returns, Quinn's salary with the Red Sox had dropped from $5,312 in 1922 to $3,647 in 1924. Both were far below his 1921 earnings of $9,895 with the Yankees, a figure that included his World Series share of $3,510.[18] Nevertheless, Quinn returned his signed contract with no record of a protest. His acceptance of such a cut may have been in part a reflection of his quiet personality and in part his realization that at his age, a Major League roster spot was appreciated.

Quinn continued to stay in shape during the off-season: "It's just a question of common sense. Some fellows go to spring training with their arms stiff from disuse and then start throwing hard too soon. So they get sore arms. I keep my arm supple all winter."[19] Early in the 1924 season, Quinn explained, "I have never had a sore arm in my life. The spitball is no harder on the arm than the curve or fastball if thrown properly."[20] More than five years later, the then forty-one-year-old Red Faber, after starting thirty-one games and hurling 234 innings, explained, "It's because I'm a spitball pitcher that I am able to keep on going. The spitter is the easiest delivery there is upon the arm. If it were not so, how do you account for the success of Jack Quinn?"[21]

Optimism, often misguided, traditionally runs high for fans of second-division teams. The press tends to feed that optimism with training camp stories of how this year's team is so much better than last year's. Of course when last year's team finished at the bottom of the league, there was a sense of "we have nowhere to go but up." This sentiment helps explain the sub-headline of Burt Whitman's *Sporting News* column just before the season opener: "Lee Fohl's Team, with Ehmke Standing Out on Pitching Staff, Has Possibilities Which Will Bear Watching."[22] With Harry Frazee gone and Bob Quinn and Lee Fohl running things, better days were ahead, Whitman wrote.

The Sox opened the season at home against the Yankees. The teams had met in eight previous openers, but this was the first played at Boston. Home attendance in 1923 had slipped to 229,688, the lowest in the team's history, but a huge and enthusiastic crowd of twenty-two thousand was at Fenway Park for the opener. Over the past several years the few fans who came to Fenway Park took great delight in belittling the home team. But at least for this one day the fans put their bitterness aside and offered the Red Sox players cheers and words of encouragement.[23]

Chosen by Fohl to pitch the opener, Ehmke responded magnificently. He took a 1–0 lead into the ninth inning—a run he himself had driven in—but the Yankees, with the help of two errors by new second baseman Wambsganss, scored two runs for a 2–1 victory. Shortstop

Dud Lee, the other half of Boston's new double-play combination, saved more runs with a diving catch of pitcher Waite Hoyt's line drive. Hugh Duffy had called him "another Rabbit Maranville," and at least on this day Lee's glovework seemed deserving of the comparison with the former Boston Braves star.[24]

When Philadelphia came to town for a Patriots Day doubleheader on April 19, the fans turned out en masse. It was to be a morning-afternoon affair, but the field was too wet to play the morning portion. It dried by the afternoon, and many fans who had watched the Boston Marathon headed to Fenway Park. The attendance was more than twenty-six thousand on a chilly, windy day. James O'Leary described the crowd at the bleacher entrances in right field as "so dense that when it surged up against one of the exit gates, the gate could not stand the pressure and gave way." Several people were trampled, although no one was seriously hurt.[25]

Backed by a ten-run second inning, Ehmke shut out the A's, 12–0, limiting them to five hits. The next time he faced the A's was May 2, in Philadelphia, and the result was much the same: a three-hit, 11–0 shutout. On May 8 he threw only a half-dozen fastballs in defeating Washington, 4–2, outpitching Walter Johnson, who had won four of his first five decisions.

"Howard keeps coming up with that underhanded curve ball, and the foe never gets a solid hold of it. They hit it into the dirt or pop up," wrote Whitman.[26] "Ehmke has the greatest assortment of stuff [of] any pitcher I ever caught," Steve O'Neill noted after catching him early in the season. "Plus, a baffling delivery makes him the toughest bird in the game to solve. I never heard an American League player say that he liked to hit against Ehmke."[27]

The day after Ehmke's opening day loss, Quinn beat the Yankees, 9–6. For eight innings he held the world champions to one run on only three hits. Will Wedge wrote, "Look what the Fenway fountain of youth has done for Pitcher Quinn. . . . Quinn gets better the longer he stays in baseball."[28] Just ten days later, this time in Yankee Stadium, Quinn went the distance in an eleven-inning loss to New York, thanks to a squeeze play executed by Yankees center fielder Whitey Witt.

An inning earlier Quinn had given up a dramatic inside-the-park home run to Wally Pipp (with Bob Meusel aboard) that erased a two-run Boston lead.[29] The usually staid *New York Times* gave a vivid account of the game and described why baseball held such a sway over the nation: "Search the records far and wide, and you won't find many better games. . . . It was packed with all the thrills of a lifetime. The crowd ran the gamut from despair to hope and then started all over again."[30]

In his first three seasons with Boston (1922–24), Quinn gave up an average of just over two runs per nine innings against his former team. "A player always likes to beat a team that turns him loose," he told umpire-columnist Billy Evans that spring, in explaining his success against the Yankees.[31]

When Quinn shut out the White Sox on May 14, James Crusinberry wrote, "Everything seems to have changed in Boston. An old man whose home is in south Chicago made them [the White Sox] look bad today."[32] The "Everything" in the quote referred to the Red Sox's winning record of 11-9. Paul Shannon wrote, "No longer is Boston the St. Helena of the Major Leagues. A player, sold or traded to Boston, now need not feel that all hope should be abandoned. . . . The dark cloud has been lifted from this burg, and baseball hopes again burn brightly."[33]

On May 28 the Red Sox, tied with the Yankees for first place, played a doubleheader against the Athletics at Shibe Park. The A's season had not started the way manager Connie Mack expected. After seven seasons of last-place finishes, the team moved up to seventh place in 1922 and sixth in 1923. Nineteen twenty-four was supposed to have continued that progression. But after splitting their first twelve games, the A's went into a tailspin and fell to last place with a record of 11-19.

Ehmke, who had an eight-game winning streak against the A's, including three shutouts and a no-hitter, started the opener. His two shutouts against Philadelphia this season had stretched his scoreless-innings streak against them to thirty-five. They also generated headlines and praise in Philadelphia. "Howard Ehmke Twirls Splendidly and Mows Down Philadelphians," was the April 20 *Philadelphia Inquirer* headline after his 12–0 win. Two weeks later the paper described a "Boston Massacre" in which Ehmke was "curving, speeding and mixing them" in his 11–0 victory.[34]

Ehmke increased the scoreless-innings streak to forty-three by shutting out Philadelphia through eight innings while allowing only one hit. He protected his 1–0 lead by retiring the first two batters in the ninth but walked Harry Riconda. That brought up right-fielder Frank

Welch, whose single had been the only hit off Ehmke. The count went to 3-1 before Welch hit his first home run of the season, a game-winner that thrilled the crowd of ten thousand.[35] Ehmke did not even turn to watch the flight of the ball. Instead, in a rare display of emotion, he threw his glove in disgust all the way to the dugout.[36]

"Ibsen could not have provided a more pulse-racing, breathtaking climax," wrote one Philadelphia reporter, evidently confident his readers were familiar with the famous Norwegian playwright.[37] Sportswriter Stoney McLinn returned to a recurring theme of why Ehmke, with all his physical talent, had not been an even more successful pitcher. McLinn hinted that Welch's home run was the result of a lack of concentration by Ehmke. "Doubtless, Ehmke, whose control was splendid and who is a heady apple-tosser, could prevent Welch from hitting a home run forty-nine out of fifty [times] under circumstances which prevailed yesterday," he wrote. "Nevertheless, Ehmke pitched to Welch's strength when he chucked that home run ball in the ninth inning. The Red Sox ace didn't do it purposely. Neither was it altogether a mental or physical lapse. It just happened that Ehmke pitched that bad ball. He could not satisfactorily explain why or how he did it."[38]

Quinn started the second game. He had continued his mastery of the Athletics when he beat them on May 1 and shut down a rally two days later when he retired the three men he faced in the ninth to save the win for Bill Piercy. Ira Flagstead, Boston's center fielder, led off the second game with a home run off Roy Meeker. Unlike Ehmke, Quinn was able to protect the 1–0 lead and salvage a split for the Red Sox. This is still the only Major League doubleheader in which game-winning home runs were hit by the last batter of the first game and the first batter of the second game.

If Howard Ehmke was one of Ty Cobb's worst trades of a pitcher, his dealing away Flagstead was one of his poorest decisions with a position player. He sent the outfielder to the Red Sox for Ed Goebel shortly after the start of the 1923 season. Goebel not only never appeared in a game for the Tigers; he never returned to the Major Leagues. Meanwhile, Flagstead had six strong seasons for Boston, averaging thirty-two doubles with a .295 batting average. He became a fan favorite, "a Boston institution," said one local sportswriter when the club honored Flagstead in 1928. "Harry Hooper was never more popular than Flaggy in Boston, and that's saying a mouthful."[39]

Like Ehmke, Quinn drew on his experience and guile. "It was evident from the stands in the 1–0 game that Quinn was relying more on his head than his good right arm," wrote a Philadelphia reporter.[40] Both games were decided by the proverbial "one bad ball," wrote another Philadelphia sportswriter.[41] The Red Sox ended the day where they had started, tied with the Yankees for first place with a sparkling 20-12 record.

Quinn beat the A's twice in May and allowed them but one run in nineteen innings, including his May 28 gem.[42] The outstanding performances by Ehmke and Quinn that month may have planted a seed in Mack's mind that these two veterans might someday be valuable assets in making the A's contenders again.

26

Back to Reality for the Red Sox

For the first eight weeks of the 1924 season, the Red Sox stunned the baseball world. As late as June 9 they held sole possession of first place, with a record of 25-17. Four days later they were tied for first with a 28-19 mark.[1] Howard Ehmke was a stalwart on the mound, leading the league in complete games (11) and tied for the league lead in wins (8). He and Jack Quinn were one-two in innings pitched, and Quinn led in earned run average (1.96).

Quinn continued to cultivate an air of mystery about his age and origins. Early in the season Will Wedge wrote, "Quinn is not Polish, as so often has been heard. He is of Welsh descent. The name he goes by, Quinn, is his mother's name. . . . Picus is really his stepfather's name."[2] A week later, when the Red Sox were in New York, Quinn told a reporter for the *Evening Telegram*, "I am forty-three-years old, not thirty-nine. . . . I was born over across the pond, which is the Atlantic Ocean, in Wales." While he may not have been sure of his exact age, Quinn surely knew that Wales was not his homeland. Then his words became more truthful as he continued: "I am a lot of things which nobody knows, and a lot of things which they knows [*sic*] about me ain't so."[3] Perhaps he enjoyed leading reporters on; he certainly enhanced the enigma with his vagueness and stories. James Isaminger summed up the situation: "Quinn is a gifted story-teller."[4] Father John Whitney Evans, a close family friend of Quinn's grandnieces in Minnesota, said in 1994, "Jack Quinn seemed to be living what spies call a cover story."[5]

While Quinn often spoke about the importance of control to his success, he emphasized the need to couple that with a knowledge of the hitters he faced: "Don't feed these hitters what they like, but pitch to their weakness. Study the batters and get control and remember there's eight other fellows to help you out when the ball is hit. That's all there is to pitching." He added, "Always keep them guessing and give them something different. Use the noodle as much as the arm."[6]

Ehmke, who had also earned a reputation for using his head as much as his arm, was the recipient of high praise from several members of the New York Yankees. "If I were to make a selection today of the greatest pitcher in the American League, I wouldn't hesitate a moment," Yankees right-hander Sam Jones told sportswriter Ford Frick. "I have my candidate picked out. He is Howard Ehmke of the Boston Red Sox."[7] Several of Jones's teammates, listening nearby, agreed, saying Ehmke had every asset of pitching greatness, including his judgment and his pitching motion.

"Probably he [Ehmke] has the slimmest pitching arm of anyone in the Major Leagues," wrote F. C. Lane. "One day, while he was conversing with the late President Harding, the President took hold of his pitching arm and said: 'I don't see where all the power comes from.' Nevertheless, there is in that long, bony right arm of his, a snap like a steel spring."[8] Writing seven years after Ehmke threw his last big league pitch, Lane called him one of those pitchers "with a lot of stuff who employed pitching psychology whenever it would serve his purpose. Ehmke had an angular windup that suggested a professional contortionist. His thin arms and legs sprawled all over the landscape, or so it seemed to the harassed batter. Ehmke had a trick of delivering the ball so that it came at the batter against this background of undulating arms and legs. . . . One of his chief assets was his aptitude in diverting the batter's mind from the task in hand—namely keeping his eyes on the ball."[9]

One such asset was Ehmke's "hesitation pitch," on which he began working at training camp with the Tigers in 1920. He said, "I had a lot of fun with it when I tried it on Ty Cobb and some of the other heavy-hitting Tigers in batting practice. . . . On and off during the past three seasons I have been working on it, and now I believe I have it under control."[10] Ed Cunningham described the pitch as a pause during Ehmke's full windup that threw the batter off stride and then a quick delivery. "The slight hesitation acts like a change of pace on the batter," Cunningham wrote. "When he is expecting a fastball, he is likely to get fooled by swinging too quickly at a slow ball."[11]

After Ehmke defeated the Yankees on June 26, New York outfielder Bob Meusel complained to the umpires about Ehmke's hesitation pitch. He claimed it was a balk, but the two umpires who worked the game, George Moriarty and Bill Dinneen, reminded Meusel that a pitcher cannot balk with no men on base, and Ehmke did not throw the pitch with runners on. Ban Johnson had been alerted to other complaints a few weeks earlier, but his lack of comment had been taken to mean he saw nothing wrong with the pitch. "I think it is a smart move," one of the umpires said after the game, "and I am surprised that a pitcher did not think of such a motion before."[12]

As the summer began, injuries to Red Sox players began to accumulate.[13] Veterans Joe Harris and Shano Collins both batted above .400 the first few weeks of the season before tailing off badly. The overachieving Red Sox simply could not maintain their heady pace; their fall was swift. Quinn lost his third straight game on June 21, 5–3, to the Yankees, as Babe Ruth hit his seventeenth home run of the year off a Quinn slow ball. Quinn had given up thirty-four hits in his last 17⅓ innings. Boston was now only two wins above .500.

Unlike some of his teammates, Ike Boone, in his first full season as a regular, did not fade as the season progressed. He finished with a batting average of .337, an on-base percentage of .404, and a slugging percentage of .491. His hitting was one reason why Boston's team batting average rose from .262 to .277 in 1924, though it was once again the league's lowest. But Boone was a liability in the field. "Ike's legs are huge, great for football, but a handicap in baseball," wrote Burt Whitman. "He is still a long way from being a good outfielder."[14]

Any dreams the Red Sox had of competing for the pennant ended when they lost ten of eleven games during a period from June 27 to July 4. The one win was on June 30, when Ehmke again defeated Walter Johnson, this time, 2–1, in eleven innings. Johnson, at age thirty-six, was having one of his best seasons in 1924, while leading the Senators to their first pennant. He won a league-leading twenty-three games and lost only seven, with two of the seven defeats coming against Ehmke.

When the Tigers beat Quinn on July 19 to complete a five-game sweep, Boston fell to seventh place, with a 38-49 record. Quinn went the distance in that 4–3 loss, but his error in the ninth inning led to two unearned runs as Detroit rallied for the win. When the club won only the second of its past eleven games four days later, Quinn got the win in an ugly 16–12 victory.[15] Both he and Ehmke would see their earned run averages for the year rise significantly following the club's surprising start.[16]

It was now becoming evident that Bob Quinn's spending spree on young prospects and trades for older players was not working out. Paul Shannon bemoaned the team's return to a familiar pattern of play: "Our Red Sox are surely going from bad to worse. Double defeats are becoming quite frequent up at Fenway Park these days."[17] Ed Cunningham was more critical: "Yes, Quinn thought he had a ball club. . . . The athletes have been going through the motions like a gang of laborers, who feel like working only when the foreman is looking. . . . There are no signs of fight on the club. . . . There is none of that fire and dash in evidence that a spirited ball club should have."[18]

Bob Quinn had talked about remodeling Fenway Park, including the building of a double-decked grandstand. But his focus would now be on building a new team. "He thought he had one, but he was mistaken," wrote Cunningham.[19]

There were few bright spots for Jack Quinn as the season wore on. One came on August 21, when his tenth-inning single against the Indians drove home the winning run in a 2–1 game that earned him his eleventh win. James O'Leary called his pitching "as fine as any he has ever done."[20] It was only Quinn's second start in more than a month, as Fohl had relegated him to the bullpen, where he made nine relief appearances.[21]

The win over Cleveland moved Quinn back into the starting rotation. On September 9 he lost a heartbreaker to the Yankees when two ninth-inning errors led to a two-run rally. New York's good-hitting pitcher Joe Bush followed the errors with a pinch-hit game-winning double. Quinn's final appearance of the season, on September 29, at home against the Senators, was also one of his best. He tossed seven innings in relief and gave up only one run. But Washington, with an early lead, prevailed, 4–2, and clinched its first American League pennant.

Alex Ferguson had bested Walter Johnson in the first of that four-game series, but the Senators defeated Ehmke the next day. As successful as Ehmke was for the 1924 Red Sox, he had the unusual experience of being booed by the hometown fans at Fenway Park. With three games to play, the Senators were battling the three-time defending champion Yankees for the title. "The demonstrations were not because of any unpopularity of the Red Sox, but simply because the game meant nothing to the home team, and the Boston fans are anxious to see the Yankees dethroned," wrote Frank Young of the *Washington Post*.[22] Walter Johnson biographer Henry Thomas wrote: "At one point they booed their own pitcher, Howard Ehmke, for striking out [Roger] Peckinpaugh in a clutch situation."[23] Ehmke suffered his league-leading seventeenth loss in the game but came back to beat Washington for his nineteenth win on the final day of the season, a day after the Senators had defeated Quinn to clinch the flag.

Quinn's 1924 statistics were remarkable for a man his age. He appeared in forty-four games, a number that was and would remain his American League high.[24] His earned run average improved by more than half a run from the previous season, and at 3.27 was almost a full run below the American League average, despite his less effective second half of the season. His seven saves were the third most in the league. And his control continued to be one of the league's best, with just over two walks per nine innings.

Grantland Rice saluted Quinn during the season in his syndicated column: "Any historian who mentions the Wonders of 1924 without chucking a collection of flowers at Jack Quinn is using a fountain pen full of soup. . . . It is always a pleasure to peg olive sprigs at a delegate who has never quite got all the widespread hip-hip that he deserves."[25]

Ehmke had been mostly a .500 pitcher with the Tigers, a strong offensive team, so his success with Boston came as a surprise to many. "Not for years has there been a more striking transformation," wrote F. C. Lane. "A pitcher commonly sinks or swims with his club. If it's a strong club, his record is good; if weak, his record suffers. But here was an amazing example that seemed contrary to all established rules. The pitcher who was merely good with a powerful club became great with a weak club." Lane asked Ehmke how he accounted for the transformation. "Last year I began all over again with a clean slate," Ehmke responded with an obvious reference to the problems he had pitching for Ty Cobb in Detroit. "I was [now] with a ball club that was weak, but always trying. I was with a manager [Lee Fohl] who was strict, but

26. Howard Ehmke, the "greatest pitcher in the American League," according to Yankees pitcher Sam Jones, who said Ehmke "had every asset of pitching greatness, including his judgment and his pitching motion." *Steve Steinberg Collection.*

fair. I was physically fit. Nothing bothered or worried me. For the first time in years I was in a position where I could do my very best work, and I did. That's all there is to the story."[26]

While he failed to reach the twenty-win mark, and his seventeen losses tied teammate Alex Ferguson and Cleveland's Joe Shaute for the most in the American League, Ehmke had his best-ever Major League season. He was the only pitcher in the American League to exceed 300 innings (315), a number that was not surprising according to the *Howe News Bureau*, the official statisticians of the American League: "Ehmke generally has been a bear for work, though somewhat frail in build and with a delivery that ball players describe as 'killing' on a pitcher."[27]

Ehmke finished second in strikeouts and had top-ten finishes in wins, earned run average, and shutouts. And for those who disdain "counting" statistics and judge performance with more analytical formulas, it should be noted that he finished seventh in walks and hits per innings pitched (WHIP) and led the league's pitchers in wins above replacement (WAR).

Jack Quinn's contract card, maintained by the *Sporting News*, notes that he was put on waivers in July 1924. The Red Sox did not release him at that time; perhaps they were seeing what interest "our ancient mariner," as Paul Shannon dubbed him, would generate.[28] Whatever the thinking behind the moves, the belief that he was finally at the end of a long career seemed widespread. Just before Christmas, manager Fohl announced he was asking waivers on Quinn as part of a move to restock the team with younger players. He explained, "I thought I could finish in the first division with a flock of stars whose brilliance was becoming dimmed. No such mistake will be made next year. We are going to build up a new team instead of patching one that is not worth patching."[29]

Jack Quinn showed up at the winter meetings in December 1924, searching for a team to sign him.[30] "For a sure-fire bet to finish games," wrote one Boston reporter during the meetings, "he will be invaluable."[31] Clark Griffith, owner of the world champion Washington Senators, claimed him.[32] But Boston had second thoughts and withdrew him from waivers in late December.[33]

The Red Sox showed limited improvement under their new leadership in 1924. They won six more games than in 1923 and moved up from eighth place to seventh. Because Bob Quinn persuaded the fans he was trying to make the team a winner again, they ended their boycott, and home attendance nearly doubled. While Howard Ehmke's future with the club seemed both promising and secure, that of Jack Quinn remained uncertain. Though he was pulled from waivers, even if he would make the team in 1925, he would be the oldest man on a young, rebuilding club.

27

A Team Going Nowhere

Boston's 1924 season started with an air of anticipation and hope based on the arrival of new owners and many new players. But after playing at a .600 clip the first two months of the season, the Red Sox played the rest of 1924 at a .364 pace, a worse rate than any in the final, desperate years of Harry Frazee's ownership. The 1925 season began under a pall of resignation and doubt. President Bob Quinn's trades and acquisitions had not panned out, and he now was abandoning his reliance on older players.

Early in the season Quinn dealt away two veteran starters from the 1924 club, outfielder Bobby Veach (almost thirty-seven) and first baseman Joe Harris (almost thirty-four).[1] Quinn explained: "We have started to clean house. Players who show they cannot deliver for us will be let go, and we will replace them with younger men. If they also fail, we will seek others. . . . We will continue to shake things up."[2] The club's president, wrote Ed Cunningham of the *Boston Traveler*, was conducting "one of the most complete turnovers of an entire squad in the history of baseball within such a short period of time."[3]

Jack Quinn approached the 1925 season cognizant his age was working against his remaining with Boston. Excitement at spring training in New Orleans revolved around a young pitcher half his age, Charles Ruffing. Known as "Ruff" before he became known as "Red," the nineteen-year-old right-hander made eight appearances for the 1924 Red Sox and spent part of the season in the low Minors.[4] In the words of Burt Whitman, he already had "one of the best natural fast balls you ever saw in a kid on his entrance into the big time."[5] The year of seasoning had brought him more confidence and control, wrote a reporter for the *Boston Globe*.[6] Would he take Quinn's spot in the rotation?

As one of the oldest players in the game, Quinn was gaining even more notoriety. On May 1 Ford Sawyer did a feature story on Quinn's

27. Jack Quinn's short stride and relaxed delivery put little strain on his arm. From 1922 to 1925, into his early forties, he averaged more than 266 innings pitched. His spitball was very deceptive; he barely touched the ball with his mouth. "His motion is so fleeting that it often seems little more than a bluff," wrote Damon Runyon. *Garland County Historical Society.*

long career.[7] The "choose-your-age-old" Quinn again reported to training camp in superb condition and told reporters, "The baseball experts have had me in the 'has been' class since 1912. . . . Tell the world that I am not at the chloroform age."[8]

Whitman noted that the longer Quinn remained in baseball, the more his value increased. As spitball pitchers were becoming fewer and fewer, their signature pitch was becoming unique.[9] Quinn threw a particularly dry spitter. Back in 1920 Damon Runyon wrote of Quinn's "wet one": "[He] barely touches it [the ball] with his mouth. His motion is so fleeting that it often seems like little more than a bluff."[10] Now in the mid-1920s little had changed. "Quinn simply moistens his fingers and heaves the ball with one and the same motion," wrote New York sportswriter Will Wedge. "It is a lovely operation to watch."[11] It was also impossible to detect. Retired Athletics second baseman Danny Murphy told a reporter in 1924 that Quinn used the same motion for all his pitches.[12]

Melville Webb of the *Boston Globe* noted that Quinn's teammate, Howard Ehmke, unlike what he had done in 1924, was not experimenting with different pitches but rather was concentrating on his underhand ball. After he pitched three innings against the Southern Association's New Orleans Pelicans in a spring training game, Webb reported the Red Sox ace "was not blazing away as he did early last Spring."[13]

As he often sounded at spring training, Ehmke was upbeat. "I expect to have the best season of my big-league career, and that is no April fool joke," he said in Mobile on April 1, while eating a breakfast of porridge and milk. Ehmke, a non-drinker of coffee, was a prodigious drinker of milk. "Yes, sir," he added, "I believe I will pitch better this season because I am strong. My stomach does not give me any trouble, and I can eat more. Naturally I have been able to put on weight (eight pounds, it was reported), and that is something new for me."[14]

Ehmke, who never missed an opportunity to denigrate Ty Cobb's leadership, continued: "It was Ty Cobb's orders that we would have an early breakfast and not have another meal until supper. . . . I could not stand working hard at the ballpark morning and afternoon and not having any luncheon. . . . And during midseason I was in poor condition due to stomach trouble." Ehmke explained that he differed from most players in preferring to eat his heaviest meal at noon. "For instance, on a day I am scheduled to pitch, I eat heartily at 11:30 o'clock, and I do not do any real work until I begin to warm up around 3 o'clock. By that time the food is digested, and I have all my strength. If I had only a light lunch at noon, I would be weak by game time."[15]

Ehmke's approach differed significantly from that of Quinn, who often attributed his fitness and longevity in part to his not eating at midday. In 1931 he said, "I haven't eaten at lunch time since I started playing ball."[16] Quinn added that he had not smoked for fifteen years.

Ehmke's wife, Marguerite, had begun coming to training camp with him in his later years with the Tigers and was there again this year. "We hire an apartment, and she cooks for me," he said. "I have found that home-cooking had been the most beneficial to me while going through spring training and especially so this spring. As a result, I am weighing 175 pounds, which is the heaviest I ever have been at this time of year."[17]

Ehmke and Quinn were also a study in contrasts when it came to weight. Quinn wanted to keep weight off his husky frame. In spring training the previous year, he proudly announced he had lost twenty-one pounds after three weeks of daily fourteen-mile hikes up the hills of Hot Springs.[18] Ed Cunningham said the weight loss made Quinn look younger—and feel as if he was getting younger.[19]

The physical frames of the two players were very different. Whereas the solidly built Quinn was 6 feet and 195 pounds, the gangly Ehmke, at 6 feet 3 inches, seemed all arms and legs and struggled to keep his weight from dropping below 175. The Old Sport described Quinn this way: "If you saw Jack get under a shower in the club house, you would know at once why he still was able to knock over hostile batsmen like tenpins. He is built like [wrestler Stanislaus] Zbyszko, and one glance impresses you with his herculean strength."[20]

Marguerite's cooking and the added weight did not prevent Ehmke from developing a case of influenza, the latest addition to his ever-growing list of illnesses and injuries. He came down with it in Louisville during the end of spring training, and it seemed to have affected his pitching shoulder, which had been sore since. A visit to Dr. Harry Knight in Rochester, New York, helped him avert a possible case of pneumonia, but he lost the weight he had gained and now had to build himself up again. (Knight, a physician who had a reputation for making "new ballplayers out of old," had become the doctor of choice for many players, especially those with injuries.)[21]

Ehmke arrived in Boston on April 15, a day after the Red Sox season opener in Philadelphia, still weak from the flu and with an ailing shoulder. Knight ordered him to stay out of uniform for a few more days. Ehmke figured he would need a week or so of practice and probably would not be ready to pitch in a game for another two weeks.

On April 17 Quinn got his first start of the season and won a five-inning, rain-shortened game against the Athletics. Lefty Grove was knocked out in the fourth inning after giving up four runs and walking five.[22] Connie Mack's Athletics had finally risen to fifth place in 1924, after finishing last in the American League for seven consecutive seasons, 1915–21. Now Mack had made a move for the top spot by purchasing two of the Minor Leagues' biggest stars, Grove and catcher Mickey Cochrane.[23]

Grove had already won 111 games in the Minors, including 96 in four full seasons (and 108 in all) with the Baltimore Orioles of the International League. He walked 625 men those four seasons and struck out the very same number. In Grove's 1975 obituary, Red Smith wrote, "He was a fierce competitor who made little effort to subdue a hair-trigger temper. His natural speed had dazzled and overpowered Minor League hitters, and he wasn't accustomed to adversity when he got to the American League. When things went bad, he raged blindly, blaming anybody who was handy."[24]

Early on, Lee Fohl said of the Philadelphia rookie, "When Groves [sic] works off some of his wildness, he will be a great pitcher, one of the greatest in the game."[25] In his first four appearances against Fohl's Red Sox, Grove walked seventeen men in 10⅓ innings. "In the beginning," said his catcher, Mickey Cochrane, "catching him was like catching bullets from a rifleman with bad aim."[26]

On April 25 Quinn went the distance for his second win, an eleven-inning affair against the Athletics. Perhaps surprised at Quinn's endurance, his effectiveness, or both, Burt Whitman called it "a remarkably fine game" by the spitballer.[27] It was also only the second win of the year for the Red Sox, whose record now stood at 2-8. When Quinn beat the Yankees on May 1 for his third straight win to raise his team's record to 3-10, Whitman wondered, "Is Quinn the ball club?"[28]

That was the day Ford Sawyer's article "Sheer Grit and Confidence Guided Jack Quinn to Fame" appeared in the *Globe*. Sawyer began, "He was only a boy of 14 years, a runaway from home, tired and dusty and hot, and O, so hungry! And perhaps he was a little homesick, if the truth were told. He had slipped from a freight train, covered with soot and grime and dust; his clothes tattered and torn, his throat dry and parched, and his stomach fairly crying out for something to eat."[29] It was in Dunbar, in western Pennsylvania, that Quinn got the break that started his baseball career. Whether this story, a version of which appeared in newspapers over the years, was mostly accurate is not known. But the embellishments contributed to what can be called the Jack Quinn legend, often told with a Huck Finn flavor.

Having missed Boston's first sixteen games, Howard Ehmke made his first appearance, in relief, at Washington on May 3. It was the first day of an arduous twenty-seven-game road trip, one that would take the Red Sox to each of the league's other seven cities. Three days later Ehmke made his first start, lasting just a third of an inning. He gave up two hits but walked five and was charged with six of the Senators' seven runs. Quinn relieved him and was almost as ineffective, giving up seven hits and four runs in 1⅔ innings. Trailing 10–1 after three, the Sox fought back but fell short, losing 10–8.

A disappointed Bob Quinn was in Cleveland, where he saw the Red Sox lose four straight games (May 12–15), dropping Boston's record to 7–18. Ehmke, this time in relief of Quinn, lost the last game, 10–7, allowing four runs in three innings. Those two ineffective outings by Quinn (he gave up six runs in each game) ballooned his earned run average to 3.89 at the end of the month, quite an increase from the 1.46 mark he had at the end of May the previous year.

"The reason for our poor showing so far this season is lack of pitching. The biggest blow is the loss of Ehmke," said the club president. Quinn's next statement, regarding Ehmke's fragility, had been heard before and would be heard again and again, even though he had pitched 631⅔ innings the past two seasons. "Unlike the average athlete, he is unable to recover from illness quickly," Quinn continued. He and Fohl had expected Ehmke to be the bulwark of Boston's shaky pitching staff. But "He was taken ill about a week before the season opened, and he has been recuperating five weeks. He still is weak and unable to work." In acknowledging Ehmke's physical limitations, Quinn did not raise the charge, made so often in Detroit, that Ehmke lacked competitive zeal. "I am satisfied that he is anxious to get in there but that he is physically unfit. When he is right, we will make a better showing."[30] Ehmke agreed. "Truthfully, I haven't got my strength back yet, and it would be foolish for me and unfair to the club to try to pitch in a weakened condition."[31]

During the Cleveland series, rumors went around that Ehmke was hoping to be traded or sold to the Yankees. "I have heard that report several times since coming to Cleveland," Ehmke said, "but there is absolutely nothing to it. I have been fairly treated in Boston, not only by the club officials but by the Sox."[32] He sought out Bob Quinn in Cleveland to tell him personally that the rumors were untrue, a gesture Quinn said he appreciated.

When Boston played in Chicago on May 23, the White Sox designated it as "Jack Quinn Day." Hundreds of his hometown friends and family turned out, presented him with a gold watch, and saw him win his fifth game of the year, 9–2. He then took delight by beating the Yankees in New York twice at the end of the month, first with a complete game 3–1 decision and then with seven innings of sparkling relief work. "With a merry twinkle in his eye, he [Quinn] will probably relate how the Yankees tossed him on the scrap heap," wrote James Harrison in the *New York Times*, "only to learn as late as yesterday that the old gentleman was still good steel."[33]

The Yankees were also struggling this season, unlike any since Jacob Ruppert purchased the team in 1915. Harrison wrote, "It is getting so now even the Red Sox can pick on the Yankees and get away with it."[34] When Quinn beat them with the sterling relief work on May 31, their record fell to 15-25. They had "folded up like an opera hat" in the twelfth inning of that game, Harrison wrote.[35] Babe Ruth was recovering from "the bellyache heard 'round the world" and would not appear in his first 1925 game until the following day.

Ehmke got his first win of the season on May 26 in the first game of a doubleheader at New York. He defeated the Yankees and Herb Pennock, 3–2. The win was the third straight for Boston—the only three-game winning streak the Red Sox would have in 1925. The streak ended when the Yanks won the second game.[36]

"Howard Ehmke is himself again," wrote Ed Cunningham. "He showed that yesterday in the overture at Yankee Stadium. Now perhaps the Red Sox can look forward to a happier career. Without Ehmke they have stumbled along, the burden of the pitching staff falling on the ancient whip of Jack Quinn and the youthful shoulders of Ted Wingfield."[37]

At the end of May Ehmke's season had barely started, and his record was 1-3. Quinn's was 7-1, and the Red Sox were 7-26 in their other games. One Boston reporter wrote that Quinn "was making a valiant effort to prove that the boys who set age limits in baseball are entirely wrong."[38] A *Sporting News* writer noted that while the Red Sox were going with a youth movement, "it would be painful to contemplate the plight of the Red Sox if [Quinn] were not around with his venerable right arm."[39]

28

From the Cellar in Boston to a
Pennant Race in Philadelphia

Jack Quinn was totally ineffective when he started against the Athletics on June 4, 1925. He retired only one man on this hot afternoon and
departed after giving up three hits and walking two as Slim Harriss
and the A's won, 12–2. Was it the heat? Lee Fohl had been trying to get
"the silly idea of hot-weather futility" out of Quinn's head, but Burt
Whitman wrote he "was beaten before he started."[1]

Philadelphia now had a heady record of 30-13 and maintained a
3-game lead over the Senators. Harriss was a big part of the team's
improvement. In his first five seasons with the A's, the 6-foot-6-inch
pitcher had a 45-76 record, including a league-leading twenty losses in
1922. Nineteen twenty-five was proving different. His win over Quinn
was his fifth of the young season, and he was on the way to a 19-12
record and his first season with an earned run average below 4.00 (3.49).
"Slim Harriss has now proved that he is one of the most dependable
hurlers in the country," wrote the Philadelphia writer whose pseudonym was The Old Sport. "A man with his stuff should go along and
twirl ten years like a house afire."[2]

There were other reasons why Connie Mack had his Athletics
winning consistently for the first time since 1914. One was rookie
catcher Mickey Cochrane. Ten days into the season, Ed Cunningham had already seen Cochrane in eight games and wrote, "Much
of the fight and spirit of these new Athletics is traced to the live
wire behind the bat. He is an effervescent young man. He keeps the
players on their toes at all times. The Athletics of recent years were
docile. . . . The modern Athletics are alert and aggressive, and they
reflect in every way the characteristics of the young man who has
stepped into major league life."[3] After the 12–2 romp over Boston,
Cochrane was batting .353.

28. Catcher Mickey Cochrane (*center*) joined outfielders Bill Lamar (*left*) and Al Simmons in Philadelphia in 1925. That season they hit .331, .356, and .387 respectively for a team that batted .308. While the A's faded from the pennant race in late summer, Cochrane and Simmons would anchor the championship teams of 1929, 1930, and 1931. Sportswriter James Isaminger called Cochrane "the motor who keeps the entire team on its toes" and Simmons "the knight errant of baseball." *Dennis Goldstein Collection.*

Mack had made another key addition with Al Simmons, a second-year outfielder. Simmons was leading the league with a .413 batting average after that June 4 game. Like Quinn, he was of East European descent.[4] "Bucketfoot Al" was known for his unorthodox batting stance in which his left foot pointed to third base. Mack did not try to change his stance. "You can hold the bat in your teeth provided you hit safely and often," he told the youngster.[5] When Simmons died in 1956, Arthur Daley wrote, "Unquestionably, Simmons was the worst looking of all the top hitters."[6] James Isaminger asked Mack in early June if he would trade Simmons for Babe Ruth. The manager answered emphatically and surprisingly, "Not in a thousand years."[7] Simmons measured his sophomore season improvement by his ability to hit safely against

Howard Ehmke, a pitcher who had handcuffed him in 1924, when Simmons batted .308.[8]

After Ehmke beat the A's on June 3, Isaminger reflected on his continued success against them. "Howard Ehmke's mission on earth transparently is to add gray hair to Connie Mack's Cicero-like head. Both in Detroit and Boston uniform, he has constantly been a railroad tie in the Athletics' path for many years."[9] Isaminger praised Ehmke's ability to use guile and intelligence to make up for a lack of overpowering natural stuff: "The lean, ascetic-looking conjurer of the peak pitched with his usual intelligence and poise. His speed didn't raise steam from the ball, and his curve didn't cause sparks to fly. But he had the Athletics hitters outguessed and hitting where the ball wasn't to use baseball code."[10]

Ehmke's 3–1 victory over Cleveland on June 8 evened his record at 3-3. Yet he remained upset at the rumors that he had delayed his return to health in the hope the Red Sox would trade him to the Yankees or some other team. "I cannot understand how that kind of talk got around," he told Ed Cunningham. "After being out longer than I expected, when I did get in there, I was bothered with a sore arm. That and my condition accounted for my wildness and lack of effectiveness. But the things said about me desiring a change are untrue." He said he was content in Boston and wanted to remain.[11]

On June 23 Quinn took a shutout against Philadelphia into the ninth inning before the A's rallied for three runs and gained their forty-first win against only nineteen losses. It was Quinn's fifth straight loss, as his record fell to 7-6. He was beaten by three unearned runs in that final inning. For most of the afternoon he showed Connie Mack he could still pitch effectively. One Philadelphia reporter wrote, "Old J. Picus was just moistening his shoots and bending 'em over, and our home talent was swinging like a gate and often just as wildly."[12]

The A's got a rare win against Ehmke the next day, when he lost, 5–4, to Sam Gray. Though his "hesitation ball" was not particularly effective in this game—Ehmke allowed fifteen hits—the pitch had become the talk of the league.[13] "Well it's a hard delivery to explain," Ehmke replied when questioned about the pitch. "When I first started throwing the ball that way, I called it the 'hesitation.' And that's the very best way to describe it—you hesitate when you pitch the ball. You see the batter starts swinging his bat, the moment you start swinging your arm for the pitch. He's up there to hit as hard as possible, and with this rabbit ball, somebody is likely to get killed if he connects. A mere change of pace doesn't help much, so I invented the 'hesitation.'"[14]

Umpire George Moriarty praised Ehmke for using brains to overcome brawn in dealing with all the free swingers in the league. "The combination of sidearm fast ones and curves, his famous fork ball, and now the 'hesitation' keeps them all worried," said Moriarty. "To my mind the 'hesitation' is the best pitching delivery I've seen in years, and I can't make that too strong."[15]

Ehmke said he did not throw the pitch often. "Otherwise the batters would get wise to it. As it is now, it keeps 'em guessing."[16] He said he discovered the pitch by accident, when he was with Detroit. While he was pitching batting practice, his arm accidentally stopped in midmotion. "Say Howard, that's a great ball you've got," veteran catcher Oscar Stanage yelled out to him. "If you can control it that thing'll be a wonder." Ehmke started perfecting the pitch during batting practice, but manager Ty Cobb refused to allow him to use it in a game. He also had trouble controlling the pitch. "Now it's different. I have the delivery under perfect control and have got so I can throw a curve ball with it. I think that is the most difficult stunt in pitching today."[17]

Ehmke also took advantage of his ability to use three kinds of deliveries—underhand, sidearm, and overhand. He thought the most effective against righties was the sidearm; against lefties, the underhand; and he would use the overhand against both, trying to keep them off stride with the change of delivery.[18]

"Bad Blood as Sox and Tigers Mix" read the headline in the *Boston Post* when the last-place Red Sox played Ty Cobb's fifth-place Tigers in a July 8 doubleheader at Navin Field. Ehmke's success with the Red Sox had "intensified the bitter feeling" between the pitcher and the manager who had traded him away.[19]

The ongoing animosity between Ehmke and Cobb erupted again in the opener, which matched Ehmke against Hooks Dauss, his friend and former teammate. Dauss defeated Boston, 5–0, but his six-hit shutout was overshadowed by what the *Sporting News* called "the renewal of the feud between Ehmke and Cobb." Detroit sportswriter Sam Greene described what had triggered the action: "In the third inning, Cobb drove a hit off the Boston first baseman's [Phil Todt] glove. Ehmke, sensing a play at first base, moved over to cover the bag. Cobb slid into the sack and dug one of his spikes into the heel of Ehmke's shoe. When Cobb rose to his feet, Ehmke kicked at him. Ehmke started for Cobb, and Cobb started for Ehmke. Both appeared willing enough to settle the issue with their fists, but Umpire [Bill] McGowan, working at first base, stepped between them, preventing further trouble."[20]

Two days later Ehmke accused Cobb of spiking him. Cobb responded, in an interview with a Detroit newspaper, by accusing Ehmke of lying. He said when he slid into first base, he neither spiked Ehmke nor ever had any intention of doing so. Ehmke, in turn, wanted to know why Cobb slid into first on a ball that had bounced through the infield. He also showed the shoe he had worn in which the leather had been cut through.[21] A writer for the *Boston Globe* echoed the sentiments of many fans when he wrote, "Howard Ehmke and Ty Cobb should at least call [a] truce during the baseball season and cut out the 'getting' of the other fellow."[22]

The incident was rehashed following a 1952 article in *Life* magazine in which Cobb claimed that despite his reputation for spiking players, he had only done so intentionally two times.[23] "Here's a play he didn't mention in the article," Ehmke told Ed Pollock of the *Philadelphia Evening Bulletin*, "and you can judge for yourself whether or not it was intentional."[24] After Cobb's ground ball to the right side, Ehmke said he ran over to cover first but stopped a yard or two from the bag when he saw that first baseman Todt would be unable to make a throw. "I had my back to Cobb, but I heard him hit the dirt [slide], and luckily I lifted my right foot. Cobb's spikes hit the heel of my shoe. If I hadn't lifted it, he would have cut off my foot. There was no play, understand. Yet Cobb decided to slide and managed to spike my shoe when I was at least a yard away from the inside corner of first base. Maybe Ty's forgotten that one, but I haven't."[25]

Jack Quinn had done well against the Yankees but not when he faced them on June 29. In the words of James Harrison, "Old man Quinn started the game with nobody out and finished his tenure with things in status quo. After pitching to five batters and retiring none of them, so far as the naked eye could detect, John Picus retired himself."[26] Three days later Quinn was rocked for six runs on eleven hits in a loss to the Senators, who had taken over the league's top spot from Philadelphia. His earned run average rose to 4.60, considerably higher than in any of his seasons other than 1912, when he was sent to the Minors.

It was Quinn's last game with the Red Sox. They put him on waivers and this time did not pull him back. On July 10 Boston's record stood at 24-54, 13½ games behind their mediocre 1924 record on that date. The worst team in baseball had decided the veteran Quinn was too old, not good enough, or probably both.

Bob Quinn, the executive who had so much success in St. Louis, could not come close to replicating that performance in Boston. Years later he told Fred Lieb, "Eventually, I lost all my money in the Red Sox, but it was due to a combination of poor breaks. Less than two years after we bought the Red Sox, my associate and backer, Palmer Winslow, died. We had some big plans, but his death forced me to go it alone."[27] Quinn could have sold but believed he could turn the franchise around and recoup Winslow's investment for his widow, wrote Lieb. "He decided to carry on—with an empty till."[28]

Red Sox historians Glenn Stout and Richard Johnson were less kind in their analysis: "All Quinn's high-priced phenoms proved to be fakes. . . . His deals, none of which worked, made those of Harry Frazee seem like the work of genius. . . . His scouts scoured the lower Minor Leagues for overlooked gems. They found mostly coal."[29] The 1924 Red Sox won sixty-seven games; the 1925 edition won only forty-seven and finished 21 games behind the seventh-place Yankees. Attendance, which had almost doubled to 448,556 in 1924, collapsed 60 percent in 1925, to only 267,782 (fewer than 3,500 fans per game).

29

Another Baseball Obituary for Quinn and a Near Tragedy for Ehmke

Connie Mack's Philadelphia Athletics dominated baseball from 1905 to 1914, winning five pennants and three world championships. In the following ten years Mack's A's were in baseball's wilderness.[1] Grantland Rice wrote of Mack during the 1925 season: "He has faced enough tough breaks to discourage a rhinoceros. . . . To keep hammering for more than a decade without an alibi or complaint deserves all the reward there is. The willowy Mr. McGillicuddy has shown more in almost unending defeat than he showed in victory, so far as inspiration fiber is concerned."[2]

During his seventh consecutive last-place finish, in 1921, Mack lamented his inability to rebuild a winner. "I will have to keep up my search for more stars. . . . I will simply have to keep my eyes peeled for youths who look to have ability."[3] With his purchase of pitcher Lefty Grove, catcher Mickey Cochrane, and outfielder Al Simmons from the Minor Leagues, Mack was admitting he no longer could sign future Major Leaguers off sandlots and from colleges, as he had done with Eddie Plank, Chief Bender, and Eddie Collins. Instead he had "joined the apostles of the checkbook, the disciples of the bankroll, and is matching dollar for dollar with his opulent foes whenever he feels that he needs a player," wrote The Old Sport in the *Philadelphia Inquirer*.[4]

Mack's 1925 Athletics occupied first place from May 4 until the end of June. They had overcome injuries, including a shattered kneecap to promising first baseman Joe Hauser and a fractured thumb to pitching sensation Sam Gray.[5] On June 15 they rallied from a 15–4 deficit to beat the Cleveland Indians, 17–15, which sparked a six-game win streak. But their stay atop the league ended on June 30, when the defending champion Senators overtook them.

On July 10 the Athletics lost their ninth of twelve decisions yet remained only 3½ games behind Washington. Giants manager John McGraw weighed in that day on the challenges a team faces the first time it competes for the pennant: "They are crossing the desert for the first time. Travelers who have crossed the sands one time can always do it better on the second attempt. They understand and appreciate the difficulties."[6]

In a little-noted deal that day, Mack paid the Red Sox the $4,000 waiver price to claim Jack Quinn. One Philadelphia reporter quoted a fan who said Mack must have been "heat-struck" to spend the money for "that old man who shot his bolt long, long ago."[7] In 1928 Philadelphia sportswriter Bill Dooly recalled that the deal generated no excitement. The Athletics, he wrote, "were grasping at straws. Even at bent and twisted straws."[8] This was not the first time Mack seriously considered acquiring Quinn. He had done so in 1918, reported Joe Vila, but balked at the $10,000 the Pacific Coast League's Vernon Tigers wanted in return.[9]

As he had done the previous December, Clark Griffith of Washington claimed Quinn, but because the Senators were in first place at the time, the claim of the second-place A's took precedence.[10] Mack gloated at winning this personnel and personal battle, an unusual reaction for the soft-spoken manager: "Let 'em [the Senators] howl. They're lucky to be in the race. If they hadn't got two veterans like [Dutch] Ruether and [Stan] Coveleski, they would have been counted out long ago. We got Quinn, and we're going to keep him."[11] The two aging pitchers to whom Mack referred had joined the Senators this season and had a combined 20-4 record on the day Quinn was claimed.

Mack said Quinn would add another weapon to his pitching staff.[12] He intended to use the old spitballer out of the bullpen, despite his six complete games for Boston this season. Quinn was also the veteran influence Mack had been looking for to settle his young club, including the petulant and moody Grove.[13] Years later Quinn credited former A's catcher and current pitching coach Ira Thomas for persuading Mack to acquire him.[14]

Once again Quinn's baseball obituary had been written prematurely. He simply would not agree: "I still have a lot of pitching left in me and expect to win for the Athletics."[15] He did not have to wait long to show he could still pitch. He started in Detroit on July 13 and tossed a five-hit, 4–1 win. "Reducing the bats of the Bengals to the impotency of pea shooters attacking the Rock of Gibraltar," wrote John Nolan, "Quinn made the Tigers look like the other animals in the zoo, meaning monkeys."[16] After the game Quinn explained to Nolan what made him a successful pitcher: "If a batter likes inside balls, pitch them on the outside. Always keep them guessing and give them something different. Use the noodle as much as the arm. Say, I don't want to talk too much. I might be getting my bumps soon."[17]

Quinn rarely had much to say to reporters. New York columnist Joe Williams described the pitcher's reserved personality and then saluted him: "He is no great conversationalist on any subject. When he says 'huh,' he is becoming verbose. Perhaps the secret of Mr. Quinn's enduring greatness is that he concentrates on pitching instead of gabbing. He may be dumb to talk to, but he is not dumb in the box. Indeed, there are times when he is eloquent out there."[18] It was unexpected when the usually reticent Quinn elaborated to Nolan a couple of weeks later: "Study the batters and get control and remember there's eight other fellows to help you out when the ball is hit. That's all there is to pitching. I don't believe in straining the arm when there's no need to. If a youngster wants to pitch for a good many years, let him learn control first, how to pitch in the pinch, and remember at all times to have something in reserve."[19]

Walter Farquhar saluted the local hero in a lengthy poem, which read in part as follows:

"Sell me a pitcher at any price"
Was the cry of Mack o'er the circuit twice.
"Since you develop men so well,
Do so now," was the league's cold yell.
Nothing to sell but sour advice,
And old Jack Quinn at the waiver price.
. . . .
So down to the A's came Ol' Jack Quinn,
With his chunky frame and his spitball fin,
With an arm still strong after forty years
And a head as wise as the Grecian seers.
"What does he want with that old man?"
Was the wail of fans when they learned Mack's plan.
"He buys 'em young, has his mind grown weak,
That he seeks to build on a rare antique?"

Down to the A's came Ol' Jack Quinn
And the Tigers laughed as Mack sent him in.
Watching the scoreboard play by play
Were the anxious Philly fans that day.
Frame by frame did the score come through
And 'twas Ty Cobb's end where the goose eggs grew.
And out on the hill was Ol' Jack Quinn
With the speed that he showed when he first broke in.[20]

Five days after his July 13 win at Detroit, Quinn held Chicago to three hits in seven innings to beat fellow spitballer Red Faber, 8–1.[21] Only now did writers begin to praise Mack's acquisition of Quinn. After he helped the A's sweep both Detroit and Chicago and take sole possession of first place, James Isaminger saluted "the pitching wonder of baseball . . . winning fresh laurels for valor on the peak."[22] The pitcher who had seemed washed up two weeks earlier was now called "one of the smartest and most dependable pitchers known in baseball."[23]

On July 27 Quinn beat his former team, the Red Sox, 2–1. Philadelphia now had won thirteen of fifteen since he had come aboard and was back in first place. Isaminger wrote that the Athletics began to improve the day Quinn joined the club: "His very presence was inspiring," this "paragon of steadiness, efficiency, and brains."[24] As the A's prepared for the stretch run, "in a goosefleshy pennant race," Isaminger wrote, "the presence of such an able, dispassionate veteran cannot be overestimated. Quinn was just the man needed to help stabilize the staff."[25] The A's seemed to be overcoming the difficulties facing a first-time contender that John McGraw had pointed out.

On August 2 the Athletics came to Pottsville, where Quinn grew up and played Minor League ball. They played an exhibition game against a local team, the Cressona Tigers. Quinn was presented with a bat and ball made of "black diamonds," the local name of anthracite coal. He pitched the first two innings of a game the A's won, 7–4. He told reporters, "I have thrown off fifteen years since I am with Connie Mack."[26]

That same day Gordon Mackay featured Quinn in the Inquirer. Mackay focused on Quinn's humble beginnings as a breaker boy in the mines and the obstacles he had to overcome as a youth. After his mother died, the youngster "didn't hit it off [with his stepmother]," wrote Mackay, a situation that led him "to quit the family hearthstone and fare forth into the great world beyond."[27] The article had a Horatio Alger rags-to-riches flavor and added to the mystique of Quinn and his indomitable spirit.

Washington was able to take over first place in mid-August, when the Athletics dropped three high-scoring one-run decisions at St. Louis. Still Philadelphia was just one game back on August 23. Then began what Fred Lieb called "one of the most agonizing two weeks in Mack's sixty years in baseball."[28] The A's dropped twelve straight games, shortly after the one-run losses in St. Louis. When they returned home on September 8, they were nine games behind the Senators, and all pennant hopes were gone.

Just a few weeks earlier Isaminger had written, "Mack has one of the grittiest teams that ever served under him. . . . The quantities of backbone and courage are no slight factors in the team's success."[29] Mack later explained this collapse: "Suddenly everything went wrong. Tired players became aware of sagging muscles. Their work became listless. Others tried to overcome this by seeking to force the breaks. They pressed too hard. The entire team lost its naturalness. I'm telling you it was a painful experience."[30]

Quinn could not help stop the slide, even though he had been through the pressure of dramatic pennant races in 1920 and 1921. In the first of the three losses to the Browns, he retired only one man and gave up three earned runs. On Labor Day he and Lefty Grove started the two ends of a doubleheader, which the league-leading Senators swept to extend their lead to nine games. Both were one-run losses, "killing all pennant chances . . . two stunning blows to the Athletics," in the words of one Pennsylvania paper.[31] Quinn went more than a month, from mid-August to mid-September, without a win.

Perhaps John McGraw was right. John Foster wrote in the *1926 Spalding Guide*, "When a team begins to feel that the breaks are going against it, it must have two qualities, one of them fight and the other no regard for what happened the days before. The Athletics had not been through the pennant mill long enough to have either, and they began to worry. Then they began to lose."[32] The Old Sport felt the A's had reached first place too soon: "There would have been no strain of holding first place against the hectic fight made by the contender," adding that "This collapse was due entirely to the strain of keeping first place so long."[33]

After his promising first month with the Athletics, Quinn's pitching tailed off. He won four games in his first thirty days in Philadelphia; he won only twice more the rest of the way. He was hindered when he strained his side in an early September game against the Senators. Once he recovered, he tossed a complete-game victory against the White Sox on September 17, ruining Eddie Collins Day in Comiskey Park.[34] The *Chicago Tribune* featured Quinn's picture with a caption that noted he "was declared to be through" when the Red Sox released him, prematurely it now seemed.[35]

The Athletics finished with eighty-eight wins, an improvement of seventeen over 1924 and 8½ games back of the repeat winners, the Washington Senators. Led by Simmons's .387 batting average and Cochrane's .331 mark, the A's led the league with a .308 team batting average.[36]

Quinn's years of experience were unable to stabilize a young team, but his control was better than ever: he walked fewer than 1.5 men per nine innings once he joined the A's.[37] That control became even more important as his velocity declined; his strikeout rate dropped as his career progressed.[38]

While he appreciated the opportunity Connie Mack had given him, Quinn felt he would not be back in 1926. After the season, he stopped by Mack's office.

"I came to say good-bye," he told Mack. "You probably won't need me anymore, will you?"

"Need you?" said Mack. "Well, I guess we will. You show up early next season. You've done wonders for us."[39]

When Quinn looked back on that conversation a few years later, he told Philadelphia sportswriter Bill Dooly, "I've never gotten that before. I don't believe I ever had a happier moment than that before in my life. . . . Somehow or other, they [my previous managers] never seemed anxious about keeping me."[40]

Mack told Burt Whitman that the change of scenery helped Quinn: "Had Jack stayed with the Red Sox, the chances are that he would never have done what he did for me."[41] And Quinn contributed mostly as a starter, rather than as a reliever.[42]

Three of Howard Ehmke's best-pitched games for the 1925 Red Sox came within a two-week span in September. The first was a 2–1 loss to the Yankees and a familiar foe, Bob Shawkey, on September 1, a game in which he allowed only four hits. His next start, also against New York, was a 5–1 victory on September 7. Not even the return of Babe Ruth from his nine-day suspension, nor a scheduled doubleheader (only one game was played) could entice a larger turnout (only four thousand fans showed up) to see these two also-rans on a cold, gloomy afternoon in Fenway Park. The Yankees' lone run off Ehmke came on rookie first baseman Lou Gehrig's long blast into the center-field bleachers.

On September 15, also at Fenway, Ehmke flirted with another no-hitter, holding St. Louis hitless through six innings as he and Milt Gaston dueled through eight scoreless innings. The Browns scored two in the ninth, and the run by baseball's worst-hitting team in the home half of the inning was not enough to prevent Ehmke from suffering his eighteenth loss of the season.[43]

A meaningless September 23 home game against Detroit turned out to be among the most memorable of Ehmke's career. He was the losing pitcher in a game the Tigers won, 15–1, but the score was not what made the game memorable. In the fourth inning one of his pitches struck the Tigers' right-handed-hitting Fred Haney above and behind his left ear. The impact left Haney sprawled in the dirt as the ball rolled toward the Detroit dugout. A distraught Ehmke, whom Burt Whitman described as "close to the breaking point," rushed to Haney, his teammate at the San Pedro submarine base during the war and later with the Tigers.

"Do you think I did it on purpose?" he asked Haney.

"Of course not," Haney replied. "I've known you too long for that."[44]

It appeared that Haney had been expecting a curve ball and was unable to duck away from Ehmke's fastball. Tigers manager Ty Cobb, coaching at third, was riding Ehmke throughout the game, though there was no confrontation between the two this time.

Several players carried Haney to the clubhouse, including Ehmke, who removed himself from the game and refused to leave Haney's side. He accompanied Haney to Boston's Peter Bent Brigham Hospital and refused to leave until doctors convinced him that his old friend was out of danger. According to a report in the *Detroit Times*, Haney had been delirious during the ride to the hospital, demanding he be allowed to return to the game. He had to be restrained from jumping out of the ambulance.[45] Ehmke was allowed to visit with him, although no members of the Tigers were granted that privilege.

Dr. Harvey Cushing, the hospital's chief surgeon, said Haney had experienced a concussion, but there were no signs of a fracture or a blood clot on the brain. A repeat of the Carl Mays–Ray Chapman tragedy of five years earlier had been averted by the margin of a half-inch, medical experts stated.

The beaning of Haney was the ninth batter Ehmke hit this season. He would hit two more in a September 26 loss to the White Sox to finish with a league-leading total of eleven. It was the fourth time in the past five seasons he led the league in hit batsman.[46] Despite missing several weeks early in the season, he also led the league in complete games (22), while his twenty losses were second in the Major Leagues to the Yankees' Sam Jones. Ehmke won only nine.

Haney, who missed the final week of the season, was traded to the Red Sox in December and was fit and ready for the 1926 campaign. Meanwhile, Ehmke checked himself into the Battle Creek Sanitarium in Battle Creek, Michigan, for rejuvenation after the season.[47]

Ellery Clark, who authored several books on the Boston Red Sox, cited a letter Ehmke sent him from the sanitarium in 1925, when Clark was a sixteen-year-old Red Sox fan. In that November 27, 1925, letter, Ehmke went into great detail in answering Clark's question about the grips he used when pitching. He told Clark he was at the sanitarium for a "little rest" and provided him with his address in Detroit, where he would be spending the winter. "Howard also took pains to answer every single letter he received [from me] during his long major-league career of 1916–1930 and later in his retirement until he died in 1959," Clark wrote. "Howard was one of the greatest gentlemen in the game and was not one to complain."[48] There were, of course, many in baseball who would not agree with the second part of that statement.

30

Quinn Gets Off to a Strong Start,
Ehmke to a Poor One

Chicago Tribune sports editor Don Maxwell interviewed Howard Ehmke
in February 1926, when the pitcher was in Chicago to visit friends. He
said Ehmke, who missed several weeks of the 1925 season due to the flu,
looked to be in splendid health and was counting on a big year. Maxwell pointed out that many of Ehmke's statistics were similar to those
of pitcher Eddie Rommel of the Philadelphia Athletics. But while Rommel tied for the league lead with twenty-one wins (he was 21-10) for the
second-place A's, Ehmke was 9-20 for the last-place Red Sox.[1] "And this
may be taken as proof that you can't rate pitchers on games won and lost,"
wrote Maxwell, echoing other observers of the game before and since.[2]

Team president Bob Quinn was pleased with what he saw of the Red
Sox when they assembled in New Orleans for the start of spring training.
"I like the spirit of the boys," he said after watching a workout. "They
look like the best collection I have gathered since I arrived in Boston. Just
think of it, there are 25 players here who were not in training camp last
spring," he noted, while singling out one who was. "Just look at Ehmke.
I never saw him in better condition. He should have a fine season."[3]

If Ehmke was frustrated at being with a club that finished last in 1925
and would finish there again in 1926, he kept it to himself. In January, while
on a business trip to Detroit, he wrote a note to the *Boston Globe* telling of
his satisfaction at remaining in Boston: "I signed my contract with the Red
Sox for the next season today, and I am mighty glad I was not transferred
to another club. Boston is my favorite city so far as baseball is concerned."[4]

Fellow pitcher Ted Wingfield, whose twelve wins (he was 12-19) in
1925 made him the only double-digit winner for the Sox, was talking
about the sore arm he had during the season. He claimed it had mirac-
ulously healed after he spent an evening bowling. Ehmke, never one
to pass up a chance to tell of his own illnesses and injuries, chimed

in. "That reminds me that I almost lost my eyesight last year," he said. "My vision was affected by the flu that knocked me cold. One eye was practically useless. I was not able to read a newspaper until about two months ago." He assured everyone that his eyes were just fine now. "I can follow the flight of the golf ball all the way," said Ehmke, an avid golfer, "and I can see the ball better as it comes to the plate."[5]

Burt Whitman also predicted a banner year for Ehmke: "He weighs 12 pounds more than ever before, is in excellent physical condition, and his arm feels so strong that he is chary of putting everything he possesses on the ball. He has been too thin for his own good."[6] Three weeks later Whitman wrote, "Ehmke is apparently in better physical trim than ever, sturdier appearing and heavier. But he is so anxious to have his biggest year that he is starting out very slowly and with high conservation."[7]

Worries about Ehmke lessened after his April 4 appearance against the American Association champion Louisville Colonels. "Ehmke has cut out all the experimental deliveries," wrote Melville Webb of the *Boston Globe*. "He has retained the best of his sidearm stuff, but also does more overhand pitching than he has done for the past two seasons, and when he does come over the shoulder, the ball has a jump which is almost as great as his best half-underhand pitch."[8]

Meanwhile, in Fort Myers, Florida, where the Athletics gathered for spring training, expectations were high. The A's were coming off an eighty-eight-win season, a jump of seventeen wins over 1924. Other teams had taken notice of Connie Mack's club as well. Yankees manager Miller Huggins felt the A's had the best chances "to come through" with the pennant in 1926.[9] Jack Quinn wrote to his friends that the spirit of the team was the best he had ever seen on any club.[10] He had reason to be pleased about his salary too; it was significantly higher than his Red Sox earnings.[11]

As the exhibition season unfolded, however, manager Mack did not like what he saw. His men were playing and talking a lot of golf, a rising recreational sport. He told James Isaminger he felt they were believing their press clippings and ripped into his team. "Witless and slovenly playing and an entire absence of snap and enthusiasm have made them look as if they were candidates to the tail end rather than the pennant," he said. "The fact that nearly everybody declares that the Athletics are pennant contenders means nothing."[12] Mack said he would repeat this message directly to his players the following day. The tirade did not create the spark Mack had hoped for: the Athletics started the season 4-10.

Ehmke's strong showing in spring training earned him his third opening day start in the last four seasons and his fourth overall. His first had been a win over the Indians in 1919, when he was with the Tigers, but the last two were losses to the Yankees, in 1923 and 1924. Bob Shawkey was Ehmke's mound opponent in those two games, as he was in the 1926 opener at a frigid Fenway Park.

For the first time Yankees manager Miller Huggins filled out his scorecard with a lineup that many historians would later call the greatest ever. Third baseman Joe Dugan was the only holdover from the infield that started the opener a year ago. Lou Gehrig had replaced Wally Pipp at first base, and two rookies, second baseman Tony Lazzeri and shortstop Mark Koenig, replaced the double-play combination of Aaron Ward and Everett Scott. The outfield of Babe Ruth, Bob Meusel, and Earle Combs remained the game's best.

The Yankees, winners of their last eighteen spring training games, jumped on Ehmke for four first-inning runs on their way to a 12–11 victory. Manager Lee Fohl replaced him after he allowed eight runs (seven earned) in four innings. In his next start, however, Ehmke was brilliant, beating Philadelphia, 6–1. Throwing mostly sidearm curves, he allowed the Athletics just two hits on another cold afternoon at Fenway Park. Because "his ancestors were Vikings," Nick Flatley said of Ehmke, "Howard didn't mind the howling gales that swept down from the North Pole."[13] Five straight losses by Ehmke followed that win, and in only one of those losses did he show a semblance of dominance. On May 10 he lost to Cleveland's George Uhle, 3–0, when the Indians broke a scoreless tie in the eighth inning with three unearned runs.

Facing the Athletics again, in the first game of a May 31 home doubleheader, Ehmke had one of his best games in a Boston uniform. His opponent was Lefty Grove, who in only his second big league season was establishing himself as an exceptionally talented pitcher. For seven innings neither team could score. In the eighth Fred Haney led off by drawing a walk. Fohl thought enough of Ehmke's hitting ability to have the number 8 hitter, Fred Bischoff, sacrifice Haney to second. As Ehmke made his way to the plate, the crowd gave him a huge round of applause. He rewarded the fans, and his manager's faith in him, by lashing a double to left that scored Haney. Ehmke later scored the second run on Ira Flagstead's sacrifice fly. He preserved that 2–0 lead, though he gave the crowd a scare in the ninth by walking the bases loaded before retiring pinch hitter Bill Wambsganss on a ground ball. "If Howard was as effective against other clubs as he is chucking to the A's," wrote Flatley, noting Ehmke's inconsistency, "he'd be the most powerful piece of baseball property extant."[14] That inconsistency was on display in his next start, on June 5, when the White Sox reached him for six hits, four walks, and seven earned runs in an inning and a third.

In his first full season with Philadelphia, Jack Quinn had quickly emerged as the ace of the A's staff. On April 24 he beat Joe Bush, now with the Senators, 4–1. Five days later he shut out his former club, the Red Sox, 4–0. One Boston reporter noted, "No club ever had a harder working pitcher or a better fellow."[15] James Isaminger wrote of the game, "Jack's flinging was worthy of being put in alcohol and exhibited during the Sezqui."[16] His next starts were two more complete-game wins to push his record to 4-0 and get the A's to .500, at 12-12.

The veteran's age was gathering more and more attention. After he beat another of his former clubs, the Yankees, James Harrison joked, "John Quinn is getting so old that pretty soon he'll qualify for the Washington pitching staff."[17] Grantland Rice again saluted Quinn that month when he wrote, "The venerable Jack Quinn doesn't gather as much ballyhoo as some of the others, but in many respects he is the most astonishing landmark of the lot. . . . Quinn has been a hard young man to discourage."[18]

Quinn had reminded a Philadelphia reporter that spring, "The whole question of pitching is control, not age. . . . My advice to any youngster is to try for control. It's more important than speed." How much control? "Be able to throw the ball to within a fraction of an inch of the desired spot," Quinn added.[19]

When Quinn beat the defending American League champion Senators, 3–1, on May 26, he raised his record to 6-2 while lowering his earned run average to a league-leading 1.65. Washington first baseman Joe Judge commented on Quinn's control: "It's marvelous the way that fellow feeds us fast-breaking 'spitters' right on the handle of the bat and keeps us from hitting."[20] While the win put the A's into a second-place tie with Cleveland, the resurgent New York Yankees were 30-9 and in the midst of a sixteen-game win streak.

Quinn's spitball was as deceptive and effective as ever this spring. When he shut out the White Sox on June 10, Isaminger wrote, "His anointed trajectories performed such odd gyrations as they sailed over the plate."[21] He won that game in Comiskey Park in just one hour and thirty-four minutes. Miller Huggins pointed out that Quinn "loaded up" and got rid of his spitter faster than any other pitcher.[22] He still was throwing a "dry spitter." As Paul Shannon wrote, Quinn "does not anoint the ball. He simply wets the tips of his fingers, and the ball is dry when it reaches the batsmen."[23]

Ed Pollock compared the A's slow start to "a convicted criminal leaving the death chamber for the gallows." The Yankees had moved so far ahead (ten games on June 15) that the chances of catching them, he wrote, "are about as slim as Mack himself."[24]

Among the reports circulating a week before the June 15 trading deadline was one that Bob Quinn was looking to swing a multiplayer deal. "I'll make any kind of a trade with anybody," Quinn said, "but I must help myself doing it."[25] Ehmke was the big prize Boston had to offer, and any of the contending clubs would have been glad to have him. "Ehmke is still a great pitcher," wrote Flatley, "but he's no youngster, and Quinn would be much better off with three or four good young players who might help along in the next few years."[26]

Quinn and Philadelphia's Mack had been in conference at Cleveland's Hollenden Hotel all day on June 15.[27] The A's players were aware their manager was working on a big deal, and many sat around the hotel that evening waiting for word of which of them would be leaving.[28]

The trade of Howard Ehmke from Boston to the Philadelphia Athletics was completed at 9 p.m., three hours before the trading deadline. Many players were discussed, but the final deal sent Ehmke to Philadelphia for pitchers Slim Harriss and Fred Heimach and outfielder Baby Doll Jacobson. "The importance of the transfer of Ehmke," wrote Isaminger, "can best be made clear by the fact that President Quinn claimed he had turned down a cash offer of $150,000 for the star made to him by a Major League club last winter."[29] Mack knew Quinn wanted Jacobson, a .317 hitter in ten seasons with the Browns, so a day earlier he acquired him from the Browns in a trade for outfielder Bing Miller.

In addition to the Athletics, the Yankees, Indians, White Sox, and Senators had also been trying to trade for Ehmke, who, contrary to his earlier statements that he was content in Boston and wanted to remain, apparently had been asking Quinn to trade him for the past two seasons.[30]

Mack had been after Ehmke that same length of time, likely impressed by how well he had pitched against the A's, winning twenty-six of forty decisions against them. (Two of his three wins this season had been against Philadelphia.) "I have always regarded Ehmke as a wonderful pitcher," Mack declared after completing the trade. "He proved he is a thinking and not a mechanical hurler by inventing the hesitation pitch. He has great control and is the type of pitcher I want."[31] In the opinion of John J. Nolan of the *Philadelphia Evening Bulletin*, the Athletics had "added one of the best right handers in the American League."[32]

After having breakfast with Ehmke the day after the trade, Isaminger described him as a tall Nordic with exceptionally wide shoulders. "He was athletic to his long finger tips. Tall but spare his movements implied energy and strength," wrote Isaminger.[33] "Well, this is a dream that I never thought would come true," Ehmke told Isaminger. "I hinted to President Quinn last winter that I wanted a change, but he said it was impossible. I decided that I would have to end my career with a weak club. I didn't have the slightest inkling of the deal."[34]

Evidently Mack was not influenced by Ehmke's last game in a Red Sox uniform, which ended in a frustrating defeat. On the day of the trade, Ehmke took a 6–4 lead into the last of the ninth inning at Navin Field before the Tigers rallied to score three runs for a 7–6 win. Ehmke allowed sixteen hits in the game; still he would have won with better defense behind him. He had two outs with no one on in the ninth when Harry Heilmann hit a routine fly ball to right that Si Rosenthal misplayed into what was generously scored as a triple. Those who had long claimed Ehmke had difficulty handling adversity could point to what happened next as proof. A walk and a triple tied the score, and a bloop single won the game for Detroit. The loss dropped Ehmke's record to 3-10.

Howard Ehmke pitched three and a half years for the Red Sox, at a time when they were among the weakest teams in the league. He compiled a won-lost record of 51-64 (.443) and a 3.83 earned run average, both significantly better marks than those of the team for which he played.

31

Ehmke and Quinn Reunited

Several Boston sportswriters were not sorry to see Howard Ehmke leave the Red Sox. Nick Flatley predicted Fred Heimach and Slim Harriss would win more games between them than Ehmke would have won had he remained. Flatley mentioned Ehmke's age (thirty-two) and the long rest he needed between starts. "Ehmke was great two years ago, but only fair last season," he wrote. "He has been an in and outer this Spring and was decidedly worried about his arm early in the year." Flatley believed Bob Quinn regretted not having traded Ehmke during the off-season. He should do better in Philadelphia, where Mack had enough starters to avoid overworking him, Flatley reasoned. In addition, Mack profited from the A's not having to face him anymore.[1]

Burt Whitman wrote, "Big Howard has not been even a fair pitcher for the Red Sox the last couple of years. It seems he had the idea in the back of his head that he simply could not win for the Red Sox. He tried hard enough, and if there ever was a conscientious player working for Bob Quinn, it was this same Ehmke."[2] Whitman continued: "That he ever worked with the thought in the back of his head to get away from the Red Sox is a rank injustice to Ehmke, whose standards are exceptionally high. But he simply could not come through here. It may be that he can deliver for Connie Mack of the soft-spoken and gentle voice and encouraging manners[,] the man with a thousand excuses for his boys when they do not come through 100 percent."[3]

The reaction to the trade in the Philadelphia press was cautious optimism. "The arrival here of Howard Ehmke may stir up the fight and punch that is needed to carry the Elephants up where we feel they belong," wrote Stoney McLinn.[4] This was the same McLinn who had hinted that the ninth-inning, game-winning home run Ehmke allowed to the A's Frank Welch in 1924 was due to a lack of concentration.

Ehmke called the trade "the luckiest break I ever got in my life. Last night I was downcast over losing to Detroit in a tight game after two were out. My support failed me, and the Tigers beat me out in the ninth, and if there's any club I like to lick it's Detroit, where Ty Cobb holds the reins."[5] Ehmke was clearly pleased now to be in a pennant race and thought, contrary to most, that the A's would be able to overtake the Yankees. "At least I'll do my part," he said. "I haven't been quite myself this year, and it has practically taken over a season for me to recover from the attack of flu I had in the spring of 1925."[6]

Ehmke was welcomed to his new club by former Red Sox teammates Jack Quinn and Bill Wambsganss and was assigned to room with Frank Welch. His new roommate triggered memories in Ehmke of one of his most frustrating defeats. In the first game of the May 18, 1924, doubleheader at Shibe Park, Welch's two-out ninth-inning home run turned a potential 1–0 victory for Boston into a bitter 2–1 defeat. "I threw him a curve," Ehmke remembered, "the same ball I had struck him out on in the seventh inning, and that cost me the game."[7]

Syndicated columnist John B. Foster wrote that unnamed teams wanted Ehmke, despite his mediocre performance with the Red Sox: "Queer record this Ehmke has pitched. He has won three games this season and lost ten, and he was valued by one major manager at $50,000, while another wanted to get him by giving up two of the best players he had."[8]

On June 15, the day Mack made the trade for Ehmke, the Yankees led second-place Chicago by 9½ games and had a 10-game lead on third-place Philadelphia. Mack felt the acquisition gave his team as good a pitching staff as any in the league, including the Yankees. "Figuring that Ehmke will win twelve games for us inside of the next three months, which is a conservative estimate, and adding to that his ability to beat New York and the fact that he will no longer be able to pitch against us," said Mack, "it would not take any stretch of the imagination to figure eighteen games as good as won."[9] "One reason for Ehmke's effectiveness," Mack noted, "is the fact that he doesn't really pitch until he is compelled to, in a tight game. He is like a fiddler tuning up. He sounds out each string for a time, and when he has to play, he cuts loose in his best style, after making sure his fiddle is in tune."[10]

Ehmke's new teammates were glad to have him on their side. He had, they believed, everything a first-class pitcher should have in his repertoire—control, speed, change of pace, a fast-breaking curve, a level head, and a knowledge of opposing batters. Additionally, he was rated second to Eddie Rommel as the best-fielding pitcher in the league. John Nolan wrote that Ehmke adhered to a regular schedule, rising at 7 a.m. and seldom staying up past 11 p.m. He neither drank, smoked, nor chewed tobacco and spent his winters negotiating sales of athletic field covers for a company based in Detroit.[11] Ehmke had sold a tarp to Mack for Shibe Park the previous winter, and in July sold one to the University of Pennsylvania for its football field.[12]

In his breakfast chat with James Isaminger that June, Ehmke defended himself against his critics, particularly those in Detroit and Boston, who had accused him of being unable to handle adversity. He did so—in a way not designed to please his former teammates—by blaming the poor defensive support he had received: "What a raft of games I have lost through punk errors. Listen, I could stay and talk to you two hours about plays that have lost me games. I don't look for perfection all the time and don't expect it now that I am with a better team, but the flock of slips that follows a pitcher hooked to a tail-end team is a curse that he is powerless to deal with."[13]

In a 1936 interview Ehmke recalled asking his new manager if he knew that his arm was in bad shape. "He countered by wanting to know if I could pitch at all," Ehmke remembered. "I said I thought I could continue if given a reasonable amount of rest between games. Mack said, 'All right, I'll go along with you.'"[14]

As the 1926 season wore on, Jack Quinn seemed to wear down. In his ten starts following his June 10 shutout in Chicago, he won only once (he also picked up a win in relief) and never went the distance.[15]

When a mid-July losing streak by the A's grew to seven games, one Philadelphia reporter showed both the superstitious nature of baseball and its racial views in the 1920s: "A colored mascot is the court of last resort in base ball [sic], and when he fails, after a few days to bring about a change, conditions become deplorable."[16]

Quinn did help stop the streak that day, against the Indians. He started and knocked in two runs with a double. After five innings he turned over a lead to Lefty Grove, who gave up the tying run before the Athletics won in the tenth inning.

29. Jack Quinn understood discrimination in early twentieth-century America. Because of it, he likely took the Irish-sounding name of Quinn rather than the East European "Pajkos" or its Americanized version, Picus. As early as 1920, Quinn pitched for the Chicago Normals, the city's semi-pro champions, against the [Black] American Giants. *Family of Jack Quinn.*

Late in the season Tigers outfielder Heinie Manush commented on Quinn's control, as well as his intelligence: "Quinn is a mighty smart pitcher. He has wonderful control of his spitter, too. Just when you're looking for one inside and back away from the ball, he gives it to you on the outside. Then, when you're expecting one outside, it pops up inside."[17] Veteran umpire Billy Evans said something similar: "Quinn depends to a great extent on the old grey matter when in the box."[18]

A columnist for the *Sporting News* revealed that Quinn kept a little book, with notes on the weaknesses of every batter. The writer reminded readers that Quinn's conditioning allowed him to pitch as well as he did for as long as he did: "Old Jack is a giant in strength. He doesn't drink or smoke and eats the plainest food."[19]

By the end of July the A's were 14 games back and only four wins above .500. Mack was unable to figure out what was wrong. On July 31 he said, "Individually, the team looks like a champion club. As a combination, it doesn't measure up."[20] Some observers questioned Mack's trading of Baby Doll Jacobson, whose bat would have helped; he was hitting over .400 his first month in Boston. Clark Griffith, the owner of the Senators, was certain of it: "Mack lost the pennant when he let Jacobson go to the Red Sox."[21]

Jacobson was the key in the Ehmke acquisition, and one sportswriter, puzzled by the trade, politely and indirectly questioned Mack. The Old Sport had noted that Mack needed to deal the slugger to land Ehmke. "Connie's reason for that is something with which we are unfamiliar, but he wanted Ehmke, and he had his own reasons for seeking the gaunt Nordic for his pitching staff."[22]

Quinn had posted an 8-3 record with a 2.21 earned run average before Ehmke arrived but finished at 10-11 with a 3.41 ERA. One thing that did not desert him, though, was his control. He walked fewer than two men every nine innings, third best in the American League. On a personal note, 1926 was a trying year for Quinn; he lost both his father and mother-in-law that year.

Howard Ehmke's first start for the A's was on June 21 against his former team, the Red Sox. He was ineffective, allowing five earned runs in 3⅓ innings, although Philadelphia won, 7–6, in eleven innings. He did, however, receive a cordial reception at Shibe Park when he batted in the home third. At that point he had pitched three innings, allowing just one run—a home run by Jacobson.

Ehmke was not much better in his second start, six days later. He went five innings at Washington and left trailing, 5–0, with all the runs coming in the fourth inning. The Senators won the game, 6–2, giving Philadelphia its fourth consecutive defeat. "To relate that Connie Mack is bitterly disappointed at seeing Howard Ehmke yanked from the pitcher's box in Washington yesterday for the second successive occasion is to put it lightly," wrote John Nolan.[23]

On July 2 Ehmke finally turned in the kind performance Mack had envisioned when he made the trade. He went twelve innings against Boston, leaving with the score tied at 3–3. The A's scored in the bottom of the thirteenth; the win went to Joe Pate, his fifth win without a loss.[24] Ehmke made occasional use of his hesitation pitch in the game, the first game in which he had employed it in some time.

Two weeks later Ehmke went the distance in beating the Browns, 3–2, while showing the Philadelphia fans his best stuff. "I've never been more anxious in my life to make good than here with the A's," he said after the game. "I guess the trouble with me is I've been overanxious. My arm feels strong and doesn't bother me in the least, although it did in the cold weather of the spring. Pretty soon I'll get accustomed to new conditions and surroundings and settle down to my normal pace."[25] When Eddie Rommel won the nightcap, it allowed the second-place A's to cut the slumping Yankees' lead to 5½ games.

At Detroit on August 2, Ehmke shut out the Tigers, 6–0, on three hits in the first game of an A's sweep. "Howard Ehmke proved to the world that Connie added an imposing magnifico of the peak in the deal that sent him here," Isaminger wrote.[26] It had rained hard the day before, but the field was in good shape, having been covered by one of Ehmke's tarps. Ty Cobb did not play but chose to coach at third base. He and Ehmke exchanged unflattering remarks throughout the game. After getting the final out, Ehmke walked halfway toward the Tigers' bench, removed his cap, and made a little bow. The gesture was uncharacteristic for Ehmke and likely aimed solely at Cobb rather than his former Detroit teammates.

Ehmke's comeback continued with complete-game wins against Chicago, 3–1, and Boston, 5–1. "The big Swede no longer weakens at the middle and the end, but twirls smoothly and consistently for full rounds," wrote Nolan after the win against the Red Sox in the first game of an August 12 doubleheader at Fenway Park.[27] Rommel shut out the hapless Sox in the second game, earning his seventh victory and his first in two weeks.

Ehmke was now 5-3 since joining the A's, prompting coach Kid Gleason to predict continued success for him. "He's got the confidence now, and the players know where to play for each batter when he pitches," Gleason said. "He may not drop another game all season."[28] Gleason was nearly correct.

The 1926 Athletics were the reverse of the 1925 club in their strengths and weaknesses. The pitching was stronger while the hitting fell off. At one point in the season, it got so bad, Isaminger wrote, that the Philadelphia pitchers would chant, "You have got to shut out a rival to win."[29]

The 1925 club hit a league-leading .308. This season the team struggled, as reflected in the fall-off of their leading hitters. Mickey Cochrane finished with a .273 batting average, far below his .331 mark of the previous season. Al Simmons hit .341 this year, far below the sensational .387 he hit the year before. It did not help the club that Joe Hauser did not come back from his knee injury as was hoped. He played in only ninety-one games and hit just .192. The A's finished with a .270 team batting average, the second-lowest in the American League. Isaminger lamented, "The team hasn't hit the weight of a Singer midget all season."[30]

The improvement in the A's pitching staff, though, was dramatic. The pitchers' combined earned run average of 3.00 was more than a run below that of the league (4.02) and a significant improvement over their 3.87 mark of 1925. Bill James called the 1926 Athletics' pitching staff of Lefty Grove, Howard Ehmke, Eddie Rommel, Jack Quinn, Rube Walberg, Sam Gray, and Joe Pate the best of the Lively Ball 1920s.[31]

Grove led the league with a 2.51 earned run average, more than two runs below his 1925 mark. He was helped by a huge improvement in his control.[32] Yankees manager Miller Huggins noticed the difference. "That boy has been taught a lot since last season," he said.[33] His control was better, but it still was not good.[34] Mack knew Grove had room for additional improvement.

After Ehmke lost three of his first five decisions with the A's, he won seven of his final eight, including a 7–2 victory over the formidable Urban Shocker and his pennant-bound Yankees on September 3. After going 3-10 for Boston, Ehmke went 12-4 for the A's, matching the win total Mack predicted for him at the time of the trade.

32

Ehmke Again a Teammate of Cobb

Despite finishing in third place in 1926, six games behind the pennant-winning Yankees, the Athletics were strong favorites to win in 1927. Frank Menke explained why he thought the 1927 New Yorkers would not repeat: "The Yankee pitching staff just staggered through 1926 . . . the last gesture of greatness. . . . If Ruth slumps—and that's very, very likely—the pennant winners of 1926 won't be remotely close to the eventful [*sic*] flag leaders."[1] Menke predicted the Athletics would win the pennant easily.

Eleven of fifteen New York sportswriters also picked the A's to win.[2] On April 11, in its last issue prior to Opening Day, *Time* magazine featured Connie Mack on its cover. Howard Ehmke was confident that come October, he would be playing in his first World Series. Ehmke thought it would be a different Athletics team, with better hitting than the 1926 bunch. "Connie Mack," he said, "discovered too late that his batters were not there."[3]

Mack upgraded the shortstop position, manned for the previous eight seasons by Chick Galloway, when he purchased thirty-year-old Joe Boley from Jack Dunn's International League Baltimore Orioles. Boley had been one of the two men (second baseman Fritz Maisel was the other) who were members of the Orioles' teams that had won seven consecutive International League pennants (1919–25).[4]

A quiet and colorless man, "Silent Joe" came from the same coal region of Pennsylvania as Jack Quinn. And like Quinn, Boley was East European; his parents were recent Polish immigrants with a family name of Bolinsky, which Joe shortened in the late 1910s. In his rookie season he finished second among the league's shortstops in batting average, on-base percentage, and slugging average.

Days into the new year Ehmke's name came up during Commissioner Landis's hearings over the controversial Tigers–White Sox back-to-back doubleheaders ten years earlier, on September 2 and 3, 1917. Rumors at the time claimed that some Tigers players had received money for not doing their best against the first-place White Sox, who were trying to hold off the defending champion Red Sox.[5] The way some Tigers performed during Chicago's four-game sweep lent credence to the rumors.[6] Shortstop Swede Risberg had testified in late December 1926 that certain Tigers players "sloughed off" during the series. Risberg was one of the eight White Sox players banned from Organized Baseball in 1920 for their roles in deliberately losing the 1919 World Series to the Cincinnati Reds.

Ehmke denied Risberg's charge and added that he never received any money. In late September 1917, when the money supposedly was delivered, he said, he was on his way to Boston to pitch in the Tim Murnane benefit game. "I don't like charges such as Risberg has made hovering over my head. . . . I have known nothing else than to play every game on the square."[7]

When it came time to testify, Ehmke followed his former Tigers teammate Oscar Stanage to the stand. "There's nothing to it," was his reply to Landis's question about the "sloughing off." "The only thing I can recall about that game is through the box score. The Sox got six hits off me in six innings. [He also walked six.] No one ever said anything to me about not pitching hard against the Sox."[8] (Ehmke is here referring to the game he pitched, a 7–5 Chicago win in the first game of the September 3 doubleheader.)

"Did you get any of the Sox pool?" Landis asked.

"I never heard anything about that money until it came out in the papers the other day," Ehmke answered. "I never got a cent of it and knew nothing about it."[9]

Landis's verdict cleared Ehmke, along with A's teammate Eddie Collins and A's coach Kid Gleason. Collins was the second baseman and Gleason a coach on that 1917 White Sox team. Three days later Ehmke, Collins, and Philadelphia Phillies catcher Jimmy Wilson agreed to spend the last few weeks of the 1926 off-season helping coach the University of Pennsylvania baseball team.

Mack had signed Collins in December 1926, a month after the White Sox released him. Collins, who would turn forty a month into the 1927 season, had starred for the A's in the early days of the team's existence. Mack sold him to Chicago when he dismantled the A's following their loss to the underdog Boston Braves in the 1914 World Series. The best second baseman of the last twenty years, Collins had batted .331 in his twelve seasons in Chicago.

The 1917 Tigers–White Sox case was not the only potential scandal with which Landis had to deal at that time. Following the 1926 season, former Tigers pitcher Dutch Leonard claimed that on September 25, 1919, he, his manager (Ty Cobb), Indians manager Tris Speaker, and Indians outfielder Joe Wood had "fixed" a game between Detroit and Cleveland. On January 27, 1927, Landis ruled that Cobb and Speaker were not guilty. Earlier Cobb and Speaker had announced their retirements, but after being cleared by Landis, both returned as players, though not as managers. Speaker signed with the Washington Senators, and on February 27, days before the start of spring training, Cobb signed with the Athletics for a reported salary of $50,000.[10]

Ehmke had hated playing under Cobb in Detroit; he had even disliked having him as a teammate before Cobb took over as manager in 1921. In his biography of Connie Mack, Norman Macht wrote: "The one player who was most upset by the arrival of Cobb was Howard Ehmke. They despised each other. . . . Cobb had no idea how to handle anyone of Ehmke's sensitive temperament. Howard couldn't take the manager's riding and talked back."[11]

As spring training got underway, John Kieran wondered how Ehmke and Cobb would reconcile their differences. Cobb claimed Ehmke had thrown at his head in 1923, Ehmke's first season with the Red Sox. "Sure," Ehmke was quoted by Kieran. "I dusted off thirty-seven batters under your orders last year. I dusted off one for myself today." Kieran wrote, "Perhaps Connie Mack will sit between them and preserve harmony."[12]

Cobb conveniently remembered the incident as if it were the one and only time he and Ehmke had clashed. "Yes, I did have trouble once with Ehmke," he told reporters. "He hit me, and I asked him if he really meant it, and he said he did, and naturally, that led to a scrap, but that was long ago and forgotten and long before I came to the A's, and everything is now very pleasant."[13]

Shortly before the 1929 World Series, Ehmke recalled how he had felt about Cobb becoming his teammate in 1927. "Maybe I had something against Cobb before that, but when he joined the A's, I just forgot about all our troubles. We both were playing on the same club then, and I wanted to win a championship just as much as he did," Ehmke said. "You need harmony on championship clubs, and there wouldn't have been any if Cobb and I had battled each other again. We just minded our own business and played baseball—and that's what a ballplayer is paid for, after all."[14]

Ehmke learned that prior to coming to Philadelphia, he was very unpopular with the players on that club because "he always seemed to use the bean ball in a pinch."[15] His reputation as a bean-ball pitcher bothered him when he was active and continued to bother him after he retired. He let his feelings about hitting batters be known after a 1937 hospital visit with Tigers catcher-manager Mickey Cochrane.[16]

When I think how I used to try to deliberately hit fellows when I was pitching, I get mad at myself all over. I was just a youngster at the time, and I did what I was told to do. In 1922 I led the leagues in hitting batters. I hit 23. I was then with Detroit. The next three in the list were also Detroit pitchers.[17] Managers forced you to throw at hitters. . . . Ty Cobb was our manager at the time, and he didn't tolerate any timidity—if that's the word. When he gave you the sign to throw at the hitter, you went through with it, or it cost you money. Every pitcher on the club knew that if he failed to dust the hitter off when Cobb gave the sign, it would cost him dough.[18]

Ehmke, who led the American League in hit batters twice with Detroit (1921 and 1922), also led the league with Boston in 1923 and 1925 and would lead with Philadelphia this season. In his career he was in the top ten for hit batters in eight seasons, and, with 137, is tied with Greg Maddux (1986–2008) for thirty-second place on the all-time list through 2019.

Cobb, still an excellent hitter at age forty, was happy to be in Philadelphia. He would be playing for a team with a strong chance at winning the pennant and for a manager he respected. He predicted the Athletics had the best chance of dethroning the champion Yankees. While not mentioning his own addition to the club, he cited three other newcomers—Collins, Boley, and veteran Brooklyn outfielder Zack Wheat—along with the strength of the pitching staff. "I look for Bob [Lefty] Grove to be the best southpaw in the league," Cobb told

St. Louis sportswriter Sid Keener. "[Rube] Walberg is another winning lefthander, and no club has four better right-handers than Sammy Gray, Ed Rommel, Howard Ehmke, and Jack Quinn." Cobb added an intangible factor he thought would help the A's, citing "the spirit to go out and win one for Mr. Mack."[19]

Observers wondered how Mack was able to afford the high salaries he was paying these veterans. "Once an economizer, Mack overnight has become a philanthropist," commented one sportswriter.[20] Bill Dooly went further: "Connie Mack, in all his years of managing, has never been so hopeful, never so anxious or so sanguine of his chances to win a pennant as he is this year. He has scattered money with a lavish and unheard-of abandon to break the drought of pennant-less years, and the outlook is most propitious."[21]

No spring training for Ehmke seemed to lack some sort of injury or illness. At Fort Myers on March 9, 1927, it was surgery to have his tonsils removed. He was out of uniform for the following week and did no pitching for two weeks. In the course of lamenting his physical condition to James Isaminger, Ehmke thought he would be lucky to be pitching by the middle of May. But on March 26 he threw four scoreless innings against the International League Buffalo Bisons before leaving after allowing two runs in the fifth. "I felt all right in this game," Ehmke told Isaminger, "and really didn't intend to pitch more than three innings. My arm is not yet strong, and I didn't bear down, but it felt good enough to make me believe that. it is much better. I want to do some pitching in the [annual city] series against the Phillies, and I want to be ready to take my turn when the championship season opens."[22] While marveling at Ehmke's quick recovery, Isaminger called him "one of the most thorough and resourceful pitchers in Christendom." He doubted if there was another pitcher who had mastered as many kinds of pitches and methods of delivering them. "He has his own ideas about pitching," Isaminger wrote. "The arm means everything in pitching, but you have only to talk two or three times to Ehmke to know that the head plays a big part, too."[23]

On April 15 Ehmke realized his goal of pitching in the A's first series of the season. He lost to the Yankees at New York, 6–3, the A's third straight loss. (There also had been a tie.) In the first inning Babe Ruth

30. A dapper Howard Ehmke sits in his new 1927 Packard. One of the major stories coming out of the A's training camp was how well he would get along with the A's latest addition, Ty Cobb. Both men promised there would be peace between them. *Steve Steinberg Collection.*

hit the first of what would be his record-breaking sixty home runs this season. Ehmke should have known better than to try to "sneak a slow curve over the outside corner," against the Babe, wrote James Harrison the next day. "He has been around a long time and has seen a few things, including the sight of Mr. Ruth belting a slow curve clear out of the park many and many a time."[24]

When asked, at spring training in 1929, what pitches he threw to Ruth, Ehmke said they were mostly slow curves. "Well, I throw him mostly slow stuff, and I try to keep it high and inside. I never would give him a low ball anywhere that he could hit it. All high for him. The idea of high, slow, and inside, of course, is that if he hits it he will pull it foul. It doesn't always work, especially with a great natural hitter like Ruth, but the best you can do is throw it where you think the least harm will result."[25]

Ruth showed the mutual respect the men had for each other in a July 1927 interview with Franklin Yeutter of *Baseball Magazine*. "I've always thought Ehmke was one of the smartest pitchers in baseball and wished many times he was with the Yankees," he said.[26]

With the Yankees at 3-0 and the A's at 0-3, the pundits who had picked Philadelphia to win the pennant perhaps were wondering if they had written off the defending champions prematurely. Ehmke and Cobb stole the headlines in Ehmke's second start, a 3-1 win at Washington. Ehmke was the complete-game winner, while Cobb stole home for the third consecutive game. Bill Dooly described the frustration of the Senators batters with Ehmke: "The tall boy served the Washington sluggers an afternoon's meal of slow stuff that had them breaking their backs with vicious lunges that only resulted in pop flies and easily fielded grounders."[27]

"I'm not quite in shape yet," Ehmke said after the game. "I'm ten pounds below weight as a result of the tonsil operation, and I can't put any strain on my pitching arm. I have to conserve my strength and try to add a few pounds. I hope to show the boys some real pitching later on."[28]

Jack Quinn had strained his arm in an exhibition game against Newark of the International League and pitched only sparingly early in the season.[29] In the A's home opener against the Yankees, he relieved Lefty Grove in the fifth inning of a 5-5 game and went the rest of the way to gain his first win. Davis Walsh featured Quinn in a syndicated article the next day. "Here is a man who has survived four separate phases of self-development in and out of the Major Leagues. . . . Quinn has lived down the vicissitudes during his twenty-four years in baseball, and that kind of thing always intrigues the fancy," he wrote. "Perhaps [Oliver Wendell] Holmes was thinking of John P. Quinn when he wrote 'The Wonderful One-Hoss Shay.'"[30]

In an article in *Baseball Magazine* that spring, Quinn explained his easygoing approach to the game: "To me it always seemed like play. . . . I compared it to swinging a pick in an underground mine chamber. It depends on the point of view."[31] He often spoke of an attitude that had at least something to do with his longevity: "Do your best, and let it go at that. Fussing and stewing and fretting is like throwing grit into the machinery."[32]

On May 1 Quinn got his first start of the season and gave up only two hits in five innings against the Yankees. But they were two-run home runs to Ruth and Gehrig, as the Yankees won, 7–3. Quinn had a rare off day with his control, issuing four walks. Two days later Ehmke defeated the Red Sox, 7–2. "Ehmke could probably have pitched a shutout if he cared to," wrote Bill Dooly, but "Ehmke was well satisfied with going the distance for the second time this season."[33] Dooly was even more impressed after Ehmke's masterful five-hit, 6–1 win at Chicago on May 22. "Ehmke's hurling was undoubtedly the best the Athletics have had this season," he wrote, "and it gave Connie Mack some degree of satisfaction and encouragement."[34]

33

Favorites Fall Short, Far Short

On May 11 Ty Cobb made his first return to Navin Field since leaving Detroit, where he was greeted by a huge crowd. Lefty Grove beat the Tigers that day, helped by two fine catches by Cobb. Jack Quinn followed with a 3–1 win the next day, with Cobb's two doubles leading the attack. Harry Bullion of the *Detroit Free Press* enlivened his account with talk of Quinn's "ancient soup bone" and "doddering old age."[1]

In the following two weeks Grove saved Quinn's third and fourth wins of the year. On June 15 he relieved Quinn again, in Chicago, with one out in the fifth inning and the score tied at four. He overpowered White Sox hitters with five strikeouts the first time through the order. But his error and a "triple" that was misplayed by Cobb in right field led to a 6–4 Chicago win. Grove erupted in anger after the game, hurling his glove against the dugout wall and shouting, "Never gonna finish another game!"[2] Despite Grove's outburst, Mack continued to use him in relief for the rest of the season, including five times in the following month.

The Chicago game was a microcosm of Grove's strengths and weaknesses. His overpowering speed led A's second baseman Max Bishop to declare, "When Grove pitched, I would say to myself, 'Dear God, thank you for allowing me to be on the same team with him.'"[3] Veteran *Sports Illustrated* reporter William Nack wrote vividly, "Grove had a Vesuvian temper that was quite as famous as his fastball, and he left behind him a trail of wrecked watercoolers and ruined lockers."[4]

Despite their erratic pitching, the A's stayed within striking distance of the first-place Yankees into late May. On May 28 Mack confided to one journalist, "Weak pitching by a good staff, and you have it all. It is the biggest mystery I have handled in my entire managerial career."[5] The mystery would continue. When the A's met the Yankees two days later, they were only four games back. After a doubleheader split on Decoration Day, including an ugly 9–8 win by Grove, Ehmke and Quinn started

Tuesday's games, the second of back-to-back twin bills. Quinn lasted only four-plus innings in the opener and left with New York on top, 6–1.

Ehmke did no better in the second game. Despite complaining of a sore shoulder in the spring, he had pitched well this year. He was 5-3 with a 4.10 earned run average before the Yankees pummeled him for eight runs and eleven hits in 4⅓ innings in an 18–5 drubbing. Tony Lazzeri had the big blow for New York, a fifth-inning grand slam, and Ruth had his twelfth career home run off Ehmke in the same inning.[6]

James Harrison was particularly colorful and brutal in his account of the day's games: "Mr. McGillicuddy's valiant lads were drawn, quartered, cooked in boiling oil, massacred and otherwise slaughtered by the champions."[7] The A's pitching staff gave up thirty-six hits on that last day in May, and the club's chances in the pennant race were fading quickly.

Ehmke rebounded from his May 31 thrashing by the Yankees with a 4–1 defeat of Cleveland. He followed with mediocre starts while losing four straight, the last of which was a dreadful performance at Boston on Independence Day. Mack pulled him after the first four Red Sox batters reached base, two on hits and two with walks. All eventually scored in Boston's 11–3 victory.

An extremely upset Mack sent Ehmke home from Boston and told him to get into shape before the club returned to Philadelphia on July 25. Mack said Ehmke had not broken any training rules and that it was not a disciplinary action. Therefore Mack did not fine or suspend him, and Ehmke would still draw his salary. "He has no bad habits," Mack explained, "but when I send him in, his pitching is pitiful. I am unable to tell if he is trying or not, but he certainly does not look as if he were. He is simply of no use to the team."[8]

Mack claimed that Ehmke told him he was not in condition, but Ehmke denied that in a statement issued from his apartment at the Mayfair House in Germantown, Pennsylvania. "I have never been out of condition since joining the Athletics," he said. "The real trouble is that my arm is not working right. . . . I had my tonsils taken out with the hope that their removal would help my arm, but the pitching wing is still in the same condition. . . . I will work out at Shibe Park every day, but I will not do much hurling but will do a lot of running.

I would like the fans to know that I was not sent home because I was out of shape."[9]

While he was in Philadelphia, Ehmke's painful pitching arm would be treated by Billy Morris, the trainer for the University of Pennsylvania football and track teams who also served as a trainer for the 1920 American Olympics teams. "Morris was just the latest to deal with Ehmke's arm problems," noted the *Philadelphia Inquirer*. "He had been treated in the past by healers all over the United States."[10]

On June 25 Philadelphia came to Yankee Stadium trailing the league-leading Yankees by 10 games. The A's swept a doubleheader to cut the lead to 8. Quinn got the start in the first game of the next day's doubleheader. He was sharp in a 4–2 win, giving up only six hits and no walks. "It was a day for veteran experience, the craft of age, the steadiness of the old timer," Monitor wrote in the *New York World*.[11] But the Yankees took the final three games of the series, and their lead was back to 10 games.

Quinn was a workhorse for his club in July. He posted a 4-1 record, including a tough 2–1 loss to the Senators. He nailed down his tenth victory on July 26 against the Tigers. Harry Bullion saluted Quinn, "hale and hearty at 42 [actually 44]," as his saliva that he "anointed the leather with not only made the enemy bats alarmingly impotent but shrunk several perfectly good batting averages."[12] He had lowered his earned run average from 4.76 to 3.34 since June 1. A Detroit reporter noted that Quinn "was standing the pace much better than the other veterans of the club."[13]

In August the A's caught fire; they posted a 21-7 mark. Quinn continued to pitch well, though he had some tough losses. On August 6 he two-hit the Browns for eight innings, but one of the hits was a Ken Williams home run. With the A's down 1–0, Connie Mack lifted him for a pinch hitter, but St. Louis won, 2–0. Five days later Quinn dropped another 2–0 decision, this time to former A's teammate Slim Harriss and the Red Sox. He was able to overcome his lack of run support in his next start, shutting out the Indians, 8–0. John Nolan credited Quinn, "who says he is a young veteran," with the "belated reformation" of the A's pitching staff.[14]

In that game at Cleveland's Dunn Field, the Athletics executed perhaps the most exciting play in baseball: the double suicide squeeze. It was a play that Connie Mack had used in the 1910s. Quinn laid down the bunt, and not only did Zack Wheat score from third, but Chick Galloway came all the way around from second. The play unsettled Cleveland pitcher Garland Buckeye so much that he could not retire any of the next four batters, capped off by a Ty Cobb triple.[15]

While Cobb still used his speed in 1927 (he stole twenty-two bases), he was caught stealing a league-leading sixteen times. This number may not have been purely a function of his slowing down; it was the sixth season in the 1920s that Cobb had been thrown out ten or more times attempting to steal. His batting eye remained as sharp as ever; Cobb finished the season with a .357 average, fifth best in the league.

Ehmke returned to action with an August 2 start at Shibe Park against Chicago. He pitched nine innings and allowed only three earned runs in a game the A's won, 6–5, in twelve innings. On August 11 he shut out the Red Sox. He claimed his sore arm had not completely healed and still pained him when he threw fastballs. Nevertheless, he performed much better after his return, winning six of eight decisions, with a 3.21 earned run average, to finish with a 12-10 record and a 4.22 ERA in 189⅔ innings.

The A's had started the month 21 games out of first, in fourth place. Their hot August merely moved them to 17 games out, albeit now in second place. The Yankees started the month at 73-27 and won their eighty-ninth game on August 31, on their way to a 110-win season.

The Athletics continued to play well in September, motivated by pride and the desire to secure second-place money. Possibly it was the knowledge that Mack was constantly evaluating his club; September baseball is often about players leaving positive impressions for the next season. On September 5 the Red Sox castoffs performed brilliantly against Washington. Ehmke won the first game, 2–1, and Quinn the second, 3–0.

It was Quinn's second consecutive shutout, the only time in his career he accomplished this feat. Just a week earlier his three-hit blanking of the Tigers had generated a *Philadelphia Inquirer* headline on August 30: "Jack Quinn Is Poison to Snarling Bengals." Michigan sportswriters were taken in by too many Quinn stories, including one that claimed he was a veteran of the Spanish-American War.[16] Just before this pitching gem, a syndicated article by Gordon Mackay appeared in sports pages across the country. Quinn told Mackay that he wanted to continue pitching for a few more years. "The old soupbone should last about three more seasons. I want to round out 30 years in baseball."[17]

Quinn earned his fifteenth win against the White Sox on September 15 and finished the season with a 15-10 record. His earned run average was a strong 3.26; the league's average was almost a full run higher at 4.14. Despite some difficult games early in the season, his control ended up being the league's best for the second time: he allowed only 1.65 walks per nine innings.[18] In Ruth's fence-busting season of sixty home runs, Ehmke and Quinn each gave up two to the Babe.

Quinn was the oldest Major League player for the first time in 1927, though he already had been the oldest full-time American League player since at least 1923.[19] During the summer W. R. Hoefer wrote in *Baseball Magazine*:

For though there's silver in his locks and age upon his wing,
When he ascends the twirling box, he makes the onion sing.
. . . .
The writers call him Old Man Quinn when he gets on the hill,
And youthful batters joke and grin and think they'll kill the pill.
But when they swing at what he's got, they find the going tough,
And fill the air with language hot and think he's got enough.
His ancient fin may creak when'er he twirls, as jokers say,
But Jack is apt to still be there when they are laid away.
For players come and players go in their ballyard endeavor,
And with the years they fade and blow. But Quinn goes
    on forever.[20]

With the Yankees holding a 17-game lead over the Athletics, with fifteen to play, Mack admitted that had everyone on his team played up to expectations, they still would not have beaten the New Yorkers. "There's no question about the Yankees being a wonderful team and ranking among the great combinations of baseball," he said. "They were the class of the league. No team could lick them this year, but we could have made a better fight if everybody had played right up to the hilt."[21] Mack praised Miller Huggins, whose fifth pennant left the Yankees' manager one shy of Mack's own total.

34

Chasing the "Greatest Team Ever"

Baseball's experts were far off with their prediction of a pennant for the Athletics in 1927. Nevertheless, as the 1928 season approached, support for Connie Mack's club remained strong, with prognosticators split between the defending World Series champion Yankees and the A's. While the young Athletics were improving and the aging Yankees' core players were a year older, a 19-game deficit was a huge margin to make up.

Philadelphia still had Ty Cobb, whose presence on the club was not without controversy. There was reported resentment among some teammates over his enormous salary. In the summer of 1927 the weekly *Collyer's Eye* reported, "It is said he [Cobb] has made the Philadelphia Athletics topsy-turvy and ruined whatever chances they had of winning the pennant. . . . There are those who will make a wager that if he sticks around Philadelphia another year that the Mackmen will take a big dive cellarward."[1]

Philadelphia sportswriter Bill Dooly said such predictions were nonsense.[2] But New York sports editor Dan Daniel wrote in 1928 that he was talking to one of the A's players when the-forty-one-year-old Cobb and forty-year-old Tris Speaker walked by. The player remarked sarcastically, "Well, there goes our strength." Daniel, who had a reputation for "telling it like it is," added, "Cobb without a doubt is through. He cannot throw, and his legs are very bad. . . . [Connie Mack] is taking the wrong course. Has-beens will not do it."[3] And when Cobb and Speaker retired after the season, Philadelphia sportswriter Gordon Mackay was blunt: "The two principal barriers to victory for the A's last season have gone. Those were Cobb and Speaker."[4]

Speaker, the aging and highly paid outfield great, joined the A's in 1928, after a season with Washington.[5] Syndicated columnist Westbrook Pegler wrote in April, "Every action of theirs [Cobb's and Speaker's] now is considered in proportion to what they would have done ten years ago, and, of course, this makes them look pathetic or comical."[6]

31. Aging superstars Eddie Collins and Ty Cobb (*left and center respectively*) were signed by the Athletics in 1927, and Tris Speaker (*right*) joined them the following season. Cobb and Speaker were liabilities in the field and sources of clubhouse unrest because of their large salaries and limited productivity. After Connie Mack benched them in the summer of 1928, the A's caught fire. *Dennis Goldstein Collection.*

Speaker confessed he was glad Jack Quinn was now his teammate. He told sportswriter Joe Williams that Quinn was the hardest spitballer for him to hit "because Quinn throws every ball alike."[7] The Athletics' backup catcher, Cy Perkins, added, "He has his two spitballs and a fast one. His slow spitter is the most deceptive pitch in the league. It seems as though it is not thrown fast enough to reach the plate. His control is second only to [Yankees pitcher Herb] Pennock's. I have seen Quinn throw a ball into a tin cup tacked up on a fence, and he stood the regulation pitcher's distance from the target."[8]

Mack made four other key additions to the club this season. He reacquired outfielder Bing Miller, who had gone to the Browns in a prelude to the Howard Ehmke deal in 1926. The consistent Miller hit

.331 and .325 in his two seasons for St. Louis and would bat .329 for the A's this season.[9]

Mack purchased Ossie Orwoll from the Milwaukee Brewers of the American Association. Orwoll was an intriguing two-way player, both a pitcher and a position player.[10] Early this season James Isaminger raved about Orwell's promise on the mound: "He has the nerves of a baby. Just remember that the fundamental principal of a money pitcher is self-control. Orwoll has that. He is so cool that he exasperates his opponents."[11]

The other two additions would prove far more important long-term for the Athletics. One was outfielder Mule Haas, whom Mack purchased from Atlanta of the Southern Association. Perhaps Mack was hedging his bet against the aging Cobb and Speaker with the twenty-four-year-old Haas. Finally, on June 1, Mack paid Jack Dunn of the Baltimore Orioles $80,000 for George Earnshaw, a 6-foot-4-inch pitcher with a fastball almost as explosive as Grove's.[12] Bill Dooly said Earnshaw's "scorch ball" was faster than Grove's fastball.[13] Norman Macht explained these acquisitions: "Like a glutton trying to make up for childhood starvation, Connie Mack was haunted by his years in the wilderness with skimpy reserves. He was loading up with reinforcements."[14]

Ehmke and his wife, Marguerite, spent the 1927–28 holiday season in California, combining pleasure with business. On New Year's Day they were in Pasadena for the Rose Bowl, where they saw Stanford defeat the University of Pittsburgh, 7–6. On the business side, Howard rented one of his tarpaulins to the University of California. The school used it to protect the field during a rainy week in Berkeley, allowing the Golden Bears to play the University of Pennsylvania Quakers on a dry field. The tarp worked so well that the university purchased it for $7,000.[15]

Ehmke received his 1928 contract offer along with a letter from Mack. "The enclosed contract will enable you to make more money this coming season than you have ever made in baseball," Mack wrote, "The only thing being required of you that you win more games than you did last season, which, with a team such as we have, should be easy for you if you are in the proper condition." Mack specified that for any game Ehmke started and the A's won, he would be credited with the victory for purposes of the contract. There was also a clause awarding him $200 for every game the A's won that he finished. "If you cannot win twenty games for our club, then you do not deserve anything like a ten-thousand-dollar salary," Mack wrote.[16] Such an incentive-based contract was not common, but it may have been Mack's approach to motivating Ehmke.

Looking forward to the upcoming season, Ehmke said: "My arm was all wrong in 1927, but I fully expect to win a lot of games in 1928. I have had it treated regularly, and I want to prove to Connie Mack that I can win for him."[17] Ehmke told a Philadelphia reporter his arm had been so sore for most of the first half of the 1927 season that he could barely raise it. It hurt so much it often woke him during the night, and he would have to get up and rub it. "The pains in his arm and shoulder have all disappeared now," the reporter wrote. "He looks much better than he did this time a year ago, when he had his tonsils removed during the training season."[18]

But as spring training progressed, Ehmke's arm trouble returned. Soreness "ran from a point in the right shoulder to the deltoid muscle. A fluid formed between the bone and the muscle," wrote John J. Nolan. "Ehmke was tortured every time he attempted to throw a ball."[19]

Questioned by a *Los Angeles Times* reporter about the upcoming pennant race, Ehmke predicted that the Yankees would not repeat in 1928, reminding everyone that all dynasties eventually fall. He was noticeably silent when asked about Ty Cobb's return to the A's.[20]

During spring training Ehmke claimed he now had mastered the "hesitation pitch," a delivery he had been working on for eight years. (The pitch had now been ruled legal when there were no base runners.) "There's really nothing to it," he said, and then the pitcher, often called the game's "brainiest," went into great detail describing what there was to it:

I had an idea eight years ago while I was in Detroit. I noticed the batters were taking a liking to my pitches and were waving their bats around in perfect cohesion with my pitching motions. I then decided it was up to me to stop them. When I figured out how the batters timed my pitches, I thought up the "hesitation" to throw them off their stride.

For instance, when a free swinger steps to the plate, he watches the pitcher closely. When the windup starts, he sets himself and commences swinging. When I pause before delivering the ball, I try to catch him with the bat half-way round and then the hitter has no power behind the poke he takes at the ball. It's largely a question of timing the batter's swing. Batters with powerful wrists like Cobb, Sisler, and others cannot be caught napping, but I always try to work it on Babe Ruth, and sometimes I have succeeded.[21]

Jack Quinn reported to Fort Myers after his usual visit to the baths and hills of Hot Springs, "as enthusiastic in training camp as a kid recruit," in the words of one Philadelphia reporter.[22] Quinn told sports editor George Daley, "There isn't any reason why a man shouldn't keep on pitching until he is fifty. . . . I am always in the same sort of condition. . . . My advice to young players is not to let themselves slip back during the winters—keep hard at something and be careful not to eat too much."[23]

After falling short of the pennant the past three seasons, Mack decided to change his luck and removed the elephant emblem from his club's uniform.[24] One thing that had not changed was his respect for his oldest player. "Jack Quinn is a wonder," Mack told Joe Vila that spring. "He's never out of shape, works like a Trojan, and seems to improve with old age. He is one of my aces and will be asked to shoulder a heavy burden this year."[25]

The A's again opened the season with three straight losses, including two to the Yankees. "Our trouble has been with our pitching," Mack said. "I am going to use Jack Quinn against Washington tomorrow. Maybe he can start us off. Jack is a great pitcher. I like the way he works. He's trying all the time, bearing down. They beat him now and then, but Jack gives his best and is always in there making a ball game out of it."[26] Quinn's best was not good enough this day, and the A's lost their fourth straight. The Senators scored six runs against him in 1⅓ innings on their way to an 11–6 win.

In discussing his pitchers, Mack said he hoped Ehmke would soon be in shape to pitch. The thirty-four-year-old Ehmke had formed a habit, according to Mack, that the manager wanted him to correct, one that was in direct contrast to his description of Quinn. Once again echoing previous critics of Ehmke, Mack told Bill Dooly that he did not think Ehmke was giving it "his all" from start to finish. He wanted him to pitch with everything he had for the entire game. Dooly agreed with Mack's criticism. He called Ehmke "one of the brainiest pitchers in the game, blessed with an unusual assortment of curves and speed." But, wrote Dooly, "Howard has formed the habit of easing up too much to conserve himself for the pinches. The result is that while he is saving himself, the other fellows are hammering his delivery for runs that beat him."[27]

In late April John Kieran wrote that the A's had two of the best pitchers in the game in Lefty Grove and Rube Walberg, but the staff fell off considerably after that. "For some strange reason [Eddie] Rommel and 'Empty' Ehmke have been off form for a full year." Kieran attributed the A's coming up short in 1927 to the ineffectiveness of those two pitchers. If they should remain ineffective, he predicted, it would severely hurt their chances of catching New York in 1928.[28] Evidently Kieran thought little of the forty-four-year-old Quinn and did not even mention him.

However, Quinn soon met the expectations of Mack and exceeded those of Kieran. The Athletics won thirteen of their next fourteen games after opening the season with the four losses, and Quinn won three of them. He shut out the Senators on April 26, a game in which fellow graybeards Cobb and Speaker had triples. "Three of baseball's fugitives from Father Time," Shirley Povich of the *Washington Post* called them.[29] "Youth today was served right on its collective chin," wrote Dooly, "while three aged figures stood over its prostrate form in pose triumphant."[30]

Grove, at 4-1, and Walberg, at 3-1, also bounced back after losing their first starts. Even Rommel won a game during the streak. Only Ehmke, among the starters, failed to contribute—or even appear. He did not make his 1928 debut until May 17, when he pitched a scoreless inning of relief against Chicago.

After Quinn shut out the Indians on May 15, John Nolan wrote, "Quinn's pitching this season has verged on the sensational."[31] It was his fourth consecutive complete game, a stretch in which he walked only one batter. Quinn explained to Dooly that he throws the ball "'in there.' He keeps the ball somewhere near the plate, rarely giving the batter a good one to strike at."[32]

Quinn would issue a career-low 1.45 walks every nine innings in 1928.[33] He often attributed his pitching success to control. "If I put the ball over, I'll put the batter under," he told columnist George Moriarty, a once and future umpire, who was now also the Detroit Tigers' manager.[34] Just after his forty-fifth birthday, Quinn explained that the key to this uncanny ability was his conditioning. Dooly marveled, "A big, burly muscular fellow is Quinn. . . . He is so broad of shoulder and deep of chest that his powerfully built frame dwarfs his six feet of height. . . . [He has] eyes that are of a faded blue and set widely apart in a strong, rugged, sun-tanned face."[35]

During that mid-May series in Cleveland, Mack made a remarkable admission to a *Sporting News* columnist. When asked what he thought of his club's pennant chances, the usually taciturn Mack replied, "I haven't got a pitcher on my ball club, barring Jack Quinn. All of them, except Jack, pitch with their arms and not with their heads. . . . Quinn alone, who is old enough to be the father of almost any other pitcher on my staff, combines mechanical ability with good head-work."[36]

On May 21 Quinn beat the Senators again, going the distance in a thirteen-inning game and delivering the game-winning hit. The A's record now stood at 18-8, but they trailed the Yankees by 3½ games. When New York took five of six from Philadelphia the following week, the lead grew to eight games. The first game of the series (and the first of a doubleheader) was a 9–7 slugfest in which the Yankees reached Grove for ten hits. A record thirteen future Hall of Famers, seven for the A's and six for Yankees, took part in the game.[37] In the first game of the next day's doubleheader, Ehmke made his first start of the season, losing to Herb Pennock, 4–2. He pitched seven innings, allowing five hits and striking out six. The game was tied at 1–1 until the seventh, when he gave up a home run to Lou Gehrig with two men on base.

Gordon Mackay saluted the seemingly invincible Yankees, "absolutely the greatest ball club in this country—one of the greatest, if not the mightiest, in the history of baseball. . . . It is almost a flawless team. . . . Nothing, save a railroad accident, earthquake, or assassination seems likely to wrest the flag from the champions in this year, 1928."[38]

Quinn was ineffective in the fifth game against New York, lasting only two innings, in which he yielded four earned runs. A positive for the Athletics was the return of Al Simmons to the lineup. Rheumatism had sidelined him for the first six weeks of the season, and as late as June 8 he was batting only .226.[39] But the biggest disappointment in the series was Grove, who dropped two games. He would post a 1-6 record with a 5.44 earned run average against the Yankees in 1928.[40] An exasperated Connie Mack told reporters in June, "It just seems that when Grove can't beat the Yankees, nobody can."[41]

Ehmke recorded his first win of the season on May 30. The biggest crowd at Fenway Park since Boston's glory days of the 1910s saw the A's sweep the Red Sox in the Memorial Day doubleheader. Ehmke won the opener, 8–1, a complete-game five-hitter, and Quinn, the other A's pitcher Mack had rescued from the Red Sox, won the second game, 9–2. "My arm felt good and strong at the finish," Ehmke said after his win. "It gives a fellow a lot of confidence to win, and I think I can turn in a few victories now and help the team make another drive at those Yankees."[42]

A loss in his next start and one in relief dropped Ehmke's record to 1-3 before he rebounded to win his next three starts. He extended the streak with a victory against the Yankees on June 29, a game that Grove finished when New York mounted a late rally. John Nolan noted that Ehmke had used different pitching styles in this game, shifting from a sidearm delivery to an underhand one. "Ehmke discarded his 'hesitation pitch,'" he wrote, "but evolved several new methods of fancy chucking. He pitched hurriedly and seldom gave the Yanks a chance to dig their spikes in and take a toe hold."[43]

Jack Quinn's 10–5 win against the Yankees on June 20 was not an artistic performance, but it was a gutsy one. After giving up five runs on five hits in the third inning, he settled down and shut out New York the rest of the way. "His superb flinging heartened his teammates," wrote Nolan, and the A's rallied with eight runs.[44]

On June 27 Connie Mack lamented what his team was up against: "I have a great club, but the Yanks are the sort of club that comes along once in a generation."[45] His A's then dropped four of five against New York in the next week and fell 13½ games back. They had now lost twelve of sixteen games against the Yankees. Mack continued to air his frustration with his pitching staff. "I give them plenty of rest. I tell them what to do, but I can't do it for them."[46]

Mack continued by critiquing each of his starters: "I'd like to know how to get them working in some kind of rotation. Quinn has pitched well for us, but really needs five days of rest between games. Grove and Walberg can pitch every four days but are better with four days off.

Ehmke—I'm lucky to get a game out him in seven days. . . . If we don't get some pitching soon, we won't even finish second."[47]

James Harrison wrote that Philadelphia still had a good chance to capture the pennant, "if Ruth contracts yellow fever, Lazzeri breaks his leg, Lou Gehrig comes down with sleeping sickness, and George Pipgras suffers complete paralysis of the right arm."[48] Many Philadelphia observers had given up. Gordon Mackay went so far as to write on July 1, "The dejection of the clan has become so pronounced that nothing short of a complete rebuilding will make the Mackmen a factor in the 1929 race. This year's battle for the flag is over."[49] Virtually every baseball fan in America believed the Yankees would win going away. They would all be proven wrong.

35

A Torrid Pennant Race

New York's doubleheader sweep on July 1, 1928, pushed the Yankees' record to 52-16, a .765 winning percentage. The Athletics then caught fire and won twenty-five of thirty-one games the rest of the month, an .806 winning clip, while New York went 18-15 the rest of July. By the end of the month the A's had closed to within 5½ games of New York.

Between June 30 and July 21 Jack Quinn won five games. When he beat the Tigers on July 16 by the score of 3–2, Mack said, "Jack deserves all the praise that can be heaped upon him. He has pitched great ball for us, and I think he is a wonder."[1] Quinn was a modest man, and while the win over Detroit pushed his record to 12-4, he told reporters, "There's nothing remarkable about my pitching. I always try to have good control, placing the ball exactly where I want it." He went on to talk about his eating habits. "Maybe my diet has something to do with my effectiveness. In hot weather, I last all day on a pint of milk and eat a hearty dinner in the cool of the evening."[2]

An editorial in the *Philadelphia Record* took note of the change in fortunes of the two leading contenders, New York and Philadelphia, and cited the play of youngsters Jimmie Foxx, Mickey Cochrane, Mule Haas, and rookie Ossie Orwoll. The twenty-year-old Foxx had played first base and caught early in the season but was now the regular third baseman and already one of the top batters in the league. The editorial writer suggested the pennant race was far from over and predicted the winner would likely be decided in September, when the teams would meet for the final time in a four-game series in New York.[3] If "the ancient arms of Jack Quinn and Howard Ehmke stand up," a New York account reported, "American League fans may yet have something to get excited about."[4] Quinn with fourteen wins and Ehmke with seven had come through for Mack.

Quinn won his fifteenth game when he shut out Washington, 8–0, on August 10, a game in which he "so nearly approached perfection."[5]

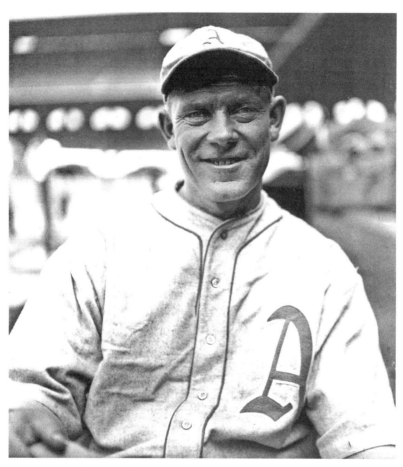

32. Jack Quinn felt Connie Mack was the best manager he ever played for. With Mack at the helm, it was like having a tenth man on the field, Quinn said, since he knew how to position fielders against opposing batters. "I have thrown off fifteen years since I am with Connie Mack," Quinn said when he joined the Athletics. In 1928 he won eighteen games, the same number he had won both eight and eighteen years earlier. *SDN-068487, Chicago Sun-Times/Chicago Daily News Collection, Chicago History Museum.*

Only one batted ball got out of the infield in the first five innings, and three of the five men who reached base were wiped out on double plays. Bill Dooly saluted "that everlasting patriarchal perennial by the name of Jack Quinn."[6] In what would be a rarity in today's game, he "pitched to contact" (to a lineup with four future Hall of Famers). He had no strikeouts and allowed no walks.[7]

Mack continued to praise the veteran he had picked up on waivers three years earlier: "He is an inspiration to the entire team, and he is always willing to help a youngster. . . . He knows baseball as few players do. He has little to say on the bench, but in a pinch, I would rather take advice from him than any other man on my club."[8]

Quinn's shutout followed Ehmke's three-hit gem the day before, his eighth straight win, which kept the A's 4½ games behind the Yankees. Al Simmons's sixth-inning bases-loaded home run led the offense.[9] "When Ehmke is right there is no better right-hander in baseball," wrote John Nolan. "He is cunning, has almost perfect control, a sweeping curve that sails upward, and he knows every batter's weakness and how to work the corners."[10]

Ehmke was clearly pleased with his performance. "My arm feels great," he said after the game. "Occasionally I get a sharp pain across the shoulder, but not enough to bother me. I haven't felt as good or pitched as well in two years as I did in the last month."[11] But this would be Ehmke' final 1928 win, as he lost his next five decisions to finish the season at 9-8. His earned run average rose from 2.62 to 3.55 over his final seven games, all but one as a starter. His 139⅓ innings pitched were the fewest in his career to date, other than his injury-plagued 1915 season with Buffalo.

Ehmke's one relief appearance was on August 30 against Boston. A's starter George Earnshaw had allowed only three hits and struck out nine through seven innings, yet the A's trailed, 1–0. Earnshaw was lifted for a pinch hitter, and Ehmke took over. After Philadelphia rallied for the lead in the eighth, Ehmke gave up two runs in the ninth, with Red Ruffing's double the key blow, as the Red Sox won, 3–2.[12]

Ehmke had been erratic all season, and according to Norman Macht, Ehmke and Mack "had an understanding: whenever the pitcher felt himself weakening during a game, he was to tell the manager."[13] If Ehmke felt he was not sharp this afternoon, he did not mention it to Mack.

"It was a dismal exhibition the slender right hander offered when he went to the mound," wrote Joe Dugan. Ehmke "apparently had nothing from the moment he entered the game," he added.[14] Mack had Eddie Rommel warming up in the bullpen but chose to let Ehmke pitch to Ruffing, after he gave up a hit and a walk. The A's lost the opportunity to cut New York's lead to a game and a half, as the Yankees lost at Washington.

The A's kept winning. Their 19-9 record in August drew them within two games of first place. The Yankees had cooled off after their blazing start and won only thirty-four of sixty games in the two summer months. A batting slump, combined with injuries, was to blame. John Kieran noted, "The rise of the Mackmen has been swift and spectacular." He captured the sinking feeling the Yankees and their fans surely had when he wrote, "There is, of course, the time-honored tale of the gentleman who fell out of a window on the twentieth floor and, passing the tenth-floor level, reported that he was all right so far."[15]

One of the keys to the turnaround was Mack's benching of Cobb and Speaker and going with a younger outfield. July 26 was Cobb's last start; he pinch-hit nine times after that and hit safely only once. Speaker's last start was on July 16; he went hitless in his seven pinch-hitting appearances after that date. An editorial in the *Philadelphia Record* cast sentimentality aside and stated, "It is easy to see the reason for this tremendous outburst of fresh enthusiasm and revived energy. The aging limbs have been benched, the senile eye gazes over the scene from the dugout; the worn legs and palsied arms resting on the laurels which they splendidly won in the long ago."[16]

Simmons (just turned twenty-six), Mule Haas (only twenty-four), and the veteran Bing Miller (almost thirty-four) became fixtures in the outfield. Simmons hit .351 in 1928, despite missing thirty-four games due to rheumatism in his legs and ankles. Haas hit .280 in the first of four solid seasons in Philadelphia. The consistent Miller hit .329. Jimmie Foxx was emerging as a dangerous hitter for both average (.328) and distance (13 home runs in only 118 games). On June 22 Ruth declared, "There is the coming long-distance hitting champion. He's only twenty years old and a natural player. He does everything right. He's the greatest young player I ever saw."[17]

After he hit .375 the first month of the season, Joe Hauser's comeback stalled. As his batting average plummeted (he would finish the season at .260), the versatile Ossie Orwoll moved from the pitcher's mound to first base. He hit .306, to go with his 6-5 record on the mound.[18] His fielding earned raves, even a comparison to Hal Chase.[19] Connie Mack declared in early August, "Orwoll is a wonder. His fielding at first base has opened my eyes. He makes plays that look impossible.

He's death on ground balls, and he covers so much territory that it's almost like having two men out there instead of one."[20]

On Friday, September 7, the Athletics swept a doubleheader in Boston, while the Yankees were outscored 17–1 in dropping a pair of games to Washington. Mack's club had climbed into a first-place tie with the Yankees. When the A's took two more games from the Red Sox on Saturday, while New York beat the Senators, Philadelphia was alone in first place. In a remarkable scene, Red Sox fans cheered Mack and his A's, perhaps in admiration of Mack and in part because they were pleased the Yankees might be dethroned. Many fans were tiring of seeing at least one New York City team appear in the World Series in seven of the past eight seasons.

The nation turned its attention to the four-game series between these top two teams at Yankee Stadium, beginning with a doubleheader on Sunday, September 9. Babe Ruth told Dan Daniel, "We can beat those Athletics any old time, and they know it and act as if they knew it. If this pennant depends on licking those birds, we're in already."[21]

New York sportswriter and future baseball commissioner Ford Frick wrote, "The man the Yankees fear most is Quinn. Old Jack with his slow stuff and his ability to mix them up is ever dangerous."[22] A's coach and former catcher Ira Thomas revealed late this season that after practicing the pitch all his life, Quinn finally had perfected a slow ball that he barely moistened, what he called "a dry spitter" and "a sort of a first cousin to the knuckle ball."[23] Bill Dooly described his delivery, which "slowly carried the ball through the air without a spin. It sailed along as though it was sliding on a greased rail. Until it reached the plate. Then it sort of hesitated, did a little shimmy, and broke away."[24]

One of the largest crowds in Yankee Stadium history, a reported 85,265, passed through the gates.[25] The *New York American* estimated two hundred thousand fans showed up, trying to gain admission.[26] Philadelphia reporter John McCullough described the scene as perhaps exceeding the tumult of any World Series game:

> Mob is the word. It pushed. It shoved. . . . It was a pickpocket's paradise and a rotten place to wear a newly pressed suit or a sprained wrist. . . . The expression, 'Sticking to the rafters,' was

quite literally true. Every beam was inhabited. The press box would not have admitted the infant daughter of a Lilliputian. . . . Above the field, like the moan of a breaking surf, was the interminable, unintelligible rumble of a baseball crowd keyed up so tight that it was on the verge of hysteria. . . . It was a real baseball crowd, nervous as a finely trained race horse, inquisitive as a terrier in a bone yard, caustic as corrosive sublimate, and utterly happy.[27]

Quinn was well-rested for this showdown series; he had not pitched since August 28. He started the first game, and "For five innings, that time-defying arm and cool calculations which came out from under Jack's cap had the Bronx blasters entirely stopped. And then the storm broke," wrote Bill Slocum of the *New York American*.[28] Quinn was touched for three runs on four hits and a walk in the sixth, when he was pulled, and the Yankees, behind George Pipgras, won, 5–0, to retake first place.

One Philadelphia writer mournfully wrote, "Old Jack Quinn worked that sorrow ball of his on the Yanks for all it was worth for five innings, but as the doctor told us after grandpa died, his age was against him."[29] James Isaminger felt the strain on Quinn was too great "after curbing the swashbucklers of the stadium for five innings," but the pitcher did not say much after the game.[30] It was Quinn's tenth loss in his last fifteen decisions against his old club.

The A's had a 3–1 lead in the seventh inning of the second game when Jimmie Foxx came up with the bases loaded. "Here was the sort of situation from which heroes emerge," wrote Richards Vidmer. "But the responsibility was too much for the 19-year-old [*sic*] kid."[31] He struck out, and the Yankees rallied for a 7–3 win, with Bob Meusel's grand slam the deciding blow. "Foxx is too young to bear up well under the strain," said Mack, "but he's too good to take out of the lineup."[32] Mack lamented after the twin loss, "I don't know why it is, our boys just can't seem to play their regular game against them."[33]

Lefty Grove took his 22-6 record to the mound in the third game.[34] He shut out New York for six innings and led, 3–1, after seven. This time the Yankees' deciding blow came from Babe Ruth (a two-run home run, his forty-ninth of the season, which provided the 5–3 final score), and the Yankees' lead was up to 2½ games. "The gaunt, troubled old man [Mack] was visibly shaken by the blast, which shattered his dreams of a baseball empire," wrote one Philadelphia columnist.[35]

The following spring, with his teammates sitting in a Washington DC hotel lobby during an Opening Day rainout, Jack Quinn told a fascinating "inside tale" to columnist Bill Dooly. Quinn said the A's had been intimidated by batting practice home runs Ruth and Lou Gehrig hit before the September 9 games the previous fall. "This is a tale of psychology that smacked perhaps of fiction," Dooly wrote, "but Jack Quinn, veteran of a quarter century of pitching, a keen observer and student of diamond happenings, related it." Quinn said, "Our fellows sat there looking at them with their mouths open and their tongues hanging out. They cowed us before we even had a smack at them. I knew it when I heard one of our boys say: 'Gee, look at those guys hit.'" He went on to say, "The Yanks were just as afraid as we were. But we showed it, and they didn't."[36]

Ehmke started the fourth game of this showdown series. He left with two outs in the eighth, with the Athletics clinging to a 3–2 lead. Earlier in the inning the Yanks had one out with Mark Koenig at second and Gehrig and Ruth due up. Ehmke struck out Gehrig and chose to intentionally walk Ruth. More likely, Mack made that decision, ignoring the baseball dogma of never intentionally putting the potential winning run on base. Ehmke hit the next batter, Bob Meusel, in the arm with a fastball to load the bases. An upset Meusel started walking toward the mound, and Ehmke moved to meet him, but umpire Bill Dinneen quickly intervened. "[Bob] didn't mean anything," Ehmke said later. "I know Bob; we were in the submarine service together. It was just part of the riding the two teams were giving each other."[37]

Up next was Tony Lazzeri, and Ehmke twisted his knee on his first pitch and limped off the field. Mack rushed Ossie Orwoll to the mound. A wild Orwoll walked Lazzeri, forcing Koenig home with the tying run. The A's broke the tie in the top of the ninth, and Rube Walberg pitched a hitless home ninth to salvage the one game. The team left New York trailing the Yankees by 1½ games.

Ehmke's injured knee would keep him out for ten days, effectively ending his season. "I hated to walk off the field," he said. "I would have

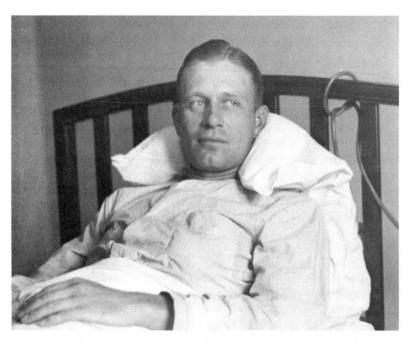

33. Facing the Yankees in a crucial September 12, 1928, game, Howard Ehmke injured his knee while throwing a pitch to Tony Lazzeri. He ended up in a Philadelphia hospital and did not return to duty for the rest of the season. *Special Collections Research Center, Temple University Libraries, Philadelphia, Pennsylvania, Philadelphia Evening Bulletin Collection.*

had [Lazzeri] breaking his back going after my curves. It's tough to be forced out of a ball game that you've just about won with only four men to retire."[38] The statement about Ehmke's injury from A's vice-president John Shibe read, "He is in the hospital now, and it will take ten days before he is able to leave. He has no broken bones, but the injury is sort of a charley horse of the knee."[39]

In a 1952 interview with Ed Pollock, Ehmke recalled an incident from the third game of that series with the Yankees. "Remember the big weekend in New York when the Yankees practically knocked us out of the pennant race? Before the [third] game . . . I saw Cobb talking to Lazzeri. That was strange, but I didn't think much about it," he told Pollock. "In one inning, Grove walked Lazzeri, and as Tony came down toward the first base line—our dugout was on that side—he was saying something, and it was apparently directed at me." Ehmke said he was completely surprised, and while he didn't hear what Lazzeri said, it was easy to determine it was not complimentary. He had no idea what had set Lazzeri off but just assumed Tony thought he had been riding him.

"More than two years later," Ehmke continued, "I was in Washington on business. The Yankees were there, too. Passing their clubhouse, I looked in. Lazzeri was sitting nearby. I asked him about the incident in New York. Lazzeri said Cobb had told third baseman Joe Dugan to tell me that you were going to knock me down, and Cobb told me the same thing himself. I don't think you can call that the act of a good team player," Ehmke concluded, while reiterating his long-held animosity toward his former manager.[40]

A week later Mack made some revealing comments to Philadelphia reporters: "All ball teams, good ones and bad ones alike, have a few players who are temperamentally unsuited to rough uphill work, but my team is over-provided with them."[41] Surely Mack was including Grove in this group. He later said, "We could have won in '28 if I had been able to handle Grove."[42] The pitcher still "doesn't capitalize [on] his abilities and his intrinsic worth as he should," wrote Gordon Mackay that summer. "He has a fatal weakness somewhere in his armor."[43] These words seem like strange criticism of a pitcher who fashioned a 24-8 record and led the league in strikeouts for the fourth straight season. But baseball people, led by Mack, saw even greater potential.[44]

While Jack Quinn did not get the job done against the Yankees, he was at his best in his next two starts, almost singlehandedly keeping his team in the pennant race. On September 15, while the Yankees lost in St. Louis, he shut out the Indians, 5–0. Isaminger wrote, "The grizzled senior of the hill . . . was never in peril, in blurring the eyes of the Indians, and keeping them tamed all afternoon."[45] This drew the Athletics to within a half-game of New York, with two weeks left to the season.

Five days later, after the A's had fallen two games back, Quinn again drew his club close to the lead. As the Yankees lost a home game in twelve innings to the White Sox, Quinn took the mound in Detroit. He beat the Tigers, 6–1, his second straight six-hitter, giving up only an unearned run. Again Isaminger led the praise when he wrote, "Jack

Quinn, the gray beard of baseball, turned in another stunning display of high-pressure pitching."[46] Harry Bullion seemed as frustrated as Detroit's hitters, but perhaps less respectful, when he wrote, "Methuselah was good, and when he is good, it is too bad for the Tigers. . . . It is exasperating to the average athlete as determined as the Tigers started out to be when a tottering wreck like Quinn squirts saliva all over a baseball and nonchalantly—that's the way it appeared—tosses it up for their inspection."[47]

Once again the A's fell back in the pennant race between Quinn's starts. When he next took the mound, on September 24, they were again two games back of the Yankees. Quinn was undone this day by four errors, resulting in a painful 6–2 loss to the Browns, while the Yankees were beaten by Cleveland. Surely he was tested to stick to one of his "Ten Tips" he shared with James Isaminger earlier in the season: "Don't let bad breaks or errors dishearten you, and never criticize members of your support."[48]

The A's were running out of games and time. They won their next four contests, but so did the Yankees. Philadelphia finished with ninety-eight wins, 2½ games behind New York. Just as Grove had little success against New York in 1928 (a 1-6 record), so too did the A's (6-16 against New York). "Connie Mack had no 'money' pitcher in the 1928 race, if you omit Jack Quinn, senior of the peak, who really did sterling work all along," wrote Isaminger as the season came to an end. "Quinn did approach the [former A's great pitchers Eddie] Plank–[Chief] Bender stencil, but he could not carry the burden alone."[49]

Quinn's 18-7 record was his best full-season winning percentage ever (.720), and his 2.90 earned run average was more than a run better than the league average of 4.04.[50] He started twenty-eight games and made only three relief appearances. In 1933 he looked back at this season as proof that "The best years of a pitcher are always the easiest." He explained, "Everything was going fine. I was starting every fifth day regularly as clockwork. . . . I was never overtaxed and so kept going consistently all season."[51]

36

A Fast Start for the A's

The torrid finish to the 1928 American League pennant race led some observers to doubt a Yankees' repeat in 1929, though the New Yorkers still had their believers. One was James Gould, who called their primary challengers, the Athletics, "perennial second-placers" in his spring predictions.[1] A survey of baseball writers by Dick Farrington of the *Sporting News* gave the edge to the Yankees, in no small part because they "always have had the Indian sign on Mr. Mack's mournful men."[2]

On January 30, 1929, Howard Ehmke and Jack Quinn were part of a group of Athletics who got an early start to spring training. All traveled by train, including Ehmke from Detroit and Quinn from Chicago. Their destination was Hot Springs, Arkansas, where they would spend three weeks before heading to the A's Florida training camp at Fort Myers.[3] An approving Connie Mack wrote George Brenner, the president of the Hot Springs Chamber of Commerce, "Have always been of the opinion that the baths at Hot Springs were more beneficial to athletes than any other course they could adopt."[4]

"He looks ready to go," said a pleased Mack in late February, after Ehmke pitched a morning session and threw curves and fastballs with no sign of trouble. "Those Hot Springs baths are going to be a good investment."[5] Ehmke's 12-10 record in 1927 and his 9-8 mark in 1928 had been big disappointments to his manager. By early April Ehmke was confident he would have a good year. He would have to if he wanted to continue in the Major Leagues, warned Mack.

This year "will make or break Ehmke as a big-league pitcher," Mack announced shortly before the 1929 season opened. "I am convinced if Howard doesn't come through for us this year, it will be because he simply hasn't got it in him. . . . I am depending heavily on Howard this season to take a regular turn in the box from the start of the season and be one of our most successful pitchers. Ehmke feels well this year.

34. Ossie Orwoll was a rare two-way player, one who could pitch as well as hit. A 1927 sensation for the American Association's Milwaukee Brewers, he batted .370 and posted a 17-6 record. Connie Mack raved about him during his 1928 rookie season, when he hit .306 and won six games for the A's. Writers spoke of his "intestinal fortitude" that year; in 1929 they were writing about his "shoddy habits." Mack released him in August 1929, and Orwoll never returned to the Majors. *Steve Steinberg Collection.*

He's strong, and he has a lot of spirit and ambition. If he doesn't win for us this season, I'll be pretty well convinced that his days as a big leaguer are about over."[6]

Mack had other reasons to be concerned about his team. Shortstop Joe Boley's arm had gone dead, and Al Simmons's rheumatism, which limited him to 119 games in 1928, had returned.[7] Moreover, the club seemed listless during spring training, and the normally mild-mannered Mack ripped into his players when he felt their intensity was missing.[8]

Mack was especially upset with pitcher–first baseman Ossie Orwoll for failing "to observe training rules." Bill Dooly wrote, "Orwoll's salvation depends wholly upon himself."[9] That salvation did not come, and Orwoll's last Major League game would be on August 21. One player Mack was especially happy with was Jimmie Foxx. In mid-March Mack told Foxx, "You're my first baseman," the position he would play virtually the rest of his career.[10]

Foxx appeared in only thirty-six games in 1925 and 1926, mostly as a catcher. But the A's already had Mickey Cochrane, the league's best young catcher. Mack was forced to find a place in the field for Foxx and started playing him at first base in 1927, when he was still only nineteen years old.

When Foxx first joined the A's in 1925, Mack said, "He's only 17 years old, and he's awkward and unpolished, but if ever I saw a great ball player in the rough, there he is. Some day, mark my words, his name will be as well-known as Ruth's, Cobb's, Collins's, or anybody else's."[11] AP sports editor Alan Gould said, "Foxxy, as Mack affectionately called his young recruit, was a player after the old master's heart, possessed of the rough natural ability Connie delighted in moulding [sic] successfully."[12]

In his spring preview article, Gould noted that one thing the A's had going for them was that Jack Quinn was still on the job. With every season, his mere presence—let alone his excellence—drew more and more attention, as did the mystery of his age. "I'm not saying how old I am," Quinn told Will Wedge in June. "I'll tell it all in time; I'll tell the truth." While we have seen above that he truly did not know when he was born, Quinn added the most important point to Wedge: "The main thing is that I can still pitch no matter how old I am."[13]

Quinn, as always, reported to the A's in top physical condition. In addition to his hikes and thermal baths in Hot Springs, he spent his winter months, as usual, hunting and hiking the hills around his cabin in Roaring Creek, Pennsylvania.[14] When he returned to his home in the

Chicago area, he worked as a bail bondsman, a job that also required a lot of walking. He also bowled every week at former White Sox catcher and manager Ray Schalk's South Side bowling alley.[15]

Quinn had a competitive fire behind his quiet demeanor. In the conversation with his teammates during the Opening Day rainout in Washington DC (discussed in chapter 35), he warned them not to count on Yankees' injuries if they wanted to wrest the pennant from them. "What we have to do is fight the Yanks, lick 'em, and make 'em like it. Forget they're the Yanks. . . . And when you feel scared of them, just remember they're only human, too: that they are just as scared as the other fellow." Quinn's demeanor, concluded sportswriter Bill Dooly, was "Fight and Guts."[16]

Quinn made his first start of the season in Yankee Stadium three days later and pitched one of his finest games but dropped a 2–1 decision to Waite Hoyt. Center fielder Mule Haas lost two late-inning fly balls in the sun that were charitably scored as doubles; each resulted in a run.[17] "It was the toughest game I ever lost in the sixteen years I've been in the Majors," Quinn said.[18]

A week later he had another start against New York, this time at home, and he prevailed, 5–2. James Isaminger wrote, "Quinn, meticulously bathing the ball with saliva, so nonplussed his adversaries that they could collect only six hits."[19] Yankees hitters were moaning afterward, "How come we can't hit that cripple ball?" said one. "It ain't got nothing on it—just floats up so big you can count the stitches—yet when you hit it, the furthest it goes is [to] the shortstop."[20] Even their manager, Miller Huggins, just a few years older than Quinn, sighed, "I wish I could still play second base the way Quinn can pitch."[21] After Quinn's two New York performances, Grantland Rice wrote, "To judge by the way he opened the new season, Quinn may be working in the big leagues when he is up around fifty, and that would be something to shoot at for a carload of generations."[22]

Despite his claim that his sore arm had healed, Ehmke did not make his first regular-season appearance until May 10, pitching scoreless eighth and ninth innings in relief in a 9–0 loss at Cleveland. The Athletics had a six-game winning streak, with a 20-8 record and a 2-game lead over the Browns when Mack chose to use Ehmke again two weeks later. In the opener of a four-game series against Washington, the Senators jumped out to an early 8–0 lead. After the A's rallied to tie the score with an eight-run fourth inning, Ehmke entered the game and held the Senators scoreless over the final five innings. Bing Miller's home run in the home fifth gave the Athletics a 9–8 win and Ehmke his first victory of the season. His first start came in his third appearance, a 9–6 win against Detroit on May 31 in which he allowed just two runs in seven innings.

Isaminger wrote, "Howard Ehmke gave a brainy display of pitching . . . was a master in diversifying his pitches and always had something on the batsmen."[23] Ehmke's braininess aside, batters were complaining to the umpires this season that some pitchers were doctoring baseballs. In particular, they cited Ehmke and Syl Johnson of the St. Louis Cardinals. "None of the batters knew exactly what the suspects do to the ball," wrote columnist Don Legg, "but they insist the accused culprits can make it sail and that you can't sail a ball unless you do something to it."[24]

The day before Ehmke's win over the Tigers, Quinn beat the Red Sox for his fourth win in five decisions; Red Ruffing took the loss to fall to 0-9. By the end of May the A's had raced to a 29-9 record, 5 games ahead of the St. Louis Browns and 8 ahead of the Yankees. At this point a year earlier, the Yankees had been 7½ games up on Philadelphia. In a fluke of the schedule, the A's already had faced the Senators and their new manager Walter Johnson thirteen times and had come out on top in twelve of those games.

Gordon Mackay felt one big reason the A's would win the pennant this season was the absence of Ty Cobb, a move Branch Rickey later characterized as addition by subtraction. "The vindictive hatred of Ty Cobb was so strong in every club that played against Connie's chattels that they virtually gave the Yankees the flag last season," Mackay wrote.[25] Outfielder Joe Hauser recalled the aftermath of Mack's benching Cobb and Speaker in July 1928, when the A's mounted their dramatic comeback. Hauser felt Cobb was jealous of him, and instead of mentoring the younger players, he began to harass them.[26]

Henry L. Farrell of the *Philadelphia Record* noted the harmony on the club that had not existed the year before. He too attributed much of the change to the absence of Speaker and Cobb. One player spoke for many when he said he resented the salaries paid to the "two old broken-downs." Farrell quoted another player saying to a friend, "Why should I go out there and kill myself for seven grand a year when those two are getting 30 and 40?"[27] Yet another player recalled an incident at Yankee Stadium, where Cobb questioned the courage of some of his Philadelphia teammates in front of several Yankees players. It is likely Ehmke was one of those whose courage Cobb was challenging.

On June 21 the A's returned to Yankee Stadium for back-to-back doubleheaders with the second-place New Yorkers, who were 7½ games back. After Philadelphia won two of the first three games, Quinn started the finale against George Pipgras before seventy thousand fans. Quinn went the distance in a fourteen-inning 4–3 loss. He allowed eighteen hits and four walks but gave a classic exhibition of strength "in the pinches." John Drebinger of the *New York Times* called it "probably one of the most amazing games ever played in the Ruppert arena."[28] After a three-run first-inning home run by Al Simmons, Drebinger noted that Pipgras set a record by leaving no men on base and facing only three men per inning the rest of the way. "Pipgras, pitching like a machine, continued his amazing work on the mound, while the old master, Quinn, squirmed deftly out of one hole only to plunge into another."[29]

It was a gutsy performance by Quinn but may have simply been too much for him, and it is surprising Mack did not pull him. Syndicated columnist Davis Walsh wrote the following:

> Quinn has sacrificed himself on the altar of team success. He pitched 14 great innings against the Yankees in the memorable series of late June, almost every inning of them a pinch that hammered at his emotions and gripped his heart. . . . Finally, beaten at last, Quinn staggered from the diamond at the end of that heartbreaker so weak that teammates had to half-carry him to the dressing room. The chances are good that he will be used less and less as a starting pitcher from now on. The part of him that he gave up out on the mound that day at the Stadium is likely to represent a permanent loss at his age.[30]

The Athletics had taken five of nine games from the Yankees thus far in 1929.[31] It was not a decisive margin, but two of the losses were Quinn's hard-fought defeats. Before the start of the season, Mack, speaking of his players, declared, "One thing may be considered a certainty. They are not afraid of the Yankees or any of the other clubs. That complex, if such it was, has been buried."[32]

Unknown at the time was that Yankees manager Miller Huggins had already expressed concern his club would not repeat as pennant winners in 1929. "I don't think these Yankees are going to win any more pennants, certainly not this one. They're getting older, and they've become glutted with success," he confided to a Cleveland reporter in early June.[33] "They read the financial pages with more interest than the sports pages."[34]

37

A Pennant for the A's at Last

In a 1936 interview with Don Basenfelder of the *Sporting News*, Howard Ehmke spoke about the meeting he had with Connie Mack after his May 31, 1929, win: "I'll never forget the morning of June 1, 1929. I walked into Shibe Park in a happy frame of mind. The day before, I had made my belated start of the season for the A's against Detroit and was credited with a 9 to 6 win."[1] The first person he saw was Mack, who informed Ehmke he had put the pitcher on waivers, and because no Major League club had claimed him, Mack was about to release him. Would Ehmke mind, Mack asked, going to Portland in the Pacific Coast League for the rest of the season and eventually becoming the manager of that club?

> Mr. Mack, I told you my final Major League days were going to be with you and nobody else. Whatever you say is all right with me. However, I've played 14 years in the majors and have never been on a winning club.[2] It looks very much as if the Athletics are going to win this year. I would like to stay with you and have the honor of being on a championship team. . . . We are going to play the Yankees in the next few weeks in a series that may have much to do in deciding whether we continue in first place. I would like to pitch the last game of the series against New York. If I don't win that game, you can let me go.

"All right, Howard, that's a go" was Mack's answer.[3]

Between his meeting with Mack and the start of the Yankees series on June 21, Ehmke made one start, against St. Louis on June 7. The Browns knocked him out in the second inning on their way to a 15–6 victory. After the A's and Yanks split doubleheaders on June 21 and 22, including Jack Quinn's fourteen-inning loss in Saturday's second game,

Sunday was the fifth game, the one Ehmke had asked to pitch. A New York win would draw the Yankees within 6½ games of first place and give them renewed hope.

"I was always an early riser, whether it was my turn to pitch or not," Ehmke recalled. "I was in the dining room of the Alamac Hotel, having ordered my breakfast, June 23, when I saw Mr. Mack peer into the room. He never ate with his players, but this time he walked up to my table and asked: 'Do you mind if I breakfast with you?' I told him I would be glad to have him. His first question was, 'Are you going to be able to pitch this afternoon?'"

"You know our agreement," I reminded him.

"Yes, I do," he responded, "and if you win today, we'll win the pennant."[4]

Ehmke, making his third start, had pitched only fifteen innings this season. "The Yankees chuckled when they saw him warming up," wrote Dan Daniel. "But imagine their surprise when in seven rounds he held them to four scattered hits."[5] The A's won, 7–4, and their lead was 8½ games.

On July 4 catcher Mickey Cochrane cracked a rib in a freak accident.[6] The loss of no other player on the club could have been as damaging because, in the words of James Isaminger, "Cochrane is the carburetor of the team."[7] When Cochrane died at the young age of fifty-nine in 1962, Arthur Daley wrote, "When Mickey Cochrane was playing baseball, he was an incendiary bomb. He exploded in such a shower of inspirational fire that he ignited those around him."[8]

The Athletics went on the road and struggled, splitting their next ten games in Cochrane's absence. A bright spot in that stretch was Ehmke at his best in a 4–1 win at St. Louis on July 10. He allowed only one hit through eight innings, but the game remained scoreless. The Athletics broke through against their former teammate Sam Gray with four ninth-inning runs. Ehmke had his first complete game since August 9, 1928.

"Ehmke was a pitching magician," wrote John Nolan. "I don't believe I ever saw a game in which there were fewer hard-hit balls," said veteran second baseman and A's coach Eddie Collins. Ehmke was more than satisfied with his performance. "This right arm feels as good as ever, but it always hurts after I put on an extra strain," he said.[9] Phil-

35. Howard Ehmke throwing underhand for the 1929 Athletics. "There are times when Ehmke doesn't appear to have enough speed to dent a pane of glass, but that's merely his deceptive style," said one sportswriter. *National Baseball Hall of Fame Library, Cooperstown, New York.*

adelphia lost the second game, Eddie Rommel's first loss after seven wins, but ended the day eight games ahead of New York.

Cochrane returned on July 14 in Cleveland, a game in which Quinn pitched five innings of two-hit relief as the A's beat the Indians, 5–3. Philadelphia won that series and swept the following one in Detroit. As the club headed home on July 21, their lead over second-place New York was 10½ games. Mack said, "I knew then I had a championship team."[10]

Quinn excelled at long relief during that road trip. Two days after Cochrane returned, he came in for Lefty Grove, pitched four effective innings, and picked up his seventh win. In the sweep of the Tigers, Quinn pitched six innings. In three games in eight days at Cleveland and Detroit, he worked fifteen innings and allowed only eleven hits.

Meanwhile, Mack was using Ehmke sparingly, keeping to a schedule that satisfied both the manager and the pitcher. Following a shaky start at Cleveland on July 15, Mack did not call on him until July 26. The thirty-five-year-old right-hander was again at his best. He four-hit the White Sox, 3–1, raising his record to 5-1 and keeping the A's 10½ games ahead of the Yankees. He did not walk anyone, and Chicago's run was unearned. Nolan wrote, "Ehmke is one of the most misunderstood fellows in baseball. He is calm and unruffled, never appears to work hard, yet he is always active, and his brain is working overtime trying to outguess the batter."[11]

"When I get a good rest between games, and I have pretty fair control, I can pitch a good game," Ehmke said. "Everything depends on control. Even if the arm doesn't feel right, I can get by as long as the ball cuts the corners. I've been pitching now for seventeen years, and I realize that control and fooling the batter is as important as whizzing curves over the plate."[12] The two veterans, Ehmke and Quinn surely exchanged ideas on pitching. "It's not the amount of stuff a pitcher has, if he doesn't know how to pitch," said Quinn. "My advice to any youngster is to try for control. It is more important than speed."[13]

By early August, with the A's first pennant since 1914 seeming inevitable, Isaminger paid tribute to the team's pitching staff. The forty-nine wins by the big three—Lefty Grove (17-2), George Earnshaw (17-5), and Rube Walberg (15-4)—represented two-thirds of the team's victories. Isaminger also pointed to the contributions of other staff members, particularly Ed Rommel, Bill Shores, Jack Quinn, and Howard Ehmke. The little-used Ehmke had taken part in only three games in May, two in June, and three in July. He compiled a 5-1 record in those eight games, with the wins often coming at crucial times. "Ehmke bobs up with a semi-monthly pitching classic that always helps his side,"

Isaminger wrote. "He doesn't do much for the team, but what he does is greatly received."[14]

Ehmke had not pitched since his July 26 complete-game, 3–1 win against Chicago when Mack chose him to pitch the opener of a double-header against the Yankees on August 7. The A's had an 11½-game lead on their always dangerous chief rival, and an overflow crowd packed Shibe Park hoping to see that lead extended. Ehmke responded with one of the worst outings of his career. The Yankees drove him out in the second inning after he allowed eight runs, climaxed by Babe Ruth's bases-loaded home run. The A's rebounded after their 13–1 drubbing when George Earnshaw notched his eighteenth win, 4–2, in the second game.

"I was disappointed in Ehmke's pitching," Mack told the press after the game. "I thought he would be in great shape after two weeks of rest, but he fooled us. I don't mind losing ball games. I have been in this game long enough to know you can't win every day, but it isn't pleasant to lose by such a score. Had Ehmke lost 1–0, I wouldn't have cared, but when he only lasted two innings and was hit hard, I can't hide my disappointment."[15]

Mack told Ehmke how disappointed he was in his effort and suggested he would benefit from some time off. When the A's headed to Detroit for their final western trip of the season, Ehmke remained in Philadelphia. On August 11 Mack wrote him a four-page letter using the stationery of the Detroit-Leland Hotel, the team's Detroit headquarters. Written in black ink from a fountain pen, the letter read as follows:

Dear Howard,

Have been giving you some thought since leaving Philadelphia and find myself still very much at a loss in regards to your pitching. You probably know as well as myself that all the clubs you have pitched for are under the same impression, and that is you can pitch if you wanted to, and the players are of the same opinion. The impression among our players are [sic] that you could pitch if you worked one game a week and would then put your stuff on the ball, otherwise they figure you are of no help to them. I have come to the conclusion that you figure too much on your soft stuff, and in my opinion you cannot get away with it without first showing plenty of speed, and both Cochrane & [backup catcher Cy] Perkins say you have the speed when you let it go. My letting you remain at home was due to your poor game against New York, having had at least fifteen days rest. Also had in mind that the players felt the same as I did—that you could have done better and for the good of all decided to let you remain at home. Am going to be frank in saying that you have me guessing regarding your pitching—dislike to think that you are thinking wholly about saving your arm and giving no thought to the club. You have been pitching a good number of years and the past few years you have not worked in many games, so cannot see any club taking you on next season. Have given you my straight opinion, don't say that it's right. As I am not a mind-reader but want you to get the view of others and myself, so you will not view your case from wholly your own views. Can you help us by working one game a week? Are you sure you can? Must not be any half-way about it, it's yes or no. If after giving the matter plenty of thought, and your decision is that you can do it as outlined and help the club by working one day a week, join club at Cleveland. In case you feel that it's better for the club and yourself to remain at home, do it and it's OK with me.

With kind regards,
Sincerely yours—Connie Mack[16]

"So far as I am personally concerned," Mack was reported to have said in a speech in Toledo, "Ehmke could stay with us, but certain of the players are bothered when they see him around. They count on him helping out. Then when he goes in and doesn't show anything, it gets them riled and dissatisfied."[17] It was common knowledge that several of the A's top players had little use for Ehmke, including Al Simmons, who was rumored to have exchanged blows with Ehmke during the season.[18] While the letter suggests Mack was giving up on Ehmke, the A's manager was a master psychologist. His letter was a last-ditch effort to coax an improved performance from his inconsistent pitcher. While highly critical, he still retained hope that Ehmke could contribute.

"As far as the rumor that the players asked that I be left home, it is a lot of talk," Ehmke said. "A few of the men may have been disgruntled at my showing against the Yanks, and in the heat of battle said a few uncomplimentary things. But that is the way we ball players often do—and it means nothing once the game is over. My arm isn't any too strong. I need about five-or-six days rest," he said, disregarding that he had twelve days of rest before his disastrous start against the Yankees. As for Mack's decision, Ehmke said, "Connie Mack is the greatest manager I ever worked for, a man who has treated me with as much consideration as I would look for from my own father."[19]

Ehmke's value to the team for the remainder of 1929 stood in sharp contrast to that of his fellow veteran, Jack Quinn. On August 8 Quinn pitched seven innings of four-hit relief against the Yankees, "weaving his mystic spell over the Yankee bats," but the A's could not overcome an early 6–1 New York lead. After the game Gordon Mackay wrote, "Connie Mack better talk brotherly to Jack Quinn and make him stick around next season."[20] Quinn had enormous respect for his manager. When rumors were swirling again that month that he would retire, he declared, "I'll retire when Connie Mack tells me I'm through, and not before."[21]

Quinn pitched yet another strong game against the Yankees on September 2, a 10–3 win in the morning game of a Labor Day doubleheader.[22] This was Quinn's eleventh and final win of the season; he would make only two relief appearances the rest of the campaign. With the pennant secure, Mack wanted him well rested for the World Series. Quinn pitched fifty-one innings against New York in 1929, more than any other Philadelphia hurler, with a 2.65 earned run average against them, more than a run lower than his season's overall average of 3.97.

Al Simmons led the A's offense in Quinn's Labor Day victory with a single, double, and home run. He was healthy enough to appear in 143 games this season. His .365 batting average was second best in the league, and he led the league in runs batted in with 157. Late in the season Westbrook Pegler wrote of Simmons's strange batting stance that he was "like an artist who paints swell pictures with his elbows. . . . He still hits wrong—wronger and better than ever."[23]

Ehmke pitched for almost the first time in a month in the afternoon game. He got the win with a strong relief performance, and the A's sweep extended their lead to 13½ games. William Brandt wrote, "The Yanks saw their prowess buffeted and strewn in the dust."[24]

Ehmke followed his relief appearance against the Yankees with a strong start against Chicago. Yet in a mid-September interview, he said he had given up hope of finding a doctor who could cure his temperamental right arm and he was contemplating retiring after the World Series. He told Raymond A. Hill of the *Philadelphia Evening Bulletin* the following:

> I haven't been able to pitch a real fast one since 1926 without pains shooting through my right shoulder. Without a good fast one, I need absolutely perfect control to pitch a winning game in my present form. . . . Just what happened to my shoulder, I don't know. It just went out of gear for no reason at all. Sometimes it feels great, but those occasions are few and far between. . . . I've seen Bonesetter Reese out in Youngstown, Ohio. He helped others, but he couldn't help me. I've gone further—to California, Hot Springs, Texas, and Detroit. No one has been able to effect a permanent cure.[25]

Ehmke took the opportunity to address reports of his impending retirement. "Well, I haven't decided anything yet," he said. "But I know I don't intend to pitch very much longer under present conditions. . . . I have a very nice business, which should be taking up all of my time anyway. . . . If I do decide to quit, it will be real soon. For I can't think of a better way to leave baseball than to retire from a world championship team. And the A's will be that after they meet the Cubs."[26]

A big reason for the Athletics' success was the reemergence of George Earnshaw as the dominant pitcher he had been with the International League Orioles. Unhappy with his situation in Baltimore, he had reported to training camp out of condition in 1928. This season, he was fit and led the league with twenty-four wins against only eight losses. Babe Ruth called him the A's best pitcher.[27] He has been "the biggest surprise of the pitching staff," said Connie Mack. "Earnshaw this year has proved one of the mightiest curvers in the two Major Leagues."[28]

Earnshaw was second in the league in strikeouts, behind Grove. He became an even better pitcher when Jack Quinn taught him the change of pace. Quinn said, "I told him if he kept on [only] with that fast one, he wouldn't have an arm after five years. So he went to work on a floater."[29] Quinn explained to him, "Just use the same motion you always do, but open all your fingers when you let the ball go."[30] After Earnshaw mastered the slow ball, "George became one of the best change-of-pace pitchers in the league," Quinn declared.[31]

Lefty Grove led the league in earned run average with a 2.81 mark. While Mack called Grove "an intelligent pitcher now," one who "no longer tries for strikeouts," he led the league in that category for the fifth straight season.[32] (He would also lead for the next two.) Humorist Bugs Baer's words still applied: Grove "could throw a lamb chop past a wolf."[33] Mack knew how to nurture his temperamental pitcher and complimented him on his progress each season, though he felt even more improvement was possible.[34]

The Athletics won the pennant by 18 games over the Yankees, who had beaten them by 19 games just two years earlier. Philadelphia took the season series from New York, fourteen games to eight. After fifteen years Connie Mack had led his club back to the World Series. His biographer, Norman Macht, wrote, "Connie Mack didn't drive them. He didn't have to. He had assembled a team of drivers. Fierce and scrappy as Cochrane was, he was far from alone."[35]

In the National League Chicago was on the way to its first pennant since 1918. After sweeping a Labor Day doubleheader from the St. Louis Cardinals, the Cubs held a 12½-game lead over the second-place Pittsburgh Pirates.[36] Looking ahead to an A's-Cubs World Series, Isaminger noted the Cubs had had great success against left-handers all season. He speculated that the A's right-handers, especially George Earnshaw, might well be Mack's best weapon. Nor did he rule out the team's other righties—Quinn, Ehmke, Rommel, and Shores—playing significant roles.

Isaminger wrote that after the New York win, Quinn was now "on top of his game." Looking ahead to the World Series, he added, "Quinn not only has a unique delivery, a style no National League pitcher possesses, but he backs this up with ripe experience. Hitters who meet him for the first time always have trouble fathoming his stuff. . . . Quinn may prove one of the pitching heroes of the series. Certainly when he is right, nobody hits him to any extent."[37]

Moreover, wrote Isaminger, in spite of Ehmke's uneven season, he should not be counted out. "Ehmke's experience this year has been an uncommon one. He is more or less in disrepute for a period and then steps in and gives a brilliant performance that wins a game for the Athletics that is vital for them to take." Ehmke was not used much, Isaminger continued, "but in a crisis he ever proves helpful, and a lot of Philadelphia fans believe that he will deal a coup for the Macks in the Series with the Cubs. It would be just like Ehmke to do this. The sage of Lehigh Avenue [Mack] has never breathed a word about his pitching plans, but he has an ace in a hole in Ehmke."[38]

Legendary sportswriter Red Smith described the story Mack would often repeat on his plans for Ehmke. Before the A's left on their last trip West, Mack called Ehmke into his office at Shibe Park. "Howard," he told him, "the time has come for us to part." Mack would then describe Ehmke looking at him, raising his right arm, and saying, "Mr. Mack, I have always wanted to pitch in a World Series," and adding, "There is one great game left in this old arm."[39]

That was what Mack was hoping to hear. "All right, Howard," he told Ehmke. "When we go West, I want you to stay here. When the Cubs come in to play the Phillies, you watch them. Learn all you can about their hitters. Say nothing to anybody. You are my opening pitcher for the World Series."[40]

On August 25 the *Philadelphia Inquirer* noted that Ehmke was in attendance and taking notes at the previous day's Cubs-Phillies game at Baker Bowl. They also reported his presence at the Cubs' final visit to Philadelphia on September 11 and 12. He skipped the final game of the series, when Mack started him against the visiting White Sox on September 13. The thought was that Ehmke was scouting the Cubs for the benefit of Mack and the A's players. Little did they realize he was scouting them for himself.

38

"The Pitcher Who Was Left Behind
May Soon Be the Hero"

How good were the 1929 Philadelphia Athletics? So good that more than a half-century later, this headline appeared on a cover of *Sports Illustrated*: "The 1929 Philadelphia A's, Not the '27 Yankees, May Have Been the Greatest Baseball Club Ever Assembled."[1] The A's (104-46) were in first place for 159 of the 174 days of the season and clinched the pennant on September 14. They finished 18 games ahead of the Yankees, while winning fourteen of twenty-two games from the three-time defending American League champions and winners of the last two World Series.

Three future Hall of Famers—Jimmie Foxx, Al Simmons, and Mickey Cochrane—led an offense that also included .300 hitters Bing Miller and Mule Haas. A's pitchers led the Major Leagues with 573 strikeouts, and they were the only American League team with more strikeouts than walks. Lefty Grove (20-6) and his fellow pitching aces—Rube Walberg (18-11) and George Earnshaw (24-8)—were all big and threw hard. Walberg was 6 feet 1 inch tall, Grove was 6 feet 3, and Earnshaw was 6 feet 4. Three other key contributors relied more on guile and "trick" pitches rather than speed: Howard Ehmke with curves and change-ups, Jack Quinn with a spitball, and Ed Rommel with a knuckleball.

Philadelphia's opponent in the World Series, the Joe McCarthy–managed Chicago Cubs, coasted to the National League pennant, 10½ games ahead of Pittsburgh. Three right-handers—Pat Malone (22-10), Charlie Root, (19-6), and Guy Bush (18-7)—led the Cubs' equally formidable pitching staff. Chicago's offense was powered by second baseman Rogers Hornsby (.380) and outfielders Riggs Stephenson (.362), Kiki Cuyler (.360), and Hack Wilson (.345). All batted right-handed. The only left-handed swinger among the starters was first baseman Charlie Grimm.

The challenge for Connie Mack, back in the World Series after a fifteen-year absence, was to devise a strategy to counter Chicago's right-handed power. In doing so, Mack and Ehmke became the central figures in one of baseball's most enduring myths—that is, that manager Mack made an "out-of-the-blue," last-minute decision to start the little-used Ehmke in the first game of the 1929 World Series. "Just as there are eight different towns in the West claiming the burial ground of Billy the Kid," wrote Norman Macht, "there are many versions of the Howard Ehmke story."[2]

Despite the legend that Ehmke's start in Game One came as a complete surprise to everyone, hints about it had surfaced a month earlier. John J. Nolan reported in September that the Cubs were well aware that Ehmke had shown up when they appeared at Baker Bowl and was taking voluminous notes. "While the Cub supporters and National Leaguers in general have been boasting what the right-hand hitters of the Cubs would do to the southpaw curves of Lefty Grove and Rube Walberg," Nolan wrote, "the one thought among the opposition is Ehmke." He added that Ehmke's role in the Series was unknown and that he would likely retire when it ended. "His pitching days are numbered, and if he would walk out of baseball in the fall, in a blaze of glory, it would bring a fitting close to his long career in baseball."[3]

Ehmke commented that reports he was ready to retire after the season were premature. "Of course, I want to beat the Cubs in a series game," he told the Associated Press, "but as to my announcing my retirement at the close of the series, why that is something else. I have made no definite decision about retiring."[4]

Three weeks before the start of the Series, Mack surprised the baseball world when he announced Ehmke could pitch any game of the Series he wanted to. "That fellow is an artist," Mack said. "Sometimes he isn't just ready to work, and it would be foolhardy to start him. But when Ehmke asks to pitch, I know he will come through."[5]

Meanwhile, the Cubs were doing some advance preparation of their own. In late September Hornsby said the A's biggest threat was their slow-ball pitchers: Ehmke, Quinn, and Rommel. McCarthy agreed and had his veteran left-hander Art Nehf throwing such pitches to the Cubs in batting practice.

Former Cubs shortstop Joe Tinker, who had been scouting the A's, was telling anyone who would listen that the Cubs would feast on left-handers Grove and Walberg. If that were true, wrote Ed Pollock, the only pitcher Mack could rely on would be right-hander George Earnshaw and he may have to turn to Ehmke and Quinn to play key roles. Ehmke needed about three weeks of rest between games, Pollock wrote. Since his last appearance, a 5–2 win over the White Sox on September 13, he was right on schedule for a World Series start. "His lazy motion and slow stuff may be a perplexing change from the speed of the three Mack aces." And, in a prescient prediction, Pollock wrote, "The pitcher who was left behind may soon be the hero on the front firing line."[6]

Ehmke had hooked up in a tight pitching duel with Ed Walsh Jr. of the White Sox in that September 13 game. The score was 2–2 until Al Simmons's three-run homer in the eighth gave the A's the 5–2 win. Ehmke had been lifted for a pinch hitter in the inning, and Grove pitched the ninth. Tinker was at the game scouting the A's, Ehmke remembered: "He reported that all I had was a lot of slow stuff. So [in Game One] I decided to show the Cubs a fast ball once in a while anyhow."[7]

The day after Ehmke defeated the White Sox, Mack again called him into his office. "What about cold weather?" Mack asked him. "Do you mean the World Series?" Ehmke replied. "Exactly," said Mack. "If you will let me train myself between now and the opening game of the Series," Ehmke told his manager, "I'll take care of it for you."[8] Mack agreed but swore Ehmke to secrecy. Ehmke abided by his oath. He told no one, not even his wife.

Red Smith recalled a conversation with Ring Lardner while covering a 1930 game between the Cardinals and the Phillies at Philadelphia's Baker Bowl. Lardner was among those who did not believe that Cubs manager McCarthy had been caught completely by surprise when Mack started Ehmke. "I talked with McCarthy late last summer," Lardner said to Smith. "He told me, 'We're not worried about Grove and Earnshaw. We can hit speed. But there's one guy on the club. . . . He's a shit pitcher. That's Howard Ehmke, and he's the guy we're going to see in the Series.'"[9] Shortly before game time, as the players were coming onto the field, Bob Paul, who covered the A's for the *Philadelphia Bulletin*,

36. Owner William Wrigley Jr., manager Joe McCarthy, and team president William Veeck Sr. of the Chicago Cubs (*left to right*). (Connie Mack occupied all those positions for the Athletics.) McCarthy expected his club could handle fastball pitchers like Lefty Grove and George Earnshaw in the World Series but was concerned how they would do against the off-speed deliveries of Howard Ehmke. *Steve Steinberg Collection.*

singled out Ehmke and wished him luck. Ehmke did not say a word, said Paul, "but there was a knowing twinkle in his eye."[10]

McCarthy expressed pleasure that his managerial foe would be Connie Mack. "Now don't go jumping to conclusions," he added. "I don't mean the American League champions are my idea of a soft touch. They're not at all." McCarthy went on to explain how kind and gracious Mack had been to a career Minor Leaguer when McCarthy signed to manage the Cubs back in 1925.[11]

Further proof that Ehmke's Game One start did not come completely out of the blue was this headline on a James Isaminger column in the *Sporting News*: "Howard Ehmke Looms as Series Dark-Horse for Mack's Champs." Isaminger based his prediction on that 5–2 win over the White Sox, citing Ehmke's eight innings without his allowing an earned run.[12]

The players' thoughts on Ehmke's participation in the Series were varied. Some thought he would play a role, even starting Game One, and some completely dismissed the idea of his even appearing in the Series.[13] Sometimes such differing opinions, at least in retrospect, were held by the same man.

In a 1942 interview Lefty Grove recalled his thoughts leading up to Game One. "I had a hunch, a few days before the Series opened, that Mr. Mack would pull a surprise," he remembered. "I knew that Howard Ehmke had scouted the Cubs before the season ended. It didn't amaze me when he announced in one of our meetings that Ehmke would open against the Cubs, and Walberg and myself were to hold ourselves in readiness in the bullpen in case anything went wrong."[14]

Grove's memories were much different in an interview he did with Donald Honig. "Remember that '29 Series against the Cubs?" Grove said. "Lots of surprises in that one. Biggest surprise was Howard Ehmke starting the first game. That sure was something. Nobody ever guessed it."[15]

In a *Philadelphia Evening Public Ledger* article, which ran a few days before the Series under Mickey Cochrane's byline, the A's catcher made his predictions concerning the starting pitchers. He expected the Game One pitchers would be George Earnshaw for the A's and Pat Malone for the Cubs. Cochrane expected Ehmke to start Game Two for Philadelphia.[16] "Ehmke, if he is right, is just the type to stop the Cubs, from what I hear. Howie has a beautiful curve ball with slow stuff and is as smart as they come. I don't believe the Cubs ever faced a pitcher that throws the same way Ehmke does," Cochrane wrote. "If Howard's arm is ripe when he takes the hill, and if he takes the hill, he is a sure bet to win. I understand he is going to retire at the end of this year, and it is his ambition to win one World Series struggle before he hangs up."[17]

Cochrane went on to write that if Ehmke wasn't the choice, it would be Jack Quinn, another veteran right-hander: "Quinn has something left in his right arm, and the Cubs will agree with me after they are through batting against him. You will recall how this spitball expert tied the Yankees into knots all through the season. And you must agree the Yanks have as dangerous clubbers—if not better—as the McCarthy pounders."[18]

Quinn had a slightly different memory of how Mack chose Ehmke. "A week or so before the Series Connie sent for Ehmke and told him he could pitch a game in the World Series," said Quinn. "He informed Howard that he could take his choice. Ehmke said nothing at the time, but the day before the Series he came to Connie and told him he would like to pitch the opening game. Connie was true to his word and started him. You know the rest."[19]

At Chicago's Congress Hotel, the press headquarters for the Series, most of the talk prior to Game One was about which pitcher would start for the A's. Mack had a history of not revealing his World Series starting pitchers. While almost all believed it would be right-hander Earnshaw, there was a persistent rumor, one based on Mack's history of playing hunches, that he would start Ehmke.

Ty Cobb, in his first year of retirement after two seasons with the A's, was among those who thought Mack would have a surprise for the Cubs. "I know the old man," he said. "If everyone picks Earnshaw to start, he'll cross the boys and start Ehmke or Quinn."[20]

A Philadelphia reporter wrote it would not be surprising if Ehmke started one of the first two games in Chicago: "This season Ehmke has enjoyed the rare privilege of making his own assignments. He was told by Mack that he would work only when he felt like pitching, and the lean leader, as usual, has kept his word.[21] He won only seven games, but each was a victory when the pitching situation was causing considerable worry. It takes no fancy imagination to liken Ehmke to the greatest 'money pitcher' of all times—Chief Bender. They are built somewhat alike, each tall and slender and in emergencies possessed of remarkable endurance."[22] In calling Ehmke "one of the shrewdest hurlers in the majors," the reporter noted "he has never stopped in his efforts to discover something new to add to his delivery. For some time, he has been working on a 'shadow' ball. Pitching underhanded, he 'throws out of his uniform.' This is when he employs his fastball. The sphere is shaded by the background of Ehmke himself and is lost to the batter's vision until it is almost upon him."[23]

Ehmke's wife was less encouraging, Ehmke said: "We left Philadelphia for Chicago and the World's Series, October 5, with the words of my wife, Marguerite, ringing in my ears, 'Howard, keep out of that series with your weak arm—let a strong-arm pitcher get in there for the Athletics.' I told her not to worry about me."[24]

Ehmke avoided the crowds that greeted the team when it arrived in Chicago. Instead he played miniature golf until after dark with his roommate, Jimmie Foxx, behind the Edgewater Beach Hotel, where the team was staying. Shortly before going to bed, at nine, Foxx revealed what he thought was a secret: "I think Mack will pitch you tomorrow, and if he does, I'll hit one for you."[25] On game day Ehmke woke up at 6 a.m. and had an early breakfast before going back to bed. After relaxing for a few hours, he packed a chicken sandwich to take to the park for lunch. He later described the moment he learned for certain, that, at age thirty-five and considered washed up, he would be pitching the opening game of the World Series. As previously noted, there are differing versions of how Ehmke came to pitch Game One. This is a summary of his, as drawn from a variety of sources over the years.

At 10:30 a.m., we were all called into a meeting by Mack in the hotel ball room. The meeting was perfunctory in nature, and nothing was said about who was going to pitch the first game. As the players filed out of the room, I walked up to Mack and Eddie Collins, who remained, watched them close the door on the last player, then asked:

"Mr. Mack, does it still go?"

"Yes," he answered, "absolutely. You'll win today."

"Who is your next choice?'" I asked.

"Earnshaw or Grove," was the reply.

"Why not keep both of them in the clubhouse with me? If I do not warm up all right, Earnshaw will start the game. If my arm is right, I'll continue to warm up." Mack agreed to the plan.[26]

Ehmke remembered arriving at Wrigley Field about eleven o'clock on October 8 and going to the A's clubhouse a half-hour before game time: "I had to laugh when I came out of the clubhouse with George Earnshaw. The photographers besieged him and ignored me. I sat there watching the Cub batters while the cameras were clicking with Earnshaw and Root, presumably the rival hurlers, posing."[27]

Ten minutes before the scheduled 1:30 start, Ehmke began warming up with backup catcher Cy Perkins. "It took me only a few minutes to ready myself. Had the game started at 1:30 p.m., as scheduled, I feel sure I would have struck out 18 Cubs. But on an order from Commissioner Landis, the start was delayed until 1:45 p.m., to enable some of the fans who arrived late to find their seats and get settled comfortably."[28]

"When I started to warm up before the game my arm ached, and there were a lot of skeptics who thought it was a stall," Ehmke said the next day. "Cy Perkins watched me anxiously, and I looked toward the bench to see if Connie wanted to know how I felt. He was laughing and paying absolutely no attention to me."[29]

Yet as time passes, even a short time, memories change, and Ehmke remembered his pregame warmup quite differently a few months later. He told William Brandt that he knew his arm was right after throwing his first two warmup pitches. "Right then, if you had asked me, I'd have said, 'Go bet all your dough on the A's.' . . . I got hold of Cochrane. I said, 'Mike, will you do what I tell you today?' He said, 'Sure, I'll eat the home plate if you say so.' . . . I said, 'Well, you and I are going to have a good time out there today. . . . Let the Cubs tighten up. We have the psychological edge on them. They didn't expect to see me out here today.'"[30]

Brandt was covering the Series for the *New York Times*. He claimed Mack had told him about starting Ehmke, and he was the only writer who hinted at that on the morning of Game One. "Most of the experts thought senility had caught up with Mack," he wrote. But Mack realized the white shirts in center field (before the ivy was planted at Wrigley Field) were the perfect backdrop for Ehmke's sidearm pitches.[31]

In the early 1940s John P. Carmichael of the *Chicago Daily News* put together a book of interviews with former stars of the early game, asking them to recall their greatest day in baseball.[32] Among them was Connie Mack, who said his greatest day was Game One of the 1929 World Series. He spoke of the secret agreement he and Ehmke had made for Ehmke to pitch that game. "You see, Howard and I sort of put a fast one over on everybody, and an old man likes to enjoy a chuckle at the expense of a younger generation."[33] Mack recalled that seeing Ehmke get ready shocked even several of his teammates:

> When it came time for the rival pitchers to warm up, Ehmke, naturally, took off his jacket and started to throw. I made sure I was where I could look along our bench, and you could see mouths pop open. Grove was looking at Earnshaw, and George was looking at Mose [Grove]. Al Simmons was sitting next to me, and he couldn't stop himself in time. "Are you gonna pitch him?" he asked in disbelief. I kept a straight face and looked very severely at him and said "Yes, I am, Al. Is that all right with you?" You could sense him pulling himself out of his surprised state, and he replied quickly: "If you say so, it's all right with me, Mr. Mack."[34]

"I was pretty sure someone was crazy," Simmons recalled thinking, "and it wasn't Al Simmons. I just stared in horror when I saw he was going to pitch, and he went out there and made 'em look silly. Made me look silly, too."[35]

39

Ehmke Sets World Series Record
in "Surprise" Start

The Philadelphia Athletics had participated in five World Series, and in each one Connie Mack started his ace in the opening game: Eddie Plank in 1905 and Chief Bender in 1910, 1911, 1913, and 1914. Mack's Game One pitcher in 1930 and 1931 would again be his ace: Lefty Grove. No wonder his selection of the little-used, thirty-five-year-old Howard Ehmke to pitch the opener against the Chicago Cubs in 1929 was such an outlier.

Yet the maneuver had its defenders, especially in hindsight. "Mack's choice [to start Ehmke] was based on sound strategy," wrote noted baseball historian Harold Seymour. "He [Mack] had every reason to believe that Ehmke, who was a right-hand sidearm pitcher with a good curve ball and good control, would be effective against the Cubs because their line-up was loaded with right-hand hitters who were particularly potent against fast-ball pitching."[1] In a 1938 article in *Collier's*, catcher Mickey Cochrane, himself a World Series–winning manager in 1935, called Mack's selection of Ehmke to pitch the opener "the most daring move I've seen a manager make in the World Series."[2]

The sight of Ehmke warming up startled many in the crowd of more than fifty thousand. This was the first World Series game played at Wrigley Field, and among the spectators was Cubs fan John Paul Stevens, a future Supreme Court Justice. Accompanied by his father, the nine-year-old Stevens recalled in a conversation with the *Chicago Tribune* eighty-five years later, "It was my first-ever baseball game, and it turned out to be one of the greatest disappointments of my life."[3]

A *Philadelphia Bulletin* reporter described one scene that was indicative of the excitement in the City of Brotherly Love: "The largest crowd ever to assemble in downtown Philadelphia watched the *Bulletin's* electric scoreboard and listened to an announcer with a direct

November 3, 2016

Mr. Steve Steinberg
Orcas Business Park
5700 6th Avenue South, Suite 214
Seattle, Washington 98108

Dear Mr. Steinberg:

My first visit to Wrigley Field in 1929 followed
a summer of listening to Hal Totten's broadcasts of
the Cubs' home games and Pat Flanagan's reports of the
away games, which had made me a well-informed fan even
though I was only nine. I had expected either Lefty
Grove or Howard Earnshaw to start the first game, but
Connie Mach caught the fans as well as the Cubs by
surprise when he started Ehmke. That must have been
the saddest day of my life because I had developed so
much confidence in the Cubs' batting order. Last
night, however, my long-suffering patience was finally
rewarded by the most bizarre finish to a world series
that ever occurred.

Sincerely,

37. In November 2016, shortly after the Chicago Cubs won the World Series, a
ninety-six-year-old Cubs fan recollected in a letter the crushing defeat Howard
Ehmke had handed to his beloved Cubs eighty-seven seasons earlier. Game One
of the 1929 World Series was the first game U.S. Supreme Court justice John Paul
Stevens had attended, and the disappointment it inflicted on the young Stevens
was finally assuaged in 2016. *Steve Steinberg Collection.*

wire to Wrigley Field. With necks craned upward, fans jammed City
Hall Plaza and the streets around the *Bulletin* building; they hung out
the windows of City Hall and its annex; bootblacks and millionaires
stood packed together talking baseball."[4]

Ehmke claimed delaying the game's start by fifteen minutes caused
his arm to stiffen slightly in the first inning. "Only my control carried
me through those first two innings," he said. "But by the third inning
I had all my stuff back. I was even fairly fast."[5] He said his arm "pained

several times during the battle, but there was so much at stake I couldn't stop. I would have pitched until my arm fell off."[6]

Through six innings Ehmke and Chicago's Charlie Root kept their opponents scoreless. The biggest threat by either team came in the Cubs' third. They had runners at second and third, with only one out and sluggers Rogers Hornsby and Hack Wilson due up. An unruffled Ehmke struck out both men. Root was even more effective, holding the A's to a mere two hits through six innings.

In the seventh inning Ehmke's roommate, Jimmie Foxx, made good on his promise to hit a home run. His solo drive into the center-field bleachers put the A's ahead, 1–0. "I really caught hold of a fast ball and sent it into the bleachers for the first run of the game," Foxx recalled. "Circling the bases in front of that suddenly very quiet crowd was my biggest thrill in baseball."[7]

In the home seventh the Cubs fought back, threatening to take the lead or at least tie the score. Singles by Kiki Cuyler and Riggs Stephenson and a sacrifice bunt by Charlie Grimm put runners on second and third with one out. But Ehmke again left the runners stranded when he retired pinch hitter Cliff Heathcote on a short fly ball and struck out Gabby Hartnett, who was batting for Root.[8]

Ehmke clung to his 1–0 lead before Philadelphia took some pressure off him by adding two runs in the ninth against Root's replacement, Guy Bush. After Cochrane opened the inning with a single, shortstop Woody English misplayed consecutive ground balls by Al Simmons and Foxx—each of which was a potential double play—to load the bases. Bing Miller's single scored Cochrane and Foxx to give the A's a 3–0 lead.

The Cubs did not go down quietly in the bottom of the ninth. Wilson led off with a sharply hit ball that struck Ehmke and knocked him down. He was able to recover and throw to first base to retire Wilson. With one out, Cuyler made it to second on a throwing error by third baseman Jimmy Dykes and scored on Stephenson's single. Grimm's single put the tying run on base. The next scheduled batter was weak-hitting catcher Mike Gonzalez, representing the potential winning run. Joe McCarthy pinch-hit for the right-handed-hitting Gonzalez with Footsie Blair, a left-handed-hitting rookie, with one home run for the season. Ehmke retired Blair on a force out of Grimm at second. With

38. Connie Mack advises a young Jimmie Foxx, who batted .354 with thirty-three home runs in 1929. Foxx promised his roommate Howard Ehmke he would hit a home run for him in Game One. He did and later called it his biggest thrill in baseball. *Dennis Goldstein Collection.*

Bush due up, McCarthy again went to his bench, sending up reserve first baseman Chick Tolson to bat for Bush. Ehmke later revealed he had no information on Tolson.[9] When he had scouted the Cubs' batters at Baker Bowl in August, Tolson never came to the plate. Ehmke recalled the following:

> He had me worried With the score 3–1, it took only one solid drive between the outfielders to tie the score. I tried to make Tolson hit a bad fastball. He wouldn't swing. I threw him five fast ones. The count stood 3 and 2. I called Cochrane out from behind the plate.

39. With two outs in the ninth inning of Game One of the World Series and the tying runs on base, manager Joe McCarthy sent reserve first baseman Chick Tolson in to bat for pitcher Guy Bush. The count went to 3–2 before Howard Ehmke struck him out for his record-breaking thirteenth strikeout. *Michael Mumby Collection.*

"Now Mike," I said, "when you go back there, remind them of my control. Get him thinking, see? Tell him this next one is sure to be over the plate. I want him swinging, see? Then when the ball gets about halfway there, you yell, 'Hit it.'"

Well, Mike yelled, and Tolson swung. But that yell kind of disturbed his timing. He swung too fast. He swung ahead of the ball and missed it.[10]

"I never felt in danger until the ninth. Then I almost saw victory fading from my grasp when Wilson's hot smack struck me in the groin. I managed to pick up the ball and toss him out for the inning's first out, but I was hurt and fell to the ground."[11] Ehmke said he remembered the game against the Yankees when he was criticized for leaving after hurting his knee. He got to his feet quickly and resumed pitching. "Once we got ahead, which was when Jimmie Foxx blasted his homer, I knew I would win," Ehmke said. "I had a hunch in the morning. It was my day, the big event for which I had waited for sixteen years."[12]

Ehmke had risen above the criticism and injuries he had endured those sixteen years to pitch the game of his life. Thought by many, including some of his own teammates, unworthy of being the Game One starter, he held the powerful Cubs to one unearned run in their own park. The strikeout of Tolson was his thirteenth of the game, setting a Major League record for a World Series game. Former Chicago White Sox pitcher Ed Walsh, who held the previous record for a nine-inning game, with twelve, was at Wrigley Field to see his record broken.[13]

Of the thirteen batters Ehmke struck out, twelve were on swinging third strikes. Twice he fanned Hornsby and Wilson back to back. Of the twenty-seven men he retired, his first pitch was a strike to twenty-six of them. At one point he struck out five consecutive Cubs, most unusual for a pitcher not known for his ability to strike out batters.[14] The only previous time in his career he had compiled double-digit strikeout totals was when he had ten, pitching for Boston against Philadelphia on May 1, 1923.[15]

Despite his high number of strikeouts, Ehmke claimed he did not have any feeling in his arm from the sixth inning on. "It feels as if it were dead from the shoulder right on down to my fingertips. . . . Winning that ball game was the greatest thrill I ever had in my baseball career. . . . I guess I'm finished. That game may be my swan song. But it was worth the price."[16] "After the game, his arm was so numb that he couldn't even hold a pencil to autograph menus in the dining room of Chicago's Edgewater Beach Hotel."[17]

Numb arm or not, Joe Williams wrote that he had never seen a pitcher work with seemingly less concern or effort. "He seemed utterly without emotion," Williams said. "He would amble out to the box and stand with his hands on his hips. . . . Then he would take the ball from one of the infielders and hold his hands clasped behind his back until Cochrane gave him the signal."[18]

"I want to say now that Howard Ehmke pitched the greatest game I have ever witnessed," Cochrane wrote the next day. "It was a pleasure to stand behind the plate, give a signal, and watch the ball zip over the plate past the Cub batters. I bet those fellows didn't know what Ehmke was throwing at them. Howie and I talked over the situation and decided how to pitch to various hitters. Howard was to pitch a certain way to each batter, and let me tell you, he did that job perfectly."[19] Cochrane was one of several players who were paid to put their names on syndicated columns for the Series.

Before opening some two hundred telegrams, Ehmke called Marguerite at home in Germantown. "Hello, I guess you know we won," he said. "Yes, she replied, but why didn't you pitch a good game while you were at it?" she joked.[20]

Mack, reveling in the work of his surprise starter, gave all the credit to Ehmke. "I felt that a pitcher of the Ehmke type, who had a deceptive side-arm curve and a dazzling change of pace, would be just the man to upset the Cubs, who for over a month have been fed up on a speed diet," he said. "I was positive Ehmke could do it if he had his control. He did, and that is the whole story."[21]

In the December issue of *Baseball Magazine*, Franklin Yeutter described Ehmke's method in baffling the Cubs' batters: "He used a slow, hesitating curve. He used a sharp-breaking, shoulder-high 'duster.' He curved a crossfire inside. He threw a floating outside curve. But not once did the Cubs get a good ball to hit."[22]

Babe Ruth, who watched from the press box, was wowed by Ehmke's performance. "I've always thought Ehmke was one of the smartest pitchers in baseball and wished many times he was with the Yankees," the Babe said. "But who ever had an idea he could throw curves like that?" asked the man who had faced Ehmke multiple times over the years. "He was a right-handed [Yankees left-hander Herb] Pennock today, and that's the greatest compliment I can pay him."[23]

Charlie Root, the victim of Ehmke's gem, was generous in praising his opponent. "Ehmke pitched a magnificent game," he wrote. "We had lots of opportunities to score, but when hits meant runs, we just couldn't seem to deliver. . . . Ehmke pitched himself out of holes as fast as he got into them—and that was the cause of our defeat."[24]

Other Cubs were less generous. "We should have won the first game, hands down," said Woody English, whose two errors in the game gave the A's two unearned runs, their winning margin. "Ehmke had been a great pitcher, but he was supposed to have a bad arm, you know."[25]

"None of us figured on batting against Ehmke, who had a three-quarter side-arm delivery," said Rogers Hornsby. "But Ehmke got the breaks, and I'm not taking anything away from him when I say that. He could have been a bum just as easily. In the first inning we got a man on base when I came up. I hit a fair ball straight for the right-field bleachers, which certainly meant Ehmke was finished in this game. But the wind was blowing in off Lake Michigan, and the ball landed foul. Then I struck out, and we didn't score."[26]

Two of baseball's elder statesmen also weighed in on Ehmke's performance. Longtime New York Giants manager John McGraw praised Mack's choice of Ehmke to start the opener: "The Cubs didn't get to bat against much sidearm pitching throughout the season for the simple reason that most of the pitchers in our league are overhand workers. Ehmke was a new and strange proposition to them, and Old Connie undoubtedly had this in mind when he started him."[27] Years later McCarthy said, "Connie taught me a lesson that time."[28]

Cy Young, who began his illustrious big league career in 1890, was also at the game. He told a reporter from the *United Press*: "I don't believe I ever saw better pitching in a World Series game. . . . Ehmke had it on the Cubs; there was no doubt about it. His tantalizing pitching—fast curves, change of paces, floaters, underhand and sidearm delivery—had the Cubs puzzled all the way through."[29] Even Ty Cobb was moved to write that Ehmke was "simply sensational." Ehmke's old foe saluted the "wonderful judgment in his pitching, continually crossing the Cubs."[30]

Philadelphia Inquirer reporter Myles Pickering wrote a poem in honor of Ehmke's brilliant Game One victory.

As through a field of wheat the moving scythe makes stubs
Of what was once an army trim and straight.
So Ehmke, with his mighty arm, mowed down the Cubs,
To take his place among the baseball great.

Not young in years, but in his heart youth's fire glowed,
And warmed each muscle and each tensing nerve;
Dropped from his shoulders all the years, while Fate bestowed
On him laurels only great deserve.[31]

The A's, behind home runs by Foxx and Simmons, won again in Game Two, 9–3, as Earnshaw (with seven strikeouts) and Grove (with six) combined to strike out thirteen more Chicago batters. Each fanned Hornsby, giving the National League's premier hitter four strikeouts in the two games. "I struck out on pitched balls that in the season I would kill nine times in ten," said an incredulous Hornsby. "When I missed them, I actually thought they must have gone through my bat."[32] Overall it was a terrible Series for Hornsby. He struck out eight times in twenty-one at bats and batted just .238.[33]

Earnshaw had pitched only 4⅔ innings in Game Two, so after a day off for travel, Mack turned to him again in Game Three at Shibe Park. He went the distance but lost to Guy Bush, 3–1, cutting the A's lead in the Series to two games to one.

With the passing of time, the fourth game of the 1929 Series has proven even more memorable than the first, as it featured the largest single-game comeback in Series history. McCarthy came back with Root, his Game One starter, while Mack chose his staff's other wily veteran, Jack Quinn. Mack had shown confidence in Quinn during the season, leading to pre-Series rumors that the forty-six-year-old right-hander would start either the first or second game.[34] "He [Quinn] has an extremely baffling delivery, especially to opponents who have seldom faced him," Mack said.[35]

The baffling delivery to which Mack referred was Quinn's spitball. The Cubs often had trouble dealing with Pittsburgh Pirates pitcher Burleigh Grimes, the National League's most renowned spitballer.[36] "However," McCarthy wrote before the Series, "Quinn is not exactly a Grimes."[37] "Quinn lacks the deception of Grimes," said Pirates third baseman Pie Traynor. Umpire-columnist Billy Evans agreed with Traynor, adding that Grimes's "jerky delivery in comparison to Quinn's rhythmic motion makes it all the more difficult to follow the ball."[38]

For the first three innings Quinn was outstanding. He held the Cubs to one hit and no runs. Grimm's two-run homer in the fourth broke the scoreless deadlock, after which the Cubs drove Quinn from the game with a five-run sixth. "He looked pretty good for three innings—before Charlie Grimm hit that homer, and I guess that staggered Quinn, for he was not the same pitcher thereafter," wrote Al Simmons the next day.[39]

The Cubs added a run in the seventh, to extend their lead to 8–0. "No club looked more hopelessly and soundly beaten than the Athletics," wrote James Isaminger. "Their chances could have been sold for one of John Rockefeller's shiny dimes."[40]

Simmons began the A's comeback with a home run to lead off the home seventh. Before the inning was over, Philadelphia had tallied ten runs on ten hits against Root, Art Nehf, Sheriff Blake, and Pat Malone, to stun the Cubs, 10–8.[41] Outfielder Mule Haas had the big blow of the inning, a three-run, inside-the-park home run on a drive that center-fielder Wilson lost in the sun. "The poor kid simply lost the ball in the sun, and he didn't put the sun there," manager McCarthy said in defense of his center fielder, who also lost another ball in the sun that inning.[42]

Chicago's crushing defeat caused owner William Wrigley to lose confidence in McCarthy. He never forgave McCarthy for the Cubs' blowing that 8–0 lead in Game Four and did not renew his contract after the 1930 season. Wrigley would make one of the great personnel blunders in baseball history the following year when he replaced McCarthy with Rogers Hornsby, who would be fired by the Cubs less than two years later.[43]

"It is too bad that Jack Quinn couldn't last in there until he could be credited with the win," Simmons wrote. "Our spitball pitcher was so very anxious to win one World Series game before he hung up his uniform."[44]

Quinn claimed he always left the ballpark when he was removed from a game and that his wife had to tell him what took place that afternoon. "I'll never forget how she tried to tell me all that had happened in the big inning. She tried to get it out in one lump."[45] Yet while Quinn did not witness the A's astounding comeback, he called it "the biggest thrill in his entire career."[46]

McCarthy named Pat Malone as his Game Five starter, while Mack said nothing. On the morning of the game, Ehmke asked Mack who would start for the A's. When Mack said he had not decided, Ehmke volunteered his services. "Well, I feel all right again, and while I don't want to change your plans, I am willing to go in."[47]

"I always had the utmost confidence in Ehmke, for when he was right he was almost unbeatable," Mack said in 1931. "Only Ehmke himself knew when he was right."[48] Mack knew Ehmke could not pitch another complete game and might not survive the first inning, but he chose to play a hunch, maybe even a bigger hunch than choosing Ehmke in the opener. Both men knew Ehmke required two weeks of rest between starts, not six days. "Mack decided to warm up both Ehmke and Rube Walberg and go with Ehmke until the first sign of trouble."[49]

When the Cubs scored two runs with two outs in the fourth, Mack brought in Walberg. Pat Malone took his 2–0 lead into the last of the ninth, when the A's staged another dramatic comeback to win, 3–2. Mule Haas's two-run homer tied the score, and doubles by Simmons and Bing Miller produced the game-winner and gave the A's their first world championship in sixteen years.

Just how fit and ready was Ehmke for that Game Five start? Was it more reckless than courageous for him to tell Mack "he was willing to go in"? In May 1930 he admitted, "In the first game of the World Series I felt better than at any time since 1926, but when I started the fifth game, I could hardly lift my arm."[50]

Sportswriter Ford Frick called Cochrane the hero of the Series. "In a series that was full of bad play along with the good, Cochrane had not a single error," he wrote. "In a series replete with mental quirks that verged on sheer stupidity, Mickey emerged without a single mark against his good judgement." Frick also credited Cochrane for the skill he showed in handling Ehmke in Game One.[51]

Ehmke's fifth-game start is little remembered, but his first-game start cemented his role in World Series history. Frick called Ehmke "the man who came back from ridicule and derision to awaken again the cheering of the multitudes. . . . His was the drama of the failure who made good—and in that role he was supreme."[52]

"To my mind winning that first game with Ehmke was the crucial stroke of the series," Connie Mack said at spring training in 1931. Ehmke had his long-deferred aspiration gratified and was the happiest man in America.[53]

40

"I Am Sorry to Have to Let Ehmke Go"

The glow of the A's 1929 World Series victory stayed with Philadelphians through the fall and winter. The city showed its appreciation for manager Connie Mack by presenting him with the Philadelphia Award, established in 1921. "A concrete expression of the city's honor," the award went to the individual who during the previous year had advanced "the best interests of the community of which Philadelphia is the center."[1]

Al Simmons voiced the esteem in which Mack was held by his players. "It was not alone the personal satisfaction of having helped to win the pennant," Simmons said. "It was the realization that at last Connie Mack, the manager and man we all so much respect and admire, had attained his ambition of winning the pennant once more. He is no longer young, and it was being said that he would never get together another pennant winner."[2]

Because of his heroics in Game One of the Series, Howard Ehmke was a popular attraction at various venues during the off-season. That fall he was the guest speaker at a meeting of a Philadelphia advertising club. When he was introduced, the club members gave him a raucous four-minute greeting that included rattles, whistles, and horns. Ehmke confirmed the story of how he came to be Mack's choice to start the opener and related a conversation he had with Mickey Cochrane before the game. He told Cochrane he "had been waiting for sixteen years for this one moment. Whatever you do, Mickey, don't get worried. Just keep smiling, we can't lose this game." Ehmke said he had his game plan all figured out: "I knew just what every batter could hit, and I saw to it that I had a ball they could not bang away at."

Ehmke talked about some strategic moves fans might have been unaware of, such as how he took advantage of the A's wearing gray road uniforms: "When Hornsby was at the plate with two men on base, I held that ball right next to my shirt. He never got his keen eye on that leather. I let the ball go without letting Hornsby gaze at it for a fraction of a second and before he knew it, the ball was at the plate."[3]

Seemingly never tired of talking about Ehmke's gem, Mack wrote the following short note to his former pitcher on December 23, 1932:

> To Howard Ehmke,
> Whom I consider the greatest pitching artist of his day. Your pitching in the first game of the World Series of 1929 when you broke all records in striking out thirteen of the Cubs gave me the thrill that will always be remembered by me.
> Connie Mack[4]

Ehmke was often a major topic of the featured speakers even at dinners he did not attend. One such occasion was a Knights of Columbus banquet to honor his teammate Jimmy Dykes. In his speech Dykes predicted that Ehmke "[will be] one of the outstanding pitchers of our staff next year. No one but Ehmke himself knows the pain and trouble he had with his pitching arm during the season," Dykes, a native Philadelphian, told the diners. "Now that his right hand [sic] has responded to treatment, I believe it will serve him well and that he will win many games."[5] (Ehmke's sore arm was treated by Dr. Charles C. Van Ronk, of Philadelphia, just before he pitched the Athletics to their Game One victory.)[6]

But it was in his hometown on the evening of January 10, 1930, where Ehmke had his most emotion-filled tribute. While he was in Silver Creek, visiting his mother, the local Chamber of Commerce sponsored a banquet in his honor at the First United Presbyterian Church. About 175 people attended, including two guest speakers: Buffalo area resident and Cubs manager Joe McCarthy and Frank J. Offermann, president of the International League's Buffalo Bisons.[7] McCarthy told the audience that Ehmke pitched the greatest-ever World Series game and that his win in Game One was the turning point of the Series.[8]

Ehmke was presented with a wristwatch bearing the inscription "From Silver Creek fans." In his remarks he remembered all his boyhood friends and teammates and many of the locals in attendance, to most of whom he was still known as "Bob." He spoke of the dreams that led to his being honored that night. "Whenever spring rolled around . . . I never could study," he recalled. "My ambition was to be a big leaguer, then a World Series hero, and some day to come back to Silver Creek and be greeted the way I am tonight."[9]

Ehmke had contemplated retirement during his regular-season struggles in 1929, but his performance in the Series made him reconsider. "I have had several chats with Connie Mack, and I have come to the conclusion I can stand another year in baseball and enjoy some success," he said. "I believe there is something left in my wing."[10]

Still Ehmke realized his days as a Major League pitcher, if not over, were surely nearing their end.[11] Looking ahead to that eventuality, he approached Mack during the winter with an idea. For several years he had been representing a Detroit-based firm that manufactured the tarpaulins that covered football fields. He now decided to open his own tarpaulin manufacturing business and asked Mack to invest in the company, and Mack did.

Reporter Henry P. Edwards, who played against Ehmke when they were teenagers, summed up what made him special among pitchers: "Ehmke is one of the select class of pitchers who can throw overhand, side-arm, and underhand, one who has a fastball, a slow one, and a still slower one, several varieties of curves, and possibly the only one who has what is termed the 'hesitation ball.'"[12]

The Babe Ruth–led evolution of baseball from that of the low-scoring Deadball Era to the long ball–style game coincided with Ehmke's Major League career. But no matter the style of play, Ehmke was always looking for ways to stay ahead of the hitters. "I'm convinced this orgy of heavy hitting which has existed in the last decade can be stopped," he said. "If a pitcher can keep a baseball in a shadow for about twenty feet of the distance from the peak to the plate, he will have the batter at a disadvantage. There are bound to be shadows or 'spots' in every park. . . . You know I have a side-arm motion which makes the ball appear to come right out of my belt. It's doggoned disconcerting to a batter to lose sight of that ball from the time I start to wind up until it starts for the plate," he explained. "And when it comes into sight from nowhere on a dull background, it's still more confusing." Likely speaking from his heart rather than his brain, Ehmke said he expected to use this knowledge to win twenty games in 1930.[13]

40. Howard Ehmke was an enthusiastic golfer who regularly shot in the low 80s. In his post-playing days he was a frequent winner of Suburban League titles around Philadelphia. *Special Collections Research Center, Temple University Libraries, Philadelphia, Pennsylvania, Philadelphia Evening Bulletin Collection.*

Before heading south to Fort Myers for spring training, the golf-loving Ehmke teamed with Johnny Farrell, the 1928 National Open champion, to win a February 13 match at St. Augustine, Florida.[14] Ehmke did not pitch an inning in any of the A's Florida exhibition games, but he worked hard and declared himself ready whenever Mack needed him.

Ehmke made his first appearance of the season on April 21, against the Senators, allowing two runs in 1⅓ innings of relief. Six days later at

Washington, he relieved Rube Walberg in the second inning and was touched for six runs and twelve hits in 6⅔ innings. Ehmke's one start in 1930 was in the first game of a May 22 home doubleheader against New York. In what was the final Major League game of his career, he allowed five runs and eight hits in two plus innings in a 10–1 Yankees win. He yielded two home runs, one to opposing pitcher George Pipgras and one to Babe Ruth that cleared the right-field roof.[15] The Yanks won the second game as well, 20–13, led by Lou Gehrig's three home runs.[16]

The official end came on May 30, 1930. The A's announced they had asked for waivers on Ehmke for the purpose of giving him his unconditional release.[17] After hearing the news, Ehmke, who had served mostly as a mentor to the team's young pitchers this spring, said, "I'll not play for any other manager except Connie Mack. I'm going to continue my workouts at Shibe Park, and if my arm comes around, I'll ask to be reinstated, and I know Mr. Mack will give me the opportunity if I tell him I can still give him some well-pitched games."[18]

Three weeks after his release, Ehmke took a job as a camp director at Camp Tecumseh, an exclusive retreat for boys on Lake Winnipesaukee in New Hampshire's White Mountains. He was in charge of several hundred boys at the camp, the same one he had attended as a youngster. Ehmke would stay there in July and August in hopes that the outdoor life would strengthen him and help his arm heal. But his heart was still with Mack and the A's. Late in the season he was spotted in the stands at Baker Bowl scouting the St. Louis Cardinals, the A's likely World Series opponents.

On September 22, 1930, less than a year after reaching the pinnacle of his career, Ehmke pitched the semi-pro Wentz-Olney club of Philadelphia to a 6–5 win over the Lancaster club. He struck out sixteen and helped his cause with two doubles.[19] A week later he switched sides and pitched Lancaster to a 9–5 victory over Wentz-Olney, whose pitcher was former A's ace Chief Bender. The game was played on a Sunday, at Shibe Park, before a crowd of more than twenty-five thousand. Sunday baseball was against the law in Philadelphia, but Mayor Harry Mackey had ordered the police "to look the other way." The game was sponsored by the *Philadelphia Record* as a fundraiser for a family of a man shot to death by the police while he was protesting the arrest of his son.[20] There was no admission fee; the funds raised were through a collection taken up among the spectators.[21]

Ehmke believed he could still pitch at the Major League level and planned to use this fall and the next spring to prove his case. Claiming his arm felt fine, he said he would pay his own way down to Fort Myers in March 1931 to try out with the A's. "Down there, I will try out the arm. If it is anything like what I expect, I'll be tossing them up for Connie Mack. I believe the complete rest I gave my arm has fixed it."[22]

Mack appeared receptive to the idea. "If Howard Ehmke says he's fit to pitch again, then he can have a job with our club," he said at spring training.[23] Ehmke, who had been working out at the University of Pennsylvania, was confident he could make it back to Philadelphia. But like so many aging athletes wanting one more season of glory, he was unable to face reality. He never made it to spring training or to the Athletics.

A day before the 1931 A's began their quest for a third straight world championship, in Washington, Ehmke was in Pennsylvania pitching for the Eighth-Ward Club of Lancaster against Allentown. "So I am ready. I got a fairly good start with the University of Pennsylvania squad, and this game helped me immensely," Ehmke said. "I will continue my training at Shibe Park and will notify Mr. Mack I am in shape again before the month is out," he said, refusing to accept the futility of his efforts.[24]

The months came and went, with Ehmke still pitching but far from the big leagues. On May 10 he pitched for Lancaster against a Black team known as the New York Stars in the first-ever integrated game played at Yankee Stadium. The Stars reached him for twelve hits and twelve runs in five innings on their way to a 16–0 win.[25] Ehmke continued to pitch in semi-pro games into 1932. Financially independent of baseball, he was doing this only as a means to return to the A's.

In the summer of 1932 Ehmke pitched for the All-Philadelphians against various Negro League teams, including the New York Black Yankees, the Cuban Stars, and the Detroit Clowns. Even after his better outings, there was never any indication that he was close to being able to pitch at the big league level. He was, however, summoned to action by an old foe. Joe McCarthy, manager of the 1929 Chicago Cubs, was now in his second season as manager of the Yankees. Prior to the 1932 World Series, McCarthy, remembering the successful scouting of the Cubs Ehmke had done in 1929, hired him to scout them again.[26]

Philadelphia Inquirer sportswriter and former big league pitcher Stan Baumgartner wrote about Ehmke's quest to return to the big leagues and pitch in one more World Series for Connie Mack.[27] Against all odds, wrote Baumgartner, the city of Philadelphia and all baseball fans were rooting for the former A's pitcher to succeed: "Time after time he has gone to the mound in independent games around the city and pitched for almost nothing, sharing the receipts pro rata with the other boys, although it was his name that drew the dollars at the gate. He has suffered the ignominy of defeat from kids who would have been pie in his hands a few years ago. He heard the cat calls of fans who two years ago waited at Shibe Park to ogle him with awe."[28] The time had come for Ehmke to admit he could no longer still pitch at the Major League level.

41

Defending Champions

The 1930 A's prepared for the new season with the same starting pitchers and position players they had in their championship season. The usually circumspect Connie Mack surprised observers at spring training when he declared, "We should win another pennant. . . . The Athletics, with their pitching and their power, should make it two straight."[1] A few weeks later he cautioned that the task would not be easy. "The past means nothing in sport. It is the living present that alone counts. Champions must fight tooth and nail to keep aspiring competitors from wrestling their honors from them."[2]

Mack expected his two oldest pitchers, Howard Ehmke and Jack Quinn, again to make key contributions. "Ehmke is going to do more pitching and win more games than he did last year," he said and added, "I never saw Quinn more serious than this spring."[3] The spitballer told reporters that his pre-spring training Hot Springs regimen started with hikes of five miles a day, working up to fifteen miles. Quinn always ended his day in the mineral baths for which the Arkansas city was known. He "sneers at a golf club," wrote one reporter, referring to the booming sport that many players enjoyed in their free time during training camp.[4]

The A's opened the defense of their championship with complete game wins by Lefty Grove and Rube Walberg. On April 20 they raised their record to 3-0 when Quinn tossed 4⅔ innings of scoreless relief in a come-from-behind win over the Red Sox at Braves Field.[5] His single to lead off the seventh inning started the Philadelphia comeback. He jokingly told a Boston reporter after the game that the first twenty-five years were the hardest.[6]

But all was not smooth for Quinn this season. He was hit hard in his two April starts, and Mack would use him primarily in relief the rest of the season.[7] On May 22, the day after an effective relief appearance by Quinn against New York, the Yankees clubbed the A's in a doubleheader sweep, as Babe Ruth hit three out of the park, one off Quinn. New York beat starter Ehmke in the first game, 10–1, and battered six Philadelphia pitchers, 20–13, in the second, a game in which Quinn, George Earnshaw, and Grove all were ineffective in relief.

Quinn bounced back on May 30 against Washington when he relieved Grove after nine innings of a 6–6 tie and pitched four perfect innings as the A's won in thirteen. When they also took the second game, they drew to within one game of the league-leading Senators.

Quinn saved back-to-back games for Grove and Earnshaw in St. Louis on June 3 and 4. "Mack is now using the veteran almost exclusively as a rescue pitcher with amazing results," wrote James Isaminger. "At an age when the majority of pitchers have long since retired, Quinn is a vital force on the Athletics' staff in the new character of relief pitcher."[8] Five days later another scoreless relief stint, this time in Chicago, earned Quinn his fifth win of the season. He retired three pinch hitters in a three-up, three-down ninth inning, and the Athletics extended their lead over the Senators to three games.

On three consecutive days at the end of June, Quinn won two games in relief and saved a third. As July began, the 45-25 A's held a 2-game lead over Washington and New York in the pennant race. Early that month he would work effectively in three straight games.[9] With iron man relief work, he had appeared in six games over eight days.

On June 27 Quinn won his sixth game with five innings of sharp relief work against the Browns. Jimmie Foxx and Al Simmons homered in the game, and so did Quinn, just four days before his forty-seventh birthday. Only Cap Anson had homered after the age of forty-five.[10] Quinn's mark stood for seventy-six years, until forty-seven-year-old Julio Franco hit a home run on April 20, 2006.[11] A reporter for Quinn's old hometown paper, the *Pottsville Republican and Herald*, wrote the next day, "Early Friday morning local time, part of Quinn's legendary career was erased."[12] He remains the oldest American League player and the oldest Major League pitcher to hit a home run.

Quinn started his first game in two months on July 23 and defeated Detroit, 4–1. He allowed only five hits over eight innings, with "captivating pitching" that "nonplussed" the Tigers.[13] Syndicated columnist Hugh Fullerton noted that whoever said "youth must prevail" would retract that statement after seeing how well "ancient" Jack Quinn and a few other aged pitchers performed that week.[14]

Ten days later Quinn pitched two innings of scoreless relief against the Red Sox. He was pulled for forty-three-year-old pinch hitter Eddie Collins, who made only three plate appearance in his final season. Collins's single helped trigger a five-run inning, and the A's rallied for an 8–7 win. This was the 3,315th and final hit of his brilliant career.

That summer *Baseball Magazine* had a feature on Quinn titled "The Oldest Veteran in the Major Leagues." In it he explained his approach to pitching: "If you can put the ball where you want to, you don't need so much stuff. . . . Some pitchers like to burn the ball over the plate when they get in a hole. I prefer to fall back on a change of pace. Slow stuff will stop a slugger more effectively than speed." He then commented on his relaxed approach to the game: "Nothing bothers me. Why should it? The undertaker will get us all soon enough. There's no need to meet him more than halfway."[15]

With their twentieth wedding anniversary approaching that fall, Quinn's wife, Jean, explained how and why her husband continued to pitch all these years: "My Jack loves baseball. I tell him it's his religion. He lives it. That's the secret to his long term in the game; he loves it so. And, too, he doesn't worry. He does the very best he can in each game, and if he loses, he says the other pitcher was better. But Jack doesn't think there is a better pitcher in the game than he is. That very self-confidence of his has been one of his biggest helps."[16]

Another "big help" for Quinn was the constant presence of his wife. One Philadelphia reporter wrote that she may have set a record "in feminine attendance at ballgames," having seen more than two thousand contests. The Quinns had no children, but their marriage seemed to be an especially loving one; they were inseparable. "Their perfectly married life has been the envy of his bachelor teammates," wrote that reporter.[17]

Quinn's final two starts of the season were not effective; he did not get past the fourth inning against the Yankees on July 29 or the Senators on August 14.[18] Yet he continued to excel out of the bullpen, not allowing a run in his final five relief appearances. His last one came on September 3 against the Red Sox, and the win pushed the A's record to 90-45 and their lead over the Senators to 6½ games. Grove was staked

41. The 6-foot-3-inch Lefty Grove got enormous speed and power behind his pitches. He was described during his career as "lanky" and "sinewy." This photo reveals his lean physique as A's trainer Doc Ebling works on him during spring training. At the time, Grove was in the midst of a seven-year run of leading the American League in strikeouts. Grove once revealed, "I throw from my spine, not from my elbow." *Steve Steinberg Collection.*

to a 5–0 lead in the game before he ran into trouble in a four-run sixth inning. Quinn pitched the final three innings, earning his sixth save and helping Grove push his record to 23-5. Mack did not call on Quinn again during the regular season, probably because he wanted him rested for the World Series.

Grove had a spectacular 28-5 season in 1930. Perhaps more impressive than his winning the pitching Triple Crown (leading the league in wins, earned run average, and strikeouts) was his control. He led the league in the strikeouts-to-walks ratio with a 3.48 mark, the best average since Walter Johnson posted a 3.63 mark in 1915.[19] His control was so good that he set a career-best mark of just 1.86 walks per nine innings. And he also set a career high in strikeouts with 209.

Ed Pollock wrote of Grove's improvement this season: "Grove has gained complete control of the temperament which led to sinking spells in the past."[20] He even was a willing relief pitcher, when needed, and led the American League with nine saves. "I'll work for you any way you want me to," he told Mack, "even if I never get credit for a game."[21]

As the Athletics prepared to meet the St. Louis Cardinals in the World Series, Quinn played a key role. The Cardinals had acquired spitballer Burleigh Grimes on June 16, when they were in fourth place. His thirteen wins for St. Louis were a big reason why they won the National League pennant, edging the Cubs by two games.[22] The A's had not done well this season against another spitballer, Chicago's Red Faber, who had beaten the Athletics three times. Quinn pitched a lot of batting practice down the stretch to prepare the A's for Grimes, "to get their eyes accustomed to the intricacies of spitball pitching," wrote Isaminger.[23]

After the Ehmke surprise start the year before, there was conjecture whether Mack would start Quinn in Game One, to "try his luck as he so astonishingly did last year with a dark horse."[24] As the rumors swirled, "Connie only smiled."[25]

But Mack made the conventional choices of Grove and Earnshaw as the starters for Games One and Two, and they each went the distance in easy wins. The Cardinals pushed across a couple runs in Game Three and held a 2–0 lead after six innings. When A's reliever Bill Shores gave up three hits and two runs to start the bottom of the seventh, Quinn got the call and pitched the final two innings. He quelled the rally without a ball leaving the infield. He did give up a run on two hits in the eighth inning. The A's could not mount a rally and went down to defeat, 5–0.

At the age of forty-seven, Jack Quinn remains the oldest pitcher to appear in a World Series, a year after becoming the oldest to start a World Series game. After St. Louis evened the Series the next day, Philadelphia pitching held the Cardinals to just one run and eight hits in the next two games to close out the A's second straight world championship.

While the 1930 season saw an explosion of offense, pitchers dominated the World Series. The A's batted only .197, and the Cardinals were only slightly better at .200. After Grove pitched just 6⅓ innings and did not make a start in the 1929 World Series, Mack was asked, "What about Grove?" Many years later he said, "I answered that in the next World Series," when the ace tossed nineteen innings.[26] Grove started two games, winning one and losing the other (a 3–1 loss, in which he gave up only five hits), and he picked up another victory in relief when Jimmie Foxx's dramatic ninth-inning home run off Grimes broke a scoreless tie in Game Five.

Earnshaw was even better: in twenty-five innings he allowed only two earned runs and struck out nineteen. Catcher Mickey Cochrane said of Earnshaw's performances, "His fast ball looked like a golf ball coming over the plate."[27] Earnshaw also set a unique postseason record: for the second straight World Series, he started two consecutive games.[28] Grimes pitched well in the Series but lost his Game One and Game Five starts to Grove.

A month after the Series the Athletics released Quinn and forty-one-year-old backup catcher Wally Schang, who had been his teammate on the Yankees a decade earlier. Stan Baumgartner wrote, "It almost broke old Jack Quinn's heart when he was notified of his release."[29] Stoney McLinn noted that Major League baseball was losing the romance of an enduring mystery: "Unconsciously, we believe, Ol' Jack stumbled over the fact that his age could become a matter of Nation-wide curiosity. So he shrouded the year of his birth in a veil of mystery that had everybody guessing. . . . The age mystery threw around him a blanket of color that kept him in the major arena."[30]

Ed Pollock wrote that Quinn "had plenty of stuff last season" but had a hard time fielding bunts and was tiring sooner. "The more fatigue, the less twist to the spitter. However, there's plenty of twist to fool Minor Leaguers."[31] Connie Mack asked Quinn if he would be willing to go to Portland of the Pacific Coast League, and that team prepared for the possibility by asking that league to exempt Quinn from the spitball ban.[32]

But Quinn, now a free agent, was not ready to accept demotion to the Minors. Reporters tracked him down at his rustic cabin in Roaring Creek. The headline of one Philadelphia paper shouted, "'Through? Not on Your Life,' Cries Jack Quinn."[33] Quinn told another sportswriter, "I still think I am good for another year. I believe I can win the quota of games allotted every good Major League pitcher, which is about 15."[34] He added, "I've been in baseball so long, I hate to give up the game. I don't know what I will do if I don't answer the spring training call."[35]

Jack Quinn finished the 1930 season with nine wins and six saves, second most in the league. His earned run average did come down as the season progressed, from 7.80 on May 24 to 4.42. It exceeded 4.00 for only the third time in his career; the other two occasions were also followed by his release (1912 with New York and 1925 with Boston). But a closer look at the numbers reveals his excellence as a reliever, in stark contrast with his performance as a starter. In six starts and 29 innings, his ERA was 7.45. In twenty-nine relief appearances and 60⅔ innings, his ERA was 2.97. Would a Major League manager see such splits and realize the possibilities even if the pitcher was forty-seven years old?

42

A New League, a New Role

Jack Quinn's career was at a crossroads after the 1930 World Series. As a free agent, he had no assurance a Major League club would sign him. Moreover, it was not clear he could pitch in the Minors, which had banned the spitball in all its leagues. While a team could request a waiver of the spitball ban, there was no guarantee it would be granted. An article in the March 1931 issue of *Baseball Magazine* had an ominous sub-headline regarding Quinn: "The Release of Jack Quinn, Oldest Player in the Major Leagues, Leaves but Three Active [Spitball Pitchers]."[1]

Quinn always emphasized conditioning his legs, to strengthen the foundation of his body. "My own recipe," he said, "is to climb mountains in the off-season. 'Going Hunting,' I call it."[2] This off-season was no different than any other and included his February routine of hiking the hills and "boiling out" in the steam baths of Hot Springs, Arkansas. Quinn did take time to go to the December winter meetings at the Commodore Hotel in New York City so that team executives could see he was in excellent shape.[3]

One of those executives was longtime Brooklyn manager Wilbert Robinson, a man with a reputation of generating success with aged pitchers who were considered washed up.[4] He won the 1916 National League pennant with Larry Cheney, Jack Coombs, and Rube Marquard, star hurlers on the downward side of their careers. More recently he almost won the 1924 pennant with the midseason acquisition of aging Bill Doak from the Cardinals.[5] Uncle Robbie, as he was affectionately known, told a *Baseball Magazine* writer, "It's a matter of diplomacy and a continual study of human nature. . . . If you work for a pitcher's good, intelligently and with some consideration for him, you have little trouble. . . . One reason for my success with old pitchers is that I give them enough time to rest up after pitching a game before trying a new one."[6]

In his history of the Dodgers, Tommy Holmes wrote that now, "More than ever, Robbie pursued his policy of collecting castoffs."[7] Robinson had a conversation with one such castoff at the winter meetings: Jack Quinn.[8] Robinson said of the forty-seven-year-old Quinn in early February, "He's just at the right age to be a great pitcher."[9]

On February 10, 1931, newspapers reported that Quinn sent a telegram from Hot Springs to Frank York, the president of the Dodgers: "Accept your offer and will sign contract." The signing generated mixed reviews in Brooklyn. "Fans were somewhat disgruntled," wrote an AP reporter, to learn that their new pitcher "was in fact just two years younger than the Brooklyn Bridge."[10] What was not known at the time was that Quinn and the bridge had come into the world the same year, 1883.[11]

Other observers saw the signing as a positive for the Dodgers. "The big right-hander boasts control, brains, and poise, as well as a moist ball delivery," wrote one.[12] When Quinn signed, he said, "The free-swinging hitters of the present era make it easy for a pitcher of my type."[13] John Kieran saluted him in his column: "It's a wonderful case of longevity. It may be genius. It may even be stubbornness. . . . A habit adhered to through a quarter of a century is hard to break."[14]

When the Yankees traded Quinn to the Red Sox a decade earlier, Joe Vila declared, "Quinn is through."[15] Another longtime New York sportswriter, Frank O'Neill, wrote at the time, "The veteran has been in the show for a long time and is making his last stand. He will at least be a good finishing pitcher."[16] Yet in the nine seasons following those predictions, only in 1930 did Quinn relieve more games than he started.[17]

At the Dodgers' training camp in Clearwater, Florida, Quinn was quoted extensively; his endurance and durability were becoming legendary. People wanted to know his "secrets"; the usually reticent Quinn obliged. "Baseball is my business," he explained in early March, "and keeping myself fit to play is an all-year-round proposition with me."[18] A week later he said, "My secret of control is keeping my eyes on the plate. I believe that shooting [clay pigeons] has helped me in this respect."[19]

Quinn was also very specific in describing his routine: "When I begin to throw in the Spring, I toss back and forth at a distance of about 35 feet. Each day I move a few feet further back, until the distance is increased to about 65 feet, or five feet further than the regulation pitching distance. Then I can start pitching to hitters, and the distance seems short to me."[20] He also gave special focus to a possible weakness in his game: "I like to have a rookie bunt to me for 20 minutes at a time, and I tell him to bunt as much as possible in unexpected directions."[21]

Quinn would be the third forty-year-old pitcher on the Brooklyn team; the others were longtime stars Dazzy Vance and Dolf Luque. Quinn would also be reunited with three men with whom he played on the Red Sox years earlier: Lefty O'Doul, Babe Herman, and Ike Boone. O'Doul, a pitcher on the 1923 Red Sox, was now one of the game's best hitters: he batted .398 and .383 for the Phillies the past two seasons. He wore out the Dodgers' pitchers, including Quinn, during workouts, prompting Holmes to write, "O'Doul needs batting practice like Bob Grove needs a fastball. . . . He'll practice as long as he can find somebody to throw a ball to him."[22] Herman, who was at spring training with the Red Sox in 1923 and 1924, hit .381 and .393 for Brooklyn in 1929–30.[23] Boone hit over .400 in the Pacific Coast League in 1929 and 1930.

But all three were poor fielders. Arthur Daley called O'Doul "the delight and despair of a generation of Brooklyn Dodger fans."[24] Holmes wrote that Boone "didn't cover much more than the ground he stood on in the outfield."[25] He would appear in only nineteen more games in the Major Leagues, and Brooklyn reporter Murray Robinson would write that Boone "will go down in baseball history as one of the greatest tragedies of them all. The King of the Minor League Sluggers, the huge Alabaman is a confirmed flop in the big leagues."[26]

The Dodgers had been the surprise team of the 1930 season. They finished just 6 games behind the pennant-winning St. Louis Cardinals, after they held first place for more than two months. The Dodgers were in first as late as September 15, when the Cardinals came to Brooklyn and swept a three-game series. With the addition of O'Doul to an already potent batting order, some observers picked Brooklyn to win the 1931 pennant. Murray Robinson wrote of the club heading into the season: "There isn't a single if or but on the club. Entire club tried and true. . . . Pitchers old, but good and plenty."[27] It was not surprising that Fred Lieb called the 1931 Dodgers "the most interesting, colorful club in baseball."[28]

But the front office was in disarray; it was bitterly split between the family of the late owner, Charles Ebbets, who supported Robinson to

42. After a long nineteenth-century playing career, Wilbert Robinson managed the Brooklyn Dodgers (often known as the Robins in his honor) for eighteen seasons, starting in 1914. The eccentric and easygoing "Uncle Robbie" had a reputation for reclaiming veteran pitchers. "Of course, he had his idiosyncrasies," said outfielder Babe Herman. "But who doesn't?" Robinson signed Jack Quinn in his last year as manager, and the pitcher responded with a sensational season out of the bullpen. *Steve Steinberg Collection.*

continue as manager, and co-owner Steve McKeever, who wanted to get rid of Uncle Robbie. Robinson was replaced as president in 1929, and 1931 would be his eighteenth and final year as the clubhouse leader. At that time John Kieran wrote, "He was not an intellectual. He knew baseball as the spotted setter knows the secrets of quail hunting, by instinct and experience. A jolly old gentleman and as honest as the sunlight."[29]

Quinn told a reporter, "They [newspapers] finally got Connie Mack to believing I'm too old. But there's many a good game left in this arm. I've taken care of it, and if I get a chance, I'll show it."[30] On March 18 in Fort Myers, Florida, he had that chance, with Mack on the receiving end. Quinn shut out the world champion A's for three innings. Mack was moved to say, "It looks as though I made a mistake. I thought I could get along this year without John Quinn. . . . And here's Quinn— well, look at him."[31]

Quinn continued to have the utmost admiration for Mack: "He's head and shoulders above any manager I ever saw." Quinn added, "The secret of his success was in knowing how to handle men. . . . Everybody who ever played for him loved him. On top of that, he knew everything that was to be known about baseball and still does."[32] Quinn predicted the A's would win the American League pennant again in 1931, in part because "when a team plays the A's, it is pitted against ten men. Mack is the tenth man."[33]

Robinson was excited to benefit from Mack's oversight: "Quinn ought to win twenty games for us this year. He is in great shape, and we were lucky to get him."[34] Quinn said five other clubs were interested in him, but he thought Brooklyn gave him the best chance to get back to the World Series. Robinson added to the fans' high expectations when he said as his club headed north after spring training, "I'm taking the strongest team to Brooklyn since I was hired as manager. . . . We can have no alibi now if we lose."[35]

Because the two leading pitchers of the 1930 club, Vance and Luque, were dealing with minor injuries, Robinson selected Quinn to start on Opening Day against the Boston Braves. "I don't care whether Quinn is 19 or 90," the manager asserted truculently.[36] Almost a century later, Quinn remains the oldest pitcher to start an opener.[37]

Another veteran of the American League, Tom Zachary, started for the Braves. He retired only one man before being pulled, as Quinn was handed an early 3–0 lead. But Quinn ran into trouble in the middle innings and departed after six-plus innings. Tommy Holmes felt Robbie should have pulled him earlier, when he tired with two outs in the fourth and a 4–1 lead.[38] Quinn was tagged with the 7–4 loss. The start would be his last in the Major Leagues.

After the Dodgers lost their first five games and ten of their first twelve, Murray Robinson wrote in the *Brooklyn Standard Union,* "They took too much stock in the advance notices they were given. . . . The 1931 pennant was won for them—in the papers—even before the umpire called 'play ball!'"[39]

Jack Quinn may have been finished as a starter, but he was not done as a pitcher. In a two-week period, from April 25 to May 8, he made five scoreless relief appearances; he saved the two games in which he inherited a lead. In the first, his two scoreless innings secured a 1–0 win over the Giants. With the tying run ninety feet away, he retired young slugger Mel Ott on an easy grounder. Two days later he held off the Phillies, and Brooklyn's winning pitcher, Joe Shaute, declared, "Jack Quinn is the best relief pitcher in baseball today, and I don't give a hang if he's older than Methuselah. I'm for him!"[40]

After a poor performance on May 23, Quinn gave up just two earned runs over 34⅓ innings in his next seventeen appearances. "The graying Quinn has been a one-man rescue squad unlike any in modern history," wrote syndicated columnist Frank Menke.[41] The National League had never seen a more dominant pitcher coming out of the bullpen.[42] Quinn told Menke, "I wanted a chance to prove that they [the A's] were wrong in their judgment. No team in the American League would give me a chance."[43] On June 14, against Pittsburgh, Quinn saved another game for Shaute. He entered in the ninth inning with the bases loaded in a 6–3 game and induced a game-ending double play on a comebacker to the mound.

Six days later "wrinkled John Picus Quinn, antediluvian spitball flinger," won his first National League game in eighteen years.[44] "Give the old boy a headline," wrote Sid Mercer in the *New York American*.[45] Babe Herman's triple in the eighth and double in the ninth rallied Brooklyn to the 6–5 decision over the Cubs. On July 5 Quinn celebrated his forty-sixth birthday (actually his forty-eighth) by beating the Giants with three perfect innings of relief. "No one worried about the mooted question of John Picus's exact age," wrote Roscoe McGowen of the *New York Times*. "It was enough that he was born on July 5 and proved himself still young enough to . . . suppress nine of McGraw's heaviest hitters as fast as they could come to the plate."[46] With the win, their fifteenth in seventeen games, the Dodgers had made a remarkable

43. Al Lopez (*right, pictured with Quinn*) was the Dodgers' regular catcher from 1930 to 1935 and was behind the plate for most of Jack Quinn's eighty-one appearances in 1931–32. Arthur Daley of the *New York Times* said of Lopez, "What he lacked in bulk, he compensated for in agility, speed, intelligence, and class." Lopez would follow his nineteen-year playing career with seventeen seasons as a manager of the Cleveland Indians and Chicago White Sox. His pennants-winning seasons with Cleveland (1954) and Chicago (1959) are the only two seasons from 1949 to 1964 that the Yankees did not finish first. *Boston Public Library, Leslie Jones Collection.*

climb to third place, within a half-game of New York and four back of the league-leading Cardinals.

Brooklyn third baseman Wally Gilbert marveled at Quinn's effectiveness: "What a man he is to have in reserve, when the going's tough in the late innings! And he seems to have the endurance of a kid. . . . Almost every pitch is a spitter. Just wets the tips of his index and second finger[s] as he winds up and lets 'er go."[47] Quinn was never one to slobber over the ball. "People think spitballs are messy things," he said. "Mine aren't. . . . Sometimes there's enough perspiration on my hand to suffice."[48]

George Earnshaw, who was still a member of the Athletics, admired his former teammate and roommate: "I used to marvel at Jack Quinn and [deceased Yankees pitcher] Urban Shocker. Those two fellows, more than any pitchers I ever saw, had the secret to taking it easy when they had a chance. Neither of them had a lot on the ball. But they were wise old owls out there on the mound. They had control, and they knew all the time just what they were trying to do."[49]

On July 17 Quinn pitched three scoreless innings at St. Louis to save a game for Luque. The next day he relieved Vance in a wild ninth inning at Wrigley Field. In the top half, Lefty O'Doul was thrown out at home and then out of the game for arguing. In the bottom half, the Cubs tied the score at two, aided by Babe Herman, who dropped "an easy fly . . . in his graceless way." With the bases loaded, three Cubs were thrown out at home, two on force plays and one on a tag play on the hit that tied the game. Quinn worked out of bases-loaded tenth and eleventh innings, the latter after the Dodgers pushed a run across that would account for a 3–2 win. Holmes said the game was "entirely a saga of old Jack Quinn's intestinal fortitude and his pitching skill."[50]

The win moved the Dodgers into third place, just a half-game behind the Giants and 5 games behind St. Louis. O'Doul, in the midst of a 32 for 51 stretch over twelve games, led the surge. At the end of July Wilbert Robinson was moved to say, "In all my fifty years of baseball, I have never seen anything to compare with the scientific hitting that Lefty has done on this trip. That goes for all the hitters I have seen in my half century in the game, including Willie Keeler."[51]

The strain of pitching six innings over two days, culminating in the drama in Chicago, took its toll on Quinn, a pitcher who (almost) never had arm trouble. "I had to bear down on every pitch in Chicago, and after the game my arm was so lame, I couldn't raise it," he said. "I'm having my arm worked on every day and night."[52] The *Brooklyn Eagle* ran a photo of Quinn with the caption "Has Father Time Stepped In?" The copy said he would be out for two weeks.[53] One account said he had a painful torn shoulder muscle. By the time he returned to action on August 4, the Dodgers had fallen 9½ games out of first place. By the end of the day, that margin had grown to 11 games.

Quinn again saved a game for Shaute on August 16. After Cincinnati scored five runs off Shaute in the ninth inning to close within one run, Quinn retired Joe Stripp to clinch the 8–7 win. Four days later he again faced just one man to nail down a victory. After motioning center fielder Johnny Frederick to move to right-center, Quinn induced the Cubs' Les Bell to hit a fly ball to the spot where Frederick was standing.

On August 23 Vance took a 4–1 lead into the eighth inning when Pittsburgh struck for three runs on five hits. Quinn got the final four outs without the ball's leaving the infield. He picked up the win when he hit a leadoff single in the ninth and came around to score the winning run. A reporter for the *New York Evening Graphic* wrote, "Probably he'll die at the age of 90 in the box hurling them . . . for he has licked age, and he has licked defeat, and he has licked adversity." The writer added, "The secret of Jack Quinn's success is his mental strength."[54] The forty-eight-year-old Quinn was in the midst of six appearances in twelve days.

The Dodgers' season played out against a backdrop of warring factions, in what one New York newspaper called "Fratricidal Flatbush."[55] Brooklyn's newspaper columnists took sides in the struggle between Uncle Robbie's supporters and his detractors. Edward Darrow of the *Standard Union* wrote that Robinson "has failed ignominiously" in handling pitchers—by overworking the veterans and overlooking the youngsters.[56] The forty-year-olds Vance and Luque won only eleven and seven games respectively. The promising twenty-year-old speed-ball pitcher, Van Lingle Mungo, was not called up until September and was impressive in the five games in which he appeared.

Quinn appeared in thirty-eight games in relief and finished twenty-nine of them.[57] His thirteen saves were the most in Major League baseball that year. Holmes noted that "his extreme efficiency" was overlooked because his club was not in the pennant race.[58] The Dodgers finished in fourth place, 21 games behind the pennant-winning Cardinals.

Edward Murphy added that "more often than not, the good work of an emergency pitcher is overlooked by the fans."[59] Quinn would return in 1932, the *Brooklyn Eagle* reported, because "Old Jack could travel at a magnificent pace for two or three innings."[60] He was "the most astonishing performer of the lot [in 1931]," wrote Holmes.[61]

43

An Extraordinary Career
Comes to an End

After eighteen years and 2,735 games, Wilbert Robinson was out as Brooklyn manager. Longtime outfielder Max Carey, who joined the Dodgers in 1926 after seventeen years with the Pirates, replaced him.[1] The difference in the management style of the two men was dramatic. "While Robbie was easygoing and gave his men great latitude on the field and off, Carey was the schoolmasterish type and would be a strict disciplinarian," wrote Frank Graham. "The fans thought he would be a good manager, but they could not have the same warm feeling they had for Robbie."[2]

Carey quickly put his stamp on the team. He brought in former Dodgers outfielder and fan favorite (and Carey's Pittsburgh teammate in 1919–20) Casey Stengel as a coach. Carey gambled with a big trade, one that would be disastrous for Brooklyn, when he dealt away Babe Herman and a young catcher and future Hall of Famer, Ernie Lombardi.[3] He signed free agent pitcher Waite Hoyt, who, at the age of thirty, was on the downward side of his career. Murray Robinson predicted the former Yankees star "will be the sensation of the National League this year."[4] The Dodgers would release Hoyt on June 7 after he won only one game and sported a 7.76 earned run average.[5]

Carey also acquired outfielder Hack Wilson, who hit a National League record fifty-six home runs for the Cubs just two years earlier. Graham wrote that the 5-foot-6-inch slugger looked "semi-heroic: He was a colossus from the knees up, but his knees seemed to start at the ground."[6] Wilson had flourished under manager Joe McCarthy that year. But when Rogers Hornsby took over the Cubs in 1931, Wilson was miserable, and his performance reflected his hatred of his manager. McCarthy, now managing the New York Yankees, predicted Wilson would return to form in Brooklyn: "He is a player you've got to coddle. . . . He is a sensitive sort of chap, and criticism cuts him in half."[7]

Unlike Wilson, Jack Quinn was a low-maintenance workhorse who did not need much attention from his manager or the press. Grantland Rice featured Quinn in a column after the pitcher's first season with the Dodgers: "The showman of sport has his place. But so has the effective competitor who can handle his job without any particular magnetic appeal to the populace at large." Quinn, he wrote, was a striking example of the "painstaking, hard-working, careful, conscientious job handler," as opposed to the more colorful sports figure, the "showman."[8]

Quinn signed with the Dodgers for $7,500, an increase from his 1931 salary.[9] A feature article that ran in many papers that summer noted Quinn wanted to round out a career of 30 years as a pro pitcher. "Old as he is," said the article, "Quinn still gets a kick out of the game. He looks forward to the thrills that come during ballgames."[10]

In his third regular-season appearance, on April 30, Quinn pitched eight innings of relief, his longest stint since 1929. He came on in the fifth with Brooklyn ahead of the Phillies, 7–5. He gave up single runs in the seventh and eighth and then pitched shutout ball until the thirteenth. A wild pitch—Quinn had a career-high seven this season—let the winning run score.

On June 8 Quinn had a similar long appearance and tough loss. He entered the game after the Cubs rallied to tie the score in the eighth inning and snuffed out the rally. He went on to pitch five scoreless innings, only to lose in the fourteenth. The *New York Times* described "a gallant pitchers' battle against Charlie Root," the Chicago veteran who pitched seven innings of one-hit relief to get the win.[11]

Two weeks later Quinn pitched six innings of sharp relief against the Pirates. Such performances led a *Brooklyn Eagle* headline to shout, just after Quinn's birthday, "Jack Quinn at 43, 47, or Even 52 Is Still a Mighty Handy Hurler." The article reported that he celebrated his birthday on the train to Cincinnati, but "What birthday? Aha!" The mystery remained, but "he's plenty old as ball players go."[12]

On July 10 a ninth-inning Hack Wilson error gave a game to the Pirates and dropped the hard-luck Quinn's record to 0-5, despite a respectable 3.35 earned run average. The 38-40 Dodgers were in fifth place but only 6½ games behind league-leading Pittsburgh.

Quinn saved two games at Wrigley Field in mid-July, costly losses for the second-place Cubs. On July 26 he picked up his first win of the season with two scoreless relief innings, when catcher Al Lopez tripled and scored the winning run. The next day Quinn squelched a Cardinals rally with one pitch by getting the last out in the top of the ninth, and Lefty O'Doul scored the winning run for Brooklyn in the home half. O'Doul was on his way to a league-leading .368 batting average.

In late July the Dodgers caught fire. During a four-week period leading up to a showdown series in Chicago starting on August 24, they won twenty-four games and lost only seven. They moved from seventh place, 12 games out, to second place, just 2½ games behind the first-place Cubs.[13] At the end of that stretch, one Brooklyn reporter gave coach Stengel some of the credit for keeping the players loose.[14] Ring Lardner wrote a fictional series about the 1932 Dodgers for the *Saturday Evening Post* and used Stengel as one of the real-life Dodgers. His warmth and patience contrasted with the traits of the prickly and humorless Carey.[15]

The Cubs swept the three-game series by a combined score of 26–11. It was "a gory shellacking," wrote Tommy Holmes in the *Sporting News*, one that probably ended "a rather desperate hope for a Brooklyn pennant."[16] Since Charlie Grimm had replaced Rogers Hornsby as manager, the Cubs had won seventeen of twenty-two games. With nine fewer losses than the Dodgers, they were in a strong position and would go on to the World Series, where they were swept by former manager McCarthy's Yankees. The Dodgers finished in third place, fourteen games back, a strong enough performance to earn Carey a return as manager in 1933.

Quinn had two excellent long outings in September. He pitched 4⅔ shutout innings against the Braves and 5 shutout innings against the Cardinals. He worked into and out of a bases-loaded jam in the tenth inning of the game against St. Louis and got the win when Lopez's bunt single drove home the winning run.

Quinn appeared in forty-two games in 1932, all in relief, and again led the league in saves, with nine. Tommy Holmes noted that Quinn warmed up in another sixty-three games and added, "He still is one of the most puzzling relief pitchers in the league."[17] His 3.30 earned run average was the lowest on the staff and more than a half-run lower

44. The Dodgers had a new manager in 1932, Max Carey (*second from left, next to Jack Quinn*), a star outfielder with the Pittsburgh Pirates for more than sixteen seasons. Dodgers favorite Casey Stengel (*seated, right*) joined Otto Miller (*second from right*), who had caught for Brooklyn for thirteen seasons, as the club's coaches. While Carey ran a far more disciplined clubhouse than Wilbert Robinson, Stengel helped keep things loose. Just two years later Stengel replaced Carey as the Dodgers' manager. *Family of Jack Quinn.*

than the league average of 3.88. Near the end of the season, he told New York reporter Edward Murphy, "If I can make it, 1933 will be my thirtieth year as an active pitcher. Naturally, since I'm so close to rounding out a thirty-year career as an active ball player, I'd be disappointed if I didn't get the chance to complete it."[18]

Before Quinn reported to Brooklyn's spring training camp in Miami in February 1933, he made his usual stop in Hot Springs, Arkansas. In an ad that month in the *Sporting News*, the town's Majestic Hotel touted the area's attractions. "Scores of famous players have found the thermal baths at Hot Springs National Park the quickest aid toward reaching mid-season form. Excess weight, winter aches and pains, shortness

45. Ever since his Boston Red Sox held spring training in Hot Springs, Arkansas, in 1922 and 1923, Jack Quinn (*front row, far left*) made the town a regular stop on his way to training camp. He hiked the surrounding hills and "boiled out" in the mineral baths. His Athletics teammate, George Earnshaw (*front row, second from right*), enjoyed the town so much that he made regular visits and retired to a farm there. Hack Wilson (*front row, second from left*) recaptured some of his late 1920s greatness with the Cubs when he joined the Dodgers in 1932. *Garland County Historical Society.*

of breath, etc., quickly vanish under treatment of these radio-active waters, with a wide choice of outdoor exercises in the invigorating Ozark mountains." Quinn's name was featured prominently in the ad.[19] "I have said it time and again and repeat it now," he said. "I never would have been able to last this long had I not come here every year and taken these baths, which boiled every element of a harmful nature out of me, kept me fit and enabled me to keep the legs in condition for the hiking over the mountain paths and trails."[20]

As Quinn prepared for his thirtieth season in Organized Baseball, he again credited his longevity to the care he took with his legs. "I'll be able to pitch a baseball as long as I can stand on my pins," he told Philadelphia sportswriter Gordon Mackay. Mackay added, "The pantalooned beauties of [movie star] Marlene Dietrich are cared for with no more attention than the dogs of Jack Quinn."[21]

Countless newspaper features tried to explain the longevity of this "Methuselah of the Mound." Tommy Holmes had written about "the masterly precision and the absolute freedom from effort" of Quinn's pitching motion.[22] The 1933 *Who's Who in Baseball* wrote of Quinn, "He'll tell you the secret of his control is the fact that he keeps his eyes glued to the plate throughout his windup. Shooting, he adds, has helped him materially, for Quinn is a demon trap artist, frequently bowling over 100 straight clay pigeons."[23] A New York reporter declared, "Probably he'll die at the age of 90 in the box hurling them."[24]

Quinn had to deal with an infected jaw in late February, and he had an abscessed tooth removed. Two weeks into the season, after not using him in a game, the Dodgers gave him his release.[25] He stayed with the club the next few days, pitching batting practice while he contacted other teams. Pittsburgh columnist James Long reported that "the touching farewells may be a trifle premature." Six clubs were interested in Quinn, he wrote, but were waiting for ten days to pass to avoid paying Brooklyn the waiver price of $4,000.[26]

A few days later, after a tryout with Cincinnati manager Donie Bush, Quinn signed with the Reds. He did not have to travel far from Brooklyn; he made his first appearance for Cincinnati in the Polo Grounds against the Giants on May 7 and pitched a scoreless inning in a 5–0 loss. On June 3 the Reds were cruising to a 5–1 victory in Pittsburgh when the Pirates struck for a ninth-inning home run followed by two triples. Bush replaced starter Ray Kolp with Quinn, who retired the next three batters for his first 1933 save. It would also be the last of his career.

In mid-June Quinn made four appearances in five days (all were Cincinnati losses) and lowered his earned run average to 1.12. On June 28 he put down a fifth-inning rally in Brooklyn and was left in the game too long when his old club scored twice off him in the eighth to give him the loss. It was his only decision of the season and the final one of his career. On July 7, a few days after Quinn's fiftieth birthday, he was effective in 1⅔ innings of relief. "Spitter of Jack Quinn Holds Game Safe," wrote Jack Ryder of the Reds' 8–5 win.[27]

But Quinn had to leave the game when he twisted his knee while batting in the eighth inning. A week later the Reds gave him his unconditional release. Newspaper articles across the country saluted Quinn and noted his long and successful career. Typical was a *Tampa Times* columnist who wrote, "His life is a remarkable study for those athletes who are 'burned out' at 30." Still "it was inevitable that he'd have to take the count from old Father Time sooner or later."[28]

The sports editor of the *Pittsburgh Press*, Chester L. Smith, put it well when he closed his column on Quinn this way: "And so Mr. Tennyson's immortal brook wins another decision, although it looked for a long time as though it would end in a tie."[29]

44

A Full and Happy Retirement

Thirty-six-year-old Howard Ehmke pitched his final Major League game on May 22, 1930. Only seven months had passed since he had promised A's manager Connie Mack that "there is one great game left in this old arm." He then made good on his promise by setting a World Series strikeout record in the first game of the 1929 Series.

As noted, for much of his playing career Ehmke represented a Detroit-based firm that manufactured canvas coverings used to protect athletic fields against bad weather. Choosing to stay in Philadelphia, he and Marguerite decided to establish their own enterprise, the Ehmke Manufacturing Company, a canvas fabricating business.

That the Ehmke Manufacturing Company developed the first infield tarpaulin was the mistaken belief of Louis Venna, whose father bought the company after Ehmke's death and agreed to keep the name of its founders.[1] "Mr. Ehmke knew there was a need for an infield cover," said Venna. "The first cover was one big canvas, and it was used for the first time at Shibe Park. Plastic tarpaulins came along in the 40s." Venna recalled Ehmke as being a "quiet, unobtrusive, and very generous man. If a friend or an employee needed anything, he'd always take care of it. He'd take money out of his pocket."[2]

Ehmke's first customer was Connie Mack. He sold his former manager on the idea of a large canvas tarpaulin that could be spread over Shibe Park when it rained to keep the playing surface dry. Other teams soon followed. At the Major League winter meetings, held at New York's Roosevelt Hotel in December 1934, Ehmke sold tarpaulin field coverings to five other big league clubs.[3]

By 1936 Ehmke Manufacturing was one of the five largest canvas makers in Philadelphia, doing over $100,000 in business annually.[4] After the Japanese attack on Pearl Harbor, Ehmke converted his tarpaulin plant to war work, making covers for anti-aircraft guns and leather bucklers to go over turrets on ships. When the war ended, the company went back to producing tarpaulins and a variety of other products for civilian use.

While Ehmke had a successful business, he felt that former players, many of whom were barely getting by, should receive some sort of pension from Organized Baseball. An editorial in the *Sporting News* summarized his position: "I believe the Major Leagues should recognize achievements of men who have given the best part of their lives to baseball. I do not say that all of them are in need of help, but most of them should be taken care of by Organized Baseball in some way." The *Sporting News* traditionally sided with the owners over the players and did so again here. "These are sentiments to which nearly everyone will subscribe," the editorial continued. "But have Ehmke and the other veterans, who have enjoyed munificent salaries and lived on the fat of the land while doing so, ever thought that maybe they owed something to the game, as well as the game owing something to them? There is a crying need for practical baseball men to assist in the regeneration of the game by taking franchises and running clubs." The editorial cited Eddie Collins, who had recently acquired an interest in the Boston Red Sox.[5]

Three years later, in 1936, the two leagues showed their "generosity" by awarding lifetime passes to every Major League ballpark to 403 retired players. Those with twenty or more years got gold passes, while those, like Ehmke, who had played from ten to nineteen years, got silver.[6]

Although Ehmke spent just over four of his fifteen Major League seasons in Philadelphia, they were the happiest of his career. His one season with Buffalo, of the Federal League, was a disaster; his six years in Detroit were marred by his dealings with Ty Cobb; and his four years in Boston, which included his career-best 1923 season, were spent deep in the second division.

During the winter of 1942–43 Ehmke was a regular attendee at the University of Pennsylvania's basketball home games. The attraction was his cousin, Jack Colberg, a 6-foot-5-inch sophomore center from Ehmke's hometown of Silver Creek.[7] Colberg, who had been pursued by Cornell and Syracuse, came to Penn on Ehmke's recommendation and prediction that his young cousin would also make a fine college pitcher. An item in the *Silver Creek Creeker* of September 11, 1941, said Howard had arranged for Colberg to try out with the Athletics.

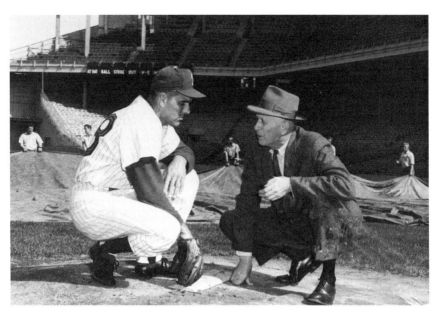

46. Howard Ehmke and Philadelphia Phillies pitcher Curt Simmons at Connie Mack Stadium in 1958. The tarp being pulled off the infield by workers in the background was fabricated by Howard's Ehmke Manufacturing Company, which was then successfully producing tarpaulins for outdoor sports venues around the country. *Special Collections Research Center, Temple University Libraries, Philadelphia, Pennsylvania, Philadelphia Evening Bulletin Collection.*

In 1952 columnist Ed Pollock interviewed Ehmke on his fifty-eighth birthday. Pollock described Ehmke as slim as ever, though his hairline had receded some, and he was graying at the temples. "I couldn't have gone to any other city and had things work out for me the way they have here," Ehmke said. "Philadelphia has been great to me and so has baseball, which gave me the entrée for business interviews."[8]

Ehmke remained close to Connie Mack and took part in many activities involving his former manager. He was among the one hundred guests who celebrated Mack's seventy-fifth birthday at a luncheon in Philadelphia on December 23, 1937. Many of them were former A's players, ranging from Chief Bender, Ira Thomas, and Harry Davis to members of Mack's early teams to several of Ehmke's teammates from the 1929 world champions, including Rube Walberg and Jimmy Dykes.[9]

Eighteen years later, in 1955, Ehmke was one of three hundred guests who gathered at the Warwick Hotel in Philadelphia to celebrate Mack's ninety-third birthday. An ailing Mack was unable to attend; nevertheless, Ehmke's remarks paid tribute to the man whom he had so long admired. "If I was rating great men," he said, limiting it to Philadelphians, "I would place them this way: Ben Franklin, William Penn, Connie Mack."[10]

Ehmke also attended most gatherings in Philadelphia that involved baseball, including old-timers' games. One such game took place on August 7, 1950, when the Athletics played an exhibition against the Harrisburg Senators of the Class B Interstate League. The game drew 3,481 to Harrisburg's Island Park. Before the regularly scheduled game, the Senators played a two-inning contest against a club of A's old-timers. Lefty Grove pitched the first inning, with Mickey Cochrane catching, Jimmie Foxx at first base, and Frank "Home Run" Baker at third. Ehmke pitched the second inning and showed surprising speed and a good assortment of pitches, all delivered sidearm. He allowed a hit and issued a walk but struck out the side.[11]

Although the A's abandoned Philadelphia for Kansas City in 1955, Ehmke continued to follow baseball to the end of his life. He was an astute observer, wrote Earl Vann of the *Baltimore Afro-American* in 1958: "If you want a keen analysis of the game of baseball, just sit next to Ehmke for nine innings as I did on opening night of the Phillies."[12]

Above all Ehmke remained an enthusiastic golfer who regularly shot in the low 80s. In his retirement he was a member of the Old York Road Golf Club, a frequent winner of both Interclub and Suburban League titles. Most winters he and Marguerite spent in Miami, escaping the cold and snow of Philadelphia. There he would play golf and indulge in another of his hobbies, attending the horseraces at Hialeah Park. Red Smith remembered him as "a big, handsome, light-haired man" and "a pretty good horse player." Smith called it a pleasure to encounter this "quiet man of warmth and charm" at Hialeah every winter.[13]

While in Miami, Ehmke was also a regular participant in the National Baseball Players' Golf Tournament, held there each February. In the 1955 tournament he shot a 76, one of only seven old-timers to break 80. He played every year, including the February 1959 tournament, a month before his death.

Along with playing golf, the retired players enjoyed reminiscing and telling tales of the old days. Often as not, time clouded their memories. One

47. Howard Ehmke's love of horse racing led him to spend time at Miami's Hialeah Park every winter. Here he is at Hialeah with *Sporting News* publisher J. G. Taylor Spink (*left*) in 1955. *Steve Steinberg Collection*.

of the participants in the 1954 tournament was Whitey Witt, the former Yankee whose questionable single on September 7, 1923, had cost Ehmke a second successive no-hitter. "I led off for the Yankees and lined a hard smash off Ehmke's chest," Witt recalled incorrectly.[14] "The ball bounced to the third base coaching box, and the official scorer [Fred Lieb] ruled it a hit. It was the only one we got off Ehmke. . . . I've always felt badly about being the man who kept Howard from pitching successive no-hitters."[15]

Meanwhile, Connie Mack's decision to start Ehmke in Game One of the 1929 World Series had become a reference point for unusual pitching choices. "Evidently a 'Howard Ehmke' has come to be recognized in baseball as a 'Corrigan' is in aviation," wrote Billy Kelly of the *Buffalo Courier-Express*.[16] Dan Daniel cited Ehmke's surprise start after Brooklyn manager Leo Durocher chose Curt Davis to start the 1941 Series opener against the Yankees. "In opening with Curt Davis, 35-year-old right-hander (he was actually 37)," wrote Daniel, "Durocher tore a page out of the book of Connie Mack. In 1929, against the Cubs, Mack had Grove, Earnshaw, Walberg, and Rommel. But he opened with the antique Howard Ehmke, whom he was reported to have quit on before Labor Day."[17]

Ehmke's name came up again two years later when a New York sportswriter criticized Cardinals manager Billy Southworth for not starting his ace, Mort Cooper, in the 1943 Series opener against the Yankees. "I used my pitchers in the order in which I thought they would do the most good," said an irked Southworth. "To say I lost faith in Mort is absurd." He reminded the members of the press that Giants manager John McGraw had twice saved his best pitcher, Christy Mathewson, for the second game and that Connie Mack showed no lack of confidence in Lefty Grove or George Earnshaw when he started Ehmke, a "62-inning [*sic*] pitcher," in 1929.[18]

In 1948 Joe McCarthy, then managing the Red Sox, figured in another controversial pitching choice. When Boston and Cleveland finished in a tie for the American League pennant, it necessitated a one-game playoff to determine the league champion. Most observers expected McCarthy would choose Mel Parnell or Ellis Kinder, but instead he chose Denny Galehouse, a thirty-six-year-old journeyman. It was an unfortunate choice. The Indians pounded Galehouse early, on their way to an 8–3 win and the AL flag.

Philadelphia Phillies manager Eddie Sawyer surprised the baseball world in 1950 when he chose his ace reliever, Jim Konstanty, to start

Game One of the World Series against the Yankees.[19] "Not since Connie Mack startled his own players by calling on obscure Howard Ehmke to pitch and win the opener . . . has a pennant winning manager taken such a chance," wrote Jack Hand.[20]

Ehmke's name came up in a different context during the 1948 season. The Cleveland Indians had brought Satchel Paige to the big leagues after his long and distinguished career in the Negro Leagues. Paige had used a "hesitation pitch" in those leagues, and observers described it "as the same style used by Howard Ehmke." But Paige ran into trouble when he tried it in a July 19 game against Washington. The Senators complained that it was a balk and that the runner on third base should have been allowed to score. No balk was called, and the Indians won the game, 7–6. The Senators appealed to American League president Will Harridge, and as a result, the league forbade Paige from throwing the pitch.[21]

A generation of fans had grown up since Ehmke retired before he again commanded national attention. When Carl Erskine of the Brooklyn Dodgers struck out fourteen Yankees in the third game of the 1953 World Series, he broke the mark Ehmke had set in 1929.[22]

After working in his factory until noon that day, Howard took Marguerite for a drive in the country. They stopped for lunch and then turned on the car radio to listen to the game. "It got so exciting," wrote a reporter from the *New York Times*, "they stopped to listen, and the car's battery ran down, so they had to get a push."[23]

"Records are made to be broken, I guess," Ehmke said of the one he had held for twenty-three years, eleven months, and twenty-four days. "My wife has taken it a little to heart. She's not crying or anything, you understand, but just sort of downhearted."[24] From what he had read of the game, said Ehmke, "I gather the background in Ebbets Field today bothered the Yankees a little bit. It was a warm day, and the crowd was probably in shirt sleeves, which means the batters were watching the ball come out of a background, which makes it harder to hit."[25]

After the game Ehmke sent Erskine a telegram that read, "Congratulations on your wonderful record-breaking game." He told Bill Roeder of the *New York World-Telegram* that he had been rooting against Erskine but not because of the strikeout record: "It's just that I'm an American Leaguer. As for the record, naturally I was proud to hold it, but this boy certainly

48. Howard Ehmke holds the October 3, 1953, *Philadelphia Inquirer* announcing that Brooklyn's Carl Erskine had broken his World Series strikeout record. "Records are made to be broken, I guess," Ehmke said of the one he had held for twenty-four years, eleven months, and twenty-four days. *Special Collections Research Center, Temple University Libraries, Philadelphia, Pennsylvania, Philadelphia Evening Bulletin Collection.*

earned it. They tell me he's a nice boy. I hope he goes on and breaks his own record."[26] Ehmke also told Roeder that he could still pitch. A month earlier, pitching for a team of old-timers against fifteen-year-olds in a side-show put on by the Phillies, Ehmke had worked one inning and struck out the side. "Even young Erskine couldn't do better than that," he said.[27]

"To tell you the truth," Erskine said after the game, "I didn't have the foggiest idea that I had broken any Series record for strikeouts. I didn't know who held it, and now that I found out that Howard Ehmke of the Athletics set the record with 13 strikeouts in the 1929 World Series, I'm still not sure that I can even spell that fellow's name right."[28]

Howard Ehmke's life ended at 1:25 a.m. on March 17, 1959, when he passed away at Philadelphia's Germantown Dispensary and Hospital. The sixty-five-year-old Ehmke had been in poor health for some time and mostly bedridden for the previous week before entering the hospital earlier that evening. His official death certificate listed the cause of death as acute meningitis (pneumococcal). The couple had no children, and Ehmke willed his entire estate to his wife.[29]

Ehmke's obituary in the *Washington Post* echoed the esteem in which he was held throughout baseball: "He was strictly a gentleman off the field, and fiercely a fighter on the field, including battles with Ty Cobb, both verbally while Cobb managed Detroit, and physically when Ehmke was with Boston."[30] Ehmke's hometown paper went further in paying tribute to the decency of its most famous son:

> Howard Ehmke will be remembered in this community not only as a famous athlete, but also as a fine gentleman, whom fame left unchanged. He typified in his life the finest ideals. He truly exemplified the goal of the athlete, a fine mind and fine body. His example is one that all youth might emulate. Neither drinking, nor smoking, he trained, and when the ultimate test came in the World Series in baseball, he had the heart and stamina of a champion. He was a pleasant, kindly, good-natured man who, in spite of all his acclaim, retained that spirit of humility that is the indication of true greatness.[31]

Marguerite Ehmke died in her Philadelphia apartment on June 27, 1966. In August 1968 Stanley Thornton, a member of the law firm that represented the Ehmkes, wrote to J. Malcolm Henderson, the president of Kirk and Nice, the undertakers that handled the Ehmkes' funerals. Henderson said Howard's ashes had been held at Kirk and Nice from March 20, 1959, until Marguerite passed away. The Ehmkes had asked that both their ashes be scattered in King of Prussia's Valley Forge Memorial Gardens.[32]

While Ehmke never made it to Cooperstown, he did receive votes from the Baseball Writers Association of America in ten Hall of Fame elections, beginning in 1938 and ending in 1960.[33]

Ehmke was enshrined in two other Halls of Fame: the Chautauqua Sports Hall of Fame, based in Jamestown, New York, in 1983, its second year of existence, and the Greater Buffalo Sports Hall of Fame in 2014. In its proclamation the Buffalo Hall noted that the Silver Creek native had had one of the most successful Major League careers ever among Western New Yorkers.

Ehmke posted a Major League record of 166 wins and 166 losses and had 10 or more wins nine times. He was a twenty-game winner for the last-place Red Sox in 1923, the season that also included his no-hitter. Four days later he followed with a one-hitter, giving him the American League record for fewest hits allowed in consecutive games.

After the trade to the Athletics, Ehmke had a winning record for the A's each season from 1926 through 1929. He gained his greatest fame as the surprise Game One starter in the 1929 World Series, when he set a World Series record that stood until 1953.

Connie Mack called Howard Ehmke a pitching artist who could do more with a baseball than any pitcher he had ever seen. There have been many who threw harder or had better curve balls, but none ever had such a variety of stuff as Ehmke. "He could develop a pitch to fool the hardest-hitting batter in the country or invent a toss to fool the keenest eye in the land," Mack said.[34] "Howard, of course, had no way of knowing what I thought of him [when Ehmke pitched for the A's]," Mack told John Carmichael in the 1940s. "Really, he was one of the most artistic pitchers of all time. He was bothered with a sore arm most of his Major League career, but he had a great head on him and studied hitters."[35]

"An indelible picture will always remain of a gallant Howard Ehmke as he stood in the center of an alien field and in a pitching epic that surprised the world earned the admiration of a hostile throng," wrote Bill Dooly. "That game, no doubt, was Ehmke's swan song. . . . Ehmke gave his all with a shadow hanging over his head, with the curtain about to drop on a career shortened by a weakened arm that was now being forced to expend every last mite of its strength in one last great effort."[36]

Before the first game of the 1957 World Series at Yankee Stadium, someone asked the sixty-three-year-old Ehmke what he would be thinking when the Yankees' Whitey Ford threw the first pitch: "I'll be thinking I wish I was Whitey Ford's age, and I was out there making that pitch, just like I did in 1929, October 8, if you're interested in the date. It was one of the nicest things ever happened in my whole life."[37]

45

———

A Sad and Bitter End

Like many athletes who spend most of their adult life in sports, Jack Quinn was facing an enormous adjustment. Unlike Howard Ehmke, he owned no business to keep him occupied. In his book on life in professional baseball, former Minor Leaguer George Gmelch had a chapter titled "When the Cheering Stops."[1] Gmelch wrote about how unprepared many players are for the transition to "civilian life" after their careers end. "All of a sudden you've gone from being a member of a small fraternity, in this highly structured environment, to being outside all on your own. And you ask what happens now," his last manager, Tony Franklin, told Gmelch.[2] Adding to the difficulty is that older players' playing days end when most men's careers are taking off. As pitcher and author Jim Bouton poignantly wrote, "You spend a good piece of your life gripping a baseball, and at the end it turns out that it was the other way round."[3]

A week after he was released by the Reds, Quinn was pitching for a semi-pro team in Detroit, in a league in which former Tigers Bobby Veach and Harry Heilmann were also playing.[4] That fall the always determined Quinn told a reporter, "You may expect to see my name on a big-league roster in 1934. . . . I feel I am still perfectly capable of acting as a relief pitcher and batting-practice pitcher. . . . I am positive I would be of great help anywhere as a coach of pitchers."[5] Around the same time, Quinn visited Rapid City, South Dakota, where he said something very different: "I'm going to stay in a baseball uniform just as long as I can. I want to locate in a small town. I have lots of baseball to play yet, but if I can find a small place to do it, I am not looking for a chance to go back to the Majors."[6]

But Quinn was neither in the Majors nor in a small town in 1934. Instead he joined the Hollywood Stars of the Pacific Coast League, where he was expected to share relief duty with a fellow pitcher with the 1921 Yankees, Tom Sheehan. The spitball was illegal throughout Organized Baseball.[7] But the league's owners made an exception for Quinn, despite the opposition of the Los Angeles Angels, who were competing for fans with Hollywood.[8] A Salt Lake City reporter spoke for many when he wrote, "Now, if baseball owes anything to anybody, it owes to Jack Quinn the best return it can make to him. No ball player has had a more distinguished career than Quinn."[9]

But there would be no more comebacks for Quinn. He appeared in only six games and was released in early May, two months before his fifty-first birthday. A Sporting News reporter noted that the aging Quinn had difficulty covering first base on ground balls hit to the right side.[10] He had a tryout with the Los Angeles Angels but was not offered a position.[11] Yet he was not ready to leave the game and soon joined the Duffy Florals, a strong semi-pro team in his hometown of Chicago. He excelled, and among his victories that summer was a shutout of the city's powerful Logan Squares. The losing pitcher was his teammate on the 1910–12 Yankees, Hippo Vaughn, another familiar face in Chicago's vibrant semi-pro baseball scene.[12]

Quinn hoped to land a coaching job in 1935 with the Chicago White Sox, where the club's player-manager was his former Athletics teammate Jimmy Dykes, but an offer never came.[13] Instead he took over as manager of the House of David team, the touring club of a Benton Harbor, Michigan, religious sect.[14] Pitching great Grover Cleveland Alexander had managed this club since 1931, but his drinking made his behavior increasingly erratic.[15]

The House of David played most of its games in the Midwest, "close enough to metropolitan areas to bring bookings with the semipro teams which flourished in proximity to big-league clubs," wrote baseball historian Jack Kavanagh. The team "pioneered night baseball in the hinterlands"; among the club's attractions was its portable lighting equipment and its warm-up and between-innings fielding routine, "the pepper game."[16] Another regular feature of the games was that Quinn pitched the first inning, as Alexander had done.

Quinn soon found a better opportunity, one that brought him back into professional baseball. He replaced Joe O'Rourke as the manager of the Johnstown (Pennsylvania) Johnnies of the Class C Middle Atlan-

49. Jack Quinn and his wife, Georgiana (known to her family and friends as Gene), had an idyllic marriage. She attended most of his games, and off the field they were inseparable. They lived in the Chicago area, where many members of her family resided. This photo was taken the morning of July 6, 1940, before a family picnic at which she suffered a tragic accident that would claim her life two days later. Jack never recovered from the loss of his beloved. The former fitness devotee began to drink heavily and died of cirrhosis of the liver in 1946, at the age of sixty-two. *Family of Jack Quinn.*

tic League in mid-July.[17] The club immediately went on a winning streak. After the Johnnies won ten straight games, a Johnstown reporter attributed the turnaround to "the magic managerial hand of Jack Quinn," who "again has the baseball populace in a state that is best described by that old favorite adjective, agog."[18]

But when the team moved into a first-place tie with the Dayton (Ohio) Ducks in early September, Quinn mysteriously resigned. Reports said a new player had created friction and was a "clubhouse lawyer" whom Quinn resented; another report said he quit because of "trouble with stockholders."[19] Quinn said that pressing business matters in Chicago demanded his immediate attention. At least one local paper was unforgiving. His "abrupt withdrawal reflects upon no one but himself. . . . Quinn simply does not have the managerial temperament. He is another of a long list of great players who have proved themselves incapable of becoming managers."[20]

In the next four years reports surfaced that Quinn was looking for another job in baseball. He again managed the House of David team in 1936.[21] After the 1939 season he interviewed for the managerial position of the Lima, Ohio, club of the Class D Ohio State League. That December he went to the baseball winter meetings, where he told a Philadelphia reporter, "All the years I pitched, I never had a sore arm. . . . I think I could show young pitchers how to take care of their arms."[22] No offers were forthcoming, and Johnstown was Quinn's last job in Organized Baseball.

Quinn and his wife, Gene, had a special relationship; they were rarely apart. She was his "first girl" and had seen many of his games.[23] They had no children and every Christmas lavished gifts on the children of fifty or so neighbors and relatives. They were looking forward to celebrating their thirtieth anniversary in November 1940.

On July 6 that year, at a family picnic in a Momence, Illinois, park, Gene ran after the children as an ice cream truck drew near. She tripped on a sprinkler and fell over a park bench. With stunning swiftness the compound fracture of her leg led to gangrene, and even amputation of the leg could not save her. She died just two days later. Her doctor wrote her devastated husband, "Gas gangrene . . . in many cases travels

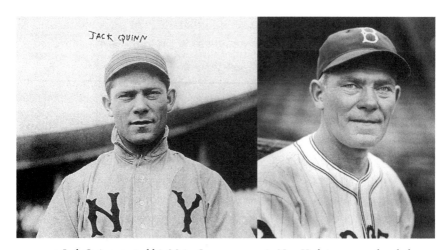

JACK QUINN

50. Jack Quinn started his Major League career in New York in 1909 and ended it in Cincinnati in 1933, though his last significant activity was also in New York (in Brooklyn in 1932). He is seen here at the "bookends" of his career. A rare combination of conditioning, control, and cunning, he won 247 games in the Majors, 348 in Organized Baseball, and many more if his semi-pro games are included. *Steve Steinberg Collection.*

very rapidly . . . and by morning had invaded the blood stream. . . . This is one of the most rapid infections we have had to contend with. . . . It had penetrated not only the blood stream but the abdominal cavity as well, causing a septicemia and peritonitis."[24]

Without the woman he loved, Jack Quinn was lost. It was a blow from which he would not recover. "He was very generous, a big gentle hunk," said one of his half-grandnieces, Sally Athmann. "He adored his wife. They couldn't have kids and didn't adopt. After she died, he was so lonesome."[25]

Quinn sold most of his possessions and returned to Pottsville, where he moved in with his half-brother, Michael Picus (1888–1965), on Mt. Hope Avenue. Michael's younger daughters, Quinn's half-nieces, lived at home at the time.[26] One daughter, Cleona, recalled Quinn chewed Elephant's Butt tobacco, which her mother said killed her plants when he spat his chew into them. Another daughter, Sally, remembered Quinn enjoyed talking to the servicemen her older sisters brought home for Sunday dinners after USO dances during World War II. They vividly remembered offering to cook breakfast for "Uncle Jack," but he demurred. He would raise his glass of liquor as he came downstairs and replied that he already had his breakfast—the clear liquid in the glass (either gin or vodka).[27] He then spent his days in Gallagher's bar in downtown Pottsville, telling his baseball stories and drinking. When the girls' older sister moved back home, Quinn moved into the Eagle Hotel downtown.

During his career and through the 1930s, Quinn drank alcohol only sparingly. Fred Lieb wrote in 1927, "Jack has been a clean liver, but he hasn't carried it to extremes. He used to like his beer when he could get it, and I guess he still likes it when he can get it."[28] This man who drank only in moderation all his life now drank heavily. Father John Whitney Evans, a family friend of the daughters when they settled in Minnesota, wrote, "He drank his sorrow—to death."[29]

Early in 1946 Quinn entered Pottsville's Good Samaritan Hospital, suffering from alcoholism. He did not want a priest, though he was born Catholic. He said his only religion was Freemasonry. On April 17, 1946, Jack Quinn passed away at the age of sixty-two. The cause of death was cirrhosis of the liver. He is buried in the non-denominational Charles Baber Cemetery in the heart of Pottsville, next to his wife and her family.

For more than a half-century, Elmer Valo, who played in the Major Leagues from 1940 to 1961, was considered the first player of any significance who was born in what was known during his playing days as Czechoslovakia and since 1992 has been the Slovak Republic. In a strange twist of fate, near the end of his life, Valo was cared for by a nurse who was one of Jack Quinn's half-grandnephews, Michael Jupina.[30] More than a half-century later, people in Pottsville, who were children at the time, remembered when Babe Ruth and Connie Mack came to the family home to pay their respects after the death of the ageless pitcher who died before his time.

Jack Quinn rose from impoverished East European origins to the top of the baseball world. Syndicated columnist Westbrook Pegler called the rugged area from which Quinn hailed "the god-forgottenest region of the Pennsylvania coal belt."[31] A health and fitness fanatic, Quinn died while still mourning the loss of the love of his life. His date and place of birth were one of baseball's enduring mysteries for decades. He added to the enigma by his vagueness and differing stories. "Apparently, he forgot his promise [to reveal his age after he retired]," wrote John Kieran in his column. "He wandered away in silence, leaving the mystery unsolved behind him."[32]

The mystery came at least in part from the fact that Quinn never knew his mother, who died when he was an infant. Despite extensive searches, the family has not been able to locate the stone of his mother, who died in 1884, shortly after the three of them reached America.[33] His father, who soon remarried, probably never talked about her again, at the behest of his second wife. As noted in chapter 1, when Jack applied for a passport in 1919, for his Social Security card in 1939, and for a Delayed Birth Certificate in 1942, he could not even provide his mother's name and wrote in the space, "Do not know."[34] He varied his date of birth from 1883 to 1884. The reality was that Jack Quinn did not know the date or location of his birth.

Other players have followed intense workout regimens and stayed in shape at all times, yet most did not play past their thirties. This prompted one New York reporter to write, "Jack must have had something on the ball besides saliva."[35] Connie Mack may have understood at least part of that "something." In 1928, when Quinn won eighteen games at the age of forty-five, Mack declared, "In all my experience, I have never found a player who works as hard as Jack Quinn."[36]

Sportswriter Frank Graham wrote in 1946, "Granted that Quinn missed greatness as a pitcher, he was a very good pitcher for a long time and, for a longer time after that, he was a real journeyman in the box, who could win a badly needed ball game every now and then."[37] More than a half-century later, Rob Neyer and Eddie Epstein wrote something similar: "He was a good pitcher for an awfully long time, and in twenty-three seasons, he was bad in only one of them."[38]

Quinn appeared in 756 games and won 247 of them, against 218 losses.[39] He is one of only five pitchers in baseball history who won two hundred or more games and saved fifty or more.[40] His control was excellent: he was in the top ten in fewest bases on balls per nine innings thirteen times, with a career average of just below two walks per nine. His resilience and comebacks are reflected in his winning eighteen games in 1910 and again eighteen seasons later, in 1928, as well as in the middle of that span, in 1920. In his *Baseball Abstract*, Bill James wrote that based on Win Shares, Quinn was the best old pitcher (over the age of forty) ever.[41]

Philadelphia columnist Bill Dooly wrote of the "remarkable epic of human endurance" of this man, who was "perhaps the athletic marvel of the age; whose career transcends those to whom fortune has been kinder, glory greater, and emoluments richer."[42] In 1933 Grantland Rice recalled how, twenty years earlier, he and a few other reporters had figured Quinn's brief Major League career was coming to a close. "We missed that guess by only 20 years."[43]

NOTES

Prologue

1. "Athletics Win First Game from Red Sox, Lose Second," *Philadelphia North American*, May 29, 1924.

1. Jack Quinn, Man of Mystery

1. Stoney McLinn, "Baseball Will Miss Jack Quinn Not for Ability as Pitcher but for Mystery He Created," *Philadelphia Evening Public Ledger*, November 12, 1930.
2. These documents include his marriage license (November 4, 1910); military registration card (September 12, 1918); passport application (November 6, 1919); Social Security application (October 7, 1939); and delayed birth certificate (May 9, 1942). Scott, "John 'Jack Quinn' Picus."
3. Jack Quinn, "Quinn Confides in 'Shag,'" *New York Evening Telegram*, April 25, 1924. In this interview Quinn claimed he was born in Wales.
4. Will Wedge, "Quinn Too Much for Yankees," *New York Sun*, April 17, 1924.
5. Necrology, *Sporting News*, April 25, 1946. Teenagers often served as drummer boys and bugle boys in nineteenth-century wars.
6. Evans, "Jack Quinn."
7. Joe Williams, *New York Evening Telegram*, March 5, 1929.
8. Joe Williams, "When It Rains, You Talk of Mr. Quinn," *Cleveland Press*, July 28, 1927.
9. Scott, "John 'Jack Quinn' Picus." Scott presented the paper at the March 2007 NINE conference in Tucson. He established that "Paikos" was the family name; that "Paykosh," "Pajkos," and "Paichus" were variations; and that "Picus" was the name's Americanization.
10. Steve Steinberg submitted this information to Bill Carle, chairman of SABR's Biographical Committee, on March 21, 2007. The official records were then changed to reflect Quinn's place and date of birth, which previously had been listed as Jeansville, Pennsylvania, and July 5, 1884, respectively.
11. An overview of Rusyn culture, religion, language, and geography was written in 1995 by Paul Robert Magocsi for the Carpatho-Rusyn Research Center. It can be found at https://c-rs.org/event-2338644.
12. These births, baptisms, deaths, and burials were all meticulously entered in the records of the Greek Orthodox church in Stefurov.

13. Zatko, "Early Beginnings of the Slovaks in America," 10. An agricultural worker earned twenty-five cents a day; wealthy landlords owned 75 percent of the land.

14. Zatko, "Early Beginnings of the Slovaks in America," 12.

15. Archdeacon, *Becoming American*, 117. Zatko notes, "Two leading steamship companies were reported to have five or six thousand agents in Galicia alone" ("Early Beginnings of the Slovaks in America," 12).

16. Wages in the mines ranged from $16 to $25 every two weeks, but the cost of living was higher than in Slovakia. Zatko, "Early Beginnings of the Slovaks in America," 18.

17. Kashatus, *Diamonds in the Coalfields*, 7.

18. Walter Licht, quoted in Ian Urbina, "King Coal Country Debates a Sacrilege, Gas Heat," *New York Times*, June 10, 2008. (Licht is coauthor of *The Face of Decline: The Anthracite Region in the Twentieth Century*.)

19. The marriage record for Anastasia and Michael had a wealth of information, including details about Maria's death and burial. Michael Scott included a copy and an English translation in "John 'Jack Quinn' Picus." Scott notes that Michael's bride was listed by occupation as "a maid" on their marriage license.

20. Lee Allen, "Baseball Methuselah—Jack Quinn Big Leaguer at 49," *Sporting News*, September 9, 1967.

21. Since a person cannot be baptized twice, a "conditional" baptism is performed when there is doubt whether a baptism had been done or was valid.

22. Breaker boys were youngsters who separated slate, rock, clay, and other impurities from coal. Boys under the age of twelve or thirteen would "break" the coal, which would then slide down chutes.

23. Gordon Mackay, "Jack Quinn Hurled the Ball Up the Hill, Winning Place on Town Team at Once," *Philadelphia Inquirer*, August 2, 1925.

24. Quoted in Thomas Holmes, "Veteran Jack Quinn Tells of His Early Days in the Pennsylvania Coal Mines," *New York Evening Journal*, July 14, 1932.

25. Quoted in Smiles, *Big Ed Walsh*, 4.

26. Quoted in "A's Stop Clowning to Win Finale," *Philadelphia Evening Bulletin*, March 28, 1928.

27. Quoted in Bill Dooly, "Jack Quinn, Hardy Perennial of Game, Has Seen 26 Years of Service on Mound," *Sporting News*, November 15, 1928. Quinn never gave the year, though he sometimes said he was almost fourteen at the time.

28. Quoted in Kashatus, *Diamonds in the Coalfields*, 28.

29. Quoted in Kashatus, *Diamonds in the Coalfields*, 40. Kashatus's book covers the many East European ballplayers who came from this region.

30. Quoted in Dooly, "Jack Quinn, Hardy Perennial of Game."

31. Frank F. O'Neill, "Jack Quinn to Umpire," *New York Sun*, July 16, 1921.

2. From Town Ball to the Big Leagues

1. Bill Dooly, "Baseball's Oldest Major League Hurler Leads Athletics," *Philadelphia Record*, July 22, 1928.
2. Organized Baseball consisted of teams and leagues that recognized the authority of the National Commission as baseball's governing body and signed its National Agreement.
3. Ford Sawyer, "Sheer Grit and Confidence Guided Jack Quinn to Fame," *Boston Globe*, May 1, 1925.
4. The fact that a player received money for playing does not necessarily mean his club was professional. Sandlot, or semi-pro, teams often collected money from the fans, especially for the pitcher and catcher.
5. Quoted in Bill Dooly, "Jack Quinn, Hardy Perennial of Game, Has Seen 26 Years of Service on Mound," *Sporting News*, November 15, 1928.
6. Necrology, "Jack Quinn," *Sporting News*, April 25, 1946.
7. Joe Hovlik appeared in sixteen games in 1909–11, and Frank Rooney appeared in fourteen games in 1914. Both were born in Austria-Hungary.
8. Two of Jack Quinn's teammates in the late 1920s did so: Joe Boley (born John Bolinsky) and Al Simmons (born Aloysius Szymanski) both came from Polish families. While newspaper linotype setters would have shortened them anyway, both men wanted names that sounded more "American."
9. Riess, *Touching Base*, 186.
10. Riess, *City Games*, 104.
11. The American Association was at the highest level of the Minor Leagues, Class A at that time.
12. News Notes, *Sporting Life*, March 9, 1907, and Condensed Notes, April 27, 1907. Quinn may have played briefly early that 1907 season in the short-lived Western Pennsylvania League, for either Connellsville or Cumberland. *Sporting Life*, May 31, 1907.
13. South Atlantic League, *Sporting Life*, May 25, 1907.
14. Quoted in *Sporting News*, April 9, 1931.
15. Quinn's letter, dated June 10, 1908, is in the Garry Herrmann Papers, Baseball Hall of Fame Library, Cooperstown, New York. "Seven years" would take his playing days back to 1900 or 1901. All these towns, except for Pottsville, are in western Pennsylvania, and all but Ursina are close to Pittsburgh. There is no indication why he was said to be a "drunkard."
16. *Sporting Life*, October 19, 1907.
17. "Supreme Court of Baseball Reports and Reorganizes," *Sporting Life*, January 18, 1908. The National Commission excused Philadelphia for "innocently" signing him, in part because of the confusion of the two names, Quinn and Picus.

18. Quinn said he won four games for Toledo, without a loss. Dooly, "Baseball's Oldest Major League Hurler Leads Athletics." Lee Allen wrote that Quinn had no decisions with the Mud Hens. "Fanning with Lee Allen," *Sporting News*, September 9, 1967. The stats from Quinn's brief stay there did not appear in the 1909 *Reach* or *Spalding Guides*. Ralph Weber says that Quinn appeared in three games and won one (*The Toledo Baseball Guide of the Mud Hens*, 95).

19. *Sporting News*, November 15, 1928. Boston sportswriter Austen Lake wrote that Quinn was "folding his thumb back in schoolboy fashion" to get extra spin on the ball. *Boston Globe*, May 1, 1925.

20. Quoted in John P. Carmichael, "Jack Quinn Rolls Back the Years," *Chicago Daily News*, July 21, 1933.

21. Will Wedge, "The Story of John P. Quinn," *New York Sun*, May 5, 1926, and June 22, 1929.

22. Quoted in Bill Dooly, Three and Two, *Philadelphia Record*, September 23, 1928. See also W. S. Farquhar, "Jack Quinn Tells of His Career," *Pottsville (PA) Journal*, December 31, 1927, and *New York Sun*, June 22, 1929.

23. Sam Crane, "Yankees Have Strong Pitching Staff," *New York Evening Journal*, April 7, 1920. See also Dan Daniel, *New York Sun*, May 19, 1919.

24. Quoted in Wedge, "The Story of John P. Quinn."

25. Quinn's memory was faulty, or he was embellishing. *Sporting Life* (August 1, 1908) said his Pottsville record was 14-4, still an impressive mark. He was again flirting with danger for joining an "outlaw" club.

26. Quoted in Dooly, "Baseball's Oldest Major League Hurler Leads Athletics."

27. Revelle won twenty-six games that season and twenty-nine the next year but never pitched outside the Virginia League.

28. *Sporting Life*, September 19, 1908. Fan support was remarkable all season: Richmond, a town of 150,000, averaged more than 5,300 fans a game and outdrew five Major League teams. See Simpson, "1908."

29. John Kieran, Sports of the Times, *New York Times*, November 6, 1929.

30. Frank F. O'Neill, "Quinn's Career Is a Romance of the Diamond," *Boston Herald*, December 28, 1921.

31. *Sporting Life*, December 26, 1908.

32. Quoted in unsourced newspaper article in the Jack Quinn family collection. Also see Wedge, "The Story of John P. Quinn."

33. "Jack Quinn Presides over No-Hit Game," *Richmond Times-Dispatch*, August 29, 1908.

34. Current Sporting Gossip, *New York Sun*, April 24, 1909.

35. George E. Firstbrook, "Quinn's Spitball All to the Saliva," *New York Evening Mail*, April 16, 1909.

3. *"I've Never Seen a Greater Pitcher"*

1. The club's manager since its 1903 beginnings, Clark Griffith, had resigned fifty-six games into the 1908 season. After second-place finishes in 1904 and 1906, the club fell to the cellar in 1908 and was there when he resigned.
2. W. J. McBeth, "Chase, Stricken by Smallpox, Sent to Pest House," *New York American*, April 9, 1909.
3. Reisler, *Before They Were Bombers*, 152.
4. Ritter, *The Glory of Their Times*, 83.
5. John Kieran, Sports of the Times, *New York Times*, February 12, 1931.
6. Quoted in Mark Roth, "Yankees Move into St. Louis Now for Series," *New York Globe*, May 19, 1909.
7. Mark Roth, "Engle and Quinn Divide the Honors," *New York Globe*, April 23, 1909. See also *New York Evening Telegram*, April 17, 1909, for more Farrell comments on Quinn.
8. Vila started at the *Morning Journal*, joined the *Herald* in 1890, and the *Evening Sun* and *Sun* three years later. By 1909 he was also the New York reporter for the *Sporting News*. H. S. Johnson, *Who's Who in Major League Baseball*, 505.
9. Joe Vila, "Up There to Stay: Stallings Has Worked Wonders with Yankees," *Sporting News*, April 29, 1909.
10. *New York Press*, April 18, 1909.
11. Ed Grillo, "Groom's Bad Start," *Washington Post*, April 16, 1909.
12. Mark Roth, "All of Stallings's Thirteen Pitchers Are Ready for the Season to Open," *New York Globe*, March 18, 1909.
13. Hauser, "Al Orth." Orth pitched only once in 1909, his final season. Known as "the Curveless Wonder," he won 204 games in his fifteen-year career.
14. *Sporting Life*, June 12, 1909.
15. "Quinn Is the Answer," *Washington Post*, June 1, 1910.
16. Ed Cunningham, "Jack Quinn Has Pitched 23 Consecutive Seasons and Never Had Sore Arm," *Boston Herald*, July 29, 1923.
17. Quoted in Lane, "The Dean of American League Pitchers," 454.
18. "New York Nuggets," *Sporting Life*, August 3, 1910.
19. "Wild Pitch Helps to Beat Yankees," *New York Times*, August 4, 1910.
20. C. E. Van Loan, *New York American*, August 13, 1909.
21. *Sporting Life*, March 11, 1910. Harry Coveleski and his more famous brother Stan, a spitball pitcher who would not become a regular in the Majors until 1916, were indeed Polish, also from a family of coal miners who lived in Pottsville. Their name is now spelled Coveleski.
22. Mark Roth, "Russell Ford Is the Great Mystery of the American League," *New York Globe*, September 17, 1910.

23. "Lajoie's Line Drive Knocks Quinn Out," *New York Times*, June 17, 1910.

24. "Yankees Lose Two Games to Athletics," *New York Times*, July 2, 1910.

25. Quinn started the second game on July 1 and the first game on July 2 and gave up three first-inning runs in both.

26. Joe Vila, "Jack Quinn Ready to Start His 25th Year," *Philadelphia Inquirer*, March 3, 1928.

27. Fred Lieb, "Prince Hal Chase, Ill-Starred Marvel at First Base, Dies in California at 64," *Sporting News*, May 28, 1947. A "stormy petrel" is a harbinger of trouble.

28. Mark Roth, "Chase Getting Them in Same Old Way," *New York Globe*, March 6, 1909.

29. James, *The New Bill James Historical Baseball Abstract*, 462.

30. "Chase Brand of Ball Surprises White Sox," *New York American*, May 27, 1910.

31. Quoted in "Highlanders Face Hard Week's Work," *New York Press*, March 22, 1909. Stallings had managed the Phillies with future Hall of Famer Nap Lajoie in 1897 and part of 1898.

32. James, *The New Bill James Historical Baseball Abstract*, 463.

33. *Sporting Life*, September 24, 1910, quoting the *New York American*.

34. "Highlanders Mutinous," *Sporting Life*, September 24, 1910. See also "Captain Hal Chase Balked in His Effort to Disrupt Yankee Club," *New York American*, September 20, 1910.

35. "Stallings to Tell of Troubles Today," *New York Press*, September 22, 1910. See also *New York American*, September 20, 1910, and Istorico, *Greatness in Waiting*, 80.

36. *Sporting Life*, September 24, 1910, quoting the *New York American*. Farrell was said to be unduly influenced by the sportswriters who covered his team.

37. "Stallings Puts All Blame on Ban Johnson," *New York American*, September 26, 1910. When Johnson organized the American League in 1901, Stallings was the manager of the Detroit franchise. Johnson felt Stallings had made overtures to move the club to the more established National League, an unforgivable act of betrayal of his new league. Stallings always denied the charge, which he felt was the story of some "inventive mind."

38. Quoted in Fountain, *The Betrayal*, 29.

39. Quoted in Fountain, *The Betrayal*, 29.

40. James, *The New Bill James Historical Baseball Abstract*, 466.

41. *New York Tribune*, September 26, 1910, quoted in Istorico, *Greatness in Waiting*, 177–78.

42. Quoted in "Chase Is Manager; Stallings Deposed," *New York Press*, September 27, 1910, and "Stallings Leaves Yanks to Talk over His Troubles," *New York Globe*, September 21, 1910. The *New York American* reported that only rookie pitcher Hippo Vaughn was with Chase, "first and last." In 1914 Stallings would manage the Miracle Boston Braves to the world

championship. They rallied from last place on July 18 to capture the National League pennant and then swept Connie Mack's heavily favored Philadelphia Athletics in the World Series.

43. Mark Roth, "Yankees Now up to Their Best Game," *New York Globe*, March 24, 1909.

4. Quinn Gets Sent Down

1. The Brook was a private social club in Manhattan. It took its name from the Lord Tennyson poem of the same name.
2. Heywood Broun, It Seems to Me, *Boston Globe*, May 25, 1926. Broun's *New York World* column was syndicated in newspapers across the country.
3. Quinn appears in the Pottsville city directory only in the 1909–11 edition.
4. "Jack Picus a Benedict," *Philadelphia Inquirer*, November 13, 1910.
5. A "Jonah" is someone who brings bad luck, a jinx (nautical, slang). A *Washington Post* reporter used this term to describe Quinn's effect on the Senators in his April 25 article, "Great Throw by Cree Kills Nationals' Hopes."
6. Damon Runyon, "All Baseball Fandom Surely Loves a Winner," *New York American*, June 19, 1911.
7. Damon Runyon, "Hal Throttles Brown Rally by Great Catch," *New York American*, July 26, 1911. See also the *New York Times* of the same day.
8. Damon Runyon, "What Is Chase Going to Do with the Yankees?" *New York American*, August 7, 1911.
9. Quoted in Reisler, *Before They Were Bombers*, 195. The next Yankees manager, Frank Chance, traded Chase to the Chicago White Sox during the 1913 season.
10. Arthur Daley, "The Tragic Figure of Hal Chase," *New York Times*, May 20, 1947.
11. Bender's name was Charles Albert. Like many Native American players, he was known as "Chief."
12. "Beating the Yankees a Frolic for the Athletics," *New York American*, September 12, 1911. "Once before" was a 1909 home run by Danny Murphy of the Athletics off the Yankees' Joe Doyle. However, the *New York Times* account of that game refers to a longer blast, hit by Harry Davis of the Athletics. His July 6, 1909, home run was described in the *Times* the following day under the headline "Record Homer by Davis Ties Score."
13. *Sporting Life*, September 23, 1911.
14. Hippo Vaughn became one of the game's best pitchers in the 1910s. Between 1914 and 1919 he won 124 games for the Chicago Cubs.
15. W. J. MacBeth, *Sporting News*, July 18, 1912, quoted in Istorico, *Greatness in Waiting*, 201. Macbeth started spelling his name with the "a" that year.
16. Cree was hit by a pitch thrown by the Red Sox's Buck O'Brien. He was hitting .332 at the time and had batted .348 in 1911.

17. "Shower of Bottles Greets O'Loughlin," *New York Times*, May 12, 1912.
18. Quoted in Murray Robinson, As You Like It, *Standard Union* (Brooklyn), March 24, 1931.
19. Damon Runyon, "Hits in Crisis Give Yanks Late Victory," *New York American*, May 11, 1912.
20. Quinn started eight of those games and gave up ninety-six hits and sixty-four runs in 48⅓ innings.
21. Damon Runyon, "Two More to the Leaders of the League," *New York American*, June 30, 1912.
22. Shortstop, On and Off the Diamond, *New York Press*, July 14, 1912.
23. Nineteen-twelve was the first year the highest level of Minor Leagues was reclassified from Single-A to Double-A.
24. Former Quinn teammates included pitcher Tom Hughes and catcher Walter Blair.
25. Ganzel hit the first-ever home run for the New York American League team on May 11, 1903. Soivenski, *New York Yankees Home Runs*, 3.
26. The first season of the International League was 1912. Its predecessor was the Eastern League, which consisted of the same eight teams.
27. The Major League team would send players to its Minor League partner, both prospects who were developing and players who were not quite good enough for the Majors. It was a symbiotic relationship but one in which the Minor League team did more giving than taking. The Yankees also sent shortstop Jack Martin to Rochester in the deal. McMillan hit only .228 for the Yankees that season and was back in Rochester in 1913. He would play in the Minor Leagues for seventeen more seasons but never returned to the Majors.
28. "Yankees Sell Quinn to Rochester Club," *New York American*, July 30, 1912.
29. "Jack Dunn Names Two of the Youngsters," *Baltimore Evening Sun*, August 7, 1912.
30. C. J. K., "Jack Quinn Successfully Uses All His Strategy," *Rochester Democrat and Chronicle*, April 18, 1913.
31. "Rochester Enters First Division," *Rochester Democrat and Chronicle*, May 25, 1913.
32. Art Ray, "Indians May Now Feel Fairly Secure in Their Lofty Position," *Rochester Union*, August 15, 1913.
33. Leo F. Kleehammer, "Ganzel Refuses to Give Up," *Sporting News*, August 28, 1913.
34. Schmidt hit .321, and Zinn hit .287 for Rochester in 1913.
35. Earlier in August the Baltimore Orioles traded Fritz Maisel to the Yankees for Bert Daniels and Ezra Midkiff. The *Rochester Union* considered this as "conclusive evidence that the 'entente cordiale' between the clubs [New York and Rochester] is a thing of the past." Art Ray, *Rochester Union*, August 9, 1913.

36. Art Ray, "Rumored That Big Deal Is Brewing to Strengthen Next Season," *Rochester Union*, August 20, 1913.

37. Art Ray, "Devlin, Former Giant Star, First to Come to Hustlers," *Rochester Union*, August 26, 1913.

38. The *Baltimore Sun* reported on May 29, 1914, that Quinn was sold for $3,500. The *Rochester Union* noted on August 23, 1913, that the draft price would have been only $2,500.

39. Before a player could be sent to the Minors, other Major League teams had an opportunity to claim him.

40. "Jack Quinn Has a Day," *Boston Globe*, September 16, 1913. Quinn stole home on the front end of a double steal.

41. Reisler, *Before They Were Bombers*, 149.

42. "The Braves Have Been Reorganized by Stallings," *Boston Traveler*, September 4, 1913.

43. Ernest J. Lanigan, Casual Comment, *Sporting News*, August 20, 1914.

44. Nineteen of those 1913 Braves played ten or fewer games for the club.

45. Alexander, *The Miracle Braves*, 22.

46. "Races Tighten in Both Big Leagues," *Mansfield (OH) News*, June 24, 1913.

5. Ehmke Hailed

1. Kipfer and Chapman, *The Dictionary of American Slang*.

2. All genealogical information for Howard Ehmke comes from Sheryl Lucas, the Ehmke family historian. Sheryl is the granddaughter of Ehmke's youngest brother, Clifford.

3. Prussia ceased to exist as a country in 1871, when the Prussian sovereign became the German sovereign, an event that created for the first time a country called Germany.

4. One son took sick and died aboard ship. He was buried at sea. The Swedish name "Hällgren" was changed to "Green" after the family's arrival in the United States.

5. Quoted in "Ehmke's New 'Shaded Ball' Pitch Designed for Shibe Park Only," *Philadelphia Evening Bulletin*, August 22, 1928.

6. Edwards, *American League Service Bureau*.

7. Edwards, *American League Service Bureau*.

8. Brother Albert followed Frank to California in 1912, then siblings Howard, Julia, and Clifford and their mother went west in the fall of 1913. At one point much of the family was in California, all except Howard's father, Charles, and his brother Harry.

9. Ehmke's mother returned to Silver Creek with daughter Julia in 1915. She died in 1940. Charles Ehmke died in 1918, and the Ehmke mill was sold in 1919.

10. Edwards, *American League Service Bureau*.

11. Quoted in N. B. Beasley, *Detroit Journal*, March 13, 1917.

12. "Banks Claims He Discovered Ehmke," *Los Angeles Evening Herald*, May 22, 1914.

13. One whom Dillon missed out on was Walter Johnson. In February 1906 he passed on Johnson because he thought the young pitcher lacked experience, couldn't hold runners on, and telegraphed everything he threw. McKenna, "Pop Dillon."

14. Snelling, *The Greatest Minor League*, 37.

15. Ehmke never graduated from high school, having dropped out of Silver Creek High in New York and then out of Glendale High in California.

16. Quoted in H. F. Weller, "Wet Grounds Sign Hung Out at Ballpark," *Los Angeles Examiner*, April 23, 1914.

17. The Tigers played in Vernon, California, in 1909–12 and 1915–25 and in Venice, California, in 1913–14. Both cities are in Los Angeles County and were natural rivals of the Angels.

18. H. M. Walker, "Tiger Veterans Badly Whipped by Youngster," *Los Angeles Examiner*, May 4, 1914.

19. "Good Records Made in 'Gym' Contests," *San Bernardino Sun*, May 5, 1914.

20. Walker, "Tiger Veterans Badly Whipped by Youngster."

21. Matt Gallagher, "Wilson and T. R. Fade before Fame of Kid Pitcher Ehmke," *Los Angeles Evening Herald*, May 22, 1914.

22. Note the hostility toward New York in that phrase and the fact that no one in Silver Creek, which is three hundred miles from New York City, spoke with what could be called a New York accent.

23. "Howard Ehmke Makes Good in Los Angeles," *Silver Creek (NY) News*, May 14, 1914.

24. "Young Ehmke Possesses All the Requirements of Great Pitcher, Declares Teammate," *Los Angeles Evening Herald*, May 19, 1914.

25. Charlie Chech pitched in the Major Leagues for four seasons, the best of which was 1908, when he went 11-7 with a 1.74 earned run average for the Cleveland Naps.

26. Quoted in "Five Brothers Helped Teach Howard Ehmke to Play Ball," *Los Angeles Evening Herald*, May 13, 1914.

27. Clark Griffith and Pop Dillon were cousins.

28. H. M. Walker, "Ehmke Blanks Seals; Drives Home Lone Run," *Los Angeles Examiner*, May 22, 1914.

29. Ernest A. Phillips, Diamond Dust, *San Bernardino County Sun*, May 23, 1914.

30. Gallagher, "Wilson and T. R. Fade before Fame of Kid Pitcher Ehmke."

31. Harry A. Williams, "Will Washington Have Two Walter Johnsons?" *Los Angeles Times*, May 24, 1914.

32. Williams, "Will Washington Have Two Walter Johnsons?"

33. W. A. Reeve, "White to Hurl Opener: Tigers Here 4 Weeks," *Los Angeles Tribune*, May 26, 1914.

34. Matt Gallagher, Off the Bat, *Los Angeles Evening Herald*, June 18, 1914.

35. In 1915 Ehmke and Chase would be teammates on the Federal League's Buffalo Blues.

36. Williams, "Will Washington Have Two Walter Johnsons?"

37. "Ehmke Value Is $1,000,000 in Home League," *Los Angeles Evening Herald*, June 9, 1914.

38. Quoted in "Ehmke Value Is $1,000,000."

39. Quoted in "Ehmke Value Is $1,000,000."

40. Quoted in "Ehmke Value Is $1,000,000."

41. Quoted in "Ehmke Value Is $1,000,000."

6. Ehmke's Tumultuous Season

1. Hub Pernoll finished the 1914 season with a record of 22-22 for the Seals. He won only one game for them in 1915, his final season.

2. Dope Fiend's Corner, *Sacramento Union*, June 7, 1914.

3. Matt Gallagher, Off the Bat, *Los Angeles Evening Herald*, June 10, 1914.

4. Quoted in *Los Angeles Times*, October 21, 1914.

5. As a youth, Ellis had played sandlot ball with Johnson in Los Nietos, California.

6. Quoted in *Los Angeles Times*, October 21, 1914.

7. "First Call on Ehmke," *Sporting News*, June 4, 1914.

8. Quoted in "Senators, Bidding $20,000, May Get Eighteen-Year-Old Coast Pitcher," *New York Evening Telegram*, June 18, 1914.

9. "Senators, Bidding $20,000."

10. Along with Griffith, the New York Giants, as well as the New York Yankees, were eager to sign Ehmke. But Washington, per its working agreement with the Angels, had the inside track.

11. Quoted in Hall Sheridan, Sport News, *Daily Capital Journal* (Salem OR), July 14, 1914.

12. Quoted in Harry A. Williams, "Mr. Griff Will Get Kid Ehmke," *Los Angeles Times*, July 11, 1914.

13. "Another Zero Is Lost in Selling Price of Ehmke," *Sacramento Union*, July 27, 1914.

14. The Federal League, which was challenging the two existing Major Leagues, was not considered a part of Organized Baseball.

15. Stanley T. Milliken, "Ehmke Is Dissatisfied with Griffith's Offer," *Washington Post*, September 1, 1914.

16. Quoted in "Howard Ehmke's Mother Wants Him to Be a Manly Lad," *Spokane Review*, September 20, 1914.

17. Matt Gallagher, Off the Bat, *Los Angeles Evening Herald*, September 11, 1914.

18. Quoted in Harry A. Williams, "Four Cracks in Coast League," *Los Angeles Times*, October 21, 1914.

19. There was also a strongly implied or suggested threat of a blacklist, that players who jumped would not be allowed back into Organized Baseball.
20. The Sporting Spotlight, *Los Angeles Evening Herald*, October 27, 1914.
21. Matt Gallagher, Off the Bat, *Los Angeles Evening Herald*, September 22, 1914.
22. The Sporting Spotlight, *Los Angeles Evening Herald*, October 29, 1914.
23. Quoted in Matt Gallagher, "Ehmke Hopes to Work One More Season with Angels under Dillon's Management," *Los Angeles Evening Herald*, November 27, 1914.

7. A Wasted Year for Ehmke

1. All Federal League teams were known by two names. In addition to the Blues, the Buffalo team was also called the Buffeds.
2. Quoted in Matt Gallagher, "Dillon Convinces Ehmke It Is Best to Remain on Coast Another Year," *Los Angeles Evening Herald*, February 1, 1915.
3. Quoted in Gallagher, "Dillon Convinces Ehmke."
4. "'Bob' Ehmke May Sign with Buffalo Feds," *Buffalo Evening News*, February 2, 1915.
5. Quoted in "Dillon Mourns Loss of Ehmke; Fears Kid Is Fed," *Los Angeles Times*, February 4, 1915.
6. Quoted in "Dillon Mourns Loss of Ehmke."
7. Quoted in "Dillon Mourns Loss of Ehmke."
8. Ehmke would celebrate his twenty-first birthday in April 1915.
9. *Sporting Life*, February 20, 1915.
10. Buffalo finished fourth in 1914, the Federal League's first season.
11. *Sporting News* quoted in Wiggins, *The Federal League of Baseball Clubs*, 181.
12. Stanley T. Milliken, Sporting Facts and Fancies, *Washington Post*, February 14, 1915.
13. Milliken, Sporting Facts and Fancies, *Washington Post*, February 14, 1915.
14. "Pitcher Ehmke Gives Promise of Being Find," *Buffalo Evening News*, March 12, 1915.
15. Buffalo manager Larry Schlafly had a brief Major League career as an infielder for the Chicago Cubs (1902) and the Washington Senators (1906–7). He was in his second season as Buffalo's manager. He played in fifty-one games in 1914 but would not play this season.
16. "Pitcher Ehmke Gives Promise of Being Find."
17. Quoted in "Pitcher Ehmke Gives Promise of Being Find."
18. The emery ball is a pitch that relies on roughening part of the baseball in order to achieve an unnatural break.
19. With the emery ball banned for the 1915 season, Ford's record fell to 5-9, and he never again pitched in the Major Leagues.
20. "Brennan Made Ehmke Great," *Nashville Tennessean*, August 5, 1917.

21. Spalding, *Pacific Coast League Stars*, 2:24.
22. Quoted in N. B. Beasley, *Detroit Journal*, March 13, 1917.
23. "Terrapins Won It, 10–4," *Buffalo Express*, April 25, 1915.
24. Quoted in Wiggins, *The Federal League of Baseball Clubs*, 219.
25. The Johnsonburg Johnnies' only year in Organized Baseball would be as members of the Interstate League in 1916.

8. Another Pitcher Joins the Outlaws

1. The Major League cities with a Federal team in 1913 were Chicago, Cleveland, Pittsburgh, and St. Louis. The league's other cities were Indianapolis and Kansas City–Covington. (The league located a team in Covington, Kentucky, just across the Ohio River from Cincinnati. But it did not draw well and was moved to Kansas City in late June 1913.) The following season, Cleveland was dropped.
2. Most owners of Major League teams earned their income from operating their teams. Many Federal League owners had wealth from their outside interests. Three of the most notable were Harry F. Sinclair, oil baron; Robert Ward, whose Ward Baking Company sold Tip-Top bread; and Charles Weeghman, who made his fortune with Chicago-area cafeterias.
3. Since 1892 the National League had been baseball's only Major League.
4. Wiggins, *The Federal League of Baseball Clubs*, 7.
5. Bill Dooly, "Jack Quinn, Hardy Perennial of Game, Has Seen 26 Years of Service on Mound," *Sporting News*, November 15, 1928.
6. *New York Times*, January 24, 1914. In an undated article in the *Sporting News*, Ernest Lanigan reported the Braves were going to pay Quinn $4,500 for the end of 1913 and the entire 1914 season. This was more than the $400 a month Quinn was paid by Rochester. Unsourced newspaper article in the Quinn family collection.
7. C. Starr Matthews, "Prominent Men to Root," *Baltimore Sun*, February 28, 1914, and "Claim of the Braves," *Baltimore Sun*, May 29, 1914.
8. Unsourced newspaper article in the Quinn family collection.
9. C. Starr Matthews, "Quinn Hero of Day," *Baltimore Sun*, April 14, 1914.
10. J. C. O'Leary, "Gaffney after Quinn," *Boston Globe*, April 14, 1914, and "Claim of the Braves," *Baltimore Sun*, May 29, 1914.
11. Quoted in Nowlin, *The Miracle Braves of 1914*, 208, and O'Leary, "Gaffney after Quinn."
12. "Jack Quinn's Career Is Marked by Victories on Opening Day Contests," *Los Angeles Evening Herald*, April 22, 1918.
13. "The Toppy Terrapins," *Sporting Life*, May 16, 1914.
14. Notes of the Tinx, *Chicago Tribune*, August 5, 1914.
15. After starting with a 22-7 record, Baltimore cooled off and played one game under .500 ball the rest of the season.

16. Quoted in Lane, "The Oldest Veteran in the Major Leagues."
17. Harry A. Williams, "Ehmke Turns Down Contract," *Los Angeles Times*, August 21, 1914.
18. Typical was the case of Phillies catcher Bill Killefer, who jumped to the Chicago Whales and then jumped back to his original team, the Philadelphia Phillies. A federal judge ruled that both sides showed a lack of scruples.
19. "Admits It Wasn't Damaged," *Sporting News*, December 10, 1914.
20. Alexander, *The Miracle Braves*, 96.
21. Guy Zinn also joined the Terrapins, while Butch Schmidt was the regular first baseman for the 1914 world champion Braves.
22. Bill Dooly, "Jack Quinn, in Harness for Quarter Century, Is Best of A's Moundmen," *Philadelphia Record*, July 22, 1928. Dooly had an article on the subject in the *Sporting News* a few months later: "Jack Quinn, Hardy Perennial of Game."
23. In late August, Rochester manager Ganzel had to deny that Rudolph would be one of the players coming his way. *Rochester Democrat and Chronicle*, August 30, 1913. Whether Rudolph would have cleared waivers is questionable.
24. Ehmke made his second Major League appearance in this game, as a reliever. It was the first time he and Quinn appeared in a game together.
25. Anderson, "Bonesetter Reese."
26. C. Starr Matthews, "Jack Quinn Will Twirl," *Baltimore Evening Sun*, July 6, 1915.
27. C. Starr Matthews, "Plank Blanks Terps," *Baltimore Sun*, August 10, 1915.
28. *Retrosheet*'s work-in-progress database shows Knabe was ejected fifteen times as a player. In his two years as manager of the Terps, he was ejected another eleven times.
29. Quoted in Phil Williams, "Otto Knabe."
30. SABR historian Emil Rothe noted that of the 286 men who played in the Federal League during its 1914–15 existence, 172 of them had previous Major League experience. However, 101 of them never returned to the big leagues. Rothe, "Was the Federal League a Major League?"
31. Neyer, "Was the Federal League Really a Major League?" Kauff led the Federal League in batting both seasons, hitting .370 and .342 respectively. He then hit .287 in five seasons with the New York Giants. The files of the now defunct online National Pastime Museum (the source of Neyer's article) have been donated to the Baseball Hall of Fame and Library in Cooperstown.
32. Seymour estimated the Federal League alone lost $2,500,000, though the league's leaders claimed their losses were far smaller (*Baseball*, 233).
33. Brooklyn's owners received $400,000; the Newark and Pittsburgh Federal League owners were paid $100,000 and $50,000 respectively. All payments were spread out over several years.

34. While he sold only seventeen players, Sinclair generated almost $130,000 from the sales.

35. George Stovall, player-manager of the Kansas City Packers; Rebel Oakes, player-manager of the Pittsburgh Rebels; and Steve Evans, Quinn's teammate on the Terrapins, never returned to the Major Leagues. All three played well in the Federal League and had solid 1916 seasons in the high Minors.

36. The other three cities were Cleveland, Louisville, and Washington.

37. Chicago White Sox owner Charles Comiskey dismissed the possibility of Baltimore's getting a Major League team, saying, "Baltimore is a Minor League city, and not a hell of a good one at that." Quoted in Wiggins, *The Federal League of Baseball Clubs*, 287.

38. The 1890 law prohibits monopolistic practices that impede competition in the marketplace.

9. Breaking Records in Syracuse

1. The settlement between the Federal League and Major League Baseball (discussed in chapter 8) permitted Major League players who had signed with the Federal League to return to Organized Baseball.

2. Ehmke had great confidence in Angels catcher Walter Boles, now a thirty-year-old veteran, who had caught him in each of his 1914 wins with Los Angeles.

3. "Patterson Planning to Have Scrappy Ball Club; Ehmke May Be with L.A.," *Los Angeles Evening Herald*, January 4, 1916.

4. Johnny Powers was a Los Angeles socialite who owned the Angels from 1915 to 1921. In 1921 the team was purchased by chewing gum magnate William Wrigley Jr., the owner of the Chicago Cubs.

5. "Ehmke Will Join L.A. Club If He Can Get Release," *Los Angeles Evening Herald*, January 8, 1916. When Ehmke jumped to the Federal League, Senators manager Clark Griffith said he never would take him back.

6. Quoted in N. B. Beasley, *Detroit Journal*, March 13, 1917.

7. Quoted in "Ehmke Will Sign Contract with L.A. Club, Says Boles," *Los Angeles Evening Herald*, January 19, 1916.

8. "Frank Chance Decides Not to Try Out Kid Ehmke: Hurler Too Weak to Hold Up," *Los Angeles Tribune*, March 4, 1916.

9. W. A. Reeve, "Seraph Tribe Given Light Workout by Manager," *Los Angeles Tribune*, March 27, 1916.

10. Henry P. Edwards, "Howard Ehmke Has Widest Variety of Mound Tricks," *Hartford Courant*, February 16, 1930.

11. Quoted in N. B. Beasley, *Detroit Journal*, March 13, 1917.

12. Matt Gallagher, Sport Gossip for Los Angeles Fans, *Los Angeles Evening Herald*, April 3, 1916.

13. "Ehmke Signs with Syracuse," *Los Angeles Tribune*, April 28, 1916.

14. Several of Mike O'Neill's brothers played in the Major Leagues: Jack (1902–6), Jim (1920, 1923), and most notably Steve, who caught for seventeen years in the American League (1911–25, 1927–28), primarily with Cleveland, and managed in the AL for fourteen years.

15. As they had done when he was with Buffalo, in 1916 Los Angeles area newspapers continued to follow the career of the "hometown" boy. A report in the *Los Angeles Evening Herald* quoted a rumor from an eastern sportswriter that claimed Ehmke's success was due to his use of the emery ball. "He Does Good Job for Syracuse Club," *Los Angeles Evening Herald*, June 15, 1916. The emery ball is described in note 18 of chapter 7.

16. Matt Gallagher, Sport Gossip for Los Angeles Fans, *Los Angeles Evening Herald*, June 24, 1916.

17. "He Goes Good for Syracuse Club," *Los Angeles Evening Herald*, June 15, 1916.

18. The Troy Trojans had moved to Harrisburg during the season.

19. "Stars Downed Harrisburg in 13-Inning Game," *Syracuse Journal*, July 25, 1916.

20. "Pitcher Ehmke Sold to Detroit Tigers," *Syracuse Journal*, July 28, 1916.

21. George Boehler went 4-4 for Syracuse in the second half of 1916. In a widely scattered nine-year Major League career, he won six games and lost twelve.

22. Quoted in L. H. Addington, "Larry Sutton, 50 Years in Baseball, Never Played Game," *Sporting News*, December 4, 1930.

23. Quoted in Addington, "Larry Sutton, 50 Years in Baseball."

24. "Howard Ehmke Wins 20 Games in East," *Los Angeles Evening Herald*, August 4, 1916.

25. Ehmke's thirty-one wins broke the record of twenty-nine set by Grover Alexander with the 1910 Syracuse Stars. Alexander's 1910 earned run average was 1.85.

10. "A Fellow to Be Reckoned With"

1. "Detroit Buys This Pitcher; Nationals Now Claim Him," *Detroit News*, August 6, 1916.

2. William Peet, "Baseball Peace Meeting Adjourns to Reconvene in Cincinnati," *Washington Herald*, December 18, 1915. Groom later joined the St. Louis Browns, but Laporte never returned to the Majors.

3. "Ehmke Is Awarded to Washington Club," *New York Sun*, September 2, 1916.

4. "Ehmke Departs to Join Tigers," *Syracuse Daily Journal*, September 7, 1916.

5. "Herrmann and Farrell Finding Opposition," *Elmira (NY) Star-Gazette*, September 18, 1916.

6. Detroit lost to the Chicago Cubs in 1907 and 1908 and to the Pittsburgh Pirates in 1909.

7. "Recruit Ehmke Looms as Pitcher to Be Prized," *Detroit Times*, September 11, 1916.

8. Ehmke made two starts with Buffalo in 1914 but completed neither one.

9. E. A. Batchelor, "Tigers One Half Game from Lead," *Detroit Free Press*, September 12, 1916.

10. The *Detroit News* reporter compared Ehmke's sidearm delivery to that of Carl Mays. However, Mays was most often described as delivering his pitches underhand; therefore it is impossible to determine from what angle Ehmke was throwing that day. Depending on the situation, he would use both the sidearm and underhand deliveries, as well as the traditional overhand delivery.

11. "Ehmke, in Debut, Never in Danger," *Detroit News*, September 13, 1916.

12. H. G. Salsinger, "It's Post-Mortem from Detroit End," *Sporting News*, September 21, 1916.

13. Ehmke's career record against Philadelphia was 26-14.

14. Quoted in Harold V. Wilcox, Looking 'Em Over, *Detroit Times*, September 18, 1916.

15. John A. Hallahan, "Red Sox Knock Detroit Tigers Down and Out," *Boston Herald*, September 21, 1916.

16. Edward P. Martin, "Red Sox Pin Another Defeat on the Tigers," *Boston Globe*, September 21, 1916.

17. Johnson's loss was his twentieth of the season (he was 25-20). It was also his third of the season without a win at Navin Field, the reverse of his 3-0 record against the Tigers at home.

18. E. A. Batchelor, "Believe Howard Ehmke Coming Baseball Star," *Albany Evening Journal*, October 18, 1916.

19. "Detroit Leader Forbids Ehmke to Play Winter Ball," *Los Angeles Evening Herald*, September 22, 1916. A floorwalker is a person employed in a retail store to oversee the salespeople and to aid customers.

11. The Tigers Take a Step Backward

1. "Bob Ehmke Signs Detroit Contract and All Is Well," *Syracuse Journal*, February 23, 1917.

2. H. G. Salsinger, "Detroit's New Year Hope Is a Pitcher," *Sporting News*, January 4, 1917.

3. Quoted in N. B. Beasley, *Detroit Journal*, March 13, 1917.

4. Future Hall of Famer Addie Joss, a Cleveland Indians right-hander, won 160 games from 1902 to 1910. He died of tubercular meningitis in 1910, at age thirty-one.

5. Beasley, *Detroit Journal*, March 13, 1917.

6. Harold V. Wilcox, Looking 'Em Over, *Detroit Times*, March 16, 1917.

7. Quoted in N. B. Beasley, "Nothing Slouchy about Way Ehmke Fields Ball," *Detroit Journal*, March 23, 1917.

8. Miller Huggins would replace Bill Donovan as the Yankees' manager after the 1917 season.

9. Quoted in Beasley, "Nothing Slouchy about Way Ehmke Fields Ball."

10. Quoted in N. B. Beasley, "Twirlers Promise Great Work for 1917 Season," *Detroit Journal*, March 26, 1917.

11. Quoted in "Ehmke a Wonder," *Duluth (MN) Evening Herald*, April 26, 1917.

12. Kofoed, "The Youngsters of 1917," 435.

13. Jim Bagby won twenty-three games (and lost thirteen) in 1917, with a 1.99 earned run average.

14. The twenty-two-year-old Ruth's 2–1 victory on May 11 raised his record to 7-0. Although he was recognized as the best left-handed pitcher in the game, this would be the final season in which he was strictly a pitcher.

15. N. B. Beasley, "20,000 Watch Ehmke Beat Shore, 2 to 1," *Detroit Journal*, May 14, 1917.

16. "Detroit Critic Lauds Bob Ehmke," *Syracuse Journal*, May 15, 1917.

17. Bill Donovan won 140 games in eleven years with Detroit, including a 25-4 season in 1907.

18. Ehmke also walked nine batters as a member of the Red Sox in a game at Cleveland on May 22, 1923.

19. Dan Holmes, "Did the Tigers Throw Games in 1917 to Help the White Sox Win the Pennant?" *Vintage Detroit Collection* (blog), May 28, 2016, www.vintagedetroit.com.

20. Holmes, "Did the Tigers Throw Games in 1917 . . . ?"

21. The three members of the Tigers were Bobby Veach, Oscar Stanage, and Pep Young.

22. E. A. Batchelor, "The Tigers Drop Both Games to Chicago," *Detroit Free Press*, September 3, 1917.

23. Batchelor, "The Tigers Drop Both Games to Chicago."

24. E. A. Batchelor, "The White Sox Beat Tigers Twice More," *Detroit Free Press*, September 4, 1917.

25. Batchelor, "The White Sox Beat Tigers Twice More."

26. Burt Whitman, "Red Sox and Stars Make Murnane Day Success," *Boston Herald*, September 28, 1917.

27. With the American League standings all but decided, others, including Chicago's Joe Jackson and Washington's Walter Johnson, were excused by their teams and allowed to take part. The all-stars' lineup was primarily American League because of the heavy National League schedule that day.

28. "Ehmke Favorite in Detroit," *Silver Creek (NY) News*, June 14, 1917.

29. Beasley quoted in "Ehmke Favorite in Detroit."

12. Quinn to the Pacific Coast League

1. Quinn posted a 9-22 record in the Federal League in 1915, with an earned run average of 3.45, almost a half-run higher than the league average.
2. Boss Schmidt continued to play in the Minors until 1924, when he was forty-three. (Schmidt was not related to Quinn's 1913 teammate Butch Schmidt.) During the spring of 1907 Boss Schmidt came to the aid of a Black couple Cobb was assaulting. See "Cobb in Fist Fight Again: Mixes with Charlie Schmidt after Beating Negro and Latter's' Wife; Insulted When Black Man Speaks to Him," *Detroit Free Press*, March 17, 1907.
3. Michal Czerwonka, "Vernon Residents Fight for Town," *New York Times*, March 1, 2011. *Forbes* had an unfavorable article on Vernon in 2007: "Welcome to Paradise." *Eraserhead*, the surreal cult classic horror film, is set in a grimy industrial landscape.
4. The city of Los Angeles was indeed "dry" at that time.
5. In 1912 the lightweight world championship fight between Ad Wolgast and Joe Rivers was held in Doyle's arena. Cecilia Rasmussen, "A Teetotaler's Bar and Boxing Mecca," *Los Angeles Times*, June 23, 1997.
6. "Quinn May Land Neat Job," *Los Angeles Times*, February 15, 1916.
7. Baseball Gossip, *Los Angeles Times*, February 26, 1916. The article stated that Quinn's Federal League contract called for $8,000 for 1916, but that is unlikely.
8. W. A. Reeve, "Tigers and Angels Ready," *Los Angeles Tribune*, May 9, 1916.
9. *Sporting News*, January 13, 1916.
10. In his playing career Chance repeatedly sacrificed his body—often his head—to get on base via a hit-by-pitch. He had blood clots on his brain that had required surgery, was deaf in one ear, and could speak only in "an annoyingly whiney tone." Ryhal, "Frank Chance."
11. The loser was Spider Baum, who won thirty games for the Seals in 1915 and would win more than three hundred in the Minors, yet he never appeared in the big leagues. Baum was a nine-time twenty-game winner in the Minors.
12. "Quinn Beaten," *Los Angeles Record*, May 27, 1916.
13. Arthur Mars, Atta Boy, *Los Angeles Evening Herald*, May 18, 1916.
14. Under Giants manager John McGraw, Crandall started 77 games for New York; he finished 128. Four times between 1909 and 1913 he ranked second or third in saves in the National League. The "save" statistic did not exist until 1969 and was computed retroactively, based on the original 1969 definition.
15. Quoted in Matt Gallagher, "L.A. Makes Great Drive to First Place; Chance Gives His Players Credit," *Los Angeles Evening Herald*, July 17, 1916.
16. Matt Gallagher, "Chance Deserves Credit for Leading Angels to Coast League Pennant," *Los Angeles Evening Herald*, October 20, 1916.

17. After Hogan's death, veteran Major League pitcher Doc White became the interim manager of the club for the balance of the 1915 season.
18. *Sporting Life*, February 10, 1917. Stovall paid $500 for his release from Toledo.
19. Snodgrass is best remembered for dropping a routine fly ball in the tenth inning of the final game of the 1912 World Series against the Boston Red Sox. "Snodgrass's muff" was blamed, somewhat unfairly, for costing the New York Giants the world championship.
20. Harry A. Williams, "Vernon Takes Two Straight," *Los Angeles Times*, April 19, 1917.
21. Dan Daniel, High Lights and Shadows in All Spheres of Sport, *New York Sun*, May 19, 1919.
22. *San Francisco Chronicle*, July 18, 1917.
23. "Quinn and Fromme Win 13 Games in 14 Starts for Vernon Ball Club," *Los Angeles Evening Herald*, August 18, 1917.
24. "Quinn and Fromme Win 13 Games in 14 Starts."
25. Harry A. Williams, "Jack Quinn Is Bad Luck Guy," *Los Angeles Times*, August 31, 1917.
26. "Quinn Wins in a Hurry," *Los Angeles Times*, September 12, 1917. Long Tom Hughes, who won 132 games in a Major League career from 1900 to 1913, is not to be confused with the Tom Hughes who was a teammate of Quinn's on the 1909–10 Yankees and posted a 16-3 record for George Stallings's 1916 Boston Braves.
27. Wolverton clashed with owner Henry Berry. Berry said his manager wanted to spend too much money on players. Putnam, "Harry Wolverton." Wolverton was replaced by Red Downs, who had played three seasons in the Majors (1907–8 and 1912).
28. Snelling, *The Greatest Minor League*, 77.
29. Matt Gallagher, Sport Gossip for Los Angeles Fans, *Los Angeles Evening Herald*, August 20, 1917.
30. Ed R. Hughes, Sports Talks, *San Francisco Chronicle*, November 21, 1917.
31. American League News in Nut Shells, *Sporting Life*, March 16, 1912.
32. Quoted in "'Through? Not on Your Life,' Cries Jack Quinn, Who Says He'll Be Back to Pitch Big League Ball Next Year," *Philadelphia Record*, November 13, 1930.
33. Levitt, "Bill Essick."
34. A "cup-of-coffee player" is someone who has appeared in ten or fewer games in his career. Essick was on the 1906 and 1907 Cincinnati Reds. He would go on to a long career as a scout for the New York Yankees.
35. Going into the 1918 season, it was not known how much impact the draft would have on baseball. So Quinn's age early in the season was not as much of an advantage as it turned out to be that summer.

36. Edwin F. O'Malley, "Jack Quinn Turns Trick," *Los Angeles Times*, April 10, 1918.

37. Quoted in "Sensational Pitching by Quinn and Martin Marks Longest Game of Season," *Los Angeles Evening Herald*, April 27, 1918.

38. O'Doul hit only .200 for San Francisco in 1918 but had a 12-8 record for the Seals. Three years later he won twenty-five games for them while batting .338.

39. Ed R. Hughes, "Jack Quinn at Last Wins One in This Town," *San Francisco Chronicle*, June 27, 1918. Future president Herbert Hoover was the nation's "food czar" during the war. He oversaw food production and pricing, as well as the supply of food to the Allies.

40. Willett won a combined thirty-six games for the pennant-winning Tigers of 1908 and 1909.

41. Nowlin, "Charlie Chech."

42. The National Railroad Board raised the round-trip fare between Los Angeles and San Francisco from $21.50 to $45 in June. Bauer, "The Year the PCL Threw in the Towel."

43. Steinberg, "World War I and Free Agency," 85.

44. H. M. Walker, An Ear to the Ground, *Los Angeles Examiner*, June 24, 1918.

45. The pitchers were Quinn and Chech, as well as Art Fromme, Wheezer Dell, and Roy Mitchell. The hitters were Tom Daley and Chet Chadbourne.

46. Bauer, "The Year the PCL Threw in the Towel."

47. The International League was the only Minor League that played its regularly scheduled season to completion.

48. Minor League historian Marshall Wright confirmed this to Steve Steinberg in an email dated October 14, 2009. He noted that Larry Jansen's 1.57 earned run average in the 1946 season (when he had a 30-6 record with San Francisco) is sometimes considered the full-season record. Yet Quinn pitched 213 innings for Vernon in 1918. Pacific Coast League historian Carlos Bauer has noted that Quinn's earned run average was actually 1.43. Email to Steve Steinberg, March 5, 2014.

13. *"The Dynamite"*

1. Many Minor Leagues disbanded during or after the 1917 season; only ten leagues began play in 1918. As noted above, the International League was the only one that completed its regular schedule in 1918. Semi-pro teams were also still operating.

2. Men of draft age (21–30) had to enlist in the military by July 1, 1918, unless they worked in an "essential industry" such as shipbuilding or steelmaking. Baseball did not get such an exemption from the government's "Work or Fight" order (first issued in May and clarified on July 20), but baseball players were given a couple of extra months to enlist—that is, until September. See Steinberg, "World War I and Free Agency," 84–85.

3. H. M. Walker, An Ear to the Ground, *Los Angeles Examiner*, May 26, 1918.

4. Organized Baseball had a "ten-day notice" clause in all player contracts that stated a club could release a player on ten days' notice for whatever reason—injury, performance, or, in this case, the decision to end the 1918 season early. This clause lacked "mutuality"—that is, players could not leave their teams on ten days' notice.

5. A very few Major Leaguers went to court to demand their full season's pay, and they won. Brooklyn's Jake Daubert was one, and he was quickly traded away. To his good fortune, he was sent to the Cincinnati Reds, who won the World Series in 1919.

6. Edward F. Martin, "Red Sox Yield to Chicago by 6–2," *Boston Globe*, August 16, 1918.

7. Matt Gallagher, Strictly Baseball, *Los Angeles Evening Herald*, July 17, 1918.

8. Bill Dooly, "Jack Quinn, Hardy Perennial of Game, Has Seen 26 Years of Service on Mound," *Sporting News*, November 15, 1928.

9. Quoted in Brown, *The Chicago White Sox*, 79.

10. "Jack Quinn Ready to Start his 25th Year," *New York Sun*, March 2, 1928.

11. The transfer of the three men was not finalized until February 1919. They were Zinn Beck, a four-year veteran of the St. Louis Cardinals; Happy Finneran, who won three games for the 1918 Yankees; and Sammy Ross, a career Minor Leaguer. Neither Beck nor Finneran ever returned to the Majors. It is possible the players were sent in lieu of cash. "Yanks Give Three for Pitcher Quinn," *Atlanta Constitution*, February 21, 1919.

12. Minor League Baseball, milb.com/content/page.jsp?sid=l112&ymd= 20060308&content_id=45943&vkey=news_milb.

13. Quoted in Dooly, "Jack Quinn, Hardy Perennial of Game."

14. "Wild Pitch Whips Yankees in 15th," *New York Sun*, August 7, 1918.

15. "Jack Quinn Helps Place Former Teammates among the Also-Rans of the League," *New York Times*, August 20, 1918. Jack Fournier, who hit .325 for the Los Angeles Angels that year, had three hits in the game. He was also in dispute, playing for New York though claimed by Chicago. Despite hitting .350 for the Yankees that August, he was back in the Minors in 1919. He was known as one of the worst fielders in the game. Greene, "Jack Fournier."

16. Fred Lieb, "Lineups These Days Seem Like a Joke," *Sporting News*, August 15, 1918.

17. Brown, *The Chicago White Sox*, 78. For an examination of the Quinn case, see Steinberg, "World War I and Free Agency."

18. Quoted in Murdock, *Ban Johnson*, 156.

19. Spink, *Judge Landis and 25 Years of Baseball*, 49, and Lieb, *The Baseball Story*, 216.

20. Leeke, *From the Dugouts to the Trenches*, 40–41, quoting *Chicago Tribune*, August 4, 1918.

21. Quoted in Fleitz, *Shoeless*, 155.
22. Ban Johnson, "Ban and Comiskey Rowed over Quinn," *Philadelphia Evening Bulletin*, March 12, 1929.
23. Murdock, *Ban Johnson*, 156.
24. John B. Sheridan, Observations of a Veteran Scribe, *Sporting News*, January 22, 1920.
25. John E. Wray and J. Roy Stockton, "Ban Johnson's Own Story," *St. Louis Post-Dispatch*, February 10, 1929.
26. Charles Comiskey, Letter to the Editor, *Cleveland Plain Dealer*, January 13, 1929.
27. Hugh S. Fullerton, "Jack Quinn Comes to New York as American Leaguer," *Atlanta Constitution*, June 17, 1919.
28. Paul Mickelson, "'The Old Roman' Figured in Greatest Friendship and Fiercest Feud of Game," AP, *St. Louis Globe-Democrat*, October 27, 1931.
29. Carney, *Burying the Black Sox*, 309n236.
30. Quinn family collection.
31. "Beloit Defeats Normals Twice," *Chicago Tribune*, October 7, 1918. In the second game of a doubleheader that day, the Fairies won again, beating Dickie Kerr. Kerr would join the White Sox the following year. The winning pitcher was not, could not, and perhaps did not want to be identified; he wore a mask. He was listed in the box score as the "Masked Marvel."
32. "Jack Quinn Best Spitball Pitcher Since Ed Walsh," *San Francisco Chronicle*, August 28, 1918.

14. Navy Service and a Return to Detroit

1. "Ehmke Lost to Detroit's Flag Cause," *Detroit Free Press*, January 14, 1918.
2. "Tigers Tops in Two Wars," *Sporting News*, March 25, 1943.
3. "Ehmke Lost to Detroit's Flag Cause."
4. San Pedro was formerly a separate city; it consolidated with Los Angeles in 1909.
5. "Rebuild Submarine Base to Make Room for Ehmke," *Los Angeles Evening Herald*, January 19, 1918.
6. *Los Angeles Evening Herald*, January 14, 1918.
7. In March 1918, while Ehmke was in the navy, his father, Charles, died in Silver Lake, New York.
8. "Billman and Ehmke Work No-Hit Game," *Los Angeles Evening Herald*, February 7, 1918.
9. "Ehmke's New 'Shaded Ball' Pitch Designed for Shibe Park Only," *Philadelphia Evening Bulletin*, August 22, 1928.
10. *Los Angeles Evening Herald*, November 4, 1918.
11. "Auto Collision Due to Pretty Companion," *Syracuse Journal*, December 5, 1918.
12. "Ehmke Quits Navy; Joins Heavyweights," *Detroit News*, March 5, 1919.

13. Steinberg and Spatz, *The Colonel and Hug*, 97. In addition to a shortened season, May to September rosters were cut from twenty-five to twenty-one players.
14. Dan Howley caught twenty-six games for the 1913 Philadelphia Phillies. He managed at Montreal and at Toronto of the International League from 1914 to 1918. He would later manage the St. Louis Browns (1927–29) and the Cincinnati Reds (1930–32).
15. Quoted in "Success of Ehmke Due to Slow Ball," *Detroit News*, April 26, 1919.
16. The Yankees, after spending 1916 to 1918 in Macon, moved to Jacksonville, Florida.
17. Quoted in M. F. Drukenbrod, "Ehmke Shows Winning Brand," *Detroit News*, April 4, 1919.
18. April 25 was the latest season opener for Detroit since 1901, the American League's first season as a Major League. The Tigers have not opened any season that late since 1919. For Cleveland it remains the latest opener ever.
19. At that time, aside from Detroit's Roscoe Miller, Boston's Win Kellum, and Chicago's Roy Patterson, all of whom were making their Major League debuts in 1901, the American League's first season as a Major League, only Chicago's Patsy Flaherty in 1903, Philadelphia's Nick Carter in 1908, and New York's Hippo Vaughn in 1910 started an American League opener without having pitched in the league the previous season.
20. "Too Much Confidence Handicap to Ehmke," *Detroit News*, May 19, 1919.
21. Harry Bullion, "Scratch Safety Deprives Howard Ehmke of No-Hit Game against Cleveland," *Detroit Free Press*, June 30, 1919.
22. I. E. Sanborn. "Tigers Take Hectic 16 Inning Battle from White Sox, 4–3," *Chicago Tribune*, September 3, 1919.
23. Ehmke would pitch beyond the ninth inning in sixteen more starts in his career but never again more than thirteen innings.
24. John C. Manning, "Ehmke Offers Help Too Late," *Detroit News*, September 3, 1919.
25. Ehmke later appeared in relief on August 27, after being out of action for three weeks with a sore arm. He pitched the final inning of a 7–5 loss at Cleveland.
26. "Yankees Shoved into 4th Place Tie," *New York Times*, August 3, 1919.
27. Curves and Bingles, *New York Times*, August 3, 1919.
28. This game was the first in which Ehmke and Quinn had faced each other since April 24, 1915, when they were in the Federal League.
29. Curves and Bingles, *New York Times*, August 3, 1919.
30. J. V. Fitz Gerald, "Tigers Rout Griffs, 9–4," *Washington Post*, September 15, 1919.
31. Letter from Howard Ehmke to his mother, October 24, 1919.
32. "Ehmke Signs His Contract with Tigers," *Detroit Free Press*, December 30, 1919. O'Loughlin died at the age of forty-two on December 20, 1918, a victim of the influenza pandemic.

33. "Ehmke Signs His Contract with Tigers."

34. "Ehmke Signs His Contract with Tigers."

35. *Los Angeles Times*, January 18, 1917, quoted in Leerhsen, *Ty Cobb*, 297.

36. Sher, "Ty Cobb," 106.

37. Quoted in Ed Pollock, Playing the Game, *Philadelphia Evening Bulletin*, June 15, 1952.

15. *"The Greatest Comeback in Baseball"*

1. Brewery magnate Jacob Ruppert and engineering entrepreneur Tillinghast L'Hommedieu ("Til") Huston bought the club from Frank Farrell and Bill Devery in January 1915.

2. "Huggins Backing Pitchers for Pennant," *New York Evening Telegram*, December 22, 1918. It is surprising that the article made no mention of Quinn's spitball.

3. Leonard and the Yankees did not agree to terms, and the club sold him to the Detroit Tigers. See Steinberg and Spatz, *The Colonel and Hug*, 379n26.

4. George Mogridge had a 16-13 record, and Slim Love went 13-12. Love would win only 28 games in his career. Mogridge was more successful, with 132 victories. He was a rare player Huggins traded away who had success elsewhere. He won 65 games for the Washington Senators from 1921 to 1924, as well as a World Series game in 1924.

5. "Trade of 4 Youths for Jack Quinn Means Veterans Are Wanted This Year," *New York Evening Mail*, February 21, 1919.

6. Hyatt Daab, "Yankees Now Have Best Mound Staff," *New York Evening Sun*, March 26, 1919.

7. Quoted in Dan Daniel, High Lights and Shadows in All Spheres of Sport, *New York Sun*, April 4, 1919.

8. George Halas famously went on to greatness as a football coach and owner of the National Football League's Chicago Bears.

9. "Yankees Have a Find in O'Doul," *New York Sun*, March 27, 1919.

10. Quoted in Dan Daniel, High Lights and Shadows in All Spheres of Sport, *New York Sun*, March 28, 1919. O'Doul appeared in five games as a pitcher for the Yankees in 1919 and 1920 and six more in 1922, after he won twenty-five games for the Pacific Coast League's San Francisco Seals in 1921. Only in 1929 would he emerge, when he hit .398 for the Phillies at the age of thirty-two. Near the end of the 1922 season, he was sent to the Boston Red Sox as "the player to be named later" in the trade that brought Joe Dugan to the Yankees that summer.

11. Quoted in Sid Mercer, All in a Day's Work, *New York Globe and Commercial Advertiser*, April 25, 1919. Henry Wadsworth Longfellow was a beloved nineteenth-century American poet.

12. Quoted in Faber and Faber, *Spitballers*, 64.

13. Quoted in Joe Vila, "Jack Quinn Ready to Start His 25th Year," *Philadelphia Inquirer*, March 3, 1928. Whether Quinn went through this routine on his hunting trips is not known.

14. For example, two weeks after the San Francisco earthquake, on Sunday, April 29, 1906, the New York Americans hosted the Philadelphia Athletics in a game to benefit victims of the disaster. Six years later, after the sinking of the *Titanic*, a benefit game between the Giants and the Yankees for the survivors was played at the Polo Grounds on Sunday, April 21, 1912. The game, attended by fourteen thousand fans, generated more than $9,000. The Giants won, 11–2.

15. Sid Mercer, All in a Day's Work, *New York Globe and Commercial Advertiser*, March 7, 1919.

16. The state law permitted each community to decide whether to allow Sunday ball. After Governor Al Smith signed the bill, New York City's Board of Aldermen voted unanimously to permit it. The *New York Sun* then observed that this "most harmless diversion" would "in no sense be deteriorating to the moral fibre [*sic*] of the witnesses" (April 20, 1919). Mayor John Hylan signed the bill a couple of weeks later.

17. Sid Mercer, All in a Day's Work, *New York Globe and Commercial Advertiser*, May 12, 1919.

18. Three times the Senators left the bases loaded.

19. Hyatt Daab, "Johnson Still the Master of Them All," *New York Evening Telegram*, May 12, 1919.

20. I. E. Sanborn, "Give Jack Quinn Horseshoe, Then Sox Put Kick in It," *Chicago Tribune*, May 23, 1919.

21. Fred Lieb, "Yankees Whip White Sox, and Quinn Rejoices," *New York Sun*, June 8, 1919.

22. Quinn applied for a passport because he went on a barnstorming tour of Cuba with other Major Leaguers that fall. There the All-Americans played a series of games against the Habana and Almendares clubs (*El Trionfo* [Habana, Cuba], November 12, 1919). Quinn looked so good in the three games he pitched, a reporter for the *Louisville Courier* declared, that he "showed as much stuff as ever in his career" (January 4, 1920).

23. "Pitching Corps in American League Will Be New York's Main Asset," *New York Sun*, April 20, 1919. Only the White Sox's Eddie Cicotte had a lower earned run average, at 1.09. O'Connor had been Huggins's pitching coach with the St. Louis Cardinals in 1914.

24. On June 30, 1918, the Yankees were just a half-game out of first place with a 36-26 record.

25. On July 31, 1918, the Yankees had fallen to fourth place, 10 games out of first, with a 47-45 mark.

26. "Leonard Blanks Hapless Yankees," *New York Times*, July 15, 1919.

27. Harry Schumacher, "Yankees Grow Worse as They Go Along in West," *New York Globe and Commercial Advertiser*, July 18, 1919.

28. Harry Schumacher, "Huggins Makes a Shift in His Batting Order," *New York Globe and Commercial Advertiser*, July 15, 1919.

29. Dan Daniel, High Lights and Shadows in All Spheres of Sport, *New York Sun*, August 1, 1919. For further discussion of the press's 1919 opinions on Huggins, see Steinberg and Spatz, *The Colonel and Hug*, 106–7.

30. Huggins traded both Pratt and Mogridge in December 1920, but he still faced clubhouse carping the following two seasons.

31. Mays walked out on his team, and Johnson did not want a player to "force" a trade in such a manner. Moreover, the New York owners charged that Johnson wanted Mays to land with a team of his choosing.

32. Harry Schumacher, "Yankees Get Pitcher Carl Mays in Trade, and Fans See Hope for A. L. Pennant," *New York Globe and Commercial Advertiser*, July 31, 1919.

33. Harry Schumacher, "Ban Johnson May Be Driven from Office Unless He Lifts Suspension of Carl Mays," *New York Globe and Commercial Advertiser*, August 5, 1919.

34. "Ruth Wallops Out His 28th Home Run," September 25, 1919. Ruth's ninth-inning blow tied the game, but the Yankees won in thirteen. Red Sox pitcher Waite Hoyt's performance made a big impression on Miller Huggins. From the fourth to the tenth innings, he did not allow a Yankee to reach base. After the 1920 season Huggins would acquire Hoyt, who joined Quinn on the New York pitching staff.

35. This was better than the league's average of 3.22.

36. "Macks Lose Another One-Sided Affair," *Philadelphia Inquirer*, June 25, 1919.

37. In his 5–2 win over the A's on September 1, Quinn threw probably the wildest of his sixty-two career wild pitches. As he was facing Cy Perkins, "the ball went off on a tangent and entered the grandstand." "World's Wildest Pitch?" *Collyer's Eye*, October 25, 1919.

16. "Not Content to Accept Fate's Decree"

1. While Ruth did start 17 games as a pitcher in 1919 (and won 9 of them), he appeared in 130 of Boston's 137 games, with 432 at bats.

2. Babe Ruth, "Babe Ruth Tells All in His Own Book of Baseball," *New York World*, January 8, 1929.

3. Quoted in Steinberg, "The Spitball and the End of the Deadball Era," 7.

4. Clark Griffith, "Ban the Spitter," *Baseball Magazine*, July 1917, quoted in Steinberg, "The Spitball and the End of the Deadball Era," 10.

5. Harry Schumacher, "New Pitching Rules Hit Big Jack Quinn," *New York Globe and Commercial Advertiser*, February 16, 1920.

6. Harry A. Williams, "Veterans Handicapped by New Pitching Rules," *New York Globe and Commercial Advertiser*, June 15, 1920.

7. Quoted in "Heydler Warns against 'Bean Ball' Delivery," *New York Evening Telegram*, February 7, 1920.

8. Harry A. Williams, "Veterans Handicapped by New Pitching Rules."

9. Frank F. O'Neill, Scribbled by Scribes, *Sporting News*, July 22, 1920.

10. Schumacher, "New Pitching Rules Hit Big Jack Quinn."

11. Damon Runyon, *New York American*, May 16, 1920.

12. "Record Crowd Sees Quinn Pitch Yanks to Victory," *St. Louis Post-Dispatch*, June 21, 1920.

13. Harry Schumacher, "Miller Huggins, Confronted by Big Task in Managing the Yankees in 1921 Campaign," *New York Globe and Commercial Advertiser*, October 30, 1920.

14. "Yanks Take Third Game from Indians," *New York Times*, August 13, 1920.

15. William B. Hanna, "Yankees Jostle Indians, 5–1," *New York Sun*, August 13, 1920.

16. Gallico, *The Golden People*, 39.

17. Ruth walked 150 times in 1920, breaking Jimmy Sheckard's Major League record of 147, set with the 1911 Chicago Cubs.

18. Quoted in James C. Isaminger, Pithy Tips from the Sport Ticker, *Philadelphia Inquirer*, August 15, 1926.

19. In his long career Quinn hit 91 batters. He ranks 115th all-time. By comparison, Walter Johnson hit 205 batters, 4th all-time.

20. "Yankees Drop Back into Second Place," *New York Times*, September 17, 1920.

21. Harry Schumacher, "Huggins Judgment Suicidal to Yankees," *New York Globe and Commercial Advertiser*, September 17, 1920.

22. Thormahlen did start the next day and lasted only two innings. He got another start two days later and could not complete four innings. Shawkey started the third and final game of the White Sox series and gave up six runs in one and one-third innings. Mays was ineffective in relief in Chicago. So much for the choices that would have been better than Jack Quinn.

23. Sam Murphy, Sports Editor's Say So, *New York Evening Mail*, September 21, 1920.

24. Joe Vila, "Yanks Must Test the Feeling of Fans in Foreign Fields," *Sporting News*, September 2, 1920. For a discussion of the press's opinions on Huggins in 1920, see Steinberg and Spatz, *The Colonel and Hug*, 159–60.

25. Jim Nasium, "They Sometimes Do Come Back Strong," *Philadelphia Inquirer*, May 18, 1920.

26. Grantland Rice, The Sportlight, *New York Tribune*, September 8, 1920.

17. Yankees Win a Championship

1. Steinberg, "The Spitball: 'Grandfathered' Spitball Pitchers."

2. Sam Crane, *New York Evening Journal*, December 15, 1920.

3. Quoted in Harry Schumacher, "Amend Ban on Spitballists," *New York Globe and Commercial Advertiser*, November 19, 1920.

4. "Bar Spitter and We Starve," *New York Evening Telegram*, May 20, 1920.

5. Quoted in Fred Lieb, "Spitballers Want to Stay," *New York Evening Telegram*, May 21, 1920.

6. Sid Mercer, Sid Mercer's Close-Ups, *New York Evening Journal*, July 7, 1920.

7. Steinberg, "The Spitball and the End of the Deadball Era," 11.

8. W. R. Hoefer, "The Reign of the Wallop," *Baseball Magazine*, July 1923, quoted in Steinberg, "The Spitball and the End of the Deadball Era," 13.

9. Joe Vila, "Sad Week It Was for Gotham Fans of Both Persuasions," *Sporting News*, May 5, 1921.

10. The Red Sox sent pitchers Harry Harper and Waite Hoyt, catcher Wally Schang, and utility infielder Mike McNally to the Yankees for Del Pratt, pitcher Hank Thormahlen, catcher Muddy Ruel, and utility outfielder Sammy Vick.

11. Joe Vila, Setting the Pace, *New York Sun*, May 23, 1921.

12. John A. Dugan, "Washington Pitchers Check Yank Maulers," *Washington Post*, May 31, 1921. In 1919 a syndicated article's headline called Quinn "Hard Luck Boy." That season he lost decisions by scores of 1–0 (twice), 2–1, 2–0, 3–0, and 3–2. *Anaconda (MT) Standard*, December 28, 1919.

13. Frank F. O'Neill, "Jack Quinn to Umpire," *New York Sun*, July 16, 1921.

14. "Yankees Give Picnic at Polo Grounds," *New York Times*, June 10, 1921.

15. O'Neill, "Jack Quinn to Umpire." Another spitball pitcher did turn to umpiring in 1922: Ed Walsh. It gave him an opportunity to stay in the game, but he hated calling balls and strikes and quit midseason.

16. "Quinn Disappoints," *Louisville Courier-Journal*, July 3, 1921.

17. "Yanks Ambuscade Speaker's Indians," *New York Times*, August 24, 1921. "Ambuscade" is both a verb and a noun. It means "ambush."

18. "Yanks Ambuscade Speaker's Indians."

19. Monitor [Daley's pseudonym], *New York World*, August 24, 1921. New York first baseman Wally Pipp had eighteen putouts, and the Yankees had nineteen assists in the game.

20. Joe Vila, "Giants and Yankees Rise Up and Knock Out the Knockers," *Sporting News*, September 1, 1921.

21. "Desperate Rallies by Hugmen Overcome Four-Run Handicap," *New York Tribune*, September 23, 1921.

22. "Detroit Snowed Under by Yankees in Final," *Detroit Journal*, September 23, 1921.

23. Quinn hit eight home runs in his career; Ehmke hit none.

24. Quotes in this paragraph are from Graham, *The New York Yankees*, 67–68.

25. "Great Ruth Leads Yanks in Victory," *New York Times*, September 27, 1921.

26. Lieb, "Ten Outstanding Games of Major League History," 27–29.

27. This was the last of three consecutive best-of-nine World Series. The first World Series of the Modern Era, in 1903, was also a best-of-nine. The first World Series in which all games were played in the same park was that of 1921.

28. Heywood Broun, "Fate Plays Big Jack Quinn a Mean Trick," *Boston Globe*, October 8, 1921.

29. "Giants Win, 13–5; Four Yank Pitchers Mauled for 20 Hits," *New York Times*, October 8, 1921.

30. Kofoed, "The Hero of the 1921 World Series," 598.

31. Broun, "Fate Plays Big Jack Quinn a Mean Trick."

32. Hugh S. Fullerton, "Yankees Must Now Do the Guessing, Fullerton Writes," *St. Louis Post-Dispatch*, October 8, 1921.

33. Hugh S. Fullerton, On the Screen of Sport, *New York Evening Mail*, October 28, 1921.

34. These pitchers were Art Nehf, Phil Douglas, and Jesse Barnes for the Giants; Carl Mays and Waite Hoyt for the Yankees.

18. "A Fellow of Gentle Soul"

1. The Tigers were one of a handful of teams that had a designated pitching coach. Owner Frank Navin had been a pioneer in using them, beginning with Deacon McGuire in 1912.

2. Coombs pitched in two games for the Tigers in the 1920 season.

3. Yawkey died from the third and final wave of the Spanish flu pandemic that killed more than fifty million people worldwide.

4. Yawkey had little interest in baseball, so Navin ran the club and made most decisions, even before he was majority owner.

5. Without Yawkey's fortune to fall back on, Navin brokered the sale of 25 percent of the Yawkey interest to auto-body manufacturer Walter Briggs Sr. and another 25 percent to wheelmaker John Kelsey.

6. Lefty Williams's three losses came in an eight-game Series. The only other pitcher to lose three games in a single World Series is George Frazier of the 1981 New York Yankees. Frazier's three losses came in a six-game Series.

7. Although an early August 1920 grand jury cleared the eight White Sox players of any wrongdoing, Landis banned them the next day for their involvement in deliberately losing the 1919 World Series to the Cincinnati Reds.

8. Cicotte was among the eight White Sox players Landis expelled from Organized Baseball.

9. Tiger Notes, *Detroit Free Press*, April 18, 1920.

10. The 1920 White Sox were the first team to have four 20-game winners: Red Faber (23), Lefty Williams (22), Eddie Cicotte (21), and Dickie Kerr (21). The 1971 Baltimore Orioles were the only other team to have four

20-game winners. Dave McNally won 21, and Jim Palmer, Mike Cueller, and Pat Dobson each won 20.

11. James Crusinberry, "Cicotte Pitches Sox to Easy Win Over Tigers," *Chicago Tribune*, April 18, 1920.

12. Quoted in Crusinberry, "Cicotte Pitches Sox to Easy Win Over Tigers."

13. The 1920 Tigers' thirteen-game losing streak to start the season remained the longest in the Major Leagues until the 1988 Baltimore Orioles lost their first twenty-one games.

14. Quoted in "Breaks Going against the Tiges," *Detroit Free Press*, May 4, 1920.

15. Quoted in "Breaks Going against the Tiges."

16. Quoted in "Breaks Going against the Tiges."

17. The *Syracuse Journal* wrote often about Ehmke following his record-breaking 1916 season with the Syracuse Stars.

18. Bob Kenefick, On the Sport Firing Line, *Syracuse Journal*, May 24, 1920.

19. Quoted in Kenefick, On the Sport Firing Line, *Syracuse Journal*, May 24, 1920.

20. John C. Manning, "Ehmke," *Detroit News*, May 25, 1920.

21. Old Timer, "Jennings Differs from His Present Lineup of Tigers," *Detroit News*, May 19, 1920.

22. For a detailed explanation of the transition from the Deadball Era to the Lively Ball Era, see Steinberg, "The Spitball and the End of the Deadball Era," 7–17.

23. Quoted in Sowell, *The Pitch That Killed*, 150–51.

24. "More Hard Hitting Wins For Yankees," *New York Times*, June 10, 1920.

25. Quoted in "Ruth Has One Great Fear," *Louisville Courier-Journal*, July 18, 1920.

26. Quoted in Bob Stevens, "Recalls Ruth Knocking Ehmke's Glove to Left Field," *Sporting News*, February 19, 1958.

27. Reisler, *Babe Ruth*, 153–54.

28. "Babe Whales Out Another of Them," *New York Times*, July 12, 1920.

29. Arthur Robinson, "Yankees Intimate Rivals Are Trying to 'Shoo-In' Cleveland," *New York American*, August 11, 1920.

30. Quoted in Hyatt Daab, Timely Views and News in the World of Sport, *New York Evening Telegram*, August 10, 1920.

31. For a more detailed description of the Yankees' "squawking," see Steinberg and Spatz, *The Colonel and Hug*, 146–47.

32. "Ruth's 49th Brings Victory to Yanks," *New York Times*, September 14, 1920.

33. Quoted in Felber, *Under Pallor, Under Shadow*, 187.

19. Playing for Ty Cobb

1. Damon Runyon, "Ty May Fool All Prophets," *New York American*, December 21, 1920.

2. Runyon, "Ty May Fool All Prophets."

3. Quoted in Hoefer, "Will Ty Make Good as a Manager?" 419.

4. "Cobb Pleased Ehmke Signs with Tigers," *Syracuse Journal*, January 20, 1921.

5. Quoted in Harry Dayton, "Tyrus Now Glad He Is Manager," *Detroit Journal*, March 4, 1921.

6. H. G. Salsinger, "Charley Navin Gets a Publicity Lesson," *Sporting News*, January 20, 1921. Charley Navin, Frank's son, was the club's secretary.

7. Salsinger, "Charley Navin Gets a Publicity Lesson."

8. "Cobb Thinks Ehmke Will Be Greatest Pitcher in the Game," *Syracuse Journal*, February 19, 1921.

9. Quoted in Jack Veiok, "6th Place for Tiges Will Satisfy Cobb," *Detroit Journal*, March 3, 1921.

10. Quoted in Veiok, "6th Place for Tiges Will Satisfy Cobb."

11. The Tigers had moved their spring training camp from Macon, Georgia, to San Antonio, Texas, where the John McGraw–led New York Giants were also training. When Cobb was named manager, Damon Runyon ("Ty May Fool All Prophets," *New York American*, December 21, 1920) noted the fiery temperaments of each, so it was not surprising that clashes between the two men occurred during several Tigers-Giants exhibition games.

12. Quoted in H. G. Salsinger, "Cobb's Tigers to Give Fans Something Different from Cut-and-Dried Stuff of Other Teams," *Sporting News*, March 24, 1921.

13. Salsinger quoted in Bob Kenefick, On the Sport Firing Line, *Syracuse Journal*, April 19, 1921.

14. Kenefick, On the Sport Firing Line, *Syracuse Journal*, April 19, 1921.

15. Hornbaker, *War on The Basepaths*, 191.

16. Harry Bullion, "Ehmke 'Blows'; Tiges Lose Sox Inaugural," *Detroit Free Press*, April 22, 1921.

17. Quoted in Bak, *Peach*, 131.

18. Bullion, "Ehmke 'Blows.'"

19. Bingle, "Poor Pitching by Ehmke Loses for the Tigers," *Detroit Times*, April 22, 1921.

20. Quoted in "Hurler Who Hit O'Neill Shows a Manly Spirit," *Baltimore Sun*, July 23, 1921.

21. By contrast, Carl Mays, who had a well-deserved reputation for hitting batters, would lead the league just once.

22. Lane, "The Extraordinary Career of Howard Ehmke," 546.

23. Sher, "Ty Cobb," 110.

24. Sher, "Ty Cobb," 107.

25. Cobb used Sutherland in just one more game and that as a pinch hitter. After the season he traded him back to the Portland Beavers of the Pacific Coast League. Sutherland never returned to the Major Leagues.

26. Hornbaker, *War on the Basepaths*, 203.

27. Ross Tenney, "Ty's Wild over Wild Hurling," *Cleveland Press*, June 20, 1921.

28. Quoted in John B. Foster, "Ehmke Picks A's to Win Next Year," *Philadelphia Evening Bulletin*, February 10, 1931.

29. Ruth's home run was the 139th of his career, breaking Roger Connor's record of 138.

30. *New York Globe and Commercial Advertiser*, July 19, 1921.

31. H. G. Salsinger, "Give Twirlers a Rest and Then Watch Them," *Detroit News*, August 22, 1921.

32. Ehmke had a 2.77 earned run average against Philadelphia and a whopping 8.32 ERA against New York.

33. Over the twenty-six games, Ruth batted .483 (43 for 89) with twelve home runs and thirty-nine runs batted in.

34. Fred Lieb, *New York Evening Telegram*, December 12, 1922, quoted in Steinberg and Spatz, *The Colonel and Hug*, 176.

35. It was Quinn's only career home run off Ehmke. As noted, Ehmke did not hit any home runs in his career.

36. Quoted in Leerhsen, *Ty Cobb*, 282. In the previous two seasons, Heilmann batted .309 and .320. Over the next seven seasons, beginning in 1921, he won four batting championships, and his average never fell below .346.

37. Curran, *Big Sticks*, 188.

20. Ehmke Endures a Season of Criticism

1. Detroit's Frank Navin had supported Ban Johnson in the 1919 disputes over Jack Quinn and Carl Mays, while Boston's Harry Frazee and New York's co-owners Jacob Ruppert and Til Huston had challenged the American League president's authority. For a fuller discussion of this split, see Steinberg and Spatz, *The Colonel and Hug*, 110–17.

2. Harry Bullion, "Yanks Expect Far Too Much from Bengals," *Detroit Free Press*, December 11, 1921.

3. H. C. (Bert) Walker, Sportology, *Detroit Times*, December 13, 1921.

4. Quoted in Burt Whitman, "Deal between Red Sox and Tigers Hangs Fire," *Boston Herald*, December 15, 1921.

5. Outfielder Ira Flagstead filled in at shortstop for the last month of the season, but Cobb wanted Scott for 1922.

6. Accompanying Scott to New York were pitchers Joe Bush and Sam Jones, while Boston received pitchers Jack Quinn, Rip Collins, and Bill Piercy, shortstop Roger Peckinpaugh, and a reported $100,000.

7. The suspension of Ruth and Meusel was for violating the rule that prohibited members of pennant-winning teams from barnstorming during the off-season without the permission of the commissioner.

8. Quoted in Fred Lieb, "Bob Veach Still Headed Here," *New York Evening Telegram*, December 28, 1921.

9. The Tigers were unable to trade Veach, who had another outstanding season for them in 1922. Meanwhile, the Yankees finally got their out-fielder when they purchased Whitey Witt from the A's, five days after their season began.

10. Hornbaker, *War on The Basepaths*, 203.

11. Harry Bullion, Sporting Views, *Detroit Free Press*, February 21, 1922.

12. Harry Bullion, "Ehmke Assures Ty of Best Endeavors," *Detroit Free Press*, March 31, 1922.

13. Quoted in Bullion, "Ehmke Assures Ty of Best Endeavors."

14. Joe Vila, Setting the Pace, *New York Sun*, July 19, 1922.

15. Leonard refused to report to Vernon and played for an independent team the next two seasons.

16. Harry Bullion, "Browns Unable to Solve Ehmke's Slow Ball and Tigers Take Opener, 3 to 1," *Detroit Free Press*, May 3, 1922.

17. Cobb was hoping to engineer a trade with the Red Sox that would send Ehmke to Boston for right-hander Rip Collins. As noted, Boston had obtained Collins in the deal that sent Everett Scott, Joe Bush, and Sam Jones to New York.

18. Harry Bullion, "Closing Game with Mackmen Halted by Rain," *Detroit Free Press*, July 15, 1922.

19. Bullion, "Closing Game with Mackmen Halted by Rain." According to historian Michael Haupert, Ehmke's 1922 salary was $8,000.

20. Bullion, "Closing Game with Mackmen Halted by Rain."

21. Bert Walker, "Bad Battery Work Beats Tigers," *Detroit Times*, July 14, 1922.

22. H. C. (Bert) Walker, Sportology, *Detroit Times*, July 17, 1922.

23. H. G. Salsinger, "Possesses Great Fast Ball, Can't Control It," *Detroit News*, July 17, 1922.

24. Quoted in A. J. Rooney, "Howard Ehmke Holds Key to Success of Detroit Club," *Boston Traveler*, July 18, 1922.

25. Lieb, *The Detroit Tigers*, 165.

26. "It Didn't Mean Anything," *Sporting News*, August 3, 1922.

27. Harry Bullion, "Pillette and Ehmke Turn Boston Crowd Back with 1 Score," *Detroit Free Press*, August 20, 1922.

28. Sisler would lead the league with a .420 batting average. Ty Cobb, at .401, was second. Sisler, in his greatest season, would also break Cobb's American League record of hitting safely in forty consecutive games by hitting in forty-one, from July 27 to September 18.

29. "Sisler's Triple Blow Brings 5 to 4 Victory," *Detroit News*, September 12, 1922.

30. This game may have cost the Browns the pennant. Sisler suffered an arm injury reaching for a throw in the ninth inning. He sat out the next few games, and in the crucial series against the Yankees the next weekend, he went 2 for 11 with no runs batted in.

31. Ehmke would later accuse Cobb of ordering him to hit or "knock down" opposing batters.

32. Alexander, *Ty Cobb*, 164.

33. Quoted in "Cobb and Ehmke, Foes Once, May Be 'Pals' Now," *New York American*, March 27, 1927.

21. From New York to Boston

1. For a discussion of this and other Yankees–Red Sox trades of this era, see Steinberg, "The Curse of the . . . Hurlers?"

2. *New York American*, December 22, 1921.

3. Peckinpaugh ran the club at the end of the 1914 season, when he was only twenty-three, after Frank Chance resigned as manager.

4. There was another issue working against Peckinpaugh. In the final game of the 1921 World Series, he made a serious mental lapse that led to the Giants' 1–0 win. Spatz and Steinberg, *1921*, 380.

5. The *New York Tribune* and the *New York World*, as well as the *Boston Globe*, were minority voices that called the trade quite balanced. They focused on the potential of Piercy and Collins and the ages of Bush and Jones.

6. Burt Whitman, "Frazee Trades McInnis, Jones, Bush and Scott," *Boston Herald*, December 21, 1921.

7. Paul H. Shannon, "Frazee Junks His Ball Club," *Boston Post*, December 21, 1921.

8. Whitman, "Frazee Trades McInnis, Jones, Bush and Scott."

9. W. C. Spargo, Speaking of Sport, *Boston Traveler*, December 21, 1921.

10. Shannon, "Frazee Junks His Ball Club."

11. Quoted in Steinberg, "The Curse of the . . . Hurlers?" 71.

12. Frank F. O'Neill, "Boston Enraged at Deal," *New York Sun*, December 22, 1921.

13. Joe Vila, Setting the Pace, *New York Sun*, March 8, 1922.

14. Sam Crane, "Big Deal Gives Yanks Strong Mound Staff," *New York Evening Journal*, December 21, 1921.

15. This total includes Quinn's 35-36 record in the Federal League.

16. Frank F. O'Neill, "Yankees in Great Deal," *New York Sun*, December 21, 1921.

17. Frank F. O'Neill, "Jack Quinn to Umpire," *New York Sun*, July 16, 1921.

18. Quoted in Burt Whitman, *Boston Herald*, December 21, 1921. In the other trade, the Red Sox sent first baseman Stuffy McInnis to Cleveland for first baseman George Burns, outfielder Elmer Smith, and utility man Joe Harris. The Red Sox finished seventh in league batting average in 1921 with a .276 mark. In 1922 they fell to last with a .263 average.

19. Sam Crane, "Duffy Well-Satisfied with Deals Made for Red Sox by Frazee," *New York Evening Journal*, December 23, 1921.

20. "Sox Get Resourceful Player in Peckinpaugh," *Boston Herald*, December 24, 1921.

21. "Former Yankees Pitcher to Play Semi-Pro Ball," *Monmouth (IL) Daily Atlas*, January (date unknown), 1922.

22. Quoted in "Jack Quinn, Veteran Pitcher, Signs with Semi-Pro Team," *New York Times*, January 21, 1922. That day's *Chicago Tribune* reported Quinn had signed with the local Marquette Manors.

23. "Quinn Quits Sox to Join Semi-Pro Team," *New York Evening Journal*, January 21, 1922.

24. Quinn's tax returns show he earned $9,894.68 in 1921 and $5.312.40 in 1922. His loser's share of the 1921 World Series was $3,510, so his base salary was $6,384.68 that year, 20 percent higher than his Red Sox salary. Quinn family collection and Baseball Almanac, baseball-almanac.com/ws/wsshares.shtml.

25. Leaves from a Fan's Scrapbook, *Sporting News*, December 22, 1932.

26. Quoted in A. J. Rooney, "Jack Quinn Likely to Pitch Opening Contest," *Boston Traveler*, April 8, 1922. Quinn went 4-2 against the Yankees in 1922.

27. A. J. Rooney, "Hendrick and Pipgras Look Good in Practice," *Boston Traveler*, March 8, 1922.

28. W. C. Spargo, Speaking of Sport, *Boston Traveler*, May 4, 1922.

29. W. C. Spargo, Speaking of Sport, *Boston Traveler*, December 21, 1921.

30. "Pitcher Hoyt Swings at Manager Huggins after Row about Passing Man," *Boston American*, April 30, 1922.

31. A. J. Rooney, "Present Pace Will Land Hub Hose in First Division," *Boston Traveler*, May 4, 1922.

32. "Jack Quinn Uses Yankees Harshly," *New York Times*, June 23, 1922.

33. Shocker had a 15-9 record against the Yankees in the four seasons since the trade (1918–21).

34. "Connellsville Beaten by Red Sox 9," *Pittsburgh Post-Gazette*, July 24, 1922. Quinn was presented with a photo of his 1900 Dunbar team. This may be taken as confirmation of the year he began his professional career.

35. Harry Schumacher, "Huggins Judgment Suicidal to Yankees," *New York Globe and Commercial Advertiser*, September 17, 1920.

36. Scribbled by Scribes, *Sporting News*, May 20, 1920.

37. A. J. Rooney, "Suspension for Players Who Unduly Delay Games," *Boston Traveler*, August 22, 1922.

38. "Rumor Nails in Bats Responsible for Heavy Hitting in Big Leagues," *Boston Traveler*, July 11, 1922. The practice was said to have been started by players to protect their favorite bats from chipping.

39. New York's Joe Bush was going for his twenty-seventh win against only seven losses. Four of those losses came at the hands of the Red Sox.

40. Quoted in Lieb, *The Boston Red Sox*, 186.

41. Nick Flatley, "Red Sox Cellar Stars Show Up N.Y. Champs," *Boston American*, September 30, 1922.

42. James C. O'Leary, "Champions Halted in Fine 1–0 Game," *Boston Globe*, September 30, 1922.

43. Paul H. Shannon, "Yankees Fail to Clinch Flag," *Boston Post*, September 29, 1922.

44. A. J. Rooney, "Open in Philadelphia with Connie's Athletics Tomorrow," *Boston Traveler*, August 28, 1922.

45. Nick Flatley, "Frazee and Grant Both Made Their Bit," *Boston American*, September 27, 1922.

22. Veteran Aces on the League's Worst Team

1. H. G. Salsinger, "Tygers Get Star Pitcher in Deal with Red Hose," *Detroit News*, September 30, 1922.

2. Alexander, *Ty Cobb*, 166; Gus Rooney, "Frazee Finds a New Pay Lode in Detroit," *Sporting News*, October 5, 1922.

3. Holling failed to show up at Boston's training camp in 1923, informing the team that he preferred to stay in California and play in an independent league. The Sox sued Detroit for $15,000 or another player in lieu of Holling.

4. "Red Sox Get Another Possible Ruth in Deal," *Sporting News*, October 26, 1922.

5. Charles E. Parker, "Red Sox Camp Throbs about Babe Herman," *Boston American*, March 16, 1923.

6. Quoted in Charles Parker, "Red Sox Camp Throbs about Babe Herman." While no one could possibly foresee it at the time, years later Herman and Quinn would be teammates with Brooklyn.

7. Salsinger, "Tygers Get Star Pitcher in Deal with Red Hose."

8. Lieb, *The Detroit Tigers*, 171.

9. K. W. Hall, "Tigers Going Back to Camp at Augusta," *Sporting News*, November 9, 1922.

10. Hall, "Tigers Going Back to Camp at Augusta."

11. "Cobb and Ehmke, Foes Once, May Be 'Pals' Now," *New York American*, March 27, 1927.

12. Quoted in Thorn and Holway, *The Pitcher*, 133–34.

13. Quoted in Thorn and Holway, *The Pitcher*, 133–34.

14. Hauser interview with William Kashatus, Sheboygan, Wisconsin, January 9, 1997, just before Hauser's ninety-ninth birthday.

15. Quoted in Kashatus, *Connie Mack's '29 Triumph*, 89.

16. Collins, "Was Ty a Bad Manager?" 493–94.

17. Fred Hoey, "Ehmke Is Pitching Ace," *Boston Traveler*, March 13, 1923.

18. Fred Hoey, "Red Sox Need More Pitchers," *Boston Traveler*, March 24, 1923.

19. "Howard Ehmke Is Due to Pitch Opening against Athletics at Fens Today," *Boston Herald*, April 30, 1923.

20. Lieb, *The Boston Red Sox*, 188.

21. Chance, who resigned shortly before the end of the 1914 season, had a 117-168 record with New York.

22. Quoted in Charles E. Parker, "Chance Nails the 'Lie' about Last Place," *Boston American*, April 5, 1923.

23. Jack Malaney, "Sox Chief Shows Socking Ability," *Boston Post*, March 10, 1923.

24. Quoted in W. J. Macbeth, "Frank Chance Sees Brighter Days Ahead for Boston Red Sox," *New York Tribune*, February 18, 1923.

25. Ed Cunningham, "Chance Will Insist on Fight and Discipline from Red Sox Players," *Boston Herald*, March 11, 1923.

26. Quoted in Ed Cunningham, "Chance Is Optimistic on Eve of Departure of Red Sox for the South," *Boston Herald*, March 2, 1923.

27. Quoted in Melville E. Webb Jr., "Ehmke's Arm in Fine Shape, Recruits Look Good," *Boston Globe*, March 9, 1923.

28. Nick Flatley, "Red Sox New Manager to Start Work Here," *Boston American*, December 14, 1922.

29. Quoted in Cunningham, "Chance Will Insist on Fight and Discipline."

30. Fred Hoey, "High Hat Harry," *Boston Traveler*, March 30, 1923.

31. John Kieran, "Chance's Team Lives Up to His Lowly Estimate," *New York Tribune*, May 6, 1923.

32. Ed Cunningham, "Jack Quinn Has Broken Bone in Pitching Hand; Ehmke to Hurl Opener," *Boston Herald*, April 9, 1923. Quinn suffered the fracture when he was at bat and hit by a pitch.

33. Quoted in Billy Evans, "Frank Chance Seems to Have a Hopeless Task," *Alton (IL) Evening Telegraph*, April 5, 1923.

34. Fred Hoey, "Regs and Yans Play Exhibition at Evansville," *Boston Traveler*, April 9, 1923.

35. Yankees business manager Ed Barrow estimated the attendance at approximately seventy-four thousand, a figure that was probably on the high side.

36. The previous record was 43,620, set at Boston's Braves Field in the fifth game of the 1916 World Series between Brooklyn and the Boston Red Sox. The Red Sox used Braves Field, rather than the smaller-capacity Fenway Park, in both the 1915 and 1916 World Series. Lowry, *Green Cathedrals*, 31.

37. Spatz, *New York Yankees Openers*, 77.

38. Quoted in Ed Cunningham, "Ehmke Gives Slow Rising Curve to Babe Ruth and Meets with Much Success," *Boston Herald*, August 12, 1923.

39. Quoted in Cunningham, "Ehmke Gives Slow Rising Curve to Babe Ruth."

40. Quoted in Cunningham, "Ehmke Gives Slow Rising Curve to Babe Ruth."

41. Ehmke and Quinn were familiar with O'Doul. Ehmke had been his teammate on the San Pedro submarine base team in 1918, and Quinn remembered him as a Yankees prospect back in 1919–20.

42. James C. O'Leary, "Quinn Invincible in 3–1 Triumph," *Boston Globe*, May 4, 1923.

43. Even after the Red Sox traded former Yankees Muddy Ruel and Allen Russell in February 1923, there were still a dozen former Yankees on the Red Sox's roster.

44. Ed Cunningham, "Red Sox Rate Win over Yanks in Same Category as Boiled Dinner," *Boston Herald*, June 4, 1923.

45. Fred Lieb, *New York Evening Telegram*, September 4, 1924.

46. Joe Vila, "Huggins Nipped in His Joy by an Upset from Red Sox," *Sporting News*, June 7, 1923.

47. "Yanks Lose Final to Red Sox, 3–1," *New York Times*, June 27, 1923.

48. "Cobb Made Mistake in Trading Howard Ehmke," *Peekskill (NY) Evening Star*, October 2, 1923. Pratt would appear in only 101 games, and because of an injury, Collins would pitch in only 17 games. He made only one appearance after June, and his win total for the season was three.

49. F. C. Lane, "Howard Ehmke's Showing with Boston Is Talk of Circuit," *Hartford Courant*, July 22, 1923.

23. Ehmke and Cobb Get Physical

1. Quoted in Ed Pollock, Playing the Game, *Philadelphia Evening Bulletin*, May 19, 1952.

2. Quoted in Green, *Forgotten Fields*, 57.

3. Herman Nickerson, Sportografs, *Boston Traveler*, May 21, 1923.

4. Quoted in Joe Williams, By Joe Williams, *New York World-Telegram*, August 14, 1941.

5. James C. O'Leary, "Howard Ehmke, Hurling Superbly, Has Laugh on Old Team Mates from Detroit," *Boston Globe*, June 17, 1923.

6. K. W. Hall, "Ty Cobb Admits His Team Is All in Air," *Sporting News*, June 21, 1923.

7. Pollock, Playing the Game, *Philadelphia Evening Bulletin*, May 19, 1952.

8. Gus Rooney, "Reason for Frazee to Raise His Price," *Sporting News*, June 21, 1923.

9. Fred Hoey, "Howard Ehmke Wonder Hurler of Big Leagues," *Boston Traveler*, June 21, 1923.

10. Bob Dunbar, By Bob Dunbar, *Boston Herald*, June 21, 1923. The four losses had been closely fought: 4–1 to New York, 2–1 to St. Louis, and 3–2 to Cleveland, twice.

11. Burt Whitman, *Boston Herald*, July 3, 1923.

12. Bob Dunbar, By Bob Dunbar, *Boston Herald*, June 30, 1923.

13. Quoted in Ed Cunningham, "Ehmke Gives Slow Rising Curve to Babe Ruth and Meets with Much Success," *Boston Herald*, August 12, 1923.

14. John McGraw, "Pitchers Big Factors in Pennant Races," *Pittsburgh Gazette Times*, June 17, 1923.

15. Quoted in "Scott of Yankees Goes Lame at Springs," *New York American*, February 28, 1923.

16. Quoted in F. C. Lane, "Howard Ehmke's Showing with Boston Is Talk of Circuit," *Hartford Courant*, July 22, 1923.

17. Lane, "Howard Ehmke's Showing with Boston Is Talk of Circuit."

18. Quoted in Lane, "The Extraordinary Career of Howard Ehmke," 545.

19. Lane, "The Extraordinary Career of Howard Ehmke," 545.

20. Ed Cunningham, "Boston Greatest Baseball City in Country—for Visiting Baseball Teams," *Boston Herald*, July 17, 1923.

21. Nick Flatley, "Frazee and Grant Both Made Their Bit," *Boston American*, September 27, 1922.

22. "Johnson Elated That Frazee Is Finally out of Baseball," *Sporting News*, July 19, 1923, quoted in Stout and Johnson, *Red Sox Century*, 160.

23. "Red Sox Reportedly Sold to Ohio Capitalist, but Frazee Denies the Deal," *Boston Herald*, May 24, 1923. It took another ten weeks for the deal to close. Stout and Johnson pegged the sale price at $1.15 million (*Red Sox Century*, 160), as did Fred Lieb (*The Boston Red Sox*, 104).

24. Ed Cunningham, Sport for Sport's Sake, *Boston Traveler*, September 8, 1925.

25. Bob Quinn was not related to Red Sox pitcher Jack Quinn.

26. Quoted in "Quinn and Fohl Make Big Impression with Newspaper Men of Hub," *Pittsburgh Gazette Times*, November 11, 1923.

27. Lee hit .340 with 210 hits for Tulsa. He had appeared in seventy-two games for the 1921 St. Louis Browns, where he hit only .167. Mitchell had come to Boston from the Yankees in the Joe Dugan deal. He ended up with Minneapolis of the American Association in 1924 before Brooklyn purchased him that summer.

28. Quoted in Nowlin, "Dud Lee."

29. Ehmke would finish with a 6-0 record against the A's in 1923.

30. John B. Sheridan, Back of the Home Plate, *Sporting News*, July 26, 1923.

31. Bob Dunbar, By Bob Dunbar, *Boston Herald*, August 31, 1923.

32. Pratt batted .310 but appeared in only 101 games. Collins had a 3-7 record in 17 games.

24. "The Toughest Break"

1. According to A's historian Norman Macht, manager Connie Mack was not at the game. He was at a Minor League game in Martinsburg, West Virginia.

2. "Ehmke Blanks Macks without a Safe Drive," *Boston Globe*, September 8, 1923.

3. It was the first no-hitter by a Red Sox pitcher since Dutch Leonard's in 1918. There would not be another until Mel Parnell's in 1956.
4. The Yankees' Sam Jones had no-hit Philadelphia on September 4, making the Athletics the first team to be no-hit twice in a season.
5. Quoted in *Philadelphia Evening Bulletin*, September 8, 1923.
6. In January 1923 the Red Sox had traded Pipgras and outfielder Harvey Hendrick, both Minor Leaguers, to the Yankees for catcher Al DeVormer and cash.
7. Fred Lieb, "Whitey Witt's Scratch Single Robs Howard Ehmke of Second No-Hit Game," *New York Evening Telegram*, September 12, 1923.
8. Quoted in Baseball By-Plays, *Sporting News*, October 4, 1923.
9. In 1938 Cincinnati's Johnny Vander Meer became the first and only (through 2020) Major League pitcher to throw consecutive no-hitters.
10. Lieb, *Baseball As I Have Known It*, 72.
11. "Ehmke Holds Yanks to Scratch Single," *New York Times*, September 12, 1923.
12. Gus Rooney, "Boston Also Resents Way of Scoring Hits in New York," *Sporting News*, September 20, 1923.
13. Quoted in "Umpires Criticize Scorers," *Sporting News*, September 27, 1923. Although the official Baseball Hall of Fame was not established until 1936, newspapers of the early twentieth century often stated that a pitcher had entered the "Hall of Fame" when he pitched a no-hitter.
14. Quoted in Weintraub, *The House That Ruth Built*, 276. Connolly was the home plate umpire for four no-hitters, including Addie Joss's perfect game on October 2, 1908.
15. Quoted in "Umpires Criticize Scorers." Howard "Ducky" Holmes, not to be confused with James "Ducky" Holmes, a Major League outfielder from 1895 to 1905, was the home plate umpire.
16. Lane, "The Toughest Break a Pitcher Ever Had," 551.
17. Frederick G. Lieb, "Echoes Lingering over Disputed Records," *Sporting News*, November 27, 1957.
18. Lieb, *The Boston Red Sox*, 190.
19. Lieb, *Baseball As I Have Known It*, 72.
20. This account of Lieb's differed from the one he wrote while covering the game. At that time, he wrote Shanks had "knocked down [the ball] with his glove hand, picked it up and threw to first baseman Joe Harris."
21. Lieb, *Baseball As I Have Known It*, 72.
22. Lieb, *Baseball As I Have Known It*, 72.
23. Lieb, *Baseball As I Have Known It*, 73.
24. Quoted in Fred Lieb, "Whitey Witt's Scratch Single Robs Howard Ehmke of Second No-Hit Game," *New York Evening Telegram*, September 12, 1923.
25. This was the first multi-hit game of Gehrig's career. He had only eleven hits for the season.

26. On August 28, 1992, the Milwaukee Brewers had thirty-one hits in defeating the Toronto Blue Jays, 22–2.

27. Dittmar, *Baseball Records Registry*, 81. That record has been tied but not exceeded.

28. The first two were Frank "Noodles" Hahn (1901 Cincinnati Reds) and Scott Perry (1918 Philadelphia Athletics). Two did it after Ehmke, in eight-team leagues: Hollis Thurston (1924 Chicago White Sox) and Ned Garver (1951 St. Louis Browns).

29. "Boston Trims Nats; Quinn Allows but a Trio of Safe Hits," *Washington Post*, July 25, 1923.

30. Newspapers reported only three previous unassisted triple plays: by Providence outfielder Paul Hines on May 8, 1878 (now disputed); by Cleveland shortstop Neal Ball on July 19, 1909; and the famous World Series play by Cleveland second baseman Bill Wambsganss on October 10, 1920. Johnny Neun of Detroit is the only other Major League first baseman with an unassisted triple play. His came on May 31, 1927, against Cleveland.

31. Billy Evans, Billy Evans Says, *New Philadelphia Daily Times*, July 28, 1923. Evans also discussed the Pirates' forty-one-year-old pitcher, Babe Adams, in the article.

32. Billy Evans, "Babe Adams and Jack Quinn Are Rated among 'Iron Men,'" *Port Huron (MI) Times-Herald*, September 21, 1923.

33. Clark, *Red Sox Fever*, 118. Clark received recognition from SABR in 1984 in the form of the "SABR Salute," which was first bestowed on Fred Lieb in 1976.

34. Allen Russell of Washington led with nine. Quinn would repeat with seven saves in 1924. All save totals, retroactively computed in 1969, are the ones listed in *Baseball-Reference* and *Retrosheet*.

35. Ehmke's career-high 316⅔ innings pitched was second in the American League to Cleveland's George Uhle. He again ranked high in walks allowed, making it the fourth time in five seasons (1919–23) that he had finished in the top three. Ehmke was beginning a three-year stretch where he would finish either first or second in the league in complete games.

36. Quoted in Ritter, *The Glory of Their Times*, 271.

25. A New Beginning for Boston

1. Herman Nickerson, *Boston Traveler*, August 14, 1923.

2. "When Quinn Dismissed Chance," *Sporting News*, October 4, 1923.

3. Fohl was let go by Browns owner Phil Ball in early August 1923, shortly after Bob Quinn left the club, in anticipation of his takeover of the Red Sox.

4. Rainey, "Lee Fohl," and Costello, "Bob Quinn." Fohl played and managed for Quinn with Ohio Minor League teams in Columbus, Lima,

and Akron. Fohl also managed the Cleveland Indians for five seasons (1915–19).

5. Fohl gave way as the Indians' manager to Tris Speaker in 1919, the year before they won the World Series.

6. Monitor (pseudonym of George Daley), *New York World*, December 16, 1923.

7. Ed Cunningham, "Extra Leap Year Day Will Make Up for Stormy Ones We Lost," *Boston Traveler*, February 29, 1924.

8. Burt Whitman, "Lee Fohl Does Not Believe in Using Up Good Pitchers as Relief Men Late in Game," *Boston Traveler*, April 11, 1924.

9. Quoted in Paul H. Shannon, "Fohl Has Had Similar Tasks," *Boston Post*, January 6, 1924.

10. Shocker had been a twenty-game winner for the Browns in each of the last four seasons. He was 79-41 the past three seasons.

11. John B. Sheridan, Back of the Home Plate, *Sporting News*, November 1, 1923.

12. Quoted in Ed Cunningham, "Howard Ehmke, Veteran, Anticipates Greatest Season; Says Sox Will Be Contender," *Boston Traveler*, February 27, 1924.

13. Boston's 1923 first baseman was George Burns.

14. Quoted in Ed Cunningham, "Red Sox Manager Quick to Change Oddities of Mound Corps with Great Success," *Boston Traveler*, March 19, 1924. Piercy came to Boston from the Yankees in the December 1921 trade that brought Jack Quinn to the Red Sox.

15. Ed Cunningham, "Former Cleveland Catcher Ready for Greatest Season," *Boston Traveler*, March 6, 1924.

16. Cunningham, "Former Cleveland Catcher Ready for Greatest Season."

17. Ed Cunningham, "Barnstorming Tour Will Give Fohl an Opportunity to Test Strength of Pitching Corps," *Boston Traveler*, March 25, 1924.

18. Quinn family collection. There was no record of Quinn's 1923 tax return.

19. Quoted in Pat Robinson, "Hypochondria Brooklyn Ailment; Detriment to Speed Ball Hurlers," *Cincinnati Enquirer*, April 14, 1950.

20. Quoted in "Hasn't Had a Sore Arm in 22 Years," *Bismarck (ND) Tribune*, June 4, 1924. When sentiment was building in the 1910s to ban trick pitches, many observers, including umpire-columnist Bill Evans, believed the spitball pitch ruined arms and shortened careers.

21. Quoted in *New York World*, December 15, 1929. Faber added, "Ed Walsh did not have to quit because of the spitter. It was overwork that turned the trick." As the 1920s progressed, critics of the ill effects of throwing the spitter vanished, as the best spitballers maintained their effectiveness as they aged. In the four seasons since the spitter was banned, four grandfathered spitball pitchers (Urban Shocker, Red Faber, Burleigh Grimes, and Stan Coveleski) won 334 games.

22. Burt Whitman, "Reconstructed Red Sox Revive Long Dormant Spirit in Boston," *Sporting News*, April 17, 1924.

23. Spatz, *New York Yankees Openers*, 80.

24. Ed Cunningham, "Veteran Sox Scout Believes the Denver Kid Will Uphold Boston's Shortstop Tradition," *Boston Traveler*, March 24, 1924.

25. James C. O'Leary, "Red Sox Send Across 10 Runs in Second," *Boston Globe*, April 20, 1924.

26. Burt Whitman, "Red Sox Give Fans Some Real Hopes," *Sporting News*, May 15, 1924.

27. Quoted in Wiggins, "1924," 45.

28. Will Wedge, "Quinn Too Much for Yankees," *New York Sun*, April 17, 1924.

29. Some accounts described it as a routine single that outfielder Ira Flagstead misplayed. Marshall Hunt, "Pipp the Pickler and Mr. Witt Contribute Their Stuff," *New York Daily News*, April 27, 1924.

30. "Yanks Defeat Sox in 11 Innings, 4–3," *New York Times*, April 27, 1924.

31. Billy Evans, "Jack Quinn Is Particular Nemesis of World's Champions," *Mitchell (SD) Evening Republican*, May 2, 1924.

32. James Crusinberry, "White Sox Kowtow to Quinn and Sox of Red," *Chicago Tribune*, May 15, 1924.

33. Paul H. Shannon, "Both Hub Teams Deliver Goods," *Boston Post*, May 15, 1924. St. Helena, the place of Napoleon Bonaparte's exile and death, is a remote island in the South Atlantic Ocean.

34. S. O. Grauley, "Slaughter Mackmen in Boston Massacre," *Philadelphia Inquirer*, May 3, 1924.

35. Sportswriter Gordon Mackay wrote about Welch's potential for greatness, but "his ambition sometimes is at such a low ebb that he spoils his chances." "Baseball Heroes Are Contrast in Ambition," *Philadelphia Inquirer*, May 30, 1924. Welch never reached that potential.

36. "Athletics Win First Game from Red Sox; Lose Second," *Philadelphia North American*, May 29, 1924.

37. "Athletics Win First Game from Red Sox."

38. Stoney McLinn, "Cash Customers See What Old Punch Can Do to Win Ball Games," *Philadelphia Evening Public Ledger*, May 29, 1924.

39. Unsourced newspaper article in Flagstead's bio file at the Baseball Hall of Fame and Library, Cooperstown.

40. "Welch's Homer Kills Ehmke As Macks Split Double-Header," *Philadelphia Evening Bulletin*, May 29, 1924.

41. McLinn, "Cash Customers See What Old Punch Can Do."

42. Game discussed in the prologue of this volume. In his first three seasons with Boston (1922–24), Quinn had an earned run average of 2.20 against the Athletics in 110 innings.

26. Back to Reality for the Red Sox

1. On June 9 Red Sox batters were among the league's offensive leaders: Bobby Veach was second in runs scored (40), Ike Boone was second in runs batted in (41), and first baseman Joe Harris had a .532 slugging percentage (fourth best).
2. Will Wedge, "Quinn Too Much for Yankees," *New York Sun*, April 17, 1924. Wedge noted that the current *Who's Who in Baseball* listed Quinn's date of birth as July 5, 1885.
3. Quoted in "Quinn Confides in Shag," *New York Evening Telegram and Evening Mail*, April 25, 1924.
4. James C. Isaminger, Pithy Tips from the Sport Ticker, *Philadelphia Inquirer*, August 15, 1926.
5. Evans, "Jack Quinn."
6. Quoted in John J. Nolan, "Quinn's Pitching Saves A's Lead," *Philadelphia Evening Bulletin*, July 28, 1925, and "40-Year-Old Jack Quinn Curves to Victory over Detroit," *Philadelphia Evening Bulletin*, July 14, 1925.
7. Ford Frick, Frick's Comments, *New York Evening Journal*, July 2, 1924.
8. Lane, "The Extraordinary Career of Howard Ehmke," 545.
9. Lane, "Some Angles of Pitching Psychology," 343.
10. Quoted in Ed Cunningham, "Lanky Red Sox Pitcher Believes New Motion Is under Control; Increases His Effectiveness," *Boston Traveler*, May 13, 1924.
11. Cunningham, "Lanky Red Sox Pitcher Believes New Motion Is under Control."
12. Quoted in Gus Rooney, "Ehmke's Hesitation Not Yet the Subject of Official Ruling," *Boston Traveler*, June 27, 1924.
13. Shortstop Dud Lee split his thumb and then fractured his elbow, first baseman Joe Harris was suffering from neuritis, outfielder Ike Boone had an ankle injury, and outfielder Shano Collins hurt his back. Wiggins, *1924*, 72.
14. Burt Whitman, "Big Ike Boone Still Has Habit of Letting a Few Good Ones Go by the Bat," *Boston Traveler*, March 10, 1925.
15. Quinn and Ehmke gave up a combined six runs on thirteen hits in 7⅓ innings of work.
16. After Quinn beat Chicago on June 7 for his sixth win, his earned run average was 1.62. He finished with a 3.27 mark. After Ehmke beat Cleveland on May 23 for his sixth win, his ERA was 1.83. He finished with a 3.46 mark.
17. Paul H. Shannon, "Bengals Chew Up Fohl's Men Twice," *Boston Post*, July 17, 1924.

18. Ed Cunningham, "Sox Prexy Abandons Plans to Build New Plant; Will Concentrate on New Club," *Boston Traveler*, July 21, 1924.

19. Cunningham, "Sox Prexy Abandons Plans to Build New Plant."

20. James C. O'Leary, "Jack Quinn Shines on Slab and at Bat," *Boston Globe*, August 22, 1924.

21. Quinn had seven saves in both 1923 and 1924. That statistic, retroactively computed since it did not exist until 1969, would have ranked Quinn second and third respectively in the American League. *Baseball-Reference* and *Retrosheet* still use the original, more expansive definition of a save as defined in 1969.

22. Frank H. Young, "Boston Fans Cheer Nats On to Victory," *Washington Post*, September 28, 1924.

23. Thomas, *Walter Johnson*, 210.

24. Quinn appeared in a career-high forty-six games in the Federal League in 1914 and forty-four in 1915.

25. Grantland Rice, The Sportlight, *New York Herald-Tribune*, June 13, 1924.

26. Lane, "The Extraordinary Career of Howard Ehmke," 545.

27. "Ehmke's 'Killing' Work," *Howe News Bureau*, December 17, 1924.

28. Paul H. Shannon, "Sox Collect Again from Indians in 10," *Boston Post*, August 24, 1924.

29. Quoted in "Boston to Release Three Veteran Pitchers," *New York Times*, December 24, 1924. The other pitchers were Bill Piercy and George Murray.

30. Unsourced Boston paper, December 27, 1924; Quinn family collection.

31. Unsourced Boston paper, December 27, 1924; Quinn family collection.

32. Frank H. Young, "Exhibition Battle Listed on March 31 at Fort Benning," *Washington Post*, December 23, 1924. Griffith liked aging veteran hurlers and had just purchased Dutch Ruether (thirty-one) and Vean Gregg (thirty-nine) and traded for Stan Coveleski (thirty-five).

33. *Washington Post*, December 26, 1924.

27. A Team Going Nowhere

1. Veach and pitcher Alex Ferguson went to the Yankees for pitcher Ray Francis, who did not win another Major League game. Harris was traded to the Senators for pitcher Paul Zahniser and outfielder Roy Carlyle.

2. Quoted in Ed Cunningham, "Passing of Harris, Veach, and Ferguson First Steps toward Active Rebuilding," *Boston Traveler*, May 6, 1925.

3. Ed Cunningham, Sport for Sport's Sake, *Boston Traveler*, May 12, 1925.

4. Ruffing had a 4-7 record with Dover (Delaware) of the Class D Eastern Shore League in 1924.

5. Burt Whitman, "Red Sox Rookie, Charley Ruffing, Has Gained Much Confidence in Past Year," *Boston Traveler*, March 16, 1925.

6. "Ruffing Looks Like a Regular," *Boston Globe*, March 23, 1925.

7. Ford Sawyer, "Sheer Grit and Confidence Guided Jack Quinn to Fame," *Boston Globe*, May 1, 1925.

8. Quoted in "Jack Quinn Scoffs at Advancing Age," *Athens (OH) Messenger*, March 11, 1925.

9. Burt Whitman, "Jack Quinn Will Try Effect of Saliva on Bears This Afternoon," *Boston Herald*, March 29, 1925.

10. Damon Runyon, "Some Umpires Just Can't Be Cheerful," *Sporting News*, April 8, 1920.

11. Will Wedge, "The Story of John P. Quinn," *New York Sun*, May 5, 1926.

12. Sports Done by Brown, *Aberdeen (WA) Daily World*, July 1, 1924. Pottsville sportswriter Walter Farquhar wrote, "His straight ball is impossible to tell from the spitter." *Pottsville (PA) Journal*, date unknown; Quinn family collection.

13. Melville E. Webb Jr., "Passes Aid Red Sox to Defeat Pelicans," *Boston Globe*, March 23, 1925.

14. Quoted in Ed Cunningham, "Red Sox Pitcher Says He Is Ready for Best Season of His Baseball Career," *Boston Traveler*, April 1, 1925.

15. Quoted in Cunningham, "Red Sox Pitcher Says He Is Ready."

16. Quoted in Bunts, *Brooklyn Eagle*, March 5, 1931.

17. Quoted in Cunningham, "Red Sox Pitcher Says He Is Ready."

18. Ed Cunningham, "Red Sox Pound Pellet All over Lot—Supply of Agates Dwindles Fast," *Boston Herald*, March 6, 1924.

19. Ed Cunningham, "Former Cleveland Catcher Ready for Greatest Season," *Boston Traveler*, March 6, 1924.

20. The Old Sport's Musings, *Philadelphia Inquirer*, May 2, 1926.

21. Louisa, *The Pirates Unraveled*.

22. Three days earlier Grove had made his Major League debut. He was also knocked out in the fourth inning of that game, in which he walked four men.

23. Cochrane came from Portland of the Pacific Coast League for five players and $35,000. Grove was purchased from the Baltimore Orioles of the International League for $100,600, the highest sale price ever, topping the $100,500 the Yankees had paid Boston for Babe Ruth.

24. Red Smith, "The Terrible-Tempered Mr. Grove," *New York Times*, May 26, 1975.

25. Quoted in "More Stuff Than I Ever Saw," *Boston Herald*, June 2, 1925.

26. Quoted in Kaplan, *Lefty Grove, American Original*, 89.

27. Burt Whitman, "Wamby Is Big Hero as Patient Sox Edge Mackmen in 11th," *Boston Herald*, April 26, 1925.

28. Burt Whitman, "Quinn Leads Sox at May Day Riots and Beats Yankees 7–5," *Boston Herald*, May 2, 1925.

29. Sawyer, "Sheer Grit and Confidence Guided Jack Quinn to Fame."

30. Quoted in *Boston Traveler*, May 18, 1925.

31. Quoted in "Ehmke Denies Hankering for Yank Uniform; Wants to Finish Career with Sox," *Boston Herald*, May 15, 1925.

32. Quoted in "Ehmke Denies Hankering for Yank Uniform."

33. James R. Harrison, "Yankees Postpone Defeat until 12th," *New York Times*, June 1, 1925.

34. Harrison, "Yankees Postpone Defeat until 12th."

35. Harrison, "Yankees Postpone Defeat until 12th."

36. "Sox Ready to Resume," *Boston Traveler*, May 23, 1925.

37. Ed Cunningham, Sport for Sport's Sake, *Boston Traveler*, May 27, 1925. Wingfield won only twenty-four games in his career, twelve of them in 1925, when he pitched 254⅓ innings.

38. "Jack Quinn Wins His Fourth Straight Game, Taming Tigers, 7–4," *Boston Herald*, May 12, 1925.

39. "When Head Proves Mightier Than Arm," *Sporting News*, June 11, 1925.

28. From Boston to Philadelphia

1. *Boston Herald*, June 8, 1925; Burt Whitman, "Harriss Smothers Sox, 12–2, in Final Contest of Series," *Boston Herald*, June 5, 1925.

2. The Old Sport's Musings, *Philadelphia Inquirer*, July 6, 1925.

3. Ed Cunningham, Sport for Sport's Sake, *Boston Traveler*, April 24, 1925. The Athletics played eight of their first nine games against the Red Sox.

4. Simmons's parents were Polish; as previously noted, he was born Aloysius Szymanski.

5. Quoted in Kaplan, *Lefty Grove, American Original*, 77.

6. Arthur Daley, Sports of the Times, *New York Times*, May 28, 1956. Simmons was only fifty-four when he died.

7. Quoted in James C. Isaminger, Tips from the Sporting Ticker, *Philadelphia Inquirer*, June 7, 1925.

8. Isaminger, Tips from the Sporting Ticker, *Philadelphia Inquirer*, June 7, 1925.

9. James C. Isaminger, "Mackmen Drop Another to Red Sox," *Philadelphia Inquirer*, June 4, 1925.

10. Isaminger, "Mackmen Drop Another to Red Sox."

11. Quoted in Ed Cunningham, Sport for Sport's Sake, *Boston Traveler*, June 9, 1925.

12. "Mack's Great Rally in Ninth Sweeps Red Sox to Defeat," *Philadelphia Inquirer*, June 24, 1925.

13. Some players called Ehmke's "hesitation pitch" as effective as Christy Mathewson's "fadeaway," Ed Cicotte's "shiner," Ed Walsh's "spitter," and Ed Rommel's "knuckler."

14. Quoted in "Ehmke Perfects 'Hesitation Ball' but It Fails to Stop Macks," *Philadelphia Evening Bulletin*, June 25, 1925.

15. Quoted in "Ehmke Perfects 'Hesitation Ball.'"
16. Quoted in "Ehmke Perfects 'Hesitation Ball.'"
17. Quoted in "Ehmke Perfects 'Hesitation Ball.'"
18. John Drohan, "But Sox Ace Made Good in Los Angeles While in High School and Forgot about It," *Boston Traveler*, September 8, 1925.
19. *Boston Post*, July 8, 1925.
20. Sam Greene, "Fourteenth Season Proving Dauss' Best," *Sporting News*, July 16, 1925.
21. "Cobb Says Ehmke Lies about Spiking," *Boston Herald*, July 11, 1925.
22. Sportsman, Live Tips and Topics, *Boston Globe*, July 10, 1925.
23. Cobb, "They Ruined Baseball"; Cobb, "Baseball Tricks That Won Me Ball Games."
24. Quoted in Ed Pollock, Playing the Game, *Philadelphia Evening Bulletin*, June 15, 1952.
25. Quoted in Ed Pollock, Playing the Game, *Philadelphia Evening Bulletin*, June 15, 1952.
26. James R. Harrison, "Yanks Are Beaten by Red Sox, 10–5," *New York Times*, June 30, 1925. The damage consisted of two doubles, a single, and a walk. Boston rallied for the win when New York starter—and former Red Sox—Alex Ferguson gave up five runs in the fourth inning.
27. Quoted in Lieb, *The Boston Red Sox*, 194.
28. Lieb, *The Boston Red Sox*, 196.
29. Stout and Johnson, *Red Sox Century*, 162, 167.

29. Another Baseball Obituary for Quinn

1. The A's finished in last place for seven consecutive years, from 1915 to 1921. They then rose one spot in the standings in each of the next three seasons, rising to fifth place in 1924.
2. Quoted in Macht, *Connie Mack*, 390. Mack was usually viewed favorably in the press, despite the fact that he made the decision to dismantle his championship team (four pennants from 1910 to 1914) after the A's upset defeat in the 1914 World Series. He sold some of his stars for cash and did not re-sign others.
3. Quoted in James C. Isaminger, Pithy Tips from the Sport Ticker, *Philadelphia Inquirer*, June 13, 1921.
4. The Old Sport's Musings, *Philadelphia Inquirer*, April 24, 1924.
5. Hauser's injury occurred during spring training, and he missed the entire season. Gray suffered his injury on May 21, when he pushed his record to 8-0, with a league-best 1.43 earned run average. He did not return until June 19. He then went 8-8 the rest of the season, and his ERA more than doubled to 3.27.

6. John J. McGraw, "Athletics' Youth and Pep Bowing to Washington's Seasoned Players," *Philadelphia Evening Bulletin*, July 11, 1925.

7. Stoney McLinn, "Quinn's Spitter Will Help Athletics Curb Adversaries," *Philadelphia Public Ledger*, July 15, 1925.

8. Bill Dooly, Three and Two, *Philadelphia Record*, May 20, 1928.

9. Joe Vila, "Jack Quinn Ready to Start His 25th Year," *Philadelphia Inquirer*, March 3, 1928.

10. Paul W. Eaton, "Steady and Heady Are Those Griffs," *Sporting News*, July 30, 1925.

11. Quoted in John J. Nolan, "Macks Look to Old Jack Quinn to Pull Them from Their Slump," *Philadelphia Evening Bulletin*, July 14, 1925. Stan Coveleski (now just days before his thirty-sixth birthday) had an 11-1 record for Washington at the time.

12. Mack noted that Quinn was his first spitball pitcher in more than a decade. Mack mentioned his earlier spitballers, Jimmy Dygert (1905–10) and Cy Morgan (1909–12). Nolan, "Macks Look to Old Jack Quinn to Pull Them from Their Slump."

13. Historian Norman Macht wrote that Grove took that "art," his hatred of losing, "to volcanic heights" (*Connie Mack*, 378). Just one week earlier Grove had what would be one of the toughest defeats in his career. He went the distance in a fifteen-inning, 1–0 loss to Herb Pennock and the Yankees.

14. James C. Isaminger, "Foxx and Krause Go Southward in Jimmy's [*sic*] Big Car," *Philadelphia Inquirer*, February 2, 1933.

15. Quoted in Athletic Shorts, *Philadelphia Inquirer*, July 12, 1925.

16. John J. Nolan, "40-Year-Old Jack Quinn Curves Macks to Victory over Detroit," *Philadelphia Evening Bulletin*, July 14, 1925.

17. Quoted in Nolan, "40-Year-Old Jack Quinn Curves Macks."

18. Joe Williams, *New York Evening Telegram*, March 5, 1929.

19. Quoted in John J. Nolan, "Quinn's Pitching Saves A's Lead," *Philadelphia Evening Bulletin*, July 28, 1925.

20. W. S. Farquhar, "The Pitching Antique," *Pottsville (PA) Journal*, July 1925; Quinn family collection.

21. Quinn was pulled for a pinch hitter in the top of the eighth inning with Chicago leading, 1–0. Pinch hitter Walt French led off with a double, and the A's went on to score six runs in the inning.

22. James C. Isaminger, "Jack Quinn Hurls Second Win in Row," *Philadelphia Inquirer*, July 18, 1925.

23. The Old Sport's Musings, *Philadelphia Inquirer*, July 19, 1925.

24. James C. Isaminger, "Revival of Macks Reveals Backbone," *Sporting News*, July 23, 1925.

25. James C. Isaminger, Tips from the Sporting Ticker, *Philadelphia Inquirer*, July 26, 1925.
26. Quoted in "Coal Region Welcomes Favorite Son, Jack Quinn; Pay Tribute to Mack," *Philadelphia Inquirer*, August 3, 1925.
27. Gordon Mackay, "Jack Quinn Hurled Ball Up the Hill, Winning Place on Town Team Once," *Philadelphia Inquirer*, August 2, 1925. Quinn's nieces confirmed that he was not close to his stepmother.
28. Lieb, *Connie Mack*, 209.
29. James C. Isaminger, Tips from the Sporting Ticker, *Philadelphia Inquirer*, July 19, 1925.
30. Quoted in Macht, *Connie Mack*, 386.
31. *Morning Call* (Allentown PA), September 8, 1925.
32. Quoted in Macht, *Connie Mack*, 388.
33. The Old Sport's Musings, *Philadelphia Inquirer*, September 14, 1925, and March 8, 1926.
34. September 17, 1925, was the nineteenth anniversary of Collins's Major League debut.
35. "In Form," *Chicago Tribune*, September 18, 1925.
36. Outfielder Bill Lamar, Quinn's teammate on the 1919 Yankees, hit .356 with 202 hits for the A's in 1925, his best season.
37. This would have been the league's best mark in 1925. For the entire season, including his Red Sox games, Quinn walked 1.85 men per nine innings, second in the league to Sherry Smith's 1.82 mark. Lefty Grove led the league with 131 walks, a rate of almost 6 walks per nine innings.
38. Quinn struck out 3.4 men per nine innings in his two stints with the Yankees. That rate dropped to 2.4 with the Red Sox. He would fan 2.25 per nine innings with the Athletics.
39. Quoted in *New York Sun*, June 23, 1928.
40. Quoted in Bill Dooly, Three and Two, *Philadelphia Record*, May 20, 1928.
41. Quoted in Burt Whitman, "Red Sox Showing Occasional Flash," *Sporting News*, July 30, 1925.
42. Thirteen of Quinn's eighteen appearances with the Athletics were starts, including his first eight. He started fifteen of his nineteen games with the Red Sox earlier in 1925.
43. The Red Sox led both leagues in fewest runs scored (640) and lowest team batting average (.266).
44. Quoted in Burt Whitman, "Near Tragedy When Ehmke Hits Haney on Head with Fast Ball," *Boston Herald*, September 24, 1925.
45. *Detroit Times*, September 24, 1925.
46. Because Ehmke's deliveries came from so many different angles, it is possible that batters had trouble picking up the trajectory of his pitches.

47. The Battle Creek Sanitarium was a health resort based on the health principles advocated by the Seventh-Day Adventist Church, most notably associated with John Harvey Kellogg. It first opened on September 5, 1866, as the Western Health Reform Institute. In his 1908 book *The Battle Creek Sanitarium System, History, Organization, Methods*, Kellogg described the Sanitarium system as "a composite physiologic method comprising hydrotherapy, phototherapy, thermotherapy, electrotherapy, mechanotherapy, dietetics, physical culture, cold-air cure, and health training" (p. 8). Among the sanitarium's most notable patients were Amelia Earhart, President Warren G. Harding, Henry Ford, Mary Todd Lincoln, Sojourner Truth, and Johnny Weissmuller.

48. Clark, *Red Sox Fever*, 95.

30. Quinn Gets Off to a Strong Start

1. Eddie Rommel pitched 261 innings, allowing 285 hits and 107 earned runs. Howard Ehmke pitched 260⅔ innings, allowing 285 hits and 108 earned runs.

2. Don Maxwell, Speaking of Sports, *Chicago Tribune*, February 5, 1926.

3. Quoted in Ed Cunningham, "Bob Quinn Gives Club Once Over and Predicts Happier Year around Fenway Park," *Boston Traveler*, March 1, 1926.

4. Quoted in "Williams, Fuhr, Boone Let Out," *Boston Globe*, January 22, 1926.

5. Quoted in Ed Cunningham, "Arm Sore Now but Thinks It Will Come Around When He Lands in Bowling Alley," *Boston Traveler*, March 6, 1926.

6. Burt Whitman, "Heavier Than Ever Before, All Ready for Best Season," *Boston Traveler*, March 6, 1926.

7. Burt Whitman, "Bob Quinn Can Get Best Smile Ready," *Sporting News*, March 25, 1926.

8. Melville E. Webb Jr., "If Ruffing and Wingfield Do as Well as Ehmke and Zahniser, Fohl Will Be Happy," *Boston Globe*, April 5, 1926.

9. "Huggins Picks Athletics to Win with St. Louis as 'Dark Horse,'" *Philadelphia Evening Bulletin*, March 12, 1926.

10. The Old Sport's Musings, *Philadelphia Inquirer*, March 8, 1926.

11. Quinn's 1926 income tax filing shows an income of $7,253. Quinn family collection.

12. Quoted in James C. Isaminger, "'Athletics Are Disappointment,' Declares Mack in Savage Attack on Macks," *Philadelphia Inquirer*, March 22, 1926.

13. Nick Flatley, "Sox Take Close Tilt with A's," *Boston American*, April 18, 1926.

14. Nick Flatley, "Hose Out to Blast A's Hopes," *Boston American*, June 1, 1926.

15. "Sportsman," Live Tips and Topics, *Boston Globe*, April 30, 1926.

16. James C. Isaminger, "Old Jack Quinn Blanks Red Sox," *Philadelphia Inquirer*, April 30, 1926. This year was the 150th anniversary (Sesquicentennial or "Sezqui") of the Declaration of Independence.

17. James R. Harrison, "Yanks Surrender to Athletics Again," *New York Times*, May 5, 1926. The 1925 Senators had pitchers Walter Johnson (age

thirty-eight), Stan Coveleski (almost thirty-six), and Dutch Ruether (thirty-two) in their starting rotation.

18. Grantland Rice, The Sportlight, *New York Herald-Tribune*, May 8, 1926.

19. John J. Nolan, "Jack Quinn's Brilliant Pitching Puts A's Back on Winning Stride," *Philadelphia Evening Bulletin*, June 11, 1926.

20. Quoted in Ross E. Kauffman, "Jack Quinn's Brilliant Pitching Beats Senators and Puts the Athletics in Third Place," *Philadelphia Evening Bulletin*, May 27, 1926. Though the A's and Indians were both 8½ games behind the Yankees, the Indians had a .553 winning percentage compared to the A's winning percentage of .550, putting the Indians in second place.

21. James C. Isaminger, "Old Jack Quinn Blanks White Sox," *Philadelphia Inquirer*, June 11, 1926.

22. Will Wedge, "Jack Quinn Checks Yankees," *New York Sun*, May 5, 1926.

23. Paul H. Shannon, "Jack Quinn Still Traveling High," *Boston Post*, May 28, 1927.

24. Ed Pollock, "A's Trade Dimming 1926 Prospects for Good Chance in 1927," *Philadelphia Public Ledger*, June 17, 1926.

25. Quoted in Nick Flatley, "Quinn Spikes Report of Red Sox Trade," *Boston American*, June 9, 1926.

26. Flatley, "Quinn Spikes Report of Red Sox Trade."

27. The A's were playing in Cleveland currently, and the Red Sox would be playing the Indians there in two days.

28. Reports had circulated about a trade of Al Simmons to Washington, even up for Goose Goslin, and another deal that would have sent Eddie Rommel to the Senators. Mack would neither confirm nor deny those reports.

29. James C. Isaminger, "Mack Pulls Biggest Barter of Season in Closing Moments," *Philadelphia Inquirer*, June 16, 1926.

30. Players then and now have often expressed a desire to remain with their current teams for public consumption while secretly asking to be traded.

31. Quoted in John J. Nolan, "Athletics Get Pitcher Ehmke by Trading 3 Players to Boston," *Philadelphia Evening Bulletin*, June 16, 1926.

32. Nolan, "Athletics Get Pitcher Ehmke."

33. James C. Isaminger, "Mack Now Boasts Best Hurling Staff," *Philadelphia Inquirer*, June 17, 1926.

34. Quoted in Isaminger, "Mack Now Boasts Best Hurling Staff."

31. Ehmke and Quinn Reunited

1. Nick Flatley, "New Pitchers Certain to Help Fohlmen," *Boston American*, June 16, 1926.

2. Burt Whitman, "A 'Miracle' Once, Hope Never Dies," *Sporting News*, June 24, 1926.

3. Whitman, "A 'Miracle' Once."

4. Stoney McLinn, "Chance of Obtaining New Morale Justifies Connie Mack's Trade," *Philadelphia Evening Public Ledger*, June 16, 1926.

5. Quoted in "Ehmke Welcomes Transfer to A's," *Philadelphia Evening Bulletin*, June 16, 1926.

6. Quoted in "Ehmke Welcomes Transfer to A's."

7. Quoted in John J. Nolan, "Mack Looks for Ehmke to Turn in Twelve Victories This Year," *Philadelphia Evening Bulletin*, June 17, 1926.

8. John B. Foster, "Mathematicians Note Yanks Have Flag Almost Half Won," *Buffalo Evening News*, June 17, 1926.

9. Quoted in Nolan, "Mack Looks for Ehmke to Turn in Twelve Victories This Year."

10. Quoted in Nolan, "Mack Looks for Ehmke to Turn in Twelve Victories This Year."

11. Nolan, "Mack Looks for Ehmke to Turn in Twelve Victories This Year." Ehmke's company served as a representative for E. I. Du Pont de Nemours, which did the actual manufacturing.

12. "Penn Purchases Big Cover for Gridiron," *Philadelphia Evening Bulletin*, July 25, 1926.

13. Quoted in James C. Isaminger, "Mack Now Boasts Best Hurling Staff," *Philadelphia Inquirer*, June 17, 1926.

14. Quoted in Don Basenfelder, "Ehmke, Three Years with Dead Arm, Tells 'Inside' of Whiffing 13 Cubs in '29 Series, Using 'Nothing Ball,'" *Sporting News*, December 17, 1936.

15. Quinn went the distance against the Senators in a 3–1 loss, but the game was called after five innings because of rain.

16. John J. Nolan, "Athletics Drop Seventh Straight; New Mascot Fails to Shake Jinx," *Philadelphia Evening Bulletin*, July 24, 1926.

17. Quoted in "Won't Use a Good Bat When Facing Jack Quinn," *Boston Globe*, September 26, 1926.

18. Billy Evans, "Age Means Little in Life of One Jack Quinn of Macks," *Appleton (WI) Post-Crescent*, August 3, 1928.

19. Scribbled by Scribes, *Sporting News*, June 24, 1926.

20. Quoted in John J. Nolan, "Earl Mack Starts Quest for New Players," *Philadelphia Evening Bulletin*, July 31, 1926.

21. Quoted in The Old Sport's Musings, *Philadelphia Inquirer*, August 2, 1926.

22. The Old Sport's Musings, *Philadelphia Inquirer*, August 2, 1926.

23. John J. Nolan, "Senators Bunch Hits on Ehmke and A's Drop Fourth Straight," *Philadelphia Evening Bulletin*, June 28, 1926.

24. Pate would finish the season with nine wins (all in relief) and no defeats. Tom Zachary of the 1929 Yankees, with twelve, holds the Major League record for most wins in a season without a loss.

25. Quoted in John J. Nolan, "Athletics Win from St. Louis Cut Yanks' Lead to 5½ Games," *Philadelphia Evening Bulletin*, July 17, 1926.

26. James C Isaminger, "Connie's Patience Sags with His A's," *Sporting News*, August 12, 1926.

27. John J. Nolan, "Ehmke and Rommel Pitch A's to Double Victory over Boston," *Philadelphia Evening Bulletin*, August 13, 1926.

28. Quoted in Nolan, "Ehmke and Rommel Pitch A's to Double Victory over Boston."

29. James C. Isaminger, Pithy Tips from the Sport Ticker, *Philadelphia Inquirer*, June 13, 1926.

30. James C. Isaminger, "Philly Optimism Is Not Easily Downed," *Sporting News*, July 8, 1926. Leopold von Singer managed a vaudeville group of little people. Some of them appeared in films in the 1930s. One was cast as a Munchkin in *The Wizard of Oz*.

31. James, *The New Bill James Historical Abstract*, 127.

32. Grove walked 3.5 men per nine innings in 1925, not a great number but better than the 4.5 of his rookie season.

33. Quoted in Ed Cunningham, Sport for Sport's Sake, *Boston Traveler*, June 1, 1926.

34. For example, between April 28 and May 28 Grove pitched three complete games against New York, winning two of them and giving up only seven runs. But he walked fourteen Yankees.

32. Ehmke Again a Teammate of Cobb

1. Frank Menke, "Athletics in Gallop Should Win Pennant," *Philadelphia Record*, April 9, 1927.

2. AP, "Base Ball Writers Consensus Favors Mackmen to Win Pennant," *Philadelphia Evening Bulletin*, April 10, 1927.

3. Quoted in John B. Foster, "Ehmke Is Confident Athletics Will Win," *Watertown (NY) Daily Times*, November 16, 1926.

4. Connie Mack had a special relationship with Jack Dunn. He purchased star pitcher Lefty Grove from Dunn's Orioles after the 1924 season.

5. Ehmke was never among those accused of having received money.

6. E. A. Batchelor: "The Tigers Drop Both Games to Chicago," *Detroit Free Press*, September 3, 1917, and "The White Sox Beat Tigers Twice More," *Detroit Free Press*, September 4, 1917.

7. Quoted in "Ehmke Is 'Peeved' at Bribe Charges," *Philadelphia Evening Bulletin*, January 7, 1927.

8. Quoted in "Score Stands 35–2 against Them After Risberg, Gandil Go to Bat," *Sporting News*, January 13, 1927.

9. Quoted in "Score Stands 35–2 against Them."

10. For a full discussion of this "fixing" incident, see Kahanowitz, *Baseball Gods in Scandal*. *Baseball-Reference* cites Cobb's 1927 salary as $50,000.

11. Macht, *Connie Mack*, 445–46.

12. John Kieran, Sports of the Times, *New York Times*, March 2, 1927.

13. Quoted in Will Wedge, *New York Sun*, March 18, 1927.

14. Quoted in Raymond A. Hill, "Ehmke, with Temperamental Arm, May Quit A's Following Series," *Philadelphia Evening Bulletin*, September 18, 1929.

15. "Cobb and Ehmke, Foes Once, May Be 'Pals' Now," *New York American*, March 27, 1927.

16. On May 25, 1937, Cochrane suffered a near-fatal beaning by the Yankees' Bump Hadley.

17. Actually it was the next two who were on the list: Herman Pillette, with fifteen hit batters, and Ole Olsen, with fourteen.

18. Quoted in "Mr. Ehmke and the Bean Ball," unsourced article from the National Baseball Hall of Fame and Library, December 9, 1937.

19. Ty Cobb (as told to Sid Keener), "Cobb Figures Macks Have Best Chance," *Atlanta Constitution*, April 11, 1927.

20. Don Q. Duffy, "Costly Material Purchased for A's," *Charleston Daily Mail*, February 23, 1927.

21. Bill Dooly, "Mack Never So Sanguine of Chance to Win Flag," *Philadelphia Record*, February 19, 1927.

22. Quoted in James C. Isaminger, Pithy Tips from the Sport Ticker, *Philadelphia Inquirer*, April 5, 1927.

23. Isaminger, Pithy Tips from the Sport Ticker, *Philadelphia Inquirer*, April 5, 1927.

24. James R. Harrison, "Ruth's Homer Aids in Yankee Victory," *New York Times*, April 16, 1927.

25. Quoted in John Kieran, Sports of the Times, *New York Times*, March 9, 1929.

26. Quoted in Yeutter, "The Man Who Baffled the Cubs."

27. Bill Dooly, "Ty Cobb Steals Home for Third Straight Game," *Philadelphia Record*, April 20, 1927.

28. Quoted in John J. Nolan, "Athletics, Back from Road Trip, Renew Feud with Champion Yanks," *Philadelphia Evening Bulletin*, April 20, 1927.

29. John J. Nolan, "Cobb Makes Record with 4,000th Safe Hit as A's Lose to Detroit," *Philadelphia Evening Bulletin*, July 27, 1927.

30. Davis J. Walsh, "Old Age Does Not Halt Baseball Leaders from Drawing Big Salaries," International News Service. In 1858 Oliver Wendell Holmes Sr. wrote a poem about a two-wheeled carriage (shay) that lasted for a hundred years.

31. Quoted in Lane, "The Dean of American League Pitchers," 453.

32. Quoted in Lane, "The Oldest Veteran in the Major Leagues," 443.

33. Bill Dooly, "Ehmke Hurls Gilt-Edged Ball against Old Club," *Philadelphia Record*, May 4, 1927.

34. Bill Dooly, "Mackmen Even Series by Downing White Sox," *Philadelphia Record*, May 23, 1927.

33. Favorites Fall Short, Far Short

1. Harry Bullion, "Jack Quinn Hurls Macks to Second Victory of Series," *Detroit Free Press*, May 12, 1927.

2. Quoted in Macht, *Connie Mack*, 469.

3. Quoted in Macht, *Connie Mack*, 377.

4. Nack, "Lost in History."

5. Quoted in Macht, *Connie Mack*, 463.

6. Ehmke's thirteen home runs allowed to Ruth ties him with Milt Gaston and Lefty Stewart for third place in yielding home runs to the Babe. Hooks Dauss, with fourteen, is second, and Rube Walberg is the leader with seventeen.

7. James R. Harrison, "Ruth Gets 2 Homers as Yanks Win Twice," *New York Times*, June 1, 1927.

8. Quoted in James Isaminger, "Connie Mack Sends Howard Ehmke Home to Get into Shape," *Philadelphia Evening Bulletin*, July 6, 1927.

9. Quoted in "Ehmke Sent Back Home to Get in Shape," *Philadelphia Evening Public Ledger*, July 6, 1927.

10. "Billy Morris Will Take Care of Ehmke," *Philadelphia Inquirer*, July 7, 1927.

11. Monitor, "Aged Jack Quinn Defeats Hugmen," *New York World*, June 27, 1927.

12. Harry Bullion, "Bengals Forced to Share Double Bill with Macks," *Detroit Free Press*, July 27, 1927.

13. "Doubleheader with Griffmen Is Washed Out," *Detroit Free Press*, July 16, 1927. Grove finished July with a 13-11 record and a 3.41 earned run average. Quinn's record at that time was 10-6, with his ERA at 3.34.

14. John J. Nolan, "A's Gain behind Good Pitching, Although Batting Marks Fall," *Philadelphia Evening Bulletin*, August 19, 1927.

15. "Ehmke Hurls First; Quinn Blanks Tribe," *Philadelphia Inquirer*, August 17, 1927.

16. Harry Bullion, "Quinn Yields Three Hits as Mackmen Sweep Series in Blanking Tigers," *Detroit Free Press*, August 30, 1927.

17. Quoted in Gordon Mackay, "Jack Quinn Expects to Pitch for Three More Seasons," *Pittsburgh Press*, August 28, 1927. The figure of "30 years" would include Quinn's seasons of sandlot ball before he became a professional.

18. The league's average was 2.73 walks per nine innings. Grove made progress with his control in 1927 but was still issuing 3.32 walks per nine innings, more than double Quinn's rate.

19. This is based on his actual age, which was not known at the time. In 1925 and 1926 Jimmy Austin of the Browns (born in December 1879) was older but appeared in only one game each season. In 1925 Oscar Stanage of the Tigers (born three months before Quinn) was also older, but he appeared in only three games. In 1924 Nick Altrock of the Nationals (born in September 1876) appeared in one game. In 1923 Austin was again the oldest with but one appearance, and Fred Carisch of the Indians (born in November 1881) appeared in two games. Even in 1922 Austin played infrequently. Pirates pitcher Babe Adams, a year older than Quinn, appeared in his last Major League game in July 1926. He was the oldest National League player his last five seasons.

20. Hoefer, "Cutting the Corners," 344.

21. Quoted in John J. Nolan, "Yankees Rank among Greatest Teams in Baseball, Says Mack," *Philadelphia Evening Bulletin*, September 14, 1927.

34. Chasing the "Greatest Team Ever"

1. "Ty Cobb, Storm Center," *Collyer's Eye*, August 6, 1927. *Baseball-Reference* has Cobb's 1927 salary as $50,000, reduced to a still high $35,000 for 1928.

2. Macht, *Connie Mack*, 470.

3. Quoted in Gentile, *The 1928 New York Yankees*, 65.

4. Gordon Mackay, Is Zat So, *Philadelphia Record*, July 26, 1929.

5. Speaker (who turned forty on April 4) hit .327 for Washington in 1927. For the tenth time in his career, he hit 40 or more doubles (43), on his way to an all-time career high of 792. He hit 22 more in 1928, but he batted only .267 that season.

6. Westbrook Pegler, "Pegler Says Laugh or Cry, Time Tells on Tris and Ty," *Washington Post*, April 23, 1928.

7. Quoted in Joe Williams, "When It Rains, You Talk of Mr. Quinn," *Cleveland Press*, July 28, 1927.

8. Quoted in "Broken Toes, Not Gnarled Fingers, Are Perkins' Catching Trade-Mark," *Philadelphia Evening Bulletin*, June 29, 1928.

9. Miller was remarkably consistent. He hit between .319 and .331 each season between 1925 and 1929.

10. In 1927 Orwoll hit .370 for the Brewers and posted a 17-6 record as a pitcher. He also played for the Milwaukee Badgers of the National Football League in 1926.

11. James C. Isaminger, Pithy Tips from the Sport Ticker, *Philadelphia Inquirer*, May 27, 1928.

12. Earnshaw's best seasons with Baltimore were 1925 and 1926, when he won a combined fifty-one games. When the Orioles fell to last place in the spring of 1928, Dunn was willing to part with him. (Pitcher Jing Johnson went to

Baltimore in the transaction; he would never return to the Major Leagues.) Other accounts reported the purchase price for Earnshaw as $50,000.

13. Bill Dooly, "Fastest Thing Game Has Seen," *Philadelphia Record*, July 28, 1929.

14. Macht, *Connie Mack*, 479.

15. Ehmke had sold tarps to almost all the Major League teams and to several football venues.

16. Undated article from the Howard Ehmke file at the National Baseball Hall of Fame Library and Museum. The A's would win twelve of the eighteen games that Ehmke started in 1928.

17. Quoted in James C. Isaminger, Pithy Tips from the Sport Ticker, *Philadelphia Inquirer*, January 1, 1928.

18. *Philadelphia Record*, March 4, 1928.

19. John J. Nolan, "White Sox Watch Macks Pile Up Fifteen Runs against Indians," *Philadelphia Evening Bulletin*, May 17, 1928.

20. "Howard Ehmke Says Yankees Won't Repeat 1927 Victory," *Los Angeles Times*, January 15, 1928.

21. Quoted in John J. Nolan, "Ehmke Conquers 'Hesitation Pitch,'" *Philadelphia Evening Bulletin*, March 26, 1928.

22. *Philadelphia Record*, March 4, 1928.

23. Quoted in Monitor, Over the Plate, *New York World*, May 1, 1928.

24. Macht, *Connie Mack*, 482. The elephant, which had adorned the left breast of the Athletics' uniforms since 1919, would be replaced with the "A" the club had worn before then.

25. Quoted in Joe Vila, Setting the Pace, *New York Sun*, March 2, 1928.

26. Quoted in Bill Dooly, "Macks' Manager Blames Hurlers for Poor Start," *Philadelphia Record*, April 18, 1928.

27. Dooly, "Macks' Manager Blames Hurlers for Poor Start."

28. John Kieran, Sports of the Times, *New York Times*, April 24, 1928.

29. Shirley L. Povich, "Quinn's Aged Arm Baffles Nationals," *Washington Post*, April 27, 1928.

30. Bill Dooly, "Old John Picus, in Form, Shuts Out His Foes with Seven Hits," *Philadelphia Record*, April 27, 1928.

31. John J. Nolan, "Speaker's Three Doubles Help Jack Quinn Defeat Cleveland," *Philadelphia Evening Bulletin*, May 16, 1928.

32. Bill Dooly, Three and Two, *Philadelphia Record*, May 20, 1928.

33. Quinn was edged out for the league's best mark by teammate Eddie Rommel, who issued a league-low 1.35 walks per nine innings in 1928.

34. Quoted in George Moriarty, "Good Control Aids Quinn to Success," *Philadelphia Evening Bulletin*, August 16, 1928.

35. Bill Dooly, "Baseball's Oldest Major League Hurler Leads Athletics," *Philadelphia Record*, July 22, 1928.

36. Quoted in Scribbled by Scribes, *Sporting News*, September 13, 1928.
37. The future Hall of Famers were as follows. For New York: Babe Ruth, Lou Gehrig, Tony Lazzeri, Earle Combs, Waite Hoyt, and Leo Durocher. For Philadelphia: Lefty Grove, Jimmie Foxx, Al Simmons, Ty Cobb, Tris Speaker, Eddie Collins, and Mickey Cochrane. Two future Hall of Fame managers, Mack and Miller Huggins, also took part in the game.
38. Gordon Mackay, Is Zat So, *Philadelphia Record*, May 28, 1928.
39. Simmons got hot as the summer progressed and finished the season with a .351 batting average.
40. Grove's earned run average against New York was 5.18 in 1927. In 1928 he had a 23-2 record with a 1.99 ERA against the league's other six teams.
41. Quoted in Macht, *Connie Mack*, 485.
42. Quoted in John J. Nolan, "Hauser's Hitting Helps A's Start New Winning Streak in Boston," *Philadelphia Evening Bulletin*, May 31, 1928.
43. John J. Nolan, "Ehmke's New Pitching Style Gives A's Victory over Yanks in Final Game," *Philadelphia Evening Bulletin*, June 30, 1928.
44. John J. Nolan, "Second-String Catcher Holds A's to Even Break with N.Y. Yankees," *Philadelphia Evening Bulletin*, June 21, 1928.
45. Quoted in Gentile, *The 1928 New York Yankees*, 133.
46. Quoted in Bill Dooly, Three and Two, *Philadelphia Record*, July 1, 1928.
47. Quoted in Bill Dooly, Three and Two, *Philadelphia Record*, July 1, 1928.
48. James R. Harrison, "60,000 See Yanks Win Doubleheader," *New York Times*, July 2, 1928.
49. Gordon Mackay, Is Zat So, *Philadelphia Record*, July 1, 1928.

35. A Torrid Pennant Race

1. Quoted in John J. Nolan, "Jack Quinn Scores Twelfth Win As Macks Divide with Detroit," *Philadelphia Evening Bulletin*, July 17, 1928.
2. Quoted in Nolan, "Jack Quinn Scores Twelfth Win." Also see *New York Sun*, July 19, 1928.
3. Sports Editorial, *Philadelphia Record*, July 30, 1928.
4. "Philadelphia May Beat Yanks Yet," *Austin (TX) American-Statesman*, August 5, 1928; the Austin paper was quoting an unnamed New York newspaper.
5. James C. Isaminger, "Veteran Allows 4 Blows in 15th Win," *Philadelphia Inquirer*, August 11, 1928. This was the fourth season in which Quinn tossed a career-high four shutouts. The others were 1914, 1919, and 1922.
6. Bill Dooly, "Quinn Grabs 15th Victory," *Philadelphia Record*, August 11, 1928. Quinn gave up four hits and hit one batter.
7. The four 1928 Senators in the Hall of Fame are Sam Rice, Goose Goslin, Joe Cronin, and Bucky Harris.

8. Quoted in Homer Thorne, Tricks with Horsehide, *New York Evening Post*, August 17, 1928.

9. Simmons was leading the American League with a .388 batting average.

10. John J. Nolan, "Ehmke's Brilliant Pitching Helps A's Stay 4½ Games Behind Yanks," *Philadelphia Evening Bulletin*, August 10, 1928.

11. Quoted in Nolan, "Ehmke's Brilliant Pitching Helps A's Stay 4½ Games Behind Yanks."

12. Ruffing hit .314 with thirteen doubles in 1928. He had a .269 career batting average with thirty-six home runs.

13. Macht, *Connie Mack*, 492.

14. Joe Dugan, "Ehmke Hesitates and Then Is Lost," *Philadelphia Record*, August 31, 1928.

15. John Kieran, Sports of the Times, *New York Times*, July 31, 1928.

16. Sports Editorial, *Philadelphia Record*, July 30, 1928.

17. Quoted in John J. Nolan, "Foxx, Picked as Future Home Run King by Ruth, Trains on Hot Cakes," *Philadelphia Evening Bulletin*, June 22, 1928.

18. Orwoll's last start was on June 25. He made nine relief appearances after that.

19. Bill Dooly, Three and Two, *Philadelphia Record*, August 13, 1928.

20. Quoted in Bill Dooly, "Mack Admits A's Have a Chance," *Philadelphia Record*, August 9, 1928. Orwoll did not prove to be as effective a pitcher as Mack expected. And with the acquisition of George Earnshaw, Mack had a starter who could replace Orwoll.

21. Quoted in Dan Daniel, "Mackmen Again Victims of Champs' Indian Sign," *New York Evening Telegram*, September 10, 1928. "Indian sign" was slang for a spell or jinx.

22. Ford Frick, "Athletics Favored to Take Series from Yankees," *New York American*, September 9, 1928.

23. Ed Bang, "Jack Not Too Old to Learn New Delivery," September 18, 1928; unsourced newspaper, Quinn family collection.

24. Bill Dooly, Three and Two, *Philadelphia Record*, September 23, 1928.

25. Steve Steinberg has a Yankee Stadium "Stadium Tours" pamphlet that lists the stadium's "record attendance" of 81,841 for a May 30, 1938, doubleheader against the Red Sox. *Retrosheet* lists that day's attendance as 81,891.

26. "200,000 Stampede Stadium; 90,000 See Yanks Win," *New York American*, September 10, 1928. The *New York Times* reported that fifty thousand fans "lingered outside to the finish."

27. John M. McCullough, "Hordes of Philadelphia Rooters Unconquerable, Vocally, Even in Defeat," *Philadelphia Inquirer*, September 10, 1928.

28. Bill Slocum, "Record Crowd of 85,000 Sees Bargain Bill," *New York American*, September 10, 1928.

29. Lynn Boyle, Close-Ups on the Sport, *Philadelphia Evening Bulletin*, September 10, 1928.

30. James C. Isaminger, "Yankees Win Two from A's, 5–0, 7–3," *Philadelphia Inquirer*, September 10, 1928.

31. Richards Vidmer, "Yankees Win Twice and Pass Athletics," *New York Times*, September 10, 1928.

32. Quoted in "Quinn Will Twirl in Detroit Opener," *Philadelphia Evening Bulletin*, September 20, 1928.

33. Quoted in Macht, *Connie Mack*, 499.

34. Grove and the Yankees' George Pipgras tied for the 1928 American League high in wins with twenty-four.

35. "Connie Mack Stands amid Turmoil to See Dream of His Later Years Fading," *Philadelphia Record*, September 13, 1928.

36. Bill Dooly, "Quinn Reveals Secret: Veteran Pitcher Declares Ruth and Gehrig Frightened Mackmen," *Philadelphia Record*, April 17, 1929. This is remarkably similar to an unconfirmed story that the Pittsburgh Pirates were similarly intimidated before Game One of the 1927 World Series.

37. Quoted in Macht, *Connie Mack*, 501.

38. Quoted in Macht, *Connie Mack*, 501.

39. Quoted in Stan Baumgartner, "Ehmke in Hospital, Is Out for Season," *Philadelphia Inquirer*, September 14, 1928.

40. Quoted in Ed Pollock, Playing the Game, *Philadelphia Evening Bulletin*, June 15, 1952.

41. Quoted in "Quinn Will Twirl in Detroit Opener," *Philadelphia Evening Bulletin*, September 20, 1928.

42. From Ed Pollock, "Lefty Grove," quoted in Walsh, *Baseball's Greatest Lineup*, 150.

43. Gordon Mackay, "Mack Lack of Money Pitchers One Reason for Lack of Success," *Philadelphia Record*, June 27, 1928.

44. Grove would have a 79-15 record over the next three seasons and 148-33 over the next five.

45. James C. Isaminger, "Jack Quinn Deals Ciphers As Macks Crush Indian Foe," *Philadelphia Inquirer*, September 16, 1928.

46. James C. Isaminger, "Quinn Quells Tigers, Haas Batters Homer," *Philadelphia Inquirer*, September 21, 1928.

47. Harry Bullion, "Jack Quinn Holds Tigers to Five Hits," *Detroit Free Press*, September 21, 1928. The headline is incorrect. The Tigers had six hits in this game, not five.

48. James C. Isaminger, Pithy Tips from the Sport Ticker, *Philadelphia Inquirer*, May 6, 1928.

49. James C. Isaminger, Pithy Tips from the Sport Ticker, *Philadelphia Inquirer*, September 30, 1928. This was an interesting comment about

money pitchers, considering that Grove had a 23-2 record against the league's other six teams.

50. In his brief stint with the White Sox in 1918 (three weeks in August), Quinn won five of six decisions, for an .833 winning percentage.

51. Thomas Holmes, "Pitcher's Best Year Is His Easiest, Dodgers Hurlers Say," *Brooklyn Eagle*, March 10, 1933.

36. A Fast Start for the A's

1. Gould, "A Forecast of the Major League Pennant Races," 535.

2. Dick Farrington, "Major League Writers Pick Yankees and Cubs to Win Pennants," *Sporting News*, April 11, 1929. As noted previously, "Indian sign" was slang for a spell or jinx.

3. "Seven Athletics Start South to Open Preliminary Training," *New York Times*, January 31, 1929.

4. Quoted in *Hot Springs Sentinel-Record*, October 10, 1930.

5. Quoted in James C. Isaminger, "Cochrane Breezes into Ft. Myers Camp, Exchanges Cheery Words with Mack," *Philadelphia Inquirer*, February 27, 1929. These accounts suggest the Athletics paid for the players' Hot Springs visit.

6. Quoted in Bill Dooly, "Ehmke Must Show or Vamoose, Is Connie's Decree," *Philadelphia Record*, April 4, 1929.

7. Boley would appear in only ninety-one games in 1929.

8. "Mack Berates His Players," *Baltimore Sun*, April 1, 1929, and Bill Dooly, "Mack Disgusted with Athletics' Form in Florida," *Philadelphia Record*, April 1, 1929.

9. Bill Dooly, "Norseman's Playing Bitter Blow to Athletics' Pilot, Who States Orwoll Doesn't Keep in Training," *Philadelphia Record*, April 3, 1929.

10. Quoted in Macht, *Connie Mack*, 513. Joe Hauser never fully recovered from his knee injury and was waived by the A's after the 1928 season.

11. Quoted in Bill Dooly, "Success of New Players Boon to Mack," *Philadelphia Record*, July 11, 1928.

12. Alan Gould, "Mack's Experiment with Stars Failed to Land Pennant for A's," *Philadelphia Evening Bulletin*, September 27, 1930.

13. Quoted in Will Wedge, "The Story of John P. Quinn," *New York Sun*, June 22, 1929.

14. John J. Nolan, "Jack Quinn Declares He Will Pitch Better Than Ever Next Year," *Philadelphia Evening Bulletin*, December 13, 1928. Rolling Hills was and still is a tiny township at the foot of Catawissa Mountain, eighty-five miles northeast of Pottsville.

15. Harold Johnson, "Round of Bowling a Week Keeps Pitcher Quinn Fit," *Chicago American*, January 21, 1929. Schalk was fired as White Sox manager in July 1928 and became a New York Giants coach in 1929; he also appeared in his final five games with the Giants.

16. Bill Dooly, "Quinn Reveals Secret: Veteran Declares Ruth and Gehrig Frightened Mackmen," *Philadelphia Record*, April 17, 1929. Among the Yankees hampered by injuries late in the 1928 season was pitcher Herb Pennock. He was still plagued with the neuritis that kept him out of the 1928 World Series. He would never come close to the form he had shown as a dominant pitcher the past decade.

17. After Haas's second misplay, Mack moved left fielder Bing Miller to center and Haas to left.

18. Quoted in James C. Isaminger, "Old Sol Blinds Haas Twice and Raps Fall for Doubles Ruining Jack Quinn's Fine Mound Work," *Philadelphia Inquirer*, April 20, 1929.

19. James C. Isaminger, "Old Jack Quinn Toys with Hug's Henchmen," *Philadelphia Inquirer*, April 27, 1929. As had been his approach in recent years, Quinn let hitters put the ball in play; he had no strikeouts and allowed only one walk in the game.

20. Quoted in Franklin W. Yeutter, "'Ole Jack' Quinn Baffles Yanks: A's Knock Out Pennock," *Philadelphia Evening Bulletin*, April 27, 1929.

21. Quoted in *New York Sun*, April 27, 1929.

22. Grantland Rice, "Talk about Iron Men," 12.

23. James C. Isaminger, "Macks Throttle Tigers, 9–6," *Philadelphia Inquirer*, June 1, 1929.

24. Don Legg, Sports Situation, *Austin (TX) Statesman*, June 21, 1929, quoting UPI sports editor Henry Farrell.

25. Gordon Mackay, Is Zat So, *Philadelphia Record*, May 27, 1929.

26. Kashatus, *Connie Mack's '29 Triumph*, 89.

27. Henry L. Farrell, "Harmony One Big Secret of Athletics' Success; Two Bones of Contention Out," *Philadelphia Record*, August 10, 1929.

28. John Drebinger, "70,000 See Yankees Break Even Again," *New York Times*, June 23, 1929.

29. Drebinger, "70,000 See Yankees Break Even Again." The Yankees had a runner on third base in each of the next three innings (twice with only one out), but Quinn held firm. Tony Lazzeri's bases-loaded single in the fourteenth won the game.

30. Davis J. Walsh, "Time Takes Toll of Stars; Several Disappear in 1929," *Butte (MT) Standard*, July 14, 1929.

31. In 1928 New York had taken eleven of fifteen games from Philadelphia by July 1.

32. Quoted in Brian Bell, "Mack Now Lauds His Team, Declaring Pessimism Gone," *Washington Post*, April 21, 1929.

33. Quoted in Meany, *The Yankee Story*, 70. The Cleveland reporter was Gordon Cobbledick.

34. Quoted in Macht, *Connie Mack*, 515. This was at a time stocks seemed to be climbing inexorably and just a few months before the October 1929 stock market crash.

37. A Pennant for the A's at Last

1. Quoted in Don Basenfelder, "Ehmke, Three Years with Dead Arm, Tells 'Inside' of Whiffing 13 Cubs in '29 Series, Using 'Nothing Ball,'" *Sporting News*, December 17, 1936.
2. Perhaps Ehmke meant he had never been on a pennant-winning club, as he had been on winning clubs with both Detroit and Philadelphia.
3. Quoted in Basenfelder, "Ehmke, Three Years with Dead Arm."
4. Quoted in Basenfelder, "Ehmke, Three Years with Dead Arm."
5. Dan Daniel, "Hoyt, Pipgras, and Pennock to Go against A's at Home," *New York Evening Telegram*, June 24, 1929.
6. When Cochrane lurched back to avoid behind hit by a pitch, the end of his bat cracked the rib.
7. James C. Isaminger, Tips from the Sport Ticker, *Philadelphia Inquirer*, July 14, 1929.
8. Arthur Daley, Sports of the Times, *New York Times*, July 5, 1962.
9. Quoted in John J. Nolan, "A's Thrill Connie As They Split with St. Louis and Gain on Yanks," *Philadelphia Evening Bulletin*, July 11, 1929.
10. Quoted in Macht, *Connie Mack*, 517.
11. John J. Nolan, "Ehmke's Side-Arm Curving Keeps the A's 10 Games Ahead of Yanks," *Philadelphia Evening Bulletin*, July 27, 1929.
12. Quoted in Nolan, "Ehmke's Side-Arm Curving."
13. Quoted in John J. Nolan, "Jack Quinn's Brilliant Pitching Puts A's Back on Winning Stride," *Philadelphia Evening Bulletin*, June 11, 1926.
14. James C. Isaminger, Tips from the Sport Ticker, *Philadelphia Inquirer*, August 4, 1929.
15. Quoted in Stoney McLinn, "Connie Mack Hints His Club May Win League Pennant," *Philadelphia Evening Public Ledger*, August 8, 1929.
16. eBay put this letter up for auction in January 2009. The opening price was $4,999.99.
17. Quoted in "Ehmke Fighting with Other Macks? Says He's Home for Rest," *Brooklyn Star*, August 10, 1929.
18. "Ehmke Fighting with Other Macks?"
19. Quoted in Stan Baumgartner, *Philadelphia Inquirer*, August 16, 1929.
20. Gordon Mackay, "Yanks Terrible in Triumph, Quinn Is Real Ball Player," *Philadelphia Record*, August 9, 1929.
21. Quoted in Stoney McLinn, "Last Triumph in Tigertown of Type to Make Elephants View World in Genial Mood," *Philadelphia Evening Public Ledger*, August 14, 1929.

22. Pennant fever gripped Philadelphia. The morning-afternoon separate admission doubleheader at Shibe Park drew thirty-eight thousand fans to the morning game and thirty-three thousand to the afternoon game.

23. Westbrook Pegler, "Al Simmons Is Hitting 'Em Wronger and Better Than Ever," *Chicago Tribune*, September 24, 1929.

24. William E. Brandt, "Yanks Turned Back Twice by Athletics," *New York Times*, September 3, 1929.

25. Quoted in Raymond A. Hill, "Ehmke, with Temperamental Arm, May Quit A's Following Series," *Philadelphia Evening Bulletin*, September 18, 1929.

26. Quoted in Hill, "Ehmke, with Temperamental Arm, May Quit A's Following Series."

27. Quoted in Gordon Mackay, Is Zat So, *Philadelphia Record*, August 5, 1929.

28. Connie Mack, "Earnshaw Big Surprise," *Philadelphia Inquirer*, October 2, 1929.

29. Quoted in Franklin Yeutter, The Sports Parade, *Philadelphia Evening Bulletin*, December 7, 1939. While Yeutter wrote that this occurred in the spring of 1930, it appears to have happened a year earlier.

30. Quoted in Walter Farquhar, Sportitorial; undated newspaper article in the Quinn family collection.

31. Quoted in Franklin Yeutter, The Sports Parade, *Philadelphia Inquirer*, December 7, 1939.

32. William Duncan, "Time Tames 'The Wild Oriole,'" *Philadelphia Public Ledger*, September 22, 1929.

33. Quoted in Red Smith, *To Absent Friends from Red Smith*, 207.

34. Grove showed significant improvement against the Yankees. He had a 2-1 record with a 2.70 earned run average against them. Those numbers were 1-6 and 5.44, respectively, the previous season.

35. Macht, *Connie Mack*, 518.

36. Chicago fans were as gripped by pennant fever as those in Philadelphia. The morning-afternoon separate admission doubleheader against the Cardinals at Wrigley Field drew thirty-eight thousand fans to the morning game and forty-four thousand to the afternoon game.

37. James C. Isaminger, Tips from the Sport Ticker, *Philadelphia Inquirer*, September 8, 1929.

38. Isaminger, Tips from the Sport Ticker, *Philadelphia Inquirer*, September 8, 1929.

39. Quoted in Smith, *To Absent Friends from Red Smith*, 330.

40. Quoted in Smith, *To Absent Friends from Red Smith*, 330.

38. "The Pitcher Who Was Left Behind"

1. *Sports Illustrated*, August 19, 1996.

2. Macht, *Connie Mack*, 528.

3. John J. Nolan, "A's Should Have Flag Actually Decided within Next Two Weeks," *Philadelphia Evening Bulletin*, September 9, 1929.

4. Quoted in "Veteran Hurler Wants to Pitch," *Austin (TX) Statesman*, September 19, 1929.

5. Quoted in Raymond A. Hill, "Ehmke, with Temperamental Arm, May Quit A's Following Series," *Philadelphia Evening Bulletin*, September 18, 1929.

6. Ed Pollock, "Cubs Propensity to Slam Portside Curves May Make World Series Ace of Ehmke," *Philadelphia Public Ledger*, September 30, 1929.

7. Quoted in Brandt, "The Pitchers' Arms," 130.

8. Quoted in Don Basenfelder, "Ehmke, Three Years with Dead Arm, Tells 'Inside' of Whiffing 13 Cubs in '29 Series, Using 'Nothing Ball,'" *Sporting News*, December 17, 1936.

9. Quoted in Berkow, *Red*, 49.

10. Quoted in Joe Williams, "More about How Ehmke Started That Series," *New York World-Telegram*, January 2, 1945.

11. Quoted in Rubenstein, *Chicago in the World Series, 1903–2005*, 107.

12. *Sporting News*, September 19, 1929.

13. Mack later said that aside from Ehmke, he took only Eddie Collins into his confidence regarding the Game One starter. Collins had broken into baseball under Mack in 1906. Traded to the White Sox after the post-1914 dismantlement of the A's, he returned in 1927 and was one of Mack's most trusted advisors.

14. Quoted in "Grove, Happy as Hunter, Would Take Shot at Comeback," *Sporting News*, December 24, 1942.

15. Quoted in Honig, *Baseball When the Grass Was Real*, 71–72.

16. We can only wonder if Mack ever considered that. Would he have started Ehmke in Game Two no matter the outcome of Game One?

17. Mickey Cochrane, "Cochrane Sees Earnshaw Facing Malone in Opening Contest of World Series," *Philadelphia Evening Public Ledger*, October 5, 1929.

18. Cochrane, "Cochrane Sees Earnshaw Facing Malone."

19. Quoted in Murray Tynan, "Ehmke Designated Himself to Pitch '29 Opener," *New York Herald Tribune*, September 29, 1931.

20. Quoted in Murray Robinson, "Speed Ball Aces Hopes of Teams in Pennant Tilt," *Standard Union* (Brooklyn), October 8, 1929.

21. Ehmke appeared in just eleven games and threw just 54⅔ innings in 1929.

22. "Miller, Ill with Cold, Insists He Will Play in Initial Contest; Homer Summa to Patrol Garden Should Bing Be Idle," *Philadelphia Evening Public Ledger*, October 8, 1929.

23. "Miller, Ill with Cold."

24. Quoted in Basenfelder, "Ehmke, Three Years with Dead Arm."

25. Quoted in Basenfelder, "Ehmke, Three Years with Dead Arm."

26. Basenfelder, "Ehmke, Three Years with Dead Arm."

27. Quoted in "Ehmke Tells How He Fooled Cubs," *Philadelphia Evening Public Ledger*, October 9, 1929.

28. Quoted in Basenfelder, "Ehmke, Three Years with Dead Arm."

29. Howard Ehmke, "'Every Fast Ball Hurt My Arm,' Says Ehmke after Great Victory," *Philadelphia Evening Bulletin*, October 9, 1929.

30. Quoted in Brandt, "The Pitchers' Arms," 130.

31. Quoted in Meany, *Baseball's Greatest Teams*, 54.

32. Ehmke is one of thirteen players whose photograph appears on the book jacket of the original edition of Carmichael, *My Greatest Day in Baseball*. He is pictured in an A's uniform preparing to throw an underhand pitch.

33. Quoted in Carmichael, *My Greatest Day in Baseball*, 218–19.

34. Quoted in Carmichael, *My Greatest Day in Baseball*, 220.

35. Quoted in Clifton Parker, *Bucketfoot Al*, 79–80.

39. Ehmke Sets World Series Record

1. Seymour, *Baseball*, 452.

2. Mickey Cochrane, "Fall Guys," 38.

3. Quoted in Jason Meisner, "Ex-Justice John Paul Stevens Coming Home for World Series," *Chicago Tribune*, October 27, 2016.

4. Quoted in Kuklick, *To Everything a Season*, 60–61.

5. Quoted in Brandt, "The Pitchers' Arms," 134.

6. Quoted in "Ehmke Tells How He Fooled Cubs," *Philadelphia Evening Public Ledger*, October 9, 1929.

7. Quoted in Gorman, *Double X*, 41.

8. The powerhouse Cubs were able to overcome the absence this season of Gabby Hartnett, who was the best catcher in the National League. A sore throwing arm limited him to only one game behind the plate and twenty-five pinch-hitting appearances in 1929.

9. Tolson batted .351 and .359 for the Pacific Coast League's Los Angeles Angels in 1928 and 1929 but never was a regular in parts of five seasons in the Major Leagues.

10. Quoted in Macht, *Connie Mack*, 538.

11. Howard Ehmke, "'Every Fast Ball Hurt My Arm,' Says Ehmke after Great Victory," *Philadelphia Evening Bulletin*, October 9, 1929. An article in the October 3, 1953, *Chicago Tribune* claimed Ehmke threw 145 pitches in the game.

12. Ehmke, "'Every Fast Ball Hurt My Arm.'"

13. Walsh struck out twelve Chicago Cubs in a two-hit, 3–0 win in Game Three of the 1906 World Series. Detroit's Bill Donovan struck out twelve Chicago Cubs in the opening game of the 1907 Series, and Washington's Walter Johnson struck out twelve New York Giants in the opening game of the 1924 Series, but Donovan and Johnson did so in twelve innings.

14. Ehmke struck out only twenty batters in 54⅔ innings in the regular season.
15. Ehmke's highest total for Philadelphia had been nine, in a twelve-inning game against Boston on July 2, 1926.
16. Quoted in Yeutter, "The Man Who Baffled the Cubs," 329.
17. Paxton, "They Stole the Series from the Stars," 96.
18. Joe Williams, By Joe Williams, *New York Evening Telegram*, October 9, 1929.
19. Mickey Cochrane, "Ehmke Calm and Cool on Mound," *Philadelphia Evening Public Ledger*, October 9, 1929.
20. Quoted in "Ehmke Tells How He Fooled Cubs."
21. Quoted in Billy Evans, "Trick Gives Mack Edge," *New York Evening Telegram*, October 9, 1929.
22. Yeutter, "The Man Who Baffled the Cubs," 305.
23. Quoted in Yeutter, "The Man Who Baffled the Cubs," 305.
24. Charlie Root, "'It Was Too Much Ehmke,' Root Figures," *Pittsburgh Post-Gazette*, October 9, 1929.
25. Quoted in Golenbock, *Wrigleyville*, 216.
26. Quoted in Golenbock, *Wrigleyville*, 216.
27. Quoted in Joe Williams, By Joe Williams, *New York Evening Telegram*, October 9, 1929.
28. Quoted in Ritter and Honig, *The Image of Their Greatness*, 116.
29. Cy Young, "Old Cy Young Lauds Ehmke," *New York Evening Telegram*, October 9, 1929.
30. Ty Cobb, "Mack's Strategy Stood Out in Opening World Series Contest, Ty Cobb Declares," *St. Louis Post-Dispatch*, October 9, 1929.
31. *Philadelphia Inquirer*, October 10, 1929.
32. Quoted in Alexander, *Rogers Hornsby*, 156–57. Hornsby also struck out in his first two at bats against Earnshaw in Game Three.
33. Chicago batters struck out fifty times, a record for a five-game Series that lasted until the 2018 Red Sox struck out fifty-three times. Nineteen of Boston's strikeouts came in Game Three, which lasted eighteen innings.
34. The only A's players with World Series experience were Quinn with the New York Yankees in 1921; reserve first baseman George Burns with the Cleveland Indians in 1920; and Eddie Collins with the Athletics in 1910–11 and 1913–14 and with the White Sox in 1917 and 1919.
35. Connie Mack, "Mack Won't Name First Pitcher until 15 Minutes before Opener," *Philadelphia Inquirer*, October 5, 1929.
36. Grimes had a 5-1 record with a 2.29 earned run average against the Cubs in 1929.
37. Joe McCarthy, "Quinn's Spitter May Worry Foe," *Philadelphia Inquirer*, October 4, 1929.
38. Quoted in Billy Evans, "Base Hits Replace Strategy As Macks Cop Third Victory," *Philadelphia Record*, October 11, 1929.

39. Al Simmons, "Power of Punch Proved in Victory," *Boston Globe*, October 11, 1929.

40. James C. Isaminger, "Macks Go into 7th Behind 8–0 and Score 10," *Philadelphia Inquirer*, October 13, 1929.

41. Philadelphia's ten runs in an inning broke the World Series record set by the New York Giants, who scored eight against the New York Yankees in the seventh inning of Game Three of the 1921 Series. The Detroit Tigers tied the A's record when they scored ten runs against the St. Louis Cardinals in the third inning of Game Six of the 1968 Series.

42. Clifton Parker, *Fouled Away*, 85.

43. Ehrgott, *Mr. Wrigley's Ball Club*, 206–7, 250–53.

44. Simmons, "Power of Punch Proved in Victory."

45. Quoted in Harvey J. Boyle, Mirrors of Sport, *Pittsburgh Gazette*, May 28, 1931.

46. "Jack Quinn Hopes to Round Out 30 Seasons as Pitcher in Professional Baseball," *Connellsville (PA) Daily Courier*, July 23, 1932.

47. Macht, *Connie Mack*, 554.

48. Quoted in "Ehmke Decided When He Would Pitch for the A's," *Boston Globe*, February 4, 1931.

49. Macht, *Connie Mack*, 554.

50. Quoted in Al Horwits, "Ehmke Feels Arm Is 'Burned Out,'" *Philadelphia Evening Public Ledger*, May 31, 1930.

51. Frick, "The Hero of the Series," 297.

52. Frick, "The Hero of the Series," 297.

53. Quoted in "Ehmke, Warming Up, Shows He Is in Trim to Pitch," *Boston Globe*, February 5, 1931.

40. "I Am Sorry to Have to Let Ehmke Go"

1. Kuklick, *To Everything a Season*, 61.

2. Quoted in Clifton Parker, *Bucketfoot Al*, 76.

3. Unsourced article in the Ehmke file at the National Baseball Hall of Fame and Library.

4. Quoted in Jack Orr, "An Oldtimer's Dream: 'Ehmke Now Pitching,'" *Philadelphia Daily News*, October 2, 1957.

5. Quoted in "Dykes Thinks Cubs Are Sweet Morsel for Macks," *Philadelphia Inquirer*, November 22, 1929.

6. "Dr. C. J. Van Ronk, 87, Treated Athletes," *New York Times*, July 22, 1975. Dr. Van Ronk treated, among others, Dizzy Dean, Tony Lazzeri, Lou Gehrig, Charlie Gehringer, Lefty Grove, and Jimmie Foxx.

7. Buffalo was only thirty-five miles from Silver Creek.

8. "World Series Hero Given Reception in Home Town," *Silver Creek (NY) News*, January 16, 1930.

9. Quoted in "World Series Hero Given Reception in Home Town."

10. Quoted in Al Horwits, "Ehmke to Pitch Again Next Year," *Philadelphia Evening Ledger*, November 29, 1929.

11. On November 1 in Baltimore, Ehmke was roughed up in a 14–7 exhibition loss by a team of Major Leaguers to the powerful American Negro League champions, the Baltimore Black Sox.

12. Henry P. Edwards, "Howard Ehmke Has Widest Variety of Mound Tricks," *Hartford Courant*, February 16, 1930.

13. Quoted in "Ehmke Develops Theory of Shadow Pitching to Aid Aging Whip," *Philadelphia Evening Public Ledger*, March 26, 1930.

14. "Farrell's 67 Ties Course Record at St. Augustine," *New York Herald Tribune*, February 14, 1930. It was Farrell who was primarily responsible for the win, as he tied the course record with a 67. Ehmke shot an 87. The National Open is now known as the U.S. Open. Farrell beat Bobby Jones in a playoff to claim his $500 first prize.

15. Ehmke gave up thirteen career homers to Ruth, tying him for third place with Lefty Stewart and Milt Gaston. Rube Walberg allowed the most (17), and Hooks Dauss was second (14).

16. The ten home runs hit by the two teams in game two of the doubleheader set a Major League World Series record, since broken.

17. With Ehmke's release, Quinn and catcher Grover Hartley of Cleveland were the only American Leaguers left who had played in the Federal League. By 1931 there were none.

18. Quoted in "Ehmke to Receive Release from A's," *Philadelphia Public Ledger*, May 31, 1930.

19. "Ehmke Whiffs 16, Beats Lancaster," *Philadelphia Public Ledger*, September 22, 1930.

20. The son's crime had been playing football in the street.

21. "Philadelphia Stages 'Outlaw' Ball Game," *New York Times*, September 29, 1930.

22. Quoted in "Ehmke Will Try Another Comeback," *Austin (TX) Statesman*, February 11, 1931.

23. "Mack Says Ehmke Can Pitch for A's," *Philadelphia Evening Bulletin*, March 18, 1931.

24. Quoted in "Howard Ehmke Says He Will Join Athletics within a Month," *Philadelphia Evening Bulletin*, April 13, 1931.

25. "New York Stars Win Two Games at Stadium," *New York Herald-Tribune*, May 11, 1931.

26. Levy, *Joe McCarthy*, 176.

27. Baumgartner pitched for both the Phillies and the A's. His last game was with the A's in 1926, just two weeks before Ehmke came to the club.

28. Stan Baumgartner, Just a Moment, *Philadelphia Inquirer*, July 28, 1931.

41. Defending Champions

1. Quoted in "Mack Favors Chi Sox [as Most Improved Team] during Race," *Altoona (PA) Mirror*, March 14, 1930.
2. Connie Mack, "Day Is Past When Champions Can Take Things for Granted," *Philadelphia Inquirer*, May 4, 1930.
3. Quoted in James C. Isaminger, "Five Young Mackmen to Stick with Team," *Philadelphia Inquirer*, March 27, 1930.
4. "Hill Climbing Helps Jack Quinn to Keep in Shape," *Hartford Courant*, February 16, 1930.
5. Because Fenway Park was located within one thousand feet of a religious edifice, Sunday baseball was not permitted there.
6. James C. O'Leary, "Jack Quinn Rescues World's Champions," *Boston Globe*, April 21, 1930.
7. Quinn gave up eleven earned runs in 9⅔ innings in those starts.
8. James C. Isaminger, "Quinn Hurls Ninth and Stifles Browns' Rally with Two on Bag," *Philadelphia Inquirer*, June 5, 1930.
9. Quinn gave up only one run in 5⅔ innings.
10. Anson did it three times in his final season (1897), at the age of forty-five.
11. Franco homered on August 13, 2005, ten days before his forty-seventh birthday. He hit a second home run in 2006 and a final one on May 4, 2007.
12. Leroy Boyer, "Quinn's Homer Record Broken," *Pottsville (PA) Republican and Herald*, April 22, 2006.
13. James C. Isaminger, "Quinn Hurls Macks to 4–1 Victory," *Philadelphia Inquirer*, July 24, 1930. Quinn walked the first two batters in the ninth and was relieved by George Earnshaw.
14. Hugh S. Fullerton, "Vet Pitchers Have Big Day against Foes," *Davenport (IA) Democrat*, July 24, 1930. The other pitchers Fullerton mentioned were Dolf Luque of Brooklyn, Red Faber of the White Sox, Eppa Rixey of the Reds, and Herb Pennock of the Yankees.
15. Quoted in Lane, "The Oldest Veteran in the Major Leagues," 444.
16. Quoted in "Baseball Helps the Jack Quinns Keep Young As They Celebrate Their 20th Wedding Anniversary," *Philadelphia Evening Bulletin*, November 6, 1930.
17. "Baseball Helps the Jack Quinns Keep Young."
18. While the losses were by the lopsided scores of 12–3 and 15–0, Quinn gave up only three earned runs in each game. The rest of the runs were charged to A's relief pitchers.
19. In the National League the Pirates' Babe Adams had better marks in 1919 and 1920, as did the Phillies' Pete Alexander in 1915 and 1917 and the Braves' Dick Rudolph in 1916.

20. Ed Pollock, "Grove Likely to Face Haines or Grimes in Series Opener," *Philadelphia Public Ledger*, September 29, 1930.

21. Quoted in Macht, *Connie Mack*, 579.

22. Cubs second baseman and leading hitter Rogers Hornsby broke his ankle in late May and appeared in only forty-two games.

23. James C. Isaminger, "Grimes May Hurl, So Mackmen Face Quinn," *Philadelphia Inquirer*, September 29, 1930.

24. Isaminger, "Grimes May Hurl."

25. Brian Bell, "Mack Baffles Experts Who Attempt to Learn His Starting Pitcher," *Elmira (NY) Star-Gazette*, October 1, 1930.

26. Mack, *My 66 Years in the Big Leagues*, 48.

27. Mickey Cochrane, "A's Catcher Lauds Pitching of Mack's Two-Man Staff," *Philadelphia Public Ledger*, October 7, 1930.

28. Earnshaw started Games Two (a 9–3 win in which he a departed in the fifth inning) and Three (a complete-game, 3–1 six-hitter) in the 1929 World Series and Games Five (pulled for a pinch hitter after seven scoreless innings) and Six (a complete-game, 7–1 five-hitter) in 1930.

29. Stan Baumgartner, Just a Moment, *Philadelphia Inquirer*, November 19, 1930.

30. Stoney McLinn, "Baseball Will Miss Jack Quinn, Not for Ability as Pitcher but for Mystery He Created," *Philadelphia Evening Public Ledger*, November 12, 1930.

31. Ed Pollock, Playing the Game, *Philadelphia Public Ledger*, November 12, 1930.

32. "Want Special Approval for Spitball Use," *Brandon (MB) Daily Sun*, December 4, 1930.

33. *Philadelphia Record*, November 13, 1930.

34. Quoted in "Jack Quinn Banks on Another Season in Major Company," *Syracuse Herald*, November 12, 1930.

35. Quoted in "Quinn to Seek Major Berth; Says He's Good for 15 Wins," *Washington Post*, November 13, 1930.

42. A New League, a New Role

1. Daher, "The Spitter Hits the Trail," 441. The remaining spitball pitchers were Red Faber, Burleigh Grimes, and Clarence Mitchell. A November 1930 article in Quinn's bio file at the Hall of Fame by St. Louis sportswriter Dick Farrington bluntly said if he was not claimed by a big league team, "Jack Quinn is out of luck."

2. Quoted in Murray Robinson, As You Like It, *Standard Union* (Brooklyn), March 24, 1931.

3. Henry Richards, "Aged Slabster Joins Robins for '31 Race," *Standard Union* (Brooklyn), February 10, 1931.

4. Although the team was known as the Dodgers for most of its years in Brooklyn, it was often called the Robins during Wilbert Robinson's tenure

as manager (1914–31) as a mark of affection for him. But as Robinson's tenure was coming to an end, the name "Dodgers" began to appear more often.

5. Cheney, Coombs, and Marquard won forty-four games in 1916. Doak won eleven games for Brooklyn in 1924.

6. W. Robinson, "How Robbie Makes Cast-Off Pitchers Win," 355–56.

7. Holmes, *Dodger Daze and Knights*, 55–56. Robinson also picked up veteran pitchers Joe Shaute from Cleveland and Fred Heimach from the Yankees. They would win a combined twenty games for the 1931 Dodgers. Holmes also wrote for the *Brooklyn Eagle* and covered the Dodgers for the *Sporting News*. His *Sporting News* byline was Tommy Holmes, the same as for his books. He was listed as Thomas Holmes in his *Brooklyn Eagle* columns.

8. Harvey J. Boyle, Mirrors of Sport, *Pittsburgh Gazette*, March 19, 1931.

9. Quoted in Murray Robinson, As You Like It, *Standard Union* (Brooklyn), March 6, 1931.

10. AP, *Abilene (TX) Morning News*, February 18, 1931.

11. Baseball's record books, including the annual *Who's Who*, still listed Quinn's date of birth as July 5, 1885.

12. "Jack Quinn Saved from Minors by Brooklyn Club," *Pittsburgh Gazette*, February 11, 1931.

13. Quoted in Richards, "Aged Slabster Joins Robins for '31 Race."

14. John Kieran, Sports of the Times, *New York Times*, February 12, 1931.

15. Joe Vila, "Ruppert Let Frazee Get Out from under Power Too Soon," *Sporting News*, December 29, 1921.

16. Frank O'Neill, "Yankees in Great Deal," *New York Sun*, December 21, 1921.

17. Even in 1929 Quinn started eighteen of his thirty-five game appearances.

18. Quoted in Edward T. Murphy, "Jack Quinn's Training Rules," *New York Sun*, March [date unknown], 1931.

19. Quoted in Thomas Holmes, "Rigid Training Rules Are Responsible for Veteran's Long Career," *Brooklyn Eagle*, March 8, 1931.

20. Quoted in Bunts, *Brooklyn Eagle*, March 5, 1931.

21. Quoted in Holmes, "Rigid Training Rules Are Responsible for Veteran's Long Career."

22. Thomas Holmes, "Brooklyn Dodgers Can Keep Nine Pitchers," *Brooklyn Eagle*, March 11, 1932.

23. Few star players had as circuitous a path to the starting lineup as Herman did. He went from Edmonton to Detroit to Reading to Omaha to Boston to Atlanta to Memphis to Boston to San Antonio to Little Rock to Seattle to Minneapolis before he settled in Brooklyn in 1926.

24. Arthur Daley, Sports of the Times, *New York Times*, April 17, 1961.

25. Holmes, *Dodger Daze and Knights*, 77.

26. Murray Robinson, As You Like It, *Standard Union* (Brooklyn), May 13, 1932.

27. Murray Robinson, As You Like It, *Standard Union* (Brooklyn), April 6, 1931.

28. Scribbled by Scribes, *Sporting News*, April 16, 1931.

29. John Kieran, Sports of the Times, *New York Times*, October 25, 1931.

30. Quoted in AP, *Abilene (TX) Morning News*, February 18, 1931.

31. Quoted in Thomas Holmes, "45-Year-Old Pitcher Outpitches Great Grove against His Old Mates," *Brooklyn Eagle*, March 19, 1931.

32. Quoted in John P. Carmichael, "Jack Quinn Rolls Back the Years," *Chicago Daily News*, chapter V, July 26, 1933.

33. Quoted in Harvey J. Boyle, Mirror of Sport, *Pittsburgh Gazette*, May 28, 1931.

34. Quoted in Henry Richards, "Luque Arrives at Clearwater; Expects Lombardi Friday," *Standard Union* (Brooklyn), March 3, 1931.

35. Quoted in William McCullough, "The Dazzler Accepts Club's $23,000 Offer," *Brooklyn Times*, March 31, 1931.

36. Quoted in *Brooklyn Eagle*, April 23, 1931.

37. The only Major Leaguer older than Quinn to play in 1931 was Cardinals manager Gabby Street. But he appeared in only one game with one at bat.

38. Thomas Holmes, "Quinn's First Effort Stamps Veteran as Strictly Relief Artist," *Brooklyn Eagle*, April 15, 1931.

39. Murray Robinson, As You Like It, *Standard Union* (Brooklyn), April 23, 1931.

40. Quoted in Thomas Holmes, "'Best Relief Pitcher in the Game' Is Shaute's Tribute to Quinn," *Brooklyn Eagle*, May 9, 1931.

41. Frank G. Menke, May 31, 1931; unsourced newspaper in Quinn family collection.

42. Firpo Marberry of the Senators had been a commanding finisher in the American League (53 saves from 1924 to 1926), and Wilcy Moore of the Yankees had a dominant 1927 season in relief (13 saves).

43. Quoted in Frank G. Menke, May 31, 1931; unsourced newspaper in Quinn family collection.

44. Thomas Holmes, "Herman's Long Hits Bring Jack Quinn under Victory Wire," *Brooklyn Eagle*, June 21, 1931. Quinn's previous National League win was for the Boston Braves on October 3, 1913, over the Dodgers.

45. Sid Mercer, "Old J. P. Quinn Finally Wins for Flatbush," *New York American*, June 20, 1931.

46. Roscoe McGowen, "Robins Win, 4–3, on Rally in Ninth," *New York Times*, July 6, 1931.

47. Quoted in Thomas Holmes, "Wally Rates Quinn and Mickey Finn as Great Robin Assets," *Brooklyn Eagle*, July 9, 1931.

48. Quoted in Will Wedge, "The Story of John P. Quinn," *New York Sun*, June 22, 1929.

49. George Earnshaw, "How to Throw a Slow Ball," *Philadelphia Inquirer*, February 22, 1931.

50. Thomas Holmes, "Jack Quinn Checks Late Rally As Mates Climb over Chicago," *Brooklyn Eagle*, July 19, 1931.
51. Quoted in Snelling, *Lefty O'Doul*, 93. After batting .398 and .383 in 1929 and 1930 respectively, O'Doul finished 1931 with a .336 batting average.
52. Quoted in Edward T. Murphy, "Jack Quinn's Arm Goes Lame," *New York Sun*, July 25, 1931.
53. "Has Father Time Stepped In?" *Brooklyn Eagle*, July 27, 1931.
54. Joseph Applegate, "30 Years on Mound and Still Stepping," *New York Evening Graphic*, August 15, 1931.
55. Murray Tynan, "Fratricidal Flatbush," *New York Herald-Tribune*, August 22, 1931.
56. Edward M. Darrow, "Poor Manipulation of Average Staff Reflects on Pilot," *Standard Union* (Brooklyn), September 16, 1931.
57. Quinn had not appeared in so many games since 1924, when he pitched in forty-four.
58. Holmes, *Dodger Daze and Knights*, 88.
59. Edward T. Murphy, "Jack Quinn's Good Record," *New York Sun*, August 25, 1931.
60. Thomas Holmes, "Robin Fledglings May Push Bressler off Flatbush Roster," *Brooklyn Eagle*, October 21, 1931.
61. Holmes, *Dodger Daze and Knights*, 88.

43. Extraordinary Career Comes to an End

1. Carey retired as a player after the 1929 season. He returned to Pittsburgh as a coach in 1930 but was out of baseball in 1931.
2. Graham, *The Brooklyn Dodgers*, 125.
3. The Dodgers, who also included Wally Gilbert in the deal, received Tony Cuccinello, Joe Stripp, and Clyde Sukeforth in the one-sided trade. Herman, who batted .340 in his six seasons with Brooklyn, went on to a number of productive seasons. Lombardi went on to a long and illustrious career that included a Most Valuable Player Award and two batting titles.
4. Murray Robinson, As You Like It, *Standard Union* (Brooklyn), April 9, 1932.
5. Hoyt did win forty-seven games after his release by Brooklyn, including a 15-6 season for the 1934 Pirates.
6. Graham, *The Brooklyn Dodgers*, 126.
7. Quoted in William McCullough, "Hack Is Leading Club at Hitting with .311 Mark," *Brooklyn Times*, June 1, 1932. Wilson did bounce back and batted .297 with 23 home runs and 123 runs batted in. Hornsby was fired as Cubs manager in early August.
8. Grantland Rice, The Sportlight, *Boston Globe*, October 1, 1931.
9. Thomas Holmes, "Patriarch of Pitchers Gets a Break at Last in Depression Time," *Brooklyn Eagle*, January 20, 1932. Newspapers did not report specific figures but said Quinn was paid a small salary in 1931.

10. "Jack Quinn Hopes to Round Out 30 Seasons as Pitcher in Professional Baseball," *Connellsville (PA) Daily Courier*, July 23, 1932.

11. Roscoe McGowen, "Cubs Down Robins in Fourteenth, 7–5," *New York Times*, June 9, 1932.

12. Thomas Holmes, "Jack Quinn at 43, 47, or Even 52 Is Still a Mighty Handy Hurler," *Brooklyn Eagle*, July 5, 1932.

13. While the Dodgers were traveling to Chicago, the Cubs won two games and extended their lead to 3½ games.

14. William McCullough, "Coach Never Too Tired to Inspire Team," *Brooklyn Times*, August 23, 1932.

15. The series was titled "Lose with a Smile," and the stories were issued as a book the following year. Goldman, *Forging Genius*, 109–11.

16. Tommy Holmes, "Brooklyn Rainbow Fades Out in West," *Sporting News*, September 1, 1932.

17. Thomas Holmes, "Manager Carey Employs Safety First Method to Assure Third Place," *Brooklyn Eagle*, September 23, 1932.

18. Quoted in Edward T. Murphy, "Quinn Hopes to Return for '33," *New York Sun*, September 22, 1932.

19. "The Baseball Players' Paradise," *Sporting News*, February 9, 1933.

20. Quoted in "One More Season and Old Jack Will Say, 'I'm All Through,'" *Hot Springs New Era*, February 16, 1934.

21. Gordon Mackay, Is Zat So, *Camden (NJ) Courier-Post*, February 23, 1933.

22. Thomas Holmes, "Quinn, Rosenfeld, Day, Lombardi, and Gallivan Make Grade," *Brooklyn Eagle*, April 5, 1931.

23. H. Johnson, *Who's Who in Major League Baseball*, 324.

24. Applegate, "30 Years on Mound and Still Stepping."

25. Thirty-five-year-old Rosy Ryan, who pitched six seasons for the New York Giants, was slated to take Quinn's place in the bullpen.

26. James J. Long, "Farewells to Slab Vet Out of Order," *Pittsburgh Sun-Telegraph*, May 4, 1933.

27. Jack Ryder, "Reds Slam Ball to Beat Braves," *Cincinnati Enquirer*, July 8, 1933.

28. Red Cole, Talk of the Times, *Tampa Times*, July 15, 1933.

29. Chester L. Smith, "A Long Career, and a Merry One, Ends for John Picus," *Pittsburgh Press*, July 16, 1933. The refrain of Alfred Lord Tennyson's "The Brook" ends with "For men may come and men may go, But I go on forever."

44. A Full and Happy Retirement

1. For more information on the use of field coverings in early baseball, see Morris, *A Game of Inches*, 2:61–63, and Steinberg, "Robert Lee Hedges."

2. Quoted in McKeon, "Ehmke Developed the First Infield Tarpaulin," 22. The company, of which Ehmke was the president, was located on the

first two floors of a factory building at Eighth and Somerset Streets in Philadelphia.

3. Seen and Heard at the Major Meetings, *Sporting News*, December 20, 1934.

4. Don Basenfelder, "Ehmke, Three Years with Dead Arm, Tells 'Inside' of Whiffing 13 Cubs in '29 Series, Using 'Nothing Ball,'" *Sporting News*, December 17, 1936.

5. "Status of Retired Players," *Sporting News*, March 2, 1933.

6. Dick Farrington, "Lifetime Passes Issued to 403 Vets, Including 17 in Majors for 20 Years," *Sporting News*, April 30, 1936.

7. "Jack Colberg Winning Laurels at Penn Games," *Silver Creek (NY) News and Times*, January 28, 1943. In a July 3, 2017, email Ehmke family historian Sheryl Lucas said Colberg was Howard's second cousin once removed.

8. Quoted in Ed Pollock, Playing the Game, *Philadelphia Evening Bulletin*, April 25, 1952.

9. In May 1954 Ehmke served as a pallbearer for Chief Bender, the A's former star pitcher.

10. Quoted in Art Morrow, "300 Toast Absent Connie at His 93rd Birthday Party," *Sporting News*, November 30, 1955.

11. Izzy Katzman, "Ehmke Shines in A's Old-Timers Contest," *Sporting News*, August 16, 1950.

12. Earl Vann, On the Vannwagon, *Baltimore Afro-American*, May 3, 1958.

13. Smith, *To Absent Friends from Red Smith*, 331.

14. A letter writer in a subsequent edition of the *Sporting News* pointed out that the ball had not been hit back to Ehmke but to third baseman Howard Shanks.

15. Quoted in "No-Hit Spoiler Witt Renews Acquaintance with Ehmke," *Sporting News*, February 24, 1954.

16. Douglas Corrigan was an American aviator. He was nicknamed "Wrong Way" in 1938. After a transcontinental flight from Long Beach, California, to New York City, he flew from Floyd Bennett Field in Brooklyn, New York, to Ireland, though his flight plan was filed to return to Long Beach. The *Buffalo Courier-Express* article was reprinted in "Local Ball Player Gains Recognition," *Silver Creek (NY) News and Times*, September 28, 1939.

17. Dan Daniel, Over the Fence, *Sporting News*, October 16, 1941. Davis was 13-7 on the season, but in choosing him, Durocher bypassed twenty-two-game winners Whit Wyatt and Kirby Higbe.

18. Fred Lieb, "Cardinals Licked on Lack of One Real Spark Plug," *Sporting News*, October 14, 1943.

19. Konstanty had appeared in a then record seventy-four games during the 1950 season, all in relief. Although he had not started a Major League game since 1946, he allowed just one run in eight innings, but the Yankees' Vic Raschi held the Phillies to two hits in defeating them, 1-0.

20. Jack Hand, "Konstanty, Biggest Series Gamble since Ehmke, Faces Yanks in Opener," *Wilkes Barre (pa) Times Leader*, October 4, 1950.

21. "American League Forbids 'Hesitation Pitch,'" *Sporting News*, July 28, 1948.

22. Sandy Koufax of the Los Angeles Dodgers broke Erskine's record when he struck out fifteen Yankees in 1963. Bob Gibson of the St. Louis Cardinals, the current record holder, broke Koufax's record when he struck out seventeen Detroit Tigers in 1968. As with Ehmke, Koufax's and Gibson's record-breaking performances came in Game One. Similarly Roy Campanella, Erskine's catcher, had fourteen putouts, tying Ehmke's catcher Mickey Cochrane's record.

23. "Battery Strikes Out While Ehmke Listens," *New York Times*, October 3, 1953.

24. Quoted in "Battery Strikes Out While Ehmke Listens."

25. Quoted in "Battery Strikes Out While Ehmke Listens."

26. Quoted in Bill Roeder, "Old Ehmke Was Pulling against Carl," *New York World-Telegram and Sun*, October 3, 1953.

27. Quoted in Roeder, "Old Ehmke Was Pulling against Carl."

28. Carl Erskine, "Erskine Eased Dodger Backs off Series Wall," *Brooklyn Eagle*, October 3, 1953.

29. *Philadelphia Evening Bulletin*, April 28, 1959.

30. "Howard Ehmke, 1929 Series Hero, Dies at 65," *Washington Post*, March 18, 1959.

31. Robert P. Galloway, "Recollections of Howard Ehmke," *Lake Shore News and Times* (Silver Creek ny), March 26, 1959.

32. Letter from J. Malcolm Henderson to Stanley L. Thornton, August 22, 1968. King of Prussia is a suburb of Philadelphia, located in Montgomery County.

33. Ehmke had his greatest support in 1960, when he received twelve votes. No players were elected that year, but Ehmke had more votes than future Hall of Famers Earl Averill, Leo Durocher, Rick Ferrell, Joe Gordon, Travis Jackson, Addie Joss, George Kelly, Ralph Kiner, Freddie Lindstrom, Ernie Lombardi, and Arky Vaughan.

34. Quoted in unsourced article in the Ehmke file at the National Baseball Hall of Fame and Library.

35. Quoted in Carmichael, *My Greatest Day in Baseball*, 219.

36. Bill Dooly, "Heroes Clad in Mufti Flit beneath Stands Now Gaunt and Silent," *Philadelphia Record*, October 16, 1929.

37. Quoted in Jack Orr, "An Oldtimer's Dream: 'Ehmke Now Pitching,'" *Philadelphia Daily News*, October 2, 1957.

45. A Sad and Bitter End

1. Gmelch, *Inside Pitch*, 173–96.

2. Quoted in Gmelch, *Inside Pitch*, 181.

3. Quoted in Gmelch, *Inside Pitch*, 188.

4. *Chicago Tribune*, July 24, 1933. In an interview in that issue of the *Tribune*, Quinn said Ty Cobb gave him the most trouble as a batter, followed by Joe Jackson. *Retrosheet*, whose pitcher-batter matchups are a work in progress, shows that Cobb hit .382 and Jackson hit .389 against Quinn. Tioga George Burns (.380) and Earle Combs (.408) also had great success against him.

5. Quoted in C. William Duncan, "Jack Quinn, the Modern Ponce de Leon," *Nebraska State Journal*, September 25, 1933.

6. Quoted in "Jack Quinn, Pitcher, Is Brief Rapid City Visitor," *Rapid City Journal*, August 19, 1933.

7. As discussed above, Major League baseball had grandfathered pre-1920 spitball pitchers after the 1920 season. By 1934 only Burleigh Grimes remained active from this group. The Pacific Coast League grandfathered a few pitchers, most notably Frank Shellenback of the 1919 White Sox, who won 316 Minor League games, more than half of them for Hollywood.

8. The 1934 Angels posted a 137-50 record and are considered the greatest Minor League team of all time, according to historians Bill Weiss and Marshall Wright. Minor League Baseball, www.milb.com/milb/history/top100.jsp.

9. *Salt Lake Tribune*, February 18, 1934. Spitballer Clarence Mitchell also was allowed to pitch in the league and won nineteen games for the Mission Reds in 1933.

10. John Connolly, "Half of Coast Spitball Dispute Ends, Quinn Out," *Sporting News*, May 17, 1934.

11. "Colonels Play Coals Today in Doubleheader," *Chicago Tribune*, June 10, 1934.

12. Both Quinn and Vaughn pitched about once a week, for which they each earned $50. "Five Former Major League Slab Stars Still Hurling," *Decatur (IL) Herald*, July 15, 1934.

13. Two more former A's teammates were on the White Sox, George Earnshaw and Al Simmons.

14. For an overview of this sect and its team, see Skipper, *Wicked Curve*, 152–57.

15. Skipper, *Wicked Curve*, 158–65.

16. Kavanagh, *Ol' Pete*, 140, 141, and 149–50.

17. "Veteran Big Leaguer Accepts Contract of Johnstown Club," *Johnstown (PA) Democrat*, July 16, 1935. Johnstown was less than sixty miles from where Quinn began his career, in Dunbar and Connellsville.

18. News, Views and Comments, *Johnstown (PA) Democrat*; Quinn family collection.

19. Lobby Notes, *Philadelphia Inquirer*, December 11, 1935.

20. George S. Cooper, "Inside Story of Jack Quinn's Resignation," *Johnstown Daily Tribune*, September 6, 1935. This account said Quinn resented the

club's addition of player Dick Goldberg, who caused leadership friction in the clubhouse.

21. "Jack Quinn, Famous Hurler, Recalls His 30 Years in Baseball," *Fort Dodge (IA) Messenger*, May 21, 1936. This article reported that the House of David had both an Eastern team, managed by Quinn, and a Western one, managed by Alexander, in 1936.

22. Quoted in Franklin Yeutter, The Sports Parade, *Philadelphia Evening Bulletin*, December 7, 1939.

23. *Philadelphia Evening Bulletin*, November 6, 1930.

24. Letter from Warren Blim, MD, August 18, 1940; Quinn family collection.

25. Phone interview by Steve Steinberg with Marcella (Sally) Athmann, December 16, 2000.

26. Michael Picus's granddaughters, Lois Nevinski and Laurie Athmann, live in Minnesota. Steve Steinberg visited Athmann and reviewed the Quinn family collection in 2006.

27. Phone interview by Steve Steinberg with Cleona Picus, December 16, 2000. Steinberg visited her in 2006 in the original family home on Mt. Hope Avenue.

28. Fred Lieb, Cutting the Plate with Fred Lieb, *New York Evening Post*, June 29, 1927.

29. Email from Father Evans to Steve Steinberg, January 31, 2001.

30. The Jupina family owned a funeral parlor in Pottsville that handled the funerals of Gene and Jack Quinn. In emails to Steve Steinberg in December 2000 and January 2001, Michael Jupina explained he was both a Philadelphia policeman and nurse, the first male RN in the United States who was also a policeman. See Acel Moore, "Nurse-Policeman Acts as Both on Duty in Emergency Wagon," *Philadelphia Inquirer*, July 7, 1968.

31. Quoted in Hanson, "Joe Boley."

32. John Kieran, Sports of the Times, *New York Times*, May 21, 1936.

33. It is possible the family could not afford a headstone. It is also possible that Quinn's mother was buried next to one of the abandoned mining camps in the area. Jack's father, Michael (1852–1926), and his second wife, Anastasia (1866–1955), are buried in the Immaculate Conception Slovak Cemetery in nearby St. Clair.

34. Quinn family collection. Quinn signed his name on these government forms as "John Quinn Picus."

35. Herbert Allan, "54 Years Old and Going Strong—in Baseball," *New York Evening Post*, December 21, 1934.

36. Quoted in Homer Thorne, "Quinn, at 43, Does Tricks with Horsehide," *New York Evening Post*, August 17, 1928.

37. Frank Graham, Graham's Corner, *New York Journal-American*, April 23, 1946.

38. Neyer and Epstein, *Baseball Dynasties*, 117.
39. Including the 101 games he won in the Minors, Quinn won 348 professional baseball games.
40. The others are Lefty Grove, Charlie Hough, Waite Hoyt, and John Smoltz. Two of the four were Quinn's teammates (Grove and Hoyt).
41. James, *The New Bill James Historical Baseball Abstract*, 863. Quinn had 111 Win Shares, Phil Niekro 110, Hoyt Wilhelm 102, Cy Young 88, and Nolan Ryan 80.
42. Bill Dooly, "Jack Quinn, in Harness for Quarter Century, Is Best of A's Moundmen," *Philadelphia Record*, July 22, 1928.
43. Grantland Rice, The Sportlight, *Atlanta Constitution*, May 4, 1933.

BIBLIOGRAPHY

Alexander, Charles C. *John McGraw*. New York: Viking, 1988.

———. *The Miracle Braves, 1914–1916*. Jefferson NC: McFarland, 2015.

———. *Rogers Hornsby*. New York: Henry Holt, 1995.

———. *Spoke: A Biography of Tris Speaker*. Dallas: Southern Methodist University Press, 2007.

———. *Ty Cobb*. New York: Oxford University Press, 1984.

Allen, Lee. *Cooperstown Corner: Columns from the Sporting News*. Cleveland: Society for American Baseball Research, 1990.

Amore, Dom. *A Franchise on the Rise: The First Twenty Years of the New York Yankees*. New York: Sports Publishing, 2018.

Anderson, David W. "Bonesetter Reese." SABR BioProject. sabr.org /bioproject.

Applegate, Joseph. "30 Years on Mound and Still Stepping." *New York Graphic Magazine*, August 15, 1931.

Archdeacon, Thomas J. *Becoming American: An Ethnic History*. New York: Free Press, 1983.

Bak, Richard. *Peach: Ty Cobb in His Time and Ours*. Ann Arbor MI: Sports Media Group, 2005.

Baldassaro, Larry, and Richard A. Johnson, eds. *The American Game: Baseball and Ethnicity*. Carbondale: Southern Illinois University Press, 2002.

Bauer, Carlos. "1918, the Year the PCL Threw in the Towel." http:// minorleagueresearcher.blogspot.com/2006/01/1918-year-pcl-threw-in -towel.html.

———. "1918, the Year the PCL Threw in the Towel, Part Two." http:// minorleagueresearcher.blogspot.com/2006/01/1918-part-two.html.

Berkow, Ira. *Red: A Biography of Red Smith, The Life and Death of a Great American Writer*. New York: Times Books, 1986.

Berry, Henry, and Harold Berry. *Boston Red Sox: The Complete Record of Red Sox Baseball*. New York: Macmillan, 1984.

Bevis, Charlie. *Mickey Cochrane: Baseball Hall of Fame Catcher*. Jefferson NC: McFarland, 1998.

Bjarkman, Peter O., ed. *Encyclopedia of Major League Baseball Team Histories: American League*. Westport CT: Meckler Publishing, 1991.

———, ed. *Encyclopedia of Major League Baseball Team Histories: National League*. Westport CT: Meckler Publishing, 1991.

Blaeuer, Mark. *Baseball in Hot Springs: Images of Baseball*. Charleston SC: Arcadia Publishing, 2016.

Blaisdell, Lowell. "Judge Landis Takes a Different Approach: The 1917 Fixing Scandal between Detroit and the Chicago White Sox." *Nine: A Journal of Baseball History and Culture* 15, no. 2 (Spring 2007).

Bloodgood, Clifford. "The Vanishing Spit Ball Pitchers." *Baseball Magazine*, June 1927, 318 (2 pp.).

Brandt, William E. "The Pitchers' Arms." *Saturday Evening Post*, August 23, 1930, 41 (4 pp.).

Broun, Heywood. "It Seems to Heywood Broun." *Nation*, October 23, 1929, 457.

Brown, Warren. *The Chicago Cubs*. Carbondale: Southern Illinois University Press, 2001. Originally published by G. P. Putnam's Sons, 1946.

———. *The Chicago White Sox*. New York: G. P. Putnam's Sons, 1952.

Browning, Reed. *Baseball's Greatest Season, 1924*. Amherst: University of Massachusetts Press, 2005.

Carmichael, John P., ed. *My Greatest Day in Baseball: Forty-Seven Dramatic Stories by Forty-Seven Stars*. New York: A. S. Barnes, 1945.

Carney, Gene. *Burying the Black Sox: How Baseball's Cover-Up of the 1919 World Series Fix Almost Succeeded*. Dulles VA: Potomac Books, 2006.

Clark, Ellery H., Jr. *Red Sox Fever*. Hicksville NY: Exposition Press, 1979.

———. *Red Sox Forever*. Hicksville NY: Exposition Press, 1977.

Cobb, Ty. "Baseball Tricks That Won Me Ball Games." *Life*, March 24, 1952.

———. "They Ruined Baseball." *Life*, March 17, 1952.

———. "What I Think of My New Job." *Baseball Magazine*, August 1921, 387 (3 pp.).

Coberly, Rich. *The No-Hit Hall of Fame: No Hitters of the 20th Century*. Newport Beach: Triple Play Productions, 1985.

Cochrane, Mickey, as told to Richard McCann. "Fall Guys." *Saturday Evening Post*, October 8, 1938, 20 (3 pp.).

Collins, Rip. "Was Ty a Bad Manager?" *Baseball Magazine*, April 1930, 493–94.

Constantelos, Stephen. "George Stovall." SABR BioProject. sabr.org/bioproject.

Cooper, Brian E. *Red Faber: A Biography of the Hall of Fame Spitball Pitcher*. Jefferson NC: McFarland, 2007.

Corbett, Warren. "George Earnshaw." SABR BioProject. sabr.org/bioproject.

Costello, Rory. "Bob Quinn." SABR BioProject. sabr.org/bioproject.

Cottrell, Robert A. *Blackball, the Black Sox and the Babe: Baseball's Crucial 1920 Season*. Jefferson NC: McFarland, 2002.

Creason, Glen. "City Dig: Vernon May Be Boring Now, but in the Early 1900s It Was Bumping." *Los Angeles Magazine*, March 2, 2016. www.lamag.com

/citythinkingblog/citydig-vernon-may-be-boring-now-but-in-the early
-1900s-it was-bumping.

Curran, William. *Big Sticks: The Batting Revolution of the Twenties.* New York: William Morrow, 1990.

———. *Strikeout: A Celebration of the Art of Pitching.* New York: Crown, 1995.

D'Addona, Dan. "Harry Heilmann." SABR BioProject. sabr.org/bioproject.

Daher, Naiph J. "The Spitter Hits the Trail." *Baseball Magazine*, March 1931, 441–42.

Daley, Arthur. *Inside Baseball: A Half Century of the National Game.* New York: Grosset and Dunlap, 1950.

Daniel, W. Harrison. *Jimmie Foxx: The Life and Times of a Baseball Hall of Famer, 1907–1967.* Jefferson NC: McFarland, 2004.

Daniel, W. Harrison, and Scott P. Mayer. *Baseball and Richmond: A History of the Professional Game, 1884–2000.* Jefferson NC: McFarland, 2003.

Dewey, Donald, and Nicholas Acocella. *The Ball Clubs.* New York: Harper Perennial, 1996.

———. *The Black Prince of Baseball: Hal Chase and the Mythology of the Game.* Wilmington DE: Sport Classic, 2004.

Dittmar, Joseph J. *Baseball Records Registry: The Best and Worst Single-Day Performances and the Stories Behind Them.* Jefferson NC: McFarland, 1997.

Edwards, Henry P. *American League Service Bureau.* New York: American League, February 1930.

Ehmke, Howard. "What a Pitcher Thinks about When He's on the Slab." *Baseball Magazine*, January 1926, 363 (2 pp.).

Ehrgott, Robert. *Mr. Wrigley's Ball Club: Chicago and the Cubs during the Jazz Age.* Lincoln: University of Nebraska Press, 2013.

Evans, John Whitney. "Jack Quinn: Stitching a Baseball Legend." Paper delivered at the American Catholic Historical Association annual meeting, Charlottesville VA, 1994.

Faber, Charles F. "Jack Quinn." SABR BioProject. sabr.org/bioproject.

Faber, Charles F., and Richard B. Faber. *Spitballers: The Last Legal Hurlers of the Wet One.* Jefferson NC: McFarland, 2006.

Felber, Bill. *Under Pallor, Under Shadow: The 1920 American League Pennant Race That Rattled and Rebuilt Baseball.* Lincoln: University of Nebraska Press, 2011.

Fleitz, David L. *Shoeless: The Life and Times of Joe Jackson.* Jefferson NC: McFarland, 2001.

Foster, John B., ed. *Spalding's Official Base Ball Guide, 1925.* New York: American Sports Publishing, 1925.

———, ed. *Spalding's Official Base Ball Guide, 1926.* New York: American Sports Publishing, 1926.

Fountain, Charles. *The Betrayal: The 1919 World Series and the Birth of Modern Baseball*. New York: Oxford University Press, 2016.

Foxx, Jimmie. "A Master Batter Discusses His Craft." *Baseball Magazine*, December 1929, 303 (2 pp.).

Frick, Ford. "The Hero of the Series." *Baseball Magazine*, December 1929, 297 (2 pp.).

Frommer, Harvey. *Baseball's Greatest Managers*. New York: Franklin Watts, 1985.

Fulton, Bob. *Top Ten Baseball Stats: Interesting Rankings of Managers, Umpires, and Teams*. Jefferson NC: McFarland, 2000.

Gallico, Paul. *The Golden People*. New York: Doubleday, 1965.

Gentile, Charlie. *The 1928 New York Yankees: The Return of Murderers' Row*. Lanham MD: Rowman and Littlefield, 2014.

Gies, Joseph, and Robert H. Shoemaker. *Stars of the Series: A Complete History of the World Series*. New York: Thomas Y. Crowell, 1965.

Ginsburg, Daniel E. *The Fix Is In: A History of Baseball Gambling and Game Fixing Scandals*. Jefferson NC: McFarland, 1995.

Gmelch, George. *Inside Pitch: Life in Professional Baseball*. Lincoln: Bison Books, 2006.

Goldman, Steven. *Forging Genius: The Making of Casey Stengel*. Washington DC: Potomac, 2007.

Golenbock, Peter. *Wrigleyville: A Magical History Tour of the Chicago Cubs*. New York: St. Martin's Press, 1996.

Gordon, Peter M. "Roger Peckinpaugh." SABR BioProject. sabr.org/bioproject.

Gorman, Bob. *Double X: The Story of Jimmie Foxx—Baseball's Forgotten Slugger*. New York: Bill Goff, 1990.

Gould, James M. "A Forecast of the Major League Pennant Races." *Baseball Magazine*, May 1929, 535 (4 pp.).

———. "Who Will Win the Big League Pennants in 1926?" *Baseball Magazine*, May 1926, 531–33.

Graham, Frank. *The Brooklyn Dodgers: An Informal History*. Carbondale: Southern Illinois University Press, 2002. Originally published by G. P. Putnam's Sons, 1945.

———. *The New York Yankees: An Informal History*. New York: G. P. Putnam's Sons, 1948.

Green, Paul. *Forgotten Fields*. Waupaca WI: Parker Publications, 1984.

Greene, Nelson "Chip." "Jack Fournier." SABR BioProject. sabr.org/bioproject.

Hanson, Darrell. "Joe Boley." SABR BioProject. sabr.org/bioproject.

Hauser, Chris. "Al Orth." SABR BioProject. sabr.org/bioproject.

Heyn, Ernest V. *Twelve Sports Immortals*. New York: Bartholomew House, 1951.

Hoefer, W. R. "Cutting the Corners: Old Jack Quinn." *Baseball Magazine*, July 1927, 344.

———. "Will Ty Make Good as a Manager?" *Baseball Magazine*, February 1921, 419 (4 pp.).

Holmes, Tommy. *Dodger Daze and Knights: Enough of a Ball Club's History to Explain Its Reputation*. New York: David McKay, 1953.

Honig, Donald. *Baseball When the Grass Was Real*. New York: Berkley Publishing, 1975.

Hornbaker, Tim. *War on the Basepaths: The Definitive Biography of Ty Cobb*. New York: Sports Publishing, 2015.

Huhn, Rick. *Eddie Collins: A Baseball Biography*. Jefferson NC: McFarland, 2008.

Istorico, Ray. *Greatness in Waiting: An Illustrated History of the Early New York Yankees, 1903–1919*. Jefferson NC: McFarland, 2008.

James, Bill. *The New Bill James Historical Baseball Abstract*. New York: Free Press, 2001.

James, Bill, and Rob Neyer. *The Neyer/James Guide to Pitchers: An Historical Compendium of Pitching, Pitchers, and Pitches*. New York: Fireside Books, 2004.

Johnson, Harold Speed, ed. *Who's Who in Major League Baseball*. Chicago: Buxton, 1933.

Johnson, Lloyd, and Miles Wolff. *Encyclopedia of Minor League Baseball*, 3rd ed. Durham NC: Baseball America, 2007.

Jordan, David M. *The Athletics of Philadelphia: Connie Mack's White Elephants, 1901–1954*. Jefferson NC: McFarland, 1999.

Kahanowitz, Ian S. *Baseball Gods in Scandal: Ty Cobb, Tris Speaker, and the Dutch Leonard Affair*. South Orange NJ: Summer Game Books, 2019.

Kaplan, Jim. *Lefty Grove, American Original*. Cleveland: Society for American Baseball Research, 2000.

Kashatus, William C. *Connie Mack's '29 Triumph: The Rise and Fall of the Philadelphia Athletics Dynasty*. Jefferson, NC: McFarland, 1999.

———. *Diamonds in the Coalfields: 21 Remarkable Baseball Players, Managers, and Umpires from Northeast Pennsylvania*. Jefferson NC: McFarland, 2002.

Kavanagh, Jack. *Ol' Pete: The Grover Cleveland Alexander Story*. South Bend IN: Diamond Communications, 1996.

———. *Walter Johnson: A Life*. South Bend IN: Diamond Communications, 1995.

Kipfer, Barbara Ann, and Robert L. Chapman. *The Dictionary of American Slang*, 4th ed. New York: HarperCollins, 2007.

Kofoed, J. C. "The Hero of the 1921 World Series." *Baseball Magazine*, December 1921, 597 (3 pp.).

———. "The Youngsters of 1917." *Baseball Magazine* 19, no. 4, 433 (5 pp.).

Kohout, Martin. "George Stallings." SABR BioProject. sabr.org/bioproject.

Kuklick, Bruce. *To Everything a Season: Shibe Park and Urban Philadelphia, 1909–1976*. Princeton NJ: Princeton University Press, 1991.

Lane, F. C. "The Dean of American League Pitchers." *Baseball Magazine*, March 1927, 453 (4 pp.).

———. "The Extraordinary Career of Howard Ehmke." *Baseball Magazine*, May 1924, 545 (2 pp.).

———. "How the World's Series of 1929 Was Lost and Won." *Baseball Magazine*, December 1929, 299 (6 pp.).

———. "The Oldest Veteran in the Major Leagues." *Baseball Magazine*, September 1930, 443–44.

———. "Razzing Uncle Robbie." *Baseball Magazine*, September 1931, 437 (3 pp.).

———. "Some Angles of Pitching Psychology." *Baseball Magazine*, January 1937, 343 (3 pp.).

———. "The Toughest Break a Pitcher Ever Had." *Baseball Magazine*, November 1923, 551 (3 pp.).

Langford, Walter M. *Legends of Baseball: An Oral History of the Game's Golden Age.* South Bend IN: Diamond Communications, 1987.

Lansche, Jerry. *The Forgotten Championships: Postseason Baseball, 1882–1981.* Jefferson NC: McFarland, 1989.

Leeke, Jim. *From the Dugouts to the Trenches: Baseball during the Great War.* Lincoln: University of Nebraska Press, 2017.

Leerhsen, Charles. *Ty Cobb: A Terrible Beauty.* New York: Simon and Schuster, 2015.

Levitt, Daniel R. "Bill Essick." SABR BioProject. sabr.org/bioproject.

———. *The Outlaw League and the Battle That Forged Modern Baseball.* Chicago: Taylor Trade, 2014.

Levy, Alan H. *Joe McCarthy: Architect of the Yankee Dynasty.* Jefferson NC: McFarland, 2005.

Lieb, Fred. *Baseball As I Have Known It.* Lincoln: University of Nebraska Press, 1996. Originally published by G. P. Putnam's Sons, 1977.

———. *The Baseball Story.* New York: G. P. Putnam's Sons, 1950.

———. *The Boston Red Sox.* New York: G. P. Putnam's Sons, 1947.

———. *Connie Mack: Grand Old Man of Baseball.* New York: G. P. Putnam's Sons, 1945.

———. *The Detroit Tigers.* New York: G. P. Putnam's Sons, 1946.

———. "Ten Outstanding Games of Major League History." In *1945 Baseball Register*, edited by J. G. Taylor Spink and Paul A. Rickart. St. Louis: Sporting News, 1945.

Light, Jonathan Fraser. *The Cultural Encyclopedia of Baseball.* Jefferson NC: McFarland, 1997.

Louisa, Angelo J. *The Pirates Unraveled: Pittsburgh's 1926 Season.* Jefferson NC: McFarland, 2015.

Lowry, Philip J. *Green Cathedrals: The Ultimate Celebration of Major League and Negro League Ballparks*. New York: Walker, 2006.

Lynch, Michael T. *Harry Frazee, Ban Johnson, and the Feud That Nearly Destroyed the American League*. Jefferson NC: McFarland, 2008.

Macht, Norman. *Connie Mack: The Turbulent and Triumphant Years, 1915–1931*. Lincoln: University of Nebraska Press, 2012.

Mack, Connie. *My 66 Years in the Big Leagues: The Great Story of America's National Game*. Philadelphia: John C. Winston, 1950.

Mack, Connie, with Al Horwits. "Winning 'Em in the Clubhouse." *Saturday Evening Post*, October 1, 1938, 20 (6 pp.).

Mahl, Tom E. *The Spitball Knuckleball Book: How They Are Thrown [and] Those Who Threw Them*. Elyria OH: Trick Pitch Press, 2008.

McCallum, John D. *Ty Cobb*. New York: Praeger, 1975.

McKenna, Brian. "Frank Shellenback." SABR BioProject. sabr.org/bioproject.

———. "Pop Dillon." SABR BioProject. sabr.org/bioproject.

McKeon, John. "Ehmke Developed the First Infield Tarpaulin." *Diehard* 10, no. 3 (March 1995): 22.

McMurray, John. "Jimmy Austin." SABR BioProject. sabr.org/bioproject.

McNeil, William F. *The Dodgers Encyclopedia*. Champaign IL: Sports Publishing, 2003.

———. *The Evolution of Pitching in Major League Baseball*. Jefferson NC: McFarland, 2006.

McPherson, Steven. "Bill James." SABR BioProject. sabr.org/bioproject.

Mead, Bill. *Two Spectacular Seasons: 1930, the Year the Hitters Ran Wild; 1968, the Year the Pitchers Took Revenge*. New York: MacMillan, 1990.

Meany, Tom. *Baseball's Greatest Hitters*. New York: A. S. Barnes, 1950.

———. *Baseball's Greatest Teams*. New York: A. S. Barnes, 1949.

———. *The Yankee Story*. New York: E. P. Dutton, 1960.

Morgan, T. Kent, and David Jones. "Russ Ford." SABR BioProject. sabr.org/bioproject.

Morris, Peter. *A Game of Inches: Stories behind the Innovations That Shaped Baseball, the Game behind the Scenes*. Chicago: Ivan R. Dee, 2006.

———. *A Game of Inches: Stories behind the Innovations That Shaped Baseball, the Game on the Field*. Chicago: Ivan R. Dee, 2006.

Murdock, Eugene C. *Ban Johnson, Czar of Baseball*. Westport CT: Greenwood Press, 1982.

———. *Baseball between the Wars: Memories of the Game by the Men Who Played It*. Westport CT: Meckler Publishing, 1992.

Nack, William. "Lost in History." *Sports Illustrated*, August 19, 1996.

Neyer, Rob. "Was the Federal League Really a Major League?" National Pastime Museum. www.thenationalpastimemuseum.com/article/was-federal-league-really-major-league. Accessed July 26, 2020.

Neyer, Rob, and Eddie Epstein. *Baseball Dynasties: The Greatest Teams of All Time*. New York: W. W. Norton, 2000.

Nowlin, Bill. "Charlie Chech." SABR BioProject. sabr.org/bioproject.

———. "Dud Lee." SABR BioProject. sabr.org/bioproject.

———. "Ike Boone." SABR BioProject. sabr.org/bioproject.

———. "Johnny Mitchell." SABR BioProject. sabr.org/bioproject.

———, ed. *The Miracle Braves of 1914: Boston's Original Worst-to-First World Champions*. Phoenix: Society for American Baseball Research, 2014.

Okkonen, Marc. *The Ty Cobb Scrapbook: An Illustrated Chronology of Significant Dates in the 24-Year Career of the Fabled Georgia Peach*. New York: Sterling Publishing, 2001.

Okrent, Daniel, and Harris Lewine, eds. *The Ultimate Baseball Book*. Boston: Houghton Mifflin, 1979.

O'Neal, Bill. *The Pacific Coast League, 1903–1988*. Austin: Eakin, 1990.

Parker, Clifton Blue. *Bucketfoot Al: The Baseball Life of Al Simmons*. Jefferson NC: McFarland, 2011.

———. *Fouled Away: The Baseball Tragedy of Hack Wilson*. Jefferson NC: McFarland, 2011.

Paxton, Harry T. "They Stole the Series from the Stars." *Saturday Evening Post*, October 1, 1949, 28 (5 pp.).

Pope, Edwin. *Baseball's Greatest Managers*. New York: Doubleday, 1960.

Putnam, Christine. "Harry Wolverton." SABR BioProject. sabr.org/bioproject.

Rainey, Chris. "Lee Fohl." SABR BioProject. sabr.org/bioproject.

Reisler, Jim. *Babe Ruth: Launching the Legend*. New York: McGraw-Hill, 2004.

———. *Before They Were Bombers: The New York Yankees' Early Years, 1903–1915*. Jefferson NC: McFarland, 2002.

Rice, Grantland. "Here Come the Elephants." *Collier's*, July 20, 1929, 16–17.

———. "Talk about Iron Men." *Collier's*, June 15, 1929, 12.

Riess, Steven A. *City Games: The Evolution of American Urban Society and the Rise of Sports*. Urbana: University of Illinois Press, 1991.

———. *Touching Base: Professional Baseball and American Culture in the Progressive Era*. Urbana: University of Illinois Press, 1999.

Ritter, Lawrence S. *The Glory of Their Times: The Story of the Early Days of Baseball Told by the Men Who Played It*. New York: Quill, 1992.

Ritter, Lawrence, and Daniel Honig. *The Image of Their Greatness: An Illustrated History of Baseball from 1900 to the Present*. New York: Crown Publishers, 1979.

Robbins, Mike. *Ninety Feet from Fame: Close Calls with Baseball Immortality*. New York: Carroll and Graf, 2004.

Robinson, Ray. *Baseball's Most Colorful Managers*. New York: G. P. Putnam's Sons, 1969.

Robinson, Wilbert. "How Robbie Makes Cast-Off Pitchers Win." *Baseball Magazine*, January 1926, 355–56.

Romanowski, Jerome C. *The Mackmen*. Baseball Padre, self-published, 1979.

Rothe, Emil H. "Was the Federal League a Major League?" In *Baseball Research Journal*, 10th annual, 1–9. Cleveland: Society for American Baseball Research, 1981. Reprint, Manhattan KS: Ag Press, 1986.

Rubenstein, Bruce A. *Chicago in the World Series, 1903–2005: The Cubs and White Sox in Championship Play*. Jefferson NC: McFarland, 2006.

Ryhal, Gregory. "Frank Chance." SABR BioProject. sabr.org/bioproject.

"SABR Salute: Ellery Clark." Society for American Baseball Research. sabr.org /content/sabr-salute-ellery-clark.

Sagert, Kelly Boyer, and Rod Nelson. "Swede Risberg." SABR BioProject. sabr .org/bioproject.

Sallee, Paul, and Eric Sallee. "Steve Evans." SABR BioProject. sabr.org /bioproject.

Sanborn, Irving E. "The Decline of Curve Ball Pitching." *Baseball Magazine*, April 1924, 483–85.

Sawyer, C. F. "Old Timers Who Are Making Good." *Baseball Magazine*, May 1919, 281 (3 pp.).

Schacht, Al. *My Own Particular Screwball*. Garden City NY: Doubleday, 1955.

Schimler, Stuart. "Ed Walsh." SABR BioProject. sabr.org/bioproject.

Scott, E. Michael D. "John 'Jack Quinn' Picus: Not Polish, Not Welsh, and Not Born in America at All." *NINE: A Journal of Baseball History and Culture* 16, no. 2 (Spring 2008): 93–106.

Seymour, Harold. *Baseball: The Golden Age*. New York: Oxford University Press, 1971.

Sher, Jack. "Ty Cobb: The Georgia Peach." In *Twelve Sports Immortals*, edited by Ernest V. Heyn, 105–28. New York: Bartholomew House, 1951.

Shoemaker, Robert H. *The Best in Baseball*. New York: Thomas Y. Crowell, 1949.

Simpkins, Terry. "Kid Elberfeld." SABR BioProject. sabr.org/bioproject.

Simpson, William S., Jr. "1908: The Year Richmond Went 'Baseball Wild.'" *Virginia Cavalcade* 26, no. 4 (Spring 1977): 184–91.

Skipper, John C. *Dazzy Vance: A Biography of the Brooklyn Dodger Hall of Famer*. Jefferson NC: McFarland, 2007.

———. *Wicked Curve: The Life and Troubled Times of Grover Cleveland Alexander*. Jefferson NC: McFarland, 2006.

Smiles, Jack. *Big Ed Walsh: The Life and Times of a Spitballing Hall of Famer*. Jefferson NC: McFarland, 2008.

Smith, Red. *To Absent Friends from Red Smith*. New York: Atheneum, 1982.

Smith, Robert. *Baseball: The Game, the Men Who Have Played It, and Its Place in American Life*. New York: Simon and Schuster, 1947.

Snelling, Dennis. *The Greatest Minor League*. Jefferson NC: McFarland, 2012.

——. *Lefty O'Doul: Baseball's Forgotten Ambassador*. Lincoln: University of Nebraska Press, 2017.

Soivenski, Mitchell S. *New York Yankees Home Runs: A Comprehensive Factbook, 1903–2012*. Jefferson NC: McFarland, 2013.

Sowell, Mike. *The Pitch That Killed: Carl Mays, Ray Chapman and the Pennant Race of 1920*. New York: Macmillan, 1989.

Spalding, John E. *Pacific Coast League Stars: One Hundred of the Best, 1903–1957*. Manhattan KS: Ag Press, 1994.

——. *Pacific Coast League Stars*. Vol. 2, *Ninety Who Made It in the Majors, 1903–1957*. Manhattan KS: Ag Press, 1997.

Spatz, Lyle. *New York Yankees Openers: An Opening Day History of Baseball's Most Famous Team, 1903–2017*. Jefferson, NC: McFarland, 2018.

——. *Willie Keeler: From the Playgrounds of Brooklyn to the Hall of Fame*. Lanham MD: Rowman and Littlefield, 2015.

——. *Yankees Coming, Yankees Going: New York Yankee Player Transactions, 1903–1999*. Jefferson NC: McFarland, 2000.

Spatz, Lyle, and Steve Steinberg. *1921: The Yankees, the Giants, and the Battle for Baseball Supremacy in New York*. Lincoln: University of Nebraska Press, 2010.

Spink, J. G. Taylor. *Judge Landis and 25 Years of Baseball*. New York: Thomas Y. Crowell, 1947.

Stanton, Tom. *Ty and The Babe: Baseball's Fiercest Rivalry: A Surprising Friendship and the 1941 Has-Beens Golf Championship*. New York: Thomas Dunne Books, 2007.

Stein, Fred. "Al Simmons." SABR BioProject. sabr.org/bioproject.

Steinberg, Steve. "The Curse of the . . . Hurlers?" *Baseball Research Journal*, no. 35 (2006): 63–73.

——. "Robert Lee Hedges." SABR BioProject. sabr.org/bioproject.

——. "The Spitball and the End of the Deadball Era." *National Pastime*, no. 23 (2003): 7–17.

——. "The Spitball: 'Grandfathered' Spitball Pitchers." stevesteinberg.net /baseball_history/the_spitball/GrandfatheredSpitballPitchers.asp.

——. "World War I and Free Agency: The Fateful 1918 Battle for Jack Quinn." *NINE: A Journal of Baseball History and Culture* 16, no. 2 (Spring 2008): 84–92.

Steinberg, Steve, and Lyle Spatz. *The Colonel and Hug: The Partnership That Transformed the New York Yankees*. Lincoln: University of Nebraska Press, 2015.

Stockton, J. Roy. "Psychology and Strategy in the Recent World's Series." *Baseball Magazine*, December 1929, 291 (4 pp.).

Stout, Glenn, and Richard A. Johnson. *Red Sox Century: The Definitive History of Baseball's Most Storied Franchise.* Boston: Houghton Mifflin, 2000.

———. *Yankees Century: One Hundred Years of New York Yankee Baseball.* Boston: Houghton Mifflin, 2002.

Sutton, Larry, talking to Hugh Bradley. "I Have Bought $1,000,000 Worth of Men." *American Magazine,* February 1933, 44 (3 pp.).

Thomas, Henry W. *Walter Johnson: Baseball's Big Train.* Washington DC: Phenom Press, 1995.

Thorn, John, and John Holway. *The Pitcher.* New York: Simon and Schuster, 1987.

Walsh, Christy, ed. *Baseball's Greatest Lineup.* New York: A. S. Barnes, 1952.

Weber, Ralph E. Lin. *The Toledo Baseball Guide of the Mud Hens 1883–1943.* Rossford IL: Baseball Research Bureau, 1944.

Weintraub, Robert. *The House That Ruth Built: A New Stadium, the First Yankees Championship, and the Redemption of 1923.* New York: Little, Brown, 2011.

Wiggins, Robert Peyton. *The Federal League of Baseball Clubs: The History of an Outlaw Major League, 1914–1915.* Jefferson, NC: McFarland, 2009.

———. "1924: The Year the Yankees Lost the Pennant." Unpublished manuscript. Charlottesville VA, 2016.

Williams, Peter, ed. *The Joe Williams Baseball Reader: The Glorious Game, from Ty Cobb and Babe Ruth to the Amazin' Mets. 50 Years of Baseball Writing by the Celebrated Newspaper Columnist.* Chapel Hill NC: Algonquin, 1989.

Williams, Phil. "Boss Schmidt." SABR BioProject. sabr.org/bioproject.

———. "Ira Thomas." SABR BioProject. sabr.org/bioproject.

———. "Otto Knabe." SABR BioProject. sabr.org/bioproject.

Wolf, Gregory H. "Howard Ehmke." SABR BioProject. sabr.org/bioproject.

———. "Sam Gray." SABR BioProject. sabr.org/bioproject.

Wood, John A. *Beyond the Ballpark: The Honorable, Immoral, and Eccentric Lives of Baseball Legends.* Lanham MD: Rowman and Littlefield, 2016.

"World Series." *Time,* October 21, 1929, 66–67.

Yeutter, Franklin W. "The Man Who Baffled the Cubs." *Baseball Magazine,* December 1929, 305 (2 pp.).

Zatko, James J. "Early Beginnings of the Slovaks in America." *Slovakia* 15, no. 38 (1965): 1–37. Middletown PA: The Slovak of America.

INDEX

Page numbers in italics refer to illustrations.

Daley, George, 126, 249, 256

Daniel, Dan, 89, 114, 252, 265, 279, 343

Daniels, Bert, 364n35

Darmody, Tom, 88, 93, 95

Darrow, Edward, 330

Daubert, Jake, 378n5

Dauss, George "Hooks," 70, 73, 78–79, 130–31, *131*, 156, 174, 214–15, 413n6, 427n15

Davis, Curt, 343, 434n17

Deadball Era, 17, 31, 135, 310

Detroit Tigers: and batting averages, 145; Donie Bush traded from, 150; and Howard Ehmke, 67–84, 104–9, 130–38, 139–47, 150–56; and late season opener, 380n18; losing streak of, 387n13; and 1916 season, 70–75; and 1917 season, 76–84; and 1919 season, 104–9, 113–14; and 1920 season, 130–38; and 1921 season, 126, 139–47; and 1922 season, 151–56; and 1923 season, 174–75, 180, 186; and 1924 season, 198–99; and 1925 season, 214, 223–24; and 1926 season, 230, 236; and 1927 season, 247–50; and 1928 season, 261, 269–70; and 1929 season, 281; and 1930 season, 316–17; and spring training, 130, 150; trade deals by, 381n3; Ty Cobb managing, 139–50, 388n11; and the war, 101; and the White Sox case, 239–41, 386nn7–8

DeVormer, Al, 175–76, 397n6

Dillon, Frank "Pop," 36–39, 41, 43, 44, 45, 47, 48–50, 366n13

Dinneen, Bill, 83–84, 112, 183, 198, 267

Doak, Bill, 123, 322–23, 430n5

Donovan, Bill, 77–79, 114, 134, 374n8, 374n17, 424n13

Dooly, Bill: on Connie Mack, 243; on George Earnshaw, 254; on Howard Ehmke, 245–46, 256–57, 347; on Jack Quinn, 218, 257–58, 262, 265, 267, 274, 355; on Ossie Orwoll, 273; predictions by, 252; on Rochester deal, 59

double suicide squeeze, 249–50

Doyle, Jack, 85–86

Drebinger, John, 276

Duffy, Hugh, 149, *159*, 160–61, 163, 168, 179, 192

Duffy Florals, 349

Dugan, Joe, 153, 160, 171, 227, 263, 269, 381n10, 396n27

Dunbar, Bob, 176, 177, 180

Dunn, Jack, 254, 411n4, 414n12

Dunn Field, 79, 145, 249–50

Durocher, Leo, 343, 434n17

Dykes, Jimmy, 299, 309, 349

earned run average: of the American League, 135; of the Athletics (1926), 237; of Burleigh Grimes, 425n36; of Charlie Chech, 92, 366n25; of Eddie Cicotte, 382n23; of George Dauss, 130; of Grover Cleveland Alexander, 372n25; of Howard Ehmke, 53, 68, 108, 126, 147, 199, 201, 230, 248, 250, 263, 389n32; of Jack Quinn, 12, 17, 22, 23–24, 27–28, 59, 90, 93, 113, 115, 118, 120–21, 163, 196, 199, 200, 208, 216, 228, 235, 249, 251, 270, 284, 321, 333–34, 336, 375n1, 401n42; of Jim Bagby, 374n13; of Larry Jansen, 377n48; of Lefty Grove, 259, 286, 413n13, 416n40, 422n34; of the Red Sox (1923), 187; of Russ Ford, 19; of Sam Gray, 405n5; of Slim Harriss, 211; of Waite Hoyt, 331

home runs: allowed by Howard
Ehmke, 147, 427n15; by Al Orth,
17; by Al Simmons, 263, 276,
304, 306, 316; by Babe Ruth, 115,
124–26, 136–37, 171, 198, 244,
246, 248, 251, 266–67, 282, 312,
383n34, 389n29, 389n33, 413; by
Baby Doll Jacobson, 236; by Bing
Miller, 275; by Bob Meusel, 155;
by Cap Anson, 316; by Charles
Ruffing, 417n12; by Danny Murphy, 363n12; by Elmer Smith, 155;
by Frank Welch, 194, 231–32; by
George Pipgras, 312; by Hack
Wilson, 331, 432n7; by Harry
Davis, 363n12; by Harry Heilmann, 114; increase in (1920),
135; by Ira Flagstead, 194; by Jack
Quinn, 24–25, 28, 57, 117, 119,
126, 147, 316, 385n23, 389n35; by
Jimmie Foxx, 265, 299–300, 304,
316, 320; by John Ganzel, 364n25;
by Julio Franco, 316, 428n11; by
Ken Williams, 249; by Lou Gehrig, 246, 258, 267, 312; by Mule
Haas, 306; and nails in bats, 162;
by Red Sox (1923), 187; by Rube
Walberg, 413n6; by Val Picinich,
182; by Wally Pipp, 137, 192; and
World Series record, 427n16; at
Yankee Stadium, 171
Honig, Donald, 292
Hornbaker, Tim, 142, 145
Hornsby, Rogers: Charlie Grimm
replacing, 333; and Cubs preparation, 288–89; and exhibition
games, 139; firing of, 432n7;
against George Earnshaw,
425n32; against Howard Ehmke,
308–9; injury of, 429n22; and
taking over for the Cubs, 331;

and the World Series (1929), 299,
302–6
Hot Springs AR, 160–61, 167, 190,
206, 256, 271, 273, 315, 322, 334–35
House of David, 349–51, 437n21
Howley, Dan, 104, 130, 380n14
Hoyt, Waite: earned run average of,
341; and 1920 season, 117, 383n34;
and 1921 season, 124, 128–29, 146;
and 1922 season, 161; and 1923
season, 174; and 1924 season, 192;
and 1929 season, 274, 331, 432n5;
trade of, 385n10
Huggins, Miller: Connie Mack's
praise of, 251; detractors of, 114;
on George Halas, 111; and George
Mogridge, 110, 381n4; on Howard Ehmke, 78; and Jack Quinn,
96, 125–27, 229, 274; on Lefty
Grove, 237–38; on Lefty O'Doul,
111; and 1918 season, 110; and
1919 season, 114; and 1920 season, 116, 120–21; and 1921 season,
125–27, 146–47; and 1922 season,
149, 161; and 1923 season, 169;
and 1926 season, 226–27, 229;
and 1929 season, 277; and Paddy
O'Connor, 382n23; replacing Bill
Donovan, 374n8; and trade deals,
110, 149–50, 157, 381n4, 383n30;
and Waite Hoyt, 161, 383n34; and
the World Series (1929), 277
Hughes, Tom, 90, 364n24, 376n26
Huston, Til, 99, 157, 389n1

inside baseball, 135
International League: and Baltimore
Orioles, 58, 239, 285, 403n23;
and Buffalo Bisons, 58, 243; and
Dan Howley, 104, 380n14; first
season of, 364n26; and George

Earnshaw, 285; and Newark, 245; and Reading, 164; and Rochester Hustlers, 27; schedule of, 377n47

Irwin, Arthur, 12, *18*

Isaminger, James: on Al Simmons–Babe Ruth trade, 212; on the Athletics (1925), 221; on the Athletics (1929), 281–82; on coal mining, 7; on Howard Ehmke, 213, 229–30, 236, 243, 275, 281–82, 287; on Jack Quinn, 196, 220, 228–29, 266, 269, 274, 286, 316; on Mickey Cochrane, 279; on Ossie Orwoll, 254; on spitball pitching, 319; on the World Series (1929), 286, 291, 305

"It Seems to Me" column, 23

Jack Quinn Day, 112, 162, 209

Jackson, Joe, 83, 121, 374n27, 436n4

Jacksonville FL, 110

Jacobson, Baby Doll, 155, 229, 235–36

James, Bill, 20, 78, 237, 355

Jansen, Larry, 377n48

Jennings, Hughie, 70–71, 73, 76, 81–84, 104–6, 130, 132, 134–35, 138–40, 150–51

Johnson, Ban, 21, 96–99, 114–15, 162, 179, 183, 198, 362n37, 383n31, 389n1

Johnson, Ernie, 36

Johnson, George "Chief," 88–89

Johnson, Richard, 216

Johnson, Syl, 275

Johnson, Walter: and 1906 season, 366n13, 373n17; and 1910 season, 17, 20; and 1911 season, 24; and 1912 season, 26; and 1914 season, 37–40, 43; and 1916 season, 74–75, 374n27; and 1917 season, 77, 81, 83–84; and 1919 season, 105, 112; and 1920 season, 117, 133–34, 384n19; and 1921 season, 124; and 1924 season, 192, 198–99; and 1925 season, 408n17; and 1929 season, 275; and 1930 season, 319; and the World Series (1924), 424n13

Jones, Fielder, 77, 88

Jones, Sam, 149, 157, 160, 185, 197, 224, 389n6, 397n4

Joss, Addie, 77, 134, 373n4, 397n14

Judge, Joe, 228

Jupina, Michael, 353, 437n30

Karr, Benn, 155

Kashatus, William, 4–5, 358n29

Kauff, Benny, 78, 370n31

Kavanagh, Jack, 349

Keeler, Willie, 14, 17

Keener, Sid, 243

Kelly, Billy, 343

Kenefick, Bob, 133, 141

Kerr, Dickie, 100, 106, 120, 142, 379n31, 386n10

Kieran, John, 12, 169, 241, 257, 264, 323, 325, 354

Kinder, Ellis, 343

Klepfer, Ed, 79

Knabe, Otto, 56, 60, 370n28

Knight, Harry, 206–7

Koenig, Mark, 227, 267

Kofoed, J. C., 78, 128

Kolp, Ray, 336

Konstanty, Jim, 343–44, 434n19

Krapp, Gene, 52

Krause, Harry, 46

Lajoie, Napoleon "Nap," 19

Lamar, Bill, *212*

Lambert, Georgiana (Mrs. J. Quinn; Gene), 23, 112, 317, *350*, 351–52, 437n30

172–73; in Jacksonville, 380n16; and Lefty O'Doul, 381n10; and Miller Huggins, 374n8; and 1909 season, 14, 363n12; and 1910 season, 17–20; and 1910 team, *18*; and 1911 season, 23–26; and 1912 season, 26–28; and 1913 season, 28–30; and 1917 season, 79, 83; and 1918 season, 95–100; and 1919 season, 110–15, 382nn24–25, 383n34; and 1920 season, 116–22, 136–37; and 1921 season, 124–29, 143–47, 385n19; and 1922 season, 154–56, 161–63; and 1923 season, 169–73, 182–87; and 1924 season, 191–93, 195, 198–200; and 1925 season, 208–10, 215–16, 223; and 1926 season, 227–30, 232, 236; and 1927 season, 243–52; and 1928 season, 256, 258–61, 263–71; and 1929 season, 274–86, 288, 420n29, 422n34; and 1930 season, 312, 315–18; and salaries, 190; trade deals by, 148–49, 157–60, 323, 363n9, 364n27, 381n3, 385n10, 390n9, 395n43, 396n27, 397n6, 402n1, 403n23, 430n7; and the World Series (1921), 127–29, 426n41

Neyer, Rob, 60, 354

Nickerson, Herman, 175, 188

no-hitters, 11–12, 20, 102, 181–84, 193, 343, 347, 397n9, 397n14, 397nn3–4

Nolan, John J.: on the Athletics (1926), 230; on Howard Ehmke, 233, 236–37, 255, 259, 263, 279–81, 289; and Jack Quinn, 218–19, 249, 257

Oakland Oaks, 26

O'Connor, Paddy, 113, 382n23

O'Doul, Lefty: batting average of, 333, 377n38, 381n10, 432n51; career overview of, 381n10; and 1918 season, 91; and 1919 season, 111; and 1923 season, 172, 186–87; and 1931 season, 324, 329, 333; on service team, 102

Offermann, Frank J., 309

Oldham, Red, 145–46, 155

Old Sport, 206, 211, 217, 221–22, 235

Old Timer, 134–35

O'Leary, James, 163, 175, 192, 199

O'Loughlin, Silk, 26, 108, 380n32

O'Malley, Edwin, 91

O'Neill, Frank, 7, 125, 158, 323

O'Neill, Mike, 66–68, 372n14

O'Neill, Steve, 144, 190, 192, 372n14

Organized Baseball: and antitrust lawsuit, 61; and Buffalo Blues, 48–49; definition of, 359n2; and the Federal League, 46, 48–49, 54, 60–61, 367n14, 371n1; and Howard Ehmke, 45–46, 339; and Jack Quinn, 8–10, 95–96; and outlaws, 54; and reserve clause, 54, 94; and "ten-day notice" clause, 378n4; and the World Series (1919), 130, 240

Ormsby, Red, 181

O'Rourke, Frank, 160

O'Rourke, Joe, 349–51

Orth, Al, 12, 13, 16–17, 361n13

Orwoll, Ossie, 254, 261, 264, 267, *272*, 273, 414n10, 417n18, 417n20

Ott, Mel, 327

outlaw teams and leagues, 8–9, 54, 61, 360n25

overhand pitches, *80*, 141, 166, 214, 226, 373n10

Owens, Brick, 74, 156

227, 233, 237–38, 245, 247, 254,
257–59, 266, 268–70, 281, 285–86,
288–92, 297, 304, 315–20, 340,
343, 403nn22–23, 406n13, 407n37,
411n4, 411n32, 411n34, 413n13,
413n18, 416n40, 418n34, 418n44,
419n49, 422n34; and Mickey
Cochrane, 207, 211–12, 217, 222,
237, 261, 273, 279–81, 286, 288,
292, 295, 299–302, 307, 308, 320,
340, 403n23, 412n16, 421n6,
435n22; and 1910 season, 19–
20; and 1911 season, 24–25; and
1913 season, 31; and 1916 season,
72–73; and 1919 season, 106, 115;
and 1920 season, 118; and 1923
season, 171–72, 180, 181; and 1924
season, 1–2, 193–94; and 1925
season, 207–8, 211, 217–18, 220–
22; and 1926 season, 227–28, 233,
237; and 1927 season, 239–51; and
1928 season, 252–70; and 1929
season, 274, 275, 276–77, 278–87;
and 1930 season, 311–12, 315–21;
and no-hitters, 397n4; and pennants, 261–70, 286; and salaries,
243; and spring training, 226–27,
271–73; and the World Series
(1914), 58; and the World Series
(1929), 288–307; and the World
Series (1930), 319–20
Philadelphia Award, 308
Philadelphia Phillies, 10, 31, 70, 324,
332, 362n31, 370n18, 380n14,
381n10, 427n27
Phillips, Ernest A., 39
Picinich, Val, 182
Pickering, Myles, 304
Picus, Michael, 352
Piercy, Bill, 157–58, 175–76, 190, 194,
389n6, 391n5, 399n14

Pillette, Herman, 153–56, 175, 412n17
Pipgras, George, 182, 260, 266, 276,
312, 397n6, 418n34
Pipp, Wally, 137, 169, 192–93, 227,
385n19
Pittsburgh Pirates, 31, 286, 305, 332,
336, 372n6, 418n36, 432n5
Plank, Eddie, 60, 134, 297
playoff game (1948), 343
Poindexter, Marguerite (Mrs. H.
Ehmke), 108, 131, 206, 254, 293–
94, 303, 338, 341, 346
Pollock, Ed, 109, 174, 176, 215, 229,
268–69, 290, 319–20, 340
Polo Grounds, 79, 107, 112, 113–14,
127, 136, 144, 154, 185, 336, 382n14
Portland Beavers, 388n25
Pottsville team, *11*
Povich, Shirley, 257
Powers, John F. "Johnny," 63–64, 95,
371n4
Pratt, Del, 114, 164, 173, 180, 383n30,
385n10, 395n48, 396n32
Pullman AC, 8

Quinn, Bob, 179, 186, 188–91, 199,
202, 203, 208–9, 216, 225, 229, 231
Quinn, Georgiana (née Lambert;
Gene), 23, 112, 317, *350*, 351–52,
437n30
Quinn, Jack: on Babe Herman, 164;
and Babe Ruth, 115; and Baltimore Terrapins, 55–62; and
barnstorming, 382n22; batters
hit by, 127, 384n19; behavior of,
89; and Boston Braves, 31, 55, 57–
59, 61, 95, 326, 333, 369n6; and
Boston Red Sox, 157–63, 168–
69, 172–73, 186–87, 190–211, 213,
215–16; and Brooklyn Dodgers,
323–30, 332–37;

430n17; strikeouts by, 407n38; on success, 218–19; and Toledo Mud Hens, 9–10, 360n18; and trade deals, 59, 157–60, 389n6, 399n14; Tris Speaker on, 253; and Vernon Tigers, 85–93; and the Virginia League, 11–13; walks by, 407n37; and the World Series (1921), 128–29; and the World Series (1929), 288–90, 292–93, 305–6; and the World Series (1930), 319

trick pitches, 116, 124, 132, 135, 288, 399n20. *See also* emery ball; spitball
tunnel ball, 102
Tzar, Anastasia, 5–6

Uhle, George, 145, 227, 398n35
underhand pitches, 38, 44, 102, 141, 166, 171, 180, 192, 205, 214, 259, *280*, 293, 373n10

Valo, Elmer, 353
Vance, Dazzy, 67, 324–26, 329–30
Van Loan, Charles, 19
Vann, Earl, 341
Vaughn, Hippo, 24–27, 349, 362n42, 363n14, 380n19, 436n12
Veach, Bobby, 70–71, 74, 107–8, 148–49, 190, 203, 348, 390n9, 401n1, 402n1
Veeck, William, Sr., *291*
Venice CA, 86, 366n17
Venice Tigers, 36–37, 86, 366n17
Venna, Louis, 338
Vernon CA, 85–86, 366n17, 375n3
Vernon Tigers, 85–93, 95–99, 377n48
Vidmer, Richards, 266
Vila, Joe, 15, 20, 121, 124–26, 150, 158, 172, 218, 256, 323, 361n8
Virginia League, 11–13, 16, 32, 360n27

Walberg, Rube: and Babe Ruth, 427n15; home runs allowed by, 413n6; and 1926 season, 237; and 1928 season, 257, 259, 267; and 1929 season, 281, 288–90, 292, 307; and 1930 season, 312, 315
Walker, Bert, 148–49, 153
Walker, H. M., 37–38
Walker, Jimmy, 112

walks and hits per innings pitched (WHIP), 201
Walsh, Davis, 245, 276
Walsh, Ed, 6, 134, 178, 302, 385n15, 399n21, 424n13
Walsh, Ed, Jr., 290
Walsh, Marty, 12
Wambsganss, Bill, 190–91, 228, 232, 398n30
Ward, Aaron, 121, 154–55, 227
Ward, Robert, 369n2
Washington Senators: and George Mogridge, 125, 381n4; and Hall of Fame members, 416n7; and Howard Ehmke, 40–41, 45–46, 50; and 1910 season, 15, 17, 20; and 1911 season, 24; and 1912 season, 26–27; and 1915 season, 48, 50; and 1917 season, 83; and 1919 season, 105, 107, 112; and 1921 season, 124–25; and 1922 season, 161; and 1923 season, 186; and 1924 season, 198–200; and 1925 season, 208, 211, 216, 217–18, 221–22; and 1926 season, 236, 410n15; and 1927 season, 245, 249; and 1928 season, 256–58; and 1929 season, 275; and 1930 season, 311–12, 316–17; and 1948 season, 344; and Organized Baseball, 48; pitching rotation of, 408n17; trade deals by, 39–40, 43–46, 160, 402n1, 409n28; and Tris Speaker, 241
Weaver, Buck, 100
Webb, Melville, 205, 226
Weber, Boots, 36
Weber, Ralph, 360n18
Wedge, Will, 3, 192, 196, 205, 273, 401n2